FRANK LLOYD WRIGHT
COLLECTED WRITINGS

FRANK LLOYD WRIGHT COLLECTED WRITINGS

Volume **3**

1931–1939

Edited by
Bruce Brooks Pfeiffer

Introduction by Kenneth Frampton

Rizzoli/New York in association with The Frank Lloyd Wright Foundation

First published in the United States of America in 1993 by
Rizzoli International Publications, Inc.,
300 Park Avenue South, New York, New York 10010
Copyright © 1993 The Frank Lloyd Wright Foundation
The drawings of Frank Lloyd Wright are copyright
© 1993 The Frank Lloyd Wright Foundation

Library of Congress Cataloging-in-Publication Data

Wright, Frank Lloyd, 1867–1959.
[Selections, 1993]
   The collected writings of Frank Lloyd Wright/
   edited by Bruce Brooks Pfeiffer.
      p.   cm.
   Includes index.
   Contents: v. 1. 1894–1930—v. 2. 1931–32.
   including a reprint of his 1932 autobiography.—
   v. 3. 1931–1939.
   ISBN 0-8478-1546-3 (HC : v. 1).—ISBN 0-8478-1547-1 (pbk. : v. 1).—
   ISBN 0-8478-1548-X (HC : v. 2).—ISBN 0-8478-1549-8 (pbk. : v. 2)—
   ISBN 0-8478-1699-0 (HC : v. 3).—ISBN 0-8478-1700-8 (pbk. : v. 3).
   1. Wright, Frank Lloyd, 1867–1959—Philosophy.
I. Pfeiffer, Bruce Brooks. II. Wright, Frank Lloyd,
1867–1959. Autobiography.
NA737. W7A35 1992
720—dc20   91-40987
                                             CIP

Printed in Mexico

Designed by Harakawa Sisco Inc

CONTENTS

INTRODUCTION

The publication of his autobiography and the foundation shortly afterwards of the Taliesin Fellowship brought Wright at the age of sixty-five to a new threshold in his life, not only because he found himself without work in the aftermath of the 1929 stock-market crash but also because he had to confront an entirely different situation from the one in which he had worked at the turn of the century. Now, as is evident from his essays of the early 1930s, he had to recognize his Midwestern isolation in the picturesque but provincial landscape of his beloved Wisconsin and the emergence of a new architectural situation that ironically enough was largely due to his own influence, as disseminated through the Wasmuth portfolios of his executed projects. All of this is at once evident from the initial essays that open this third volume of his collected writings, beginning with a typical complaint as to the way he had been misunderstood by Europeans, who had, in his view, already taken his reformist zeal too far and turned it into the kind of stripped abstraction that he abhorred, as he put it in his first essay of 1931, the cult of "the straight line and the flat plane." What he had in mind of course were all those avant-garde practitioners of the International Style, a term that he seems to have coined prior to its adoption by Henry-Russell Hitchcock and Philip Johnson.

This was not the only change he had to confront, however; for apart from the abstractions of the European avant-garde, there were anathemas closer to home: the emergence of the mega-skyscraper, as exemplified by the Chrysler Building of 1929, and the transformation of the American Beaux-Arts tradition into the compromise of the modernistic Art Deco, a monumental ornamental manner that was obviously somewhat too close to home as far as Wright was concerned, although he would never admit it. Thus the early 1930s will find him railing against two different manifestations; first, the Parisian Exposition Internationale des Arts Décoratifs of 1925 that had brought legitimacy to what he called the Mexicano manner; and second, the forthcoming "Century of Progress" exhibition scheduled to open in Chicago in 1933, a Midwestern fête from which Wright had been pointedly excluded. One of the main figures in all this was the then Art Deco master Raymond Hood, about whom Wright felt ambivalent, since Hood was a man of talent, wit, and charm, as Wright freely admits.

Architecturally speaking, Hood was also anathema to Wright, as was architect Joseph Urban, who was largely responsible for the Babylonian manner of the Century of Progress exhibition: a floodlit, theatrical display that Wright saw as exploiting the vulgar sensibility of the mobocracy. Caught in the Depression between the Scylla and Charybdis of popular American taste, Wright could stand neither the neo-colonialism of middle America, as it was then being sponsored by the federal government, nor the pseudo-modern, Eldorado manner of the Jazz Moderne. At the same time he could not align himself with what he regarded as the *neutered* manner of European functionalism, particularly as this was then being propagated by the Museum of Modern Art (MOMA) under the curatorial guidance of Hitchcock, Johnson, and Alfred Barr. By way of compensating for having accepted this critical patronage, Wright would continue to denigrate these tyros of the East Coast throughout the 1930s. What irked Wright the most was that they were the only figures aside from Lewis Mumford who recognized the continuing importance of his contribution. This explains the awkward explanation that he felt he had to make with regard to his participation in the 1932

MOMA exhibition. Perhaps the most surprising thing about this self-serving anti-apology is the fact that, notwithstanding his pan-German affinities, he would regard Oswald Spengler as the ultimate *neutering* demi-urge of the Western avant-garde. Thus we read in "Of Thee I Sing," published in *Shelter* magazine, April 1932:

> I know the European neuter's argument: The Western soul is dead; Western intelligence, though keen, is therefore sterile and can realize an impression but not expression of life except as life may be recognized as some intellectual formula . . . . We are sickened by capitalistic centralization but not so sick, I believe, that we need not confess impotence by embracing a communistic exterior discipline in architecture to kill finally what spontaneous life we have left to circumstance. . . . So we need no *Geist der Kleinlichkeit* touting a style at us. No, Herr Spengler, we are not yet impotent.

Here once more we encounter the implication that the curators of the 1932 MOMA show were, with their *Sachlich* taste, quintessentially *asexual*, aside from their even greater sin of having included Raymond Hood in the show.

Sequestered in a country that in his view was bankrupt both economically and spiritually, Wright focused his critical acumen on one target after another, first on Hood for taking "a heavy header into the blood and thunder mass known as *modernism*," second on Albert Kahn "for putting on the architecture" in his nonindustrial work, and finally on Hood's RCA building, which between the lines one feels Wright ultimately envied. The first break from this constant carping came with the prospectus "The Hillside Home School of the Allied Arts." This, the most substantial text of 1931, throws an intriguing light on Wright's promise to his then deceased aunts, Jane and Ellen Lloyd Jones, to reopen the abandoned Hillside Home School, which he had built for them in 1902. Wright's intent was to restore the existing ruin and turn it into a school for applied art, featuring classes in architecture, painting, pottery, sculpture, glass- and metalwork, dance, and drama. This curriculum and its financial prospectus was painstakingly elaborated and at one time, as Bruce Pfeiffer informs us, it looked as if it would be sponsored by the University of Wisconsin. However, support was not forthcoming and one year later the Wrights shifted their energy to a similar proposal under a different name, namely the more modest program of the Taliesin Fellowship. "The Hillside Home School for the Allied Arts" thus became the first draft of the Taliesin Fellowship prospectus, which would then be cast in a number of different versions between 1932 and 1933. In an early draft, however, Wright entered a *mea culpa* plea made on behalf of the American people:

> We have no superstructure, that is to say no culture above the matters of behavior, commerce, industry, politics, and an unsure taste for objets d'art. . . . We are a nation rich beyond the bounds, even of our own avarice, living in abundance with a creature-comfort undreamed of in the World before. We are ingenious, inventive, scientifically, commercially progressive and, as the whole World has occasion to know—uncreative. . . . Nor will more than three-fifths of our people know what is meant by the assertion that the American is "uncreative."

However coincidentally, Wright's Hillside Home School prospectus was in part as a response to the challenge of the Finnish architect Eliel Saarinen, who after a decade as resident architect and ideologue was in 1932 appointed director of the newly founded Cranbrook Art Academy in Bloomfield Hills, Michigan. Wright had been nursing a similar idea for some time as his 1928 *Architectural Record* series, "In the Cause of Architecture," makes clear. Certainly it had been in the back of his mind ever since the first *Gesamtkunstwerk* triumph of his career: namely, the realization of Midway Gardens, when he had a number of different artists collaborating under his direction. The Hillside Home School prospectus had its students studying all branches of applied and fine art while at the same time earning their keep through communal constructive and agrarian work, thereby sustaining Wright's self-subsistent Arts and Crafts, land-based economy. The Wrights also envisaged augmenting this rustic *modus vivendi* by selling the artworks produced in the school:

> Thus belonging to the school would be each month a very considerable product of modern beautifully useful or usefully beautiful things ready for markets and influence. Stuffs, tapestries, table linens, new cotton fabrics, batik, with special emphasis on tapestries, table glassware, glass flower holders, lighting devices of glass, and glass dishes of all sorts, ashtrays, window glass, and glass mosaics, necklaces, decorative beads, and objects of glass.

However, this was not the only feature that the prospective Hillside Home School would have shared with its German predecessor, the Bauhaus. For both institutions would eventually attach great importance to music, drama, and dance. Above all, in Wright's case, Wagner's music-drama was the ultimate vehicle for the total work of art.

Surprisingly enough, given his Arts and Crafts bias, Wright would enter into the subject of town planning in his curriculum for the Hillside Home School, and this is the theme to which he will return in his book *The Disappearing City* of the following year (initially drafted under the title *The Industrial Revolution Runs Away*). Wright declared that the future city will be everywhere and nowhere, and that it will be a city so greatly different from the ancient city or from any city today that we will probably fail to recognize its coming as the city at all! Elsewhere he stated, "America needs no help to Broadacre City, it will build itself haphazard." On the one hand Wright thought that one should consciously establish a new system of dispersed land-settlement, throughout the country, while on the other he thought that such an anti-metropolitan condition would come into being by itself. As Bruce Pfeiffer points out, by the late 1920s he had experienced the nascent disurbanization of America first-hand, habitually driving back and forth across the country between Wisconsin and Arizona. Thus, after condemning, at length, the dead and dying metropolis of rent and victimization, Wright turned to the impact of the mobilization and mass communication as brought about by the mass ownership of the automobile and by the concomitant convenience of modern telecommunications, including, all too prophetically, television. All this meant that the dense city of capital was no longer the essential instrument of technological and economic progress. For Wright in 1932 there were five agencies that were jointly responsible for bringing this about: (1) electrification; (2) the internal combustion engine, not dependent on any form of fixed track; (3) electro-mechanical refrigerating and heating that could operate independently of the metropolis; (4) the existence of new lightweight materials that Wright saw as facilitating economic forms of low-density, residential land settlement; (5) mechanized production in general, which since his 1901 lecture "The Art and Craft of the Machine" Wright had seen as the prime mover of a democratic, deurbanized American civilization.

At the same time Wright acknowledged that none of this would achieve its fully liberative capacity without certain political changes, although as to the exact nature of these he remained somewhat uncertain. As with Ebenezer Howard, he thought Henry George's *Progress and Poverty* of 1879 held the key; although like Howard he had serious misgivings about the "single tax" theory. He was nonetheless extremely positive about the promise of George's social vision:

> Democracy reintegrated as the systematized integration of small individual units built up high in the quality of individuality is a practical and rational ideal of freedom: machine in hand. Division of the exaggerated commercial-enterprise into more effective small units and reintegration over the whole surface of the nation—this is now no less practical. Communal ownership by way of taxation of all communal resources is not necessarily communism, as Henry George points out with complete logic. It may be entirely democratic.

Later he would write about his automotive utopia in terms that, in retrospect, seem almost Futurist:

> . . . spacious landscaped highways, grade crossings eliminated, "by-passing" living areas, devoid of the already archaic telegraph and telephone poles and wires and free of blaring billboards and obsolete construction. Imagine these great highways, bright with wayside flowers. . . . Giant roads, themselves great architecture, pass public service stations, no longer eyesores, expanded to include all kinds of service and comfort.

Wright is so enamored with this megalopolitan vision *avant la lettre*, that he is quite willing to accept automobile commutation of up to one hundred fifty miles one way as a normative standard. In this text Wright already outlines many of the ideal building types of his Broadacre City model of 1934, including freestanding low-rise Usonian homes, tall free-standing towers for migrants and bachelors, silent, smokeless, small-scale factories, and resort hotels such as Wright had projected for San Marcos in the Desert. One of the key types of Broadacre City was the Walter Davidson model farm unit, exhibited at the Museum of Modern Art, New York in 1940. Designed to facilitate the economic management of both home and land, this unit was critical to the economy of Broadacre, where every man would be allocated his acre of land at birth. Apart from George's economic theory, Wright patently based his ideal city on Peter Kropotkin's *Fields, Factories, and Workshops* of 1899. Wright, like Henry Ford, refused to recognize the inherent contradiction of such a proposition, namely, that an individualistic, quasi-agrarian economy would not necessarily guarantee a regionally urbanized populace either its subsistence or the benefits of Taylorized production, since the latter still demanded a certain concentration of both labor and resources. Kropotkin himself acknowledged the need to centralize the processes of heavy industry. Wright's vision of smallholders driving to rural factories in secondhand Model-T Fords suggests that a permanent, "sweaty equity" labor force would have been an essential aspect of the Broadacre economy.

Aside from continuing his diatribe against the hegemony of Hood et al., as in his *Architectural Forum* review of an Art Deco architectural show staged in Macy's department store, Wright encountered an entirely new protagonist in 1933, namely the Soviet Union, which in the form of a wayward *Pravda* correspondent first contacted him in the fall of that year. Wright was asked to comment on the fate of the American intellectual and intellectual life during the Depression, to which he responded:

> No radical measures have been undertaken in the New Deal but there has been a great deal of tinkering and adjusting and pushing with prices to bring the old game alive again. Something more is needed than an arbitrary price system to re-awaken capitalistic confidence in the spending of money. . . . It is now proposed among the more sensible of the intelligentsia that all absentee-ownership be declared illegal. . . . In the course of the next five years a real demand for such "repeal" of special privilege may come to pass. This is the feeling of the minority among intelligentsia but they are doing nothing about it. They are spectators, by birth, breeding and habit. Meantime all are getting on with about one tenth of their former incomes.

Seemingly dissatisfied with this, Wright wrote *Pravda* again soon after, arguing that the Depression had virtually eliminated the profession, which had in any event been previously reduced to the mere decoration of real estate, and that the entire capitalist system had done nothing but perpetuate a makeshift society. While praising the Soviet Union for its heroic attempt at a society based on human values, he nonetheless expressed his fear that it would degenerate into state capitalism and into a world solely dominated by the Stakhanovite standards of Taylorized production. For him the issue was how to allow for individual creativity while still providing social justice for all.

Soon after this exchange Wright received a further questionnaire from the magazine *Sovietskaya Archi-*

tectura, touching not only on socio-political issues but also on his working method. The questions ranged from technological constraints to conceptual development and from the role of drawing to the future place of the classical tradition in modern architectural production. These questions already reflected the imposition of Stalinist cultural policy and the emergence of a Socialist Realist party line in architecture as in the other arts. Wright's reply is one of the most concise and lucid statements of his career:

> The solution of every problem is contained within itself. Its plan, form and character are determined by the nature of the site, the nature of the materials used, the nature of the system using them, the nature of the life concerned and the purpose of the building itself.

Needless to say, while he was against any notion of composition in architecture or any kind of classical allusion, he often made use of classical composition in his own more extensive layouts. As to the role of drawing, he insisted that it was only a means to an end. Committed to the idea of the *Gesamtkunstwerk*, Wright thought that painting and sculpture should be fully integrated into the work, under the architect's control. He went on to stress the importance of site supervision and his general antipathy to last-minute refinements. He wrote: "Corrections, additions should be as few as possible. If sufficient study has been devoted to the development of the project they should be unnecessary."

When the "Century of Progress" exhibition opened in 1933 Wright denounced it yet again for being a miscarriage of modern architecture. Once more he would lay the ultimate blame on the Exposition Internationale des Arts Décoratifs, which he saw, somewhat self-servingly, as an assimilation of his own Prairie manner and, more objectively, as a distortion of the organic architectural tradition of the Midwest. Feeling let down by his fellow architects and abandoned by the society, Wright wrote:

> The cause of an organic architecture as a living tradition is here betrayed just as the same old eclecticism has betrayed the dying Gothic tradition [a reference to Hood's Chicago Tribune Building of 1922] and as it has betrayed the dead pseudo-classic. It should not wholly betray the Renaissance because the Renaissance itself, where architecture was concerned, was a Roman holiday—a "Fair"—you may see the deeper and more profound work that is indigenous to their own country betrayed by way of its own countenance, used as a mask by the expedient eclecticism of unfair architects and sold as ballyhoo to the public in the name of "Progress."

In the last analysis, Wright regarded the entire exhibition as a parody of his vision; as the proliferation of a pseudo-style similar to the White City classicism that, with the single exception of Louis Sullivan's Transportation Pavilion, had dominated the Chicago World's Columbian Exhibition of 1893. Even the colored floodlighting of the 1933 fair earned Wright's disapproval, for he saw it as a parody of Sullivan's polychromy.

In December 1933 Wright wrote the most "critical" version of the Taliesin Fellowship prospectus, wherein aside from claiming the manifest virtues of a hands-on apprenticeship system he also attacked the academic degeneracy of the professional architectural schools. Needless to say it was also an advertisement for what the fellowship had achieved to date. Among many other achievements, both real and fictive, the reader is informed of the film archive that Wright had started to assemble in order to overcome the isolation of his Taliesin stronghold:

> In the Taliesin Playhouse there has been and will be seen a series of five films projected by the excellent Western Electric sound equipment, films composed by such masters as Eisenstein, René Clair, Murnau, Chaplin, Disney, Pabst and other productions of fine character. The sound system is wired to speakers in other buildings of the group, in the living rooms and in

the balcony of the central studio. Pianos are located in the studios and living room for apprentices to play. Facilities exist in the Playhouse for amateur theatricals. The Playhouse has a flexible stage, dressing rooms, rooms for designing and making sets and is adapted to concerts, lectures and fellowship gatherings as well as theatre and cinema.

Wright concludes the 1933 prospectus by discussing how all the other arts will be integrated into the culture of Taliesin, including painting, sculpture, and music. Following the lead of the Bauhaus, he also envisages branching out into photography, printing, and publicity.

Throughout Wright's fallow period of the first half of the 1930s, when he had little work, he will occupy himself at Taliesin on designing and fabricating a large demonstration model of Broadacre City that, ironically enough, will be first exhibited in Hood's Rockefeller Center in 1934. At the same time he will write a series of articles that while going over old ground, as in his attack on the International Style and Le Corbusier, will also open up new themes, such as his "Two-Zone House" article published in 1934 or his essay on architectural sculpture of 1935. In this last case he will reveal his longstanding admiration for the artists of the Viennese Secession: Messrs. Klimt, Wagner, Hoffmann, and Olbrich. Written as a review of *The New Architectural Sculpture* by Walter Raymond Agard, this short notice began a series of reviews that he will write at the time, including a generous appraisal of Paul Frankl's *Form and Reform: A Practical Handbook for Modern Interiors* and a more critical reading of Hugh Morrison's *Louis Sullivan: Prophet of Modern Architecture*. While Wright finds in Frankl yet another native Viennese genius in the field of decorative art, he will deliver a fresh account of the Adler and Sullivan partnership, in which he not only defended Sullivan against what he regarded as Morrison's misrepresentations, but also came to Adler's defense, as Sullivan's functionalist teacher. With a display of misplaced loyalty rather than critical acumen, Wright will repudiate Morrison's thesis that H. H. Richardson had exercised an influence on Sullivan. Finally, in an essay of 1936 entitled "To the Memorial Craftsmen of America," he will condemn the American cult of venerating the dead through vertical tombstones and monuments. He will advocate instead the conversion of existing cemeteries into horizontally terraced parks, paved with commemorative marble slabs, very much like the cemetery that he designed for the Martin family in 1928, the so-called Blue Sky Burial Terraces.

As his Two-Zone House essay would indicate, published in the first issue of the lavish *Taliesin* magazine, Wright had by now evolved his concept of the fully modernized American home into a new plan type in which the kitchen will be treated as a "work studio" partially open to the living space and the services will be condensed into a central core dividing the house into its quiet and active zones. Wright would finally synthesize these ideas in his first Usonian L-plan courthouses of the mid-1930s; his Malcolm Willey House in Minneapolis of 1934 and his Herbert Jacobs House built in Madison, Wisconsin in 1936.

While Wright would receive two important commissions in 1936—Fallingwater for Edgar Kaufmann and the S. C. Johnson Administration Building—he was more aware than ever of the deepening economic depression and of the reconstruction policies then being pursued by Roosevelt's New Deal. In such a climate he became increasingly concerned that capitalism had reached an impasse and that only a fundamental change would enable the United States to restructure itself and to recover its former energy and direction. As to the political form that this change should take Wright remained uncertain, except that it should conform to some kind of neo-capitalist, social democracy, which accounts for his evident sympathy for the Netherlands and Scandinavia. This also explains the empathy he felt for the Soviet Union when he visited it with his wife, Olgivanna, in June 1937.

Despite the enforced collectivization and the purges of the Soviet elite, Wright felt that the Soviet Union was on the right track politically—or at least moving in a direction that would soon prove to be more effective than that of the United States. That Wright's view of all this was naive, not to say confused, is suggested by his breezy dismissal of the Trotskyite claim that the revolution was being betrayed. At the same time he remained acutely aware that an equally radical change would have to be enacted in the United States if an organic modern society worthy of democracy were ever to be realized. In 1937 he wrote "The Russian spirit in this new way of life over there, where 90 per cent of the people are still what we call illiterate, is vigorous and healthy beyond any nation on earth. As I walked the streets among them I felt, God help any nation or nations either undertaking to interfere with this." Such enthusiasm together with his categoric attack on land and money speculation, as made in his address to the Chicago Real Estate Board in 1938, were sufficient to render him a radical suspect in the paranoid McCarthy era of the 1950s.

Notwithstanding his political sympathy, he would dissociate himself from the pompier classicism of Stalinist Russia, seeing it as a betrayal of the revolution in architectural terms. In his 1937 *Izvestia* article he wrote: "The buildings of a democracy will first know and love the nature of the ground upon which they stand. They will realize that the humble horizontal line is the line of human life upon this earth." At the same time, he understood only too well why the abstract, Constructivist architecture of the Soviet avant-garde should have been rejected by the Soviet state, for this once again was the international "neutered" functionalism against which he had been campaigning since the early 1930s. In a rather repetitious text of 1937, entitled *Architecture and Modern Life*, Wright, together with the philosopher Baker Brownwell, attempted to further justify his radical proposals for reconstructing America. Hood's Radio City was again seen as symptomatic of all that was wrong with the vertical metropolis of New York as opposed to the low-rise horizontal city of Broadacre. The familiar diatribe aside, the most intriguing aspect of this book is the Socratic dialogue between Wright and Brownwell, in which Brownwell generally plays Boswell to Wright's Johnson, but is at times decidedly more astute.

1938 will see Wright generally sympathetic to the achievements of the New Deal and in the *Architectural Forum* monograph on his work published in January, he will itemize the nine essential precepts of the Usonian house as a general principle for future low-rise, low-cost suburban development. Thus he would advocate the minimalization of the roof, the provision of a carport, the elimination of the basement together with radiators and as much freestanding furniture as possible. As far as he was concerned, seating, like storage, should be built-in. This was Wright's "natural house" in the making and as a result he came out against plastering, painting, gutters, and down pipes. By 1938 Wright could set forth his modernized organic architecture as a total program from the smallest prefabricated house to a total deurbanization strategy as the ultimate model for future development. This was the message that he took to England when he was invited to give the George Watson lectures at the Royal Institute of British Architects (RIBA) in London in April 1939. Appropriately enough, this volume concludes with the edited transcript of the four lectures, published in England, in that year, under the title *An Organic Architecture: The Architecture of Democracy*. Wright rose to the royal occasion of his appearance at the RIBA by making an iridescent presentation of his life's work, complete with films of Taliesin West under construction. While covering the familiar Broadacre argument, he pointedly referred to a categoric stand against commodity speculation and usury. This messianic stance brought about an intelligent and sometimes aggressive response that Wright mostly managed to field with wit and sagacity. However, when once pushed into a corner, he was forced to concede that he did not recommend dismantling the historic urban centers of the world where they existed and were justly revered.

Shortly after the lectures were published, the whole of Europe was at war for the second time in twenty years. One year later, in 1940, when he was seventy-three, Wright would be honored *in absentia* with the Gold Medal of the Royal Institute of British Architects for the year 1941, the eighth in the line of such similar honors, as he wryly remarked in the postwar edition of his autobiography.

K.F.

FRANK LLOYD WRIGHT
A BIOGRAPHICAL SKETCH:
1931–1939

Frank Lloyd Wright survived a long period when little of his work was built. From 1924 to 1934 there were designs made for all manner of great projects—a world's fair, skyscrapers, hotels, city planning, a cathedral of immense proportions—but none was constructed. There were a few exceptions to this barren period: a summer home for his friend and client Darwin D. Martin (1928), a home for his cousin Richard Lloyd Jones (1929), and a home for the Malcolm Willeys in Minneapolis (1932–1934). In the late 1920s, to compensate for the lack of architectural work, he began writing his autobiography. At about the same time he also started writing about city planning, decentralization, and the plight of urban life. This culminated in the book *The Disappearing City,* which was more than an attack on current urban ills—it was a broad offering of social, economic, and architectural alternatives for living in the twentieth century.

The message Wright most clearly conveys in *The Disappearing City* is the relationship of man to nature. In this regard what Wright was promulgating—in 1932—was a profound regard for the environment and conservation—words that at that time had little or no currency, but would be vitally pertinent later in the century. He believed that it could be nothing but beneficial for man to associate closely and reverently with the natural features around him, and any so-called city must be immersed in this continuum of "green."

The following two years, still without commissions in the office, he devoted his time and effort to putting the ideas expressed in *The Disappearing City* into a more concrete form, a model city plan that he called "Broadacre City." Many of the articles he wrote and published at this time had Broadacre City as their theme. Broadacre City placed the salvation of the American family in the hands of the architect; utilizing the benefits of modern methods and technology, the decentralized city would respect human needs and the environment and enhance the features of the landscape. He believed that Broadacre City expressed not only a plan for living in the United States, but a plan for living in a democracy.

In his definition of the democratic faith, he placed most emphasis on the health of the individual, what he often called "rule by the bravest and the best," not the strongest or most political. The bravest and the best were, to him, those individuals who rose in the ranks by their own merits and accomplishments, earning trust and honor not as something conferred on them, but rather as qualities that grow from within them. Exactly the same principles that governed his thinking about organic architecture applied, in his way of thinking, to a true democracy.

Following the making of the Broadacre City model, along with some related models, such as a service station, a theater, and several homes, came a surge of new work. The long dry spell was over, and into this new work he poured himself with renewed creative energies. From Paul and Jean Hanna and Edgar and Liliane Kaufmann came requests for house designs.

"Fallingwater," the famous weekend house Wright designed for Edgar J. Kaufmann, is built over a series of water cascades, anchored to a cliff at one side, cantilevered over the water on the other. It is perhaps the greatest blend of building and environment ever achieved in domestic architecture. The moment it was completed, in 1939, it was exhibited as a solo project in New York's Museum of Modern Art. The Hanna house of 1935, constructed in Stanford, California, was Wright's first application of the hexagon as a unit system for architecture. Accordingly he named it "Honeycomb House." It also was an early prototype of construction methods he developed, the following year, into a building system he called "the Usonian House," an innovative building system aimed at providing for a moderate income family a home befitting the ideology of a democratic nation, not one harking back to the period styles of imperial Europe. The Herbert Jacobs house, built in Madison, Wisconsin, in 1936 was the first of the Usonian houses. It was published in the 1938 January issue of the *Architectural Forum*, with an accompanying text by Wright explaining how the system worked. From 1936 to 1939, Wright designed 38 Usonian houses, based on the Jacobs model, of which 17 were constructed. These homes were built across the nation, from Massachusetts to California. The Usonian houses varied in size and plan according to each client's requirements and budget. But the basic construction method was the same for all of them. Wright regarded the Usonian houses as his most valuable contribution to architecture.

In 1936 Wright was given the commission to design a large administration building for the S.C. Johnson & Son Company in Racine, Wisconsin. He hoped with this building to revolutionize the design of industrial workspaces. "Organic architecture designed this great building," Wright wrote, "to be as inspiring a place to work in as any cathedral ever was in which to worship. It was meant to be a socio-architectural interpretation of modern business at its top and best."[1] The pure excitement of receiving a commission of such size and scope compelled him to describe how he felt when Herbert Johnson, president of the company, sent Wright a note and a retainer for his services after visiting the architect at Taliesin:

> And, the pie thus opened, the birds began to sing again below the house at Taliesin; dry grass on the hillside turned green and the hollyhocks went gaily into a second blooming. The orchard decided to come in with a heavy crop of big red harvest apples and the whole landscape seemed to have more color; Iovanna [Wright's daughter] rode more fiercely through the Valley; both Olgivanna's [Wright's wife's] responsibilities and mine were doubled—with smiles. Work was incessant. Taliesin galvanized into fresh activity. . . .What a release of pent-up creative energy—the making of those plans! Ideas came tumbling up and out onto paper to be thrown back in heaps—for careful scrutiny and selection.[2]

The Johnson building, like the Larkin building thirty years earlier, was Wright's solution to the problem of creating an inspiring workplace in an industrial environment. The office building was lit from above by a series of skylights running between the lily-pad dendriform columns that rose from the floor to become the ceiling and roof at the same time. In style and design, as well as engineering, the Johnson building was distinctly different from the work Wright had done up to this time and heralded a generation of daring new public buildings to follow, including the Guggenheim Museum.

Wright termed "Wingspread," the sizable house he built for Johnson in 1937, the last of the prairie houses. He further described it as a "zoned" house, an evolution of the zoned plan he had used for the Avery Coonley house in Riverside, Illinois, in 1906. With the Johnson house, he extended four wings out from a central three-story area called "The Great Hall," which served as living room, entry, library, and dining room—each section with its own fireplace but all radiating out from one central fireplace mass. The extending wings contained bedrooms for the Johnsons, their children, and guests, with the fourth wing for kitchen, pantry, and servants' quarters.

Three years after the Hanna house was built, in 1938, Wright furthered his search for more flexible planning, moving from the hexagon to the circle. In the Ralph Jester house every room was a circle, the entire grouping of circles separated and spaced by an open, but roofed, patio: the total abolition of angles in a free-flowing plan. Unfortunately this project was not built.

Wright had contracted pneumonia in December 1936, while the Johnson building was in construction. Fortunately, his apprentices, Edgar Tafel and Wesley Peters, were able to continue supervision of the project. But once Wright recovered, his wife, Olgivanna, prompted him to take a few weeks off to travel to Arizona, where he recuperated in the warm sunshine and dry air. They had been in Arizona during the winter of

1933–1934, when Wright and the Taliesin Fellowship built the Broadacre City model. At that time, they rented space in the Hacienda Inn, at Chandler, Arizona, some miles south of Phoenix. In 1937 the Wrights roamed the area looking for land to build on. Finally, to Eugene Masselink, a Taliesin apprentice who also served as Wright's secretary, Wright sent this wire:

WEATHER WARM. BEAUTIFUL SITE IN HAND. COME JOKAKE INN SOON YOU ARE READY. BRING SHOVELS, RAKES, HOES AND ALSO HOES. EIGHTEEN DRAFTING BOARDS AND TOOLS. WHEELBARROW, CONCRETE MIXER, SMALL KOHLER (ELECTRICAL PLANT) AND WIRE. MELODEON, OIL STOVES FOR COOKING AND HEATING. WATER VIOLA, CELLO, RUGS NOT IN USE AND WHATEVER ELSE WE NEED.

Wright purchased the property at the foot of the McDowell Mountains, and 32 Taliesin Fellowship members arrived from his studio in Wisconsin to begin construction of the winter home, studio, and workshop that Wright called Taliesin West. He claimed that the desert was such a revelation and inspiration to him, that the design of this desert camp came, as well, in the nature of a revelation, a religious experience. The building of the desert camp, great masonry walls topped with canvas, was an exhilarating adventure not only for the apprentices who carried on most of the construction, but also for Wright and Olgivanna. Out on the desert floor they lived in tent-like structures for several winters until the building was habitable:

That desert camp belonged to the desert as though it had stood there for centuries. And also built into Taliesin West is the best in the strong young lives of about thirty young men and women for their winter seasons of about seven years. Some local labor went in too, but not much. And the constant supervision of an architect—myself, Olgivanna inspiring and working with us all, working as hard as I—living a full life, too full, meanwhile.[3]

What were the elements that helped to nurture, if not directly cause, this renewed activity? Two inspirations were prominent in his personal life: his wife and the Taliesin Fellowship. Olgivanna saw it as her duty to create a beneficent environment for her husband, to assure that he would be in an atmosphere conducive to creative work. She well remembered the first several years of their life together, hounded by police, the banks, his former wife Miriam Noel, and the press. More and more she took charge of his personal and social life, to the extent that he took to calling her not by her first name, but "Mother." "I ruled him," she once admitted to this author, "but I ruled him with love."

Although born in Montenegro and educated in Russia, Olgivanna was no stranger to the English language. Beginning at the age of nine she had an English governess, and she was steeped not only in the language but the literature as well. Later, at the Gurdjieff Institute in Fontainebleau, her friends and colleagues were English and American men and women of letters: Alfred Orage, Jane Heap, Margaret Anderson, and—especially—her close and devoted friend Katherine Mansfield. All of this background in literature served Wright well. She not only encouraged him to write his autobiography, but worked alongside him and edited his writing herself, making suggestions and asking for clarifications.

To help develop the conditions she believed essential to his creative life, she encouraged him to found a school for architects, the Taliesin Fellowship. He was now surrounded by young men and women who admired him, admired his work, desired to be part of that work as well as the communal life at Taliesin, and generated the type of energy he fed upon. Speaking of the aim and goals of the fellowship, he said:

Now we are not educational. We are, we hope, cultural. We do feel that unless we turn you out better looking, better thinking, better able, when you get through your term with us here, we haven't done much for ourselves, have we? Because it is a true statement. I have been looked upon as a wise old gentleman who succeeded in setting up a system whereby he got his work done for nothing. Well, all it cost me to get my work done for nothing was all I ever earned in life, all I will ever earn, all I could possibly earn and all I can do is to share that with the boys and girls who want to come in here along a quest for something I myself haven't finished with. You see, I am in it still, just the way you are. So is Olgivanna. We are working and learning. And it occurred to me the other day—I don't know what brought it up—something that made me feel that I could still learn faster, learn quicker, and by way of the years that I have lived, learn more, faster than anybody here. And that I was getting more out of this fellowship than any of you were getting in just that way of learning. I think, of course, that this is the richest thing that could possibly have happened to us, that we have opportunity to learn by way of your learning. That is the great benefit in it.[4]

The apprenticeship method was the core of training at Taliesin, what today we call experiential learning. The apprentices worked with Wright on all the designs he was creating in the drafting room; many had previous training in engineering, foremost among them William Wesley Peters, married to Wright's adopted daughter, Svetlana. Peters, along with Mendel Glickman, was able to translate Wright's innovative structural concepts into the language engineers understood in order to get the buildings built. They worked on "Fallingwater," with its far-reaching cantilever terraces, and the Johnson building in Racine, with its dendriform columns that form the ceiling of the main workroom.

The fellowship was proving that Wright's educational system worked: all the great designs of Wright's that were realized during this period were built from working drawings prepared by the apprentices, from specifications worked out by them, and with their on-site supervision, often in the role of general contractors, especially in the case of the Usonian houses.

By no means all of Wright's time was spent at the drafting board. In 1937 the Wrights went to Russia, where he had been invited by the All-Union Congress of Soviet Architects. Wright could never condone communism. As a way of life it was anathema to him, considering his deeply felt belief in democracy and what he called the "sovereignty of the individual." But he held the Russian people in high regard, ever since his first close encounter with them in Tokyo. Following the Revolution, in 1917, many of the nobility fled Vladivostok and migrated to Tokyo. Wright had a piano in his apartment in the Imperial Hotel Annex (a temporary structure he designed and built to accommodate the hotel's guests while the new building was in construction.) Several Russians came to his apartment to enjoy musical evenings. He also admired Russian literature: Tolstoy, Dostoyevski, Gogol, and Pushkin. When he first met Olgivanna in 1924 he thought she might be a Russian princess. She continued to bring into his life the culture and romance of Russia, where she had received her education. Beginning in the early 1930s he collected films from the Russian cinema; he felt that they had made advances in cinema art beyond even the contributions of Hollywood. He particularly admired the work of the director Sergei Eisenstein. His 1937 trip to Moscow further confirmed his assessment of Russia as a nation of fine-spirited and talented people. Two years later he was invited to England by the Royal Institute of British Architects. From his four lectures at the Sulgrave Manor, in London, came his book *An Organic Architecture: The Architecture of Democracy*. The trip to London and his address to the Royal Institute of British Architects earned him the King's Gold Medal for Architecture.

Among Wright's writings about architecture, the environment, and people is a gem all its own and unto itself. "The Man Who . . ." series is an unexpected sampling of Wright's purely fictional writings—almost like a series of fables—and demonstrates in yet another way Wright's versatility as a writer.

B.B.P.

1. Frank Lloyd Wright, *An Autobiography* (New York: Duell, Sloan and Pearce, 1943), p. 472.
2. Ibid., pp.468-469.
3. Ibid., p.454.
4. Frank Lloyd Wright in a talk to the Taliesin Fellowship, December 20, 1955. FLLW Fdn AV#1014.055. pp. 9-10.

FRANK LLOYD WRIGHT
COLLECTED WRITINGS

1931

TO MY CRITICS IN THE LAND OF THE DANUBE AND THE RHINE

In response to a minority of writers, who had criticized aspects of an exhibition of his work that traveled to Holland, Germany, and Belgium in 1931, Wright composed this rebuttal and sent it to the Frankfurter Allemagne Zeitung, *a leading German newspaper. For the exhibition in Berlin, Wright had prepared drawings for the layouts and had sent his draftsman Heinrich Klumb to supervise the installation. The tremendous publicity and subsequent honors Wright received as a result of this European tour led the next year to an exhibition at The Museum of Modern Art in New York City. The architect Philip Johnson, who was the director of the exhibition in New York, was greatly impressed by the installation in Berlin.* [Unpublished essay, 1931][1]

READING MANY CRITICISMS OF MY PLANS AND MODELS, now among you, by Mendelsohn, Behrendt, Behne, Donath, Schmidt, Fechter, Friedrich, Deri, Biebrzhnski, G. L., Reidrich, Gramatki, Canske, Meissner, Bie, N. V. N., Meunier, Alemann, Embell, Dulberg, Stein, B. Y., H. W. R., Sholz, Scharfe, H. A., H. S., Osborn, V. Brockhusen, Paulsen, Dargel, m. a., and others, I realize I should not have sent plans and models to you, but have come to talk with you myself.[2]

The New Theatre (Project). Woodstock, New York. 1931. Section. Pencil on tracing paper, 27x16". FLLW Fdn#3106.017

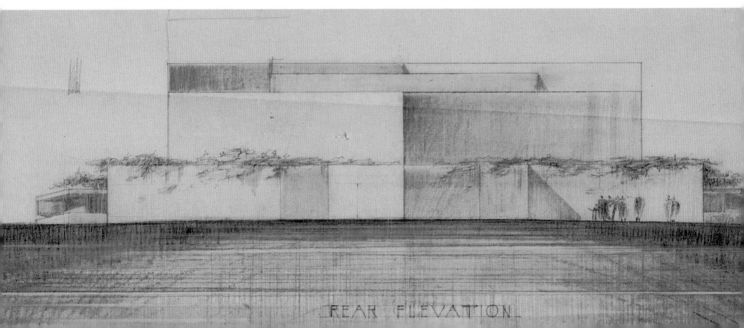

REAR ELEVATION

Appreciation from you is not lacking, nor generosity, my Germans . . . I am not ungrateful.

But a mystery is made of what is extremely simple. I should explain that I let the small fragment or remnant of my work go abroad to you because I felt the force of its example confused or no longer clearly felt. And because I have noticed of late years, in Germany, a concentration upon an appearance that does not grow outward into manifold richness of expression but that does tend to concentrate on the barren bands and box-outlines of a calculated style.

Any tyro may emulate this calculated superficial style. While much talk of principles goes with this calculated effort it is a rationalizing after the fact. Principles, if involved, do not fructify creation.

What has happened?

The usual abuse has happened.

The straight line and the flat plane—the necessary basis of forms for our Machine-age have been capitalized as something by, for and in themselves.

The T-square, triangle and the flat of the paper have been "stylized" and there the matter stays—a negation and sterile!

Negation is good, for a time.

But, affirmation of more than the negation is needed if human life is going beyond its own machinery. So this friendly warning and brotherly protest against the protestant who protests the human riches involved in creative endeavor of all kinds.

Do not imagine, my architects and critics, that mathematics is music, although music is sublimated mathematics.

No more is the geometry of the straight line and flat plane of the Machine-age—architecture.

Once the rejection of former insignificance, waste and lying by way of functionless ornament is effected, the matter seems to rest with you. You get no farther on. You seem content.

And some of you seem to imagine by renouncing such individualities you possess you may calculate a style for the future. Nothing could be more absurd.

While the machine is become the tool of the age a new ideal has grown up beside it. We call that ideal Freedom! An interior evolution of the individuality. That evolution is the human core of such culture as the age has developed.

Now must man, to be free, triumph over you and your new abstraction made by way of the machine? Or is man to triumph, by your help, over all machinery and over all abstraction?

A style is no longer necessary except as it is individual and therefore free.

An international style is a horrible nightmare; again a mistake; the sensibilities and potencies of human life imprisoned by the narrow vision and impotence of small men.

Life can not be straightened out and tipped up edgewise to be surveyed "in the flat" for longer

The New Theatre (Project). Woodstock, New York. 1931. Elevation. Pencil on tracing paper, 32 x 16". FLLW Fdn#3106.018

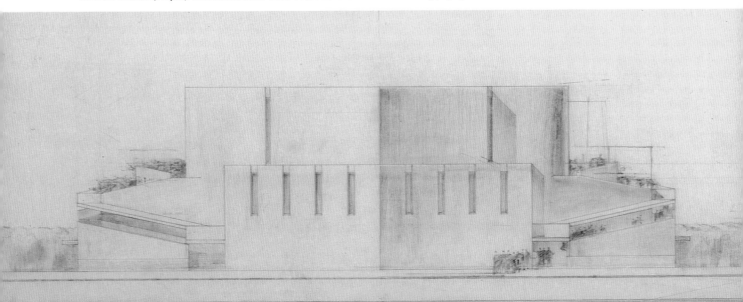

than a brief period while novelty is a satisfaction.

The wellsprings of human activity are as deep and more thirst-quenching than ever before.

The thirst for life is at once intensified and denied by the engine we now live by, the Machine.

As Artists it is our office not only to overcome the machine by intelligent use of that engine, but by means of it, used as a new tool, to gratify the natural thirst of the human soul for beauty.

For sentient, living beauty, I say. Not for mere plain "effects," compositions, gestures, affectations and lies, however pretentious of common sense they may be. So the thought at the center of the plans and models you have just seen is wasted on you if you gauge the worth of that thought by the negation you have mistaken for affirmation.

I have seen and used the straight line and flat plane only as humble and new means to a greater end. But that end is not an "International Style" nor any style at all. All that I have shown you is aimed at greater individuality by way of greater imagination because of greater resources and the demands of a deepening sense of life. So do not strand life in shallows just beneath the surface by way of the box, the flat plane and the unmitigated straight line. All these are good but all three are abstractions.

So in any new freedom for life all are to be regarded with doubt and suspicion and held in their places. Not by way of the momentary thrill of discovery are they to be made into a style. Emulation by way of any such abstraction has put the world into the prison-house.

Why not liberate the world by way of greater imagination, new and better technique, mastering new and greater resources in order to make no more prison-houses.

Such liberation means no more emulation. No emulation of emulation by emulation, such as we used to call a style.

No, the matter is more truly simple now.

Liberation means only the free exercise of what resources of imagination may happen to be your individual gift, disciplined by your new tool, the machine, but not mastered by it, and such wealth of form as the world never saw before will belong to our coming of age.

Do not take from one another more than common knowledge.

Do not take from any source more than inspiration.

Do not try to take from life more than you can put into it because the natural thief is always severely punished by nature herself.

I say this to you out of the depths of an intensely joyous personal experience.

Great appreciation I have given to life and received from it. Life is no niggard except to the niggardly. The more anyone gives to life in free spirit, the more he will receive from life. Strength increases by way of exercise of strength, never by way of keeping an eye on the other fellow, to do as well or even better than he does.

In the arts of life—emulation is cowardice. To be a coward is to die continually and never be quite dead because one never was quite alive.

If the plans and models I have sent to you for an hour have any significance to you—such appreciation is that general significance. But, there is much to help the young man in the way of technique because he may see form taking shape out of the nature and character of materials and material conditions as a flower takes shape from the principle committed to its seed.

My good friends in the land of the Danube and the Rhine, criticize me as I am. Do not criticize me as you would have me. Because I would not be as you would have me and unless you change we could not have each other.

And realize that I am still at work with greater appreciation of life.

What you have seen from my hand is yet unfinished.

1. Although we do not have a date of publication, Wright's letter was submitted to the editor of *Frankfurter Allemagne Zeitung* on July 23, 1931, copies being sent to Th. Wijdeveld, Erich Mendelsohn, and Heinrich Klumb.
2. This essay was drafted in response to the numerous signed articles that appeared throughout Germany during the week of June 18, 1931, in response to the exhibition of Wright's work that opened in Berlin on June 17. Heinrich Klumb apparently forwarded them to Wright, as copies are on file in the Frank Lloyd Wright Archives. Among his "critics": Erich Mendelsohn (architect), Walter Curt Behrendt (architect), Adolf Behne (architect), Adolph Donath, Paul Schmidt, Franz Dulberg Fechter, Max Deri, Richard Biebrzhnski, Otto Riedrich, Willy Ganske, Carl Meissner, Oscar Bie, F. Meunier, Max Osborn, Robert Scholz, Siegfried Scharfe, and F.A. Dargel.

CONCERNING SKYSCRAPER

Wright abhorred the skyscrapers being developed in crowded urban centers such as New York City. As promulgators of rent income, the tall buildings enslaved their occupants; placed in close proximity to each other, skyscrapers reduced the streets around them to a dark, cavernous series of alleys. This article, never published, criticizes these skyscrapers. Later, in his design for Broadacre City (1934), Wright offered his own solution to the skyscraper and its uses for humanity: "This type of structure would enable many to go to the country with their children who have grown so accustomed to apartment life under serviced conditions that they would be unable or unwilling (it is the same thing) to establish themselves in the country otherwise. These prismatic metal and glass shafts riding from the greenery parks in which they would stand would be acceptable units in the Broadacre City. Many of the advantages of the countryside could still go to them."[1] Wright continued his thesis on the skyscraper some twenty-six years later, when he wrote: "A tall building may be very beautiful, economical, and desirable in itself—provided always that it is in no way interference with what lives below, but looking further ahead than the end of the landlord's ruse—by inhabiting a small green park. That is humane now. The skyscraper is no longer sane unless in free green space."[2] [Unpublished essay, 1931]

MY DEAR NATION:
Speaking of the skyscraper—why sentimentalize over a silhouette? Why thrill with the glint on an aluminum erection?

Why not recognize the glint on gloom?

Look at the thing—not as it says it is or as it would like to be, but see the thing as it is—an unethical monstrosity. A robber, going tall to rob the neighbors. Were the neighbors to go tall, too, all would be worthless because all would be stalled. Dead. No thrills. The thing has the same "picturesque" as has any piling up of wreckage by way of blind forces. To admire, you must forget what is happening to humanity. This space-enclosure to the "Big Buddha"—otherwise the banker's mantrap is rooted in greed. It rises regardless of human life or human scale to impose exaggeration on a weak animal. To keep it on him by persuading him it is his own "greatness" is no good. The herd instinct of the human animal is easy to exploit. The deserted agrarian areas of the United States testify to that. And this tall monument to the white-collarite is also testimony.

No, as a minor point, skillful engineering in-

Century of Progress, Skyscraper (Project). Chicago, Illinois. 1931. Elevation. Pencil and color pencil on tracing paper, 36 x 27".
FLLW Fdn#3103.002

side and stone draped on it outside by the architectural-tailor is not architecture except by grace of such sentimentality for lies as has "built" the Nation to a standstill.

Cathedral? All the little houses round about the cathedral each itself trying to be a cathedral? And the Nation! Tell the super millions to go back home and get to work on their human inheritance.

1. Frank Lloyd Wright, *The Disappearing City* (New York: William Farquhar Payson, 1932), see p. 71 of this volume.
2. Frank Lloyd Wright, *The Living City* (New York: Horizon Press, 1958), p. 52.

I WILL

In 1931, in a talk at Town Hall in New York City, Wright proposed three designs for the pending 1933 Chicago World's Fair, an exposition officially titled "A Century of Progress." He described a skyscraper, a series of floating barges on Lake Michigan, and a group of glass and steel pavilions. Each was meant to be a permanent construction, to continue functioning after the fair closed. These were entirely impromptu descriptions that he then recorded as architectural designs in his studio. This ability to create with such spontaneity, clarity, and finality was one of the marks of his genius. The ideas outlined here were also later incorporated into his autobiography. Objecting to the "architectural fakery," as he wrote, that the fair organizers were bound to commission, he sent this criticism to the Chicagoan *magazine. [Published in the* Chicagoan *magazine, May 23, 1931]*

MY LANCE IS FREE.

But I did feel at the Town Hall meeting in New York that I should not criticize the next fair unless I had something better in mind. So, spontaneously, for the listeners on that occasion I built three fairs that might properly be called modern and got myself so interested that soon designs for the three will be published—caption: "Three Chicago Fairs for One"—because I believe all three could be realized for the cost of the next one.

Constructive criticism is fair criticism?

This publication is rebuke to the all-too-happy smile European Modern Architecture is indulging because a few lucky—or unlucky—American eclectics are all afraid of ideas, all in a huddle over "a cross-section of something or other"(the phrase is the eclectics). With plenty of room for individuality, if the huddle is sure individuality is without originality.

Why another fair as a foolish endeavor to prove that the nineteenth can not yet be the twentieth century in architecture?

Why again show the old Columbian fair with its face lifted—if not its seat saved—in the name of progress?

The fountain, the lagoon with a couple of miles of buildings wrapped around it, terraces more than ever and more shrubs in tubs, more fake mass-architecture, this time Babylonian.

Why, by way of the skyscraper-minded (mark the progress?) is the old Chicago fair next time going to "look more like New York seen from one of its own high buildings"? (The fair's own fair-language). This done by the skyscraper-pilots, adding a few more decks—swapping stairs for ramps and ordering many—so very many cheap elevators. But since we all have her to look at—anyway, temporarily—why build a fair to imitate New York? It is easy to out-new New York?

What progress this? And how fair?

I submit that face-lifting in architecture does not make Modern Architecture. Modern Architecture is young architecture—thought-born and thought-built—less expensive—even for a fair—than sham.

So, why in the name of Progress does Chicago make more ensemble of fake-mass-architecture falsified to Babylonian, just to "impressively" interfere with the interesting individual exhibits expected to pay for it. It looks too much the way the same sort of thing sounds over the radio nowadays, only the other way around: instead of the advertising interfering with the music, the architecture interferes with the advertising.

Why advertise with the same economic crime to get the same ugly civic kickback we already know so well.

Why more of the architectural fakery that is another curse of the same stripe of culture that has sickened us in five or six failures heretofore, no matter how fancy its new "vest" or "up-lifted" its equivocal face.

And, why it is so hard to get sensible Americans interested for the seventh time in that old fair just because it is to have a more constrained (strained) smile due to plastic surgery is not so hard to see—except as they may come on in from the country on a load of poles or—"something or other."

The old fair killed architecture for America. The next one will bury the corpse. Organic architecture may then flourish on American ground.

I hope.

Hall of Science, Chicago World's Fair (Paul Phillipe Cret, architect). 1931–1933. Hedrich-Blessing photograph, courtesy the Chicago Historical Society

CHARACTER IS FATE

Although submitted to Cosmopolitan *magazine in October 1932, this article was never published. It scourges the capitalistic system in a way that led many Americans to accuse Wright of being "un-American." Nothing could have been further from the truth. Wright certainly condemns the system:*

> *I look upon the late unpleasantness we like to call "depression" . . . as really the end of an epoch. I believe the best thought has left capitalistic centralization rampant to die of its own habit and is flowing into channels more normal to the life of the human being.*

But he also offers a glimmer of hope for the future:

> *And if by chance, or grace of whatever gods there may be, we should ever again have a statesman in this country he would be the architect of a social order that would be a fit basis for the architecture that is going to give new and more livable form to our homes, forms that will express a broader and better life than we have known.*
>
> *[Unpublished essay, 1931]*

IN THE SAME SENSE THAT CHARACTER IS FATE, THE FUTURE is the present in this machine-age civilization that is making the city into a triple slum, lower slum, middle slum, and scum: the skyscraper meantime jumps from pig-pile to pig-pile some more. To make money more grand. Notwithstanding this degradation, our future is being modeled out of our present by the extraordinary mechanical leverage we call the machine—become so ordinary that we forget, if ever we knew, what the thing means.

We have seen a gambling, capitalistic autocracy blind drunk with vicarious machine power as a consequence. The Romans were similarly drunk but with manpower. And as, out of machinery, we are able to create nothing but more machinery so we will fail as the Romans fell: gambling on science to save us all at the last.

No, I look upon the late unpleasantness we like to call "depression" (as we call wiping out the buyer's equity in what he buys, "re-possession") as really the end of an epoch.

I believe the best thought has left capitalistic centralization rampant to die of its own habit and is flowing into channels more normal to the life of the human being.

An entirely new set of ideas, more organic

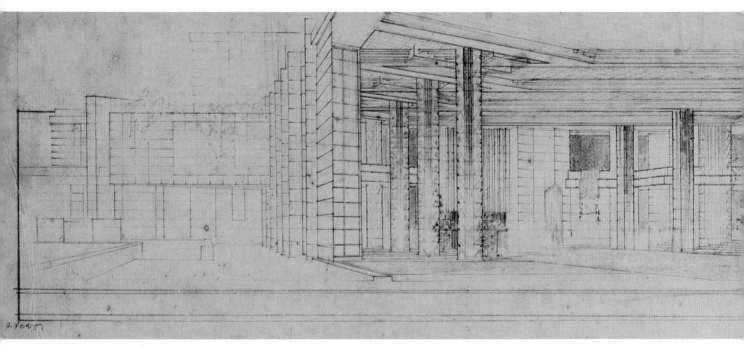

San Marcos in the Desert (Project). Chandler, Arizona. 1927. Lobby perspective. Pencil and color pencil on tracing paper, 23 x 6". FLLW Fdn#2704.051

than those of the era now in anguish, are being prepared for a coming era to enable the use of such by-products of accelerated centralization as are worth having for man—just as the past era used man as a by-product.

The systems and practices of the passing era nor even the ideals that made them and gave them right of way—will be buried overnight. But when the most vital thinking of the day has left them, these systems and practices only take time to die.

"The machine"—as economy or leverage, as even the enamored Russians have recently awakened to declare—is for man, not man for the machine. So Russia, too, is in time, as we may not be in time, to realize that all values are human values or must lack validity whatsoever.

Big corporate business and machine worship has all but wiped out human values. So big corporate business itself will be wiped out and the human habitation as a "home" will become the just "center" of human interest once more. Individual homes will be the only centralization that democracy will tolerate because any rational interpretation

of that ideal must mean exactly that.

But we have come by new ways and means in our machinery to enable us to make the supreme home superlatively useful and make that usefulness beautiful. Machinery will place a good home within reach of everyone.

Do not imagine the landlord is going to be allowed to "handle" the new home of the new era as he has handled the old one in the era that is passing. There will be no chance for the new one in his hands. But to tell why would be too long a story.

At the moment it is enough to know that in spite of him human habitation is about to find new forms and a new effectiveness. I know we can't have a great architecture while it is only for the landlord. I know we must have architecture out of the man and for the man and we may have it by way of such modern improvements as machinery has already made or will soon be making or we will go spiritually bankrupt. I know these new forms which will bear the same relation to the old as a sunlit strand to cave will be more delightful than pseudo-Tudor or pseudo-classic or Camden-gothic or Mediterranean

or anything the Colonials had with them when they came over. I know they will be more satisfying than the commonplace elegance we cherish now between a cellar and an attic. Modern houses are going to have as genuine an enclosed space significance as they had as sculpture in Greece and Rome.

Compare a streamlined motorship of the line with the Spanish caravel in which Columbus managed to get here and you will be making the comparison that will be just as valid between the modern home and the popular one of the fifty-seven periods. You will be able to drive a motorcar up to the new house and not spoil the picture. You can't do that to the fashionable ones now if you are sensibly eye-minded. These new houses will be modernistic? No, because modernistic, too, is just another kind of style-mongering. There would be but little progress in that. Organic? That they will be! And individual, too, notwithstanding the fact that severe limitations will be natural to any freedom the house will know in its method of production.

And, speaking of production, I don't believe big corporations are going to turn out these modern homes in toto as Henry turned out the busy Model T. The American people are too much themselves to buy them. But when real architects design the machine-made houses they will have such benefit of machinery as will make them more useful, infinitely more reasonable and appropriate to the life we love to live than even the ones our proficient decorators designed and that this new house will supplant as architecture.

When we come to understand architecture as the essential nature of all harmonious structure we will see that it is the architecture of music that inspired Bach and Beethoven, the architecture of painting that is inspiring Picasso as it inspired Vélazquez, that it is the architecture of life itself that is the inspiration of the great poets and philosophers. And if by any chance, or by grace of whatever gods may be, we should ever again have a statesman in this country he would be the architect of a social order that would be a fit basis for the architecture that is going to give new and more liveable form to our homes, forms that will express a broader and better life than we have known.

RAYMOND HOOD

The following two articles appear here for the first time in their entirety. In each, Wright continues his attack on the state of architecture in the United States. "Apology for the Decorator" harks back to his early articles of the 1890s, in which he wrote that his contemporaries all too often designed a house as a shell, papered and painted in the eclectic period tastes of the interior decorator.

His criticism of Raymond Hood, the New York architect, is a different matter, however. There is a certain tongue-in-cheek jocularity about it. Although they were in different camps, the two architects were good friends. During the mid-1920s Hood once asked Wright, "Frank, what do you do when you get to the top of the building?" This was at a time when the tops of skyscrapers had little, or grand, architectural monuments at the top—mock temples, arches, cupolas, shimmering art-deco chrome turrets. Wright simply replied, "Just stop, Ray—cut it off!"

When Hood died in 1934, Wright remarked, "Ray Hood was a good egg. Architecture needs about ten first-class funerals of the higher-ups more than it needed his."[1] [Unpublished book review, 1931][2]

AS AN ARCHITECT, RAYMOND HOOD, THE SUBJECT OF A second Whittlesey House brochure is a type of the designing partner; and his work is a symbol of what is the matter with architecture in the United States.

"Ray" himself is another matter. I am criticizing his attempts at picturesque architecture, partly because I have heard him say he wanted criticism of architects to be made by architects.

Well, here is one, regarded as an architect in certain circles, about to read the "language" Hood uses and look at the work called Hood's for what it seems worth, with no unfriendly feeling toward Ray but I am, by birth, training and conviction hostile to the Hood-type of "architect" and to his work as "architecture."

And I began making no secret of this, whatever, when the Tribune Building happened to be built, as Raymond Hood, himself, well knows.

The language of the "designing partner" of Howells, himself a designing partner and the designing partner of Mr. Godley and now Mr. Fouilhoux—

as might be expected—is language chiefly with an eye on the ear of the "prospect."[3]

For instance: Purport 1: Architecture is a "product" which Mr. Hood "analyzes" as possessing properties of "maximum usefulness, adequate strength and durability—all combined with considerations of obsolescence."

His architecture, then, he confesses is a "product" on a par with pots and pans—combined with a sense of when they are worn out? Good sense. But architecture ends, for him, then, where it should only begin. It should begin as pots are pots and pans are pans.

And he says: "*It can be no more than this.*"

Purport 2: "Every kind of building comes within the scope of this concept." And having just said, "architecture can be no more than this," he immediately jumps to the assumption that "contemporary architecture is disclosed and established as 'logic.'" In which case I do not see how Mr. Hood makes sense when he builds or can build when he makes sense.

Purport 3: Defining architecture in general, his advocate Mr. North[4] avers, "Mr. Hood believes it to be a business of manufacturing" and that Hood has "exemplified this belief in a convincing manner by his work." He doesn't say manufacturing what. But by what Mr. Hood says as well as by what he has done, I am myself convinced, with Mr. North, that this "business of manufacturing" when it comes to "effects" is true of him and of his work. But I, for one, would hesitate to take that view as significant of modern architecture. Building on that basis would be neither modern nor architecture.

Purport 4: Again, Mr. North assuring us that Mr. Hood "maintains an open mind, ever ready to study and adopt new ideas if practicable and appropriate." Being willing to adopt (or adapt, I suppose) whatever may be shown to him as worth his while; "always according a courteous consideration of the opinion of others, he exercises a freedom of opinion that is indicated in his work."

But I fail to see what all that has to do with having ideas himself or with any creation of his own. This language may mean, probably does, that R. H. exercises a freedom of choice as to whatever R. H. sees and hears in the words and works of others as most useful to R. H. and he appropriates them, as indicated by R. H.'s work?

Purport 5: Concerning the rampant New York "success standard." This, of course, is well aimed at the ear of the landlord: "The *success* of a building is measured by the degree of satisfaction to its occupants— and if it pays—and if it is acceptable to the public."

"Architectural ability," so Mr. Hood goes on to say, "lies in the production of a 'successful' building on these lines." We have here a certain feature of an architect's "ability," certainly. But again going a little beyond Mr. Hood, by these terms present popularity would be the test of all art. The intelligence of the purchasers or tenants today (they may not know what art is, but they know what they like) is not only "tomorrow" but it must be the horoscope and horizon of all art and architecture whatever. Apparently, in common with his landlord, Mr. Hood often mistakes such success for architecture. And, as contemporary thought runs, this mistake is good business—but only for a short time. This is the "quick turnover."

Purport 6: Concerning construction: "The several acceptable types of building construction," Mr. Hood goes on, "are those which provide for commercial contingencies." Because, he says, "no one can tell what is going to happen to the building." So, something like the sideboard converted into the folding bed seem to be the ideal here. Any landlord would like that, because as I gather from the language of this section of his "credo," construction should be "mixed"-up as much as possible. The more mongrel construction is, the easier it is to tear the building down, or to make it over into something else. This is the "expedient."

Thus sound engineering passes out, and the makeshift comes in to take its place.

This is one reason, I suppose, why Mr. Hood's "architecture" is designed to go on outside or on top of the construction in any style preferred by the client. It all has to come off again anyway.

Purport 7: In "publicity" as a feature of architecture Mr. Hood has a lively and timely interest. "Publicity" has influenced all his designs, he says. Expert in this, he cites examples of his success. All of which seems sensible expediency and might account in no small degree for his career.

"Magnitude" is such an advertising feature, it seems, and so are "hanging gardens," "meteorology" especially. And "height." Whereas I grew up in the belief that architecture might be great in the little and little in the great. But Mr. Hood talks somewhat like an advertising expert, who, somehow, got into architecture. And as the "contemporary thought" of which he speaks, runs, this is praise for him, not blame.

Purport 8: This is philosophical. "Logic and knowledge have always been the road to beauty." Thus the language. But if this is a true statement then Art is replaced by Science. The scientists replace the artists. And I say it serves the artists right. But I suspect they are being replaced by high-power salesmen.

Let Art look to herself if Beauty is really contemplating a divorce by way of "logic."

Purport 9: What R. H. here gleans from his experience with himself as "the ideal architect" must be satisfying to him, but dangerous is this language if he is still facing the client—"he possesses the spirit of creation, adventure, independence, determination, and bravery." Also, "a large measure of humanistic instincts." He is long on "ordinary common sense," which is the saving clause. Just the same, possessing all the others, R.H. leaves out important colors in the spectrum of the architect ideal: imagination and ability to create. But to the landlord that would only render the architect suspicious.

Purport 10: Color. Mr. Hood has discovered—speaking of color—that "striking effects may easily be obtained in this way." He says, "applied with taste startling advertising effects may be created." But he does get around to mentioning that "the architect should be limited by proper consideration of form, proportion, and color." This last from Owen Jones's *Grammar of Ornament*.[5] No less good on that account, but medicine to be taken more seriously by Mr. Hood himself I should think after looking at progress-fair sketches.

"Architecture"? Well, in all this, so far as I can see, architecture itself is still a "purport" waiting outside. It has been and is to be dealt with as an "outside."

The language of the peroration concerns habit. And I find myself wholly in accord now, as at no other point. I have written the same screed on "habit" myself.

Leaving this opportunist language of salesmanship—and getting down to performance. First the Tribune Tower: he does not dare omit to mention it as exemplar. "Constructed of stone" from him must be misquoted. Surely he saw the building standing there splendidly naked in steel before they began to hang Hood and Howells' Gothic terra-cotta drapery[6] all over it?

This "conception" (Gothic stonework for steel buildings) Mr. Hood says, "was considered generally appropriate." Logic where art thou now!

Second: "Mr. Hood," so Mr. North says, "employs latitude in materials and in designing." For instance, terra-cotta imitating stone, stone imitating feudal masses over steel framing, etc. This "latitude" as to design is evident in the camouflage at Ossining;[7] wherein a clumsy clump of domestic and private buildings is thinly veiled with pink camouflage, the attempted veil publicly aggravating what might otherwise have passed for mere private indiscretion. Where is the "public" now?

Third: Many too many bridges to Manhattan.[8] We see here in this Hooded dream, huge skyscraper frames masquerading as huge blocks of masonry cut off

from their moorings, at the street level, to walk a tightrope across two rivers, taking the traffic problem right along with them. My contemporary Hood's logic is now what? Sheer travesty, I say. And here hangs, clear, the apotheosis of all pictorial building like Raymond Hood's. And here, unfortunately, is what this pragmatic advertising language means when we get down to actual performance. Yes, "expediency" hangs, but clean, in this voluntary caricature and shows what is the matter with so-called American architecture.

But, trying to steal the rivers and rent them for residence purposes, ought to appeal to the Hoodish landlord. But, if "courteous to the ideas of others," Mr. Hood should acknowledge Charles Morgan of Chicago who thought of stealing the river first, and stole it much better.

Unhappily any architect, once grown accustomed to the ethics of ghost-building and grave-robbing, grows careless if not utterly callous when he comes to helping himself to origins still living. He sees in them not a tradition, but he does see a "crib."

The illustrations jump thus, over page to page, from Gothic imitation, or ghost-building, to mildly modified jumbo-classic, or grave-robbing, to suddenly take a heavy header into blood and thunder mass as "modernism." This last opportune eclecticism, advertised as "modernistic," seems to me as gratuitously false as it is premature. But it may be only the eclectic's "independence, determination, adventure, and bravery" getting the better of "common sense" by way of the "humanistic instincts," after all.

Being myself born in, trained in, and having lived all my life in what we have turned to, over page, as Mr. Hood did overnight—modern building—I believe it is not only indiscreet on his part, but impossible—his eye on the "public"—for him to build good buildings by way of his latest fortuitous election on his part. Architecture must be born, not made. It grows slowly. Unfortunately there is not yet enough modern architecture ready-made to go around the eclectic's circle. Then what shallow effrontery for a man—clever and popular as Raymond Hood is clever, or I should not be criticizing him here—to suddenly seize it for show purposes and self-advertising.

I know by the internal evidence of Hoodish language, no less than by the way Hood does what he does, that he cannot know what organic architecture is as distinguished from any other kind except as to classifying certain effects as desirable or undesirable appearances. Nor do I believe he nor his "scuola" feels it necessary to care what it is. Were it expedient (R.H. would say practical), he would build a Gothic church tomorrow. He would build a classic temple for any purpose if such were opportune. He would build anything a likely client wanted, and so he is the beaux-ideal architect. In other words, architecture, Beaux Arts or Modern, to Raymond Hood, is just one more expediency.

Architecture to his kind is not rooted in his unconsciousness as a spiritual conviction for which he would suffer defeat and fail, if need be. But modern architecture must be a feature of "success" as his apostasy now, alone, would indicate. And there are as many like him as there are eclectics engaged in designing pictorial prevarication in the name of advertising; the Chicago show which now illustrates a page or two of the brochure under consideration is a case in point. But the design of this "eclectical" group, such as it is, by no means can be considered by R.H. in any sense, I believe, except as the curate's egg—"in the worst parts." That is to say—after deducting the original sources of inspiration.

Such expedient exploitation, for self-seeking advertising of the "the cause of an organic architecture" is why I am hostile to Raymond Hood as an architect.

A good fellow in company, and with charm, he is in architecture, however charming, a liar, a cheat, and never sincere. He stands for most of what I have openly fought against all my life. Have I fought the flu-flu bird (he flies backward because he doesn't care where he is going, just so he can see where he has been), to find the cuckoo on the nest?

No one born and bred eclectic can become a modern architect, in any practical application of the exacting term, overnight if, indeed, he ever can be one. An eclectic would not be capable of more than mere exploit of some original.

But "big business" cannot be asked or expected to go beyond expedience in these more or less serious matters of culture. They may be entirely beside the point. The fads would seem to indicate that they are. So I won't say that the Raymond Hoods may not serve a useful purpose, were they content to pass for what they are. But they aggravate the impotence of our tragic situation in architecture when they clown or indifferently pretend their expediency to be the real thing itself and pass it off as genuine in their "jobs": to the cause of architecture their value is as much less than little as their makeshift pretension is recklessly followed by others when opportunity comes to advertise by way of more imitation and more caricature. That is where the whole eclectic-imitation thing goes rotten—"lousy," to use Mr. Hood's favorite aphorism.

Architecture can be no form of expediency whatever. Architecture is "pot and pan" only as pots are pots and pans are pans. And it is self-advertising only as one of the lowest attributes of its character; a misfortune into which it has fallen due to our commercial circumstances.

Any good architecture is the genuine expression of the realities of life by way of genuinely practical building. The integrities spiritual, mental, physical are the stake of architecture, not the pretensions and lies of life that make money to make life lie "smooth."

And finally let me express the belief that in our country such architecture and architectural careers as Raymond Hood's—and we have hardly any other kind—are only proof of how shallow is any demand for integrity of any kind in this culture we have made impotent by way of too much "good taste," and too little honesty.

Wherever principle concerns a purpose, career will always be a poor substitute for creation where life is concerned.

1. Frank Lloyd Wright, letter to Paul Frankl, August 20, 1934.
2. Raymond Hood, *Raymond M. Hood* (New York: McGraw Hill, 1931).
3. John Mead Howells (1868-1959) invited Hood's collaboration in the 1921 Chicago Tribune Tower competition, which they won (Howells & Hood). Hood worked with Frederick Godley and Jacques Andre Fouilhoux on several projects from 1924 to 1931 (Raymond Hood, Godley & Fouilhoux; later Hood & Fouilhoux).
4. Arthur Tappan North, New York architect and associate editor of *The Architectural Forum*. North wrote the foreword to the 1931 book *Raymond Hood* published by McGraw-Hill.
5. Owen Jones's *Grammar of Ornament*, published in 1856, illustrated historic styles.
6. The Gothic reference in the Howells and Hood entry was explicit both in the terra-cotta ornamental design of the building as well as in the flying buttresses making the transition from the lower vertical block—of modern steel construction—to the tower above. Wright deplored what he saw as the dishonest use of modern methods and materials; in this case, the sheathing of a modern building in "feudal" garb.
7. Possibly a reference to Hood's design (with Howells) for *Daily News* publisher Joseph Medill Patterson (1930) in Ossining.
8. Presumably a reference to Hood's 1929 "Manhattan 1950" design for huge skyscraper bridges with setback housing blocks spanning the rivers of New York City.

APOLOGY FOR THE DECORATOR

[Unpublished essay, 1931]

OVER THE GINZA SHOP IN TOKIO,[1] IN GLARING GILT LETTERS, a foot high on a black background, I saw the sign "In And Out Decorator." Next door was the sign "Shimidzu, Fashions Maker." And in smaller gilt letters on the glass entrance door, "Ladies have fits upstairs."

It was not the fashion maker but the "In" decorator I had in mind in this apology I am forcing upon him. He is doing too well in these United States on account of his running mate, the "Out" decorator.

A recent drive across the country from Los Angeles to New York convinced me that the country was 97 percent the decorators' in one form or another wherever culture persisted—such is madame's "taste." Now, for the sake of argument: of course, from any standpoint of an organic architecture, the decorator as such and "as is," has no right to exist.

And the apology I offer for the "In" decorator is the architect, himself the "Out" decorator.

Because the architect is not what he ought to be, the decorator "as is" is what he is. And the "In" decorator per se as such has risen and flourishes as a culture in the building world to supply the architect's defects. In fact it is the architect himself who is the "Out" decorator, in more ways than one. So,

"In and Out," it is the "decorator" who has done the country.

No . . . the "In" decorator could not exist unless the architect had become merely an "out and out" decorator. If the architect were creative and went clear through with his work to button at the back there would be no place for the so-called "decorator" as we have him, or her, or it, now.

It was a bad day for our culture when it became thus reduced to a matter of applied taste. It was a worse day and woeful "waste" when an outside for the thing we call life got well set up in business, and an inside for the thing got set up separately in business.

But, face it! That is the kind of culture we've got or that has got us by way of madame and her decorators.

As these rival decor establishments make the most of our cultural defects, I blame the architects.

If they were good, culture might have, by now, a soul of its own.

They are not good. The "Out" is satisfied with a picturesque outside on anything either in periods, commas, semi-colons—or well—what have you? Someone has to pictorialize the inside of the architect's buildings after he has pictorialized the outside?

Meet the Interior Decorator. He will make all habitable and charming by way of the arts and crafts, such as they are.

So the interior decorator or "In" is a lapse of the architect or "Out."

Now by simple working of a law of nature, so much nearer and more useful to the life involved is the interior decorator than the architect, that on the terms of the architect's "appliqué outside" the interior decorators "appliqué inside" is getting just as capable of doing the outside too and he often does it, and does it as well, or better. It is the natural consequence of the circumstance of "applied taste."

And throughout the country from coast to coast and from wet-line North to wet-line South the inside man can now develop the whole "appliqué" establishment and deliver it to "madame" in any style she selects. The "In" can hire draughtsmen and engineers just as well as the "Out" can?

Madame is the milk in the decorator's coconut and the riot of madame's taste is thus encouraged and gratified. But there is just a blankety-blank-blank hole where a genuine culture, if we had any at all, would demand architecture as a genuine expression of our own life. Culture as thoroughbred instead of culture as mongrel.

I submit, that "In and Out Decorator" applies with particular force and good reason to all we can call American Architecture, as things are. I think I can prove it, after this little story and its plans are unfolded.

So why, any longer, the deceptive division between "in" and "out," without any real distinction? Why the outside man and the inside man?

Why not, Ladies and Gentlemen—both "In and Out" get together?

Since by way of the architect himself architecture has thus come to be 97 percent a matter of madame's taste, or an applied matter of her taste, I see no reason why the interior decorator can't thrive outside by extending his establishment a little or perhaps taking in the architect on some partnership basis for the sake of such technical knowledge as the architect may happen to have. The difficulty with the scheme is that such technique as the architect doesn't possess, the contractor would as soon deliver to the "In" as to the "Out." And it might be enough. In

which case, where would the architect be?

But, the contractor aside, were this merger effected, we would then have but one type of establishment to support. Overheads might be cut. Also wasteful interferences with this business of getting the country "dressed up" for a part—or a funeral.

What does it matter?

Yes, the architect is a decorator.

Well, the decorator is such an architect?

And more, for the sake of more argument, how are you going to divide the spoils without constant trouble unless by some such merger as I here propose? What discounts, eligibility, etc., etc.

The merger would be more honest and make madame more profitable to all concerned. She is not so profitable now, by and large. Decorators, both "Out" and "In," are all poor in several senses but for a streak of luck—now and then in her exuberance—her extravagance. . . .

I respectfully submit that the only question as the matter stands between "In" and "Out" at present is, which is whose? and whose is which? And the nice question gives rise to some pretty bad acting and hard feelings. I have seen both, coming and going as I have travelled. I remember a little incident in point. I was building the Dana house[2] in Springfield—I used to get down there from Chicago early enough in the morning for breakfast. We were sitting at breakfast this morning when the doorbell rang. Mrs. Dana went to the door—and I overheard—"I am so and so interior decorator from Chicago . . . (must have been on my train) a friend told me of your new house and I thought we might do your interior for you." Brightly and pleasantly, "By the way, who is your architect?" Mrs. Dana said, recklessly, "Frank Lloyd Wright."

"Oh!" came back, cold and short.

Mrs. Dana said he lifted his hat, but I heard him say "good bye" in the tone employed in the slang "good night" of that period. I heard the gate slam as he went on his way. Those were parlous times.

But it is easier now to commercialize the present product on its own basis of applied taste, outside or inside, and specialize no further than at present. In fact were the merger effected all the parts would soon be interchangeable. The commercial ideal of the age thus attained. "Service" improved.

Why not then begin the work of merging the architect or "Out" with the decorator or merging the decorator or "In" with the architect?

It is the only hope I see for the continued commercial success of the popular architect as he runs. Otherwise he is doomed.

Now, with proper apologies for this desperation—my turn to desecrate—to all of you, really this is not so far-fetched or fantastic a picture of the present situation between architect and decorator as it exists in our country?

The architects, of course, won't admit it except as the curate admitted his egg to be, "good in parts."

The decorator knows it but is afraid to admit it except when the architect is not looking and he thinks he is not listening.

Well, what is to be done?

I have offered the architect as the apology for the present ascendancy of the decorator. The decorator could not put him out if he would, but he should be grateful to the poor architect and take him into the business.

This magnanimity would be the first step toward clearing the ground for the slow growth of an organic architecture. I say "slow growth" because this matter of an organic architecture is no get-rich-quick business at all, nor an overnight, or "during the night" turnover. This organic ideal and this ideal of an organically qualified architect are the only means that can fundamentally change the existing situation at all. The only means that can effect the desired merger by more natural methods than the commercialization I have just, half-seriously, suggested. But if methods are noncommercial, slower methods—and they are—the results would be profound and permanent.

But the more I see of the popular transformations constantly taking place in the applied "styles" we have already had, the more I see that madame herself is out of hand, as another natural sequence of appliqué, and regardless of any decorator is going to be supplied with whatever she likes by way of the department stores, even if the "In and Out" decorators were to get together soon. It is too late to "head her off." Her head is hers. You see this captious matter of applied taste is after all—naturally a free for all. It has no organic base or character or rhyme or reason, or sense or knowledge or even science.

It is, by now, nearly impossible to imbue madame with any coherent ideal or deepen her understanding while the license of eclecticism runs riot as decoration in the place of architecture. "She" was hopelessly demoralized by her experts at the beginning. It is too late to turn to stop her now. And the great difficulty in saving either her from herself or saving her from her experts, or saving her experts from her, lies in the simple disconcerting fact that the necessary desire for creative art and architecture is in the nature of an inner experience. It is a depth of culture.

Genuine serious culture alone can make that deeper desire for creative life a fact and make it a factor in our coming factorialization of the universe.

So what hope of culture in this deeper organic sense in this crass, pretentious, and yes—utterly commercialized competition for madame's capricious, unfounded—confounded—ignorant "taste"?

Were the decorators to conclude to acquire culture and make the attempt to educate her as things are, they would educate themselves out of the job they themselves made of her, the job they have now learned well how to sell. Were the architects seriously to acquire genuine culture and attempt to educate her, as things stand, they would be educated out of their job *tout de suite* by the interior decorators who would be just as quick to cater to madame as they have ever been. It is only necessary, now, to give the lady what she wants or "steer" her a little.

Yes . . . there is no use blinking the fact: if we had this deeper culture the whole system would change, and probably a new type of individual would appear in the general abolition of commercial degeneracy in the arts to take the matter away from both the "In" and "Out" decorator and by way of awakened integrity put it all up to a regenerate architect. An architect that had no sense of outside as distinguished from inside, knowing where both come from and how they are each of each other.

Then, such "decorative" talent as we now have, employed in both "In" and "Out" fields, would be released to industry.

Would that be such a bad outcome for all concerned?

It might be a little hard on industry at first. But such undoubted talent as I confess the decorator possesses would soon be at home in that fundamental field. The decorator would become a determinator—integrated and happy.

I believe that outside the few individuals really capable of educating madame to look beneath the decorated surface of her present life nearly all our present undoubted talent and skill in decoration should be drafted—into industry. I genuinely admire this undoubted talent and, often, I myself envy this extraordinary skill. It should be at work making the things that madame buys at the department stores, making them worth buying and making them worth having, while those, competent and willing, are helping to make her worthy of having such things. This important work in the industrial field should not be left to France and our industry left to prostitute to imitation of French models as it is at present, and decoration left to consist in merely assisting madame to choose between the imitations of these models—and combinations of them. The decorators should go to work on the general source of supply and let madame vegetate or gravitate or oscillate for a time in a quandary of her own, while education prepares to save her soul alive. She herself should go to school. How many decorators are fit for the task of saving her soul alive in such schools would depend on how many now had souls of their own, alive.

Judging from what I've seen in the various quarters of this activity I should say there would be a good many such. Probably one-fifth of our decorators, interior or exterior, would be capable of rising above the current of eclecticism and really getting inside the thing to be done. If this more serious and creative fifth were to get in touch with each other by way of common sense, and begin to work on madame, and with her, while the remaining four-fifths were digging into industry—something

might happen that could never be called by so shallow a name as "decoration." Were madame left to shift for herself for a time, "taste" might decline to the point where a genuine life of our own might begin to revive by way of such natural integration as I propose.

But this is probably an impractical suggestion because now the commercial turnover on another appearance is already here. The eclectic spies another "style," and the turnover must be quick.

The amount of the American turnover in any case, on any style, is enormous.

The amount of money that passes through the hands of the surface decorator, "In" or "Out" in the course of a year in these United States is colossal. A staggering total. I do not know, nor does anybody, just what the total of millions is, but it is only fair to admit that it is nearly all spent with intent to make something beautiful. A picture of some kind is aimed at and often very pretty pictures result. This pretty picture is the poison of the future. This meretricious picture is the stumbling block on the path. The good-looking "picture" is about all architects as decorators or decorators as architects ever think about except the more and more important business of selling the picture to the inhabitant. Given enough over-stuffing and cushions and free floor space the pictures can be made habitable and, as we all know quite generally, though incongruously, they are inhabited.

For instance, take the modernistic "picture." It is, not yet, the least expensive picture—but it is, at the moment, the quick "turnover."

Madame has been through the "great" styles pretty well backward and forward these past thirty years. This new appearance seizes her.

The decorators seize this new appearance as it has seized her. But the new appearance, originally, was the countenance of an organic simplicity founded by rational thinking, founded on principles well in hand in our own country.

The look of the new thing got abroad to become even more emphasized to look at, and our decorators seeing it at the Paris exhibition first seriously noted it a "possibility."[3] The principles had got lost on the way abroad, but the Paris decorators made a good deal of the "look of the thing" in many very clever ways. By virtue of being "the fount of fashion" Paris was in a position to sell it to our "madame." She came back home, to its home, with the look of it in her eye. And soon our decorators saw the new appearance as "the handwriting on the wall."

Hundreds went modern overnight!

And now the "new appearance" has become the look of something few of the hundreds really know the meaning of at all. Few care to know. They take another appearance, *"fait accompli."*

There is a studio phraseology in decor circles that goes with the new appearance—talk of the machine and modernity. Various new aesthetics vie in the making, made to apply to more surface and mass effects. Soon another "style." The FACTORY supersedes the HEARTH! HEARTS become suction pumps—writing becomes staccato specification—but—decoration is still decoration.

The functioneer is here. But notwithstanding his rationalizing he is stuck "on the surface" no less than he was before he began to functioneer. Rather more stuck on the surface in fact. And from the position of vantage I occupy by virtue of having dug away at getting the principles established in actual work years ago, I see fresh demonstration of how unnecessary it is to know anything at all to be a tasteful decorator . . . "In and Out." I continue to see how an appearance is all an eclectic ever can see or will ever desire or, as things go, may ever need. But with discouragement I see and say too, a great good is going up in commercial exploitation once more by way of "studios" and plan-factories[4] and the same good old poison of madame's goddamn taste.

If the decor establishments inside and the plan-factories outside can do Mexicano, they can do modernistic?

And they all do. It is all that easy.

The discouraging thing to me, and I am sure to anyone who thinks at all, in this latest repetition by way of competition, is not that the new mode is here. In common with others I have waited long enough to see a more simple appearance in our country, but I have worked long for the end of sen-

timental make-believe for an organic simplicity.

But so far as any real grasp goes of the significance of such forms as modernism is taking—this hoped-for reality is more lacking in the modernistic "taking" than it was lacking in the other "takings."

The greater shame lies in this fact: that here at last is something really different; in this latest eclecticism America has something really to lose.

There was no principle at work in the great "styles" so far as our life went or goes and so not much to lose.

There is a principle at work behind the appearances from which the "modernistic" is deriving its "style." There is an underlying form that is appropriate to our age and life. Those underlying principles and forms can save the day for our art and industry only if decorators abandon desecration long enough to get down to these principles and learn the technique that is able to work them, independently.

The gist of the thing—the *geist*, let's say—that is so thoughtlessly copied and recklessly improvised as modernistic—is not, essentially, decoration at all. The gist of the thing is not decoration in the old sense either as plain surface cut to shape—or applied ornamentation. It is a way of life and thought and fine feeling that gets inside materials and conditions to get to work. It means no fixed style for America any more. That is centralization, and centralization is monarchianistic and dead. It means a man's own style is his very own. It means the integration that is enlightened democracy. And it means as many genuine significances for every line, plane, and pattern as there are individuals. The whole psychology of the eclectic who would again "stylize" the world is stagnation to what should and must give meaning and value to the modern. The modern, or young, must be seen as true integration without centralization of any kind or the machine is doom instead of destiny.

But, again the eclectic is "pseudo." This time "pseudo-modern." And, with no such intention, I am sure, he will temporarily destroy or greatly hinder the virtue of the *geist* of the modern as it was born and as it must continue to develop if it is to grow. As art and decoration it is only damned. As appliqué inside or appliqué outside for anything at all we make

Grouped Towers (Project). Chicago, Illinois. 1930. Perspective. Pencil on tracing paper, 29 x 20". FLLW Fdn#3001.001[1032]

with our hearts and hands, it is simply damnation.

I sometimes despair of seeing any great expression of the great ideas that were originally back of this new appearance so long as present "Art and Decoration" sees it as a new style. The proposed Chicago Fair is an obvious instance in point. There the appearances are played with as a mere mask to be staged with theatrical lights to play upon the sensibilities of the ignorant.

I have conscientiously looked for one single use of the ideas that originally built such appearances as are extravagantly employed there for scenic effect. And I have looked in vain.

There is no single thought in it all that goes within to the spirit of the modern for relief or for honest expression.

Inferior in taste and sense even to the Columbian Fair with not so good an excuse for such superficiality—the proposed fair to advertise Chicago is the same but more inexcusable type of the old shallow make-believe.

So, if I am to be serious, and I have been serious and am now, with you to get inside the ideas that originally founded and promoted the modern appearance you now call "modernism." Foster these original ideas, even if decoration per se as such dies and the decorator per se as such—dies with it. He will be born again. Something finer and larger in spirit, firmer on its base will take place—in industry itself. And when that awakening takes place in industry, architecture will weave all the arts again into a consistent whole with the help of a regenerate and knowledgeable madame.

The architect will no longer be apology for the decorator or his architecture be decoration. His work will apotheosize the life he serves. "Success" and "profit" will take on a new meaning for all concerned.

1. Wright used both spellings of Tokyo (or Tokio) throughout his life. Until the 1920s Tokio was probably the more common. These volumes reproduce the original spelling.
2. Susan Lawrence Dana house, Springfield, Illinois (1902).
3. Exposition International des Arts Decoratifs et Industrielle Modernes, held in Paris, 1925.
4. Wright defined "plan-factories" in the 1930 article "Architecture as a Profession Is All Wrong." He decried the "great corporate enterprise"—"broker-builders" who were taking over the architectural profession, bringing in young individuals to follow the company program and promote the firm rather than practice the noble profession of architecture.

Hillside Home School. Spring Green, Wisconsin. 1903.
FLLW Fdn FA#0216.0009

Classroom, Hillside Home School. Spring Green, Wisconsin. 1887. FLLW Fdn FA#8703.0009

THE HILLSIDE HOME SCHOOL OF THE ALLIED ARTS

The Hillside Home School, founded as an alternative school by Wright's aunts Jane and Ellen Lloyd Jones in 1886, was closed in 1915. However, the Lloyd Jones sisters extracted a promise from Frank Lloyd Wright: somehow he was to continue the work in education that they had carried on for many years in the school buildings he had built in 1902. Following their deaths, in 1917 and 1919, respectively, Wright acquired the property, partly in view of his promise not to let it fall out of the "family" and partly to protect his own property, Taliesin, which was situated on a nearby hill in the same valley.

For many years the closed buildings were vandalized. The diamond-patterned leaded glass windows were smashed, the roofs leaked in several places, and the floorboards rotted. But the main structure, built of hard sandstone and oak, withstood these ravages. By 1928 Wright and his wife, Olgivanna, decided to repair the damage and to reopen the school, which they renamed the Hillside Home School of the Allied Arts. Consulting with such academicians as Franz Aust, a landscape architect and professor at the University of Wisconsin, and Ferdinand Schevill, chairman of the History department at the University of Chicago, they garnered great enthusiasm for the school. It was even considered that the University of Wisconsin would act as sponsor.

The school curriculum was to feature architecture and to include painting, sculpture, pottery, glasswork, metalwork, dance, and drama, as well as history and philosophy. A long list of teachers and visiting lecturers was prepared. In 1931 a prospectus describing the program was sent out, but no financial support could be mustered for the project.

Although the Wrights then elected to abandon the idea, it would soon come alive again, in a much modified form, as the Taliesin Fellowship, which opened almost one year to the day after this prospectus was distributed.

An interesting feature of the original concept was the plan to offer for sale decorative objects and designs produced by the school, not unlike the practices of the Bauhaus, which opened in Germany in 1919. Wright was not one to turn his back on a good idea, and the notion of a school that served art and industry at the same time was most attractive to him. Further, he saw his own work and principles evolving—through education, training, and manufacturing—into a viable "market" through which he could exert a beneficial and lasting influence on the American arts. [Published brochure, The Hillside Home School of the Allied Arts, 1931]

Sporting activities (golf), Hillside Home School. Spring Green, Wisconsin. 1887. FLLW Fdn FA#8703.0014

WHY WE WANT THIS SCHOOL

AMERICA HAS PROVIDED INNUMERABLE SCHOOLS, ACADEMIC, vocational, or free in which to educate its children. Americans are proud of the results with good reason. America, too, has trade-schools and a few industrial schools of a more or less formal or sentimental pattern.

A minority report is needed at this psychological moment. It seems high time to plan for the superstructure we are to rear upon the elaborate educational preparations we have so expensively and laboriously made, from Kindergarten to University, for a past century or more.

We have no superstructure, that is to say no culture above the matters of behavior, commerce, industry, politics, and an unsure taste for objets d'art. It may even appear that the preparation or foundation was inadequate and in the wrong place.

We are a nation rich beyond the bounds, even of our own avarice, living in abundance with a creature-comfort undreamed of in the World before. We are ingenious, inventive, scientifically, commercially progressive and, as the whole World has occasion to know—uncreative.

We have had many sympathetic critics, some of them worthy of attention, who repeatedly and pointedly call our attention to this fact.

Nor will more than three-fifths of our people know what is meant by the assertion that the American is "uncreative." Another fifth would deny the allegation pointing to our magnificent machinery and scientific accomplishments to refute the charge.

About one man in a hundred would agree with the stricture and admit it. But he would apologize on the ground that we are a pioneering people, with a continent to make habitable and workable, while as a Nation we are digesting not the best elements of the Nationalities of the World.

Like the Chicago Captain of Industry at the dinner given C. R. Ashbee,[1] famous London Arts and Craftsman and architect, when Ashbee arrived in Chicago some fifteen years ago and criticized the City for its ugliness.

The Captain sat it out as long as he could, then got his feet under him to say that: "Ashbee may be right, Chicago isn't much on Culture now. . . maybe. But when Chicago gets after Culture, she'll make Culture hum."

But, as a matter of fact, "Culture" all the time is bound up with commerce and industry. Culture can't be made to "hum" at will "when we are ready."

Seriously inclined to "get after Culture" we'll find Culture ready to unfold naturally out of these everyday matters—commerce and industry. We will have Culture only when and because we want it enough to be patient and more generous of our other resources in that direction than it has yet occurred to our donors to be in memorializing themselves.

Culture is struggling as a minority report even now to get itself born for Americans. We call evidences of this struggle Modern Art. Out of everyday commonplaces in which we will soon excel all other nations, as things look now, our own Culture will be born. But it will not be seen as these commonplaces themselves, nor as anything much like them.

Meantime all America has borrowed from Europe what she had, readymade. She is still ready to buy the Modern readymade, at the moment, from France. But unless we will now "get after" Culture as this enlightened interpretation of our own and Modern, Culture will be long in coming, if it should ever come.

During thirty years past the United States has developed a system of taste for the Antique, which should teach her something now—and perhaps does.

But the entire country lives in little "picture" houses, little decorated plaster caverns patterned upon the transient stylistic periods that rose and marched and fell in the procession of time.

The shame of thus giving ourselves away as well as the folly are both becoming apparent, because European countries have, lately, shown us many things that were America's very own in point of Culture. Europe, herself profiting by them, has brought these very things which were thoughts, and deeds back here to start a fashion among us by way of our system of "taste." Our eclecticism.

Show us a new appearance and it is our habit to fashion appearances rapidly into a nation-wide cult in lieu of genuine culture.

A pity to let this original interpretation of the internal content of America's own Nature be commercially exploited by any such habit. Such exploitation of this original source would set American Culture back again another thirty years, at least. Perhaps poison its culture permanently.

Why not, then, take hold ourselves of this interior native content awaiting deliverance as Culture in our own minority report and ourselves gradually build with it a Nation where no commodity can hope for success except as it contributes not only to the ease and wealth of the Nation, but contributes as well to the integrity of the Nation considered as created for the spirit of Man—not merely for men.

We may then produce work outranking the products of the civilizations we copy. We copy them because we say, "a good copy is better than a poor original." Thereby falsely declaring to our shame, that we have no originals, and if we had they would necessarily be inferior.

To end this era of systematic "taste" by way of eclecticism the time has come when Art must take the lead in Education. Fundamental Education must enter this more subjective human field, wherein so many seeds or germs of indigenous culture have been struggling for recognition. But it must enter more humbly than in other fields, because what we seek is more simple at the same time that it is more subjective than in other fields. What we seek, now, is the soul of the thing itself.

The soul must be wooed if it is to be won. It cannot be *taught*. Nor can it ever be *forced*. To be more specific this means that the nature of our livelihood, commercial industry, both by machine and process, must be put into experimental stations where its many operations may come into the hands of sensitive, unspoiled students inspired by such creative artists as we can obtain to help them.

The very name for commercial industry as we know it in this country is the Machine.

America is yet the unqualified Machine, although recently its most outstanding success in a machine-way, had to stop his machine to get a little more of the thing we call "beauty" into his product. It is becoming axiomatic in Business, that "beauty pays."

Now to put the machine to any extent into young hands in any such practical and inspirational way as we have described may properly mean what is called a school.

To make this school an integral part of the great industrial system of America would be desirable, but it should not yet be a part of the present educational system. To keep the school free certain donors would have to be found to cooperate and contribute to the extent of say dollar for dollar with those immediately concerned in manufactures who would contribute funds or property or tools to the needed school.

To establish and put into operation in private hands a "Style-center" or experiment station of the character proposed would only mean that when those hands fell lifeless, the school might perish. So there is desirability or necessity of some foundation in perpetuity to insure to all contributors a reasonable continuance of the work.

The original donors of this foundation should elect the president of "Hillside Home School of the Allied Arts." (A suggestion for the name by which the school would be known, thus memorializing a worthy original.)

The funds of the School would be administered by a secretary and treasurer, appointees of this appointed president.

Although such a school would justify its existence were it to be written off as a total physical loss in three years, yet, were this desirable foundation effected, the raising of funds to any necessary extent to insure the life of the school for a half century or more should be easy to find to the extent of $250,000, the sum needed for the plan here outlined.

WHAT THE SCHOOL WE WANT WOULD BE LIKE

Naturally such a school would be an art-school but also a hive of industry in which all the arts, having by nature an architectural background, and so allied to industry would be at work.

Machines would be the tools of study, the machine meanwhile reacting upon design and the design acting upon the machine until both became more suited to each other. Valuable inventions and adaptation and simplification would be sure to result from such cooperation and inspiration.

The fine arts, so called, should stand at the center as inspiration grouped about architecture. Architecture properly understood (of which landscape and the decorative arts would be a division) should take direction. Another division Painting, another Sculpture, another Music, Drama and the Dance in their places as divisions of architecture. The fine arts thus grouped under architecture would stand at the center of the work for the purpose of inspiring designers for the various machinery-using crafts to interpretation in the making of useful machine-made things. The workers might then discover possibilities existing in the nature of the particular machines or processes in any particular craft and design work these particular processes or machines could better express. The tool would not only become more suited to the effects it might artistically produce, but new effects would be continually obtained.

So, in this new School of the Fine Arts, would serve machinery in order that machinery itself, in the future might honestly serve what is growing to be a beauty-loving and appreciative country now borrowing or faking its effects because it knows no better and has none other.

Architecture leading in this School would mean the study of the nature of materials and such systems of construction as get most out of both men and materials. Architecture in this School being that practical expression of contemporary life in terms of building best suited to each and every material, true to purpose, environment and materials. A comprehensive study of town-planning should go with such intensive Nature-study as this interpretation would mean. Painting, outside the Mural for Architecture and the abstraction seen as pattern would again mean interpretation. Architecture in terms of the process or print, all modern processes known to the modern publisher, as well as what is known as "painting" should receive special attention. Characteristic Printing and reproductive processes as they are at work would be in the school work.

Sculpture, as related to architecture and materials, would mean the bas-relief and inlay, sgraffito and fret, as well as play with light and shade in various mediums. Interpretation of form in terms of casting and various mechanical forms of "reproduction," therefore again Architecture.

Music would mean the fundamental study of sound and rhythm as emotional reaction both as to original character and present nature. Tone-weaving in general. Subsequently, tone and rhythm as the expression of human moods, and feelings—again the Nature-study that is Architecture.

Drama would be studied as the essential structure of all great Literature, and concerned primarily with the "patterns" of human Life—Architecture.

Dancing in this school would be actual cultivation of rhythm in the correlation of mind and body to make both together a perfect instrument. Dancing should be allied with the physical direction of the work done by the students in the buildings and the fields—as well as in itself a poetic form of expression.

Now, to bring all these matters in the sense of architectural interpretation properly into a school, artists truly creative in their work should and would either contribute their services as visitors or be drafted from all over the world as paid workers.

Artists have universally been waiting for a school of this character and the effort would be one to which they would surely and generously respond.

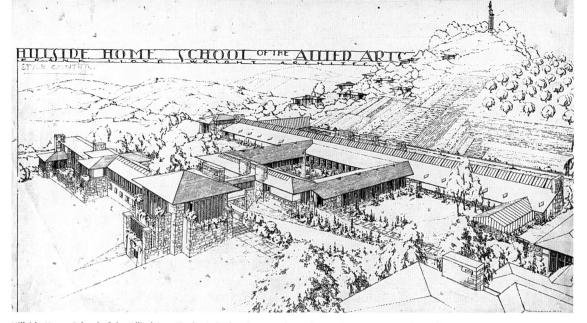

Hillside Home School of the Allied Arts (Project). Spring Green, Wisconsin. 1928–1931. Perspective. Ink on tracing paper, 20 x 13".
FLLW Fdn#2703.003

I am certain many of the greatest among the artists of the world would respond to any demand that might be made upon them, to any extent possible to them by such a school.

In addition and allied to the general inspirational architectural group would be—to start with, say seven branches of the industrial arts—glassmaking, pottery, textiles, the forge, casting in all materials, woodworking, sheet-metal working. Each of these branch-industries would, through contributions from various great successful enterprises out in the world of industry endow the craft represented, at least endow its own craft so far as the machinery needed to establish it as an experiment station at the school was concerned. Say these seven industries were to contribute the equivalent of $150,000 in machinery and plant for experimental purposes. These industrialists approving the foundation and president might contribute with the understanding that they would have first right to purchase from the school any design or processes that would originate in their particular branch of industry and also have the first right to draft the services of a competent worker developed by the school—if approved by the school director.

Manufacturers bringing their problem to the school might also have the research organization of the school available to them as well for special purposes of their own.

WHERE THE SCHOOL SHOULD BE AND WHY IT SHOULD BE THERE AND WHAT PRICE

The school site proposed is that of the Hillside Home School, formerly the Lloyd Jones Sisters' Coeducational Home School, which is falling into decay.

The beautiful grounds are located well into the country among the Southern Wisconsin Hills about an hour's drive on hard roads from the state capital. Such a school should be properly organized and directed, get its own living as far as possible from the ground itself.

So such a school should be a farm-school and should be none too easy of access. A certain isolation together with the necessity of labor out of doors are both indispensable to the Spirit and "morale" of work to be done indoors, if such work is to be *creative*. Physical property of the Hillside Home School is offered for this school-purpose with ten acres of ground for the sum of $25,000. The central building, a piece of modern architecture is alone worth five times the sum. The other buildings existing about this central building represent additional investment of about $50,000. Together with this ground and these buildings would go my own architectural services in making plans and superintending the completing of the plant proposed according to the accompanying design or one to be approved by the school organization.

To complete the plant as tentatively planned herewith and temporarily furnish the buildings, $90,000.00 would be needed for rehabilitation and new construction. For farm equipment, stock, machinery, refrigeration and tools—$7,000. Materials for use in the first year's work—$3,500. Fuel—the first year and light—$1,500.

Also a total required contribution from Industry would be needed for building purposes and building equipment of about $140,000. Machinery, furnaces and equipment to be contributed by Industry.

In addition to this initial contribution Industry might be asked to guarantee the first year's salary for the paid workers as herein before specified, but that sum could eventually be repaid by the school. Should donors be found to establish a foundation beneath these donations by Industry to match this outlay by Industry of say, $250,000, including plant and machinery there would be the interest of 6% on that sum or about $5,000 per year to help carry the deficit in salaries and operating expenses that would probably occur the first year and that income would be available, guarantee and extend the powers of the school each year thereafter as deemed advisable by the president and directors.

For the first year only, that sum would be required to meet a deficit because thereafter, the sales and services account of the school should swell this income. The school should soon have adequate funds for all experimental work and a constantly increasing residue. There should soon be a substantial profit to show on production.

There is no reason why an institution, small as this one would be, should not produce articles easily worth fifty thousand dollars a year above cost, as compared with the less favorably situated factories themselves. Each article would be of the quality of a genuine work of art, a missionary, and should therefore eventually bring a fair price as such.

And in return for this donation of a foundation fund of $250,000, the foundation would own, in perpetuity, the physical plant of the school and all its products, guaranteeing to the contributors from the various industries only that the purpose of the school should remain as herein described: That every effort would be made to keep the school as broad and free as the specifications herein for the individuals in charge would indicate, so that the school might be and remain the experimental school of the Free Spirit, in purpose and in deed.

WHAT THE SCHOOL WOULD PRODUCE

Only an item of $3,500—for temporary furnishing of the school is included in the foregoing cost of plant for the reason that only temporary furnishings would be required, and of the simplest character.

The workers themselves should design and make all of the furnishings of the buildings, and certain additions to buildings and repairs, of whatever nature and do the planting around the buildings. All pottery, furniture, textiles, ironwork, glassware needed in the furnishings should be the school's own making. The grounds should also be planted, graded, terraced, walled and gardened by the workers themselves.

This work should continue for several years and might go on for many more, better work being substituted for earlier work as that earlier work of the school might be included and sold in the sales and exhibitions, which should take place periodically—traveling from city to city throughout the country.

Above the time necessary—two hours each day for each worker—to carry on the physical work of insuring the living of sixty students and the resident group of paid workers themselves at the head of the school (say fourteen in number and two more in direct charge of student body and farm—adding to this number a reasonable allowance for the families of the paid workers—say in all 124 people)—there would remain to this entire working force of seventy-six people, seven hours per day, six days of every week to unite in producing power. This would represent a large well directed *creative power* with modern machinery to produce superior articles of every kind in the crafts, articles to be sold and exhibited. Sunday only would be visitor's day.

Thus belonging to the school would be each month a very considerable product of modern beautifully useful or usefully beautiful things ready for markets and influence. Stuffs, tapestries, table linens, new cotton fabrics, batik, with special emphasis on tapestries, table glassware, glass flower holders, lighting devices of glass, and glass dishes of all sorts, ashtrays, window glass, and glass mosaics, necklaces, decorative beads, and objects of glass.

Well-designed modern furniture of all kinds for all purposes.

Wrought-iron screens, light standards, light fixtures, gates, fire-irons, and tools. Light decorative forms in beaten metal to be enameled as jewelry and in which precious stones might be set. Enameled iron for various decorative purposes in house and garden.

Cast-iron and concrete sculpture for houses and gardens, special hardware, outdoor furniture, gates and doors, sheet-metal objects in copper, silver, tin, also enameled in color for ornaments.

Large decorative and practical flowerpots, water jars, pottery from baking service to sculpture.

Modern details and designs themselves for all these things for sale or for purely decorative purposes themselves to be sold.

Decorative drawings and paintings in free modern spirit to apply to walls or hang on them. Sculpture, the same.

An orchestra recruited from workers, paid or student, available for paid concerts as propaganda for progress in music. Plays, after given at the school, might be repeated at the nearer universities.

A group of dancers recruited from the school illustrating elemental exercises of body-rhythm, practical as mind and body exercises.

Sets for the cinema.

Newly published music.

Designs for the theatre. Designs for farm homes, farm buildings, gardens, town-cottages, towns and villages, industrial towns, the gas station, country homes, factories of various sorts for the crafts—as, involved in the school itself. And all these designs for the various materials.

Brochures, illustrated on all these subjects for distribution printed on the school presses. Designs of every kind for furnishing and decorating these buildings. Landscape designs for various localities and regions and plans in detail for typical planting to be done about them.

Landscape studies and brochures, also illustrated, on landscape conservation and treatment. City planning.

All work produced in the school would be the property of the school and, under proper auspices, would be marketed where it would have the most beneficial effect.

In short, the school would be a hive of industry, a group of seventy-six or more workers comprising the most competent artists and craftsmen to be found either in Europe, America, or the Orient. And these again advised and inspired by such great creative artists, as would be their guests from time to time by invitation.

Such a product as this would have tremendous effect on Industry in these United States within a few years and might swing the tide of production toward new and genuine significance in all the design forms of American Industrial production.

The exhibiting and marketing of these results should, therefore be another feature of the "school work." Traveling exhibits, annually or semi-annually, fall and spring made a feature at least, of every American University.

Now this school could be no university where thousands must be herded or cradled and handled together. It would have to remain small, capacity, say, at most sixty students. Of necessity it would be isolated, mobile, sensitive, specialized, and free. But it could serve mass-production well as antenna for proper methods of teaching and might provide desirable teachers.

As an alcove, or adjunct, or experimental station in connection with university or art institute courses in the allied arts, it would be an ideal resource.

There would be of course no examinations. No graduations, no diplomas. But so soon as any worker showed special ability for a position and marked competence in any line of the industrial arts that worker would be available for a position in a factory-industry as designer. Those manufacturers having contributed to the School should have first choice of such students at all times—or they might be supplied as teachers at the various universities or similar schools of which, I believe, there soon would be many more.

It might be reasonable to expect that each such worker reaching such position to contribute for three years a fifth of his salary for the commercial position thus secured—to the endowment fund of his school. He would be continually drawing fresh inspiration and ideas from it during the period of probation. He would therefore not be fully released from his school until three years after he had left it.

HOW THIS SCHOOL WOULD BE OPERATED, BY WHOM, WHAT PRICE

A school of this nature should be international in its resources. A resident director should occupy the Cottage A shown in the sketch. This man should be an Architect chosen for his association with the crafts—consequently he would have to be found in Europe. A man like Herr Wijdeveld of Amsterdam, Holland,[2] a member of the Royal Academy, whom Holland has made a Knight of the House of Orange, Nassau, and whom France has made a chevalier of the Legion d'Honneur. He is editor of *Wendingen,* the famous European fine art publication and is himself a tireless worker in the Arts. His living should be assured and in addition a salary of $5,500 per year.

Around him, as directors should be the fine art group—say an architect, a sculptor, a painter, a musician, a teacher of rhythm as practiced by D'Alcroze, at Hellerau, or by Gurdjieff at Fontainebleau, France.[3] These should all be men of international reputation and creative significance. All should have mainly their own food and lodging assured together with their wives and children and a salary of $2,500 per year. To enrich and reinforce the services of these resident workers the Guest house is provided to entertain artists of creative consequence who may be passing through the country or who may come by invitation from Europe or distant parts of America from time to time to minister to the students either by lectures, criticism or entertainment or all together. Traveling expenses and food and lodging while at the school, only would need to be provided for them out of school funds.

Next to this inner-group would come seven resident foremen of experience in their particular lines knowing their machinery well. Such men as these are now foremen in many industrial establishments of America, Europe, and Japan. These industrial foremen would be released for this purpose by various leaders in industry—sympathetic to our purpose, say like P.M. Cochius of Leerdam Glasfabriek, and each foreman should receive a living for himself and family and a salary of say $1,000 per year. It might be well to change these foremen yearly—thus accumulating a greater fund of technique for the traditions of the School and such processes as would be

by this means recorded by the School historian.

There should be another guest-system of visitation, consultation and criticism arranged to reinforce this "foreman-group" also. Expenses paid each and living provided while the "expert" guest is at the school.

The providers of the endowment fund should elect the president for the Hillside Home School of the Allied Arts. The president should provide the administration of all funds. The school director, governing with a board of directors, called by him as a cabinet, should be responsible to the president for the conduct and work of the school. All paid resident artists and foremen and the Historian himself should sit in this cabinet or board of directors and such others as might be elected to the cabinet by the cabinet itself.

Philosophy and psychology should be available in some form to this school—by extension work. The men in charge of those branches at the nearest universities should do extension work here on, say one day of each week.

And the relation of religion to Art—the fact that every ritual preserved as a religious rite today was preserved for its aesthetic worth—should be presented by some competent churchmen to the students.

Saturday afternoons there might be a forum in which all matters would be discussed, attended by the entire student body. On Wednesday and Saturday afternoons—entertainment, music, the cinema, drama, rhythm.

On such other afternoons as might be convenient—lectures by guest artists.

To secure the paid workers such as we shall name and guarantee the salary account above the amount already secured by tuition and interest on the endowment fund for the first three years, the necessary sum should be guaranteed by industry. Available as income, $15,000 would be available from the endowment fund or "foundation" and the total of sixty tuition fees of $300—each contributed by the workers. A total income therefore of $33,000 could be used to pay this total salary and expense list of $33,000 leaving whatever deficit might arise the first year to be thus guaranteed by industry. This accounts for nothing made and sold meantime. And if board were paid by 60 students at $7 per week about $10,000 more would be added to income to reduce the deficit to $3,000 per year. Probably not more than a portion of the first year's incidental deficit ever need be claimed owing to the high character of the services directly employed in producing utilitarian objects of great value.

The tuition fee might be raised to abolish this possible deficit if deemed advisable. And there would be the small kindergarten and perhaps considerable day-pupil fees to add to this fee as it stands.

By building this coming Spring and taking proper steps toward an organization, the school could be open for work September 15th, 1932.

Looking toward this organization, the director has been suggested—Herr Wijdeveld, who, also, would have direct charge of Architecture.

Supplemented by myself, Frank Lloyd Wright, as chairman of the board, "Taliesin," just over the hill from the school would be available as a tributary atelier.

Visitors: H. P. Berlage, Holland—Mallet Stevens, Paris, France—Erich Mendelsohn, Berlin—J. P. Oud, Belgium—Le Courbusier, Paris, France—Lewis Mumford, New York—H. de Fries, Munich, Germany—Claude Bragdon, New York City.

For Landscape: Franz Aust of Madison, Wisconsin, supplemented by Jens Jensen, of Chicago. Visitors: Geddes, London; W. C. Pitts, Pittsburgh.

For Painting and Sculpture: Guira Stojyana, Los Angeles; or Joseph Stella, New York. Visitors: Paul Manship, New York; Elie Nedelmann, Paris, Bourdelle, Paris.

For Music: Ernest Bloch of San Francisco. Visitors: Eugene Goosens, Harold Bauer, Pablo Casals, Leopold Stokowsky, Igor Stravinsky, John Alden Carpenter.

Rhythm: Count and Countess Lubiensky of Tokio; also resident assistants in classroom in all branches. Visitors: Sent. Mahesa, Lithuania.

For Drama and Cinema: A man of the type of Somerset Maugham or Eisenstein. Visitors: Eugene O'Neil, Ernest Lubitsch, Murnau, Pudowkin, Carl Sandburg, Sherwood Anderson, Max Rheinhardt, Ernst Toller, Munich; Lee Simonson, New York; Alexander Woollcott, New York City; Joseph Urban.

For Historian: Ferdinand Schevill, Chicago.

For university extension in Philosophy and Psychology, Professors Henry Otto, and Hart.

For Religion in relation to Aesthetics: William Norman Guthrie, Rector of St. Mark's in the Bowerie, New York City.[4]

OPERATING EXPENSES

Farm Supt. House Mother, two cooks	$ 3,000.00
Masters' Group—Salaries	$18,000.00
Foremen—Salaries	$ 7,000.00
Historian and Secretary	$ 1,500.00
Total	$29,500.00

Additional cost above all farm production of feeding 124 people for one year at 26¢ a day each, or about $100 per year each: $12,500.00

Total	$42,000.00
Fuel, Light	$ 1,500.00
Grand Total	$43,500.00

AS TO THE MANAGEMENT OF THE STUDENTS

In keeping with the traditions of Hillside Home School the school should probably be coeducational. Entry open to boys and girls from 11 to 21 years of age. Test for fitness to enter as a student being those of sensitiveness, correlation and, especially, of predilection as already suggested. There should be in addition to those entering a waiting list to take the place of those going into industry. As one worker found his proper niche, another could step into his place.

The Farm superintendent, and Housemother would be in direct charge of all students but there should be self-government by the student body with appeal to the director only.

The students themselves would have power to expel one of their number by unanimous vote approved by the director or power to punish a fellow student.

The entire work of feeding and caring for the student body so far as possible should be done by itself; Tolstoy's "What to Do," a textbook in this connection.

Work in gardens, fields, animal husbandry, laundry, cooking, cleaning, serving, should rotate among the students according to some plan that would make them all do their bit with each kind of work at some time.

ADDENDA

A small Kindergarten of day pupils from three to nine years of age might be arranged. A small inner-circle of children incidentally related to school work. Parents wishing a child to have this advantage of the inner circle could take up residence in the neighborhood. Several cottages are already available for the purpose and room for many more.

The Principles giving rise to pure form and natural rhythm should be put in elemental exercises for these children who would be taken only as special aptitude for such expression as shown by them at play or at work.

Valuable workers might be developed for the school in this kindergarten. Tuition would be the same as for the regular pupils.

The body of talent represented by this school would naturally attract hundreds of more mature students who would like to have points of contact with the work going on there, especially with the group at the center of its activities and the constantly occurring lectures and entertainments by great artists.

Advanced day pupils might therefore be admitted to day work coming each day to school and might be admitted in such numbers as deemed advisable by the director. Tuition same as for regular pupils.

WE BELIEVE

We believe the time has come when Art should take the lead in Education, because we believe creative faculty is the birthright of Man—the quality in him that has enabled him to distinguish himself from the brute—but that owing to his betrayal of himself by tricks played upon himself by means of his brain or what he self-consciously styles his "intellect"—and by means of his collection of abstractions which he has turned into a system of so-called education—he has all but sterilized himself. And commerce merely as commerce cannot reproduce as Life.

In Modern Education there has been, and still is too much Science and Philosophy and too little of that inner experience of the Soul we call Art and Religion.

Art—this creative faculty in a man, is, we believe, that quality or faculty of getting himself born and born again and again, into whatever he does, into whatever he really works with or in or for. By means of this faculty he has the gods if not God.

Imagination is the tool by which this force and faculty in man works. By putting a false premium upon will and intellect, men have done injury to themselves falsely in the name of Man. And this deadly work is only begun in what we call education.

Now how to get back again by way of Youth—to Man, this essential quality of Manhood? How may we shield, preserve, or develop what little there is left glimmering of this man-quality in our own form of social contact? This is our concern in this school—our first thought. It should be the first thought of every thinking man in our country today. We should like to be first among those that would initiate steps that would put a little experiment station at work here at Hillside where this thing might be wooed and won, if only to a small extent. We know it cannot be taught.

In this school the ego should be allowed natural scope and the privileges, social and in work, insisted upon that are fair recognition of the qualities of manhood or womanhood.

Creative Impulse is the very soul of this natural ego—the fruit of the struggle and the triumph of what we call work. Inhibitions that impose upon this essential ego meet hypocrisy and are educational unwisdom. To allow the ego its natural salt and sanity is wiser. Walt Whitman was foremost among those who rebelled against this unwisdom.

So we are working for constructive steps to be taken *now*, not sometime, to save this precious quality

Design for teacup (Project). 1930. Plan and elevation. Pencil on tracing paper, 7 x 14". FLLW Fdn#3003.007

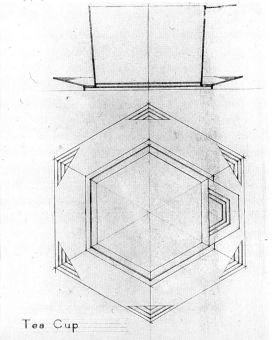

Tea Cup

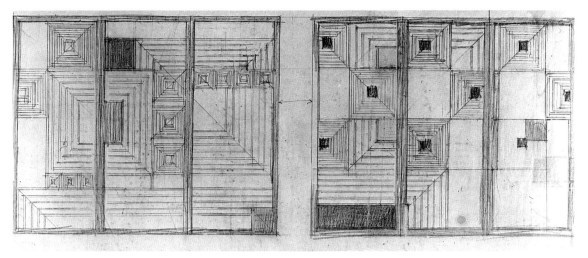

Design for metal and wood screen (Project). 1934. Elevations. Pencil and color pencil on tracing paper, 38 x 15". FLLW Fdn#3405.001

within the soul of Man himself from further atrophy and decay—from greater degradation at his own hands. Enough mischief has already been done in the name of misconceived and selfishly applied *Democracy*.

Even the "best" of us may now, all too plainly, see in our country the evil consequences of a sentimentalized singing to Demos as a god. We see the evil consequences of this patting of the "common denominator" on the back and ascribing to him the virtues of deity.

This hypocrisy has become so expedient for political purposes and "economic" reasons as to be obstructive if not destructive. The hypocrisy necessary for such expediency as a point of view or as a basis for conduct is already so imbued in the 100% Americans as to be like the color and curl of his hair, the shape of his nose, or the timbre of his voice.

We should love Man more and men less in order to hasten the time when a natural Art shall take the lead in all true education and natural character be the natural consequence.

Isolation, concentration and sympathetic inspiration in the natural correlation of the whole man in such work in a school as we propose may induce this now-rare inner experience as more common experience. In such a workshop for the whole man as we have tried to describe the individual ego should be strengthened and restored to sanity by *consciousness of creative power* and to such an extent that puerile "egotism" such as we know it as bred by such education

as we now have, would only be a sickly disease of consciousness, highly improbable.

If Democracy means anything at all it means that each man is entitled to the growth of a true individuality, his very own, that no man can take from him.

True Democracy means that Man should be himself, too modest or ashamed to try to be someone else.

And the ego of the creative Man in this sense will always be the salt and savor of sanity itself.

What we often thoughtlessly call God or the Infinite or Divine Principle would then continually be proved afresh by what the Man himself could do and would do and alive in the Man—be expressed by means of his own manhood in his own work in some true form as his own vision of Reality.

Thus only do Men become a vital medium, through which the Infinite may appear to Mankind.

1. Charles Robert Ashbee (1863–1942), architect, is best known for his association with the English Arts and Crafts movement. He met Wright in 1900 and the two became lifelong friends.
2. Hendrik Theodor Wijdeveld (1886–?) was a Wright enthusiast and was instrumental in directing the course of architecture in Holland mainly through articles that he published in the journal *Wendingen*.
3. Georgei Gurdjieff, founder of the Institute for the Harmonious Development of Man in Fontainebleau, France, in the early 1920s. Olgivanna Wright had been a member, and his influence would surface in the organization of the Taliesin Fellowship.
4. Among the names listed here are close friends of Wright's as well as prominent names whom he wanted included in this program. Among his friends and acquaintances were J. P. Oud, Lewis Mumford, Erich Mendelsohn, Claude Bragdon, Jens Jensen, Carl Sandburg, Alexander Woollcott, Ferdinand Schevill, and William Norman Guthrie.

AMERICAN ARCHITECTURE TODAY

In this address, delivered on February 21, 1931, to his colleagues and fellow architects, Wright is once more urging them to leave the styles and tastes of the past and to embrace modern architecture. In fact, he begins the talk with a toast, "To our supreme mistress, Architecture! May she ever be modern! And that means young." After the assembled company was seated, he called for a second toast, this time for his "Lieber Meister," Louis Sullivan, for whom he worked at the start of his career.

It is obvious that Wright was enjoying the occasion, even though he admonished his colleagues about imitation of the past and urged them to look to the character of the nation, and to express its democratic and free life in terms of architecture: "I have been surprised to see how hypnotic the truth is. How little you have to argue if you have principle on your side! How little trouble you have with an intelligent American businessman if you really have a workable idea!" [Speech delivered to the annual convention of the Michigan Society of Architects and the Grand Rapids Chapter of the Institute of Architects and published in two parts in the Weekly Bulletin *of the Michigan Society of Architects, July 14 and July 21, 1931]*

(The assembled company rose at the banquet tables to greet the speaker.)

MR. WRIGHT: DON'T SIT DOWN FOR A MOMENT BOYS, please! We are all standing?

Here's to our supreme mistress, Architecture! May she ever be modern! And that means young.

One sip? It is, at least, "Clear."

(And the assembled company sat down to the tables.)

Mr. Wright: I am going to ask you for another moment.

I don't know how—otherwise—we can best express it—why not stand up again? Just to show that hero-worship on our ground is not yet dead. Will you all stand up to the memory of Louis Sullivan?

(The banquet stood—silently—lifted glasses again and sat down.)

Mr. Wright: Thank you.

This has been so delightful a "get-together," so far, that I don't know why you should want to introduce the subject of architecture at all. This is my first convention.

I did not know they were such fun.

And I did not know architects were such good fellows when they got together to play. It has been most charming to me to see you all having a good play time. I am proud to be here with you. And it was awfully nice of you to ask me to come.

I will try not to be offensive.

But Modern architecture as a topic is a disagreeable subject. You have given it to me, here, tonight.

I think, yes as a matter of fact, it was your witty chairman who said that architecture was one of the "lively arts."

Would to God architecture were. It will be. But I don't know how soon, or where.

Of course what we call architecture—you won't mind my being frank with you, that is what I am here for—if I can be of any service to you at all it will be in telling you what I believe to be the truth?

Well—I really believe that architecture and architects, in the old, noble sense of both words are dead.

You see architecture is, now, blacksmithing, iron work, engineering. Most of you have been busy putting such architecture as you had on the outside of these new things—putting it all over the surface. I do not blame you so much because it had been going on for nearly five centuries before we took hold here in this country.

I think the great catastrophe that has really befallen our supreme Mistress, Architecture, is that she is no longer young—that is to say—no longer modern. She is old—senile. A Renaissance, at best.

Now, Art with a capital "A" is something that never was reborn, never will be reborn. So if only we could let architecture die as old and get the life principle in her born again, get it born without all of these bad precedents, without all of this corruption brought over to us, dignified by association, hallowed by all the sentimental academic phrases the human mouth can utter, we should have a chance at an architecture of our own. Architecture, already old, was brought over here by Thomas Jefferson himself. He brought his Georgian with him, as he brought his clothes, because he had none other. Nevertheless there with *his* architecture is where we stand.

Even officially in our country our president Hoover recently recommended senility—that is to say—to go on building our public buildings as we have been building them. Already—T-square and triangle in hand—most of our able architects are standing still, at Thomas Jefferson's grave. Whereas I am sure that were Thomas Jefferson himself alive today—were he standing here at this table tonight to talk to you, he would be "modern."

He was modern when he lived? He was the advanced "modern" idealist of his time. And do you really believe that if he were living today he would be building the buildings now that he built then? You know he wouldn't. He would be modern now.

Entering into our life in this great country is a struggle to be free—God knows it is a struggle. And it looks as though we were sinking deeper and deeper with every struggle into the morass, to mention prohibition only as one vexed feature of anti-free-dom. We are ignoring all our new, great riches, and our new materials. Do you realize that we, today, are the richest nation in material-resources in the world? To make new inventions, create new materials that are really super materials, of such quality the entire world will be changed and we will change it if we, as architects here tonight, will think, with understanding, of the significance of these materials and new processes and learn just what they mean to modern life. One of these super materials is glass. I do not need to tell you about glass.

The new spiritual concept of architecture which we call Modern Life is architecture. And architecture is life. I think that what is the matter with us in architecture is that architecture is no longer life. Such architecture as we have is something *on* life not *of* life.

All Art with us has come to be some form of mere eclecticism. But, especially, our leading architects are all heavy eclectics. And I think American architecture today is impoverished due to this license which we call "eclecticism" and which, after all, is only a form of "taste." Taste never was individuality. Taste is poison if you substitute it for creative impulse or allow it to take the place of knowledge, judgement and art. "Taste" is the individual idiosyncrasy, cultivated.

No Nation can build a great life for itself nor can any nation develop great art—which means it cannot develop a great life—on any such basis as selective "taste."

Now, what we all need—and we must have it—is new grasp on fundamentals. New grasp of what constitutes American life and American character.

We can afford to throw away everything that has happened and begin again. Begin anew.

I don't think it would be too much to say that in America today there is not a single public building and very few private buildings owned by the very rich, that could be characterized as a thought-built, genuine product of American thought or of American Life. We have had with us dead things that we have sentimentally taken as live traditions. For one, Thomas Jefferson's architecture that he brought with him to the East. And—for another, that which Father Junipero brought up from Mexico into California—Southwest.

In the East—Georgian.

In the Southwest—Mexicana.

In the Middle West—what have you?

But this is getting to be a little to much like a speech. Don't you think it would be more in the spirit of this occasion if we were to get into discussion here together. Since these insulting remarks must have aroused some resentment in some honest bosoms by now, I will give you a chance to say so.

(No one responded.)

Mr. Wright: Why not rise up and defend yourselves?

Why should we not have an argument?

I would like to have you take part in this affair this evening and discuss this matter with me. Let *me* "answer back."

Is there anybody here who does not know all about architecture?

(Laughter.)

Well—what is it that somebody in particular does not know about architecture and would like to know, because maybe I can tell him. I am placed here where I must pretend that I know.

No response.

Mr. Wright (aside to Mr. Allen,[1] lifting his coffee cup to finish it): My wife told me when I came here tonight to be careful not to spill coffee on my shirt front . . . You know the old definition, don't you, of a genius . . . "a man who knows all about everything and scatters his food down the front of his clothes"? She told me that I need not make that demonstration here tonight just because I was going to pretend that I knew all about everything.

Mr. Wright (appealing to the audience—right and left and then to the speakers' table): Well. Isn't somebody kindly going to enter into this situation with me, to make it really easier for me?

(Mr. Sukert rises at the speakers' table to question Mr. Wright.)

Mr. Sukert: Mr. Wright, how would you express American life in architecture?

Mr. Wright: That? And all in one evening, Mr. Sukert? Recently Mr. Einstein asked for three days in which to explain the relatively unimportant and far less pressing matter of relativity!

But . . .well . . . first of all. Any such expression is a matter of the American Ideal. We have one in this country haven't we?

Of course, I know the "Success" ideal of America. But there is another Ideal in this great country that makes it what it is. What is it?—(The thing to do seems to keep you all talking when I get on my feet).

(No answer, so Mr. Wright continued):

That Ideal is freedom, isn't it?

We, as a people, desire freedom?

It was the ideal of the men who founded our country, Thomas Jefferson for one and George Washington for another, although I am afraid George was too good a business man to have had perhaps as strong an Ideal of freedom as some of the others. At any rate, we are dedicated, our ground itself is dedicated to freedom? Is it not?

Now, are we free?

Of course we are not . . . and I don't think any of our forefathers were much more free than we are.

But they were not foolish enough to imagine that freedom is something that can be handed to any man or assume that it is something that can be brought home ready-made or that it is a question of government or any question at all but the question of the interior life of the individual man.

Freedom for any man must be a development from within as seen crystallized in past life and as it will be seen, fluid, in present forms of government.

Our Ideal of Democracy characterized such freedom as the basis on which all nations would have to obtain or recover their liberty.

I believe that the founders of America were wise.

I believe that in every heart here tonight, in every soul, is that sense of freedom as growth of the power and privilege to develop from within. This is, as a possession of the man, the greatest thing we have got.

Now, on the surface, there are lots of other things. But let us begin with this. Brother Sukert has started something deep here. Let us begin our explanation with that fundamental thought of "freedom."

We have no free architecture, because such "license" as we have practiced in architecture is not "freedom": nevertheless we are privileged. But, as privilege, we have pillaged the store house of the world in the name of Tradition and have proudly encumbered the land with the results. But I understand freedom, the great American Ideal, as something quite above that and something quite different. Freedom means the entire character of our civilization developed from within. And that is the only true expression of our life whether it is in our architecture, or our sculpture, or our painting or our living.

Now, then, starting with that as the basis for our architecture. What architecture?

All right—

The answer to that question is that this ideal of development from within restores the life of character, gives you what motive you have to build with and tells you how you are going to build.

In keeping with this old, yet new ideal comes a new science of life, and there comes, too, a new integrity. A great new integrity comes to make a new conception of what a building should now be like.

This interior or organic ideal is not "new" because it was innate in the simplicities of the carpenter of Nazareth. In his thought this character and quality of the within must be developed into whatever might be called good life. And five hundred years before he lived there was a great Chinese sage, Laotze, with an organic philosophy to similar purpose.

So why say our ideal of freedom is natural thought. Natural expression of the nature of the within.

Then this ideal will be what we now call "Modern." And notwithstanding its ancient origin we may call it modern. To Modern Architects this organic "interior" Ideal in building is the building seen as enclosure of interior space. Walls in the old sense do not exist for the new concept. The interior space itself is the reality of the building. The room itself must "come through" or architecture has not arrived.

The ancient ideal, of course, was some block of building material, a great heavy block, the heavier the block the better it was. Buildings were built like ancient fortifications. They had to be. Life, then was different. You had to fight for your life, instead of for your living.

But—seriously—we say we are, and I believe we are on the road to freedom. So we are not chattel slaves any longer. We are not serfs, but free men. And so these formidable house walls may now vanish.

Glass, Steel (steel like the spider spinning) is making the new buildings all the while lighter and stronger. And by means of glass we are making the environment and the building itself all grow together as one natural thing.

Does that ideal sound modern? Have I made my logic and supported it so you all may understand?

At any rate, in words, that to me is the basis of the new architecture. And you can see without any prompting from me that this is the expression of a better and finer integrity of life than making things conceived by the indirection and individual license called taste. I believe that architecture and architects may become true prophets of our future.

I believe this would soon come to be if the architects themselves got solid grasp on these new concepts of architecture: because while the Spirit of architecture has not changed, its forms must absolutely change. As we ourselves have had to change.

I think if architects would get that thought into their souls it would not take very long to reconstruct our life, because things in our country (they do the same in other countries) come from the top down. Architects are supposed to be the head of the body of this great republic in the matter about which we are talking? And, honestly I believe that architects are all aware that what is the matter with architecture in our country is that it is not Architecture.

No, I am not exaggerating or making an epigram—I say it because architects themselves do not yet know the modern from the "modernistic." If, even now, they are willing to become "istic": or an "ism" or an "ite," they have risen up only to drop low. And we still have the adopted standards of Mrs. Gablemore, Mrs. Plasterbilt, and Miss Flat-top, the three American graces in our architecture. All is still, the shallow Hokum of "taste."

Of course at this point I could get into difficulties with you up to my neck and at that not add enough wisdom so that any of us would be very much the wiser. But I will say that this matter of modern architecture is no superficial matter at all.

This new ideal isn't something I have read about. It is something I have tried to live. I have been true to America as I see America.

And I am going to continue to be true to America no matter what America thinks about it.

I do believe that all of you here tonight would better yourselves and so better your country should you get this inner-experience, this new ideal of architecture as organic. Because that would mean a great architecture for a great life.

Never mind a few mistakes! Be true to these simple "specifications." Eliminate anything or all else as you please, but modern architecture as organic is still in the nature of a spiritual conviction.

When you have got the conviction something is going to happen.

Until you have it nothing will happen.

Just as absolutely nothing has really happened in architecture in America since America was born.

This last is insulting and if I knew how to insult you more deeply and to a greater purpose I would do it in order that I might see some of you defending yourselves right here and now.

Do you, as architects, all propose to sit quiet down there and let me put myself in a situation where I seem to have beaten you into insensibility?

Professor Rousseau: Mr. Wright, won't you tell us something about the essential contribution of Louis Sullivan?

Mr. Wright: The essential contribution of Louis Sullivan was one of heroism, one of faith and an ideal—an architectural ideal which after all, is an expression of that life-within of which we have just been speaking. His work was tentative. He got on the wrong side of the social ledger. He abused himself. But he was more mightily abused by his own country. He was wasted and thrown away by ignorance; not designedly. Simply run over by the juggernaut of selfish ambition and greed which characterizes our great country. And the significance of his work lies in the fact that he, fundamentally, courageously, like a prophet, set about his ideal and did his "damn'dest" until he died.

Now the significance of his works I have said.

What more would you?

The fact that Louis Sullivan's buildings were imperfect manifestations of his own ideal is no weakness of his, nor to be regarded as such by anyone. An ideal that can be realized by any man in a lifetime is not worth striving for as an ideal. But his work in behalf of that ideal is forever valuable to his country. For God's sake let us be grateful. He, the first in American architecture, was true to his country to the death.

Architecture to him was really the life and beating heart of his own country. Now, what does it matter that we can build better buildings today than the buildings he built? Every great worker, every great man must be taken, in connection—in relation—to the time in which he worked and sweated and was bled. And by any standard whatsoever brought, by intelligence, to bear upon his work or his life—he was a great man. He was a genius.

Is that fair to your question?

Mr. Cordner: Mr. Wright, a while ago you said that, so far, America had produced no public building that was purely American. We have been disposed to think of the skyscraper as such, and I wonder what your comment on that would be?

Mr. Wright: It would hardly be fit for publication in these happy circumstances this evening, I am afraid. But—well—you all know, as well as I know, that the skyscraper is only a commercial expedient?

The skyscraper is a special pet invention of the "space-maker-for-rent" to please the landlord. The spacemaker has carried the pleasing very far. But the poor devil has neglected architecture in the whole matter. He has not yet realized that masonry-mass, as such, was the necessary result of the crude stone building of a feudal architecture. Some day he can come into his own. Steel forming the skyscraper. But now of course the "scraper" as the architect's is an absurdity: As the engineer's it is an anomaly. Tons and tons of stone go up on high to be held up there on steel, by wire. These tons and tons have got to come down again. No one has decided just how the superfluous tons will come down or just when.

I think that a tall building may be a beautiful building.

I do not see why we should not have tall buildings. But I would be hanged before I could see why we should have any more big monuments to landlord–ism, to swell the rent-roll, add to congestion and contribute to all that is subversive and that defeats the purpose of human life, wherever the attempt to build any more, as they are, may be made. You are witnessing in the skyscraper a collision between the mechanistic factor and the mechanistic device: between the automobile and the skyscraper. On which would you bet?

You will have to take one or the other.

I would take the automobile.

Wouldn't you?

I see no reason why any tall building cannot be beautiful—say—dignified as a tree in the midst of nature.

But, we would then have, instead of a monumental–mass, significant outline. We now have to try to find that desirable substitute. Such skyscraper–architecture is all thrown away to make "fake" architecture. One of your members, Albert Kahn,[2] drove me through the streets of Detroit not so long ago. I had seen his Ford factory. I had seen the industrial buildings which he had designed and for which I have always had a great respect. But when I saw him self-consciously "putting on" architecture I could only tell him I wished to God he would forget about architecture and stick to industrial buildings. This, because in the industrial building he was honest, he was respectable. But when it came to putting architecture on to the engineer's skyscraper, like the Fisher building, and other buildings downtown there in Detroit, he was just as big a liar as anybody else. And so it goes in our skyscraper architecture.

Mr. Allen: How are you going to get a new architecture until you get a new literature?

What do you think of Carl Sandburg?

Mr. Wright: I think, Mr. Allen, you have got the cart before the horse. Literature comes after a fact, not before. All literature is to some extent history—unless it is actually poetry. But we have not yet reached true poetry. Such poetry as we had by way of nineteenth-century sentimentality and degenerated into ornament. And Carl Sandburg is still quite sentimental in spite of being hard and rough. But he is a sentiment poet and very interesting to me. Carl is a greater poet now. He is my friend and I am his. But I have no need to lie about him on that account?

Mr. Steffens: Will the World's Fair in Chicago in 1933 represent the freedom that you have in mind?

Mr. Wright: 1933? Well, one might think it back in past centuries.

So far as I have seen or read and talked with the boys who are doing the Fair, the Fair is going to be just an exaggerated case of antique Babylonian license. I mean it seriously. It is.

Architecture, that is to say, true modern architecture is a slow growth. Modern architecture, of course, must grow. It is not a form of eclecticism. The eclectics have turned to the modern, I think, over night?

Now all of the designers concerned with the Fair in Chicago, are our "foremost" business architects. Yesterday they were eclectics building medieval pseudoclassic buildings. The modern architecture appeared on the horizon. I don't know just where they saw it—ask them. But it must have seemed to them like the handwriting on the wall, or, oh well, I don't know what. Perhaps they were already tired of the many choices they had been able to exercise. Here was new choice, here was a new appearance. Here then was the "style" for the next "Fair"?

The French had already had a fair in Paris in 1925, where were seen these new appearances. Therefore in the next fair we have, I say, merely got a new eclecticism.

The new Chicago Fair belongs literally, as the old one did, although it is younger, to the nineteenth century. It is exactly the same thing as the Columbian Exposition, stated in a little different terms. The old pseudo fair taken in, thought unchanged, washed behind the ears and set up as new. Truly an outrageous senility this name of the Modern? No you have got it.

Unfortunately a fool will always tell you the truth. So why ask him?

Professor Rousseau: What do you mean when you say that a building should be beautiful?

Mr. Wright: Did I say that?

Professor Rousseau: I thought you said that.

Mr. Wright: Then more indiscretion on my part. Like the reference to our friend, Albert Kahn.

I really think no one should talk very much about beauty. No I don't think anyone should talk much about beauty. Especially not to his client. I never do.

I think an architect should talk to his client in terms of practical, hard, common-sense. You have got to give him the facts and then he will know really what you are doing. He will see that what you are doing, you are doing on principle.

I have been surprised to see how hypnotic the truth is. How little you have to argue if you have principle on your side! How little trouble you have with an intelligent American business man if you really have a workable idea!

I believe that America is less bound by tradition than any great country in the world. But unfortunately, just the same, in this day of concrete—there is a good deal of concrete placed where it does not belong. Notwithstanding that misplacement as misfortune I think that there is a great chance for the Architect in America. America is a proving ground in which this new idealism, in which this organic architecture we've been talking about can be born.

Here's hoping!

Mr. Allen: Well, at least, the banquet audience has gotten a fair break. If they did not like what Mr. Wright said, they could get up and argue about it.

Mr. Wright: And they were too nice to argue.

Mr. Allen: I would like to know if there are any other questions that any one of you would like to ask?

Mr. Wright: Really I am, informally at the service of all here.

Mr. Ruppell: Mr. Allen, I would really like to ask Mr. Wright whether in this architecture of the future, the architecture of the future will draw on the services of the sculptor and the painter as it has done in the past.

Mr. Wright: Yes, my dear boy. The architect will. And to a greater extent than ever before. This architecture of the future is the only hope the sculptor and the painter have. They got a divorce from architecture when architecture became moribund. They could not hang around there to die, so by way of the Renaissance, they tried to set up for themselves. And they have been having a very good time ever since. But they have been getting nowhere in particular.

They both naturally belong with the architect. The interior ideal of which I spoke, when put to work, is the ideal that makes a building natural, a true expression of contemporary life. There is the painter's chance. There is the sculptor's chance. Both co-operatives of the modern architect.

Mr. Hughes: Mr. Wright, you said something about having a choice between the automobile and the skyscraper. Would you speak a little more about that?

Mr. Wright: Yes. Take the automobile city. Detroit. Well . . . I really think Detroit wants to know what to do with her own automobile.

I believe the automobile has brought into American life, anomaly, because of the conflict with another mechanical invention, the skyscraper. And the automobile is unwittingly widening the horizon and providing a new means of distribution. It is an agent of de-centralization.

Keep your eye on the little gas station.[3] That is the advance agent of de-centralization, a new integration made by the advent of the automobile. That is what it is going to do for the country—de-centralization—re-integration. Specifically, the automobile, of course, has changed all American life without Americans knowing very much about it.

All of America is now in a state where we may in a day go from here to anywhere else we want to go, pretty much. Now we have here, in reserve, the mobilization, when it gets to working and comes fully into being that will change the whole situation in regard to landlords. The new freedom brought by the machine is not going to be centralized and imprisoned forever just to pay somebody excess profits on a "lucky" piece of ground. Is it? Do you think so?

The American people have already had a widening of their physical horizon. I believe if they can only get something wider now by way of the spirit to go with that widening, they will get the characteristic changes that are past due. Then you fellows won't build skyscrapers any longer. I am sure of that.

Personally, I think Hetty Green, the crafty New York millionairess, pretty wise. Nobody could sell her any stock in a skyscraper. No, not any. Even she had vision enough to see the skyscraper supertaxed. The mechanical successes of today carried fairly afield to benefit human life, and the city will not remain.

Too strong language?

Yes . . . strong words.

But look back 25 years from now.

Professor Rousseau: Mr. Wright, what do you think of the theory which is getting such attention in Europe right now in which they exclude any kind of decoration of a building? I refer to the group of architects headed by Le Corbusier.

Mr. Wright: Thank you. That question concerns a phase of our subject I had overlooked. I have the greatest respect for my European colleagues. I think that in Europe are perhaps a dozen who are among the greatest architects and among the greatest men who have lived in our time.

I believe they are doing magnificent work. I think they got some original inspiration from us, here in America. But I think, they use it pretty well. Better than we do. And what does it matter that for the moment ornaphobia takes the place of ornamentia?

Of course, the protestant has never been beautiful, but he has been useful. And I believe Le Corbusier and the group around him are extremely useful. Extremely valuable, especially, as an enemy, able to demonstrate the depravity of our own very best ornamentia.

And I think that for us to build any more ornamental buildings, as such, is just criminal waste, now. But, on the other hand, some of the so-called mechanistic buildings in the name of the straight-line and the flat-plane have become fetish or a fad in the name of aesthetics. You get not much nearer to ultimate truth with these new buildings than with the old ornamental buildings. Because when you get below the surface no matter how plain "modernistic" is—it is still merely ornamental. You are in the istic of the ism, and in just the same fix as the fellow who sticks to his ornament in the definite old-fashioning of his building.

Does that answer your question?

Professor Rousseau: Partly.

Mr. Wright: If you will tell me what it doesn't answer, I'll try again.

Professor Rousseau: Do you think the result of that work expresses the life of Europe, the actual life? I mean the work connected with the life of Europe?

Mr. Wright: No. I don't think it does. I think it is reaction. I think the pendulum generally swings too far in the other direction and gets to be too much the other thing. I think it all a little intemperate. But since we must have intemperance I think it is the kind of intemperance we should have. Le Corbusier's dictum that a house must be utterly "plain" is minus a greater architectural truth.

Here is the point: We are concerned with the housing of the complete human being. In the house that we are concerned with as architects the home itself can be no machine. Architecture enters when and where the element of machinery ceases to be. Now,

that idea, for the moment, is heresy because it is dangerous. And it is dangerous because it may be abused. It may be better for a time for everybody concerned to take everything as turned away from ornamentality. That, at least, is now, characteristically, the European architect's viewpoint.

Mr. Cordner: Mr. Wright, I think that the average person's impression of all this matter of which Professor Rousseau speaks is that they regard the home as a sort of museum piece which the man himself would not want to live in.

Mr. Wright: Why should he want to live in it? How can any man make a "change" of his building on the future? I think he shouldn't. I see no reason for his doing it.

A great many of these buildings, in their reaction to machinery, are crudities. Nothing else. I think that when the country runs across some of these things 10 or 15 years from now the people will have them moved down to the highways, set up on wheels and sent on their way—out of sight.

I remember when the Larkin Building[4] was built. It was protestant.

I designed it in 1903 and 1904. That building had some ornamentation. But the entire building was set up in plain brick surface and straight lines. It was a simple cliff of brick and stone. At the time the Larkin Building was being built that protest was innovation. But we are a very young nation. No protestantism is going to last with us very long. We want affirmation. We are not satisfied to keep on protesting. I soon tried to go deeper than the Larkin Building went and I am trying to go deeper now. I have tried to find something I have not touched on here tonight, because I was sure I would get it wrong and be misunderstood. And that something is ornament as integral feature of building: Ornament, seen . as the pattern of the structure itself.

A Chinese sage has said that poetry is the sound of the heart. This is a beautiful, uncommon saying.

We say, instead, integral pattern, integral ornament is the expression of the nature of the within. Unluckily we have a clumsy language. It is very difficult to find the right thing in speaking when we touch upon subject matter of this nature, but more difficult to make it all clear, as I understand it. It is hard, I find, to make others understand.

The Japanese have a very different language in that respect. I wish we could try theirs. They could by three words say all I want to say. They have one word for instance, *"edaburi,"* which means, well . . . as I said it will take four or five sentences to translate the meaning of that one word. First the word means the interior scheme or habit of growth of any growing thing. We will take this thing, say (picking up a tulip bloom from the table decoration). It is rather clumsy but it will serve. *Edaburi* means that when this leaf comes out of the stem this comes in relation to this and to this and all to each other (illustrating by touching the stem, the leaf, and finally the flower). *Edaburi* is the habit of growth within the life of this thing that makes it a tulip. It is the same thing in a pine that makes the pine tree "pine," as distinguished from a willow tree. A pine *edaburi* always makes a pine. And a willow *edaburi* always makes a willow. You see?

Well, it is *edaburi* then, or interior nature-expression that we call integral ornament. . . . Is it still unclear? . . . Because that interior nature-expression is architecture. And in that subjective expression lies all the essential difference between building as engineering and building as architecture. It is the great thing we do not try to talk about any more, because it is poetry; because it is beautiful. We have got to keep quiet about beauty now for quite a while. We have forfeited . . . yes, we have forfeited the right to use the word as we have lost the exercise of that quality in things which makes them beautiful as they are, for what they are.

Beethoven's Fifth Symphony was founded on four notes . . . you know? And on a rhythm a child can play with one finger on the piano. Now, out of these simple elements came great revolution, probably the most revolutionary thing the mind of man has expressed or ever produced. And I suppose, really, all said and done, the noblest edifice ever reared by the mind of man. That tumult and splendor of sound is the result of the working of what I have called integral-ornament. I know that this elemental means will be an influence in the further development of the machine age, in our common architecture.

But we talk too much about our new opportunities in operation and we talk about our scientific ideals. But we do not say anything about this magnificent tool, this tremendous power that has been given to us to work with as a tool—the machine—as an instrumentality for new beauty.

The Greeks had only a chattel slave. Civilization in Feudal times had hands, fingers and could do things by guild we cannot do. We have been trying all along, trying to do by machinery for ourselves, things they could do for themselves better by hand. Now, these things that we have been talking about, our new ideals, this new tool, this new use, this idea, is, perhaps the greatest power, the most tremendous force that has ever entered into the world. But unqualified, savage, implacable, this power has been destroying everything in the name of this ancient art ideal we have sentimentalized over. And it is our job now, as I see it, to take this tool—this instrument we call a machine—and give it work to do by way of these new systems of ours that it can do so much better for our life and do so supremely well as to make the ancient architecture look to you as it looks to me—unbeautiful as imitation.

Mr. Allen: Are there no further questions? I am sure that we would all be glad if there are any further questions, because I am sure Mr. Wright could continue in the same entertaining manner, indefinitely.

Mr. Wright: I think you have all suffered enough.

Mr. Allen: In behalf of the Michigan Society of Architects and the Grand Rapids Architects, I want to thank Mr. Wright for one of the most inspiring evenings we have ever spent. I am sure that all of the guests and likewise the architects have this same tribute to Mr. Wright's group of speeches.

(Applause.)

If there are no further matters we will stand adjourned until 1932.

1. A number of those who appear in this article were officers or directors of the Michigan Society of Architects, including Roger Allen, Lancelot Sukert, and G. Frank Cordner. As this address was part of their annual convention, the others were presumably Michigan architects.
2. Albert Kahn (1869–1942), German-born architect, best known for his industrial designs. Among his buildings are two factories for the Ford Motor Company (1908 and 1917), as well as buildings for the campus of the University of Michigan, Ann Arbor.
3. Wright has great plans for the "little gas station" in his decentralized Broadacre City. See *The Disappearing City*, p. 70.
4. The Larkin Building (1903) of Buffalo, New York, was Wright's first completed commercial commission.

RADIO CITY

In 1926 Frank Lloyd Wright designed for an urban environment a group of tall buildings—a project that he called "Skyscraper Regulation." Although he intrinsically disapproved of multistoried buildings in cities, he recognized their inevitability. His scheme, therefore, allows the structures height but staggers the towers so that sunlight falls to the street below, thereby abolishing such dark caverns as New York's Wall Street.

Wright's skyscrapers were to be built of glass and steel, the rooftops to be garden parks. Pedestrians were to be provided with mezzanine networks separated from the traffic routes below, while the avenues were to have medians planted with trees and shrubs and interspersed with occasional fountains. In all, it was a solution to an existing problem, making the best of circumstances.

The proposed design by Raymond Hood for Radio City (Rockefeller Center), some five years after the regulation project struck Wright as nothing more than a continuation of the existing evils of the skyscraper: "Radio City simply exaggerates—for money—the worst elements of our economic, industrial and aesthetic situation." It was, in his words, but "space for rent," enriching landlords using construction methods as dated as those of the nineteenth century, the citizen sacrificed to the powers of wealth and greed. In a photograph illustrating his book The Disappearing City (p. 70) smoke and soot rise up from a dense forest of skyscrapers. Wright captioned the illustration, "Find the Citizen." [Published in New York Evening Post & New York Tribune, 1932]

"MR. ROCKEFELLER IS NOT BUILDING A MONUMENT," SAID Dr. Corbett, apologizing for the new model for Radio City.

No, Mr. Rockefeller is in need of money. And space-makers-for-rent are arranging the little drama for him. When that is all right they will talk to you about architecture. If you want to talk about it.

But why talk about it?

That is only the public's concern. Neither Mr. Rockefeller or his doctors are concerned, unless afterward. [See The New York Times, March 6, 1931.]

The typical situation in our great United Experiment . . . sacrosanct.

Any fair criticism of Radio City should begin with Mr. Rockefeller and include his hired men. Because his "architects" confess that is what they are. And rather proud of it they seem to be.

He ought to be proud of their service. Because as "architects" [The New York Times, March 6, 1931] they reject any inference of architecture, modern or modernistic.

They are just making more money for Mr. Rockefeller.

Salesmanship is making it. Salesmen are to sell it when it is done.

What is it precisely that is to be sold?

Can it be the patient public?

And wherein is Mr. Rockefeller public bene-factor in Radio City? Is he not exaggerating by common means and common standards the mask that rent wears to get itself rented?

I think there is no higher Ideal behind the whole performance.

Radio City is then the typical product of the New York Functioneer.

A great opportunity for co-relation of the kinetic energy of this Age, its industrial and eco-nomic power put at work on our new wealth of materials, is wasted. It is wasted to match the char-acteristic urban waste in which it stands.

In Radio City what seems to be "Opera" is a bank and shops. I suppose a bank is modern "opera."

The theaters are units concealed in office buildings. But the monotony of the cubicles for the busybee is unrelieved by this recreation for him when he is tired.

The office buildings are feudal towers—"busi-ness" the baron. A feudal tower on the right. A feu-dal tower on the left. A nondescript office tower—"too young to name"—official for broadcasting, is seen between them.

Broadcasting then has no possible distinction or characterization? Radio is just "business," too? It is then as we suspected. This interpretation proves it is.

The three towers are placed tit, tat, toe.

And the ovular opera is "tum."

Imaginative?

There is no theme but "space for rent." No interrelation of parts to make a stupendous whole.

The whole work of making the exterior "as good looking as possible" has failed to dramatize even itself with all the false means at its disposal.

As the usual last resort Hugh Ferris should be called in to render the opus "at night," in the cus-tomary New York manner. "At night" might help save it for advertising purposes. Otherwise it utterly lacks distinction.

So this greatest privatistic manifestation of pri-vatism, and maybe privateering, of our great exper-iment in democracy is devoid of all but "space for rent." To make it intelligible a lettered, gigantic ground plan painted on the flat faces of the four sides, window holes disappearing in the black paint, would be necessary to identify anything whatsoever as to what is which or which is what. If the func-tioneer's privatism is to be made intelligible this is not only advisable but necessary.

But these signboards would succeed in con-veying only the fact that so far as architecture goes it is all unintelligent waste.

Mr. Rockefeller does not know waste in this sense, when he sees it. Because waste "pays." And his employees are not going to tell, if indeed they know, that exaggeration in any form is not great-ness.

Radio City simply exaggerates—for money—the worst elements of our economic, industrial and aesthetic situation.

Why and how Modern Architecture?

So far as its own idea of a "good-looking out-side" goes, Radio City is haphazard composition. Composition is a nineteenth-century term for a nineteenth-century mental process discarded by modern artists. So the city is old-fashioned before it starts upward.

Even as old-fashioned "composition" it has no correlation. No coherence. No interesting scheme.

Take off a chunk of New York anywhere you please, of similar area, where congestion is greatest and you will have another and perhaps a better Radio City, on its own old-fashioned terms of old-fashioned composition, lacking only the little park down in the dark.

Radio City, of course, is a lie.

Its "feature," as architecture, is masonry mass in masonry materials entirely, falsifying the actual materials and the nature of its construction: a series of tall steel frames designed by the structural engi-neers. The steel framing might have great beauty in itself.

But now, all set up and waiting, "architec-ture," please!

Here come the doctors of appearances, the functioneers, T-square and triangle in hand to dra-matize Mr. Rockefeller's private enterprise for

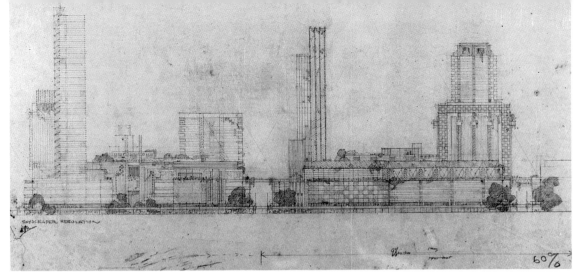

Skyscraper Regulation (Project). 1926. Elevation/section. Pencil on tracing paper, 35 x 20". FLLW Fdn#2603.002

profit and make it a gift to the public.

And how?

By pretending that steel is not steel. By believing the fortification of feudal times is still ideal architecture to put on steel stilts.

By falsifying nature to make another chunk of New York, just like New York. As though there wasn't too much of New York already on those terms.

And all they mean is not architecture but exaggerated scene-decoration for the sinews of the machine age.

How should Mr. Rockefeller know?

Why should his architects care?

And what does it really matter. Radio City is just "another one of those things" to come down in thirty years—paid up and paid out.

"Radio City is New York style, cut loose from the styles of the past and too young to have a name of its own," says Mr. Rockefeller's spokesman, Dr. Corbett.

No, not too young!

How would "Functioneer" do?

"The engineer," says Hood, "comes first, the elevator man and expert in light and air come next. And then comes the "work"—work is right—"of making the outside as good looking as possible."

And Mr. Hood himself has told you what is the matter with Radio City. Why it cannot be architecture. Why it betrays its opportunity. He tells you this by way of showing you how sensible a hired man he is and how reconciled to his job of making the outside, yes, any old outside as it happens to come—"as good looking as possible."

Radio City is therefore not intelligently designed.

It is not necessity growing by virtue of inner life into a fine integral pattern of the materials and construction that make it stand there where it is.

Not in the least. So the city within the city has no genuine vigorous beauty.

It has instead of beauty what is found in the New York skyscraper, a shallow scene painting that belongs in the Hollywood studio of a movie magnate.

It has no place at all in the great culture of a great architecture.

Perhaps, right here, I should build the right kind of a Radio City for Mr. Rockefeller. But since he is going to make so much money by building the wrong kind, I think that would be "giving" Mr. Rockefeller more than he deserves.

But I will explain.

Modern, or young, architecture, is Organic Architecture.

Organic Architecture says just what it is, and says it by way of being its own natural self.

For instance, Brooklyn Bridge is organic architecture. A blemish, the Gothic arching of the stone pylons carrying the cables. A functioneer touch. Why Gothic arches? Nevertheless the bridge is true modern building.

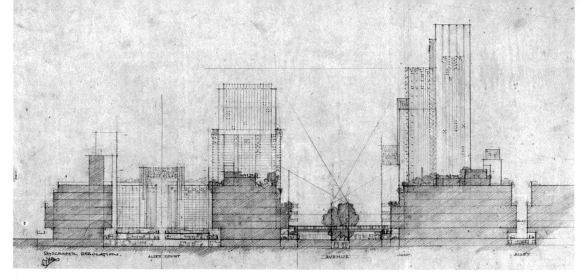

Skyscraper Regulation (Project). 1926. Elevation/section. Pencil on tracing paper, 35 x 20". FLLW Fdn#2603.003

The Crystal Palace in London was mainly modern and organic. A blemish, the manufactured ornamental detail.

The Eiffel Tower was modern and organic but not in form adapted to the medium of construction. It was difficult to build and ugly unless modified by atmospheric conditions.

Our grain elevators[1] have the simplicity and force that is a modern idea, but they are not yet architecture. Their purpose is primitive.

A steamship is an instance of modern construction until functioneers get hold of its "insides" and "decorate" them.

Motor cars are becoming more modern in appearance as in effect. The Cord[2] was a leader along this line.

In short, the Modern is a protest against the sentimentality that ignores reality to find comfort and respectability in sentimental make-believe.

Apply this to our buildings:

And a hotel won't look like an office building.

A railway station won't look like a palazzo.

A gas station won't look like a Colonial diminutive.

A school won't look like a factory.

A factory won't look like a museum etc., etc.

To be modern simply means that all materials are used honestly for the sake of their own qualities and that the materials also modify the design of the building.

For the instance in hand, a steel building won't look like a masonry building. In the purpose of the structure itself, in the way it is built, and in what makes it stand there where it is, modern architecture is found and developed into an outside.

Architecture *is not made on the "outside" of anything,* as the functioneers shamelessly say they make it after the thing is all arranged and set up.

Modern Architecture happened in all these things I've mentioned, except in Radio City.

So, Radio City is not Modern Architecture in any genuine sense. To reiterate: as architecture the "City" is the shallow scene painting that belongs in the Hollywood studio of a movie magnate. It has no place at all and will have none in the great culture of a great architecture.

1. Chicago, as "stacker of wheat," was the catalyst for the development of the grain elevator in the mid- to late nineteenth century, and these giant structures, numbering 22 in the city in 1898, would certainly have been familiar to Wright. Although Wright does not often mention them, later European modernists admitted to being greatly inspired by them.
2. Body styling in automotive design did not become a major consideration until the 1920s; "streamlining" was not a factor until the 1930s. The Cord, manufactured by Auburn Automobile Co. of Connersville, Indiana, was among the forerunners of a new design aesthetic and in its ascendancy in the early 1930s.

BOOKS THAT HAVE MEANT MOST TO ME

Of all the arts, music Wright considered to be the closest to architecture. He wrote that he saw a great similarity between the mind of the architect and the mind of the composer in the creation of structure, rhythm, scale, and melody:

> *Beethoven's music is in itself the greatest proof I know of divine harmony alive in the human spirit. When I build I often hear his music and, yes, when Beethoven made music I am sure he sometimes saw buildings like mine in character.*[1]

In this article, ostensibly devoted to literature, Wright concludes with the praise of music.[Published in Scholastic *magazine, September 1932]*

I SUPPOSE THE BOOKS ONE HAS CHOSEN OR HAS HAPPENED to read are important. Everybody makes a more or less natural selection, I should say, notwithstanding suggestions or commands. And the book fodder for which we have a natural taste does most to feed the thing we call ourselves.

The Arabian Nights fascinated me as a boy. Aladdin and his wonderful lamp—"imagination" was the lamp as I see now—was one of the tales that never tired me. My father threw in Edward Everett Hale's *The Man Without a Country* and that made a deep impression. I remember *Don Quixote* was with me early, almost as early as *Gulliver's Travels* and *Robinson Crusoe*.

I should mention *Wilhelm Meister*. I got to that through Carlyle, after *Sartor Resartus*. I owe a lot to Shakespeare because of Carlyle, and to Goethe, the

"great liberator." And I should be ungrateful if I omitted to mention Victor Hugo, the great modern in my boyhood, who declared for romanticism as a new freedom. He wrote the best amateur essay on architecture ever published. It is in *Nôtre Dame de Paris*.

In early manhood I was a Meredithian to the bone for years—am yet. When I discovered Samuel Butler, William Blake came to stay, and in Blake I found the source of the Pre-Raphaelite movement in England. Rabelais came along about that time. But Shelley lifted me higher than was my wont in middle life, and strange to say I became one of Walt Whitman's lovers about the same time. I see no chasm between Shelley and Whitman, though Old Walt is much more with me now. So are Thoreau and Emerson.

I have read with enthusiasm the great Russians. They early on got inside me, from Tolstoy and Gogol to Gorky and Dostoyevski. Lately, finding the Bible in print by Cobden-Sanderson, I've found it entirely fresh reading and inspiring. I like Carl Sandburg, Edna St. Vincent Millay, Ring Lardner, Westbrook Pegler, Alexander Woollcott, and the editorial observations of *The New Yorker*.

Mine is a catholic taste, which probably means a hearty appetite, and I find much to admire in books that do not touch my own work. When I get to those, I find too much pretended or missing.

But, to me, the greatest literature, after all, is not words but notes. Bach, Handel, and Beethoven, Stravinsky, Scriabin, Debussy, and sometimes the Negro spirituals and jazz. Music gives me more now.

My son Lloyd once took me to task for swinging so wide an arc in my appreciation, taking it for a lack of distinction and discrimination. So here I make my confession, with an uneasy feeling that I have probably omitted to mention the most important, if incidental, book-factors in my making because they were so thoroughly digested as to be utterly forgotten now.

1. Frank Lloyd Wright, *An Autobiography* (New York: Duell, Sloan and Pearce, 1943), p. 422.

Malcolm Willey House, Scheme 1 (Project). Minneapolis, Minnesota. 1932. Perspective. Pencil on tracing paper, 35 x 18".
FLLW Fdn#3204.001

TO THE NEUTER

This rather caustic—in fact, sarcastic—assault on the International Style, finds Wright characteristically issuing a plea for a more humane, and therefore more natural, approach to architecture. [Unpublished essay January 13, 1932]

THE EUNUCH HAS CERTAIN ADVANTAGES BY WAY OF HIS operation. The urge of his pro-creative power, let's say, if his character is good, gives way to a calm attitude of intellectual appreciation. Himself now vicarious, if at all, it is the "formula" that intrigues him, or else, desire still alive, he is maddened and envious. In a sad case, sterilized to the point of "intellectuality" as substitute for creative power, his resources are those of apperception instead of feelings.

So it is not surprising at this juncture that the "internationalist" should so soon go off virility of spirit and try to substitute, for feeling in action, a vicarious mental formula as habit.

This equivalent of the consequences of the operation—impotence—is the result of overindulgence, sentimentality, or the practice of self-abuse—eclecticism.

But, Nature (the creative mind) her custom holds, let shame (the style internationalism) say what it will.

The human spirit still has a soul that will not be made impotent. Nor consciously nor subconsciously will she make a neuter. She will make the man of her choice claim his human birthright, however the herd may turn. Let's shamelessly call the birthright "individuality" for one thing and be sus-

pect by all those whose attributes of character have never risen above personal idiosyncracy: Neuters.

We have prohibition because a few fools can't carry their liquor. We have internationalist formula for art because we have sentimentality and eclecticism.

The vicarious attitude turns the matter over to society's intellectual appreciation. To take the abuse of the thing for the real thing, condemn the reality and exalt the formula. This, it is, to be a neuter.

What we call Art and Architecture are love affairs. It has not yet been given by nature that all men should function above the belt to the same degree. And this quality of love in men or the capacity for it, perhaps, has been growing small while the capacity for lust is much the same in all men as in animals. It is over this blind instinct of lust the eunuch has the advantage of being unable to act.

And I believe that, speaking to the profane figure we started with, it is a too-long-continued rendezvous with lust that has made the manhood of our century neuter, as eunuch.

Though rendered impotent the neuter is not a total loss. He has his uses as has the eunuch as mentor. But do not let him imagine Love is dead because he has ceased to function. The twentieth century, notwithstanding the prostitution of the nineteenth, still has men with capacity for love who will create anew and fructify the future refusing vicarious trading whatever, in and upon the immediate present, as any formula.

It would be surprising if this probability were recognized by the neuter and placed among his intellectual appreciations—because he would not then be neuter. Though vicarious, desire not dead, he would still be on the side of life for others, at least.

But to a neuter all men are neuter. His impotence accords only envy to the potent. The impulse of neutrality (or impotence) when it comes to this love affair that is creative art is naturally willing to transfer the creative function to society as a mental matter, and say "it is better so." But only quieter so for them—as far as they go, I should say. And since

they are now the grand majority they may be right enough to temporarily serve the purposes of the age we are about to try to live in.

Such human nature as excess of success with the prostitute (the nineteenth century) has left us, may be content with the neuter and neutrality for a time. The rendezvous with the prostitute has incapacitated the majority for the love that is art and architecture. But nature is recuperative beyond anticipation or belief. She will have her way with the neuter by way of the potent individual and not the neuter his way with her.

Learning him, so soon as he attempts her with his formula, she will cast him forth, intellectually *sans culottes*.

Do you think he will then be really happier with his "operation" than the man of feeling who, falling in love with nature, succeeds with her?

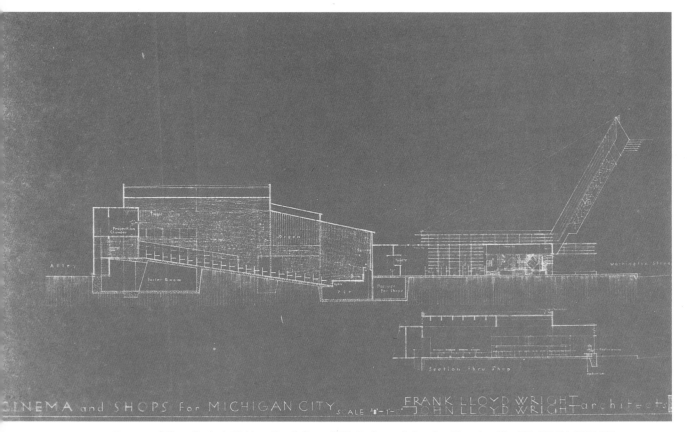

Cinema and Shops (Project). Michigan City, Indiana. 1932. Section and elevation. Blueprint, 38 x 20". FLLW Fdn#3203.015

THE FROZEN FOUNTAIN

W right's affection for Louis Sullivan, combined with a profound understanding of his life and work, prompted him to write this comment on Claude Bragdon's 1932 book, The Frozen Fountain *(New York: Alfred A. Knopf). This unsolicited manuscript, sent to* The Saturday Review of Literature *on February 18, 1932, was accompanied by a note to the editor, Henry Seidl Canby: "My dear Mr. Canby: Bragdon's book seems to me fearfully superficial but here is a criticism if you care to use it." [Published in* The Saturday Review, *May 21, 1932]*

THE FROZEN FOUNTAIN IS, PRINCIPALLY, A TREATISE ON ornament as an abstract element—something in itself, which of course it may be as snow or mineral crystal are. Or as Louis Sullivan's system of ornament was. But Louis Sullivan devised a system of ornament out of himself with a sense of organic unity warmly exponent of the individuality of one Louis Henry Sullivan.

Mr. Bragdon devises a formula or a system for devising geometrical patterns, which is not the same thing and in which there is very little room for Mr. Bragdon's individuality or anyone's.

That may be a virtue as things are with us. At any rate Claude Bragdon, necromancer, has well written another entertaining book. It is a beautiful book and if the author could letter the drawings as well as he draws, the draughtsmanship of the work would be faultless.

In this affair of cutting out the head of the drum to find where the sound comes from C. B. is an enthusiast with no equal. And, be it said, although he doesn't find out where the sound comes from he does discover all sorts of curious and interesting things on the inside wall of the drum and excites more speculation as to what became of the sound when the head of the drum was cut out.

But this is the fate of all attempts to especially adapt geo-astro-labery to incidental façades and effect coincidences with the features of building elevations.

Such coincidences can only bore one who has dealt directly with proportion and gone into it directly enough to know that great buildings never happened that way.

Proportion is nothing in itself but is a matter of relation to environment modified always by every feature-exterior as well as interior. Le Corbusier, hard as nails and sane as a hammer up to this point, goes as superstitious as a milkmaid lost in the mist of a moonlit night.

But in meticulous, abstract, geometrical analysis there will always be fascinating room for the astrological, geometrical mind. And sometimes the long arm of coincidence will find a pretty circumstance in its hand. I should say the laws lie deeper and in the realm of relativity. Were the abstract so easily made I should distrust the validity of the laws.

But Claude Bragdon and I have much in common in this book because he came as a visitor and friend to reverently sit at the feet of my old master Louis Sullivan. I first met him there. And the Master's worth can not be exaggerated for me by his lively sense of gratitude. Nor do I resent his tying me so closely to the Master's side, refusing to let me stray. Though in regard to Louis Sullivan's direct European influence he is mistaken. European reactions were not Sullivanian but by way of the straight line and flat plane as abstractions—with which Louis Sullivan did nothing. Mr. Sullivan himself has said that I was his apprentice but never his disciple. This last sentence as against the Bragdon reference to me as Sullivan's disciple.

And I think C.B., as his disciple, applies to him more of the fourth dimension than necessary if he will take the simple third we now have and give it spiritual interpretation. That is to say take "thickness" and see it as depth.

Architectural depths are seldom if ever plumbed by geometrical devices. Certainly not Louis Sullivan's. They were too human.

Coming to the concrete analysis of architecture there is much sense in this book. Some wisdom. But I cannot agree with the Bragdon category of "Significant, Dramatic, Organic"!

Were a building genuinely organic the word "significant" might be forgotten and the word "dramatic" be forgiven. Because the term "organic" implies the others as the term manhood implies health and beauty.

He adds "ecstatic" for good measure. Dangerous because this is not a quality of a building, but of the beholder.

It is characteristic of him, however, because he characterizes a building as a frozen fountain, going back to agree with Ruskin's "frozen music," I suppose. A term Ruskin successfully applied to Gothic architecture.

But the Bragdon simile would be much more true were it applied to the sources of creative inspiration that build the building. Fountains they certainly are and, unhappily, frozen. They are the only fountains I can connect with the thought of a building: the fountains of creative energy that cultured the building into being. Spires should be less inspiring than depths and breadths of integral character. The superficial skyscraper did not begin our American architecture. The simile of "fountain" applied to the building and "the Chrysler" becomes the ideal building when it is, as are the skyscrapers, inorganic, utterly.

The buildings that deserve the term "organic" are streamline with the horizon, marrying the features of the terrain, upstanding as the trees. No matter. The danger of any simile is a deadly danger. He is a brave man who makes one.

Notwithstanding these seemingly fundamental disagreements with Mr. Claude Bragdon's thesis—there is much to admire in his book as there is in him. But books call for books.

THE DESIGNING PARTNER

This short manuscript is a personal reflection by Wright on the nature of the "designing partner." He refers, at its conclusion, to the structure of the firm of Adler and Sullivan, for whom he worked for nearly seven years before establishing his own office. [Unpublished essay, 1932]

AFTER WORKING HOURS TODAY AND OUR DINING TOGETHER in the little dining room on the hill, I went alone into the deserted working rooms with time to reflect a little.

Looking about over the drafting boards I wondered what, at the moment, would please me most. The most pleasurable thing I could imagine was that I might go into some shop where fine colored pencils were kept and gather several of every color I had ever seen and perhaps see some never seen before. Perhaps a more gorgeous red—a truer blue—a warmly green. And I would lay them all out in a row—abuse the white paper on the board at which I sat—and sit looking at them—several of each and every possible color. Enough to use and last some time for once. I suppose the recent scarcity of some of the most desirable colors—because we use those most and can't buy more at the moment—led up to this organic desire.

But I love colored pencils. They are intimately associated with my sense of happiness—and have been since childhood.

And what has all this to do with the designing partner? Nothing at all except that the word "design" always brings colored pencils to mind just as the pencils bring the idea of design to mind.

The designer is a happy fellow. Ordinarily the happiest of all but it is hard for me to see him as a "partner."

Nevertheless most of our architectural "firms" are made up of a designer—and a builder or a business getter or all three.

And I wonder how the thing works out. Is the designing partner a happy fellow working for the builder and business getter or is it the other way around?

It is hard to think of a real designer managing a partner. It is easier for me to imagine a partner managing the designer—perhaps because Louis Sullivan was the designing partner of Adler and Sullivan and there I saw the relationship at work, at its best no doubt.

Mr. Sullivan tackled the problems presented by Mr. Adler (who was splendidly equipped as a constructor and planner) and the client—who was usually Adler's client—because Adler established the practice, needing help in matters of design—believing Sullivan had genius along that line and annexed him.

THE DISAPPEARING CITY

During the late 1920s the Wrights made several trips by automobile across the nation: twice from Wisconsin to Arizona and back, and several times from Arizona to California, New York, or Washington, D.C. Prior to these trips, Wright had voyaged across the United States, but always by train. Now his perception and perspective of the depth and breadth of the nation was intensified. He experienced the enormous sweeps of land and the varied landscapes—in sharp contrast with the ever more crowded urban centers. Thoughts of city planning as an antidote to the general lack of design that he witnessed everywhere formed in his mind. In this book, The Disappearing City, published in the same year as An Autobiography, he put on record his observations as well as his vision and solutions. His autobiography contains a section entitled "The Usonian City," in which he attacks the existing idea of the city and how cities have grown steadily more and more inhumane. He then describes the potential features of a city that is more related to the landscape, more dedicated to the individual human being. Open space, decentralization, humanization, privacy, and association with natural features of the terrain are all now possible, he writes, because of the benefits of modern technology and modern inventions, including automobiles, a growing network of great road systems, and expanding communications. In very sketchy form, the chapter of his autobiography laid the groundwork for this much more detailed treatise. Two years after The Disappearing City was published, Wright formulated his architectonic solution to the city, Broadacre City. [Published with four illustrations by William Farquar Payson, New York, 1932]

ON EARTH

THE VALUE OF THIS EARTH, AS MAN'S HERITAGE, IS PRETTY far gone from him now in the cities centralization has built. And centralization has over-built them all. Such urban happiness as the properly citified citizen knows consists in the warmth and pressure or the approbation of the crowd. Grown Argus-eyed and enamoured of "whirl" as a dervish, the surge and mechanical roar of the big city turns his head, fills his ears as the song of birds, the wind in the trees, animal cries and the voices and songs of his loved ones once filled his heart.

But as he stands, out of machines he can create nothing but machinery.

The properly citified citizen has become a broker dealing, chiefly, in human frailties or the ideas and inventions of others: a puller of levers, a presser of the buttons of a vicarious power, his by way of machine craft.

A parasite of the spirit is here, a whirling dervish in a whirling vortex.

Perpetual to and fro excites and robs the urban individual of the meditation, imaginative reflection and projection once his as he lived and walked under clean sky among the growing greenery to which he was born companion. The invigoration of the Book of Creation he has traded for the emasculation of a treatise on abstraction. Native pastimes with the native streams, woods and fields, this recreation he has traded for the taint of carbon-monoxide, a rented aggregate of rented cells up-ended on hard pavements, "Paramounts," "Roxies," and nightclubs, speakeasies. And for this he lives in a cubicle among cubicles under a landlord who lives above him, the apotheosis of rent, in some form, in some penthouse.

The citizen, properly citified, is a slave to herd instinct and vicarious power as the medieval laborer, not so long before him, was a slave to his pot of "heavy wet." A cultural weed of another kind.

The weed goes to seed. Children grow up, herded by thousands in schools built like factories, run like factories, systematically turning out herd-struck morons as machinery turns out shoes.

Men of genius, productive when unsuccessful, "succeed," become vicarious, and except those whose métier is the crowd, these men, who should be human salvage, sink in the city to produce, but create no more. Impotent.

Life itself is become the restless "tenant" in the big city. The citizen himself has lost sight of the true aim of human existence and accepts substitute aims as his life, unnaturally gregarious, tends more and more toward the promiscuous blind adventure of a crafty animal, some form of graft, a febrile pursuit of sex as "relief" from factual routine in the mechanical uproar of mechanical conflicts. Meantime, he is struggling to maintain, artificially, teeth, hair, muscles and sap; sight growing dim by work in artificial light, hearing now chiefly by telephone; going against or across the tide of traffic at the risk of damage or death. His time is regularly wasted by others because he, as regularly, wastes theirs as all go in different directions on scaffolding, or concrete or underground to get into another cubicle under some other landlord. The citizen's entire life is exaggerated but sterilized by machinery—and medicine: were motor oil and castor oil to dry up, the city would cease to function and promptly perish.

The city itself is become a form of anxious rent, the citizen's own life rented, he and his family evicted if he is in "arrears" or "the system" goes to smash. Renting, rented and finally the man himself rent should his nervous pace slacken. Should this anxious lockstep of his fall out with the landlord, the money-lord, the machinelord, he is a total loss.

And over him, beside him and beneath him, even in his heart as he sleeps is the taximeter of rent, in some form, to goad this anxious consumer's unceasing struggle for or against more or less merciful or merciless money increment. To stay in lockstep. To pay up. He hopes for not much more now. He is paying his own life into bondage or he is managing to get the lives of others there, in order to keep up the three sacrosanct increments to which he has subscribed as the present great and beneficent lottery of private capital. Humanity preying upon humanity seems to be the only "economic system" he knows anything about.

But all the powerful modern resources naturally his by use of modern machinery are, by way of human progress, now involuntarily turning against the city. Although a system he, himself, helped to build, capitalized centralization is no longer a system for the citizen nor one working for him. Having done its work for humanity, centralization is centripetal force beyond control, exaggerated by various vicarious powers. And it is exaggerating more and more in its victim his animal fear of being turned out of the hole into which he has been accustomed to crawl only to crawl out again tomorrow morning. Natural horizontality is gone and the citizen condemns himself to an unnatural, sterile verticality— upended by his own excess.

Notwithstanding, sporadic housing, slumming, and profit sharing to build him permanently into bondage as he stands, but for this involuntary war of mechanical factors he is all but helpless now, cursed by the primitive cave dwelling instinct: the shadow of the wall of the ancestral tribe.

PRIMITIVE INSTINCTS

Time was when mankind was divided between cave dwellers and wandering tribes. And were we to go back far enough, we might find the wanderer swinging from branch to branch in the leafy bower of the trees insured by the curl of his tail while the more stolid lover of the wall lurked in such hidden holes and material cavities as he could find.

The cave dweller was the ancient conservative. But probably he was more brutal with his heavy club, if not more ferocious, than the wanderer with his spear.

The cave dweller became the cliff dweller and began to build cities. Establishment was his. His God was a statue more terrible than himself, a murderer, and hidden in a cave. This statue he erected into a covenant.

His swifter, more mobile brother devised a more adaptable and elusive dwelling place, the folding tent.

From place to place over the earth following the law of change, natural law to him, he went in changing seasons.

An adventurer.

His God was a spirit, a wind devastating or beneficent as himself.

These divisions of the human family, having the herd instinct in common with other animals, made God in their own image. Both set up an enmity, each of the other.

The cave dwellers bred their young in the shadow of the wall. The mobile tribes bred their young under the stars in such safety as seclusion by distance from the enemy might afford.

So we may assume the cave dweller multiplied more swiftly than his brother. But more complete was his destruction, more terrible his waste when his defenses fell. His walls grew heavier as he grew more powerful. When he ceased to find a cave he made one. The fortification became his. Cities were originally fortifications.

The cave dweller's human counterpart cultivated mobility for his safety. Defenses, for him, lay in swiftness, stratagem, physical prowess and such arts as Nature taught.

As ingrained instinct of the human race now, in this far distance of time, are both these primitive instincts, though the wandering tribes seem, gradually, to have been overcome by the material defenses and the static forces of the material establishment of the cave dweller.

But I imagine that the ideal of freedom that keeps breaking through our establishments setting their features aside or obliterating them is due in some degree to the original instinct of the adventurer. He who lived by his freedom and his prowess

beneath the stars rather than he who lived by his obedience and labor in the shadow of the wall.

However that may be here two human natures have married and brought forth other natures. A fusion of natures in some. A straining confusion in others. In some a survival, more or less instinct, of one or the other salient, archaic, characteristic instinct.

Gradually the body of mankind, both natures working together, has produced what the body of mankind calls civilization. Civilizations become conscious, insist upon, and strive to perfect culture. In this matter of civilization, the shadow of the wall has seemed to predominate, though the open sky of the adventurer is far from disappearing. As physical fear of brutal force and any need of fortification grow less, so the ingrained yearning for the freedom of the mobile hunter, surviving, finds more truth and reason for being than the stolid masonry or cave dwelling defenses erected and once necessary to protect human life and now slumbering in the manufacturer, the agrarian and the merchant. Those defenses, in any case, modern science and war have made useless and a man's value may again depend not so much on what he has as upon what he can do. So, by way of modern resources, a type is developing capable of changing environment to fit desires and offset losses to the type sinking permanently into the "shadow of the wall"—the big city.

It is already evident that life now must be more naturally conserved by more light, more freedom of movement and a more general spatial freedom in the ideal establishment of what we call civilization. A new space concept is needed. And it is evident, in this need, that it has come.

Modern mobilization, as a leading factor, is by way of modern means of transport, having its effect upon the nature of the cave dweller—this city brother who submitted obedience to man to be well saved by faith and not by works. But it is only a natural means of realization returning to his brother of the wandering tribe.

So, the "Machine" is at work moulding as well as destroying human character.

But survivals of human habit wait long for burial.

Man, mobile or static, is first a creature of habit.

The habits bred by primitive instincts resist change, however reasonable the change, and will wear away as the dropping of water wears away stone.

All that any change in the conditions of life produces in the conglomerate man-mass at first is reaction toward the old order. Increased sentiment for the old, violence to the new.

But certain long subconscious desires rooted in these primitive instincts and never yet realized in the present dense order of centralization gradually find release and new means, in the new order of the machine age, to realization. As always, this new release and dawning realization acts positively in favor of the new and eventual destruction of the old life. Such is the order of change in the human habits bred by instinct.

A present instance: for generations the rural youth of Usonia[1] longed for the activity, the sophistication and prizes of the City. There he sought his "fortune." The great prizes were still to be had in accelerated human intercourse as well as in the human excitements to be found in the city. So when, by mobilization, he was made free to move he was by that aid moved cityward to gratify his longing.

THE UNECONOMIC BASIS OF THE CITY

Such human concentration upon the city has been abnormally intensified because, as hangover from traditions having their origin in other circumstances, three major economic artificialities have been grafted upon intrinsic production and grown into a legitimate economic system. Two of the three now uneconomic "economics" are forms of rent and are artificial because they are not intrinsic. Both are extrinsic forms of unearned increment. The third artificiality, unearned increment also, is so by way of traffic in machine-invention: another, less obvious, form of rent.

By the leverage of a mechanical acceleration never existing in the world before, the operation of these economic systems have been abnormally exaggerated and intensified.

The first and most important form of rent contributing most to poverty as a human institution and to the overgrowth of the cities is rent for land: land values, created by improvements or the growth of the community itself held by the fortuitous individual whose claim to a lucky piece of realty is good-fortune "by law." The profits of this adventitious good-fortune create a series of white-collar satellites all subsisting by the sale, distribution, operation and collection of the various unearned increments arising from traffic in more or less lucky land. The skyscraper is this adventitious fortune's modern monument. The city is its natural home.

The second artificiality is rent for money. By way of the ancient Mosaic invention of "interest," money, in itself, becoming alive to go on continuously working to make all work useless. The profits earned by money as a premium placed upon the accretions of labor, create another adventitious form of good-fortune. More armies of white-collar satellites are created busily engaged in the sale, distribution, operation and collection of this form of increment, unearned except as the gratuitous, mysterious premium placed upon earnings earned it.

The modern city is its stronghold.

The third artificiality is the unearned increment of the machine: the profits of this now great common invention of mankind, by way of traffic in invention, captained and placed where they do not belong except as capitalistic centralization itself is a proper objective. Inevitably by this means, the profits of imaginative ingenuity in doing the work of the world are almost all funneled into the pockets of fewer and fewer captains of industry. Only in a small measure— except by gift from the captains—are these profits yet where they belong—with the man whose life is modified, given or sacrificed by this new common agency for doing the work of the world.

Armies of high-powered salesmanship came into being to unload the senseless overvalues and overproduction, inevitable to this common machine-facility, upon the true owner of the machine; the man himself. In this third form of good-fortune another series of white-collar satellites arose, "selling." Selling by financing and collecting by threatening and foreclosure, or refinancing and "repossession." All, as a natural tendency, concentrating in fewer and fewer hands these various unearned increments, by the inevitable centripetal action of capitalistic centralization.

Now, to maintain in due force and legal effect all these various white-collar armies deriving from the

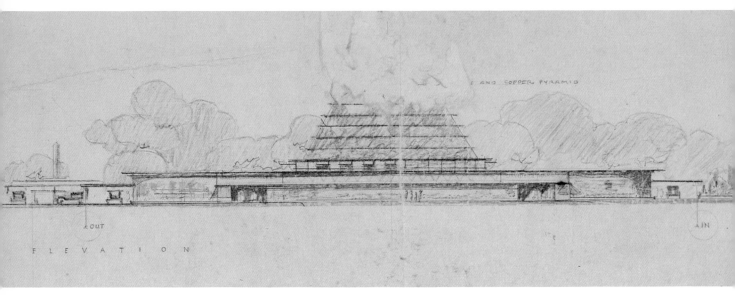

Prefabricated Wayside Markets (Project). 1932. Elevation (above) and section (opposite). Pencil and color pencil on paper, 14 x 12". FLLW Fdn#3205.002/3205.001

three artificial "economic" factors and keep all dove-tailing together smoothly, has inevitably exaggerated a simple natural human benefit. Government.

"That Government is best Government that is least Government" was the Jeffersonian ideal of these United States of America. But to keep peace and some show of equity between the lower passions busily engaged in getting money by these extraordinarily complicated forms of money-getting, legitimized by government, government ran away with government and itself became extraordinary. Another army of white-collarites to add to the other armies was the consequence. Major and minor courts, petty officials and their complex rulings themselves became this official army.

And now the multifarious laws enacted as complex expedients to make all function together bred, finally, still another white-collar army: the lawyers. It soon became impossible to hold, operate or distribute land, sell money or manufacture anything safely without the guide and counsel of these specialists in the extraordinary rules and regulations of this now involute game called machine-age civilization. No wonder the interpretations of these specialists, themselves, are often in conflict.

These satellites of rent in its several forms, too, are natural minions and mentors of cities.

This group of artificialities, naturally depending upon a strong-arm status-quo and, too, upon an expedient religion wherein men were to be saved by faith rather than by their own works, taken all together constitute the traditional but exaggerated and unsafe substitute for a sound economic basis of human society in the United States. They subsist as the substructure of the outmoded city; the inorganic basis of the inorganic city now battening and feeding upon all intrinsic sources of intrinsic production.

These intrinsic sources are the men who by manual toil or by concentration of superior ability upon actual production, physical, aesthetic, intellectual or moral—render "value received" to human life.

THE VICTIM OF THE BATTLE OF INCREMENTS

Meantime, what of the subject, or object or living man-unit upon whom, by his voluntary subordination this extraordinarily complicated economic superstructure, has been imposed, erected, and functions as government and "business"? What about the man himself? The man who labors out of the earth essential sustenance for all and the material riches for industry? Where, in all this, is the agrarian, the mechanic, the artist, the teacher, the inventor, the scientist, the artisan, hewers of wood and drawers of water?

All are pretty much in the same caste, no longer masters of fortune. Fortunes being engendered and controlled by schemers employing artificialities of a complex economic system resting upon no sound, broad basis in intrinsic production nor in the nature of man's relation to his earth. And these three false systems of false fortune place a false premium upon ignoble traits of character. Moreover, the three systems of good-fortune being thus necessarily maintained by the strong arm of a forced legitimacy, that arm—however strong—must tire and periodically come down for a rest while confusion and misery descend upon all or all become confused and in alarm, seek cover of some kind—somehow.

Where then is the genuine artifex in this tower of an economic Babel that finds its apex and ideal in exaggerated buildings and exaggerated enterprises in exaggerated cities?

Well, centralization has conferred certain human benefits upon him by stimulating machine development and expert mechanics while meantime, the essential rightmindedness and decency of humanity—the artifex—has gone on working with the machines trying to cultivate beauty, justice, generosity and pity: worshipping the one god, no longer a statue hidden in a cave but a great spirit ruling all by principle.

This god of the artifex is now a free spirit allowing man choice between what is good for him and what is bad for him, so that in free exercise of individual choice he may himself grow to be godlike.

THE EXPERIMENT

Out of this confused life has come, gradually, the modern conception of God and man as growth—a concept called Democracy. And out of this concept, too, came the foundling: this nation conceived in liberty where all men were to have equal opportunity before the law; where vast territory, riches untouched, were inherited by all the breeds of the earth desiring freedom and courageous enough to come and take domain on the terms of the pioneer.

This new experiment in government soon became a great federation of states: these United States. A great nation harboring within its borders the adventuresome, the outcast, the cheated, the thwarted, the predatory worst and the courageous best, deserting previous nations.

With no corresponding revisions of traditional "property rights" the new country was founded upon this more just and therefore more complete freedom for the individual than any existing before in all the world: a government that should be "best government because least government." And a Thomas Jefferson crossing an Alexander Hamilton, a George Washington hand in hand with an Abraham Lincoln, a William Lloyd Garrison, a John Brown, an Emerson, a Whitman and a Thoreau, a Louis Sullivan, a Henry George—such were her sons. In them the original ideal was held, still clear. Then came, quickly, extreme private wealth by way of the three fortuitous money-getting systems, and soon com-

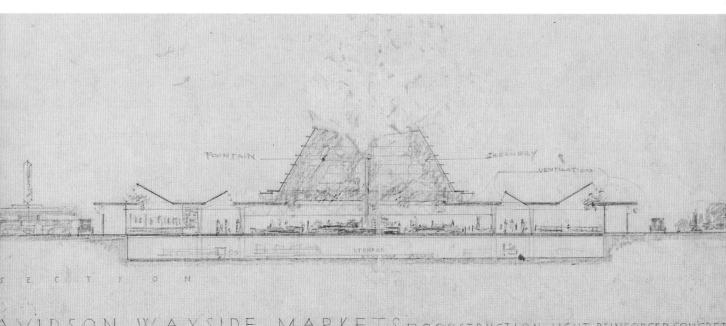

mercial ascendancy and power outran culture. Unnatural reservoirs of capital made of little or no value such cultural understanding as the new country had. It was so easy to grow or gather or discover in the freshness and the first spoils of a new ground, that fortunes piled up overnight in hands least fitted to administer either power or wealth, and both were willing to buy whatever they liked and what they should have grown. The suddenly rich needed a culture that could be bought or taken ready-made. The original idea grew more and more impractical. And such arts as had come to the new country with the decency of the early colonials naturally took ascendancy for a time. But, soon, with the advent of many nationalities came eclecticism in art and architecture. Ready-made art and architecture became a pressing need as the nation itself rapidly became the greatest eclecticism of all time. As culture, ready-made thus became a necessity, the expedient became a virtue.

Here for the first time in history a self-determining people subscribing to an ideal of new freedom sprang into being as a nation with a collection of ready-made cultures to piece together as best it could into a makeshift composite. The incongruities were enormous and begot abortions. Abortion became convenient, therefore desirable. Culture as a convenience consisted, at best, in a form of rebirth of rebirths until nothing was, or could be, born. All culture came to be selected, artificially adapted and soon was, by way of education, arbitrarily applied by academic advice to growing power and to developing resources. Inevitably such applied culture failed to qualify as impregnator of new life or as adequate interpreter of the new ideal on which the life of the country was originally founded.

So, as the new nation arose in might and riches, its crude natural resources, as culture, aborted strange, borrowed or "adapted" forms. Perversion or pretension became everywhere manifest. The new life itself outgrew the old forms, making them unnatural, but there seemed to be no imaginative power to impregnate life with new and natural forms because no constructive lessons could be learned by eclectic imitation. All was by way of personal likes or dislikes—a form of license in the name of the "classical."

Culture, impotent while power was enormous, itself became enormity, took refuge and committed enormities in the name of classic conformity. Names and styles had authority. Fashion ruled. Impotence became honorable. It was safe.

At length, parasiticism was raised to the level of an academic culture in the "new freedom" as the consequence of such utter confusion of choice by way of what selectious taste could buy. This was inevitable because the God of principle that was to rule the rulers of the country founded upon a more just expression of human liberty than men knew before did not inspire the people with a more sensible interpretation of life in the arts and crafts of that life. And now, into this vital department of the human mind, "Tradition" itself has entered as itself—an eclecticism. Art and architecture that had previously existed as parasite for five centuries imitated by parasites. Religion, too, sank to the level of eclecticism. This was necessary to maintain the general artificiality. The exploitation of the "formula" in all religion as well as in all art had the right-of-way.

Any nation, eclectic by nature, perhaps, could only, in matters of culture thus breed "tastes" that could only turn to "taste" as culture.

And the "academic" mistook a setting sun for dawn! The "pseudo," by official and academic order, ruled the mind. "American Culture" became a following after into the general darkness. What could it do except stumble or fall away where life insisted upon life?

There could be nothing in any such culture that could grow anything genuine out of the new soil if it would, except, as wealth and vicarious power increased, to overgrow centralized cities upon the ground upon which we were so newly founded. The Ideal was so quickly betrayed by sudden-riches.

The Jeffersonian democratic ideal, inspiring in the beginning, lacked nourishment in culture and so languished. Except as a mask might be imposed by the draper and haberdasher functioning as artists and architects, and high-powered salesmanship could sell both them and their product to the "successful," the facts of power and the surge of life of the new country were left to stand unqualified and ugly as mere necessity. But that naked necessity was better than their cultural mask.

Meantime Youth went to the professional eclecticism of the greatest colleges to be hopelessly confirmed as spiritual parasites.

Thus has such culture as we have in the United States set itself up as something beautiful on life because we could not, or would not, learn how to be of life.

And life itself, as it is, goes on its subconscious and natural way in the channels of necessity performing the miracles to which culture itself now points with pride and wonderment . . . astonished that such things can be. Culture itself had to be rejected in order that the miracles might be and the scale of man-movement be utterly changed.

These miracles of technical machine invention with which culture has had nothing to do and that in spite of misuse and abuse are forces with which culture and life itself have now to reckon, working toward a new freedom, are the internal combustion engine working as various forms of mobilization; various forms of electric intercommunication; steel, glass and automatic machines; modern architecture.

Given electrification, distances are all but annihilated so far as communication goes. Given the automatons of machinery, and human labor, relatively, disappears.

Given mechanical mobilizations, the steamship, airship, automobile, and mechanical human sphere of movement immeasurably widens by way of comparative flight.

Given a modern architecture, and man is a noble feature of the ground as the trees and streams are such features. An architecture for the individual becomes reasonable and possible. The individual comes into his own.

THE CASE FOR THE INDIVIDUAL

Buddha believed that only non-vicarious, that is to say individual, effort might reach the ultimate.

Jesus taught the dignity and worth of the individual developed from within as an individual, although Christianity perverted the teaching.

The Catholic Church discounting this ideal as every man for himself and the devil for the hindmost, emphasized the desirability of the utter disappearance of individuality which is more or less the politics of all agrarian peoples—but not their practice. The Protestants brought individuality, partially, back again. As a confused ideal. But some 500 years before Jesus the philosophy of the Chinese philosopher Laotze had a sense of individuality as achieved organic unity. Our own ideal social state, Democracy, was originally conceived as some such organic unity—that is to say—the free growth of many individuals as units free in themselves, functioning together in a unity of their own making. This is the natural ideal of democracy we now need to emphasize and live up to in order to regain the ground we have lost to the big cities centralization has overbuilt.

The "rugged individualism" that now captains our enterprises and becomes the "capitalist" is entirely foreign to this ideal of individuality. The actual difference between such "ism" and true individuality is the difference between selfishness and selfhood; the difference between sentiment and sentimentality; the difference between liberty and license.

And such individual "ism," literally "every man for himself and the devil for the hindmost," aggravated by the misuse of vicarious power has got native individuality into bad repute. Like the abuse of any good thing it is likely to bring on reactionary consequences. Signs of this reaction are not wanting. No counteraction can come from such culture as we have assumed because in such art as we know the personal idiosyncrasy as personality is too easily and generally mistaken for individuality. Sterility is the natural consequence of the vicarious exercise of power that is our modern characteristic, where creative ability should be concerned as individuality.

As a matter of fact until Usonians recognize that individuality is a high attribute of character, seldom common, always radical, and so always truly conservative, a matter of the soul: we have no defense.

Personality run to seed is not individuality. The will and the intellect working together for desire cannot make individuality. They can only make a human monster.

True individuality is, above all, an interior quality of the spirit or let us say individuality is organic spirituality—to couple two words almost never joined in our conversation or philosophy.

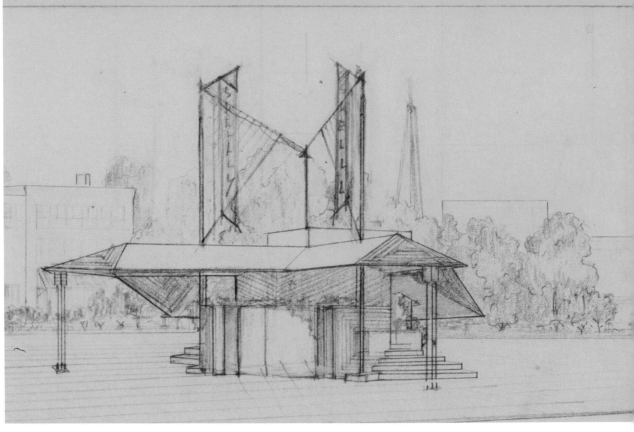

Standard Overhead Service Station (Project). 1932. Perspective. Pencil and color pencil on tracing paper, 19 x 16". FLW Fdn#3206.005

But it is a popular weakness or error to speak of spirituality as apart from the body, instead of its essential significance. Any true significance can only be the spiritual indication of whatever is material. If such significance is lacking, then life itself must be lacking. Wherever there is life there is significance. The insignificant is without life.

Individuality then may be said to be the organic significance of any person or any soul as distinguished from mere personality. So the true man is, always, from first to last concerned with significance in this sense and recognizes its integrity. Individuality, then, is such integrity whether of persons or of things.

Without individuality in this fundamental sense as a human integrity what life may there be but vicarious life only? There can never be great Life, so there can never be great Art.

Therefore we should be careful how we turn upon individuality sickened by flagrant abuses in its name. Capitalism may be individualism run riot. But individuality is something else. Necessarily it has nothing to do with capitalism, or communism, or socialism. The "ism" in any form has no individual-ity. The Formula has already taken its place when the "ist," the "ism" or the "ite" may be applied. And that was why all the great religious teachers—Jesus, Abdul Bahai, and Laotze especially—wanted no institutionalizing, no officialdom, not even disciples except as "fishers of men."

But human nature, by way of the human head, is yet weak and can only function on civilized lines, it seems, by way of the groove or the rail. Or more probably the rut.

So the rut is respectable and advised as "safe." And the rut is too often called law and order, when it should be seen and recognized as only the rut. Individuality soon becomes a menace to any form of rut-life. So rut-life turns against Individuality.

THE BROADACRE CITY[2]

We are concerned here in the consideration of the future city as a future for individuality in this organic sense: individuality being a fine integrity of the human race. Without such integrity there can be no real culture whatever what we call civilization may be.

We are going to call this city for the individual the Broadacre City because it is based upon a minimum of an acre to the family.

And, we are concerned for fear systems, schemes, and "styles" have already become so expedient as civilization that they may try to go on in Usonia as imitation culture and so will indefinitely postpone all hope of any great life for a growing people in any such city the United States may yet have.

To date our capitalism as individualism, our eclecticism as personality has, by way of taste, got in the way of integrity as individuality in the popular understanding, and on account of that fundamental misunderstanding we, the prey of our culture-monger, stand in danger of losing our chance at this free life our charter of liberty originally held out to us.

I see that free life in the Broadacre City.

As for freedom; we have prohibition because a few fools can't carry their liquor; Russia has communism because a few fools couldn't carry their power; we have a swollen privatism because a few fools can't carry their "success" and money must go on making money.

If instead of an organic architecture we have a style formula in architecture in America, it will be because too many fools have neither imagination nor the integrity called individuality. And we have our present overgrown cities because the many capitalistic fools are contented to be dangerous fools.

A fool ordinarily lacks significance except as a cipher has it. The fool is neither positive nor negative. But by way of adventitious wealth and mechanical leverage he and his satellites—the neuters—are the overgrown city and the dam across the stream flowing toward freedom.

Broadacre City. Model. 1934. Detail. FLLW Fdn FA#3402.0082

It is only the individual developing in his own right (consciously or unconsciously) who will go, first, to the Broadacre City because it is the proper sense of the dignity and worth of the individual, as an individual, that is building that city. But after those with this sense the others will come trailing along into the communal-individuality that alone we can call Democracy.

But before anything of significance or consequence can happen in the culture of such a civilization as ours, no matter how that civilization came to be, individuality as a significance and integrity must be a healthy growth or at least growing healthy. And it must be a recognized quality of greatness.

In an organic modern architecture, all will gladly contribute this quality, as they may, in the spirit that built the majestic cathedrals of the Middle Ages. That medieval spirit was nearest the communal, democratic spirit of anything we know. The common-spirit of a people disciplined by means and methods and materials, in common, will have—and with no recognized formula—great unity.

Already the centripetal city is itself an "ism" for ists and ites. Individuality has no longer a place in it more important than a burrow. Individuality is driven into nooks and corners or thwarted or aborted: frustrated by the mass-life only competing with, never completing, life.

So no healthy human-soul may longer grow or long survive in the vicarious life of the machine-made city because life, there, must be a surrender of true correlation of the human faculties to the expedient in some form; expedients imposed senselessly upon every soul in it to no purpose at all—except as they may be found to be some form of rent.

Voluntary self-sacrifice may be constructive. But to be condemned to the servile sacrifice of a voluntary life-long use of petty expedients to get by to, eventually, nowhere, is quite another matter. The human soul grows by what it gives as well as by what it feeds on. But the soul does not grow by what is exacted from it. Urban life having served its term is become a life-sentence of vicarious acts and the petty exaction of the expedient. A life outmoded. The big city is no longer modern.

CHANGE

Let us say that before the advent of universal and standardized mechanization, the city was more human. Its life as well as its proportion was more humane.

In planning the city, spacing was based, fairly enough, on the human being on his feet or sitting in some trap behind a horse, or two. Machinery had yet brought no swifter alternative. And a festival of wit, a show of pomp and a revel of circumstance rewarded life there in the original circumstances for which the city was planned. So, originally the city was a group life of powerful individualities true to life, conveniently enough spaced. This better life has already left the modern city, as it may, either for travel or the country estate. And such genius as the city has known for many a day is recruited from the country: the foolish celebrant of his "success," as such, seeking the city as a market, only to find an insatiable maw devouring quantity instead of protecting quality—eventually devouring himself as it is now devouring itself. "Fish for sale in the marketplace" but none in the streams. Frequent escape is already essential to any life at all in the overgrown city which offers nothing to the individual in bondage he cannot better find on terms of freedom in the country.

What, then, is the overgrown city for? The necessity that chained the individual to city life is dead or dying away. It is only as life has been taken from him and he has accepted substitutes offered to him that the "citizen" now remains.

The fundamental unit of space-measurement has so radically changed that the man now bulks ten to one and in speed a thousand to one as he is seated in his motor car. This circumstance would render the city obsolete. Like some old building the city is inhabited only because we have it, feel we must use it and cannot yet afford to throw it away to build the new one we know we need. We will soon be willing to give all we have, to get this new freedom that is ours for our posterity, if not for ourselves.

Devouring human individuality invariably ends in desertion. Eventually, as history records, it invariably ends in the destruction of the devourer.

Instead of being modern in any phase the devourer is senile in every phase.

Standard Overhead Service Station (Project). 1932. Model. FLLW Fdn FA#3206.0005

THE WHIRLING VORTEX BUILT FROM THE TOP DOWN

The overgrown city of the United States stands, thus, enforced upon our undergrown social life as a false economy.

Like some tumor grown malignant, the city, like some cancerous growth, is become a menace to the future of humanity. Not only is the city already grown so far out of human scale by way of commercial exploitation of the herd instinct that the human being as a unit is utterly lost, but the soul, properly citified, is so far gone as to mistake exaggeration for greatness, mistake a vicarious power for his own power, finding in the uproar and verticality of the great city a proof of his own great quality. The properly citified citizen, reduced to a pleasing inferiority in the roar of congestion and terrific collision of forces, sees in this whirling exaggeration, his own greatness. He is satisfied to have greatness, too, vicarious.

But who, coming into New York, say, for the first time, could feel otherwise than that we were a "great" people to have raised the frame of such a relentless commercial engine so cruelly high, and hung so much book-architecture upon it regardless, at such cost?

Such energy, too, as has poured into a common center here to pile up material resources by way of riches in labor and materials and wasted attempts at "decoration," cramming the picturesque outlines of haphazard masses upon the bewildered eye peering from the black shadows down below? We see similar effects wherever irresistible force has broken and tilted up the earth's crust. Here is a volcanic crater of blind, confused, human forces pushing together and grinding upon each other, moved by greed in common exploitation, forcing anxiety upon all life. No noble expression of life, this. But, heedless of the meaning of it all, seen at night, the monster aggregation has myriad, haphazard beauties of silhouette and reflected or refracted light. The monster becomes rhythmical and does appeal to the love of romance and beauty. It is, then, mysterious and suggestive to the imaginative, inspiring to the ignorant. Fascinating entertainment this mysterious gloom upon which hang necklaces of light, through which shine clouds of substitutes for stars. The streets become rhythmical perspectives of glowing dotted lines, reflections hung upon them in the streets as the wistaria hangs its violet racemes on its trellis. The buildings are a shimmering verticality, a gossamer veil, a festive scene-drop hanging there against the black sky to dazzle, entertain and amaze.

The lighted interiors come through it all with a sense of life and well-being. At night the city not only seems to live. It does live—as illusion lives.

And then comes the light of day. Reality. Streams of beings again pouring into the ground, "holing in" to find their way to this or that part of it, densely packed into some roar and rush of speed to pour out somewhere else. The sordid reiteration of space for rent. The overpowering sense of the cell. The dreary emphasis of narrowness, slicing, edging, niching and crowding. Tier above tier the soulless shelf, the empty crevice, the winding ways of the windy, unhealthy canyon. The heartless grip of the selfish, grasping universal stricture. Box on box beside box. Black shadows below with artificial lights burning all day in the little caverns and squared cells. Prison cubicles. Above it all a false, cruel, ambition is painting haphazard, jagged, pretentious, feudal skylines trying to relieve it and make it more humane by lying about its purpose. Congestion, confusion and the anxious spasmodic to and fro—stop and go. At best the all too narrow lanes, were they available, are only fifty per cent effective owing to the gridiron. In them roars a bedlam of harsh sound and a dangerous, wasteful, spasmodic movement runs in these narrow village lanes in the deep shadows. Distortion.

This man-trap of gigantic dimensions, devouring manhood, denies in its affected riot of personality any individuality whatsoever. This Moloch knows no god but "More."

Nowhere is there a clear thought or a sane feeling for good life manifest. In all, even in the libraries, museums and institutes is parasitic make-believe or fantastic abortion. But, if the citizenry is parasitic, the overgrown city itself is barbaric in the true meaning of the word. As good an example of barbarism as exists.

How could it be otherwise?

Some thriving little village port driven insane by excess: excess of such success as current business ideals or principles knows as such. And it is nothing more than much more of much too much already.

The finer human sensibilities become numb.

And even the whole callous, commercial enterprise, pretentious as such, stalls its own engine!

Otherwise the interests that built the city and own it, and spend millions upon it and devote such prowess in the arts as we have to making its purpose—rent—acceptable to the millions, are in immediate danger of running each other down in the perennial race for bigger and better building bait for bewildered tenants, as the factual forces that built the city out of this competition for swarming tenantry in one form or another, built it only to tear it down.

THE FORCES THAT ARE TEARING THE CITY DOWN

Let us turn, now, to these forces that are thrusting at the city to see how they will, eventually, return such human nature as survives this festering acceleration, body and soul to the soil, and, in course of time, repair the damage cancerous overgrowth has wrought upon the life of the United States.

As one force working toward the destruction that is really emancipation, we have already mentioned the reawakening of the slumbering primitive-instinct of the wandering tribe that has come down the ages and intermingled with the instincts of the cave dweller.

The active physical forces that are now trained inevitably against the city are now on the side of this space loving primitive because modern force, by way of electrical, mechanical and chemical invention are volatilizing voice, vision and movement-in-distance in all its human forms until spaciousness is scientific. So the city is already become unscientific in its congested verticality and to the space-loving human being, intolerable. The unnatural stricture of verticality can not stand against natural horizontality.

As another force—a moving spiritual force—the fresh interpretation to which we have referred as a superb ideal of human freedom—Democracy comes to our aid. Our own new spiritual concept of life will find its natural consequences in the life we are about to live. We are going to move with that new spiritual concept the nation has been calling Democracy only half comprehending either ideal or form. This ideal is becoming the greatest subconscious spiritual moving force now moving against the city with new factual resources.

Surviving instincts of the freedom-loving primitive; these new instruments of civilization we call the machines working on new and super materials, together with this great new ideal of human freedom, Democracy: these are three great organic agencies at work, as yet only partly conscious but working together to overthrow the impositions and indirection that have fostered and exaggerated the city as an exaggerated form of selfish concentration. No longer do human satisfactions depend upon density of population.

Let us glance at these new agencies at work as machines upon the super-materials that are forcing changes upon this "best of all possible worlds" and go, more in detail, into this new sense of freedom already at work as Modern Architecture.

THE NEW STANDARD OF SPACE MEASUREMENT

In previous times, too much legwork being objectionable, and as human intercommunication could only be had by personal contacts, integration, commercial or social, was difficult—if it was not wholly lacking except as the city was a close built mart, a general meeting place and a distributing center. So, cities originally grew that way to serve a human need. Human concentration was once upon a time, a necessity and not unmixed evil. Cities grew, as said before, as some organism within the organism that is our body grew, a non-malignant, fibrous tumor, say. The acceleration of circulation and activity characterizing the parasitic tumor characterized the centralized concentration called the city, as compared with the normal course of life in relation to natural environment and agrarian or industrial work over wide agrarian areas. The cities of ancient civilization so grew, originally, to relieve a lack of such integration as is now modern and they have all perished. European cities have resisted skyscraper exploitation and are, still, nearer to human scale. But now, owing to organic change, assuming malignant character, our skyscraper exploited cities must continue to grow as symptoms of disease that is relieved by fever and discharging matter. Or death.

But to take a less abhorrent view, cities were the centralization needed by the unorganized life of the country and on terms of concentration necessary then, they served and, resisting exploitation, survived. But our American cities accepting such exaggeration with pride, have sucked the substance and the spirit of the very life they "centralized." The country once needed the city just as the city needed the country because of the physical inabilities of overcoming distance owing to the necessities of such primitive communications as were then at work. But more and more as those primitive limitations disappeared by way of developed invention, the new discoveries of science and the increasing use of labor-saving devices upon super-materials, these new devices and resources perverted the city, and enabled the city to absorb more and more from the country life what the city could never repay.

Finally, by force of thoughtless habit, the principal effect of all these powerful, fundamental, new physical resources which humanity itself has developed has been, in confusion, to exaggerate the no longer necessary city into a threat against life itself.

Owing to the pressure of these fundamental changes the fever and the excitation of the urban ganglia have not only grown phenomenal. They have grown deadly.

To look at the plan of any great city is to look at the cross section of some fibrous tumor. Seen in the light of present space needs there is unnatural concentration of tissue, an accelerated but painfully forced circulation.

Out of essential concentration centripetal centralization became the industrial economic force at work, unchecked. Unchecked. What force can check centralization?

Centralization, the social force that made kings, is the economic force that overbuilt cities. Centralization, by way of the leverage of the vicarious power of machinery, has now proved to be something that, winding up space tighter and tighter, is like a centripetal device revolving at increasing speed until, out of control entirely turning centrifugal, it is ended only by dissipation or destruction. Centralization as a centripetal force knows acceleration. What other control?

Government? No.

Only human intelligence grasping machine-power exaggeration and interference in behalf of humanity in order to employ machines as organic agencies industrial, social, moral, of a new freedom: in this lies the only salvation from such urban centralization as the big city has become and the future of the machine age if the machine age has any future.

THE NATURE OF MODERN RESOURCES

We have already mentioned these machine-age agencies of the new freedom which centralization itself has done much to bring to efficiency and that have immeasurably widened the areas of man-movement. But to reiterate:

Agency number one. Electrification: so far as communication is concerned, the city may now scatter. There is little advantage in a few blocks apart over ten miles apart or a thousand miles so far as communication went or goes. Human thought has long ago been rendered ubiquitous by printing. But now not only thought but speech and movement become volatile. First the telegraph, then the telephone, then mobilization, now the radio, soon television and safe flight.

Agency number two: Steam had congested and coupled as short as possible all human devices for living comforts. Enters, the internal combustion engine that might safely ride anywhere, smoothly working as it went. The motor-ship, the automobile, and the airplane came along; and so far as human movement by transport went, a few hundred feet had little advantage over a mile, and a mile not much advantage over ten. Hard roads began to be developed as avenues of swift, continuous motor communication.

Agency number three: Mechanical systems of refrigeration, heating and lighting make dependence upon the centralized service systems of the city unnecessary and of small account or economy.

Agency number four: The new materials, steel-in-tension and concrete, glass and broad, thin, cheap sheets of metal and similar sheets of insulation make a new type of building possible by way of machinery that may open to environment and broaden the life of the individual in relation to the ground.

Agency number five: The mass production of the machine, shop fabrications can now make expensive utilities and accommodations cheap for all concerned instead of questionable luxuries for the few.

So, naturally enough, here come the means to take all the real advantages of the centralization known as the big city into the regional field we call the countryside and unite them with the features of the ground in that union we call modern architecture in that native creation we call the beauty of the country. The disadvantages of the city may all be left behind, for "finance" and prostitution until they too become regenerate.

Modern architecture now comes with its new demand for a finer integrity to unite "modern-improvements" in the service of the individual. Integration as against centralization is the true corollary of the ideal "Democracy" and decentralization and integration come in as architecture to go to work over the whole land to create a better basis and re-create the framework and background of a modern life run too far out of human scale. Man must now be brought back to his inheritance that he may be a whole man. Nor is there longer excuse for him to be the parasite that centralization has been making of him.

But all these new forms of liberation are not yet working freely for mankind in this way. They are not yet owned by the man. They are owned by the forces of centralization that own the cities and mechanically so far as may be they are warped to triplex economic distortion instead of being devoted to the conservation of a growing human life.

Nevertheless, we may be sure that "all one does for or against the truth serves it equally well."

It is well within the internal nature and power of these forces, themselves organic, to destroy these systems that blindly usurp and warp them and deprive humanity, for the time being, of all but a small fragment of the benefits of new resources in machine power and super-materials.

The practical solution is a matter of social structure. But it is more a matter of what we call architecture. It is modern architecture that must lead the way out of this blind collision of forces and away from the perversions of our democratic ideal. End a waste of life not natural to our experiment in civilization.

Let us learn to see life as organic architecture and learn to see organic architecture as life. Be sure that great life will have a great architecture.

WHAT THE TRAFFIC PROBLEM REALLY MEANS TO THE MAN IN THE STREET

In art or architecture any imitative eclecticism, however sophisticated, is only some form of sentimentality. At best it can be no more than some exploitation of something ready-made. At worst it is a kind of thievery. The jackdaw, the magpie, the cuckoo. The monkey.

The "Experiment" has consciously known the artist only as a sophisticate sentimentalist. The sentimentalist, at the moment, be it said, is trying hard to see himself as a functionalist. But the sentimentalist's faith learns no such lessons and, to date, his effort is only another form of his usual expediency—imitative eclecticism.

Too long the artist has tried to pick and choose his "effects" ready-made and opportunely lead his life instead of letting life lead him, and teach him how to work and live honestly and effectively.

The artist's faith still lies, as it has since the birth of the republic, in expedients. So long as he remains "unnatural" how can he build for the future?

Only the radical faith that keeps faith with radical life itself is practical where any true building is to be done.

So, let us approach the traffic problem as a human problem—that is the essential problem the congested city now presents—not as mere tinker or as some garage-mechanic, nor childish, try to tear the out-moded city down to get the green pastures in and set the city up in them again on its old site—feudal towers only a little further apart.

Vested interests once invested cannot be divested except by agreement. They will not agree.

With an architect's vision, let us observe the natural law of organic growth at work upon the city as change: seeking the sequence to provide for inevitable consequences.

Enough blind-alley nonsense has been talked about congestion, by skyscraperites, obscuring the simple issue. Of what practical use is this expedient imagery of super-spacemakers for rent? To enable super-landlords to have and to hold the super-millions in super-concentration to make super-millions of superfluous millions?

For organic reasons the "traffic-problem" as we call the more obvious problem of the city streets is insoluble for the future on any basis satisfactory to human life within any busy city we have.

The instincts of the amorphous human herd exploited by the city, swarm with the swarm in the erstwhile village streets, but the swarm is taking wing—or to wheels which is much the same thing because increased facilities of lateral movement are comparative flight. A fond human dream is about to be realized.

By means of the motor car and the collateral inventions that are here with it, the horizon of the individual has immeasurably widened. It is significant that not only have space values entirely changed with the new standard: It is more important that the new sense of spacing based upon the man in his motor car is now at work upon the man himself. Any ride high into the air in any elevator to-day only shows him how far he can soon go on the ground. And it is this view of the horizon that gives him the desire to go. If he has the means he goes. He has the means—his car—and his horizon widens as he goes.

This physical release is at work upon his character.

His selfish interests might easily multiply and pile him up senselessly in tiers of cells, ad infinitum when he got his release and may still do so. Still dazed by his new freedom, he is like some bird born in captivity to whom the door of his cage has been opened. Sometime, soon, he will learn that he can fly and when he learns that he is free, he is gone.

After all he is the city? So the city is going where and as he goes, and he will be gone where he may enjoy all that the centralized city ever really gave him plus the security, freedom and beauty of the ground that will be his.

That means that the citizen is going to the country with his machine by means of the machine, in larger sense, that is opening the way for him to be a better citizen in a better city in a better country.

Considering this traffic-problem, reflect that the present city is yet only about one-tenth the motor car city it will be, if machine made promises to the man tied to the machine are ever kept. Any dutiful devotion to the machine on his part to-day should mean a motor car, comparative flight—or it means a moron for a citizen. Or a maniac. The citizen and his increase either have a car or dream of having one, envying the neighbor the one or two or three which he already has.

If grid-iron congestion is crucifixion now, what will the "grid-iron" be like when multiplied within a few years as many times by "success" as is inevitable?

Roughly calculate the mass of machines that machine-age "success" must mean to the overgrown city of one of several to six million people. More than one half the number of private cars; perhaps one twenty-fifth as many trucks and as many delivery machines, one fiftieth as many buses displacing street car tracks and unwholesome subways; thousands of taxi-cabs cruising about meantime. With room enough for each incidental transient, in his machine-bulk, to function at all lengthwise, the mass would fill the busy city channels above the tenth story.

Allowing for the criss-cross on the gridiron, making every street only half-time efficient and the mass would double and pile up over the skyscrapers themselves. Call this exaggeration and cut it in two—then cut it in two again, to be rash. There will be enough left, at the rate of increase "success" will bring, to put Manhattan and its kind out of commission with its own motors and those of inevitable transients in streets that can at best be but fifty per cent efficient owing to the crisscross of the gridiron.

And reflect upon the fact that the motor car has just begun on the cities. Then why deck or double deck or triple deck city-streets at a cost of billions of dollars only to invite further increase and eventually meet inevitable defeat?

Why not allow citizenship to keep the billions it would have to pay for "decking" to buy more motor cars and get out and get more out of living in a more natural and fruitful life as freedom dawns on the citizen as for him? As the new freedom of our ideal dawns, the utility of the city vanishes by way of the machine that built it.

Yes, democracy means just that freedom for the citizen, by machine, if the machine is going to work for the citizen; and who can stop it now from going to work for him voluntarily as it is working involuntarily?

Let us repeat: monarchy was the ideal of centralization . . . the unit—no emphasis upon individuality—compelled to revolve around about a common center, so democracy is the ideal of integration . . . many units free in themselves built up high in the quality of individuality, functioning together in freedom.

Consider that monarchy has fallen. It mortified democratic individuality. And our capitalistic system, if it persists as a form of centralization, stands to fall for the same reason. Electrified mechanical-forces employed in building our modern world are now, by nature, outmoding it and turning upon it to destroy it.

Centripetal centralization, whether as the city, the factory, the school or farm, now not only has the spiritual forces of democracy to work against, but by way of this traffic-problem has the enormous power of the machine-age setting in, dead against it because it is in the nature of universal or ubiquitous mobilization that the city spreads out far away and thin.

It is in the nature of flying that it disappears.

It is in the nature of universal electrification that the city is nowhere or everywhere.

Centralization, by way of the Usonian city, has had a big day but not a relatively long day. As a matter of course it is not dead yet. But it is easy, now, to see that it is no longer either a necessity or a luxury. Universal mobilization of the human animal, volatilization of his thought, voice and vision are making the city as troublesome an interference to human life as "static" is troublesome to radio.

Already the man may get more out of his new release, by way of increased facility for lateral movement, than ever came to him before in the history of his race. Imagine, then, what is coming to him in the next twenty-five years!

Democracy reintegrated as the systematized integration of small individual units built up high in quality of individuality is a practical and rational ideal of freedom: machine in hand. Division of the exaggerated commercial-enterprise into more effective smaller units and reintegration over the whole surface of the nation—this is now no less practical. Communal ownership by way of taxation of all communal resources is not necessarily communism, as Henry George pointed out with complete logic. It may be entirely democratic.

So the Broadacre City is not only the only democratic city. It is the only possible city looking toward the future. Exaggerated vertical lanes of transport impinging upon congested, narrow horizontal lanes; tall channels as "courts" ruinous to privacy, makeshifts for light and air in offices or habitations, towering concrete shelves and pigeonholes for human dwellings, these are landlord expedients to have done with. They are no human solution of any "traffic problem" because there is no life in them. There is only rent. As for the proposed improvement, "by modernism," securing privacy by hermetically sealed and blinded buildings, hot air circulating between two glass surfaces opaque or transparent, that proposed expedient means to heat the inside and the outside impartially—50-50—with no gratitude from the outside. And 1,000 people to the "hectare" (two and a half acres) is looking not so far ahead. That is, now, 990 too many.

THE NEW IDEA OF LUXURY

None may say how far man's liberation may go by proper use of the mechanical resources developed in the past century and by proper use of the new materials like steel and glass in the new spirit of an organic architecture.

Trained imagination of the same mind is needed to harness modern machines to higher uses, in order to get out of them what they have to give to expand human life.

A new idea of luxury and beauty is needed and must grow up, naturally here among us.

Power directly and simply applied to purpose is the clear basis of any such aesthetic expression now as is either utile or operative in this twentieth century. Machine-age luxury will consist more and more in the appropriate use and intelligent limitation of the machine at work in the making of the new patterns for the new life.

But why try to make buildings look as hard as

machines? That means that life is as hard as machines, too. Why confound romance with sentimentality and so destroy both? Modern buildings should have the beauty that any well-balanced machine has, but before all, that is only the basis for beauty, however novel at the moment, the assertion of the negation. Machine-power directly and simply applied to purpose is only the basis for buildings because it has been discovered that a single mechanical unit may be indefinitely repeated in construction or use, and yet infinite variety of form and scheme may be the given result in hands guided by creative imagination.

It has been discovered, too, that severe standardization is no bar at all to even greater freedom in self-expression than was ever known before, if by self-expression we mean genuine individuality and not personal idiosyncrasy. And these two discoveries are the Magna Charta of the new liberty into which the architect may now go by way of machinery and go in his own machine into a modern architecture. And the man himself may go to join the more natural group of the more natural buildings of the more natural Broadacre City of the Twentieth Century.

All unknown to the citizen, that city has already begun to be built on the ground where he belongs.

Only short-sighted interests can deny that the present-day city, in the light of our new opportunities, has become a stricture in distribution and transport; a handicap in production; an imposition upon family life. And the family holds within itself the seeds of the future! The traffic problem is not a symptom of urban success but evidence of urban failure. Make the ground available by modifying the terms of ownership to the man that can make good use of it, and the new city will grow fast. Otherwise it will grow but grow more slowly and by greater suffering. What then is the thought that is modern and working for the organic change that is growth?

WHAT THOUGHT—AS MODERN— IS BRINGING RELIEF?

Well—certainly not the same old thought that made our American cities a landlord's triumph.

Certainly not the same old thought that has impoverished our agrarian areas . . . and offers— "relief"?

Certainly not the same old thought that turns America's youth into white-collar men, and sends them to the city in search of a job . . . a job where at least one hand may be kept in the pocket!

Certainly not the same old thought that has made of our economic system a legalized "strong arm" that must weaken periodically to come down for a "rest" while we all gravitate toward starvation in the midst of plenty.

Nor can we imagine it to be the same old thought that looked for freedom by way of arbitrary laws having no foundation in basic economic structure nor in the character of our ideal, resulting only in senseless reiterations by political cowardice, of falsehood: drifting again toward the same old impotence or cataclysm of centralization of which all civilizations, hitherto, have died.

That same old thought has made of this form of centralization we call the city a conspiracy against man-like freedom just as it made American architecture a bad form of surface-decoration; and just as, now—a typical if minor instance of impotence—it can offer for the fifth time only the same old Columbian Fair of 1893 with its face lifted, as progress, to mark our greatness in 1933.

That same old thought, as we may now see, places most of its premiums upon baser qualities and by way of privileges in property held out, always just ahead of him, tends to make the man a form of property himself.

The "same old thought" continues to standardize him as a piece of property in behalf of property, or breaks him.

That "same old thought" drives our universities to deprive the American youth of such correlation as he has, turning his mind into an empty tool box by throwing books at his head.

That "same old thought" makes the banker a wary professional acquisitive, by banking on Yesterday stalling or betraying Tomorrow.

That "same old thought" immures the man in the same old man-trap . . . the skyscraper Bedlam . . . where machine power emasculates him to the consistency of the machine-made moron, when machine power can have no meaning whatever ex-

cept to help make him a man and set him free.

That "same old thought," simply stated, is this: the mistake that everything or anything at all worth any man's time can be made to happen by outside means or be the result of some external idea of form. And it is the confusing survival of such exterior ideal as characterized the pagan civilizations upon which we have nurtured our youth and after which we have patterned our institutions. From this we have derived the pretentious Usonian culture we try to apply on the surface. All, inorganic.

What then is this idea we call modern?

Life as organic architecture and organic architecture as life.

The enlarged means of today employing supermaterials and machine power, allowed to be today, not yesterday, is modern.

But more important still the new democratic conception of man-freedom where life or land or humanity itself is concerned, is modern.

The dignity and worth of the individual as an individual—not the mere personal idiosyncrasy—ancient as the ideal is, as basis for life or art is modern.

The sense of the within unfolding, by interior content to achieve genuine expression as individuality, ancient as Laotze at least, is modern . . . modern in manhood, modern in government: but especially modern in education and slowly and painfully becoming modern in art.

True simplicity seen as the countenance of organic-integrity in all man-made life-concerns: that, as it ever was—outward form, only, now changed—is modern.

Infinitely these new integrities have new possibilities in making a modern life for the machine-age.

And modern architecture, it must be, will grasp the integrity of this modern demand of modern life for a new and higher spiritual order of living: perceiving finer integrity in a more livable human simplicity than was the necessary basis for such architecture as we have had.

The new enlarged means of today used to increase spaciousness in human living and bring back appropriate sense of space in human life itself will give us the Broadacre City, complete. Modern.

If you can see the extended highway as the horizontal line of Usonian freedom, then you will see the modern Usonian city approaching.

And it is now modern to hate the waste of power and be suspicious of this opportunity to be vicarious that is forced upon the human being by the senseless reiteration of insignificance we call the city.

It is now modern no longer to build or consent to live in the prettified cavern or take pleasure in the glorified cave. Such vainglory is not only antique, but worse, it is now false. Improved conditions of life make it not merely an expedient but an impediment.

So it is modern to believe in, to see as new, and to seek for organic simplicity and see it as the fine countenance of this machine age in which we live.

Modern architecture sees this new simplicity working up out of the ground into the sunlight as no box, no boxment, nor any burrow in any overgrown city whatever. When the citizen himself sees this, the modern Broadacre City has come into being for him. He is "on his way" there.

MODERN ARCHITECTURE
Modern architecture sees all of life in terms of this future city although modernism can not do so.

Nevertheless, walls as solid-walls, everywhere building is sensible, are vanishing.

The heavy bulks of building material, hollowed out as caves to live in, are gradually disappearing with the fortifications that protected the might of feudal estate, just as shadows vanish.

No free man in a modern America needs to "box up" or "hole in" any longer for "protection" in any building or burrow in any city whatever. Our country, notwithstanding "vested interests," is gradually becoming as free as our own ideal must eventually and naturally make it. I see all the resources in power and material we have, working now to make our ideal of freedom come true in these United States. What need have we, longer, for master or slave however disguised? Or for lord and serf? Where is the need for more imitation of

the exaggerated feudal-masonry defenses of a foregone, outlived human enmity by whatever name urban "interests" may choose to call them? Or for whatever purpose they may be thought to be appropriate decoration.

In a genuine democracy, in modern circumstances, no man needs longer to live as the savage animal as man was once compelled to live. Any man may now live as the free being the best of him has always dreamed of being and as our experiment declared he would have the opportunity to be.

Modern architecture then simply reinterprets our own ideal of human freedom and naturally seeks the spaciousness, openness, lightness and strength that is so completely logical that it is bound, on its way, to scatter a diseased urbanism first into the regional field and then—as inadvertent disease is absorbed—into the circulation of the healthy body that is the whole country.

These modern gifts of glass; these modern gifts of steel-in-tension; these modern gifts of electro-magnetic science—all these gifts begin for us a new era as soon as we begin to use them in the light of ancient principles but new ideals of form. So simple and fundamental are the natural agents of this new freedom for mankind that they are already all in the citizen's hands. If he will take them, as they are, they are his means to modern life.

Facility to roam the sky or ground and yet live with the perfect freedom of vision that will relate him to the ground and all that the ground should still mean to him, is already possible.

Architectural values are human values or they are not valuable. So any true modern building is born of organic integration and rises, as the modern city rises, enemy to centralization in whatever form. Both building and city are now true sun-growth and true sun-acceptance or not modern. The building itself may be a shaft of light flashing in the sun. And both building and city be no less true defense against time and against the elements than ever.

Modern architecture may be no less true shield for whatever privacy humanity desires or needs, but it may be indestructible machine-made fabric of light metals, woven in webs of turquoise, blue or green and gold and silver or the deep hues of bronze. Or the building may be visible as all together and as the integral patterns of a free life.

But organic architecture does demand the ground be made available on some fair basis to those who can use it as an intrinsic human value as are all the other elements. Once emancipated from the tyranny of the "lucky lot" area wherever it may lie, the building will stand free or lie long and lie low, flowing lazily on the mesa or upon the ledges of the hillsides. Any building public, private or industrial may now be a shaft or a streak of light, enmeshed in metal strands, as music is made of notes. But what is any building, as architecture, without intimate relation to the ground? No more than a man-trap or a landlord's ruse.

Organic architecture, as life itself, can no longer allow the man himself to crawl toward any dubious, impotent past, blind to the forces that ruined the past and to the new constructive forces that waken for us in our age of the machine.

Why should stupid faith—in the name of loyalty—in doctorial facts of sentimentalized academic culture result, for him, only in an afterglow of feudalism?

Why, still fearful, must he go along with the academic "interests" that have betrayed his own life in our own age by way of sentimentalized abuse of all noble traditions? Modern architecture, only, is true to tradition.

THE ARCHITECT

America cannot afford to believe that great art, as her interpreter, is moribund. And the logical interpreter, perhaps the only one who can now show us the way is an organic modern architecture. The other arts are not yet awake, though they have lately shown signs of awakening.

We must believe in our country, and that means, we must believe that the ancient power that built great civilizations, to die, still lives to build a greater one, to live. We know that ancient cities are dead because of the exterior ideals of an external life that prevailed and withered away such life as they had.

But we know, too, the same human power that was theirs, multiplied infinitely now by the new leverage of mechanical forces may build a new city for us that will live indefinitely as the new architecture of a greater ideal belonging to the new ground of a fresh life.

This "new" ideal, having lived in the human heart two thousand five hundred years, finally founded this great Union of States. An experiment. If the "Experiment" is to succeed this union must now turn from centralization that was monarchic to the segregation and integration that is democratic. That means to turn toward the greater freedom of a life for the individual as individual, based squarely with the ground, some such life as life would be in the Broadacre City.

In the Broadacre City of modern architecture the individual home of the individual family group, more directly related to transport, distribution and publicity than in the present city will enjoy in the country a freedom, a richness of life, no city ever yet gave, because it never had it to give.

So, the present city, feudal terms and feudal thinking now changed only to terms of commerce, has nothing to give the citizen, even commercialized, because centralization having no vital forces of regeneration, is grown old. This survival of the feudal type of city, the only one we have, seems only to conspire, as a hang-over of habit, to beguile the man from his birthright in freedom the high-priests of our culture singing false hymns to vicarious power in hypocritical language never understood and comprehended, least of all, by those who sang the hymns. Manifestly theme songs are now out of key, false in the singing and to the singers, as impotence slowly imprisons the citizen. Impotence is the price of his mistaking an artificial machine-power for his own. And impotence is the price of his artificial career and his habitual practice of an artifice without art.

The false atonement "big" centralization has asked of him in the name of "big-business" is inability to create. Impotence.

THE TRUE ATONEMENT

When man shall build a building, a society, a life, as himself, inspired by nature in this modern interior sense, training his imagination to see life as the architect trains his imagination to see the nature of glass as glass, to see the nature of steel as steel, and see the nature of the time, the place, and the hour, eager to be himself, harmonious with nature, as the trees are native to the wood or the grass to the field, then the individual as a citizen, will rise high in the communal life of a civilization. And, supreme to all about him he can not fail to make the communal life the richer for his own riches. That faith is the faith of Democracy. Human values are life giving not life taking.

GENERAL VIEW OF THE BROADACRE CITY OF THE FUTURE BASED UPON THE NEW SCALE OF SPACING

In the City of Yesterday ground space was reckoned by the square foot. In the City of Tomorrow ground space will be reckoned by the acre: an acre to the family. This seems a modest minimum if we consider that if all the inhabitants of the world were to stand upright together they would scarcely occupy the island of Bermuda. And reflect that in these United States there is more than 57 acres of land, each, for every man, woman and child within its borders.

On this basis of an acre to the family architecture would come again into the service, not of the landlord, but of the man himself as an organic feature of his own ground. Architecture would no longer be merely adapted, commercialized space to be sold and resold by taximeter—no more standing room than competition demands.

Ground space is the essential basis of the new city of a new life.

The present form of the motor car is crude and imitative compared with the varied forms of fleet machines, beautiful as such, manufacturers will soon be inclined or be soon compelled to make.

The flying machine is yet a more or less extravagant, experimental form, unwieldy in scale, and with its exaggerated wings imitating a bird it is yet a hostage that gives itself to the mercy of the elements. No more than a primitive step in evolution.

Teletransmissions of sight and sound, too, are not only experimental they are in their infancy as is the intelligence to which their operation is entrusted.

We are justly proud of the great network of highways, the hardroad systems of the country. But they too are in their infancy. We are only just beginning to build them.

Young as the highway system is, however, it requires but little imagination to see in the great highway and see in the power of all these new resources of machines and materials a new physical release of human activity within reach of everyone . . . not only as adventure and romance with nature but a basis for safer, saner, less anxious life for a sane and dignified free people. A longer, happier life waits, naturally, upon this changed sense of a changed space relationship.

Any man once square with his own acre or so of ground is sure of a living for himself and his own and sure of some invigorating association with beauty. Not only is the city itself a stricture, a handicap in production: the contributing railroad itself is too limited in movement, too expensively clumsy and too slow in operation. The end of the day of the long or short back and forth haul demanded by centralization is in sight. The end, too, of mass transport by iron rail.

Imagine spacious landscaped highways, grade crossings eliminated, "by-passing" living areas, devoid of the already archaic telegraph and telephone poles and wires and free of blaring bill boards and obsolete construction. Imagine these great highways, safe in width and grade, bright with wayside flowers, cool with shade trees, joined at intervals with fields from which the safe, noiseless transport planes take off and land. Giant roads, themselves great architecture, pass public service stations, no longer eyesores, expanded to include all kinds of service and comfort. They unite and separate—separate and unite the series of diversified units, the farm units, the factory units, the roadside markets, the garden schools, the dwelling places (each on its acre of individually adorned and cultivated ground), the places for pleasure and leisure. All of these units so arranged and so integrated that each citizen of the future will have all forms of production, distribution, self-improvement, enjoyment, within a radius of a hundred and fifty miles of his home now easily and speedily available by means of his car or his plane. This integral whole composes the great city that I see embracing all of this country—the Broadacre City of tomorrow.

It is because every man will own his acre of home ground, that architecture will be in the service of the man himself, creating appropriate new buildings in harmony not only with the ground but harmonious with the pattern of the personal life of the individual. No two homes, no two gardens, none of the three-to-ten-acre farm units, no two factory buildings need be alike. There need be no special "styles," but style everywhere.

Light, strong houses and workplaces will be solidly and sympathetically built out of the nature of the ground into sunlight. Factory workers will live on acre home units within walking distance or a short ride away from the future factories. Factories beautiful, smokeless and noiseless. No longer will the farmer envy the urban dweller his mechanical improvements while the latter in turn covets his "green pastures."

Each factory and farm would be within a ten mile radius of a vast and variegated wayside market, so that each can serve the other simply and effectively and both can serve that other portion of the population which lives and works in the neighborhood of that market. No longer will any need exist for futile racing to a common center and racing back again crucifying life just to keep things piled up and "big."

Without air, sunlight, land, human life cannot go on. Recognizing this principle, as we are all beginning to do, the home life of tomorrow will conform. It will eliminate no modern comforts, yet keep the age-less healthgiving comforts too. Steel and glass will be called in to fulfill their own—steel for strength, durability and lightness; translucent glass, enclosing interior space, would give privacy yet make of living in a house a delightful association with sun, with sky, with surrounding gardens. The home would be an indoor garden, the garden an outdoor house.

Tall buildings are not barred, but having no interior courts, they must stand free in natural parks. A "co-operative" apartment house might be eighteen stories, perhaps: tier on tier of immense glass screen-walls golden with sun, on shining steel or copper-sheathed frames, each tier with its flower and vine festooned balcony terrace, an iridescence of vivid color, the whole standing in generously parked and blossoming grounds.

The principles of architecture are simply the principles of life. Just as a house built on makeshift foundations cannot stand, so life set on makeshift character in a makeshift country cannot endure. Good and lasting architecture gives or concedes the right to all of us to live abundantly in the exuberance that is beauty—in the sense that William Blake defined exuberance. He did not mean excess. He meant according to nature, without stint. Thus, also, must good and lasting life yield up that right to all of us. And the only secure foundation for such life is enlightened human character which will understandingly accept, not merely ape the organic relation between the welfare of one and the welfare of the whole. Only that sort of character is fit for and able to create a permanent and universal well being.

And good architecture and the civilized architect of the future are necessarily modern, because life itself continually changes and new forms of building are needed to contain and express it sincerely without waste, loving beauty.

To put it concretely again, architectural values are human values or they are not valuable. Human values are life-giving, not life-taking. When one is content to build for oneself alone taking the natural rights of life, breadth and light and space, away from one's neighbor, the result is some such monstrosity as the pretentious skyscraper. It stands for a while in the business slum formed by its own greed, selfishly casting its shadow on its neighbors, only to find that it, too, is dependent upon their success and must fail with their failure.

What life to give has the toll-gatherer the big city has become, to the worthwhile citizen now that the motor car stands at the door: the great, hard road systems of the country beckoning?

Voices and vision everywhere are penetrating solid walls to entertain and inform him wherever and as he goes, and when general and immediate distribution of everything he needs is becoming convenient to him wherever he may happen to be and or choose to live. I see his buildings modern, sanitary, living conveniences, his wherever he is or wants to be, and as economically as his motor car is his—by a few hours' devotion to machinery. I see the factory too, divided and operated in humane proportions not far away from him in the country; the time spent in any ceaseless to and fro from the office, senseless and waste time that may be well spent in the new individual centralization—the only one that is a real necessity, or a great luxury or a great human asset—his diversified modern Home. I see that home not so far away from the diversified farm units but that they may bring him, at the highway wayside markets, as he passes, food, fresh every hour.

I can see "going places" a luxury and a pleasure to him and to his; and beautiful places to which he can go. I see his children going to small and smaller individual garden schools in parks that are playgrounds as their parents live individual lives that enrich the communal life by the very quality of its individuality in a beauty of life that is appropriate luxury and superior common sense.

Transport, buildings, all life spaciously intimate with the ground, all appropriate to each other and life to each and every man according to his nature or his need and love of life. Woods, streams, mountains, ranges of hills, the great plains—all are shrines, beauty to be preserved. Architecture and acreage seen as landscape.

Imagination is our human divinity. It alone may distinguish the human herd and save it from the fate that has overtaken all other herds, human or animal. All this leads the way to the realization of a new civilization with an architecture of its own which will make the machine its slave and create nobler longings for mankind.

ARCHITECTURE AND ACREAGE SEEN AS LANDSCAPE

The architectural features of the Broadacre City will arise naturally out of the nature and character of the ground on which it stands and of which it is a component if not an organic feature.

The individual architectural features themselves would naturally harmonize with the nature features; therefore no two could ever be precisely alike except as the city might be built on some featureless plain

which again has a certain beauty of its own and might well bear repetition of pattern. But the Broadacre cities would seldom be so built, because a feeling for beauty of terrain, in the city builders, would be seeking for beauty of feature in the landscape. A great variety of architecture would be the natural result of a varied topography in the organic architecture which would be inevitable because natural to the thought building the new cities.

Twentieth-century architecture it is that is destined to comprise all the features of construction and design going to make up the framework, background and physical body of the machine age. Because it is the architecture of painting, of sculpture, of music, of life itself that is most vital, architecture is most vital because it is the essential structure of them all.

And as architecture was in ancient times, so it will be again if the organic correlation that is essentially a high ideal of beauty is to belong to twentieth-century life.

So the various features of the Broadacre City we are about to describe in more detail are primarily and essentially architecture. From the roads that are its veins and arteries to the buildings that are its cellular tissue, to the parks and gardens that are its "epidermis" and "hirsute adornment," the new city will be architecture.

The time has come when the whole man must be reflected in the creative idea of his city, the city as free and organic in itself as man is in himself and as he will be in his thinking and his free institutions in this rendezvous he will make by way of nature-interior with nature-exterior.

So, in the Broadacre City the entire American scene becomes an organic architectural expression of the nature of man himself and of his life here upon the earth. This native expression of himself will be his in abundance, chiefly by intelligent use and restraint of his gigantic leverage, the machine.

Nevertheless, the ground will determine the shape and even the style of the buildings in the Broadacre City, so that to see where ground leaves off and the buildings begin would require careful attention. With this—the ground motive—variety in unity will be infinite. The architect himself, his ideal of organic unity held firmly in his mind, will become more equal to his opportunity with new materials and new machines. The ever-growing intelligence of the artifex itself, a desire for a whole life, will make the new city into which the old one disappears a great human work of art in every sense. Petty partitions and defacements of nature, everywhere irritating now, will no longer be excused or tolerated. No mechanical shrieks or smoke or grinding noises. No glaring abortions set up as super-salesmen to fight each other for the desired eye to sell anything. Not anything at all.

THE SUPER-HIGHWAY AND THE TRIBUTARY HARD ROAD—THE LAKES AND STREAMS

The regenerate architect first enters upon the native scene as the master roadbuilder, the super-highway and the tributary hard road now architectural factors of fundamental if not greatest importance. In the new dispensation is a new sense of order, throughout.

Sweeping grades, banked turns, well considered cuts and fills healed by good planting of indigenous growth may have supreme beauty. Sympathetic moving lines that are the highways threading the hills and plains with safe grades will be, wherever they occur, elemental features of the landscape. So will be sightly road protection, well studied; well-designed culverts, bridges. Where concrete walls were prohibitive, there would be dotted lines along the banks of every turn. Evergreen masses would be lined up along the roads for snow protection, instead of unsightly snow fences. Masses of native growth would sweep over the banks of the cut or fill, not the usual collections of many different kinds of shrubs and trees called landscape architecture, but broad sweeps of a single species at one place with an eye to bloom and to color in the changing seasons.

No hard road in the new city would have less than three lanes. The super highway should have no less than six lanes. The fueling and servicing-station units would be developing in ample parks at appropriate points at desirable highway intersections. This road construction and planting, both as engineering and architecture, will be naturally under the control of the state, with the best supervising architects and landscape architects and structural engineers not only

the state affords, but the country or perhaps the world affords. Each section receiving special attention by forces common to all.

An architect's trained sense of the harmonious "altogether" in the several matters of road construction, planting and bridge building, from beginning to end, would be indispensable to the integrity of the whole conception and so take place.

There is no more important function looking toward the city of the future than to get the best architects of the world interested in road building. They should see road building as great architecture.

The Romans built great roads that remain to this day. But with reinforced concrete as we now practice it and our modern machines, we could build better and more lasting roads and make them noble modern architecture. What greater, nobler agent has culture or civilization than the safe, open road made, in itself, beautiful?

Along these grand roads as through veins and arteries comes and goes the throng building and living in the Broadacre City of the Twentieth Century.

The lakes and streams too, now available by motorization, contribute no small element of transport or pleasure. The motor boat has done for bodies of water in relation to the land what it has done for the land itself.

THE GREAT TRAFFIC STATION

The form of centralization that built the great railway station as the gateway of the old city will be gone. Exaggeration, conspicuous waste in any form will bore or insult society. There will be many minor stations instead of a few major ones because the great station will no longer be possible or desirable. Aeroplane depots, as flight develops, will be connected with the rights of way on which once lay the hard rails of the old, cumbersome railroads. And the new traffic "station" may occur as a minor feature, again ten for one, wherever one may be needed for purposes of general convenience. The big terminal and the storage capacities will disappear except at ports of entry or export. The major part of the business of gathering or distributing is, of course, from hand to hand or from factory and farm to family or from producer to exporter or from importer to distributing center by way of the universal traffic lanes to which all units of either production or consumption now have quick and easy access. The back and forth haul will no longer be necessary. It will be absurd. Distribution is direct.

There will always be a special concentration at ports and mines. A port-city will differ from an inland city as in fact every city will take on the character of its special environment and situation and differ from every other.

These differences would naturally be accentuated and developed as to their individuality except where uniformity of standardization and mass-production entered as substantial human benefit into the warp of the fabric. But the ultimate weaving need show no less imagination and individuality when the woof began to be stitched on to the warp. The finished whole should have an individuality now genuine, therefore, far greater than any the United States has ever known. It is this individual differentiation that would be interesting entertainment, no longer pretense or academic affectation as before, but genuine not only in cities but becoming so in people as well. And it is that human quality of individuality— strange to say—that the United States will find most difficult to preserve or to develop. As things are going with us we have all but lost it in the vicarious life of a vicarious means to live.

POWER UNITS

In the Broadacre City it is inevitable that fuel be turned into electricity at the mines and wherever water power may be found, relayed from station to station to the consumer.

Electrification will easily become universal by this means; and current being produced at original centers of supply, like the mines or the dams or the oil wells and owned by the citizens, electricity will be able not only to compete but to abolish all but oil as a source of heat and power for the city. Oil itself might well be used at the source to produce electric power.

These great power units—they would be the same miracles of modern engineering as those we already have—would develop where natural resources were. Improved methods of conducting power

would take the conduits underground, as the oil pipelines already are underground, with small loss of voltage.

A general sentiment for the beauty of the landscape would take advantage of developments in wireless telegraphy and telephone already available to make poles, trestles and wires a memory only of the disappearing city.

It is easy to realize how the complexity of crude utilitarian construction in the mechanical infancy of our growth, like the crude scaffolding for some noble building, did violence to the landscape. But this violence will disappear as power and traffic find avenues of distribution in more conservative and economical channels. The crude devices now called construction are already being swept away out of sight. Into the discard with poles and wires and rails will go track elevation, gas plants, coal burning power houses, train sheds, roundhouses, coal yards, lumberyards. There need be and there will be no unsightly structures in the Broadacre City of the future. The crude purpose of pioneering days has been accomplished. The scaffolding may now be taken down and the true work, the culture of a civilization, may appear.

THE ORGANIC ARCHITECTURE OF THE VARIOUS NEW BUILDINGS

We now have, in bare suggestive outline, the general topographical, traffic and power features of the new city that integration has already begun to build and that begins to absorb the city built by centralization. The stem of the new city as we have seen will be the mobilization already well under way. A matter of "traffic."

We have already glanced at the changing ideals that will make the new city a finer, freer city by way of new ideals of what constitutes culture, according to our ideal of freedom—Democracy.

Let us now see how the buildings themselves as units of the plan in the construction of that city would be built into it as expressions of these new ideals: built into it as modern architecture by way of these new resources of industry and materials.

Let us now see how the new standard of spacing we have mentioned as necessary and at work will affect the arrangement or general plan of the city we call the Broadacre City and appear in every building feature of it. New forms for a finer concept of life. The new integrity of the individual as an individual must take effect in these constructions.

We might call this modern architecture an architecture for the individual as distinguished from the attempt at re-classification called an "international style," say, or any preconceived, impecunious or impertinent formula for appearances whatever.

In any conception of organic architecture, style is an expression of character. Character is an expression of principle at work. In this sense only will the new city have style. It will have style as something natural, not something exterior forced upon it by any outside discipline or academic attempt at classification whatsoever. Architecture and acreage will now again be seen together as landscape, as the best of architecture has ever been. If our principles are working and we are using our industrial means and new materials to good advantage with a sense of their fitness to purpose, we shall universally arrive at forms that are "good style" and perhaps—who knows?— though we need not bother much about this, a Twentieth-century Style.

The thing most important at the moment is the fact that a more livable life demands a more livable building under the circumstances of a more livable city. To make all more livable by our new means enters naturally, now. In all this conception of city plan and the plan of any buildings of whatever kind, enters this new sense of space. The old standards of spacing went out when the universal mobilization of the individual came in. The individual has secured for himself comparative flight. By vicarious power he has secured this, it is true. But his power now if he seizes it and enlarges his life with it and develops his own power correspondingly, using this power as a tool and not ignorantly mistaking it for himself and passing out by its exaggeration and abuse.

To develop thus, he must appropriately use machine power to make for himself a new world of pure and noble form in which to live the new life that is inevitable, consistently with the new powers of motion that widen his physical horizon.

THE NEW SCALE

Several times the idea of a standard, necessarily new, of scale or measurement has already appeared in these pages: the man seated in his motor car with its powers being the unit of that standard rather than the man standing on his legs or his limitations in a trap hitched to a horse. His movement in a motor car is a far different thing from his movement on his legs or in any horse-drawn vehicle. This new standard of measurement is standard for all general plan-spacing in the planning of the new city. But, greatly important also, a new space concept now enters that directly applies to the buildings themselves: the sense of the lived-in space of the building itself as the real building. This is a new concept of architecture as new. But it is an essential implied by any true ideal of Democracy.

And along with steel and along with the use of a variety of indestructible thin insulated sheets of metal comes still another demand for the economical and appropriate use of these new materials. This demand is for lightly and widely spanned spaces closed to the elements but not closed, except at will, to human sight itself. Here enters the supermaterial, glass.

Here the old sense of architecture as heavy enclosure or the survival of the fortification disappears. A building appears as of the landscape. And the human life living in it is less separation from nature than ever before. The hard and fast lines between outside and inside disappear. The outside may come inside and the inside go outside, each seen as part of each other. This difference is a great difference, and the basis of a new world of effects.

The new building itself may now be as free in its space relations as the new city itself is free, and free as the circumstances dawning in the man himself. The developing sense of individuality as communal organic expression of the man within has here something worthwhile to work with. Traditional forms can only interfere with this new freedom because all the traditional forms we know were mass-concepts for a mass-life under conditions where congestion was no unmixed evil. But it now becomes evil under present changed conditions, if not soon impossible. The fact is here that immense, significant freedom for the art of building serviceable beautiful buildings is now new economy. Economy may be beautiful. Economy and beauty are, at last, harmonious and primarily human.

SIMPLICITY

Just as the present city is direct interference to the growth of modern life, so is the traditional form of a building not only interference in all building, but demoralizing. We have suffered from a surfeit of things not only within our buildings but from the buildings themselves. The same much too much of more as the city is itself. Our factory buildings alone are exempt from this criticism. And we suffer most of all from the results of property ideals too narrowly and meanly held and wrongly based. As the acquisitive jackdaw lines his nest, or monkey psychology glorifies the antique, so is this "to have and to hold" cult of things inorganic waste.

Not only was the fashionable house a heavy box-mass of some kind of building material punched with holes "à la" some pre-elected previous fashion, but the collector's mania for the antique made of it, inside, a bazaar or a junk shop gathering dust or disgrace in the shadow of the wall.

As the new era dawns in sunlight the fashionable American home appears as the graveyard of the impotent soul. Vicarious power by push-button or lever was here reflected in the vicarious expression of a taste for incompatible luxury. "Possession" may be seen here sunk to its lowest terms. For a sense of life that sank to mimicry there is ample punishment in this realization and confession of an inferiority that mistook itself for refinement.

Backward-looking, outworn styles were all the average householder possessed to inform him concerning his own possibilities in his own age until regenerate, capable of consecutive thought, he takes hold of his modern problem in new light and thinks his way through to the beginning of an organic solution.

This beginning, for him, is found in the significance of the word "organic."

The architect and his client have tried all phases of affectation and pretense. They have tried in their better moments, in better homes, for a pictorial simplicity. Let them now try for an organic simplicity, or let's say, simplicity as organic. A sense of life as organic architecture or architecture as a form of organic life, that is the sense we need now.

THE NEGATION THAT IS AFFIRMATION

From where and how is this needed change in thought to come?

Probably the source nearest to our understanding: our machines. And, likely enough, turning to this source we will fall to imitating them in our buildings. Inspired by steamships, automobiles, aeroplanes, bathtubs, refrigerators and kitchen sinks, we will at first lay hold of simplicity as negation.

Not fatal, such negation? But not necessary either. And only pictorial simplicity, again, after all. We will eventually understand that organic simplicity is as far beyond that as the lilies of the field are far from a washtub or a clothes-wringer. But, as a beginning, it is enough, for it will serve to clear away the rubbish heap for us that encumbers our life now.

The citizen's bathtub is more nearly beautiful than his house dressed up as it now is.

The necessary act is his renunciation of the stuffy house à la mode for a new one with more sunlight and simplicity. His search for intimacy with the ground will result eventually in his search for principle. The realization of principle will result in competence in place of impotence. And with the song in him, not yet dead, he will begin to build as the songmasters wrote, out of the man.

No, not all of him, but such inevitable intelligent eclecticism as would follow him who could, would be nearer life in our own time than anything the eclectic had before by way of taste unless he should fall into the same pretense of art, assume without the ability the prerogatives that belong only to creation and again stultify himself by stultifying others as himself. But the negation is good medicine and likely to do something to the culture fakir himself by way of awakened desire for true simplicity, if not on his part, then on the part of his attempted victim.

The passing order has left us with an inheritance of peddlers, brokers, "designing" partners, decorators and "esses" doing brokerage between the homeowner and the homebuilder for moderate fees, but exorbitant results. These will become the "modern" eclectics afresh. No matter. Instead of crying "aloud" for the exterior discipline that can only make more weaklings acceptable, let us put a premium upon the essentially organic quality in the human being that is individuality, not personality. Let us put this premium upon this quality in philosophy, in religion, in art and science. Let us demand that all be organic as all of life; and by such interior discipline as this would mean not only will we live in rubbish heaps no more, but the rubbish that builds them be swept away with them by a finer common sense encouraging the super-sense of the creative artist. The creative artist is one who is himself more society than society is itself. This means that he is, by nature, the naive interpreter of the best in the social order in which he lives, and society itself by way of the "next in line" must soon see him as a way-shower.

Society in this age at this period seems afraid of the radical mind of the creative artist because the values, economic and social, are so badly tipsy and twisted all down the line, too easily topsy-turvy if the strong arm relaxes. And were the true conception of the term organic applied, as a test, to the rubbish heap or the rubbishers themselves is all that is needed to set the United States on the road to a finer and higher order, social, economic, artistic. The word organic, if taken in too biological a sense, would be a stumbling block. As we are using the word here it applies to a concept of living structure. That would be a concept of structure wherein features and parts are so organized in form and substance as to be, applied to purpose, integral. Integration is used in this sense of the word integral, with this quality of thought in mind. Such is the quality "organic."

WHAT, THEN, IN GENERAL DETAIL WILL BROAD-ACRE BUILDINGS BE LIKE?

Well, let us first take the poor.

That means the "housing-problem" receiving so much philanthropic attention at the moment which, beneficent though it is, can only result in putting off by mitigation the day of regeneration for the poor.

THE TENEMENT

The poor are those damaged most by the progress of unearned increment as it piles up into vast fortunes by way of rent, or they are the lame, the halt and the blind.

Where is their place in the city built by triple rent?

See the salvage effected by the latest and best "housing" developments all over the world for your answer. Improved slums doubtless. But the slum quarter now changing to a region of the mind: standardization reaching for the soul. Poverty is being made a "decent" institution. The "row" is as inevitable to it as it is inevitable to any army.

Rows behind or beside rows of cubicles on shelves, hard, orderly and remote from nature as any coffin. Decent? Yes, but damnable straight jackets in which life is to be beneficiary but not blessed. Ingenious officering, this, of the army of the poor built in to stay "decently" poor. Institutionalized. The machine triumphant.

There is some dignity in freedom, even though "one's own way" may sink to license in filth. But what dignity in the cell of a soulless economic repetition of spiritual poverty, even though some posy be stuck in a flower box, gratuitous, for each?

Why not make more free to "the poor" the land they were born to inherit as they inherit air to breathe and daylight to see by and water to drink? I am aware of the academic economist's reaction to any land question. Nevertheless, Henry George clearly enough showed us the simple basis of poverty in human society. And some organic solution of this land problem is not only needed, it is imperative. What hope for stimulating a great architecture while land holds the improvements instead of the improvements holding the land? For an organic economic structure this is wrong end around, and all architecture is only for the landlord.

By some form of exemption and subsequent sharing of increase in land values, make his acre available to each poor man, or more according to his ability to use the land, and what house for him? And where and how may he go to work to build it?

Well, mobilization is already his, too, by way of a fare in a bus or a secondhand Ford or more or less. Emancipated from the rent he must now pay the city in order to work at all the machine-worker goes back to his birthright in the ground, as his birthright in the air to breathe and water to drink, with his family and goes to work in the factory and for himself as he can, both factory and family now on their own ground. He goes to work for his manufacturing employer in some factory unit nearby. Ten miles is nearby now by any modern standard of spacing.

The poor man—the man at the machine— buys the modern, civilized, standardized privy (it is a bathroom) manufactured and delivered complete in a single unit, even as his car or bathtub is manufactured, ready to use when connected to a septic tank or a cesspool. He plants this first unit on his ground as a center unit to which a standardized complete kitchen unit similarly cheap and beneficial may be added. As the months go by, the rent saved may buy other standardized units, or as soon as he earns them by his work on the ground. The units would be suited in general scheme of assembly either to flat land or to hillside and designed to make a well planned whole. These various standardized units are the machine-workers' cheaply, by way of his labor in the factory unit nearby and as the automobile is his by the cheapening power of mass production in standardization. His ménage may grow as his devotion goes along with time, buying each unit in a group-scheme that has had the benefit of expert study, in design and production, by the world's best minds. Not only may this group of units be variegated and so harmonized to purpose as to do no outrage to the landscape, but be so cheap that his rent for three months, in the present city bondage, would buy him the first units.

In a year or two he would own a house scientifically modern and complete along any one of a variety of lines and plan-schemes and his establishment be good to look at, hooked up in his own way with such a garden as he could make and such outbuildings—also standardized units—as he would need. Fruit trees, shade trees, berry bushes, vegetables, flowers, hot and cold running water, a modern fireplace, cookstove and heat-unit all combined. With some proper aid in the way of tax exemption here is a home of his own that would be within reach of the man by way of his devotion to the machine. And the machine itself did this, say, five-hundred-dollar house for him as it did his automobile now standing in his fifty-dollar garage. Electricity for light, heat and power he might have cheaply by voluntary co-operation. And co-operation could simplify and bring life nearer to him in many ways.

There is nothing remarkable about this opportunity as a physical product. It is already accomplished. But what is remarkable is the fact that the whole establishment may have, the mass-product notwithstanding, the proportion that is order and the order that is beauty. The finished whole, as an expression of himself need not be lacking in individuality. Characteristic choice might be freely his in appropriate designs and devices where before he could exercise only a choice of abortive sentimentalities or be compelled to accept housing as an "institution."

Where is your "poor" man now? No longer poor. Because his soul again grows to be his own. It grows to be his own because opportunity has opened natural ways for him to be free to exercise his own faculties as well as the faculty of some machine. And the next erstwhile "poor" man is beside him a block away, or more, on his own also; but owing to the quality of mind in design and device, he is there differently in plan and scheme according to his individual needs and tastes. Birds sing, the grass grows for him, rain falls on his growing garden while the wheels of standardization and invention turn for him not against him where he lives. Because his devotion to the machine in these circumstances means increased life and opportunity for him, so it must mean increased life and opportunity for all concerned with him.

His children would be growing up making first-hand contact with all the freshness and sweetness of their birthright that any "rich" man's children can know, and not by grace of some municipal-minded landlord as a goldfish inhabits a glass globe, with a pebble and a reed.

He is planted square with his fellow-man to grow as he may grow on his own ground.

Individuality is his. So he, too, is aristocrat in the true democratic meaning of that word.

Now integrate his small garden production whatever it may be, and relate this factory service of his, so this aid by his family out of his ground, such as it may be, is related to the great, universal neighborhood markets opened by the great highway—

perhaps as added features of the service stations. The family produce to be regularly called for each day in some such plan as that of the Walter V. Davidson[3] markets. Each day the family receives in cash one half the value of what their free time on the ground has raised and everyone in the new city may have "produce, fresh every hour," reinforcing the larger, more standardized farm units, not only affording still greater variety to the consumer but some additional money earned by the machine-worker's household.

Where, now, would be your city slums?

Integration by way of neighborhood schools, entertainments, hospitals for sickness, insurance for old age, all take from the machine-slave the anxieties that bore him down and out at an early age. Society would soon have an individual for a citizen instead of a herd-struck moron. Instead of another cultural weed gone to seed in good-style municipal barracks or filthy slums to raise more weeds, here would be a valuable human asset. Nonetheless a man because machine-man. No, much more—a man.

What would this establishment of his look like?

THE EMPLOYEE ON HIS ACRE

Well, so far as it went, it would look like a house to live in as his car looks like an automobile to ride in. The two would look well together—if you can imagine it. I can, and soon so can you and anyone although, now the automobile and the house are utterly out of feeling—incongruous in every case.

The various units of the house would be fabricated of sheet metal or composition slabs or both together, say, and permanently "finished" as is his car in any texture or color he preferred, but no "bad" color or unsuitable texture to be "preferred." Much glass he might have—but not to wither him—shaded above by thin, sheltering metal projections. The various units would be in one scheme rectangular, in another scheme hexagonal, in another circular in form. In other schemes, combinations could be made of these forms, infinite in variety. He might soon achieve the enclosure of a central court-garden and much greenery and flowers. Perhaps a pool. His establishment would grow as he grew, he would be earning it himself as he grew able.

The roofs he might leave flat and use as a roof-garden under an awning. Or he could slope the roof and use the ground to save expense. His furnishings become part of his house now, and are as good to look at inside as his house is good to look at outside because he got his furnishings as he got his house, designed for him by the best talent the world affords with perfect knowledge, not only of his problem, but of the capacities of production. And there is a range of choice wide enough in which he may find his own.

He works, now, on ground that cannot be taken away from him for it could not be his by way of debt, that is, mortgage but by way of improvement. There can be no landlord but society. A social unit will grow up independently on his own ground as he is able. The house is his own. He is no soulless unit, officered in the rank and file of the standardized army that is the "poor." No longer is the "poor" man a reproach to fortuitous good fortune in the form of rent unless enough rent is set aside to make him "look" decent.

No, here now may be a manly man, in Usonia, living in manlike freedom. On his own together with his own. Like the bravest and like the best.

In bare outline, of course, all this (essentials not all drawn). But here, in outline, is a sketch of the feasible "tenement" in the Broadacre City: the only possible city of the future.

THE TILLER OF THE SOIL AND THE HUSBAND OF THE ANIMALS

What establishment would be the farmer's as a suburban citizen in the new city?

He is suffering from rent in its most oppressive form, any improvements he may make are only a gamble adding to his burden of rent. Should his labor be insufficient to pay rent for money, rent for his own improvements or rent for land and government goodbye to all his improvements. But at least so long as he can keep his ground under his feet and able to work he and his need have no fear of starving.

But farming is the hinterland of economics, if not the borderland of despair, because the farmer was not taken into the present scheme of increments except as a source. Let us take the farmer in the more thickly settled regions of the country where he is trying to compete against the grain and beef-raising of machine-farming on the almost endless and nearly free acreage of the great Western open spaces of the United States. Grain raising is against him. Nor in cattle and sheep raising can he compete with the ranges of the great ranches on western land with no improvements, taxed at fifty cents per acre, if at all, while the cost of his "improvements" only works dead against him on his land taxed at fifty dollars or more per acre.

Modern sanitation, the motor car and the radio have already brought the farmer's life a little nearer to the luxury of the sons and daughters he too has lost—voluntary deserters to the prevailing white-collarite army. But he is alone on the farm often. And sometimes an inmate of the poor house, or better off if he were, at the end of his labor on the ground, whatever may have been his energy and thrift.

This ground is so seldom his own ground, now, except by some slender show of equity. The farmer East, Middle West, or South, is no winner of the game of increment as the game is played for high stakes with the three false rules of the game. The dice are loaded against him by the very circumstances in which he is placed to "find" himself.

And it is amusing or exasperating, as you may happen to get the view, to see the empty political gestures his would-be saviors make to "relieve" him.

Not a statesman's voice nor a sensible legal move made to free him from the inequalities that grip him for no other purpose, it seems, than to give the white-collarite army a free ride on his back. That army rides to some extent on the farmer's back because the farmer's labor is intrinsic. A source.

His labor on the land contributes to the various vicarious powers—power by lever and push-button—of city life. But his labor contributes not much to his own life. Parasites are parasites because they batten down sources, live upon origins but never live by originating. So here in the tiller of the soil is good life, and genuine, in deep trouble.

Cities are great mouths. The farmer is essentially food for humanity. It is his job to feed the cities. And the raw material for clothing is his job also.

Without the farmer the cities would starve and go naked. Now the Broadacre City comes to him

not only to be fed but also to take him in and share with him the luxury that the very nature of his service to the city has hitherto denied him. And his new establishment is a most welcome and perhaps the most attractive unit in all the structure of the city of the future.

Feeding the multitude being naturally his job, it is clear that the produce of intensive farming as varied as possible will be his advantage over the great grain- and beef-producing areas competing with him, and this produce is as direct to the consumer as possible. Dairying, fruit growing, truck gardening, raising the rarer meats and fowls, eggs, in all of which freshness is a first condition, though the tin-can has increasingly become the resource of our civilization—as life itself, became, more or less, canned.

The little-farmer who will take the place of the big-farmer by intensive methods needs a greenhouse and less than one tenth of the land he tries to farm now. And he needs an establishment that makes his life a more decent and bearable association with the animals he husbands, tending, breeding and feeding them, primarily, for the urban millions who have educated, therefore artificial, tastes as compared with his own more simple ones.

The farmer too, and most of all, needs the organic architecture that will end his wasteful to and fro about the inefficient group of crude, ill-adapted buildings now habitual to him, to turn all into a compact, efficient, correlated single unit for his purpose: considering his life as worthy of high conservation. The little-farmer needs his living comforts assured. He needs less in some ways than before when he was "big." He no longer needs a haymow, the thing that exaggerated his barn. He no longer needs machine sheds, but he needs a workshop and tools. He does not need many fences except those that are a part of his buildings.

His energy would be conserved by having, under sanitary conditions, his animals a step away, his car reached by opening a door, his crop proscribed and sold before he raises it by some such plan of integration, now of larger units, as the one referred to as being worked out by Walter V. Davidson in the plan for farm markets. This plan is of the type—integration of small units into great ones—that is destined, and inevitably soon, to take the place of present overgrown centralizations.

Such a composite farm building as this one might be would be assembled of units consisting of a garage, a dwelling, a greenhouse, a packing and distributing house, a silo, a stable and a diversified animal shed. The whole would be practical architecture and as such could be delivered to the little-farmer at low cost by benefit of machine standardization. Again architecture would be his by way of the best brains in the world, to simplify, dignify and make his life effective as his own.

This composite farm building would be a group-building not of one type only, but of as many types in various materials as there are modifications of the farmer and his purpose.

In this modernization of the basis of farming is a true and important phase of farm relief.

Well-designed farm life grouped in units of three-, five-, or ten-acre farms, production proscribed and all related to highway traffic markets, produced fresh every hour, is radical farm relief. And the design of that great traffic market as another feature of this rural integration is another important building among the service features along the highways of the Broadacre City.

A single community tractor could plow and harrow the soil for all. Community centers provide not only power and pooling of certain labors and interests in sickness or in health but entertainment for all.

Again here is but a suggestive sketch, in outline, of "farm relief," and "relief" also for so many white-collarites who are still capable men and women but now unhappy as city parasites. They would by this division and reintegration of the smaller units, up-building living conditions on a better basis, find means to live well by their own labor on their own ground in an independent life. No longer rented but owners of themselves.

In every Broadacre City there would be plenty of room for many thousands of such integrated, yet independent farm units.

FACTORY DECENTRALIZATION AND INTEGRATION

The factory too is now to come to the countryside, the employees themselves small gardeners as outlined in "The Tenement." Already the factory is so well organized and built and managed in our country that it needs less re-designing than any institution we have. Although its product is sadly in need of organic design, it needs only the ground available or comparatively free to its workers. The big factory already needs dividing up into smaller units, spaced in the countryside according to the new standards of space measurement. This ideal of re-integration, in this division of the big factory into smaller units, is now at work in many places. Instead of scheming for the greater and greater centralization that, as we may now see, defeats life and even defeats its own purpose by meaningless back and forth, the factory will be the first to end the expensive waste motion of to and fro. The factory, except for exaggeration of its size—due to over centralization—is in itself the one best thing America has done. The best thing we have ready to divide and reintegrate as sightly features of the country.

THE OFFICE IN THE NEW CITY

Financial, official, professional, distributive, administrative: offices may now all go where they belong to function as units of whatever industry they represent and be found there where actual production is taking place. Volatilized, instantaneous intercommunication make this return to origins reasonable and practical. Once the movement is started, this correlation of offices and manufactures would be desirable and efficient conservation of time and energy. It will be easier to work forward from the plant than it is to work backward to it or to and fro from it.

The offices of public officialism, petty or major, should all center at the police and fire-stations at certain road junctions, and, owing to lack of congestion as a contributor cause of disturbance, might be cut to one of the ten needed now. The district court would be found at this point, and all functionaries be established there in appropriate quarters, not in the braggadocio buildings now customary. These functions are utilitarian. Not necessarily grandiose in a democracy. Appropriately, the reverse.

The offices of the "professional" man should develop for his especial work in connection with his own home-grounds as a shop, either a studio, a clinic, a hospital, or a gallery suited to his purpose: "show-off" place, if he is like that. Such individualized units added to homes would enrich the architectural aspect of the whole, save human wear and tear in the "back and forth haul" and be more available under such conditions of modern transport as are fast approaching than they are under the present attempts to reach them in the positive traffic hindrances that do violence to the time and patience of the professional and his client, alike, in the present form of centralization. The professional man needs more time for service and study in a better atmosphere. Less of his energy consumed in the vain scramble in and scramble out would give it to him.

The bank is an "office," too, but as a quasi-public one it should be found with the public official-buildings at some important junction, in itself an integrated unit in various strong financial chain systems. It would no longer need to put on airs as a temple or place of worship to hold its importance or to get business.

A bank is a machine. A cold, calculating business institution. And it is a strongbox. So it might properly take on the air of a typewriter or a filing system in a steel box. Grandomania in the construction of banks, as in safes or locks, would no longer be direct invitation to thieves by useless glorification of money-power. The grand temple of the unearned increments might well shrink to the strongbox of intrinsic earnings.

THE NEW STORE: OR DISTRIBUTION OF MANUFACTURED MERCHANDISE

This integration of mercantile distribution as it will be natural to the Broadacre City would occur upon the great arteries of mobilization, or traffic. This feature of the future city is already appearing neglected and despised—but as the roadside service station the distributing centers, in embryo, of the future are appearing.

In the gasoline service station may be seen the beginning of an important advance agent of decentralization by way of distribution and also the beginning of the establishment of the Broadacre City.

Wherever the service station happens to be naturally located, these now crude and seemingly insignificant units will grow and expand into various distributing centers for merchandise of all sorts. They are already doing so in the Southwest to a great extent. Each of these smaller units might be again integrated or systematically chained together over large areas, thus cutting down costs of buying and distribution to add to the economies of mass production and standardizing. They would become, in the little, distributors of all that Marshall Field, Sears-Roebuck, or Wanamaker now find to distribute in the large.

Fresh architectural opportunity is here: the most diversified single modern unit to be found in all the features of the Broadacre City. With the service-station would be found generous parking facilities and various schemes for automatic parking; beguiling entertainments; cabarets, cafés, and restaurants, and comfortable overnight accommodations for transients. There would be individual competition between the various centers and individuality would soon develop. From every stream of traffic one might turn aside and pick up, at these stations, in natural to and fro, anything needed or desired at home. To not too suddenly deprive the age of its characteristic art, advertising, the purchaser might be subjected to the same temptations by salesmanship and by means of effective display as is now the case in any of the highly specialized city stores. Proprietors, salesmen and managers all living nearby, within twenty-five miles say, and living in country places of their own, their children going to the Broadacre schools. Themselves now "landed gentry."

These are only slight changes for the better of an ideal that is already doing its work; and that ideal—reintegration of decentralization—must, to go on working, follow the law of change as Marshall Field followed when he established stores at outlying suburbs. And as Sears-Roebuck followed in establishing a chain of stores in small towns. And as Woolworth and his followers followed. So, ahead of their merchandising, now comes the next step in decentralization and the integration that is Democracy. This is for the inland towns. The port towns would naturally enough be subject to special concentrations.

Modern inventions and machine resources, now destructive interferences to city life, not only point in this direction but are compelling the merchant to take it.

THE MAINTENANCE OF THE MOTOR CAR AND THE PLANE

The garage will naturally be found as expansion of the roadside service stations.

Probably some of the stations will become "union-stations" merchandising all oils on some basis as drug and department stores now handle various brands of the same merchandise. Or they may subsist as individual units—co-related as now.

FOR THOSE WHO HAVE BEEN EMASCULATED BY THE PRESENT CITY

The tall apartment building will go to the country. It will be among the first steps toward rescue . . . this infirmary for the confirmed "citified." The Broadacre City unit here may be of the type proposed for the apartment tower in the small park of St. Mark's on the Bouwerie in New York City.[4]

An arrangement in quadruple of say, thirty-six indestructible duplex apartments built, furnished, complete. The buildings would stand in a small park of, say, thirty acres with its own garage beneath, and playgrounds and gardens for each tenant arranged as features of the park.

This type of structure would enable many to go to the country with their children who have grown so accustomed to apartment life under serviced conditions that they would be unable or unwilling (it is the same thing) to establish themselves in the country otherwise.

These prismatic metal and glass shafts rising from the greenery of the private parks in which they would stand would be acceptable units in the Broadacre City. Many of the advantages of the countryside could still go to them. And they might own the "apartment" in which they lived in the country on the economical terms of the age we live in.

THE HOTEL, THE MOBILE HOTEL AND THE PREDATORY HOUSE

As a matter of course, there would be fewer hotels. Each would probably be a group of small cottages related to a general unit comprising the rooms for the use of all as seen in better planned establishments like the Arizona Biltmore,[5] or the San Marcos in the Desert at Chandler, Arizona.[6] And these would be found where Nature had "staged a show" with which they might harmonize and which they could well employ for recreation and recuperation by wise building.

But a new manifestation of hotel life would be the hotel on wheels. The mobilized hotel.

These commodious cars with sleeping accommodations and cuisine aboard would tour the country with parties. They would go from North to South and from East to West. With attendant trailers or lorries they would be found in the scenic marvels of the great plains and mountain ranges where no other hostelry could survive.

As the nature of transportation is developing, there is no reason why such mobile hotels should not be safe, comfortable and profitable in some such form as already developed by the McArthur brothers at Phoenix, Arizona, and intended as a feature for the Arizona Biltmore Hotel itself.

If the scheme is feasible for a hotel, it is certainly feasible for a house. And this mobilization applies to the lakes and streams by way of motorization.

Artists, pleasure-seekers, explorers, the modern gypsies, could all have road-traveling or floating houses of perfect convenience and, by way of superior design facilities, be presentable, as sightly as a plane or any car. More so, naturally, than most of them are now.

These motor houses could go about, at the householder's will, from place to place, from mountain to seashore or rivers or lakes as the nomad once drifted over the desert with his camel and tent.

THE BACHELOR

A new phase of domestic arrangements enters the picture here that might take the curse off domesticity for many who cannot tolerate it now, and so perhaps reclaim many a life dissolute because establishment means too great monotony.

And as a suggestion to this gregarious product, our heritage from the disappearing city, as the children came they could be accommodated in trailers, behind, nursery and all. Inasmuch as little trains will soon trickle along the highways anyway, why not the domestic arrangements of the now unwilling husband?

The slogan of this element . . . "Give the children a ride."

The art of fashioning the trailer has already gone so far there would be no difficulty whatever in appropriately "trailing" any feature of life whatsoever, anywhere.

THE HUMANE HOSPITAL

Efficient and humane as it is, the present hospital is too large and too obviously an institution. The Broadacre hospital will be several sunlit clinics scattered in a spacious garden, to every large unit we have now. Homelike quarters where no disabled or sick person need ever see another disabled or sick person unless he so wills. The resources of modern therapeutics, surgery and medicine would be in their places as the plumbing, electric lighting and heating of the home are a part of the house, but not visible as fixtures.

In short, the emphasis should be on normality and not on the paraphernalia of abnormality. Death's head shows at once in the present hospital and grins incessantly at any and every unfortunate inmate. Why not a hospital as humane in effect as in its purpose?

THE UNIVERSITY: UNIVERSAL

The present university, specialized, is the mass production of specialists in book knowledge. As the antenna of the insect is a feeler for the life of the insect, so a modern university should be the antenna of the life of a society and able to communicate its "findings."

Here in quiet retreats made beautiful and appropriate for reflection and concentration there should be rendezvous for groups of developed individuals in noble storehouses where all that mankind has produced in science, art and philosophy would be a matter of record, or model available for free study.

There need be no "professors," nor large groups. Only several father confessors and their recorders. One elected by the scientists, one by the artists, and one by the philosophers of each state, respectively, and, if one could be found, a statesman

should be added to the group. The best chosen by the best.

All others would be privileged students accepted by the father confessors and employed in research concerning the correlation of these matters of the social soul. No privilege of the novice, this. Only those having given proof of inner human experience in some one of these qualities of human life would, of course, be accepted.

The old monastic institution, liberalized, made free and related to social progress by research work where contemporary life—modern materials, modern industrial circumstances and association with performances as well as ideas—would be inspiring. No preparation for teaching or practicing anything should be a feature of these "universities." This renunciation of vocational training would of course come along slowly, even in the Broadacre City. It is so much harder for us to de-limit the sacred institutions of "learning" than any of our institutions.

THE COMMUNAL CENTER

Of course such centers would be features of every new city and each would be an automobile-objective situated near some major highway or in some nook of the countryside where views are inspiring and nature lovable.

Golf courses, racetrack, zoo, aquarium and planetarium will naturally be found at these places grouped in architectural ensemble with a botanical garden. Of clubs there would still be many, but the community center would be something else. It would be the great common club, but avoiding commonplace elegance. The community center would be an educational factor as well as an amusement center. The art gallery, the museum, would be there. And as all would be laid out in harmony with each other and the ground, each center would take on the individuality of its circumstances. Scattered over the states these centers would embody and express the best thought of which our democratic ideal is capable. There would be no commercial bustle or humdrum here. All common excitement could be reached, further on, at the service stations. But the various community centers should be quiet places for study, reflection and introspection, in comradeship.

THE THEATRE

Where nature has been raised by art to the level of greater nature, the new theatre, no longer a peep show but a circumstance, the building itself an automatic machine rivalling in plasticity the cinema, would be a sanctuary for emotion and aspiration, rivalling the church in the old city. Architecture in these civic centers would be worked out in native materials.

The cinema would, like the theatre, go direct from camera to the home. Sound and vision. But at the community center there would be special creative features maintained by the community not by big business as a sales agency.

THE NEW CHURCH

Assuming that religious sentiment has deepened by way of the ideal that builds the Broadacre City, and a false sentimentality as oppressive to enlightened democracy in religion as it would be in social economics or art, the surviving church would be likely to take on some non-sectarian devotional form. Here would be a great opportunity for a true symphony, as building. The church might, in the new city, be a church as a song without words is a song. The Broadacre church would be a rendezvous with beauty in the depths and breadths of the soul, a refuge no less individual because more profound and comprehensive, for the stained and worn and skeptic. Harmony complete might in this church again descend to refresh a mortal weariness. This skeptic ego of our more sophisticated age needs spiritual recreation. No theology, now, can ever be essential. The unhistorical cathedral as a feature of the Broadacre City would be erected by and for the spirit of man to evoke again in terms of our machine-age life an organic ideal of the organic social life and new faith in the nobility and beauty of which human nature itself is capable.

THE DESIGN CENTER

The machine as it exists in every important trade, by way of capable artist interpreters, should without delay be put into the hands of the young architects. Reluctantly I admit that to put the machine, as the modern tool of a great civilization, to any extent into the hands of a body of young students, means some kind of school; naturally such a school would be called an art school, but one in which competent interpreters of fine art would not only be allied to the industries they would now try to serve, but would stand there at the center of an industrial hive of characteristic industry as inspiration and influence to younger talent in the design problems of inevitable and desirable mass production.

Sensitive, unspoiled students (and they may yet be found in this unqualified machine that America is becoming) should be put in touch with commercial industry in what we might call industrial design or style centers. The centers would be workshops equipped with modern machinery, endowed by the industries themselves, where the students would remain domiciled and spend the better part of each day working in the shop itself.

Machinery-using crafts making useful things might through such experimental centers discover possibilities existing in the nature of their craft, which the present industries know nothing about and might never discover for themselves. In such a school it would be the turn of the fine arts to serve machinery in order that machinery might better serve them and all together better serve a beauty-loving and an appreciative United States.

Let us say that seven branches of industrial arts be taken for a beginning (a number should be grouped together for the reason that they react upon one another to the advantage of each).

Let us name glass-making, textiles, pottery, sheet-metals, woodworking, casting in metal, the "process reproduction." Each industry so represented should be willing to donate machinery and supply a competent machinist and to a certain extent endow its own craft, provided such industries were certain of proper management under proper auspices, and assured of a share in results which would be directly their own, sharing either the benefits of designs or presently in designers themselves, both adapted to their particular field.

Such experimental centers intelligently conducted could do more to rationalize and vitalize our industries than all else, and soon would make them independent of France, Germany, Austria or any other country, except as instruction by international example from all countries would help work out our own forms. There is no reason why an experiment center of this character, each center confined to one hundred students or less, should not make its own living and produce valuable articles to help in "carrying on the growth of style in our industries." As compared with the less favorably circumstanced factories, and owing to the artists at the head of the group, each article would be of the quality of a work of art and so be a genuine missionary wherever it went.

Such a school should be in the countryside on sufficient land so that three hours a day of physical work on the soil would help to insure the living of the students and the resident group of seven artist workers, themselves the head of the student group. There would remain, say, seven hours of each day for forty-seven individuals in which to unite in production.

A well-directed force of this sort would very soon have considerable producing power. Thus belonging to the school each month there would be beautifully useful or usefully beautiful things ready for market and influence: stuffs, tapestries, table linen, new cotton fabrics, table glassware, flower holders, lighting devices, window-glass mosaics, necklaces, screens, iron standards, fixtures, gates, fences, fire irons, enamelled metals for house or garden purposes, cast metal sculpture for gardens, building hardware. All sorts of industrial art in aluminum, copper, lead, tin. Practical flower pots, architectural flower containers on large scale, water jars, pots and sculpture. Paintings for decoration suitable for reproduction and designs for new media, for process reproductions. Modern music, plays, rhythm, designs for farm buildings, the characteristic new problems like the gasoline station, food distribution, town and country cottages and objects for their furnishings. And factories, too, of various sorts.

The station might broadcast itself. Issue brochures, illustrated by itself, of pertinent phases of its work. Devote a branch to landscape studies on conservation and planting and town-planning. In short, the station would be a hive of creative industry. Architecture, without hesitation or equivoca-

tion, should be the broad essential background of the whole endeavor, again strong in modern life as it ever was strong in ancient times. It is desirable to repeat that architecture again must be the logical background and framework of modern civilization.

Such style stations or culture centers could be alcoves in connection with standard college courses in the history of art, architecture and archaeology. And it would not matter where the centers were located, were they sufficiently isolated in beautiful country. They should not be too easy of access.

No examinations, graduations or diplomas. But so soon as a student worker showed special competence in any branch of industry he would be available as teacher in the Broadacre schools or for a place as designer in that industry. Manufacturers who were contributors to the school would, however, have first right to use him, or her. The body of inspirational talent and the trade machinists should be of such character that outside students would enjoy and seek points of contact with the work going on at the school, helpful to them and to the school as well.

These units, directly dedicated to practical style culture, would be essential to the organic growth of the organic Broadacre City.

THE NEW SCHOOL: THE TEACHER AND HIS FLOCK

More teachers and smaller flocks would be the natural thing in the organic integration that challenges centralization.

The big knowledge-factory was always a self-defeating institution. How like a factory it looks and is, as one passes through the towns and villages. How unimaginative and impotent the vicarious product. How many prison houses for the mind are its abstractions. Armchair ethics, philosophy, science and art. Bookology is their science and their craft.

But any school in the Broadacre City would be, first, a park in the choicest part of the countryside, preferably by a stream or by a body of water. It is not only small as a whole, but that small could divide again into smaller so far as possible. Each school building is never more than one story high, fashioned of metals and glass for young life in sunlight. Divided into smaller buildings, each unit might contain not more than ten children. Say, forty children would be a large school. A gymnasium and a common hall, a modelling and a drawing room, a kitchen and a dining room. The group in composition materials and glass, or perhaps metals, arranged about interior and exterior courts. Standardization could here, again, be used, but give way to more individual treatment. Enough ground for a flower and vegetable bed for each pupil would be alongside, with large play-spaces beyond that. Each pupil would learn of the soil by working on it and in it, and he would educate his hand to draw what his eye might see, and learn to model it equally well. Eye-minded is modern-minded. So the school building should be developed by artists and architects as, in itself, a free work of art.

To learn to draw well would civilize the faculties as a whole once more and more than any other means correlate the growing faculties.

Perfect correlation of all the faculties is the most important aim of the new education. The eye and the hand, the body and what we call the mind. And the just relation of this just correlation directly to the growth of the earth, as natural to the pupil. Thus getting a working sense and appreciation of the rhythm that is life itself.

In these sunlit buildings, beautiful in themselves, and in these garden courts, the child would be working, preparing food and learning how to eat it, learning to see accurately, by drawing what he sees, gradually taking the steps to learn how to make two blades of grass grow where one or none grew before. Physically and spiritually. Boys and girls here would become true co-efficients of a spiritually potent, therefore naturally creative humanity. Individuals, in communal individualship, becoming a certainty. An average of a teacher to a group of not more than ten would not be too much and the teachers themselves would be qualified as human beings to help develop or qualify an individual.

Here again is only a rough sketch of the smaller school buildings of the Broadacre City of which there would be ten such organic units for every inorganic one now attempting to function on hard pavements in overgrown, outdone centralization or new ones built on the model of the circus.

THE NEW HOME IN THE BROADACRE CITY

We come, now, to the most important unit in the city, really the center and the only centralization allowable. The individual home. Integration here is voluntary and so far only as it is free individual choice.

Luxury may enter as gratification of developed sensibility. The home has grown in dignity and spiritual significance by this concept of the free city of Democracy. Not every man's home his castle, that was a feudal concept. No, every man's home his sunlit strand and no less, but more than ever, a refuge for the expanding spirit that is still his. And in his home the Broadacre citizen is, himself, true exponent and expression of his true place and relation to other men: his fellows. He inculcates high ideals in others by practicing them himself and insisting upon opportunities for others to do likewise.

The opportunity of men made equal before the law of the land as promised in the charter of Independence, and therefore the artificial economic structure dissolved or abolished, communal life may be based upon a sound economy of machine resources. Improvements of the ground are free to those who improve their ground. It is economic sense for the house owner to surround himself with such expression of himself as seems ideal to him, paying no penalty for so doing. Advantages have flowed in upon this house of his. He is becoming aware of these advantages. The significance of much he never realized before is coming clear to him. Physical changes in his situation have rendered obsolete most of his education and nearly all of his traditions. Then to what may he hold fast now, as he stands to go forward to new life on new ground with power never dreamed of until he began to dream?

THREE WORDS

Let him learn their meaning well.

The word "democracy."
The word "integration."
The word "organic."

They have never been interpreted and applied as ideals in this or, consciously, in any other culture up to now. The significance of these watchwords should be his guide. And as understanding opens to him the Old will naturally fall away. He will come face to face with the New.

The vicarious power that has left him and his home-making, too, spiritually stranded—aground on sterility—will have a new meaning. In a new direction new forces will open to him that will make machine power no longer vicarious but a match for his own. He will build with that power the new house of a new world.

HIS MODERN HOME

In this modern home the hitherto painfully and expensively acquired utilitarian conveniences and sanitation may now be integrated in a single unit standardized for all. And ten for one in point of convenience and economy they may be his now to do for him what he could not ask of them ten years ago. Toilet convenience and sanitation and kitchen complete may be delivered to him as his car is delivered. In the standardized units composing his house, the new materials, glass and sheet metal, will let him out into the grounds and gardens around him as he lives within and open to him the vistas of the landscape.

The man himself has now a new ideal of living, in this new space concept of the machine age. Free space, in sunlight, ten feet or a thousand where one foot was his limit is now within his reach. His luxury consists, first, in that new sense of freedom, however simple the house may be otherwise. The home-maker will exercise this new sense of space freedom in the new space concept of his home. The reward and refuge of his life is this enlarged opportunity to build and live in a shelter of his own making.

This new standard of space measurement—the man seated in his automobile—affects him everywhere he goes, but most of all the new sense of space affects him here where he lives his family life. Vista, breadth, depth not only in his philosophy but in simple reaches of the building he calls home may now belong to him, not by way of mortgage or the "financing" that only leads to refinancing and eventually to "repossession."

Extended lightness, spacious openness, a firm cleanliness of line make satisfying appeal to his awakened imagination. And in the quality of surface, breadth of plane and length of line, he may see the simplicity of the flower. In all his home will be a feeling of free space to be lived in and enjoyed, even as the fields, the hill slopes, or the ravines and forests themselves. At home, he is lord of a free spacious interior life. Elemental spaciousness a reasonable possession. As a new significance physical and spiritual, this is in itself tremendous.

LET IT WORK

As a creative product of this sense of spaciousness, machine-age luxury will be more truly a concrete freedom than the Greek ever knew, the Goth ever felt or any man before except, perhaps, the Nomad. In sweep, simplicity and quality, no architecture ever rivalled what may now be the American home-unit: the only centralization in the new city in the American scene.

And characteristic also of this machine-age comes the increase of space by conservation of space. Such conservation makes all furniture either a part of or appropriate to the building. And takes all appurtenances for heat or light into invisible, but effective cooperation of the building itself.

A NEW AND AN ORGANIC SIMPLICITY

This sense of life as organic architecture and architecture as organic life reacts upon this man's sense of everything. He grows in breadth and health of mind. And his new freedom in his own home makes freedom dear to him, for others no less than for himself. He demands it as his right. Moreover, as the meaning of the word "organic" dawns upon him, he demands true significance in all about him. His awakened eye searches forms he once took for granted. Finding them false he rejects them. He will have truth of form or he will have none. And this goes out from him to establish itself in his relations with others in the communal life.

The communal life, too, must rest squarely and naturally with the basis for all human life, the ground for all.

Political science, too, he now sees as organic. Legitimatizing artificialities for crucifying life to feed ambition is no longer for him. Philosophy he has come to see as organic. The simplicities of Laotze and Jesus dawn afresh for him as he sees them, tangible, at work as modern art and religion. The interior discipline of a clean ideal of a simpler but more scientific and spacious life in true freedom of individual expression is set up within him and grows tall against the very roof of his mind.

Potentialities undreamed of begin to work in him.

Soon he may walk abroad, a man among men.

When his power is no longer a vicarious power, he will be eager to share the work of the world, invigorated by the happiness and vitality of his life at home with the ground. The Usonian Citizen no longer growing impotent. Creatively he will be competent.

TYPICAL EXAMPLES

Here set up in descriptive outline is the sketch of an ideal. The graphic arts must come in to show you what such a house would look like. And the different buildings described here already have graphic form. But the outline of an ideal is better than any specific plan for any house. . . . The ideal once fixed, the plan will come.

IN CONCLUSION

These outlines of the appearing city—the disappearing city must really be the appearing city—may seem to the patient reader who has come with me so far, another Utopia to join the many, come and gone. I am not trying to prove a case. My interest lies in the nature of the elemental changes we have been discussing and there is plenty of evidence. Here, at least, is a study based upon an architect's experience in trying to get an organic architecture born for these United States.

I now realize that organic architecture is life, that life itself is organic architecture or both are in vain.

I see that the principles working in the one are at work in the other or must be. There can be no doubt that we are sacrificing the greater efficiency of humankind to put all into the lesser efficiency of the machine. I believe it is useless to go on working for the machine or the landlord on any general basis of any great future for a noble architecture because a noble architecture means a noble life. The landlord, as a hangover from feudal institutions, is not intrin-

sic, nor is the machine itself. What perversion to allow land to hold the improvements instead of improvements holding the land and the machine to own the man instead of the man owning the machine!

We have reached the point where all is more or less makeshift where human life itself is concerned or at best more or less adventitious. It must be, so long as the basis upon which life as architecture and architecture as life must function together is not fundamentally strong and genuinely free. The valiant special case alone is free. Freedom is a dangerous adventure, as things are with us.

Out of my own sense of an organic architecture, observing the principles of that architecture at work as the law of natural change in the life of our country comes this tentative outline of the Broadacre City as I see it growing, as it must grow, from the ground up: a city to utilize for the human being the forces that built the present whirling vortex from the top down.

I confess that I have never been more than tolerant of reform. It is true form I am seeking. And no such form will ever be had by any alteration upon any old building or upon an old order. The new forms our modern life desperately needs will grow up from the ground, from within the nature of our common life. As Nature always grows her forms, so human nature must grow them, too; roots in the soil that is nature.

Cruelty, misfortune and poverty may be mitigated and should be, meantime. Honor to those so engaged in reform.

But I believe we have learned enough from the specialization that is centripetal centralization and have made enough ready, to go to the root for construction and do radical work with the law of natural, therefore of beneficent, change. The equalization, emphasizing individuality, that we call integration is that change. Why try to stand longer against it? "To have and to hold" is all very well when having and holding with nature. Both are disastrous when giving and taking against nature. And all that is written here is in line with that normal law of organic change as I have observed it beginning to work throughout our country.

The important new machine factors we have been discussing should be made no more than the scaffolding of our civilization. But we have been taking them for granted, high and low, as civilization itself. Therefore these factors are becoming forces of destruction. As forces of construction they have had little intelligent recognition in our plan. In our culture—the elevation of the plan—none whatever. But adventitious increment derived from centralization as an incentive or premium has not been wholly wasted. These mechanical forces of our age having been more rapidly developed to a higher degree of efficiency than would ever have been the case otherwise these gains should now be utilized in the architecture of our states, economic, social, moral, aesthetic. The time has gone by when such development as centralization has brought with it can justify the immense cost of its "efficiencies."

The time is here when something must be done with these new resources in a larger way for humanity in order to relieve the centripetal pressure inordinate centralization has become or we will leave a record of the shortest life of any civilization yet attempted. These new machine-and-material resources and humanity itself are fast growing apart as enemies to destroy each other although both are by way of each other, capable of new and true forms. Denied the new forms, degradation and misery will deepen.

Why not see the new forces openly thrusting at the old form or at the lack of any form, in all these agencies we have enumerated as beginning to decentralize the city? And see that we must subdivide the immense aggregates and build up individuality in order to re-integrate in larger scale and in the true individual freedom we desire, the life of our States.

Compelled by the organic force of these new resources the skeptical may see our big cities already splitting up into several centers; our big mercantile establishments already building distributing centers on the edges of the congestion. Our more advanced big manufacturers have already confessed the big establishment no longer necessary; the motorbus and motor truck have already cut the now senseless back and forth haul of the too many competing railways to the heart. The new centers of distribution serving mobilization—the roadside service station an important one among them—are everywhere rapidly growing in importance and range, especially Middle West and South, Southwest and West. Manhattan alone lost hundreds of thousands of citizens last year. Many other big cities lost heavily also. Density of population must decline.

So greatly has mobilization already changed human values, modified human character and needs and altered the circumstances, that most of our buildings and our cities, both in plan and in style, are obsolete when they are built. Almost all of our present architecture and structural equipment—outside certain industries—is obsolete. Too old. The machine-age has made the old arrangements of which the architecture of the city itself was perhaps the most important, already invalid.

IT IS TIME

Therefore it is time not to dream of the future but to realize that future as now and here. It is time to go to work with it, no longer foolishly trying to stand up against it for an eleventh-hour retrenchment.

Super-sense soon becomes common-sense. The Broadacre City is already super-sense, needing only to realize the forms that best express it in our daily life to make it valid. Those needed forms we already have. And they are all organic architecture. But we need organic economics and we need an organic social contract in order to make the new forms effective for all.

Our pioneer days are not over. Perhaps pioneer days are never over. But the frontier has shifted. Our American forebears took life in their hands and, efficient, went in their covered wagons to clear the ground for habitation. It seems they blazed the way for another efficiency that, by way of a rugged individualism that was only an exaggeration of their own great qualities, could only become exaggerated centralization. The strength of will and courage of our original pioneers was native forerunner to this type of domination we now see building its own mortal monuments, the skyscrapers in the cemetery that is the old city. They mark the end of an epoch.

Pioneering now lies along this new frontier: decentralization. Encumbrance and interference and danger again are there to be cleared away by the pioneers of a more humane because, at last, of an organic culture [*sic*]. Excess "success" must perish into promised opportunity for all to live as the bravest and best. Why, longer, should men be compelled to live according to the baser qualities of their natures would they live at all successfully? Why not a simpler natural basis for men to live according to their better selves—and not only survive but, actually, thrive? As "pioneering" on this new frontier, then, is scraping off the too full bushel, while ignoring the complex impositions that overfill it, statesmanship? Then the tinker is the best maker, the imitator the best creator and vicarious power is the best power of which we are capable.

We now know that politicians are not statesmen. A statesman is an architect of an organic social order. The reforms proposed and effected by our political governing powers are no more than little shifts in the complex rules of the game. Makeshifts have been tried. But no interpretation in the changed circumstances of the ideal we have professed but have ignored has yet been tried. The by-products of any process whether of life or manufacture react and require constant modification. Are we thus stultified because we have really lost that ideal and so are unable to recognize or meet organic change?

There is no question whatever in the enlightened mind that includes a heart, as to the rightmindedness and humane instincts of humanity when humanity is free, but . . . in what does equitable human freedom actually consist in a modern society?

Let us discuss that and its underlying economics as intelligently and frankly as we discuss science—biology for instance—and this fundamental cause to which we have dedicated our lives may work more intelligently to allow these new forces we have raised to be released that we may come nearer our own Ideal.

What is the meaning of life in a democracy—developed machine power a factor—as distinguished from life in other forms of social contract? What is true human efficiency? What is true human economy?

Let our bravest and best seek the answer and although perhaps in other terms, whatever the terms may be, they will find the answer in life as organic architecture, as I have found it in organic architecture as life.

EVOLUTION

We all know that the present basis of our life is inorganic—therefore unsound and dangerous just as such architecture as we have is two-fifths inorganic waste. We should also know that the inorganic has sporadic increase but can not possibly reproduce as life because it lacks the correlation essential to organic growth. Centralization, as centripetal force has no interior, informing, expanding principle of life. Its efficiencies are all involved and narrow: involution not evolution.

So, because our economic system has been inorganic, inorganic our social system must be also and so our arts and our religion be uncreative. Our politics are absurd because our status quo is a strong arm. Our fortunes are largely false.

We have drifted into fatal exaggeration, and are being drawn inward toward impotence by way of a thoughtless use of vicarious power to make money as, itself, more vicarious power.

Let us have an intelligent interpretation of democracy—our own ideal. And then let us have an honest appraisal of our direction as we stand. And then?

With what we have accomplished let us go in the direction we intend.

1. Wright's acronym for the United States of America. He always asserted the word originated with Samuel Butler.
2. Broadacre City was Wright's solution to the problems of urban decentralization. The plan was first introduced here; a model, built by the Taliesin Fellowship, followed in 1934.
3. Roadside markets to be incorporated into the Broadacre City plan. Spaces were provided for fresh fruit and produce, a delicatessen, bakery, flower shop, and restaurant. See FLLW Fdn#3205.
4. A design commissioned by William Norman Guthrie, Rector of St. Marks in 1929.
5. Arizona Biltmore Resort (1927), Phoenix, Arizona.
6. San Marcos in the Desert (project, 1929), Chandler, Arizona.

OF THEE I SING

This article is a commentary on the exhibition Modern Architecture: International Exhibition, *held at New York's Museum of Modern Art and curated by Philip Johnson. The article was prefaced by Wright's own "An Explanation":*

> *Feeling that the so-called "internationalist" exhibition as it developed, was more propaganda than exhibition and totally in disagreement with the premises of the propaganda, I desire to withdraw entirely.*
>
> *But being in some degree essential to the propaganda as the promoters of the exhibition see it, I have consented to go with them if I might state my own feelings in plain terms alongside their own statements.*
>
> *"Of Thee I Sing" is that somewhat ungracious statement. I am a sincere admirer of all but several of the men whose work is included in the exhibit. And I can only feel respect for the liberality which the promoters show in taking me along on my own terms.*

Wright refers to Philip Johnson and to Lewis Mumford, who urged him to remain in the show despite his obviously strong opposition to the inclusion of Raymond Hood and Richard Neutra. [Published in Shelter, *April 1932]*

I FIND MYSELF STANDING NOW AGAINST THE "*GEIST DER Kleinlichkeit,*" to strike for an architecture for the individual instead of tamely recognizing senility in the guise of a new invention . . . the so-called international style.

No unusual vision is required to see in this alleged invention an attempt to strip hide and horns from the living breathing organism that is modern architecture of the past twenty-five years and, by beating the tom-tom, try to make the hide come alive, or, in despair, tack the "skin" on America's barn-door for a pattern.

Such, I believe, is the nature of this ulterior "invention."

Architecture was made for man, not man made for architecture. And since when, then, has the man sunk so low, even by way of the machine, that a self-elected group of formalizers could predetermine his literature, his music, or his architecture for him?

I know the European neuter's argument: "The Western soul is dead; Western intelligence, though keen, is therefore sterile and can realize an impression but not expression of life except as life may be recognized as some intellectual formula."

But I think such confession of genital impotence, while valid enough where this cliché is concerned, a senility that healthy youth North, South, East, or West is bound to ridicule and repudiate.

Youth is not going to take its architecture or its life that way.

Form, and such style as it may own, comes out of structure industrial, social, architectural.

Principles of construction employing suitable materials for the definite purposes of industry or society, in living hands, will result in style. The changing methods and materials of a changing life should keep the road open for developing variety of expression, spontaneous so long as human imagination lives.

The imagination that makes a building into architecture as mathematics is made into music is not the quality of mind that makes a professor of mathematics or makes a building engineer or makes a short-cut aesthete. *Nor is it ever a matter of a "style."*

Mass-machine-production needs a conscience but needs no aesthetic formula as a short cut to any style. It is itself a deadly formula. Machinery needs the creative force that can seize it, as it is, for what it is worth, to get the work of the world done by it and gradually make that work no less an expression of the spontaneous human spirit than ever before. We must make the expression of life as much richer as it is bound to be more general in realization. Or, by way of machine worship, go machine mad.

Do you think that, as a style, any aesthetic formula forced upon this work of ours in our country can do more than stultify this reasonable hope for a life of the soil?

A creative architecture for America can only mean an architecture for the individual.

The community interest in these United States is not communism or communistic as the internationalists' formula for a "style" presents itself. Its language aside, communistic the proposition is. Communistic in communism's most objectionable phase: the sterility of the individual its end if not its aim and . . . in the name of "discipline"!

Life needs and gets interior discipline according to its ideal. The higher the ideal, the greater the discipline. But this communistic formula proposes to get rid of this constructive interior discipline's anxieties (and joys) by the surrender that ends all in all and for all, by way of a preconceived style for life—conceived by the few to be imposed upon all alike.

Such communistic "ism" belongs to inverted capitalism. Some good, undoubtedly, the inversion if only to demonstrate the cruelty of both capitalism and such communism. Out of any sincere struggle, something comes for the growth of humanity. But, for a free democracy to accept a communistic tenet of this breed disguised as aesthetic formula for architecture is a confession of failure I do not believe we, as a people, are ready to make.

Centralization (a form of every man for himself and the devil for the hindmost) is what is the matter with us. We are suffering from an abuse of individuality in this virulent form, instead of enjoying the ideal of integration natural to democracy.

We are sickened by capitalistic centralization but not so sick, I believe, that we need confess impotence by embracing a communistic exterior discipline in architecture to kill finally what spontaneous life we have left in the circumstances.

As for discipline?

Do you know the living discipline of an ideal of life as organic architecture or architecture as organic life? Those who do know the interior discipline of this ideal look upon surrender to any style formula whatever as dead exterior discipline. Imprisonment in impotence.

"Besonnenheit?"

"Entsagung?"

Well . . . if an effect is produced at all in organic architecture, it must proceed from the interior of the work. It must be of the very organism created.

Try that for discipline in our democracy!

It is an inflexible will, bridling a rich and powerful ego, that is necessary to the creation of any building as architecture or the living of any life in a free democracy. Call it individual. And it is ever so.

And any great thing is too much of whatever it is: it is a quality of greatness.

"Excess of contrast, in genius, brings about a mighty equilibrium."

But *Geist der Kleinlichkeit* will take the excess and capitalize it as a "style." Never will it take the principle or its essence. But it will take the excess and prescribe a *pattern*. In this case an excess of the original protest.

Styles are anterior, posterior or ulterior.

Why should pretentious formalizers worry about the discipline of a "style" for Americans before either they or America yet know style?

The methods, materials and life of our country are common discipline to any right idea of work. Allowed to exercise at our best such whole-souled individuality as we may find among us, the common use of the common tools and materials of a common life will so discipline individual effort that centuries forward men will look back and recognize the work of the democratic life of the twentieth century as a great, not a dead, style. The honest buildings from which this proposed internationalist style is derived were made that way. We can build many more buildings in that same brave, independent, liberal spirit.

So we need no *Geist der Kleinlichkeit* touting a style at us. No, Herr Spengler, we are not yet impotent.

We will, given our own principle, with no self-conscious effort make a great one.

By force of circumstances freely acting upon what is great and alive in us—and that is our democratic principle of freedom—we will make our own.

It is true that we understand imperfectly our own ideal of democracy, and so we have shamefully abused it.

We have allowed our ideal to foster offensive privatism that is exaggerated selfishness in the name of individualism. Selfish beyond any monarchy. But do you imagine communism eradicates selfishness? It may suppress it or submerge it.

Nor can socialism eradicate selfishness. It gives it another turn. Democracy cannot eradicate it. No, but democracy alone can turn it into a noble, creative selfhood.

And that is best of all for all.

So out of my own life-experience as an architect, I earnestly say: what our country needs in order to realize a great architecture for a great life is only to realize and release a high ideal of democracy, the ideal upon which the new life here was founded on new ground, and humbly try to learn how to live up to its principles.

I am sure, too, that the work of an organic architecture, for the individual, had gone so far in the work of the world before this self-seeking propaganda came up, as to enable anyone with ordinary vision to see it coming naturally as our future architecture, propagandists aside. So why, now, as a self-appointed committee on a *style*, do promoting propagandists imagine they can steal the hide and horns of this living, breathing, healthy, young organism and vaingloriously parade the hide and shake the horns to make Americans think it is the living creature?

Granted they are sincere: having confessed impotence, do they urge others to confess too?

Granted they are ambitious: they wish to be inventors as a eunuch might wish to be a father.

Granted they are impecunious: do they wish to get work to do under false pretenses?

Granted they are aesthetes: they are superficial and ignorant of the depths of nature.

Granted they are as intelligent and hard and scientific as they think they are: they are miscarriage of a machine-age that would sterilize itself, if it could, to avoid continuing to propagate the race.

Youth asks for life, and the *Geist der Kleinlichkeit* would hand out a recipe in the form of a pattern of itself?

The letter is more than the spirit only to artists of the second rank.

It is the thing said that is more important, now, than the manner of saying it.

Our pioneer days are not over.

CARAVEL OR MOTORSHIP

The caravel was a small sailing ship of the Spanish (Columbus's) and Portuguese era of exploration, charming in itself, but obsolete in the current era of the ocean liner, a vessel that Wright refers to as the "motorship." In this short essay a choice is offered to architects to embrace either the caravel, picturesque, but out of step with the modern era, or the motorship, part and parcel of the twentieth century. [Published in The Architectural Forum, *August 1932]*

THE FATE OF THE ARCHITECT IS LARGELY IN DOUBT. NO longer an essential factor in our civilization, he is now a "designing partner" or an employer of "designing partners."[1]

And this dismemberment has happened to him at a time when his services are as necessary as ever, if not more so, and because as "architect" he has preferred to sail or tow a caravel, instead of investing in a streamlined motorship of the line.

That caravel is picturesque but no longer practical. Until he can see the streamlined motorship as more beautiful than the caravel, 99 out of 100 American architects will continue to "design" their way to complete oblivion.

If this machine age needs an architect at all it needs him in the same place now as he was in former civilizations, and that place was the interpreter of the industry of his epoch, the builder of the buildings natural to their day.

Now, it may be that the buildings natural to our day may be only plain or fancy masks, and a masquerade may be all our undereducated, overtutored people have coming to them. In that case the function of the architect is that of a decorator and chiefly important to women who do not know what architecture is—but do know what they like.

The business of industry is not one thing and architecture another thing. If it is, then the God of things as they are will have done with both.

And when the matter gets down, as it has, to a struggle as to whether architecture is to be "modern" or "antique" there is a laugh in it somewhere at the "business" as well as the "art" of architecture.

Why do we have "modern" architecture?

Just because it seems necessary to *insist* that the motorship is more natural to us, more native than the caravel—that is all.

The "academic" can't remodel the old caravel into the new motorship without sinking, so there "architecture" is, for the time being—at sea in a caravel.

That means if we are going to have architects at all, in any vital sense, we will apprentice them, not to academics or the landlord or to business, but, humbly, to the industry of our time.

The place for the architect, adolescent or adult, is in this field directly connected with the making of things the way we now make them in order to show us how to make them better by making them more appropriate and significant.

Architectural education as it stands must be abolished and this apprenticeship substituted before we can get our architects back again where they belong.

But perhaps it is too late.

The caravel is a prideful institution.

1. See "The Designing Partner," p. 69.

FOR ALL MAY RAISE THE FLOWERS NOW FOR ALL HAVE GOT THE SEED

This article was written while the exhibition Modern Architecture: International Exhibition *was on view at New York's Museum of Modern Art. Although Wright acquiesced to his inclusion in the show, the whole affair still rankled him (see "Of Thee I Sing," p. 113) as this article, published in a professional architecture magazine, clearly demonstrates. The eclectic imitation of period architecture and the importation of the International Style from Europe he saw as anathema to the culture of the United States. He concludes the article on a more positive note: "The man wants to see the principles he loves, live. He wants life to go on growing, not by emulation but by depth of individual experience. Not by peddling but by working." [Published in* T-Square, *February 1932]*

IT IS A WEAKNESS OF OUR AMERICAN SYSTEM THAT ANY energetic, unscrupulous individual with something of the instinct of the salesman, may get a fortune in a few years.

With no culture, but much will and desire, power comes with money. He gets himself "fixed" with "makings" as no one of his quality could do in any other country.

His ability to sell lands him in an incongruous self-made shell. His ability to use his power is all out of drawing with his ability to administer it as his money systematically comes alive and goes on, itself working, to multiply itself.

He knows nothing of the real meaning of what he now gathers. He does not know what art is, but he knows what he likes. It is ready-made. The country is free.

So here is the cultural weed.

He goes to seed. And more weeds by way of "ready-made."

Exaggerated power is aggravated by such ready-made culture as he can (or will) provide.

The salesman is . . . "Success."

Now, salesman cuts salesman. In architecture—and it is the culture most important to him—it is his counterpart that sells it to him by way of similar success.

It is only ready-made culture that he will buy.

And, to him, that is European. Europeans themselves come and find this out and soon become expert salesmen in the American scene by the American method.

This salesmanship we call propaganda.

The propagandist at the present moment is the "internationalist."

Is architecture "modern" because alter-egos need some formula to follow any individual initiative and overtaking it, as they imagine, may thus manage soon to ride the initiative to death? How much is being written and how little built and how little sense in cause or contra shows clearly *why* the straight-line and flat-plane (both abstractions), and the single curved-surface added to make of the whole another abstraction, have come to be expedient "modern" architecture.

Why is the formula expedient? Is it in order that original impotence—eclecticism—may be now "improved" as modernistic—or modernism—and function as the inevitable ism, ist, or ite, to make a *"movement"*? A movement of this sort depends upon the obvious and easy for the nearsighted near-great, the smaller and small men to play up for selfish purposes in small ways to again kill such initiative as lives, or might live, in our architecture.

A "movement" is usually exploitation, not initiative. Taking all this together, it becomes personal to me because the cause of an organic-architecture runs well beyond the yard-stick and plain-plaster by which busybodies, in their extremity, obscure a simple issue as "modern."

A bee in their bonnets!

They are doing some harm, I believe, and unless there is enough vitality in the great cause of architecture itself to rebuke and shake them off, they intend doing not only more but all the harm there is in them. It may not be so much in the long run, but it discourages all true creative initiative meantime.

But trust the reactionary alter-ego—anyone's alter-ego—to make the great small, the little big and both of not much consequence so far as his own ability goes.

I said doing harm.

Let's be specific.

Poor Japan, who eagerly copies the latest in Western haberdashery or art—impartially—not knowing what either is all about, and . . . gets kicked out!

I loved Japan and reverently took off my hat to its nativity when asked there to build a building. The Japanese are Oriental, not Occidental, hard as they may try to be Occidental. They are trying pitifully hard, but there is a chasm between the races where art is concerned wholly in favor of the Oriental.

Yet, see all the internationalists busy over there encouraging that ambitious, industrious nation to belie and stultify itself by an aggravated architectural version of the Derby hat, kimono and Boston gaiters. Tokio is becoming a profane sight in consequence. To any-

one who loves these sensitive, ambitious people who call Tokio capital, here is deplorable butchery.

The East still thinks the West knows what it is about and promptly gets after whatever is after the West, too quick to grab and fall in line. Japan's national weakness.

Some day the East will learn that the West itself is a formula-chaser or an imitator, instead of a culture builder. Any formula derived from its experimental civilization can only be a brand, or a fraud, upon the East.

The Japanese will some day wake to curse the abuse they were encouraged to practice upon themselves.

The Japanese house—a perfect expression of organic architecture—is being made over into a Western garage, instead of being organically developed into a suitable place for the same life rising from its knees to its feet.

On the verge—another instance.

Rio de Janeiro[1]—the capital of a romantic people in love with loveliness.

There I found some seven hundred art students of the Bellas Artes on "strike"—as they built our word into their Portuguese language. These students wanted to go forward instead of backward, and the Beaux-Arts armchairs couldn't allow that, so they couldn't get the students back to work. These high-spirited young people were regarding "the formula" as it had found its way there overseas by way of a Russian working for a German on the tropical mountain-side, at Copacabana.[2] A good "internationalist" example. As good as any.

These young people were regarding it proudly but uneasily. Something was out of "drawing."

In tropical sunshine, the flat-faced hard-head was glaring shamelessly at a high-spirited romantic people regardless of climate or environment, and they were trying to see it, whole, as the right thing. Not quite so gullible as the poor Japanese where the West is concerned, they were suspicious.

The students had gathered there and invited me to tell them if that was "modern architecture."

I said the equivocal term might mean that it was, probably did. But it wasn't architecture at all where they were concerned, because it ignored their natures, their climate, and the character of their environment.

A cheer went up, and smiles broke out. They were relieved. As I told them why, in more detail, the sky cleared for a moment.

But propaganda is at work on them, too. They have no models otherwise. They have no one directly to stimulate their imaginations along lines natural to them, unless Lucio Costa or Araujo.[3]

What are they to do?

Here is our own nation.

Eclecticism, a form of self-abuse too long practiced, has rendered us impotent. Such architecture as we have, we got that way. We are prostitute to any formula because we are prostitute to the machine.

Now comes this "internationalist" formula deduced from such initiative as we have had in our own architecture. Such as it is, it is all too easy for eclectics to seize it. And soon—regardless of native characteristics and fitness to climate or environment—we may see the formula in Miami, Minneapolis, Alaska, Arizona, the Philippines, and Texas.

And this is what the little minds of the propagandists for "the international" call success.

All formulae have pedigrees. Yes . . . this one, as many pedigrees as there are peddlers.

This one has bad ones from the time it became a formula.

The creative artists, whose initiative is capitalized and exploited in this formula, would none of them own it. They would, and they do, abominate it.

And they would, and do, despise the peddlers whose "pedigree" it is to trade in it or on it regardless of depth or quality or fitness to purpose just because they can only "elect" some style or pass up an exploit in salesmanship.

If these busybodies would get down to work, put up more, and shut off propaganda for a while I, for one, might have some belief in their sincerity and the character of their effort, half-baked though it must be.

H. Th. Wijdeveld recently told me of "a propagandist" who got to Amsterdam and, asked to speak, wore out the "audience" with 62 out of 76 lantern slides of a by-no-means unusual or remarkable "internationalist" house built by himself. He will probably not lecture again in Amsterdam. But he is by no means unusual. In this busybody propaganda wherever it is found, the cackling outdoes the egg.

No genuine art ever sought expression by way of such calculated selfishness.

Now it is another weakness of our American system

School for the Rosenwald Foundation (Project). Tennessee. 1929. Elevation. Pencil and color pencil on tracing paper, 28 x 20".
FLLW Fdn#2904.006[1032]

that the national mind seems never to believe that a man may be actuated by principles to speak his own mind, loving principle more than himself and willing to eat the dirt thrown into his mouth every time he opens it rather than let the principle in him go by default. No. The instinct of the salesman immediately places him as not "having got his." To a salesman, all men are salesmen. So where financial interests have any concern in architecture (and where are they not concerned?)—it is all the man's socioeconomic life is worth to voice dissent where money is tied up or tied in. There is but one voice where there is "investment." Hence the default, or the combined ballyhoo of salesmanship to drown the voice.

One of those unfortunate men who live to be the envy and the reproach of the alter-ego, I often have occasion to reflect upon the disadvantage I offer—by being alive and more productive than ever—to callous or flighty disciples or perhaps callow apprentices now full-fledged and eager to fly. As somebody said at the "League" last year—was it "Little Napoleon" number three?—"We always come to the realization that Wright is alive with a kind of shock."

And I am writing this with an enemy in each eye. Two extremes.

The predatory eclectic in the right eye.

The predatory "internationalist" in the left eye.

The one elects forms "ready-made" from an architecture dead.

The other elects a formula derived from an architect living, or just beginning to live, and kills the architecture.

I am not at the moment cross-eyed because both the old and improved eclectic come from the same stock and amount to the same thing. I can see straight through both eyes, because the "internationalist" is only the modern improvement on the old eclectic. He is the up-to-date eclectic.

Now, eclecticism, unimproved, was obnoxious to me. And eclecticism improved seems no less obnoxious because, while the unimproved peddled the dead, to peddle the improvement the living must lose its life.

Special activity, now, to juggle and fake history by warped and twisted pedigrees by specialists important in Europe, according to themselves, when in America and important in America, according to themselves, when in Europe . . . until "modern" architecture is a bone for any stray dog to gnaw. But the bone holds its shape. Contention or no contention.

Architecture is architecture.

Standards as they go about with the predatory "internationalist" are weaknesses all too near the weakness of our own American socioeconomic system to be lightly encouraged for personal profit.

What creative mind wants emulation? What he-architect wants disciples?

Not one.

He wants work.

The man wants to see the principles he loves, live.

He wants life to go on growing, not by emulation but by depth of individual experience. Not by *peddling* but by *working.*

The man may be kind, easily flattered and fond of the mirror in personal matters.

But the very life in him is the honor of his art if he is an architect.

And any man's art is dishonored by imitation.

Any nation's life is dishonored by seizing formula instead of perceiving principles. And, especially, it will pay a hard price for any formula in the freedom that we, as Usonians in America, must learn to see as democracy.

I love my country, and I would that my country love me. But not by way of flattery or imitation, coming or going, will I give or accept love.

To such I, now, prefer hate.

If only our country would "*raise the flowers, now, that all have got the seed,*"[4] from seed: principle, the seed, transplanting not preferred . . . what a country!

1. Wright went to Rio de Janeiro in September 1931 to serve as one of three judges for the Christopher Columbus Memorial Lighthouse competition. Eliel Saarinen and Horacio Acosta y Lara also served on the panel.
2. Wright's reference here must be to Gregori Warchavchik (1896–1975), a Russian émigré to Brazil via the Fine Arts Institute in Rome, who, with Lucio Costa (see below), would pioneer functionalist architecture in Brazil.
3. Lucio Costa (b. 1902) was appointed head of the National School of Fine Arts in Rio de Janeiro in 1930; there he introduced the functionalist theories of the Bauhaus and Le Corbusier into the established Beaux-Arts curriculum. Upon his dismissal a year later, the students went "on strike," the situation Wright refers to above.
4. Wright has taken a slight liberty here with the fifth stanza of a poem entitled "The Flower," by Alfred Lord Tennyson; "Read my little fable: He that runs may read. Most can raise the flowers now, For all have got the seed." See *The Poetical Works of Tennyson,* Cambridge edition, ed. by G. Robert Stange (Boston: Houghton Mifflin Co., 1974) p. 264.

TASTE AND AUTOBIOGRAPHY

This brief article is in the nature of an apologia by Wright, who explains why he wrote his autobiography (New York: Longmans Green, 1932). Perhaps this was written in response to a particular criticism of the book. Yet, for the most part, the critics praised the work for its candor and his struggle to develop an architecture more in keeping with the precepts of a democratic faith in the United States. [Published in The Chicagoan, *April 1932]*

I AM INCLINED TO BELIEVE THAT AUTOBIOGRAPHY SAYS good-bye to "taste." The nature of the genuine thing is not and will not be in keeping with our best standards of private life—no matter how reticent. Why Autobiography if reticent? Why not leave the matter to such Biographers as come along?

A man's "reticent" Autobiography would be, really, only Biography biased by himself, or an essay on himself. The least any autobiographer can do to square himself with his readers or himself is to lay his cards—his life in this case—on the table, so to speak. No light matter. His opus must have the authority of his own intimacy with his own experience—not only pro but con.

No doubt the poor man who writes about himself would do well not to inform the general reader of personal matters in which only intimates know he is askew or aslant or he himself knows how ignoble or inglorious he is . . . . And harder, by far, others are involved the moment he takes his pen in hand, even though he concerns himself only with the ambiguity he is pleased to call his own soul.

I do not mean the autobiographer should bawl the truth. No, the poor dupe is chiefly familiar with facts anyway. He is, in spite of himself, in his readers' hands so far as this affair goes with truth, but he should be fair with his facts or not start. That is what is the matter with Autobiography as a work of art. And why usually it is, instead, recitation, defamation, expurgation or dramatization with some axe to grind.

All this together in some degree, is autobiography, seldom simple, never quite candid.

Then why write one?

Well, I think only one who has been gratuitously twisted and maimed by publicity, or deliberately misrepresented to his fellows, and in consequence has had to hunchback his way through life, or one who has given his life, freely, to a great cause, or one who can make his life, such as it is, honestly interesting, useful or beautiful to his fellows, should be allowed to try.

If he can do all these—and this is true autobiographic ambition—his enterprise is ruined by the "taste" that runs as the product of pride and current social standards unless his life has been lived in "taste."

Mine has not.

Social standards, even as to decency, change.

They are always changing.

The genuine Autobiography stays.

As for the squirming of the victims, victimized by propinquity, relationship or imagination with the hapless one urged to unseemliness and indiscretion to get the hump off his back, or get it on straight, or get an idea over, or simply make something beautiful, well, if he has been careful with his sense of proportion in the circumstances to be just to them, what can they do but squirm and sue, the autobiographer being what he is? The shame of any hurt is not theirs. It is his. They suffer through him.

Good taste!

Ruefully this unwilling penman conscientiously bids you good-bye. When my own taste would move me to leave something out, my conscience would say, put it in. When conscience would prick and say "take it out," the artist in me would say "no, it is essential to the balance of the whole."

And I confess the artist has so far run with the man that when I, that man, protest, I stand a small chance of winning in any argument as to ways and means or even ends. To sustain this attempt there is only the artist's sense of right, that has destroyed so many a man, good and bad, and a feeling that perhaps is no more reliable where Autobiography is concerned than in matters of Art and Architecture.

Taliesin. Spring Green, Wisconsin. Hedrich-Blessing photograph, courtesy the Chicago Historical Society. FLLW Fdn FA#2501.0232

THE HOUSE OF THE FUTURE

From 1915, when Frank Lloyd Wright first designed a series of homes to be built by means of prefabrication, the concept of a systems-built house occupied his thought and design. The 1915 project was realized, to some degree, beginning with a series of drawings in 1917 entitled "American Homes," or "American Ready-Cut System Houses." All wooden members—beams, rafters, studs, etc.—were to be cut in the factory or shop and assembled on site; exterior and interior walls would then be plastered. In 1932 Wright predicted the prefabrication of entire units of a house: kitchen, bathroom, bedroom, and living room. Here, addressing an assembly of realtors, he advises them to seek a new direction in real estate: to broaden out and expand, to decentralize, to take advantage of the automobile and to "make spaciousness more characteristic of modern life." [Excerpt from speech delivered to the 1932 Convention of the National Association of Real Estate Boards in Cincinnati, published in National Real Estate Journal, *July 1932]*

I SHALL CALL THE THING THE "ASSEMBLED HOUSE." I DO NOT think there is a big concern in the United States that has not been flirting with it more or less, that has not done some research work along the line of a standardized, machine-made house.

At first, of course, the house itself is going to take on some of the characteristics that Henry's Model-T took on when it was in Henry's hands, when it was in the inventor's hands. An inventor is not an architect. The house will be ugly in the beginning, but it will get into the hands of the creative architect or the artist who can evolve a scheme or a plan by which it can be made a harmonious whole. There is no reason why the assembled house, fabricated in the factory, should not be made as beautiful and as efficient as the modern automobile.

You will see a few appearing, and will turn away from them and say: "My God, anything but that." But that is the way everything that is new and effective has found its way into civilization.

When we have established a few models that are usable, beautiful, and livable, there is no question but that the people will like them.

There will be as great a difference between this new house and the old house as between the old caravel in which Columbus discovered America and a beautiful stream-lined rotor ship.[1] You will see that a new element esthetically has entered into modern life by way of the very things that are now doing more to destroy that life than to make it.

There will be a new simplicity, a machine-made simplicity. Now, a good machine is good to look at. There is no reason why a house should look like a machine, but there is no reason why it should not be just as good to look at as a machine, and for just the same reason.

That is an entirely new basis for architecture and for thought and for life.

Now, in working out this "assembled house" we have already the bathroom as a single unit to draw upon. We will call it unit No. 1. You can now get a bathroom with a bath tub and the bowl and the water closet in one fixture, and all that is to be done is to make the connection to the sewer we have provided, and screw it up. There it is.

Now, your kitchen has been worked out in many ways. I think there are at least five now available where you can get a complete and a more practical, a more beautiful kitchen, than almost any architect could himself design. Unit No. 2. And in connection with that unit you have the heating of the house—the heat which you use for your kitchen for cooking—an immense economy. All that needs is a single connection, screwing it up and putting it together.

The appurtenant systems in any house are more than one-third of the cost of the house. As the cost of the building comes down the proportion rises. Once we have those things completely established as certain parts are established in your car, and they have nothing whatever to do with the general effect of the house as a whole, we have established one very essential economy, and we have then something at last toward the building of this modern house.

Now, in addition to that it is just as easy to standardize a bedroom unit which is ideal and which does not have the old stuffy closet. We do not have closets any more in the older sense. We architects, in spite of our impracticability, have seen the consequences of providing the housewife with a hole in which to chuck things. Our closet is not essential any more and we do not have it. We have the wardrobe instead, which is a ventilated affair, which can be easily kept in order.

The bedroom unit can be in various sizes; it can be assembled in various ways with the other units.

Then we can have a living room unit of two or three sizes. In fact, all the features which are characteristic of modern life and modern living, we can buy on some standardized scheme of arrangement.

These can be laid out on a unit system so that they all come together in an organic style, and the design of these things in the first place can be of such a character that in the final assembly no wrong or bad thing can happen.

In putting these units together according to your means, you may be able to have a three-unit house. You will probably have to have a bathroom, a kitchen unit, and a bedroom—three units at the minimum. Then you can go on and you can amplify that house until you have it surrounding an interior court. And this thing can all come knocked down to you in metal, metal slabs pressed on each side with some heat-resisting or cold-resisting insulation. In fact, you can have the slabs 10 feet or you can have them 12 feet long and 8 to 9 feet high in the knock-down shape and put together on the job with a B. T. U. resistance equal to that of an 8-inch brick wall.

Now, in connection with this assembled house a man need not go so heavily into debt to own his house as he has to do now. He will not have to encourage the mortgage banker to quite such an extent. As his means grow and his family grows, his house can grow. And I can demonstrate to you with perspectives and models, which are being prepared, that none of these houses in any way you can put them together will be other than good to look at.

They are characteristic of the age. You can drive a car up to the door of one of these little houses, or big houses, however they may be extended, drive into the garage, and it will all look as though it belonged together—as the costume of the modern woman as she is dressed today also belongs to that house and to that car. The men's costume does not simply because the women won't let us change. We ought to have something simpler than we are putting on in order to be modern. We are dreadfully old-fashioned when we hook up about 43 buttons and go through all our pockets, and finally take stock of the gadgets which go to make us complete.

Simplification is the slogan of the machine age, a new significance for the car, for the house, for madam's dress, for monsieur, eventually, but we have got to fight for that freedom; it is not coming unless we do fight for it.

Well, now, I have laid before you a simple outline and the gist of this thing that we call modern. I have given you an outline here of the main characteristics and the thought behind modern architecture. It is not well to laugh at it, and it is not well to put it aside. You can't. I have seen it during the 30 years which it has been my pleasure and privilege to try to build houses for people. I have seen it growing and growing, going abroad, becoming the characteristic thing in Holland, in Germany, in Switzerland, Czecho-Slovakia, Poland, and France. Our own country has been the only country satisfied with its own little plaster caverns, its own gadgets, its own little pretty things which it is willing to set up in some style or other and try to live in.

Now, it seems to me that the most valuable thing for a body of Realtors to get into their systems is the idea, first, that we have got to make spaciousness more characteristic of modern life. It is the natural thing for democracy to get space. The modern city works against it. All of you Realtors have worked against it all your lives. The finer you could get the thing, and the smaller the pieces you could pass around, why the more successful you were. That time has gone by, I believe.

There is a lot of ground in this country. In fact if all the people of the world were to be put together on the Island of Bermuda, they would not cover it standing up—I do not know about sitting down. And there is just about 53 acres, at any rate about 50 acres in this country, for every man, woman and child in it if it were to be divided up on that basis.

Now, it is senseless getting the thing in a heap, pig-piling, to pig-pile some more. Believe me, it is old-fashioned. It is not in the keeping of our modern opportunities. It is not in the keeping of our modern thought. It is dead.

Probably you do not even know now when you see the little gas station out there on the prairie that that is the advance agent of decentralization. Distribution is changing. Whole agencies are changing. Your telephone poles could be down tomorrow if it was not for the investment in them. The whole expression and guide of modern living has gained fluidity, spontaneity. What before took 10 years is now spontaneous.

Have we got to go on building buildings, partitioning ground, setting up institutions along these dead old lines, and crucifying human life to make a little money? We are all where we are now, flat on our backs, gasping for a little sustenance—I guess we call it cash—just because we can't keep pace with the modern thought that is building the modern world. We have had before us a spectacle of what we call depression. I suppose we call it a "depression" to be nice, just the way the car people when they take your car call it "repossession."

But I do not believe that this is a depression. I believe that we are at the end of an epoch, and I believe that unless real-estate men put their ears to their own ground and get this message: Decentralization—Reintegration—Organic Architecture—The Use of Our Other Resources—we are faced with a very serious situation. Those things seem insignificant, but God knows what they can do. Glass, steel, the automobile, mobilization of the whole community. Why, it has changed the entire face of civilization and the universe.

And until we can grasp that, until we can interpret it, until we can capitalize it for the people, we have not got a civilization.

1. See "Caravel or Motorship," p. 116.

THE HOUSE ON THE MESA/
THE CONVENTIONAL HOUSE

A *model for Wright's design for the "House on the Mesa," described here, was prepared and exhibited in The Museum of Modern Art's exhibition* Modern Architecture: International Exhibition *in 1932. The "House on the Mesa" is obviously a luxury residence, somewhat understated by Wright as a house "for a moderately wealthy American family." In juxtaposition to this ample home, Wright designed a moderate-cost house, which he entitled the "Conventional House." Wright was referring to the type of dwelling that could be built on the average one-hundred-foot-wide urban or suburban lot. The system of building, as the essay describes, is related to methods and materials Wright deemed appropriate to the machine age. In a later drawing, that Wright entitled "A Colonial Equivalent," he again relates this design to what the average American family could afford without resorting to the typical Colonial boxes that were proliferating across the nation during and following the Depression. Both the federal government and lending agencies favored the Colonial style. More affluent Americans have generally preferred eclectic styles dredged up from the past. Thus both of Wright's designs remain unbuilt. [Unpublished notes to drawings, 1932]*

House on the Mesa (Project). Denver, Colorado. 1932. Perspective. Pencil on tracing paper, 36 x 11". FLLW Fdn#3102.015

THE HOUSE ON THE MESA

THE HOUSE ON THE MESA WAS DESIGNED FOR A MODERately wealthy American family of considerable culture—master, mistress and four children, cook and two maids, chauffeur and gardener.

Their architect intended to help them make something of machine-age luxury that would compare favorably in character and integrity with the luxury of the Greeks or Goths, within the limits of an expenditure of some $125,000.

The site, comprising several acres, is nearly flat, extending along a motor highway. The general scheme is simple. A concrete blockshell wall toward the highway; an extended toplit arbor or sunlit loggia, itself a continuous living-room, open to the grass planes of the garden and the small lake to the south, sequestered by the house and the surrounding wood. This sun-loggia connects the various individual groups of rooms.

Each fireproof group of rooms has articulation according to function. The family quarters with large fireplace are grouped at the garden end of the sun-loggia for privacy and semi-detached by sitting-room or loggia from the series of rooms for the children. Two guest-rooms, to be used singly or together, are placed nearer the entrance and dining-room. These rooms are directly lit, above the sun-loggia, and are screened from the loggia by a perforated copper wall-screen.

The living-room, billiard-room, beneath, and a pool, sheltered by a perforated copper canopy attached, is the main group, and it is managed as a large, free-standing sun-pavilion with a great fireplace. This living-room stands free on the concrete roof-slab level. The adjoining concrete roof-slabs are all related to the living-room as roof-garden terraces.

Standing near on the same roof-slab level, across the concrete slab of a broad roof-terrace, is another smaller pavilion with its fireplace, to be used as a tea-house and breakfast-room. This upper level and its pavilions, as in the sun-loggia below and its rooms, are all directly related to the garden and the lake.

The kitchen is so placed at a level midway between the dining-room below and the breakfast-room and tea-room above that it connects directly with both and connects also with a kitchen roof-garden and the dwelling place of the servants. The kitchen roof-garden slab makes a broad cover for the automobile entrances and exits.

The motor car is, in this plan, the feature of American life it is fast becoming. The group of family motors and those of visitors have ample space in the garage courtyard. The garage, chauffeur's and gardener's dwelling place and dwelling place for the servants surround this court.

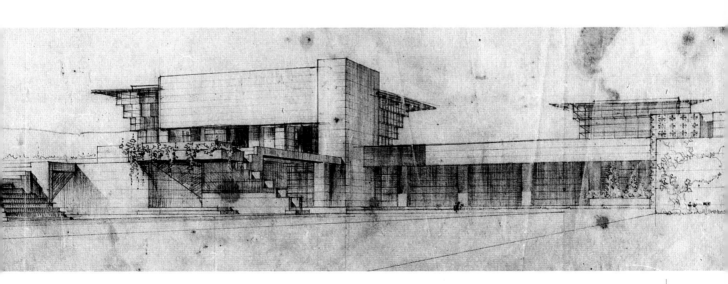

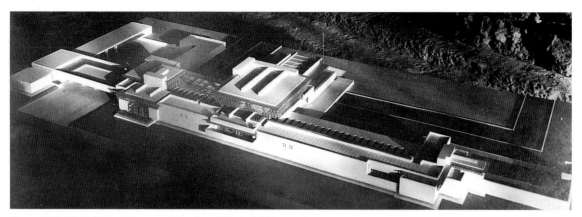

House on the Mesa (Project). Denver, Colorado. 1932. Model. FLLW Fdn FA#3102.0005

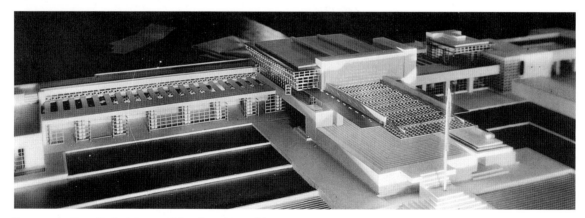

House on the Mesa (Project). Denver, Colorado. 1932. Model. FLLW Fdn FA#3102.0006

Thus the features of American family life, the motor car, service, family life and social life each have appropriate and convenient grouping. All are individualized and integrated with air, light, vista in the sense of freedom characteristic of our new resources: steel in tension, glass, concrete and the motor car.

The style of this fireproof house grows naturally from this sense of space arrangement definitely related to a modern scheme of a construction. That scheme of construction is the cantilever slab hung from above by cantilever beams projecting from the masonry chimney masses. The light, enclosing copper and glass screens hanging from the cantilever slabs are offset to place the opening sash in the horizontal ledges. This general type of construction and

the offset concrete-block wall to allow ventilation at the floor levels, gives the house its individual grammar.

The sweep of the mesa with the magnificent views of the Rocky Mountains is felt in the arrangement and, as a foil, comes the sheltered bathing pool pouring into the "lake-for-swimming," its surrounding glass planes sequestered by the surrounding masses of trees.

The house itself, as a whole, becomes a complete garden, open or sheltered at will. A good time place . . . it has what might truthfully be called twentieth-century style.

The enclosing screens are horizontally offset or inset, so the opening sash may lift up from the flat ledges, thus made to render the winds of the region less objectionable.

The reinforced concrete-block wall is offset, likewise, at the level of the main floor-slab. Screened openings in the floor itself afford cool circulation of air over the floors. The best way to keep a house cool in hot weather.

Thin, projecting overhangs of sheet copper protect the glass screens from streaking and leaking and modify the sun-glare on the glass. These horizontal plates of metal form a border of copper around the ceiling of each room, appropriately completing the copper wall-screens.

The reinforced concrete cantilever construction itself is exposed above the reinforced cantilever roof slabs as architecture. The cantilever beams themselves are wide at the bottom and narrow at the top, according to stress. Changing to shaft-supported beams at the top over the living-room, they become wide at top, narrow at bottom, according to stress.

The masonry chimney masses are all used for anchorage and support to secure the cantilevers and leave the main walls entirely free.

The roof-slabs are all insulated against cold or heat. The sheet copper projections added to them are insulated likewise.

The enclosing screens, being hung from the cantilevered slab above, may be inexpensive and extremely light.

Privacy is had by interior hangings wholly of copper mesh to be drawn as blinds over the glass surfaces anywhere at any time. For warmth or coolness another tapestry hanging may be·used inside of this one, harmonizing with interior furnishings. The hangings themselves thus become a beautiful architectural feature.

Standardization in this house is perfectly utilized without prejudice to free imagination so long as imagination sees steel as steel, glass as glass, and concrete as concrete. The whole fabrication becomes, notwithstanding severe limitations, a light, strong expression of the new materials of this age, and uses these for our American life as it almost is and might readily be: that is, genuine and free in point of culture and scientific art.

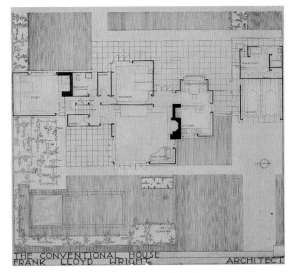

Conventional House (Project). 1932. Plan. Ink on paper, 28 x 26". FLLW Fdn#3201.002

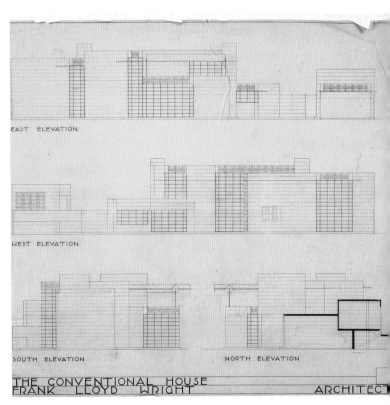

Conventional House (Project). 1932. Elevations. Ink on paper, 28 x 26". FLLW Fdn#3201.003

THE CONVENTIONAL HOUSE

The conventional house—as we live in the United States it might be built nearby the House on the Mesa—is a solution of the more conventional house problem of the well-to-do American family paying $12,500 to $15,000 for a home: master and mistress, several children, one servant and a Ford or two.

The type of home built by hundreds in a thousand or more American towns.

Here is the average town lot 100 feet wide of usual depth and regulation of building line. The lawn toward the street is so managed as not to destroy the general effect characteristic of the American town but to conserve a forecourt to the living-room against the garage next door.

A study or workroom for father or mother, a gathering place for the family with court to the front and garden to the rear; a simple arrangement for a menage managed by the help of a single servant or none; a separate room provided in the semi-detached garage for a servant or man about the place to insure greater privacy in the house; a dining nook off the kitchen to be ordinarily used, but the large table in the living-room, almost as convenient, may be used as a dining table on occasion. The workroom or study then becomes the withdrawing room.

This fireproof house is no less a genuine expression of construction.

The walls are a single shell of reinforced concrete blocks inset at each opening to strengthen the thin wall.

The broad openings from floor to ceiling are filled with metal-sash, opening in series.

The roof-slabs and floor-slabs are reinforced concrete.

In this scheme, also, there is a general lightness, openness and relation to the garden, combined with privacy when desired, that is modern and that makes natural the quiet simplicity of the early "Colonial" that is now merely artificial. The fabrication of this "Conventional house" again utilizes standardization in a light, economic expression of concrete, steel and glass, doing no violence to the "conservative" tastes that prefer Colonial by adding the advantages of plan and free space naturally belonging to the life of our modern times.

This house would be worthy of a place, notwithstanding its more simple extent, next door to the House on the Mesa. Quality and character are more important in such association, in our country, than extent.

WHAT DOES THE MACHINE MEAN TO LIFE IN A DEMOCRACY?

In this article, written for but not published by Pictorial Review, *Wright elaborates on the thesis put forth in his book* The Disappearing City *(pp. 70–112). His thoughts on city planning go far beyond the scope of architecture, extending to politics, social studies, and economics. He sees the problem of urban density as an issue that the architect must solve by creating an entirely new environment. He repeatedly emphasizes the need not for* reform *but for* form. *The idea of design underlies all his thinking in this arena of urban problems, suburban sprawl, and the position of the American family in the American landscape. While working on these articles in tandem to his book* The Disappearing City, *he was working at the drawing boards on the design for Broadacre City, his solution, in line and form, to the ills and sicknesses he had been addressing in his writings. [Unpublished essay, 1932]*

I NOW REALIZE THAT ORGANIC ARCHITECTURE IS LIFE AND life itself is organic architecture or both are in vain.

The principles that are working in one are working in the other. We are sacrificing the greater human efficiency to put all into the lesser machine efficiency. It is useless to go on working for the landlord on any general basis of a great future for a noble architecture. The landlord is not intrinsic. What perversion to allow land to hold the improvements instead of the improvements holding the land?

All is more or less makeshift where life itself is concerned, because it must be, so long as the basis upon which life and architecture must function is not free. The valiant special case alone is free. Out of my own sense of an organic architecture and observing the principles of that architecture at work as the law of natural change, in our own country, comes a basic outline of a future city growing from the ground up to utilize for the human being the forces that built the whirling vortex from the top down.

The vortex was built on the space measurement most appropriate to the man on his legs or sitting in a trap behind a horse. The plan, even so, was faulty. But how utilize that plan now when the standard of space measurement has changed to the man seated in his motor car, vicarious power in the throttle at his feet, his hands on a steering wheel—not to mention the cigar in his mouth? One mile has little advantage to him over ten miles. But he bulks in space requirements, movement aside, ten to one, as compared with his former self.

We have been too tolerant of re-form. It is true form we should now be seeking. It has never been had by any alteration upon any old building or will it be had by any alteration upon an old order: it will grow from the ground up as nature always grows her forms, roots in the soil that is nature. And

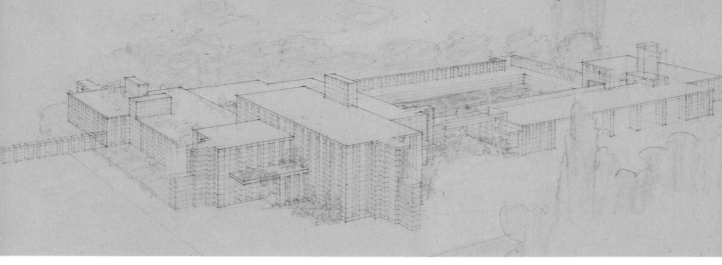

"Westhope," Richard Lloyd Jones House. Tulsa, Oklahoma. 1929. Perspective. Pencil and color pencil on tracing paper, 19 x 10".
FLLW Fdn#2902.002

that means a new layout of a new city upon free ground for a new sense of freedom in space.

In the present city cruelty, misfortune and poverty may be mitigated and should be, meantime. Honor to those so engaged.

But we have learned enough from the specialization that is centralization to go to the root for construction and by way of evolution work with the law of beneficent change. The generalization that is integration is that change. Why longer try to hold what we have against it? "To have and to hold" is all very well when having and holding *with* nature, both are disastrous when *against* nature. And in line with that normal law of change as I have observed its working throughout our country will come the disappearance of the Moloch that knows no god but more: the big city, the big establishment, the big fortune, the big business. Except as bigness is in a general group of individual units and not in any particular overgrown unit it is no longer humanly economic. All will be absorbed into the body of the whole country, circulation, once more healthy and efficiency again genuine where humanity is concerned.

The important new factors, electrification, mobilization, modern architecture, have been taken for granted by high and low, therefore they have had no intelligent recognition in our industrial plan or in our culture.

But factitious increment as a premium put upon centralization has not been wholly wasted because the mechanical factors of our age have been more rapidly developed to a higher degree of efficiency than would have ever been possible otherwise. This mechanical power, as leverage, should be utilized. But the time has gone by when this efficiency can justify the immense cost of its efficiencies to life itself.

Time is here when something must be done with these new powers in a larger way, for humanity, to relieve the cruel centrifugal pressure inordinate centralization has become. These new resources and humanity, fast growing apart as enemies to destroy each other, wasting each other meantime, are both by way of each other capable of a new form.

And the new form is openly thrusting at the old in all these factors. Their new forces are beginning to decentralize the city, subdivide the immense aggregates, and build up individuality in order to reintegrate all in larger unity; an entirely new space measurement demanded by volatilizing of thought, voice and sight, the widening of the horizon of physical movement by means of the motor car and a true individual freedom in the life of the United States. Compelled by the organic forces of these new resources, our big cities are already splitting up into several centers; our big mercantile establishments are already building distributing centers on the edges of the big cities; our big manufacturers have already confessed that the big establishment is no longer necessary; the motor bus and motor truck have already cut the wasteful back and forth haul of the too many competing railways to the heart. The new centers of distribution serving mobilization, the gas station one of them, are rapidly growing in importance and range, especially Middle West and South, Southwest, and West. Manhattan alone lost hundreds of thousands of citizens last year.

So greatly has mobilization already changed human values, modified human character and altered the circumstances, that most of our equipment is obsolete when it is built. Almost all our present architectural and structural equipment is obsolete or old. The machine age, while exaggerating them, has made the old arrangements of which the city was the most important already invalid and soon inoperative.

Decentralization is inevitable.

It is therefore time not to dream of the future but to realize the future as now and here. It is imperative to go to work with it, no longer foolishly trying to stand against it.

Super sense is soon common sense.

To decentralize is already common sense, needing only to realize the forms that best express it in our daily life. Those needed forms are all organic architecture, organic economics and an organic social contract.

Our pioneer days are not over, but the frontier has shifted. Our forebears took life in their hands and, efficient, went in their covered wagons to clear the ground. It seems they blazed the way for an efficiency that could only become exaggerated centralization by way of a rugged individualism: an exaggeration of their own great qualities. The heroic sacrifice of the original pioneers was forerunner to this type of selfish domination we now see as exaggerated centralization.

This later pioneering, our inheritance, is now the frontier to be cleared away again by the forces of a more humane, because a more organic, culture. Only by regaining appropriate humane use of the new resources derived from pioneer "success" may democracy flourish. "Excess" as "success" must perish into opportunity for all to live as the bravest and best. No longer should men be compelled to live—would they succeed at all—according to the baser qualities of their natures, but "success" according to their better selves. And survive.

On this new frontier, however, is scraping off the too full bushel while ignoring the sources that overfill it, statesmanship? Then the tinker is the best maker, the imitator the best creator, and vicarious power the best power.

Politicians are not statesmen. A statesman is an architect of an organic social order. The *re*forms proposed and effected by our governing powers are little shifts in the rules of the game that have been tried; but no interpretation in the changed circumstances of the ideal we have professed, and have ignored, has been tried.

Have we, then, really lost that ideal?

There is no question whatever as to the rightmindedness and humane instincts of humanity, when humanity is free, but . . . in what does this freedom actually consist?

Let us discuss that as intelligently and frankly as we do science—biology for instance—and this fundamental cause to which we have dedicated our country and ourselves may come a little nearer realization.

What *is* the meaning of life in a democracy—developed machine power a factor—as distinguished from life in other forms of social contract? What is true human efficiency? What is true human economy?

Let our bravest and best seek the answer and they will find it in life as organic architecture, as I have found it in organic architecture as life.

The present basis for life is inorganic, unsound and therefore dangerous just as such architecture as we have is inorganic waste. The inorganic has sporadic increase but has no possible life because it lacks the correlation essential to growth. Centralization is *ingrowing*. Even with all its increase, it has no interior, informing, expanding principle of life. Its efficiencies are all too narrow.

Inorganic, our economic system, our social system, our arts, our religion. Our politics are absurd. Our status quo a strong arm. Our fortunes false.

We have drifted into exaggeration and toward impotence by way of a vicarious use of a vicarious power to make money as, itself, another vicarious power.

Let us have an intelligent interpretation of our own ideal, democracy, and then honest appraisal of our direction as we stand. And then?

With what we have accomplished let us go in the direction we intend.

WHY I LOVE WISCONSIN

*"*W*isconsin has put sap into my veins," Wright wrote. "Why, I should love her as I loved my mother, my old grandmother, and as I love my work." With descriptions of pastoral landscapes, farming, and the red barns that proliferate throughout Wisconsin, Wright here tells of his love for his native state, where he was born and raised and to where he returned to live from 1911 to 1959. He proudly notes some of the progressive and radical people Wisconsin nurtured. But it is to the soil and to the agrarian life the article returns, as it opened. [Published in* Wisconsin *magazine, 1932][1]*

I LOVE WISCONSIN BECAUSE MY STAUNCH OLD WELSH grandfather with my gentle grandmother and their 10 children settled here nearby. I see the site of their homestead and those of their offspring as I write. Offspring myself, my home and workshop are planted on the ground grandfather and his sons broke before the Indians had entirely gone away.

This Wisconsin valley with the spring-water stream winding down as its center line has been looked forward to or back upon by me and mine from all over the world, as home.

And I come back from the distant, strange, and beautiful places that I used to read about when I was a boy, and wonder about; yes, every time I come back here it is with the feeling there is nothing anywhere better than this is.

More dramatic elsewhere, perhaps more strange, more thrilling, more grand, too, but nothing that picks you up in its arms and so gently, almost lovingly, cradles you as do these southwestern Wisconsin hills. These ranges of low hills that make these fertile valleys of southwestern Wisconsin by leading down to the great sandy plain that was once the bed of a mightier Wisconsin River than any of us have ever seen.

I doubt if that vast river flood were more beautiful then, however, than this wide, slow-winding, curving stream in the broad sand bed, where gleaming sandbars make curved beaches and shaded shores to be overhung by masses of great greenery. Well, it is not quite like any of the more important rivers of the world. It is more what specialists in scenery would call "picturesque." It is, however, unique.

So "human" is this countryside in scale and feeling. "Pastoral" beauty, I believe, the poets call it. More like Tuscany,[2] perhaps, than any other land, but the Florentines that roamed those hills never saw such wild flowers as we see any spring, if the snow has been plentiful. The snow usually is plentiful and the cold too. The kind of cold that has always tempered the man of the North as a conqueror of the South.

And the Wisconsin red barn! Wisconsin barns

are mostly all red, and everywhere make a feature of the landscape missing in most states. A farmstead here is somehow warmed and given life by the red of the barns as they stand about me over the green hills and among the yellow fields with the sun on them.

And then Wisconsin is a dairy state. That means herds of pure Holsteins or Guernseys, or what have you, occupying the best ground anywhere around, making pictures that go with the one made by the red barn. Wisconsin, fond of passing laws, should pass another law compelling every farmer to paint his barn red. Another that will compel him to pasture his cows by the highway and his pigs back behind the barn.

I've found out, too, that we are known abroad as a "progressive" state. They know about Ross and Commons, Reinsch and Glenn Frank: names that help to make Wisconsin scientific, agrarian and political to the outside world. The name of La Follette distinguishes our political history, I find, wherever I go. And I, too, always speak of Wisconsin as "progressive" when I talk about her away from home. Not understanding very well just what the word means, I suppose, any more than other Wisconsin people, in general, do. But that is what Wisconsin would like to be anyway, and what she means to be. Which is most important after all.

A good solid state, our state. Physically very beautiful, a veritable playground for humanity in summer as Arizona is in winter.

Next to Wisconsin, "gathering of the waters," Arizona, "arid zone," is my favorite state. Each very different from the other, but something individual in them both not to be found elsewhere.

I am glad, too, "Wisconsin" is an Indian name. European people interested in architecture have learned to say "Wisconsin," in Japan, in Germany, in Holland, Austria, and Switzerland more often probably than any other American name except "New York."

Just now on my table is a Lloyd's Reisebureau advertisement proposing excursions to America from Switzerland. The program is given by days, what is to be seen each day. When the "West" is reached, *Dienstag und Mittwoch* are to be devoted to the *Landhausen Wright*.

Taliesin has received architectural pilgrims from all over the world. They have helped Taliesin a lot and the pilgrims have gone home and written in European newspapers and magazines and books, about America as they discovered it hidden away in a rural nook in southwestern Wisconsin.

In this rural nook in southwestern Wisconsin is our busy workshop. Out of it have come plans for buildings that have established new ideals in life and architecture and carried new principles in engineering into effect. They will never again build buildings in earthquake zones as they did before the Imperial was built in Tokio.

They will never again build the skyscraper quite so wastefully and foolishly whenever St. Mark's Tower is completed.

They will not long continue to make little scene paintings of houses in Arizona and California as they now do after San Marcos in the Desert grows up out of the desert as an indigenous human plant.

The American people only need to know they *can* build *real* buildings. We would like to hold and consolidate all these gains for Wisconsin as the Cardinals hold and consolidate their football gains on the gridiron. We are trying to do this by establishing a larger industrial workshop near here for the young people who want to be American artists; something in which the state university itself might well take an interest. Students are awakening to a lively interest in this matter. But that interest on the part of a great university might, after all, stultify our own enjoyment in a fresh endeavor and get us mixed up with senators and assemblymen and committees and regents and wear us all away with nothing done. Our social system is like that, unfortunately; yes, even in Wisconsin.

Why does any real progress have to overcome so much resistance? Why do we need, always, so many first-class funerals in order to get anything sensible done, if it is "unusual." Some day Wisconsin will be so progressive that she will consider the

Overleaf: **"Wisconsin Red Barns"** (destroyed), mural for Hillside Home School. Spring Green, Wisconsin. 1933. Elevation. Pencil and color pencil on tracing paper, 18 x 17". FLLW Fdn#3404.003

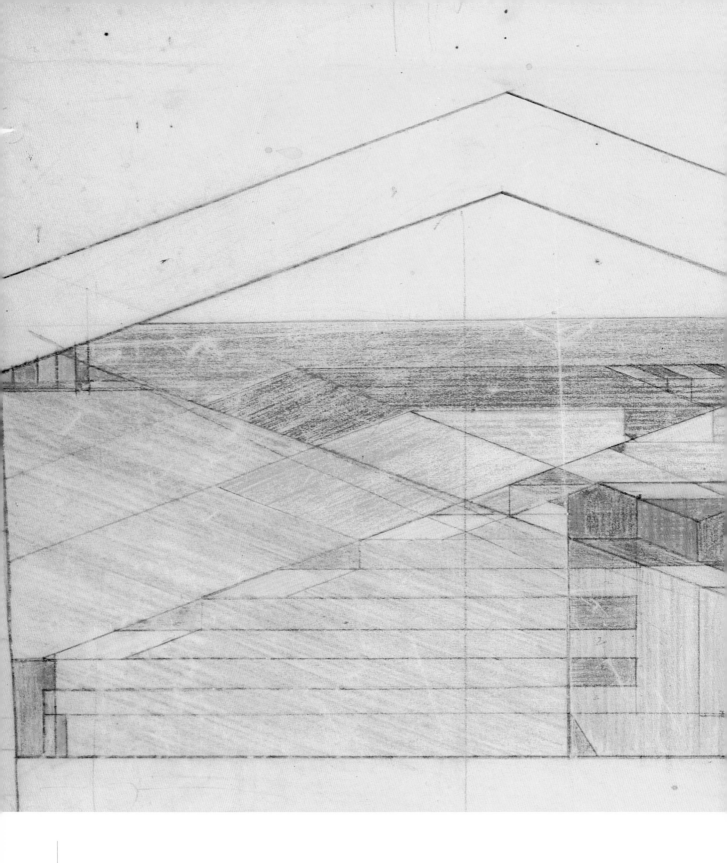

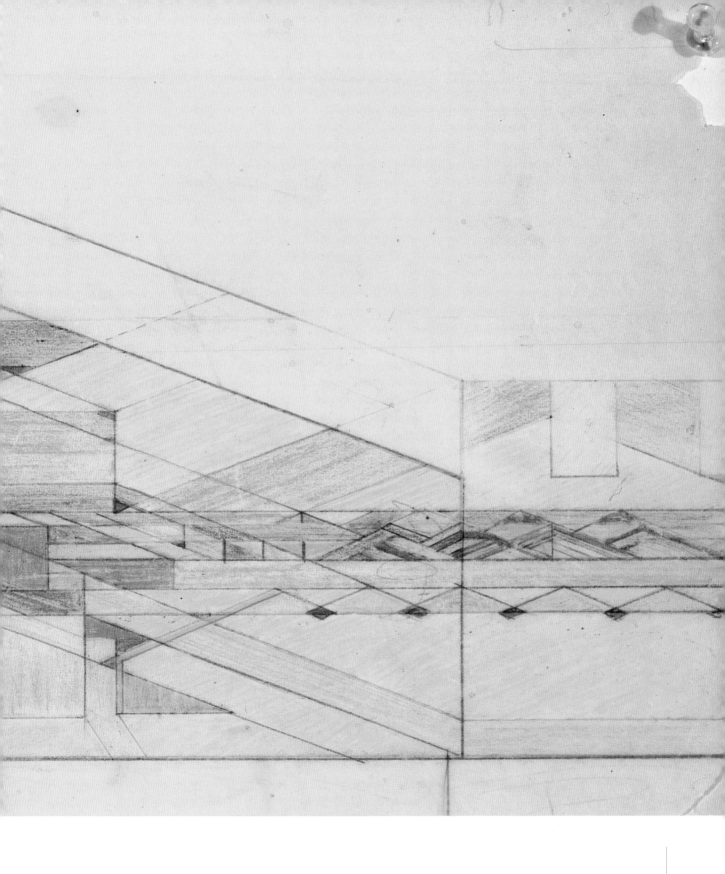

WHY I LOVE WISCONSIN

fine arts not only essential as science, politics, or farming, but even more fundamental to any state that would live "above the belt."

Getting back to why I love Wisconsin . . . .

I love Wisconsin because of her Meiklejohn experiment at the university, whether it succeeded or not. And because of every sincere forward-looking experiment the state itself has ever made; because of her courage; her love of independence; her true belief in individuality as essential to immortality. I love her because she will spend her money to grubstake prospectors for future benefits to her posterity, even though some of her too, too substantial citizens call her foolish for that—and I love her because she has not so very many snobs.

I love her because she has so few highbrows. They are men educated far beyond their capacity, so my old master Louis Sullivan used to say. And I love her because most of her was for the temper-ance of the Declaration of Independence instead of for the prohibition that violates temperance.

Without taking myself too seriously, I hope I love her because I, too, am by birth and nature a Wisconsin radical. Radical is a fine word, meaning "roots." Being radical I must strike root somewhere. Wisconsin is my somewhere. I feel my roots in these hillsides as I know those of the oak that have struck in here beside me.

That oak and I understand each other.

Wisconsin soil has put sap into my veins. Why, I should love her as I loved my mother, my old grandmother, and as I love my work.

1. This article was actually first published in *Industrial Wisconsin*, April 1930.
2. Wright spent time in Italy during his European sojourn in 1909–1910.

FIRST ANSWERS TO QUESTIONS BY "PRAVDA"

On October 19, 1933, Frank Lloyd Wright received the following letter from Moissaye J. Olgin, American correspondent for Pravda.

> *Dear Mr. Wright:*
>
> *A year ago the* Pravda *asked your opinion about the position of the intellectuals in the United States in connection with the economic crisis. Your opinion was then forwarded to Moscow. Today the* Pravda *editors, wishing to acquaint their readers more thoroughly with the changes wrought in the life of the intellectuals, during the last year, solicit your opinion on the following questions:*
>
> *1. What change, if any, has taken place in the life of the intellectuals (engineers, technicians, architects, artists, writers, teachers, etc.) during the last year?*
>
> *2. How has the prolongation of the crisis influenced the creative activities in this country in the realm of technique, art, literature and the sciences?*
>
> *3. Do you see improvement ahead for the intellectual groups?*
>
> *An early reply will be highly appreciated.*
>
> *Yours sincerely,*
>
> *Moissaye J. Olgin*

As early as 1933 Wright was recognized by Russian intellectuals as a leading figure not only of architectural thought in the United States, but also of social and political thought.

Beyond the scope of politics, Wright was drawn to the music and arts of Russia—both traditional and contemporary. The Russian cinema had appealed to him, from the late 1920s on, as a great revolution in that particular art form. Beginning in 1932 he started collecting Russian films to show at his own playhouse at Taliesin. Some of these he rented, others he purchased outright. The Frank Lloyd Wright Archives still contains a sizable collection of these films, which he bought from 1933 to the mid-1950s. On his visit to Russia in 1937, Wright met Sergei Eisenstein and returned to Taliesin with a long, uncut and uncensored version of the film director's Ivan the Terrible *for a private showing; the reels were later sent back to Russia. [Letters to* Pravda, *1933]*

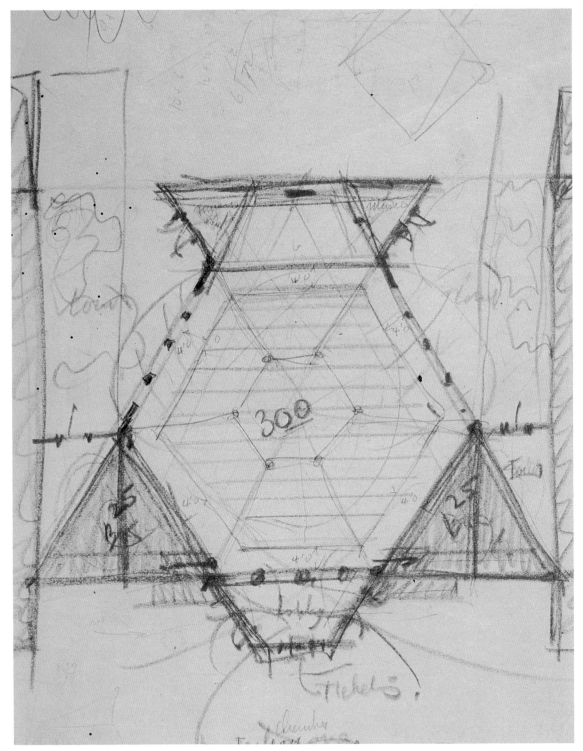

Cinema and shops (Project). Michigan City, Indiana. 1932. Conceptual plan. Pencil on paper, 9 x 10". FLLW Fdn#3203.001

MY DEAR MR. OLGIN:

Little visible change in the life or the attitude toward life of the intelligentsia of the United States is evident. No clear thinking is possible to them. They are all the hapless beneficiaries of a success-system they have never clearly understood, but a system that worked miracles for them while they slept. The hardships of the last three years have left them confused but not without hope that more miracles will come to pass in their behalf. They are willing to wait for them to happen.

The capitalistic system is a gambling game. It is hard to cure gamblers of gambling and everybody high and low in this country prefers the gamblers chance at a great fortune to the slower growth of a more personal fortune.

It is true that the educational system of the country has for many decades been breeding inertia. It aims to produce the middle-class mind which is able to function only in the middle of the road, boulevard preferred. It is the "safe" mind for the system as set up.

Machine power is vicarious power at best and breeds a lower type of individuality, it seems, the longer it functions. Action of any sort becomes less and less likely. So creative activity is a thing of the past—so far as it goes with machine power in these United States. Little art of any but the most superficial kind—the formula or the fashion—now characterizes the life of the States. The capacity for spiritual rebellion has grown small and the present ideals of success are making it smaller every day. No radical measures have been undertaken in the New Deal but there has been a great deal of tinkering and adjusting and pushing with prices to bring the old game alive again. Something more is needed than an arbitrary price-system to re-awaken capitalistic confidence in the spending of money.

The capitalistic system has evidently come to the necessity for a radical change that no tinkering can effect.

It is now proposed among the more sensible of the intelligentsia that all absentee-ownership be declared illegal by legislation.

The far-reaching consequences of such an enactment are hard to forecast but certainly the stranglehold of capitalism would be cut by such a measure and a freedom would ensue that would soon make Democracy a reality instead of the pretense it is. There is little chance however for any such measure until all the expedients have been tried and have failed in plain sight of everyone.

In the course of the next five years a real demand for such "repeal" of special privilege may come to pass. This is the feeling of the minority among the intelligentsia but they are doing nothing about it. They are spectators by birth, breeding, and habit.

Meantime all are getting on with about one-tenth of their former incomes.

I believe all three of your questions are answered in this answer to the first question.

1. The present economy has practically eliminated our profession, such as it was.

2. An entirely new set of ideas more in keeping with the principles of architecture are needed before thinking men can be inspired with sufficient confidence to go on building any more buildings. In the epoch now painfully closing—disguised as "economic depression"—architecture was only bad form of surface decoration: landlord bait for tenants. If the profession of architecture has any future it must get the building more directly and sensibly out of nature for the native.

3. Nor do I see any possibility of any return to the abnormality which has become normal, without some serious recognition of such organic integrity as a matter of means as well as an end to be achieved. Capitalistic centralization was content to employ the makeshift. Its economic structure was a makeshift. Its buildings were makeshifts. Its social life was an economic anxiety to makeshift. And finally its devotion to the makeshift is sterilizing all human creative power. There is left but ingenuity and scientific research.

4. I view the U.S.S.R. as a heroic endeavor to establish more genuine human values in a social state than any existing before. Its heroism and de-

votion move me deeply and with great hope. But I fear that machine worship to defeat capitalism may become inverted capitalism in Russia itself and so prostitute the man to the machine. Because the heart beats of the human soul are not like the ticking of a watch creative art is essential in any up-building of any social order worthy to be called organic and to endure. Individuality is a precious asset of the human race where it rests upon a common basis fair to all and should be rewarded according to its just value. This just reward is no less the problem of Russia now than of every other sincere attempt to enable all to rule and be ruled by their own bravest and their own best.

Yours sincerely,
Frank Lloyd Wright

CATEGORICAL REPLY TO QUESTIONS BY "ARCHITECTURE OF THE U.S.S.R."

In 1933 Wright received a list of nine questions from the editor of Architecture of the U.S.S.R., a magazine of the association of Soviet architects. The nine questions dealt not with the political and social questions that Pravda had asked (pp. 140–142), but with the workings of the architect's mind, from preliminary conceptual design to final work on construction and "polishing up."

Wright's reply presents a concise picture of how he regarded the architectural process, from start to finish, as it applies to the design and construction of a building. Consistent with all his thinking, the process itself cannot be easily divided into parts. Rather, it issues from the same general principle he applied to his work—from within outward:

Dear Sir:

We are mailing you today the first issue of our new magazine "Architecture of the U.S.S.R.," and wish to inform you that we wish to have the pleasure of your kind collaboration.

We consider one of our main objects an exchange of experience between prominent Soviet and foreign architects and your collaboration would be of particular value to us.

In the next issue of our magazine an exchange of opinions is organized between the most prominent architects of Russia and foreign countries on the subject:

"MY METHOD OF ARCHITECTURAL DESIGNING"

(Method of work and the course of creative process).

Owing to the considerable interest your answer to this question presents for us, we would ask you in particular to take up the following problems:

1. Preliminary working out of an architectural assignment, study of technical and economic conditions;
2. Composition work, how in the course of designing a certain artistic idea is born and worked out in detail;
3. Part played by drawing and sketching;
4. How to make use of classical and modern architectural monuments; how to utilize them;
5. Forms of collective work, collaboration with other architects while working out a certain design. Role of one's assistants;
6. Collaboration with sculptors, artists;
7. Final work on the design;

8. *Work following completion of design, work on the construction site;*

9. *Corrections, additions, polishing up.*

It goes without saying that the above-mentioned questions are of an estimating nature and may be, should you deem it necessary, altered, amplified, and also replaced by any other questions you will find of interest.

We would request you to answer us in the way you will find most advisable and, if possible, to illustrate it with photographs of your works, drawings, sketches, etc.

Considering that all the material relating to this subject will appear in our next issue, we should get your answer not later than on October 10th.

Thanking you in anticipation of your kind collaboration, we beg to remain,

Sincerely yours,

Editor in Chief

[Letter to Architecture of the U.S.S.R., *December 7, 1933]*

Fire screen (destroyed), Hillside Home School. Spring Green, Wisconsin. 1934. Elevation. Pencil and color pencil on tracing paper, 38 x 18".
FLLW Fdn#3404.004

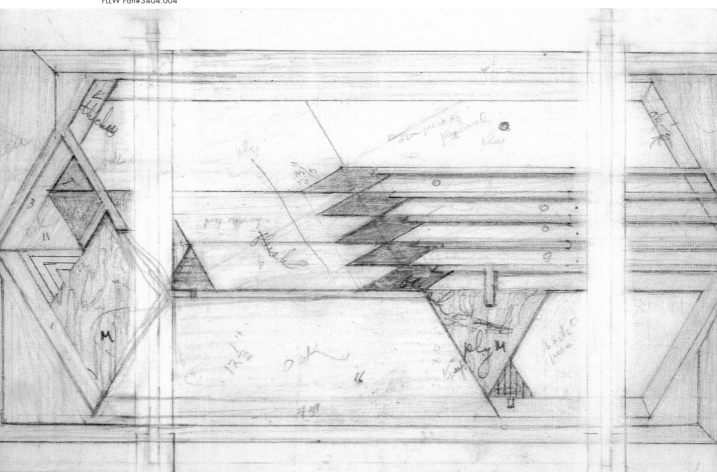

TO SHOW HOW THE WHEELS GO ROUND IN THE CREATIVE mind of an architect is none other than creation itself. But to answer your questions as may be:

1. The solution of every problem is contained within itself. Its plan, form, and character are determined by the nature of the site, the nature of the materials used, the nature of the system using them, the nature of the life concerned and the purpose of the building itself.

2. In organic architecture composition, as such, is dead. We no longer compose. We conceive the building as an entity. Proceeding from generals to particulars by way of some appropriate scheme of construction we try to find the equation of expression best suited, that is to say most natural, to all the factors involved as enumerated in above answer to question number one.

3. Drawing and sketching are merely a means to clarify and to record ideas. In themselves they should play this minor part. As a means of communication between architect and client or between architect and builder they are necessary language and as such should say as simply and directly as possible, and as truthfully, what requires to be said and no more.

4. The only way classical or modern architectural monuments can be helpful to us is to study that quality in them which made them serviceable or beautiful in their day and be informed by that quality in them. As ready-made forms they can only be harmful to us today. What made them great in their day is the same as what would make great buildings in our own day. But the buildings we should make would be very different, necessarily.

5. It is seldom that collaboration can enter into truly creative work except as one man conceives and another executes. But, even so, the highest is not attained. In the art of architecture conception and execution should be a self-contained unit. An architect's assistants should be like the fingers on the architect's hands in relation to the work that he does. The "committee meeting" never produced anything in architecture above the level of a compromise. No architect's competition ever resulted in anything above an averaging of averages. Where creative work is concerned competitions are devastating.

6. Sculpture and painting are integral features of architecture and the architect himself should be sufficiently master of both to enable him to visualize and embody these features where and as they belong in his creation. Architecture, sculpture and painting should be one synthesis, as sympathetically executed as the composer's score is executed by the orchestra directed by the composer himself.

7. Final work on the design should merely be completing the harmony of the whole by justifying all details, checking up on and changing such as may not be digested in the sum total of the project. Little "polishing" should be necessary if the project has been well conceived and is a natural solution well worked out and if it was properly recorded.

8. Work on the construction of the site should be directly under the supervision of the mind of the man that conceived the building in its completeness: the architect. And such organization and assistance should be given him as will ensure the completion of the work to his satisfaction.

9. Corrections, additions should be as few as possible. If sufficient study has been devoted to the development of the project they should be unnecessary. But sometime in the final construction of any work a better way of accomplishing the desired result may appear and a better way which should not be lost. But the architect should be the final judge in any such event and he should be free to make the necessary changes to the best advantage of the whole work. Plans and specifications are made to educate the architect and his assistants. Progress in this educational process should not stop as experience goes on after the structure has been begun except in so far as the process may complicate the system executing the building. For this reason it is better to have flexible means of execution with as little financial penalty for changes as possible and, in the work, as little confusion or waste as possible. Nevertheless, and before all, any good building is the proper working out of a definite system of construction which should be fully grasped and understood—that is to say "mastered"—by the architect before he begins to plan his building.

IN THE SHOW WINDOW AT MACY'S

This article is Wright's response to eight residential designs by rather fashionable architects of the time, who traditionally designed tall buildings and office structures. While they believed themselves to be in line with the so-called modern movement, Wright suggests that they would be better off sticking to the eclecticism in which they were especially well-versed: "Dear boys—your senior speaking . . . why not go back to eclecticism and, safely, stay there? You do not know what lies beneath the countenance of organic architecture and you wouldn't like it if you did know because you couldn't use it." [Published with eight illustrations in The Architectural Forum, *November 1933]*

A WELL-MADE BOOKLET, IN THE GOOD STYLE TO WHICH THE *Forum* is becoming accustomed, informs me that the men who made the New York Skyline have designed a house for me. Eight houses—exactly, from which, by code word, I may order one, or order two, if not direct then from my local architect.[1]

I may take my choice of the eight houses, as a "modern" home is seen by the tall skyscraper minds of New York City; the minds of eight of the men who have covered the skyscraper bones of the engineer with a good many million tons of much too much flesh.

These architects, in good standing with the A.I.A., may not advertise. No, but they may be advertised. And why not Macy's? From functioneer faces to tail-pieces the department stores are now willing where the academies are rot. And wherever anything modern goes they are rot.

I remember standing up before a jammed crowd at "that Sears and Roebuck's" department store last summer on the occasion of the exhibit of Phil. Johnson's traveling "Punch and Judy" for European modernism, because the Art Institutes and the Museums were willing to be unable.[2]

The show had proceeded from the Moscow of Modern Art to tour the U.S.S.A. I received two hundred and fifty dollars as my share of the "come down." So we are all "come downs." We are in the department store at last for better or for worse and I don't see how it could be worse.

Dignified by the *Forum* is this latest department store event. Between a self-portrait and a small tail-piece of a Master-work utterly otherwise we see the plan and a photograph of a model of some "Forward" house. To distinguish the "Forward" houses from each other they have been differentiated as "Hospitality"—"Outdoor"—"Sun"—"Next Year"—"Common Sense"—"Ground"—"Garden" —and "Individual": good code words in the accepted advertising manner. The code words might be more appropriate but are interchangeable, except the last, which seems to have little or no application elsewhere and is therefore ideal for the purpose. In fact these colleagues of mine, obviously, definitely

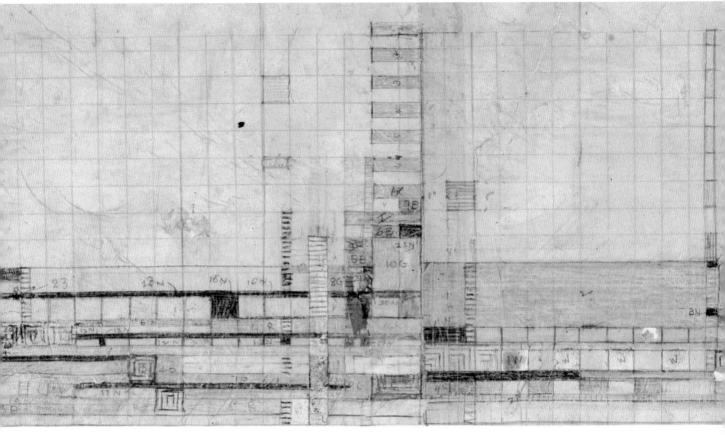

Hillside Theatre curtain #1 (destroyed). Spring Green, Wisconsin. 1934. Elevation. Pencil and color pencil on paper, 27 x 18".
FLLW Fdn#3302.001

are high up in the air where modern architecture is concerned. Each would need only twenty-five to forty thousand dollars to functioneer any house at all. They must see what the modern house looks like from high above and far away. Their little come-downs do resemble somewhat the cliché's with which our department stores are becoming familiar as "modernistic."

But, "Hospitality," for instance, is just a Colonial house with the shingles left off and the corners wrecked to cover a plan that wastefully chases around a big central stairway to an utterly banal conclusion.

Better stick to the Telephone Company, Ralph!

"Outdoor" may be a proper name for a house that by elevation doesn't seem in the least to belong there except as a clumsy intrusion in which none of the three stories belong together. The plan would be better but for the incident of dining with a big

pier between the eyes or should I say—square in the esophagus? Blind walls are perhaps best for a dressing room, too? Anyhow they are no bar to the use of floor space in a skyscraper except for toilet purposes. But I admire the "nothing-for-a-top" skyscraper, Ray. Your little tail-piece.

As for "Sun"—Sunny Harvey's house—I like "Sun" best because it affectionately leans toward the sort of thing that has grown up in my own mind as a more modern type of exterior. But the plan is a wall-and-window plan. That is to say an old-fashioned plan. A glorified pantry like Harvey's may blind the wall of a dining room and in many houses one does do work with one's back to the light. The antecedent likeness of the architect shows keen eyes but, like the one who would try to live in this house, he must see from the top down. Too far away, Wiley?

We arrive at "Next Year" to find a house that

"defies all the scourges that a house is heir to"—except the one touch that makes the whole world kin. I mean vulgarity. Van has seen homes similar to this one but has never seen one that showed a rotund backside to the passer-by more deliberately. To make the effect perfect the watercloset should change places with the washbowl.

Here, backed by huge green pylons, we have the originality usually achieved by the eclectic who would differentiate. Stick more closely to your precedents, Van! And watch your scale.

What better name to disarm criticism at the outset than "Common Sense"? Great crimes have been committed in that name. But Ely's house is no great crime, it is just a "little" house he says, but must think so only because he builds so many huge loft-buildings. This little primrose invites you to "bust in" between the garage and the lavatory into a "Hall." Is a Hall common sense in any small house? I ask you. Also I am sorry I ever started the wrap-around corner window on its International career. It makes nonsense here. But Ely, you know your women . . . that good second floor is proof.

If we may have a Ground-hog why not a "Ground House" with someone in it "before it is built"—Yes, but preferably someone wise enough to escape before it is under way.

What a conception skyscraperites must have of a "limited income" in this plot 150' x 200'—150 on the street. And there where the buzz wagons all live happily together in the family circle. One mass and one harmony achieved by Harmon. A good old-fashioned plan but for this noisy innovation. And for this plan a good old-fashioned exterior. A performance as recklessly conservative as this one shows modern architecture still sound (and little but sound) at the core. A safe man, indeed, Art!

The "Garden House" is no mere place for tools and the hose, nor for tea. No, it's a place for a proper New England family that hates the country but is forced to live there. Were it not for bathrooms and garage this sanctuary would be Tradition, inviolate. The world does move, somewhat, however, and Mr. White says he moves with it. Why then does he leave his "Forward" house behind him. The Colonial "tradition" splits the house

in the center; as to the right so to the left. No reflexes—they are defection. No eclectic and proud of it should ever tantalize progress, Mr. White!

Finally the house "Individual." And a good idea, too, "individual"—if possible. In plan this house is somewhat so. In exterior we have here a sad case of mixed personality struggling, finally, with five style complexes. An ingenious plan this, by Schultze. But somewhere down the line, even before that undigested terrace enters, the co-relation that is architecture is missed. Here are too many sides . . . periphery too great. And Leonard—your self-confessed "semi-modern" is automatically non-individual. Any semi is and you should know it.

However, it was Bernard Shaw who once said one might do anything if only one talked strongly enough the other way and one might say anything provided what one did was strongly enough the opposite.

It would so seem throughout this topical, tasteful and tidy little advertisement for the New York Skyline—the *Forum* standing by.

In no single instance is the thought of an organic architecture felt in the plan of any one of the houses.

"Modern" remains a matter of "styling" an exterior for some plan or other.

Dear boys—your senior speaking . . . . Why not go back to eclecticism and, safely, stay there? You do not know what lies beneath the countenance of organic architecture and you wouldn't like it if you did know because you couldn't use it. Had you this inner experience now, the experience would use you and unmake your success. With it you never could have made the New York Skyline what it is today.

1. Macy's and *The Architectural Forum* undertook an exhibit of house designs in 1933. The following architects (primarily commercial) were represented, each one of whom Wright chastises: Ralph Walker (1889–1973), Raymond Hood (1881–1934), Harvey Wiley Corbett (1873–1954), William Van Alen (b. 1907), Ely Jacques Kahn (1884–1972), Arthur Loomis Harmons (1878–1958), Lawrence Grant White (son of Stanford White), and Leonard Schultze.
2. A reference to The Museum of Modern Art exhibit *Modern Architecture: The International Style* organized by Philip Johnson and Henry-Russell Hitchcock. The exhibition traveled extensively and was on view at Sears and Roebuck in Chicago, June 9–July 8, 1932. See *International Style: Exhibition 15 and The Museum of Modern Art,* Terence Riley (New York: Rizzoli, 1992), Appendix 5, p. 222.

THE CITY OF TO-MORROW

At about the same time that Wright's book The Disappearing City *(pp. 70–112) was published, several articles Wright wrote for different journals reiterated the ideas published in that work. Some articles were excerpted directly from the book, while others, such as this one, are variations on his particular thesis of decentralization. Removing man from the congested evils of the city is a recurrent theme in Wright's writings. In a most eloquent passage he envisions man "tanned, muscular, and supple from his invigorating life, replete with sun and air, with work in wholesome surroundings, with exercise and play accessible to both his purse and his house." [As told to Catherine Brody, published in* Pictorial Review, *March 1933]*

THE MOLOCH THAT HAS KNOWN NO GOD IS CRACKING AT its huge joints. It sickens in its giant maw. The big city and all that made it big are being destroyed by its own cruel voracity.

That offering of the American city to the world as the height of progress—the skyscraper—is really only an example of extremity in the wrong direction. It points away from the common, human welfare toward a void of futility piled on futility, the whole poised merely on the shifting sands of excess gold. Our cities are not modern. They are outmoded.

Long ago a close group of huts or houses hugging the shelter of a city wall had the excuse of fulfilling definite human desires—the desire for safety and for convenient association with one's kind. In our time these desires no longer depend for satisfaction upon nearness of residence and density of population. The city, as we know it, has ceased to answer our needs, and has thus lost its true excuse for being.

Instead it has framed an artificial excuse, guaranteed just as good as the real. Why must cities be built for people to live in, anyhow? Cities are only real estate, are they not? And real estate exists only to be "developed" and rented and made profitable for the owner. Therefore build cities for rent and profit alone!

And so they were built. The more houses that could be squeezed into a plot, each cutting off light, space, and air, the essentials of serenity, from its neighbor, the more houses could be rented, the greater the gain. The taller the buildings grew, each thrusting itself farther and farther above its neighbors, regardless of the latters' comfort, the greater the rentable space, the higher the profits.

Rising daily to huge towers which coined our air into money for others, jostling each other in narrow streets for every inch of foot room, fighting for our very lives the motor traffic, which should be the mechanics of our pleasure and convenience, we, too, lost sight of the true aims of our existence and accepted what was only a substitute.

We thought, not horizontally, not in terms of the man beside us at the level of our eyes, not in terms of interrelated humanity, each dependent on all, all drawing common subsistence from the earth which bore us. We thought vertically.

Like our skyscrapers, each of us clutched our own little plot of appetites and ambitions and shut out the rest. Each of us reached, so we thought, up—up, each toward the highest profits. The few who attained them fled from the cities. They bought for themselves the grassy soil, the trees, the restful space which the earth offers to all for growth and peace, but which only the few could afford.

There was one inalienable though forgotten reason why this state of affairs could not go on forever. The human soul, in order to preserve itself, must and will rebel against the unendurable. However falsely we may think, our bodies and souls know that they cannot be divorced from the benefits of earth. They must have room to turn in and pure air to breathe and an unobstructed heaven to muse upon or they perish.

The skyscraper city has been trampling sanity and dignity underfoot. It has forced people to eat and sleep and have their being in miniature apartments fit only for closet space, never free of the interference of life in abutting cubicles. It has compelled them to inhabit jerry-built houses, either too close or too cold in winter, and ovens in summer. The even less fortunate have had to live in rooms harassed by the incessant roar of traffic. City dirt clogs the lungs, city noise deafens the ears.

The horror of being pushed underfoot and stamped upon in the rush of the sheeplike crowd, each particle of it driven uncontrollably by a similar horror, has strained the nerves and deadened the heart. But at last the tortured body, feeling what it must have, has turned instinctively, fear giving place to a battling rage for survival. And then revolt sprang up against enslavement to stone and steel and money as against any other ruthless masters.

Zoning laws and setbacks in our high buildings were the first concessions of Moloch to the revolt of his idolaters. But they did not stop the flight toward self-preservation.

Manhattan alone lost hundreds of thousands of citizens last year. In the larger cities, especially in New York, the newest and greatest skyscrapers, the newest and biggest apartment houses, stand half or two-thirds empty. It is doubtful if these towers built for rent will ever be rented. Greed has at last defeated itself.

It never occurred to the property owners that the higher they built the greater would be the expense both of construction and of upkeep; the further one district was "improved" and made the latest center, i.e., the latest source of congestion, the higher the taxes the landlord must pay. In this way, year by year, the return which an owner had to get from his property in order to pay for the congestion to which he had added and to take his reward for having added to that congestion, mounted.

Year by year buildings had to be higher, the last drop of profitable space had to be squeezed out of taxable space. Yet, as buildings multiplied and grew, as more offices and apartments were added to yet more offices and apartments, there was produced a mighty supply of space far exceeding demand. Space, such artificial space as that, everywhere—and not enough tenants to fill it!

The very machine power which formed the supercity makes it, on the one hand, more and more dangerous and time-consuming, and, on the other hand, becomes the means of escape from it. Transportation is already easier and better, and every day it is swifter.

The motor car, the airplane, the bus, the commuters' trains, even the extension of subways, those products of the cities, permit all classes to go farther and farther afield. They enable them to satisfy the growing desire to get disentangled from the crowd, to live, to play, and even to work in the country without losing a single advantage urbanism can offer.

These modern means of transit also cultivate in our current citizen the new sense of spacing. When our present cities were laid out the man on his legs or behind a horse was the standard of space measurement. This standard is utterly obsolete.

The future city must be planned in terms of that speedy annihilation of once immense distances

Broadacre City (Project). Model. 1934. FLLW Fdn FA#3402.0083

brought about by the plane, the automobile, and the various forms of electrical intercommunication. It is in the nature of motoring and flying that the city should spread out, intimate with the ground.

In the city of yesterday ground space was reckoned by the square foot. In the city of to-morrow ground space will be reckoned by the acre—an acre to a family.

Does this seem like the dream of another Utopia? Yet if all the inhabitants of the world were to stand upright together they would scarcely occupy the island of Bermuda. The United States alone contains more than fifty-seven acres of land for each man, woman, and child within its borders. An acre to a family is only a modest minimum.

As my dream of the spacious future I see land-scaped highways, devoid of the already archaic telegraph and telephone poles and wires, free of blaring billboards, bright with wayside flowers, cool with shade trees, joined at intervals with fields from which the safe, noiseless transport planes take off and land.

I see giant roads swinging past public-service stations no longer eyesores, through a series of diversified units—the farm, the factory, the roadside market, the garden school, the dwelling place— each home on its acre of individually adorned and cultivated ground—with garden space for pleasure and leisure.

These units will be so arranged and integrated that each citizen of the future will have all forms of production, distribution, self-improvement, enjoyment, within a radius of a hundred and fifty miles of his home, easily and speedily available by means of his car or plane.

Because every man will own his acre of home ground, architecture will be in the service of the man himself, creating in harmony with the personal tastes of the individual. No two homes, no two gardens, none of the three-to-ten-acre farm units, no two factory buildings need be alike.

There need be no special style, but style everywhere. Light, strong houses and work places will be solidly and sympathetically built out of the nature of the ground into sunlight. Factory workers will live on acre home units, within walking distance of, or a short ride away from, the future factories—beautiful, smokeless, and noiseless. No more will the farmer envy the urban dweller his mechanical improvements, while the latter in turn covets the farmer's green solitudes.

Each factory and farm would be within a ten-mile radius of a vast and variegated wayside market, so that each can serve the other simply and effectively, and both can serve that other portion of the population which lives and works in the neighborhood of that market. No longer will any need exist for futile racing to and from a common center.

Without air, sunlight, land, human life cannot go on. Recognizing this principle, as we are all beginning to, the home of tomorrow will conform. It will eliminate no modern comforts, yet it will also keep the ageless, health-giving comforts of light, freedom, and air.

Steel and glass will be called in to fulfill their own—steel for strength, durability, and lightness; translucent glass will give privacy, as well as access to the sun and sky. The home would be an indoor garden, the garden an outdoor house.

Tall buildings are not barred, but they must have no interior courts. They must stand free in natural parks. An apartment house might be nine or ten stories, perhaps; tier on tier of immense glass panes golden with sun, on shining steel foundations, each tier with its flower and vine-festooned porch composing a medley of vivid colors, and the whole set off by spacious blossoming grounds.

If the machine age has any future, the type of city that I have described is the only possible city. The principles of architecture are simply the principles of life. Just as a house built on a makeshift foundation cannot stand, so life set on a makeshift character in a makeshift country cannot endure. Good and lasting architecture gives or concedes the right to all of us to live abundantly in the exuberance that is beauty—in the sense that William Blake defined "exuberance." He did not mean excess. He meant according to nature, without stint.

Thus, also, must good and lasting life yield up that right to all of us. And the only secure foundation for such life is enlightened human character that will accept, not merely mouth, the indissoluble relation between the welfare of one and the welfare of the whole. Only that sort of character is fit for and able to create a permanent and universal well-being.

To put it concretely, architectural values are human values or they are not valuable. Human values are life-*giving*, not life-*taking*. When one is content to build for one's self, taking the natural rights of life, breath, and light and space away from one's neighbor, the result is the pretentious skyscraper. It stands for a while in its business slum, formed by greed, selfishly casting its shadow on its neighbors, only to find that it, too, is dependent upon their success and must fall with their failure.

Only the golden rule can bring in the golden age, the age of the many living in an abundance, in a freedom and ease, now reserved for the few. In that day the skyscraper will have become as horrid an example of past barbarism as medieval instruments of torture are to us.

Every prophet has his own vision—and each prefers his own. I like to think of my citizen of tomorrow living—if he is to progress and live instead of deteriorate and die—in his great cities of giving that extend throughout the land—the Broadacre Cities of to-morrow.

I like to think of him within the sheer, sunlit panes of his house, his routine and the routine of his wife and family interwoven with the outdoors in a way that the present city resident can never imagine, with every duty of the day providing contacts with nature—his own trip to and from the nearby office or factory; his work in his own garden; his wife's daily marketing at the roadside markets, where produce comes fresh from the farms every hour; his children's daily attendance at the small schools set in parks that are playgrounds.

I see him tanned, muscular, and supple from his invigorating life, replete with sun and air, with work in wholesome surroundings, with exercise and play accessible to both his purse and his house. Wherever he is or wants to be, his home and all modern conveniences are as economical as his motor car. Voices and vision—radio and television—penetrate solid walls to entertain and inform him.

And when he wants to "go places," he will drive over the great hard-road systems of the country, with their magnificent bridges and viaducts, through the charm of a diverse, but gracious, architecture, along flowing rivers, up winding mountain highways, where he can look down upon a world grown beautiful again. Or his plane, resting in the field, will await his bidding, carrying him across the continent in twenty-four hours, bringing him back again to a home that enriches the communal life by a fitting abundance.

THE CHICAGO WORLD'S FAIR

Although its formal title was "The Century of Progress," the Chicago World's Fair of 1933–1934 seemed to Frank Lloyd Wright to represent anything but progress. Here he recalls the World's Columbian Exposition of 1893, which occurred at the same time that he opened his architectural practice, and he somewhat excuses the classical picture-making that affair was (see also p. 156). Late in the nineteenth century, he argues, architects were still pitifully ignorant of the methods and machinery that the twentieth century would soon offer. But now, forty years later, he sees no excuse for the continued "picture-making," especially under the guise of a century of progress. [Published in Architect's Journal, *July 13, 1933]*

To SEE THE CHICAGO "PROGRESS" FAIR OF 1933 IS TO remember its original, the Columbian Fair of 1893, and to realize how much better the Columbian Fair was in every respect, as an eclecticism—even as novelty. At the Columbian Fair the provincials of the United States saw for the first time Architecture as co-ordination on the grand scale. Thrilled by its orchestral effects the provinces, aided by the group of eclectics responsible for the ensemble, went heavily pseudo—and imagined they went "classic."

There was some excuse for their debauch of sanity by way of academic taste because they yet knew nothing of the scientific organism of architecture. The building, to them, was a picture. The pictorial in any form was the art they knew. They were Victorian. And there was much to be said for the eclecticism of 1893 as a picture for the United States. The architecture of the Fair became epidemic and five times since the same thing has broken out in various parts of the country, modified somewhat each time but the thought wholly unchanged.

There was only retrogression in the repetition and each was confessed a failure. No progress.

Came 1930. The Dawes family of Chicago counted it time to go to another Fair and called up by telephone several eclectics they considered prominent and nominated them to choose others of their kind, altogether to finally lay out a scheme for a fair to celebrate progress in honor of the City of Chicago. There was hope of profit to Chicago business and increased prestige estimated also as profit.

Chicago had not yet recovered from the blaze of glory in which she found herself in '93 and which had been emulated on the grand scale by rival St. Louis, by distant San Francisco and San Diego and by several other ambitious Usonian cities.

But progress, a dubious matter at best, is difficult to celebrate. And the chief failure of the Fair lies in this choice of the "progress-motif" for the 1933 celebration. They might have called the thing anything else! But Chicago was vainglorious owing to past triumphs and the cliché, serving so faithfully and so ill so many too many times already—that is to say, the lagoon with several miles of temporary picture buildings dedicated to various industries wrapped around it, the fountain still at one end of it, the buildings named for the various industries they were intended to advertise by aesthetic inference and to exploit by façade, in short the same Victorian idea that made the Columbian Fair was taken out, dusted off and adopted complete. But then, a pause. What progress? As I happen to know this question threw the designers of the Fair into temporary confusion for progress must be evident in a Fair celebrating Progress? Well then, what progress?

At the French Fair of 1925 a new appearance had been seen. The appearance resembled to a startling degree some work that was indigenous to the United States. But that indigenous work was not well known in its own country and being done some quarter of a century ago might be disregarded—though still living—and become a fresh appearance with a view to indicating progress to the country at large. Any fresh appearance might be taken by the people for progress? As for the tyro and the fashion, France had endorsed the new appearance and there was an increasing wave of appreciation from Middle-Europe. Why not seize it and name it Progress? Once an eclectic—always eclectic; so it was done.

And came another thought: the Columbian Fair with one outstanding polychromatic exception had been in the white. "Let's paint this one in gay colors like the solitary outstanding exception at the Columbian Fair." It was done. More progress.

The new appearance was characterized by the long horizontal line and the extended flat plane, both broken as little as possible. Originally the straight line and flat plane had been seen in the obscure indigenous architecture—now the skeleton in the closet—as a means to an end: the sincere use of the machine as a new tool in building and the development of an organic architecture for our country. The original had been a faithful development of structure. The effects were honest, clean, bold and striking by way of elimination of the insignificant and affirmation of structural principles. They were as distinctive in style as the Gothic, the Greek or the Indian. But being themselves specialists in the various styles it was a simple enough matter for the Dawes group of eclectics to take on overnight one more specialty as the latest style. This was easy because the art of building was, to them, merely getting something in some style set up. No need to change the thought. That would be impossible anyway because an eclectic must not really think. He

must run the outside on the thing somehow, simulating the outlines surfaces and contrasts. These new effects could all be simulated by leaving the familiar pseudo-classic plan-structure where and as they understood it—and arriving at the elevations, by scraping off capitals, cornices, pilasters and ornamental detail. By omitting all window openings less interruption of flat effects could be had, but as may be seen although the buildings did shut their eyes the countenance they had taken on could not fail to be recognized?

The net result: Ideas? None. Scheme? Bad! Messy and commonplace even from their own standpoint. Features? Commonplace repetition in the glare of publicity of effects now merely superficial that had already appeared in out of the way places as genuine. Style? Faked again. On the whole here was constructed decoration in the new quarter-century-old mode.

"Changed" is not necessarily "progress" and here comes no reality as "progress." Here is only fanciful change: the black and white poster of 1893, republished in the same old vein but colored now in 1933. In some few effects a fetching poster—but when the effects are good they are not new and when they are new they are not good. They are not good because they are merely superficial imitation of something not understood. Here is a desperate and depressing attempt to visualize progress in Architecture by rejecting the old not as *honor* to dead or dying tradition but rejection as *insult* to a living tradition by patterning after a new appearance that can only be a seeming to the patterners. Of what it is that originally appeared this Fair knows nothing and cares less.

It is the privilege of any architect to inebriate himself at a Fair. And it is well to remember that any one of the architects who set up this apparition could as well set it up Gothic, or turn it over to pseudo-classic or make it go Chinese. And all would have much preferred to do any of these things had they not seen the handwriting on the wall: "the old styles at the end of their tether." So the same lack of respect for tradition now characterizes this "Progress" effort in their hands that has heretofore characterized any effort to work in any style. The same insincerity damns the work for any future reference except as an eclectic's latest scrap-pile to add to those already known as "Americana."

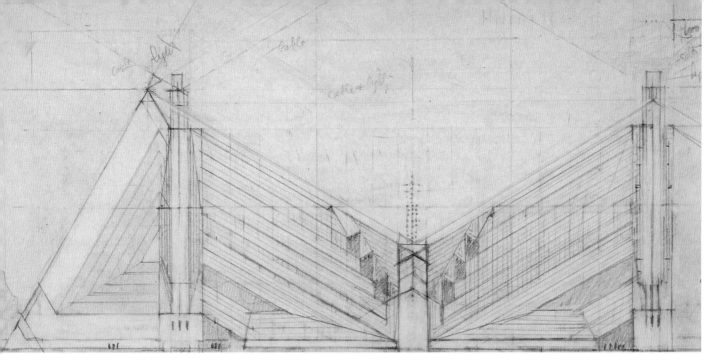

"Century of Progress," Fair Pavilion (Project). Chicago, Illinois. 1931. Detail, elevation. Pencil on tracing paper, 36 x 24". FLLW Fdn#3103.001

No architect really understanding good work will copy that work or trade in it nor will he act on its appearances. Understanding should and would make him master of his own work. This ambitious show as a whole, would if it could betray a hope belonging by nature to those whose deeper understanding of life an organic architecture expresses.

By premature but habitual exploitation here is the betrayal of an organic architecture for our country to make a Dawes holiday for a people already bought and sold way beyond their own generation or the next. Yes, or the next. The cause of an organic architecture as a living tradition is here betrayed just as the same old eclecticism has betrayed the dying Gothic tradition and as it has betrayed the dead pseudo-classic. It could not wholly betray the Renaissance because the Renaissance itself, where architecture was concerned, was a self-betrayal. So here to make the newest Roman holiday—a "Fair"—you may see the deeper and more profound work that is indigenous to their own country betrayed by way of its own countenance, used as a mask by the expedient eclecticism of unfair architects and sold by ballyhoo to the public in the name of "Progress."

What consequences?

Well, let's admit that the departure in itself may help to break the fixture in the popular mind of epidemic classic and "the periods." Let's suppose that demand for the "modernistic" becomes even more department-store popular than it already is. It will automatically be damned the quicker.

At any rate the camp of the eclectics will be badly broken up if not stampeded.

I see no such effect upon the never more fair-jaded public of today as was produced by the original fair. An unhappy people at a despondent period may welcome diversion. But in the confusion resulting from the division in the eclectic's camp the people may see the refreshing values of simplicity—simple surface and the single line singularly significant—and be moved—the better among them—to go deeper into the causes of these "new" effects. Architecture can't be made to grow much by bally-hoo or propaganda unless in this way.

Let's forgive the expediency of these shallow architects for their exploitation of appearances belonging by nature to work deeper than their understanding. Let's say these men did the best they knew how to do with their newest eclecticism.

But the fact remains that the whole as architecture is false. It is not architecture, however gaily painted.

And what is false is more than likely to be damn'd when the excitement is all over.

ANOTHER PSEUDO

Wright here criticizes the 1893 World's Columbian Exposition at Chicago and the devastating influence it had on the nation at that time: "By this overwhelming rise of grandomania I was confirmed in my fear that a native architecture would be set back at least fifty years."[1] In this second article for a commercial publication (see pp. 153–155), Wright again criticizes the 1933 Chicago World's Fair, but for different reasons: "By aping modern architecture, the fair became somewhat theatrical, "pseudo-modern," and represented a complete failure to understand the principle underlying good modern building. Wright maintained that if the 1893 fair killed good architecture in the United States, the 1933 fair buried it. [Published in The Architectural Forum, *July 1933]*

WHEN I AM ASKED TO WRITE OR SPEAK ABOUT THE DAWES FAIR at Chicago—and continually I am asked to do one or the other—my feelings are curious. Mixed. Perhaps something gets to me like the sensations of the woman who longed for a child and, one day, found one gratuitously laid on her doorstep, only to discover the child to be a doll.

In this instance, the hoax goes so far as to forge in this foundling on the doorstep a resemblance to myself. Let's look at the doll.

Eyes closed but features nonetheless recognizable. Pinned to the dress is the familiar label—"surface and mass," but, by countenance, the manikin acknowledges as sire the straight line and flat plane of the machine age that first appeared in our country some thirty years ago. The doll, as an illegitimate offspring, is amusing but equivocal and wakens a rueful train of recollection as I look upon its features to see that where they are new, they are not good; and where they are good, they are not new . . . .

This latest inflation testifies afresh to how little the "artistic" really have in their lives. How fussy-feeble their desire is. How little power is in them. To have enough synthetic "forms divine" to go around the select eclectic circle may be desirable.

But no synthesis is involved in this Fair except wholesale imitation, hit or miss, of the genuine new forms that occurred in our country in out of the way places many years ago. A formula has now been deduced from them that may be made to pass for a new style for a while. The "public," whatever that is, may be partially weaned from pseudo-classic only to find another "pseudo" thrust into its arms. How stale it all is where the spirit is hungry for reality, any artist, yes and it seems to me even the artistic, must at least see.

To me, of course, the whole performance is petty, strident and base. Great repose, belonging by nature to the spontaneous, genuine originality which almost all of the superficial forms helplessly or craftily resemble, are nowhere.

Genuine art must come from the inside. Never from the will. And here is no inside. Only an "I will," or an empty artifice. I am no pontiff. But still youthful in creative energy I feel all these ignoble satisfactions to be contemptible waste, if no worse. Of course, they are far worse because impotence is the consequence. Something deeper than the artistic perpetrators of this latest eclecticism could understand has passed through the place where great art should have been. In that place there was only the "artistic." Therefore, again, nothing has happened except gesture and gaudy— sometimes bawdy—self-indulgence. Viewing the Fair, one cannot help wondering what might happen were the "system" in its present extremity to break? Something genuine in Creative Art might then get a break.

1. Frank Lloyd Wright, *A Testament* (New York: Horizon Press, 1957), p. 57.

THE TALIESIN FELLOWSHIP

A *proposal for a school for architecture and the allied arts had been drawn up as early as 1928. More fully developed in 1931 (pp. 39–49), the scheme was still too ambitious and therefore not carried out. But early in 1932 the idea of a school was revived by Wright, encouraged and assisted by his wife, Olgivanna, who reminded him, "It is not enough to leave behind you monuments of buildings, you owe it to future generations to leave monuments of human beings." The Taliesin Fellowship was conceived as an education based on apprenticeship training. Combining both their backgrounds in independent education, his through the original Hillside Home School, and hers through her training at the Gurdjieff Institute, the Wrights founded the Taliesin Fellowship and opened its doors to the first apprentices in October 1932. The prospectus that was sent out to architectural schools and friends clearly outlined the program and the intended plan for expanding the Taliesin complex. Various rooms and sections of Taliesin itself were remodeled to accommodate the new apprentices, several of whom arrived with their wives. A plan was drawn up to expand the original Hillside Home School buildings that Wright had designed for his aunts in 1896 and 1902. But, as with the plan of 1928–1931, it proved more than the Wrights could afford. Only the new drafting room was added to the north section of the existing building. In addition, the original gymnasium was converted to a theater-playhouse and several classrooms were converted into dormitory rooms for apprentices; these conversions did not take place all at once, but over a period of years.*

A second text was published in London Studio, *in December 1932, although parts were reprinted from the prospectus sent out from Taliesin beforehand.*

At the same time that the brochure of the Taliesin Fellowship was sent out, a list of "Friends of the Fellowship" was assembled, as an endorsement of the proposed school plan. Included among the two hundred names were Charles Robert Ashbee, Sophie Breslau, Albert and Elsa Einstein, Buckminster Fuller, Walter Gropius, Josef Hoffman, George Howe, Albert Kahn, Ely Kahn, Eric Mendelsohn, Lewis Mumford, Georgia O'Keeffe, Dorothy Parker, Diego Rivera, Eliel Saarinen, Carl Sandburg, Edward Steichen, Alfred Stieglitz, Leopold Stokowski, Mies van der Rohe, and Alexander Woollcott. The text for the prospectus was revised several times during 1932 and 1933, and again in 1943, when it was incorporated into Wright's revised and expanded An Autobiography.

Of the various "editions" of the Taliesin Fellowship prospectus, the one dated December 1933 and reproduced here contains the most text, especially a section on the ills and crimes of the educational system for architecture at work in the nation at that time—a harsh criticism still seemingly appropriate today.

A few paragraphs of historical background dealing with the Hillside Home School were originally published by Wright in 1941 in a revised brochure for the Taliesin Fellowship. The text, however, seems more appropriately inserted here and takes its place as a meaningful introduction to Wright's description of a new school, but with a philosophy strongly based on that of 1886. [Prospectus, published by the Taliesin Fellowship, December 1933]

Taliesin Fellowship Complex. Spring Green, Wisconsin. 1932. Aerial perspective. Pencil and color pencil on tracing paper, 21x18".
FLLW Fdn#3301.001

⟊ TRUTH AGAINST THE WORLD, WAS A DRUID SYMBOL CUT into a block of sandstone set by an old Welsh stone-man into the walls of the Lloyd Jones Sisters' Home School—the first co-educational home school anywhere to be found. Later the ancient symbol appeared on the stone gate posts of the family chapel in the "Valley."[1] Later still it appeared in sandstone walls of the new school buildings built for "the maiden sisters" by their nephew.

The old Welsh stone-man carved the symbol in the stone but it was there by wish and will of the spirit of the sisters and five brothers. It was the Lloyd Jones family crest, as a matter of fact, and came over from Wales with Grandfather Richard Lloyd Jones. This unique home-school founded on democratic non-sectarian lines had Francis Parker for patron saint. And Francis Parker bowed his head to John Dewey. Liberal faith—liberal thought, teaching liberality and trying to live it. Within severely restricted means they lived on their old homestead of 160 acres of rolling farmland surrounded by five other farms—their brothers'. "The girls," as their brothers called them, carried on this brave enterprise to the point, so some said, where there was no intolerance quite so intolerant as the Lloyd Jones' intolerance of intolerance. Of course they couldn't make any money. As the years went by they gradually sank deeply into debt for one reason or another, but principally, I imagine, because of the "Truth against the World." They took about sixty boys and girls at a time, pupils ranging from eleven to nineteen years of age (some younger), and, of all things, undertook by maintaining there some thirteen teachers to fit most of them for college.

Mary Ellen Chase was one of their teachers, and she has given us their priceless portraits. Well, the usual took place. Divorced parents and other unfortunate people sent their children into the care of these noble women. For several years the children's tuition and board would be paid. Some mighty fine folk entrusted their young to the Hillside Home School. Mothering these youngsters they became like their own. Payments ceased in too many cases as the years wore on, but the children stayed. The Aunts couldn't send them away just for that. Beloved and loving, they managed along somehow until 1910. The accidental death of Uncle James, whose ambitious paper they had co-signed, ruined them. They never quite recovered from the loss of Uncle James.

I was their favorite nephew and from the very beginning came to the school to spend a few days with them now and then. Some of the happiest days of my life. I got some of my clients interested in helping to build the new school buildings which were their pride and glory. A client, Susan Lawrence Dana, built a little chemical laboratory and an art room for them. All had gone on again pretty well until 1915 when again the too many teachers were unpaid and the amount of the uncollectable tuition fees had mounted into many thousands. The beloved aunts had grown old without knowing it. No one would place any confidence in the two lone old ladies under a hopeless burden of debt, and their alumni were helpless or strangely indifferent. Somebody had to rescue them from a second "proceedings." Fortunately, I could do it.

I could borrow the money and the aunts, now retiring, gave the school buildings and grounds to me. But neither of them survived long after the beloved work was gone. Both passed away about 1917–1918. I promised them before they died that I would see the work they had begun in liberal education carried on in some fashion. So when misfortune overtook me, too, in 1927 and there were no buildings to build anywhere anymore for me, or anybody else, I turned to the 1902 buildings fast falling to ruin and the promise I meant to keep somehow, sometime, and wondered. . . .

Why not make architects while there was time to do it? I would bring the buildings back by putting young people to work on them, using what money they could pay as tuition to buy materials to work with and food for us all. In this matter of food I thought the farm would be a great help. So the Taliesin Fellowship of apprentices to Frank Lloyd Wright was born. Some 19 responded, paying $650.00 that year. Fortunately I had found in my wife, Olgivanna, a partner in sympathy with all this. What we did with their labor and their money for the first several years until my own earning power came back, you will glimpse in these pages.

The Fellowship is still very young, born in 1932. But the Fellowship still has the background of liberal education established by the Lloyd Jones sisters. ⁄ι\ (Truth against the World) has a new lease of life for another lifetime—the generation after theirs—perhaps to continue the generation after mine. In any form, truth has all the persistence there is. The old school neglected by me for many years is coming back to young life again working along another line toward the same end—indigenous culture for our democracy. The line of endeavor is somewhat changed, that is all.

I often wish those grand old grey heads—my mother's with them and her grey bearded stalwart brothers, my uncles, could come in and sit down by our new fireplace in the new draughting room—we are most proud of that draughting room—and how proud they would be too. Their satisfaction I know would be greater than mine. I could look at them all on such good terms with myself now for having kept faith with them—the nephew looked upon by all but his mother and his maiden aunts as a kind of unknown quantity probably coming to no good end and "what a pity." Bless them all.

OUR CAUSE

Paper inflation and overproduction have characterized education in our country for a half-century or more. We have manufactured white-collarites, both sexes, by the million, and they are on our hands now, "for better or for worse." Textbook and classroom education by way of "credits" and "degrees" has inflated utterly commonplace intelligences far beyond their merits. And this inflation of the unfit, this mass production of the candidate for a white collar job somewhere, somehow, is more serious than we seem to imagine. I do not know how far the machine, once man's slave, has conquered its master, but I do know the old traditions are broken or breaking down and thousands of young men and young women are wandering about the States with little hope of the good life enjoyed by their forefathers. Every day it is becoming more difficult to be a decent failure, the prevailing success is so outrageous. By "new deal" and ultimatum, to get the system started again we are trying hard to make all the sad

mistakes all over again and at the slightest sign of improvement there is a selfish rush to play the game once more. The "game" has many angles and incidents, but only one net result: as the result of the gamble in education—more impotence, and as a result of the economic gamble—more poverty.

Taliesin is concerned with the impotence that is the consequence of the gamble in education, believing young America over-educated and under-cultured: sex overemphasized, present sex social differentiations absurd or obscene. Nor does Taliesin believe the "artist" has any special claim to divinity such as he arrogates to himself. As the usual "graduate" is educated far beyond his capacity, so the "artist" sacrifices manhood to a bag of tricks, a mere pose or seeming. Both are insignificant—there is no health nor any strength in them. Personality gets in the way of the quality of individuality genuinely divine in man and that relates him nobly to all men. The being that is unconcerned with seeming has found in our life little soil in which to grow. As the "American" people our ingenuity is unquestioned. Intellectually we function in the glittering generality pretty well and for certain specific purposes very well. But where the deeper needs of men are concerned (we speak of these needs as Art and Religion)—we beg or borrow or steal what we have and assume the virtue we have not. Nor do I

Frank Lloyd Wright and apprentices working on model. Chandler, Arizona. 1933. FLLW Fdn FA#6606.0004

doubt that, in the large, we have been cut off from the life-giving sources of inspiration by the very means we take to find and reach them. Take youth away from the ground, put growth on hard pavements and pigeon-hole it in the city—and the first step has been taken toward future impotence. Herd youth in schools and colleges, text-book and classroom the growing period, and what have you but vicarious power in the hands and a cigarette in the mouth? Send the more self-indulgent, egotistic youths to Art Institutes and again the vicarious life and the insignificant "me." Technique and nothing to do with it. Men of vision? Men of deep feeling? Men to create life anew and the strength to meet defeat in that cause? Not much of any of these qualities. Our youth runs more and more to journalese and the wisecrack. Stimulants an inevitable craving. And youth will have to function in fashion, the critical faculty stimulated with no valid basis for criticism; choice predetermined in various shallow or narrow grooves; personality more and more mistaken for individuality; mechanical horse-power or kilowatt mistaken for personal power. Noble selfhood run down into ignoble selfishness. The salt and savor of life that is joy in work soon runs stale in any academic formula whatsoever or in any attempt at "institution." A stale sap is the consequence. How can this knowledge-factory-education really culture any individual for the wrestle with machine-leverage owned by selfish interests, or encourage in man the interpretation of life in an era unprecedented in all the essential factors of the artifex? Education has gone on until, dropped from the present scheme of things, are these two great inner experiences, fructifying sources of good life—Art and Religion. Both, by way of education, have gone to seed. Seed on the barren soil capitalistic centralization has become where man-growth is concerned.

Architecture is the harmonious nature of all structure whatsoever, and a sense of valid structure in our culture is what we most lack. In steel, pulp, glass, and in the multiple powers of machinery and the basis for life they should bring with them, we have greater resources for new form than ever existed before and greater facility for failure. And it is a knowledge of architecture in this broad, organic sense that is essentially not only the salvation of twentieth-century life but

An apprentice cutting stone.1933. FLLW Fdn FA#6501.0126

it is the natural opportunity for a great culture. The very basis of our future as a civilization. An architect of an organic social order would then be our statesman. The poet and philosopher would be an architect of an organic social life. The architecture of sound it was that intrigued Bach and Beethoven as music and this will inform our musicians. The architect himself on this natural or organic basis is necessarily the useful interpreter of the life of his era. Search for new forms is particularly his because we live in them and we live by them. If we had them we would be only too happy to live for them. Painting and sculpture are features of such architecture. As for literature, the writer committed to the literal knows less of architecture in this sense—and unfortunately this writer is almost the only writer we have. By way of him the liberal has invaded, confused, and corrupted the plastic arts. In all artists must lie these deeper appreciations and realizations that, consciously or unconsciously, have always recreated, refreshed and lifted life above pleasure into joy. Our society knows pleasure but knows how little joy; knows excitement but knows no gaiety; has lost innocence of heart in exchange for an arid sophistication that may debunk anything but can make nothing but machinery. Reverence is dead. Even reverence for money is dying. To machine-power we do reverence, still, but essentially human powers and human values are in the discard while we pretend to do them honor, expecting to get around to them again some day—somehow.

Well, Taliesin believes the day has come for art in this more simple organic sense to take the lead in this thing we miscall "Education"; believes the time over-ripe for a rejection of the too many minor traditions in favor of great elemental Tradition that is decentralization; sees a going forward in new spirit to the ground as the basis for a good life that sets the human soul free above artificial anxieties and all vicarious powers, able and willing to work again as the first condition of true gentility. Taliesin sees work itself where there is something growing and living in it as not only the salt and savor of existence but as the opportunity for bringing "heaven" decently back to Earth where it really belongs. Taliesin sees art as no less than ever the expression of a way of life in this machine age if its civilization is to live. Yes we must go forward, feet on the ground, with all our mechanical leverage made more simple and effective, to a new realization of human values in everything. By simple measure of the man as a man and new standards of human values in "success" it expects to measure the man for a nobler environment and beget in him a better correlation of sense and factor. Taliesin is not a back-to-the-land movement. No. Nor is Taliesin interested in art for art's sake. Not at all. But means to go forward, feet on the ground, seeing art as man's practical appreciation of the gift of life by putting his sense of it into the things he makes to live with and in the way he lives with them. When he makes them he must make them his own and make them worthy of his spirit. When he does that he will know well how to live with them to greater purpose and with greater satisfaction of the demand real men make upon themselves.

The language of an ideal? Guilty. The moth, rust and corruption that have broken in and stolen are not so easily defeated? Yes, easily defeated, but not by Utopia. It takes only faith and the ideal to defeat defeat where there is good work to be done and the capacity definitely to do it. Neither Faith nor Ideal are yet dead in our country although we have done our academic dollar-minded best to kill them, seeing both as the sentimentality they have mostly become. But Faith and the Ideal are alive at Taliesin in spite of "the system" and in some ways more alive because of it; not insensible of what has been achieved in the way of useful tools but determined to make better use of efficiencies for the humanity that has bought them at a terrible price. As a people we may see, now, that they have cost too much. The Fellowship is an experiment? Inevitably an experiment. But one that knows direction definitely from experience. The experiment may fail but if a failure, even so more valuable to life in our extremity at the end of this epoch than so many of the successes we have acclaimed or achieved in the past. A few more such successes and we will know no future!

As to the young men and women who are voluntary apprentices: watching their work—I was about the new group of buildings when several apparently well-educated people came up and, all together asked: "Can you tell us what they are building here?" "Yes, they are building a refuge from the universities. There is now no place to lay one's head," and walked away to let them figure it out for themselves. And I suppose the impertinence does come to something like that. A group of volunteers: no courses, no credits, no examinations, no teaching. A work in progress and many refugees from "Education" doing always all they can do to help it forward wherever the work lies and whatever it may be. Meantime they are being as natural and kind as is possible to intelligent social human beings designing and creating a new integrity in the atmosphere of environment conscious of the design of the whole as organic. Conscious of the design of the whole together with old masters in their craft, they are felling trees, sawing them into lumber, quarrying rock and burning lime to lay the rock in the wall. Laying the hewn stones in the wall. Sculpturing likely stones and carving likely blocks of wood. Turning the sawed lumber into structure, trusses and furniture. Plastering walls, frescoing them. Digging ditches, working in the fields with the ground. Washing dishes, caring for their own rooms. Planting and harvesting. Making roads. Farming, planning, working, kitchenizing and philosophizing in voluntary co-operation in an atmosphere of natural loveliness they are helping to make eventually habitable. A consistency seldom seen in any country. Here is building, painting, music, sculpture, motion as good work. All together working out a greater correlation than they have known, toward an end dimly foreseen, it is true. But why not relax, work hard, and enjoy the journey? What worthwhile ideal was ever reached except to find realization still—beyond. It was the poet and philosopher Cervantes who said—"the road is always better than the inn." So Taliesin is a way of life. Action is a form of idea and idea is, as surely, a form of action in that life.

But action in the sense known at Taliesin is unthinkable as "academic." Good correlation, a good background, sane feeling for what we call the work of art and ability to work with some initiative are the essential qualifications for the apprenticeship which is a practical form of the co-operative competition that is growth. Individual initiative must awaken in the apprentice or he will lose himself in unaccustomed freedom and become a nuisance or a betrayal. And yet in this freedom—sometimes seeming chaotic—here are being made better plans for all the special buildings needed by the farm, factory and countryside so badly, if we are ever going to get started again; rational, appropriate forms and better and more sensible furniture and utensils. More honestly significant painting and sculpture and music. We must have a better use of our industrial achievements where the user is concerned and more sane and beautiful ways of using our tools and synthetic and natural materials and we must have true and more rhythmic and free interpretation of life in all these things we live with and live by, most of all in ourselves. Fellowship at Taliesin is either making the necessary new forms or is going to make them soon, not blind to the sociological changes necessary if they are to become properly effective to society.

Music is architecture at Taliesin just as architecture is a kind of music. Music, being modern, is necessary to existence. Perhaps music as we already know it is the only modern among all the arts.

And Taliesin has a Tradition—that of an organic architecture for America. A center line for a valid culture. Love, Sincerity, Determination, and Courage not reserved for heroes but the common-sense basis of any life worth living. As for economic basis this relaxed and more or less spontaneous activity in which the novitiate may be lost or find himself, the Fellowship has a two-hundred-acre farm, and as another there are yearly fees fixed at about what a medium-grade college education would cost plus work the apprentice can do. Eventually, paid services to Industry in architectural research will contribute substantially to put the tools needed into the hands of the workers and reduce or eventually abolish the fee so worthwhile young men and women may work for their living not as education but as culture. Out of this endeavor is coming an appropriate—somewhat cosmic—place in which to live and in which to work for and with America. And play, although when work is play—mere play becomes rather irksome at times. The margin of leisure here is no problem, nor is overproduction, nor is the length of the working day. Competition is a form of voluntary co-operation. Institution and routine is avoided where possible. Here is a workplace, rather, and a decent way of life as spontaneous as still may be so that growth may be joy—not the too much pain it has become in current effort. Our textbook is the one book of creation itself. Our classrooms are the various workshops of the artist.

OUR PLAN

An extension of the work of Taliesin to include seven and seventy workers in the arts. Frank Lloyd Wright Architect and a group of six honor men having the status of seniors in music, painting, sculpture, drama, motion and philosophy together with a group of seventy qualified apprentices chosen for work to be done. These with technical advisors in the various crafts constitute the Taliesin Fellowship. Leaders in thought from many countries visit the Fellowship some residing here temporarily.

INTEGRATION

Fundamental architecture is the first essential of organic living and fruitful culture in this work at Taliesin. The generation of life and art alike cannot be taught, only experienced. Social, industrial, and eco-

Living room, Taliesin. Spring Green, Wisconsin. 1925. Photograph by Hedrich-Blessing, courtesy the Chicago Historical Society. FLLW Fdn FA#2501.0241

nomic processes must be integrated with life. In no other way can life be harmonious. Left to their own selfish devices both devastate the whole fabric of creation. No compromise between what we call art and commercialized industry can ever be creative. If we are eventually to have appropriate organic forms as worthwhile expressions of our machine-age life the original work will be done where workers themselves have as a way of life spontaneous recourse to practical modern machine-shops and general modern working conditions; and have at the same time the benefit of inspirational fellowship in the arts and machine crafts. Voluntary apprenticeship and work provide this in the desired measure.

The Taliesin Fellowship is an apprenticeship to a work, itself a living tradition, in this constructive sense, and chooses to live and work in the country where constant contact with the nature of the ground and with nature growth are the most valuable of texts when the contacts are forms of experience directly related to work.

The Fellowship buildings practicing what the Fellowship preaches are a simple expression of indigenous architecture and are being constructed by the Fellowship itself. All are located in a group on State Highway 23 in southern Wisconsin near the Wisconsin River upon a two-hundred-acre farm about forty miles from Madison and three miles from the nearest village. The integrity of this architecture is an important feature in the life of the Fellowship

and although many of the buildings are completed or are well along every apprentice will have a share in extending the group of buildings. The way of life is simple; meals in common; fixed hours for all work, recreation and sleep. Rooms for individual study and rest. Imaginative entertainment is a feature of the home life. Music, drama, literature, the cinema of our own and other countries. Evening conferences with musicians, writers, artists and scientists who visit the Fellowship or are invited to sojourn. The beautiful region itself is a never-failing source for recreation and inspiration.

The Fellowship aims, first, to develop a well-correlated, creative human being with a wide horizon but capable of effective communication of his faculties upon the circumstances in which he lives.

There is no age limit qualifying Fellowship as long as the quality of youth and the spirit of co-operation of the apprentice is characteristic. There is no specific time for entering or leaving the Fellowship except that no apprenticeships are accepted for less than one year. But qualifications of each applicant—(good background and correlation of faculties foremost among them)—will finally be decided upon by Mr. Wright after a month's trial in actual work. To learn to draw well what he sees as the best means to further develop and maintain necessary correlation is a primary requirement. The first experimental units are those of architectural construction and design, research in technical industrial engineering, the philosophy of architecture, the

Living room, Taliesin. Spring Green, Wisconsin. 1925. Photograph by Hedrich-Blessing, courtesy the Chicago Historical Society.
FLLW Fdn FA#2501.0240

construction of models of architectural projects. And with a more complete consciousness of the design of the whole materials are taken directly from their sources: felling trees, sawing them into lumber, turning lumber into structure, trusses, furniture, block carvings; quarrying rock and burning lime to lay the hewn stones in the wall; sculpturing them; plastering; digging; working in the field, planting and harvesting; making roads. Planning, working, and philosophizing in voluntary co-operation in an atmosphere that has the integrity of natural loveliness. In the Taliesin Playhouse there has been and will be seen a series of fine films projected by the excellent Western Electric sound equipment, films composed and directed by such masters as Eisenstein, René Clair, Murnau, Chaplin, Disney, Pabst and other productions of fine character. The sound equipment is wired to speakers in other buildings of the group, in the living room and in the balcony of a central studio. Pianos are located in the studios and living room for apprentices to play. Facilities exist in the Playhouse for amateur theatricals. The Playhouse has a flexible stage, dressing rooms, rooms for designing and making sets and is adapted to concerts, lectures, and fellowship gatherings as well as theater and cinema.

Music making. The spirit of creation at work for the time when music will be made directly for a perfect "interpreter"—not human, perhaps, but humanly devised. At Taliesin is already the beginning—the becoming—of a natural simple music made unaffectedly for joy: imagination in terms of sound—from voice and instrument treated as integral with our architecture, indigenous with it as are all other arts. Inspiration in the making and playing of music, by the making and playing of music of the great living masters. Initiative by the apprentices in preparing music as self-expression. Demonstration by an enthusiastic co-operative manufacturing and collecting of simple instruments, a resource of great variable qualities. Not only group-playing but group-singing.

Painting, drawing, sculpture and motion. Experiments to bring these expressions closer to the architecture of life, or life as architecture. Arts must reveal themselves as essential living and culture both, spontaneous as may be.

Among present activities also are the designing and making of furniture to complete the Fellowship buildings. These furnishings are done by the apprentices together with masters in the crafts. Weaving will start a new supply of textiles and fabrics for use here. As soon as possible other units will be in operation in the Fellowship: Photography and Printing among them. Publishing is projected. Monographs, books, music, drawings, block prints, etc. These first units are to be followed as soon as possible by the shopwork of actual glass making, pottery, modern reproduction processes in many forms as we may find the help to establish these units so that men of Industry in the United States may find it worthwhile to co-operate with us or employ our research work.

After having had several years acquaintance with the actual performance of an apprentice, should the apprentice desire to leave the Fellowship a personal testimonial only will be given. The length of any apprenticeship beyond the initial year will be determined by the circumstances. During each working year a holiday of six weeks for each worker may be arranged if the worker so desires and the work permits.

Inasmuch as we are not a "Foundation," but to preserve direction, initiative and prompt action, an individual enterprise, the revenue for the first several years must come mainly from apprenticeship fees and the sustaining work of the apprentices. As the work grows, added to this may be compensation from industries for services rendered, sales of completed art objects, subscriptions to the various publications to be printed by the Fellowship and the contributions by the friends of the "Fellowship"—the equivalent of scholarship—or gifts of equipment from "Friends of the Fellowship," a group organized among those who believe in our work and are able to add scope to our usefulness. Fellows with sufficient experience in architecture may, if approved by the senior architect, bring individual commissions into the work of the Fellowship and sharing the work with the Fellowship, retain personal contact with the client. But the work will issue as the work of the Fellowship, not merely as the work of the individual. Compensation for such commissions to go fifty percent to the fellow and fifty to the Fellowship after deducting the cost of the work. Under the circumstances of such co-operation, the fee should be ten percent for Residence work, six percent for commercial work. Superintendence in every case is to be carried out by the individual architect, if he so elects, but satisfactory to the Fellowship.[2]

1. Sometimes called the Helena Valley, it is located three miles from Spring Green, Wisconsin, forty miles from Madison.
2. Seven hundred people have been Taliesin Fellowship apprentices since 1932.

Hillside Home School. Spring Green, Wisconsin. 1903. FLLW Fdn FA#0216.0003

934

ARCHITECTURE OF INDIVIDUALISM

When this article was published in the March–April issue of Trend, *it was accompanied by a preface from the editors:*

> *This is the first of a series of articles to be written by leading American architects, and which will appear in successive issues of* Trend. *Each writer will answer, in his own way, a number of questions similar to the following which Percival Goodman,* Trend's *architectural editor, asked Mr. Wright to answer in the accompanying article:*
>
> *1. What relation exists between the social, political and economic forces of our time and the architecture that is being created? In a planned society would there not be a restriction of individual taste?*
>
> *2. What is the future of architecture under mass production? Or a less general way of putting the question would be: mass-produced housing on the basis of a scientific study of structure, convenience and the like seems a most definite possibility. Mass design of buildings exists (the tremendous habitable areas of our skyscrapers equal to many square blocks of older type structures and mass designs of towns in Russia). Will not a few architects be sufficient to design the type-houses? Would architecture become a problem of engineering only, with the elimination of the individual as artist and the substitution of a new industry in which the laboratory and the testing machine become the symbol and the fact?*
>
> *3. Where does the school in Taliesin stand, in this connection? (Frank Lloyd Wright's School of Architecture.)*
>
> *4. If the answer to question two is that "taylorization," "Machines for living in" and the like are mere phrases or temporary phases; that the architect as artist, as philosopher, will remain—if you believe that architecture is an individual expression—what objection do you have to the works called "Internationale style," especially those of Le Corbusier?*

[Published in Trend, *March–April 1934]*

I. IS AN ARCHITECTURE BEING CREATED? I SUPPOSE IT IS, inevitably. Buildings are being built, which of course means that they must take some form. But the thought entering into the process is so exterior and so ignorant or unaware of nature—so superficially concerned with forms as a style that nothing can really grow out of the circumstances except more affectation of styles—the machine-modernistic being the latest affectation. I can only see that—such as it is—our architecture bears the same relation to the social, political, and economic forces of our time that confusion bears to confusion or affectation bears to chaos.

Yes. In a "planned society" there would be a restriction upon individual taste. And since individual taste is utterly insufficient to develop an architecture this would mean not so much loss so far as a creative architecture was concerned. But a formula would necessarily be substituted for individual taste and be enforced. What formula? How derived? By whom enforced? Would any formula be nearer the desired source, creation? I think not. Russia is an example of the consequences to date. Only as true sources of inspiration are open to artists and they are free to work upon the knowledge of principle they must possess can any people create a living architecture for itself. By way of taste would then mean not much more than the personal idiosyncrasy.

And in this organic sense the creative artist has always been more his epoch and his people than the epoch and the people are themselves because he is principle—articulate. They are not articulate. Nothing therefore that tends to deprive him of liberty and facility is wise where anything creative is sought because it must arise within the heart and mind of the race. The creative artist has always been, where expression in concrete terms is concerned, the heart and mind of his race. A planned society putting the artist—in this deeper sense—where he belongs in the plan might look for such an architecture in course of time.

II. Also, under any form of mass, say mass production, Architecture has a future only upon the same terms. Therefore the chance of creation in mass production is small because the planning and the production would necessarily tend to be merely or formally scientific. Or expedient. By merely or formally scientific I mean intellectual imagination exercised for its own sake or upon facts as a prime motive. By expedient I mean the same thing exercised for profit. "Realistic."

I think mass production need be no bar to creative effort if creative effort could give direction and control to production. In the present circumstances of capitalistic production such might be the case were capitalistic control aware of the need and was a fair judge of results. The same condition applies to any other form of society.

But "Mass design" is no design. No such thing can live. There may be design for mass or mass production certainly. But mass design would be only repetition of some formula. Design in this sense is precisely what the scientific process mentioned in your second question would get: a reiteration of form according to formula with no power to so inform the product that the true variety of life necessary to reproduction—or vitality—might issue.

So your question really is, as it seems to me, can individual feelings and ideals find individual expression or realization in the mass? And I should say Yes if the individual human feelings and ideals came first and the mass came afterward by natural addition and multiplication. The Interior Ideal, Development, Reality. If the mass is to come first—then how is it to be qualified? By division and subtraction from without? An unlikely process because who would there be to make either except by force? And what and whose force? The exterior ideal again. Enforcement. Realistic.

A single artist, great enough master of principles, could issue the mandates in accord with which a living architecture might function for the mass if enough latitude were given the artist and enough competent interpreters could be found to realize them. The quality of inspiration however would not be numerical in any case.

So to eliminate artistic individuality as the inspiring element in favor of the test tube and the mechanical laboratory would be to reduce art to an affair of the brain; music to mathematics, architecture to engineering, poetry to rhyme, philosophy to intellectual cerebration, religion to ritual, etc., etc. That is to say to leave the human heart and mind, typified by the creative artist, out of its own.

Now the mathematics of sound might be preferable to bad music. Good engineering certainly is, from my standpoint as an architect, preferable to the bad architecture of the moment, etc., etc. But why pose the situation? Is it not merely the age-old circumstance of rich and poor—great and small—high and low—alive and dead?

The position is, simply, do we prefer our architecture dead—our music dead—our philosophy and religion dead—prefer mechanistic symbols rather than the sentimental and foolish thing ignorance of scientific development has caused our art to become? But testing machines and tubes and machinery we would find poor enough symbols except as they symbolize more power for a richer, nobler and more humane life for mankind.

And the human feelings and ideals of great individuals, then, must they symbolize this life for the mass? Yes—more and more. For what mass can live as human growth when the quality, as individual, of the units that compose it is suppressed or dead?

III. Taliesin believes in putting the man before the mass: believes in qualifying him as an artist and by natural addition and multiplication—reaching the sum total—mass. Why not, then, more life in the mass—because the mass is consequence characterized by this developed quality in the individual? And the Taliesin view of the artist is that he is the mind and soul of this thing we call human life wherever its concrete expression of its growth is concerned and believes that insofar as the true artist as a valid interpretation of life exists in any man just so far will his life be valuable to Life. Aware of the necessary social changes implied—Taliesin sets quality before quantity believing the only salvation of any mass to be the quality of its units; and believes this as applied to every department of human endeavor or experience. Architecture thus becomes a natural feature of the natural life of a great Nature. Creative Architecture.

IV. Believing in Architecture as essentially the greatest of all human documents and the most reliable record of time, place, and man—naturally I believe that architecture should be an expression disciplined by ways and means peculiar to itself and to man in its time and place. That is to say disciplined from within. I believe also that this discipline should reach the point in its development where, in any fair retrospect the buildings that compose it may be said to definitely belong to that era—and so, in the large, might be referred to as a style. But I still believe that this mass product would only be seen as "creative" were the effect of a style subordinate and subsequent to the individual perceptions that gave each building composing the whole its own great individuality; good building in itself unconscious of itself as a feature of any style whatsoever. Style should be the architect's aim, not a style.

Into this category of individual works might fall Le Corbusier et al., until an attempt would be made to make Le Corbusier a style or the style. Then the growth of architecture would stop and such life as it had would depart from it. This was the case with the "Style Internationale." It soon became a formula any tyro could cliché and it soon became abhorrent to the feelings of the free man everywhere. Only academies and governments could ever look upon such narrow abstraction with tolerance. And in their case they would so look upon it only because, otherwise, they are impotent. It is from them that the compelling formula must come were the mass to come first.

After all, the gist of the argument is simply this: only from within can mass be truly qualified as life. All else is the Expedient.

WHAT IS THE MODERN IDEA?

In self-consciously simplistic terms, Frank Lloyd Wright here poses and qualifies the question, "What is the Modern Idea?" and then proceeds to answer it. The qualifications include his views of urban and rural life and a description of the "nature of materials." Once again he condemns the missed opportunities of the 1933 Chicago World's Fair, which he believes was nothing more than the 1893 fair with a facelift. Most of his explanations are rather broad, but the essay includes a very precise definition: "Actually, the modern idea is a definite turning away from the artificial, from the extreme, from the synthetic and back to the simple, the wholesome, the natural." [Published in Liberty *magazine, February 10, 1934]*

A REALLY GREAT AND SPLENDID REVOLUTION IS SWEEPING through this country. It is a bloodless revolution, but before it is over it will see the death of the city and all that the city stands for as a dwelling place.

Idleness and privation have given the American people a lot of time for thought and a lot to think about—but they started thinking about these things long before the Depression. They started thinking about them when the word "modern" came into common use.

There is probably no word in the English language today more misused, more misunderstood. To the average mind it suggests the extreme in everything. Extreme artificiality. Extreme efficiency. The result of straining men's minds and men's bodies to produce something new, something different.

Actually, the modern idea is a definite turning away from the artificial, from the extreme, from the synthetic and back to the simple, the wholesome, the natural. And in no way is this more clearly reflected than in the present style of interior decoration and modern architecture with their severely simple lines, their total absence of ginger-bread trimmings, their natural grace and their reaching out for sun and air.

The ever-increasing migration of city people out into the country and suburbs where there is no false premium on fresh air, sunshine, green grass, trees, and all the wholesome natural simplicity that they stand for is another symptom of the modern idea. So is the popularity of roof gardens and penthouse apartments.

Modern life is beginning to see, in the far-reaching motor highways, a horizontal line leading to freedom for human life here on earth. By means of this simple release through the machine power that made the automobile you are going to see the death of the city.

It is no longer modern to build or to consent to live in any prettified cavern or take pleasure or pride in any glorified cave, however grand. All that is old.

Freedom is the keynote of the modern idea. And soon every man will have the facility to roam the ground or sky with a perfect freedom of vision that will relate him to the ground and all that the ground should mean to human life.

The modern gifts of glass, of stressed steel, of electromagnetic sciences began a new era. All are the simple natural agents of a new freedom for mankind. They are at work. No power can turn them aside now.

Whole walls through which the sun and light may pass can now be easily made of glass. It is replacing cumbersome and costly metals in the manufacture of countless articles.

In many instances, as an aid to beauty, glass has no equal.

Another of man's supermaterials—steel—is another direct means to this same liberation. Still others are the new textiles which, as shimmering robes, clothe the interior spaciousness within the shells of glass and metals that are replacing the offending hulks of masonry in which we have been living.

Working with these supermaterials for twentieth-century freedom are mobilization, teletransmission, widespread publicity, and the power of the machine.

So the modern building, an enemy to the city, is fast rising—true sun acceptance; a shaft of light flashing in the sun; still a true defense against time and the elements; no less a true shield for privacy.

All of this beauty of modern architecture is going into the country, its true and perfect setting. And when emancipated from the metropolis, then let the new buildings lie long and lie low, flowing lazily on the mesa or upon the ledges of the hillsides—streaks of light enmeshed in metal strands, as music is made of notes.

Great art as interpreter of twentieth-century life is not yet dead. But the only interpreter to show America the way now is what we may call great architecture when we understand the meaning of the term. We have great artists living today who are capable of giving to the world the utmost in beauty, but before we can appreciate their gifts we must first know the beauty that is simplicity. And the truth that is freedom.

The ancient man power that built the least and the greatest of decadent and dead civilizations still lives. That same ancient man power, multiplied infi-

nitely now, may build for us a civilization that will live forever because the drive comes from our interior ideal of an interior life, externalized as the great architecture of a great life. That is the thought which we call the modern idea.

To preserve, amplify, and make use of the gifts of our own time no matter what the effort, is the business of this new life of freedom—and is the modern idea.

All that has made our cities a landlord's triumph—is not the modern idea. The impoverishment of our agrarian areas—is not the modern idea.

The turning of splendid American youth into "white-collar" men by sending them into already crowded cities in search of soft jobs where at least one hand may be kept in the pocket—is not the modern idea.

The periodic weakening of our economic system is because the modern idea is ignored or misunderstood.

The modern idea does not permit the city to exist as a conspiracy to destroy man's freedom. Nor does it propose to let American architecture remain the bad form of surface decoration that it is—offering the same old Columbian Fair of 1893, with its face lifted, as "progress" in 1933.

The modern idea refuses to make man himself a form of property, resents any attempt to standardize him as a piece of property, or power to "break" him.

The modern idea does not allow the universities to deprive the American youth of such correlation as he has to turn his head into an empty tool box.

The modern idea sees the banker as no more than a snubbing post, banking on yesterday, betraying tomorrow.

The modern idea today is Freedom with a large F. Only today is modern—with its enlarged and increasing machine power working for man's freedom.

The ideal of the dignity and worth of the individual as an individual is modern.

In other words, a sense of the *within* unfolding by interior content to genuine outward self-expression—that is the gist of the modern idea.

Life is learning to see itself as free.

THE TWO-ZONE HOUSE—SUITED TO COUNTRY, SUBURB, AND TOWN

In 1934, Wright designed and issued a magazine, Taliesin, *that contained several articles and illustrations about the work and events at Taliesin and in the Taliesin Fellowship. Printed in two colors, the general texts were written by fellowship members, with further articles by Heinrich de Fries and Stamo Papadaki. A running text by Wright, printed in red ink, serves as the editorial leader. Wright discusses many issues and events as well as general philosophical views on architecture. The feature article, if it can be called that, is devoted to "The Two-Zone House—Suited to Country, Suburb, and Town." In answer to a challenge by Dorothy Johnson Field, who later amplified the same ideas in her book* The Human House, *Wright designed the two-zone house discussed in this selection. Mrs. Field's main point: a house has two centers, a center of activity and a center of quiet, and should be designed accordingly. The text is illustrated by plans and views of the three types, based on one idea, that constitute this prototype for housing for the United States. Out of this early project of 1934, Wright's Usonian house, his solution for the modern dwelling of the American of moderate means, would evolve in 1936. [Published in* Taliesin, Journal of the Taliesin Fellowship, *1934]*

THIS LETTER FROM HOUSEWIFE FIELD CAME AT AN OPPORtune moment. I read it to the apprentices—the council ring that gathers at tea time in whatever seem appropriate circumstances at the time. And it provoked much discussion. Much good sense characterized both letter and action. Here was something valuable. Testimony from the field of action. I decided to work upon the idea and in the folder herewith devoted to the Two-Zone house you have the result of the studies provoked by the housewife who seemed to take "housing" more seriously and intelligently than most architects do or can do.

The letter from housewife Field is directly responsible for the germ plan of the Two-Zone house. New facilities make it desirable to lay aside the provincial squeamishness that made the American parlor and designedly make a beautiful circumstance to take the place of the kind of kitchen that should now go where the parlor went sometime ago. With modern kitchen appurtenances what used to be the kitchen can now become a high spacious "work studio" opening level with the garden. Therefore the zone of activity may be a natural get-together place in which to live while at work. In this "Two-Zone plan" the utility-stack has economically standardized and concentrated within it all appurtenance systems entering into modern house construction: oil burning boiler and fuel tanks—air compressors, oil and gasoline supply for car, heating and air conditioning units, electric wiring and plumbing, vent and smoke flues. This enlarged hollow chimney—about six by eight feet on the ground—is accessible from the coat-room and so placed that only one short run (the horizontal pipe or wire run to the study) is necessary. Each bathroom, entire, is a one-piece standardized fixture directly connected to the stack. Kitchen sink, ranges and refrigeration likewise. Here as the nexus of the arrangement is a complete standardization in factory-production of the wasteful tangled web of wires and piping at present involved in the construction of the ordinary dwelling. Thus the cost of about one-third of the usual home is here reduced to a certainty and one-half of one-third of the cost is saved.

The carport has been "entered" as integral feature of the dwelling, convenient and not the gaping hole it usually is as built in now. The features that distinguish the Two-Zone house from the Norm of the early One-Zone house given out from the same source about 1901 are the utilities concentration called the utilities stack, the development of the kitchen into the real living room completely furnished as part of the whole, and the segregation of space called the study. A third zone—call it the slumber zone—is introduced as a mezzanine with a balcony opening into the living room or "work room." While the children are young, each member of the household has a dressing room and "sleeps out." When they grow up, by a few simple changes, indicated in mezzanine number two, each has a private room. Here are self-contained econo-

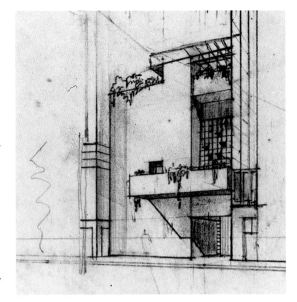

Zoned Houses (Project). 1934. City House perspective. Pencil on tracing paper, 13 x 9". FLLW Fdn#3502.003

mies for the family as a self-contained unit in society, more natural and yet more orderly than is possible under conditions popular at present.

This germ-plan would easily adapt itself, as indicated, to the several standard conditions of the small house in suburb, town and country. The suburban house is shown lighted largely from above—to avoid the more or less indecent exposure most suburban houses suffer from because they try to be little country houses on lots 50 feet wide on the street.

Zoned Houses (Project). 1934. Suburban House perspective. Pencil on tracing paper, 7 x 5". FLLW Fdn#3502.009

The town house is tall, all rooms having high ceilings. The entire house is to be hermetically sealed from dirt and noise, and air conditioned with opportunity to go out to view the passing show on occasions, but viewing only when moved and also opportunity to live outside "up top" where greenery can see the sky. The utility-stack and bathrooms, workroom, segregated study and segregated slumber rooms of this townhouse all keep to the scheme of the suburban house.

The country house keeps to the same scheme. Its outer walls are mostly a matter of metal and glass screens and the plan is opened wide to sun, air and vista. More a spreading good-time-place is possible in country life.

The designs could utilize different materials by modifying structural details, only. The simple type of exterior we have indicated would lend itself either to synthetic sheet, to slab construction or to wood frame with plastered metal covering. Were brick or stone to be used the walls would be thicker, reducing floor space somewhat without any other necessary changes because the upper story is, in every case, mostly glass and would need the protecting roof planes for protection. The roofs in suburb and country also might be utilized if surroundings and circumstances made it desirable. There is no basement. It has disappeared. The main floor is made directly upon a concrete mat laid over dry filling well drained.

This Two-Zone suburban house complete with standardized utility-stack built in synthetic sheets of metal, wood and plaster, or other materials should not cost over six thousand dollars for garage, three bedrooms, two bathrooms and commodious living quarters. Probably where conditions are favorable and prefabrication possible such a house could come within a four-thousand-dollar cost limit where no slabs would be taken from the appropriation by "financing" charges or too large a profit taken by the system.

The servant has no domicile in a house of this type. The whole idea of "servant" would vulgarize the kind of life suited to the house. Outside help coming in at stated times—being more professional and should be all the labor the modern housewife would need with her modern labor-saving devices and a proper regard for bringing up the young to accept normal responsibilities in the household.

Zoned Houses (Project). 1934. Country House plan. Pencil on tracing paper, 19 x 8". FLLW Fdn#3502.016

THE BAD LANDS

Frank Lloyd Wright wrote extensively on the beauty and inspiration to be derived from nature, which he invariably chose to spell with a capital N. In this extraordinary letter to his client Robert Lusk, published in the newspaper that Lusk edited, Wright gives a most dramatic and poetic description of the beauty of America's natural features that he saw on a trip through the Badlands of South Dakota. [Published in The Evening Huronite, *Huron, South Dakota, September 28, 1935]*

DEAR BOB: I HAVE BEEN LAID UP FOR 3 DAYS BUT AM FIT once more. You are a good soldier and I too hope I can come out to see you all again. I am writing a note to "Spitz" thanking him. Publicity might be such a worthy power in a place like the U.S.A. if it were in the hands of worthy men; well, like you, of course. Or anything else? But think of Hearst *et al.!*

Speaking of our trip to the Big Bad Lands, Black Hills, and Spearfish Canyon: I've been about the world a lot and pretty much over our own country; but I was totally unprepared for that revolution called the Dakota Bad Lands. From Mitchell, Paul Bellamy was driving a fair seventy over the brown Dakota prairie to reach the Bad Lands before sunset. About four, afternoon, something came into view that made me sit up straight and look at Bellamy to see if he saw what I saw. "Oh," said he,

"you've seen nothing yet." But I had. What I saw gave me an indescribable sense of mysterious otherwhere—a distant architecture, ethereal, touched, only touched with a sense of Egyptian, Mayan drift and silhouette. As we came closer a templed realm definitely stood ambient in air before my astonished "scene"-loving but scene-jaded gaze. The streamline working on a vast plateau of solid cream white clay, something like "calichi," had sculptured this familiar world into one unfamiliar but entrancing.

Endless trabeations surmounted by or rising into pyramid (obelisk) and temple, ethereal in color and exquisitely chiseled in endless detail, they began to reach to infinity, spreading into the sky on every side; an endless supernatural world more spiritual than earth but created out of it. As we rode, or seemed to be floating upon a splendid winding road that seemed to understand it all and just where to go, we rose and fell between its delicate parallels of rose and cream and sublime shapes, chalk white, fretted against a blue sky with high floating clouds; the sky itself seemed only there to cleanse and light the vast harmonious building scheme.

Of course I am an architect and that ride through the land of pure line and evanescent color affected me strangely. Here was the element, architecture, cut of the body of the ground itself, beggaring human imagination, prostrating the simplicities of man before the great cosmic simplicity. Reverence, yes, awe. Deep satisfaction, harmonious like great music drifted over the senses until a new sacred realm was born of light, delicate color and ever changing but immaculate form wherein not even the senses could touch bottom, top, nor sides of its vast repose.

Here, for once, came complete release from materiality. Communion with what man often calls "God" is inevitable in this place. It is everywhere around him and when the man emerges to the brown plateau and looks back, as I did, the sun now setting, a pale moon rising in darkening rose and blue sky as rays of last light drifted over, linking drifting water lines of dark rose in pallid creamy walls, gently playing with the skyline, with mingled obelisks, terraces and temples more beautiful than thought, eternal, who knows, a strange sense of inner experience will come to him of a crisis in his perception of what he has termed beauty. He will leave that place a more humble, seeking soul than when he went in to this pure appeal to his spirit. He will know baptism in its higher than sectarian sense. Let sculptors come to the Bad Lands. Let painters come. But first of all the true architect should come. He who could interpret this vast gift of nature in terms of human habitation so that Americans on their own continent might glimpse a new and higher civilization certainly, and touch it and feel as they lived in it and deserved to call it their own. Yes, I say the aspects of the Dakota Bad Lands have more spiritual quality to impart to the mind of America than anything else in it made by man's God.

I turned to Bellamy and finally said, "But how is it that I've heard so little of this miracle and we,

toward the Atlantic, have heard so much of the Grand Canyon when this is even more miraculous?"

"Oh," said he slyly, "we are not on the through line to the coast."

"Never mind," I said, "all the better eventually." And we drove on to the famous Black Hills which the fame of Borglum's work had already brought to my attention.

Next day, Bellamy again at the wheel, from fine little Rapid City, well set in low hills (what could not that town do for itself if it knew how to live accordingly), several of us drove up another finely laid-out road that seemed to know what the region was all about, through scenery I had often heard of as beautiful. But a more flesh and blood kind of beauty. The beauty that appeals surely to a human being because he is human and brother to the tree and respects individualistic rock formations. Here they are great but not too great. All has the charm of human scale, which many great Western scenes lack, and invites the wanderer to enter into the spirit of it all and rest. No home for man the Rocky Mountains; no, nor perhaps the Bad Lands, yet; but an ideal home; these Black Hills. Do not think from this that the Hills are unexciting. They are exciting but they stir a different region of the soul; we call it the heart probably. There are stone needles, stone spires, stone piles and stone blades, artificial lakes, tall beautiful pines, wooded gorges, more free-standing and sculptured rock masses in nature's own style than one has ever seen before grouped in one area. So it seems fitting that some hand of man should brush aside the realistic veil of a stained, weathered rock and let the mind of man himself envision his own greatness and his fate alongside the titanic handiwork of nature. Human nature, let us hope eventually nature's higher nature, found its hand for this in Gutzon Borglum's masterhand and the face of the great leader of his country. The noble countenance emerges from Rushmore as though the spirit of the mountain had heard a human prayer and itself became a human countenance. The countenance haunts you as you ride rises; winds and falls with you as freight through depths of pine woods; huge rocks standing about you, themselves statues of a more elemental

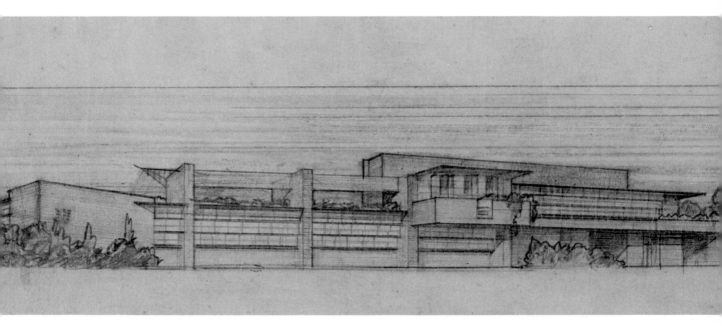

Stanley Marcus House (Project). Dallas, Texas. 1935. Perspective. Pencil and color pencil on tracing paper, 13 x 5". FLLW Fdn#3501.002

thought than Gutzon Borglum's: the cosmic urge.

We passed by a quiet land-locked lake (Stockade Lake) that seems to be there with a man-made white sand shore to invite you to get out and stay and rest and drink in the breath of the pines as the breezes print themselves on the surface of the placid water. This Black Hills country has charm, inviting you to get out and go about or stay about. It is a lingering kind of human satisfaction for the soul, hungry of a tired body, the recreation of any jaded mind compelled to live by the abacus, money.

You may think all this the feeling of the moment, a mood, and because I was in good company. But no! I am an old soldier of the spirit, a veteran in time, place, and man. I could not be mistaken. Go and see.

We wound on upward to Sylvan Lake, a gem spot in the Hills where South Dakota plans to entertain her guests. It may be that South Dakota sees a body of water so seldom that her citizens overvalue it for the lake is artificial and small, but what a setting! Here a sweeping mountain resort, with the lake as a vignette seen below, could be a masterful thing of the kind, woven in with the great rich rock and tree foreground, framing the vistas of this spot;

another and a higher kind of nature understanding well and loving the earth from which it springs, loving it too much to imitate it.

Harney Peak loomed to one side. Turning from the little rock-defended, rock-bound lake your gaze travels away along blue ridges ornamented by great rock piles to distant blue mountain tops, as far away as the human eye can go beneath the clouds. Round about you, rugged strengths, forest depths, primeval earth at best; well, an architect is speaking.

There was a hotel there once but nature disposed of it in her inscrutable way, for cause. It was ugly.

Notwithstanding the expenditure of riches, so far, there were wonders left for tomorrow. And "Spitz," as I felt like calling him by now, came with Ted Lusk's car to drive me to Spearfish Canyon. I felt a little dull toward Spearfish. I had seen two marvels unique in the scenery of the world. I felt headed in for an anticlimax and said so. The boys said, no. These South Dakota boys by now had me where I believed that they knew their stuff. They couldn't have built those superb roads in the Bad Lands and Black Hills if they didn't know. So I patiently waited and visited with "Spitz" as we rode away. We stopped at Homestake, of which everyone has heard, and saw how a primitive gold mining operation has been turned over to the power of the machine and remains primitive just the same. The resources of machinery couldn't change the original steps or even the original way of mining except to cut down the manpower involved. By afternoon we got in by Spearfish, a mountain torrent beginning a canyon 26 miles long. Not very interesting at first, I had seen so many; the Western States are full of them, as everyone knows. The road here is haphazard as hazard was and is none too good. "Spitz" drove well, fortunately. And the stream itself was something but after a half-hour things began to happen. We would be headed straight for gigantic white walls trabeated in ledges from which pines sprouted and grew in precisely the manner of the pictorial dreams of the great Chinese painters, the greatest painters who ever lived. We were in the land of the Sung and Ming masters. Whoever knows their idealizations of nature in the Chinese landscape painting of those great periods, and they were mostly landscapes, can see the character of the Spearfish ensemble.

Great horizontal rock walls abruptly rising above torrential streams, their stratified surfaces decorated (it is the word) with red pine stems carving stratified branches in horizontal textures over the cream white walls, multiplied red pine trunks and the black green masses of the pine rhythmically repeating pattern, climbing, climbing until the sky disappeared or was a narrow rift of blue as the clear water poured over pebbles or pooled under the heavy masses of green at the foot of the grand rock walls. Well, here was something again different. As different as could be from Bad Lands or Black Hills or anything I had actually seen, a stately exposition of what decorated walls on enormous scale can do and be. The Chinese predicted and depicted it. This continued for miles and miles without palling or growing in the least stale. We drove out, finally, and turned away from Spearfish town to get back, two architects drunk with primal scene painting, to Gutzon Borglum's little dinner. A third type of

earthly marvel was now added to the two. All unique and unparalleled elsewhere in our country.

But now came an unexpected experience. That drive from the Canyon "Spearfish" to Rapid City. Does anyone who knows California and Arizona know that in the softly modeled brown surfaces of South Dakota binding these three wonders together is a terrain greater in charm than any to be found in either? A sweep of modeling and a tender color (it is early September) and a variety of aspect matchless anywhere?

No, I shall be burned for a heretic when I make the statement. But I should be thanked as a prophet and hailed as a discoverer by that jaded public who have "seen everything" and stick to the "through lines." The greatest scenic wonders of the world I know now are touched on grand safe highways but not on railroads. My hat is off to South Dakota's treasures and the men who made them.

We got back in time for a whisky; no soda, thank you; and Gutzon's little dinner, where some Rapid City folk were gathered together to welcome a stranger. He, Gutzon Borglum, of course, is master in more than one medium. The way he handled his dinner, the guests (among them Congressman Harry Gandy), and handled me too, was a masterpiece. Ask anybody there. Gutzon broke down. I like him for it, and anyway, I like those South Dakota folk; I want to see them all again sometime if I can.

Go to South Dakota, but drive there. It is so near to us all and yet I never knew, nor had ever heard much about its southwestern treasure house until Gutzon Borglum went out there to work and Senator Norbeck invited me to see it.

I hope the noble inheritance, for that is what it is, won't be exploited too much and spoiled as lesser beauty spots in our country have been spoiled and will not continue to be marred by the nature imitator with his "rustic" effects, piled boulders, peeled logs, and imitation of camp-style primitive gabled buildings. Nature seeds from man not imitation but interpretation. It is quite another story, as you may learn.

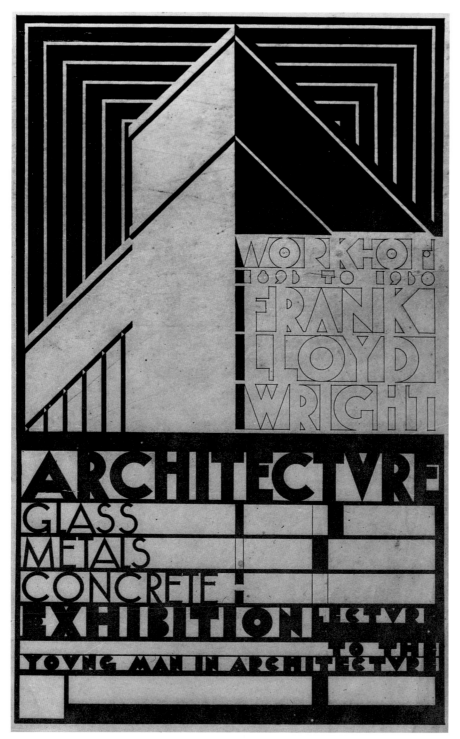

Exhibition poster. 1930. Ink on tracing paper, 16 x 29". FLLW Fdn#3000.003

Overleaf: **"The Old-Fashioned Window (Fugue),"** designed for *Liberty* magazine
(Project). 1926. Pencil and color pencil on tracing paper, 12 x 13". FLLW Fdn#2604.011

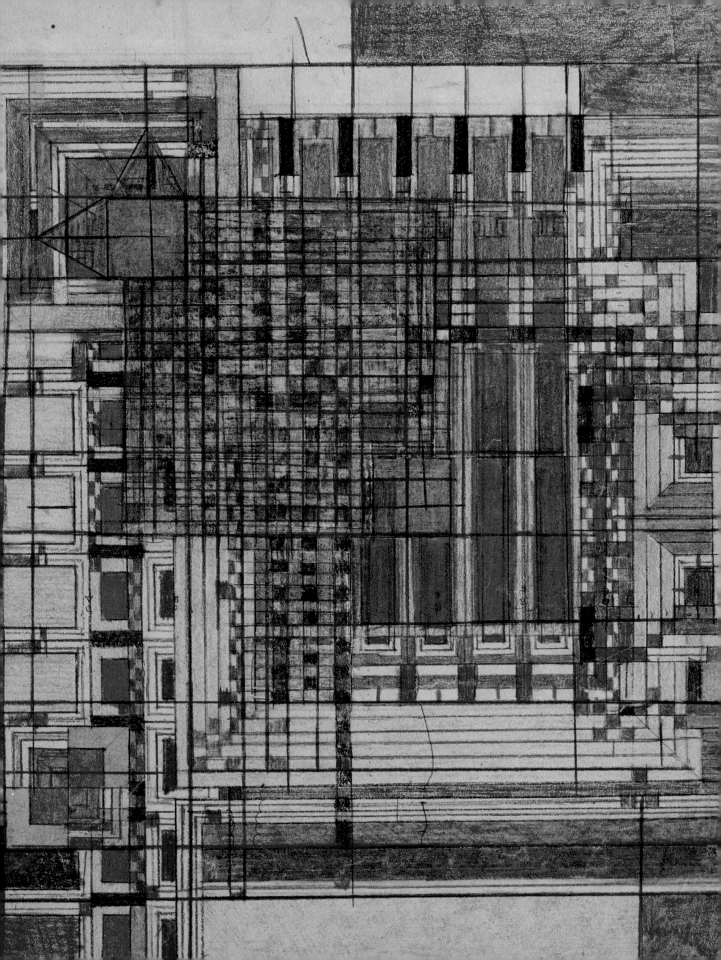

THE NEW ARCHITECTURAL SCULPTURE

I*t is apparent from this review that Wright viewed* The New Architectural Sculpture *by Walter Raymond Agard (New York: Oxford University Press, 1935) as lacking in any true understanding of either architecture or sculpture. But the article is informative in that it puts on record Wright's admiration for the artists and architects associated with the Secession movement in Vienna, among them Gustav Klimt, Otto Wagner, Josef Hoffman, and Josef Olbrich. As the text progresses, Wright attacks American scholasticism: "A 'scholarly' book, it seems, need be no more now than some college man's thesis upon any subject of which he is sufficiently ignorant in practice but concerning which he has read or has traveled and viewed, meantime gathering contemporary opinions." He therefore brings up his persistent nemesis, formal education, which he believed suffocated creativity, especially in architecture and the fine arts. [Published in* The State Journal, *Spring Green, Wisconsin, October 11, 1935]*

THIS BOOKLET, "THE NEW ARCHITECTURAL SCULPTURE," touches me as an architect.

The jacket advertises that "Professor Agard writes from a wide acquaintance with the contemporary architects and sculptors and their work."

Exactly that is what ruined his enterprise. The "acquaintances" were all eclectics but one. And they have robbed his book of any historical validity whatever except as a record of false and narrow contemporary opinions. An eclectic himself, our author comes out of this huddle with the eclectics with Bert Goodhue as his star and with his masterpiece, the tower of the Nebraska State Capitol, firmly held in both hands as he proceeds to kick goals with it.

Goodhue of course was not a modern architect in any sense. This by internal evidence anyone may see to whom modern architecture is more than merely architecture, *à la mode*.

Nor—apparently—had the wide Agard acquaintance ever heard of Otto Wagner, the greatest native force at the base of European modernism. No, nor of Klimt, nor of Olbrich or of the Viennese Hoffman: the greatest moderns of the Secession from whom the Martels and most of those he illustrates—stem. One of the greatest American sculptors, Gutzon Borglum, whose "Lincoln" transcends anything Bourdelle ever did and who is hewing the history of his country into mountainous shapes, and several other Americans— Manship among them—are not even mentioned. Karl Knappe, the greatest modern European sculptor of them all is passed by with a casual reference. He did, somehow, pick up Hans Panger, and the Martels and Carl Milles—(good enough sculptors all)—although he didn't realize their proper significance because he didn't know where they came from. He is looking for modern sculpture by way of the antique. All his illustrated architects are derivators and his illustrations show what the derivators derived and from whom but do not seem to have shown it to Walter Agard. He brackets Sullivan and Wright without wanting to raise the dust by properly placing either. What American eclectic would want to? Or could?

Why eclectics shun originals (they do if, and so far as, they can) is clear enough. Any original is a reproach to them or a danger and they don't go in for damage. The derivatives are far safer. They would prefer St. Paul to Jesus and they would consider the preference conservative. They prefer the thing, always, diluted by once removed at least from any source whatsoever. It is rough to call them cowards but cowards they are unless running together in the pack. Eclecticism in art turns out to be no more than stupid soon or late or just plain thievery.

Now why Agard had the presumption to go and commit more eclecticism to paper can only be accounted for by the fact that he is a professor of Greek and an amateur student of Greek sculpture. If he had to write a book just because he was professor, the circumstance simply goes to show how indirect it is to "profess" anything at all. Why, otherwise, should he thus want to join the endless procession of eclectics sitting all over the country in judgment upon matters of art that are greater than they can know and lie far deeper than any eclectic could ever go beneath the surface in one lifetime. As for the shallow books which the tribe will persist in writing, they might pass for a harmless little ventilation of the ego on their part were education not as it is. As education is, these paper brain-children enter the brain stream called education (mostly paper anyhow) by chance corrupting the mind of a youth or two, or one may blow like a blinder over some popular eye, adding to public confusion concerning the truths which should lie open and clear to all, uncorrupted by opinionated interference or twisted by left-handed interpretation.

Think of a man with Russell Hitchcock's experience, for instance, yes, or with Phil Johnson's either, or a dozen others sitting in liberal judgement upon Modern Architecture, passing "judgements" along to the uninformed! And Walter Agard tries now for that same class by way of another paper brain-child.

I wish I might encourage someone to write a book to end the writing of all books on art like these: end the writing of any book whatever upon so meager a basis of fundamental knowledge in the practice of a great subject. As American scholasticism multiplies these superficial performances its utter sterility and shabby weakness shows more and more. Eventually such exploitation will take the life of the subject unless somehow checked.

I see the end but shudder to see confirmation after confirmation of the haphazard way in which, by the tyro for the tyro, history of any sort is made today. A "scholarly" book, it seems, need be no more now than some college man's thesis on any subject of which he is sufficiently ignorant in practice but concerning which he has read or has traveled and viewed, meantime gathering contemporary opinions. Such authors may be sincere enough—I've no doubt Walter Agard himself is sincere—but sincerity is not enough. It burned the Salem witches at the stake and frequently turns might into spite and turns spite into what seems right.

As for the illustrations in this book on sculpture and architecture, the architecture is merely sculpture—not architecture at all in the modern sense—especially the Nebraska tower kicked for goal. And almost all of the sculpture is of the kind that has nothing of its own to say, content with living as a travesty upon a glorious past or imitating the style of something it really doesn't seem to understand below the belt or above the nose.

All any architect or sculptor need do to qualify in the Agard book is to keep his "classic" thinking unchanged while he sandpapers all the tell-tale details flat and smooth or merely changes them on the surface. As to the profound and elemental forces working this apparent change in the countenance of things and that now bear along toward a great triumph over all eclecticism whatsoever—a change in the thought of the world—there is nothing. There could be nothing.

Another author has merely prepared his conservative's seat with the derivators—now more smugly derivative than any. For this seat, of course, he wrote the book and I hope he finds the company he is in to his taste. But, skyrocketing opinions by way of some book on art in due course only to come down like the stick: that is really the modern art of our author, *à la mode,* you know.

FORM AND REFORM

In writing this book review of Form and Reform: A Practical Handbook for Modern Interiors *(New York: Harper and Bros., 1930), by Paul Theodore Frankl, Wright was kinder than usual, probably because the book's subject was not architecture. He did not hesitate to lash out at the current art scene and disdainfully claim that "to write books about art is now everybody's pastime." He exonerates his friend, the writer Paul Frankl from this dilettantism. [Published in* The Daily Cardinal, *1935]*

FOR ME TO WRITE A CRITICISM OF A PAUL FRANKL BOOK IS for a friend to sit in judgment upon his friend. But a friendly review is no nearer wrong than one hostile. Having both, the truth is probably nearer the friendly one.

Paul is prolific. He designs, manufactures, sells, writes, is a talented painter, a good teacher, and like most of the Viennese who come here to help us get our "artistic" on straight he has a gift for being socially agreeable and personally entertaining.

He has several books to his credit. The first one, *New Dimensions,* he asked me to write a preface for. I wrote declining on principle as all prefaces are odious. If a book is good it needs no preface. If the book is no good it doesn't deserve a preface. And Paul used the note itself for a preface.

That cleverness is his—this Fifth Avenue pioneer in getting the American rich of rich America interested in the effects we call, with some reason, modern.

I think he has done a good work in that. In this, his second book, *Form and Reform,* he has tried to live up to the title and reform the form in the format of his book. It is quite in the mode as it now

goes. His heavy lines and black bands and balancing black masses are all intended to correlate the text and illustrations into a more cogent whole than is usual in the current book.

Now that he has written a third book, *Machine Made Leisure,* he doesn't like *Form and Reform* so well as when he did it, he says, but I thought that on the whole the idea was good and the way he executed it worthwhile. Paul is like that. Nothing is final—for him. He has chosen his illustrations too much from among the work of the so-called "interior architects," but these examples are among the best to be found.

No decorator or interior architect among them all has a clearer or more sensible grasp upon what the "new" means in furniture and decoration than "Frankl." No one, I think, has more consistently put everything he has in him or on him—or coming to him—into this thing we call modern art.

His way of saying the thing to be said is interesting.

And while he is a good salesman of what he makes and knows how to get a good price for it—his ideals are high as his capabilities are high. He doesn't sell *them* out so far as I can see.

Stanley Marcus House (Project). Dallas, Texas. 1935. Perspective. Pencil and color pencil on tracing paper, 12 x 5". FLLW Fdn#3501.001

To write books about art is now anybody's pastime. Paint a little, carve a little, compose a little, get some little something built somehow and then write something about it. That is the prevailing fashion. To publicize soon and do it continuously is the secret of such success as most of our modernistic artists, themselves graduates from the ranks of advertising experts, know. That is the mode. So the American public gets almost all it knows or can stand of art that way. But Paul has a better right to write a book.

He can beat most of the successes at their own game and in this book *Form and Reform* he throws in something of real value out of himself. Being an artist. He is easy to read for one thing because he does talk most of the time out of his own experience. He knows good stuff when he sees it because he can make it. An author of that type is rare, and, a book on any subject being a sort of indexed guide to the author's tastes and characteristics, here in this book we have laid out in cold type, and flat blacks, not only Frankl's hope and abstract choice but his abilities as well. In none of these is he, mean, negligible—or untrustworthy.

935

LOUIS SULLIVAN'S WORDS AND WORK

In 1935 Wright wrote two articles about his "beloved master," Louis H. Sullivan, after reading recent books published by and about Sullivan: Sullivan's own book, Kindergarten Chats, *published posthumously by the Scarab Fraternity Press (Lawrence, Kansas) in 1934, and Hugh Morrison's* Louis Sullivan: Prophet of Modern Architecture, *published by W. W. Norton & Co. in 1935 (see pp. 187–188).*

Wright reiterates the futility of trying to "honor" Sullivan: "No university ever honors any man until by recognizing him as an honor it honors itself." Instead, he makes the observation that "I am certain that where Louis Sullivan matters now is where his love, sincerity and courage gave him to his kind while he lived, by way of his creative impulse." [Published in The Architectural Record, *March 1935]*

IT IS ALWAYS PAINFUL TO ME TO SEE WHAT LESSER MEN WILL do to a great man when they feel him on their hands as such. One will assume to erect a monument to him by way of one's own appreciations: really, such monuments are attempts to shine in reflected light. Another will, gratuitously, place him "securely" in the Hall of Representative men, where the great man would not care to be at all. Another will sob into his own kerchief at the thought of the suffering ascribed to the great man when his country passed him by—when really his country did not pass him by; the great man simply passed his country by.

There are many variations of the aftermath— the most abominable being, so it seems to me, designing in the great man's own manner to commemorate him. A form of commiseration not intended as insult—but gross insult, nevertheless. Nature her custom holds, let shame say what it will, and runs thus true to form here and now where

Louis Sullivan is concerned in the preface and criticism of his *Kindergarten Chats.*

This posthumous affair of honor—what really does it matter? A spirit has come and is with us, still, in spite of his words and work because he belonged to those he was like and because they are him and he is themselves. It is only for them he could either write or build. They see nothing remarkable in that he expressed what they felt and knew—and love him as they love themselves because he was what they were and he knew it as they know it.

Why not, then, let it go at that?

Well, I suppose it is this provincial matter of making the most of, or being on good terms with, ourselves by "honoring him" as we say.

But "honoring him" can't be done. No university ever honors any man until by recognizing him as an honor it honors itself. Nor has anyone the power to do honor to any great man. The great man

Ornamental design for plaster panel (Louis Sullivan, architect). McVickers Theater, Chicago. 1885. Pencil on paper, 11 x 7". FLLW Fdn#7116.031 (AV1038.019)

has become a sentimentality to the living citizens. None really have anything concerned with him. He was. He is. He will be—a mystery.

Why look the gift-horse in the teeth? And then to "suppose" again, I suppose that, from him, post-mortem we are expected to deduce a moral or profit of some kind. What post-mortem moral or profit by way of Louis Sullivan? Certainly none by poking at his remains. His carcass was as troublesome to him in life as it would be to me in death. Certainly none in his buildings. They were the troubled carcass of his thought, shared and troublesome to him alive as to us when he is dead. I am certain that where Louis Sullivan matters now is where his love, sincerity and courage gave him to his kind while he lived, by way of his creative impulse. And it is for that we must read his words or view the fragments that are his work. Before either

words or work can mean anything great to us we too must be or become as he was. And then we won't value his words overmuch, nor feel other than sad that he couldn't have lived to carry his thought further in his work; glad that both words and work escaped being standards of measurement by way of which immaturity *assumes* maturity and so defeats youth; glad we thus escaped in order that the spirit that lived in him might continue to live and work—unobstructed by him as he stood, now that we see that inside he stood very tall indeed—up against the roof of his own mind.

Heed his own words in the *Chats:* "Let it suffice that he has lived to point it out to you."

"Now begin."

It is the only honor you can do him. A great man is a great gift—but only in this sense, because "it is our time for willing."

FORM AND FUNCTION

In this review of Hugh Morrison's book Louis Sullivan: Prophet of Modern Architecture,[1] *Frank Lloyd Wright is strongly critical of the secondary role that the author assigns to Dankmar Adler in the firm of Adler and Sullivan: "'Form follows Function'? Has it occurred to no one, then, that Dankmar Adler, not Louis Sullivan, deserves the credit for that dogma? It was Adler's contribution to his young partner when he was teaching him practically all the young man knew about architecture below the belt? As an architect Louis Sullivan went to school, not to the Beaux Arts, but to Dankmar Adler. Out of his association with Adler came Sullivan's whole sense of building as a functional experience in Function." Wright himself, of course, went to Sullivan for his apprenticeship. [Published in* The Saturday Review, *December 14, 1935]*

THE IMPENDING SUCCESS OF MODERN ARCHITECTURE HAS excited critics and incited them to look the gift-horse in the teeth. Mr. Morrison's book goes beyond other recent critics' post-mortems concerning modern architecture in drawing its information from a single person (my understudy while "serving my time" with Adler and Sullivan) and the critic dedicates his criticisms to that personal source. Not much honor have I seen among gratuitous enlighteners of the public where modern architecture is concerned. I've lived long enough to see it through and see through it.

But it is only fair to say that the gathering together of Adler's and Sullivan's important work in the beginning of our new architecture is useful and, but for reducing the grand old chief—Adler—to an appendix, the inclusion of a building neither ever saw (the Heath House[2]), and many neither of them cared to even look at—that part of the work is well done.

If only these gratuitous critics would confine themselves to effects they can see with their own eyes and would steer clear of causes they would have a better chance to be honest with themselves and so with others. When Morrison makes selections and infers he goes to pieces badly. His judgements are exactly wrong. The case against eclecticism is well presented but the real Louis Sullivan in his relation to time, place, and man is thrown entirely away to make a case for him as the forerunner of a functionalism for which neither then—no, nor now, would he have ever had more than a curse. His biographer foolishly takes pains to defend him against the very thing that he was and that no critic has yet been able to see as his true greatness.

"Form follows Function"? Has it occurred to no one, then, that Dankmar Adler, not Louis Sullivan, deserves the credit for that dogma? It was Adler's contribution to his young partner when he was teaching him practically all the young man knew about architecture below the belt? As an architect Louis Sullivan went to school, not to the Beaux Arts, but to Dankmar Adler. Out of his association with Adler came Sullivan's whole sense of building as a functional experience in Function.

Morrison should have appended Adler's paper on "The Influence of Steel Construction and Plate Glass on the Development of a Modern Style," etc., etc., and moved the chief up as teacher of the young poet and artist whose efflorescence he adored because it went beyond him to a realm he coveted.

A just biographer should know that to honor Adler is not to dishonor Sullivan. To underrate the chief, Adler, is to lose Sullivan as Morrison has lost him. Morrison's Sullivan is more Adler than Sullivan. None seems to see the master as he was and is so plainly written in his works. He put into my hands just before he died his own complete collection (hundreds) of the drawings (he had dated them) that represented him to himself at his best and said—"Frank, this to you for you'll be writing about my work some day." And "some day" I will give the world the figure of the great creative artist as he was and as he saw himself.

Sullivan is so much greater than his postmortems would have him. He is essentially a lyric poet-philosopher interested in the sensuous experience of expressing inner rhythms, evolving a language of his own—his ornament—in which to utter himself: unique among mankind. The Wainwright, the Guaranty, and the Bayard buildings, the Getty Tomb and the Golden Door will tell. But what crass impertinence to put Richardson's influence upon Sullivan where ornament is concerned just because of similarity in the edges of certain leaves which if all children were to draw they would draw similarly: specious inference worthy of R. Hitchcock[3] at his merriest and maddest.

I can explain, for Mr. Morrison, the "mystery" of the oriels of the Stock Exchange Building. The "oriels" are nine bays projecting about two and one half feet over the sidewalk below them; projecting on nine floor levels. Calculate the floor space stolen, by ordinance, from the street and see "why" they were there! Then consider that such bays were preferred by tenants because they could look up and down the street without sticking their heads out of the windows, etc.

Bah! Sullivan's decline was not as Morrison says—due to the fact that his contemporaries did not recognize his talents, but more because they did and built a defense wall of gossip around him, to isolate him from their own possible clientele which meant, to them, these United States.

The later work shown in the book is backwash or, as in the case of the Bradley House—Elmslie.[4] The Getty Tomb, Wainwright, Guaranty and Condict and Schesinger-Meyer buildings were unadulterated Sullivan—his best buildings. The Condict (Bayard) building he loved best. It was nearest to his desire. Among the later ones, the Owatoma and Columbus banks are the only works in which the master shows himself.

When Morrison says there is little or nothing known of the late years of Louis Sullivan's life he destroys the great significance of the tragedy of a great life in its helpless relation to the time in which and to the people among whom Louis Sullivan, the great creative artist, lived. And this is biography? No. No more biography than good criticism!

1. Hugh Morrison, *Louis Sullivan: Prophet of Modern Architecture* (New York: Museum of Modern Art & W. W. Norton Co., 1935).
2. W. R. Heath residence, Buffalo, NY, 1905.
3. Henry-Russell Hitchcock (1903–1987), a prominent architectural historian, lecturer, and critic.
4. George Grant Elmslie (1871–1952) was Sullivan's chief draftsman from 1894 to 1909.

936

AN ARCHITECT SPEAKING FOR CULTURE

Wright read this address to the Woman's Congress, at the Palmer House in Chicago, on February 14, 1936. It was a well-considered address, arrived at after nine revisions. In studied sequences he underlines the ills and problems facing the nation in 1936 and then explains the significance and meaning of organic architecture. By way of example for solutions to urban problems, he cites the idea and thesis of Broadacre City, a decentralized city plan he first designed and modeled in 1934. He warns of the threat and danger of overemphasizing the importance of the machine—of allowing the machine to dictate the life and needs of people instead of serving them. He envisions a culture that takes its roots in the ground rather than placing its faith in congested, ill-planned cities:

> *Any civilization wherein exaggerated urbanism rules the mind—as it rules ours—is sure to lose sight of its birthright—the ground. No Art of any life heretofore or hereafter begins or ends anywhere else. . . . This means that no house is a machine for living in except as the heart of man is a suction pump. But it does mean that the house, if it is a home, is the epitome of the entire resource of this expert mechanical era; those resources put to work to secure more life for more individuals as individual life ever held for the individual before. More freedom, better quality—more colorful in effect so far as individuality goes. I tell you that is of the true nature of true American Democracy.*

[Unpublished speech, January 26, 1936]

SPEAKING OF CULTURE—WHAT WOULD YOU SAY WAS THE matter with a great new country—most powerful on earth—that put its Supreme Court to work where it was lost in a monstrous monument to Rome, and not see it as ridiculous; where government marked its public buildings with a symbol of authority that always was false architecture: the dome; whose better fold dwelt in little stage settings pleased and proud to imitate foreign dwellings; whose art institutions were museums directed by picture brokers—and whose museums were really its art institutes; where "learning" was housed in pseudo-cathedrals and higher teaching was stale: pseudo-academic post mortem; where the church was an alibi; whose popular music was a gift from the Negro and the photograph was the great medium of popular expression; whose business men, pulled up and let down by wires, got up into feudal towers of fake masonry, and the busier they were up there the more often they had to come down to destroy what they had done in order to keep on being busy, meanwhile building more towers; a country where the channels of news and policy were popular entertainment privately owned and no one could do anything about it; a country where every several to seven years government must take hand over the people and tax the future to feed the present else its workers would starve; a country where cultural endeavor must be false or stand square against the current of available ways and means, sincerity being a quality for heroes; where the greatest of inventions—the radio—was a peddler in the parlor and, in order to peddle there, made the country's finest talent a huckster and society did nothing about it; a people unable (because it had never learned by honestly trying to be itself) to make any proper use of its strength in order to make its enormous strength a blessing—helplessly allowing its powers to become an unmitigated curse; this people so busily ingenious that apparatus multiplied, and the necessity for anything except more machines to run more money-making machinery was beside the mark; where the push-button was becoming the symbol of power whether of hostess, wife, overlord, or the citizen; therefore a country wherein all power was becoming vicarious—proxy being the machine.

In short, a country trying to outwit life and take a short cut to somewhere—with no idea whatever where, mistaking nervousness for emotion, restlessness for energy, believing progress to consist in getting work done by machinery.

What besides sex and more of it; harder and harder liquor; more and better selling, wisecracking and town crying; more and swifter travel, would you say the infallible eventual resource of such a country would be? Over-riding all its minorities it would be war—wouldn't it? More war and better, or revolutionary, wars—the final war a war between the sexes—probably fought with guns.

That nation would be without art—no matter how inventive and industrious, and so with no cultural power to reproduce itself. Looked at impartially you would say such a country would go under as the shortest lived civilization in History.

Who then is going to say no to such aims if not the artist—conscience of the country?

Quietly opposed to the growing danger of such sterility in our own enormous country, is the ideal of an organic architecture for the life of our people: an ideal—first finding approximate form out here where the country was most coarse (but not most superficial) only to encounter pseudo-academic pretenses and be rewarded first by ridicule and then hostility. Being a matter of super-common sense the practice of this ideal might have appealed to the American business man. But the rich wife of American business had been abroad. Her pampered sons

and daughters had been to fashionable Harvard—Princeton—Yale—the great cultural electioneers, themselves helpless eclecticisms. Consequently, over-educated, undercultured—all became fashionable eclectics. Nothing out of the ground for them—plenty was in sight ready made now, and how!

Came the Chicago Fair of 1893. Eclecticism won that day—there was so little to put against it—and the debacle began that has lasted to this moment. The apostles of integral culture: Louis Sullivan foremost, Richardson, Root, and previously our Whitman, Thoreau and later Veblen, all became voices crying in the wilderness. Here was life ready made. And what life! Only reproduction by machine was needed to turn "magnificence" over to the country at a profit. And there was nothing to be done for the turn of the turbulent tide but wait. I, for one, waited by going on working as I could. My old master in his field somewhat tired by then, kept on as best he could. And strange to say to you now—that working went back to our cultural creditor—the Continent of Europe to change the thought of Europe itself where the new forms needed for a new life were concerned and Europe began to talk of modern architecture, acknowledging a debt to us. Certain European voices of her own, unheeded until then, found reinforcement in this vital fresh performance and went forward. Not far away, on these prairies you may still find surviving examples of this vitalizing thought put into approximate practice by way of the few American men and women willing, by way of their own discernment to be laughed at—maybe—for living their own lives in their own way in unfashionable houses. These scattered lucky, unlucky buildings have had a great influence in the world of advanced thought.

Now precisely, what is this thought.

I have been asked to come to this conference to tell you.

The thought is simple. *Not* new except in specific application to architecture. It goes back 500 years B.C. to the Chinese philosopher Laotze at least—came to him probably from the great motherland—and comes by way of the man Jesus more directly to present view.

The thought is simple but difficult to grasp because it is a complete change in what we call "reality." The change places *life-emphasis* where it belongs, not upon artifice but upon nature, upon *growth* from forces within, not upon aggregations shaped by outside forces.

The new thought is for this integrity first—therefore the thought sees any building, any life or any individuality, not as walls and roof nor as some projected appearance nor as some assumption of character but sees the reality of any building as the room within, to be lived in—sees life as actual experience—sees individuality as the development of the true character of a man: and sees all this as subject to the law of change we call *growth*.

To be modern therefore, culture, in this new-old and deeper sense, is of the nature of the thing, never merely *on* it.

The form of the building now takes its shape by way of the nature of the materials according to purpose and building forms change as circumstances change.

Now only a small fragment of the world's architecture had this integrity because that architecture was the exterior approach. That is to say made with little sense of the within as determining factor. Antique Architecture was made, rather, by the power extant in the world around and about it as determining factor—merely Fashion, you see—in a somewhat broader application. The Greeks could give the world the Vase on this basis—a perfected elegance—but could only give the world a false Architecture. A stumbling block for us, now.

With this—to us—new sense of culture, individuality in the nature-sense of character itself, becomes inviolable.

Again, *character* is beauty but all the more is harmony essential. All the more is co-relation to be cultivated because again we know that nothing has any value unless part is to whole as part is to part and as the whole is to the great entirety.

In short, entity is at last, as at first—cultural ideal.

It is in this sense that we of the modern movement use the word organic. Organic means—therefore the integrity that alone enables a thought, a building, or a person to be true to itself.

So in the 20th century Modern Architecture begins at the beginning to search for synthesis—tries to arrive at complete harmony of outside and inside: its sense of space not the exterior sense of the Greeks but more that of Einstein. Not a search for the elegant so much as the organic solution. You see—then—how false this mere "seeming" must be, that we (ourselves "mostly seeming to be") are lost in? You see then, how this self-conscious being that academic education has erected upon the human ego is without reality. True being lies deeper—substratum to it all.

You see, too, how any achievement square with this organic sense is timeless. Fashion ceases even to exist.

How difficult any application of such an ideal would be where all is thoughtless waste of life, much of the waste a kind of academic consecration, is easy to see.

You will see, too, how the first requirement of life would be the harmonious integrity of Art. Art *would be integrity* wherever the nature of work was concerned and that would be everywhere. Where any form was concerned, the thing itself would be according to the way the thing is made and related to every other thing going to make up its total use and environment.

You may think how hopeless such an endeavor.

But it is not hopeless.

Grasp firmly the near end of this thought of integration I have called "organic" and the false will become evident as false. The true will come true.

The tragedy of our unpreparedness to meet life on any such invincible basis is clearly seen in emergencies like the present, when government must step in to perform the functions that a democratic society should perform for itself—and civilization must again see freedom of choice and speech set aside to make "jobs." A progressive people must stand by to see the fruits of labor politically characterized by mediocre groups rather than by the super common sense of Art—see the nation's bravest and best idle, equality of meals the emergency forcing the country to stay down rather than the highest good by means of which the country ought to be inspired and enabled to rise. Our government—and it is our own fault—is where it must put a premium upon the mediocre—in order to live! And perhaps that is the only thing any government so politically founded as ours can ever do. But if so, see only the travesty of an ideal of Democracy originally the expression in government nearest to the ideal of an organic architecture: Now that the time has come to atone for success such as ours, instead of Democracy see a sort of mobocracy as the nearest possible approach.

And you must see too that it is all just the same thing in social economics that you see around you in the housing of Supreme Court justices; the popular fashionable housing of yourselves; the shallows of your entertainment; this riot of choice wherein choice is itself a riot and wherein education is not even on speaking terms with true culture. Meantime, riches go on fashioning a way of life wherein old age is deadly disqualification instead of the dignified qualification it is in older, wiser civilizations.

Of course such lack of integrity must result in confusion and the confusion result in a waste of life and in unhappiness throughout the social fabric we so strive to maintain. A stiff price for a great people to pay for the excess we have called success.

Where our culture is concerned we are a fat, gaseous aggregation; too much of everything; no good digestion of anything wholesome.

Too much education—mostly the wrong kind in the wrong place.

Too much money—most of it in the wrong places.

Too much food—most of that in the wrong places at the moment.

Too much machinery—the right kind in wrong places.

Too much science—even in the right places.

Too much salesmanship of mechanical artifice in the name of Art.

No indigenous Art because of too little concern for the present or future of human sensibility: property rights being no longer human rights: Our ambitions have been satisfied to climb upward upon the miseries and credulities of mankind.

This country was and still is the world's white hope for a better future but it is evident now that some true center line is needed for a life-line here in the United States. Somebody must go to work. And that somebody is the creative artist.

Now for some comfort: the structure of whatever is—is architecture. The ideal of an organic ar-

chitecture, an upshoot on the prairie in the tall grass not far away is in a profound sense the needed center-line for indigenous American culture. But this ideal demands of you a new and different idea of "*success.*" If you were to begin to say *organic architecture* a thought would enter with the term itself to enable you to set up a new standard according to the greatest constructive thought that has come to us through all the ages probably from the motherland itself—to make of Art the vitalizing integrity in the life of our time that Art ever was in the life of great times past.

In speaking of the new center line, however, let us not say "Modern" Architecture for that is only architecture "à la mode" and Architecture à la mode means eclecticism of some kind, means going on electing the selection of the work of some man dead or— no matter—alive. Furthermore, it is Art in this integral sense that must, now, take the lead in education.

But I should say we would be likely to take the look of this new thing, too apt to apply it on the surface of the same old thought, seeing it only as a new and the latest appearance. Just this was done at the recent Chicago Fair.

But comfort again comes from the thought that we can't go on with that folly because recent pressure has made a certain contingent among us see the folly of grandomania in any form, recognize the idiocy of present exaggerations, realize the crime of further herd concentrations. We are now seeing decentralization upon some organic basis as a way forward— out of the impasse we have created for ourselves. And I am happy to believe our president is so minded.

Any civilization wherein exaggerated urbanism rules the mind—as it rules ours—is sure to lose sight of its birthright—the ground. No Art of any life heretofore or hereafter begins or ends anywhere else! We have neglected our ground as the basis for our culture and tried to get culture from the pavements and factories of the world. The factors and their factories have had whip-hand over our art and culture— so why, indeed, wonder that our cultural endeavor should take on the character of the factory—knowledge factories, news factories, war factories, picture factories, relief factories—as well as shoe factories?

But well-planned decentralization by way of intelligent new use and fresh interpretation of the

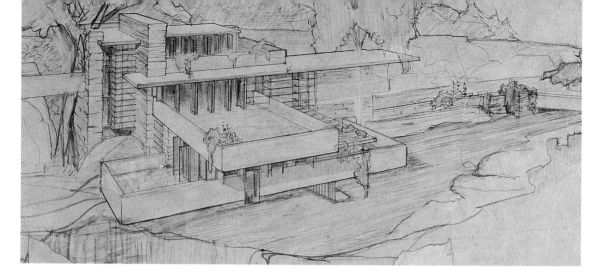

"Fallingwater," Edgar J. Kaufmann House. Mill Run, Pennsylvania. 1935. Perspectives. Pencil and color pencil on tracing paper, **30 x 19"**. FLLW Fdn#3602.001/3602.003

ground itself, does loom ahead and sanity may be restored to culture if we will begin to plan for more human use of our new machine advantages instead of letting the present owners go on to further use *us* and destroy themselves.

In this connection Broadacre City was planned and modelled by the Taliesin Fellowship because no complete scheme for such advantageous human use of our advantages had yet been designed. By way of 20th-century assets Broadacre City takes the principle of decentralization to a humane beginning. Moreover the work puts that beginning in such form that it may be touched and seen by anyone intelligent enough to study it. Like any factory because of the invention of better machines—obsolete overnight—our cities are distinctly dated and dying. The city it-

self was not planned to use our new advantages so it can never qualify now unless the growth of our mechanical advantages is stopped or turned back.

Henry Ford—most shrewd among our factors—sees this and is openly an agent for decentralization but as a car man would be he is for a ribbon or highway city which is again bad.

An entire change is coming over this old urban set-up we once regarded as progressive just as it came over factory-better ways of making things. The nation will now have to pay that price.

The new thought put to work will destroy much but create more as every great concentration except government is decentralized and individualized and government is simplified; the university sent to the people instead of the people herded in any universi-ty. The herding of humanity will decrease and so will the back and forth haul as traffic and markets grow more and more spontaneous and the great rights of railway will go back to the people for fluid continuous traffic directly connected to collateral highways.

Congestion in the name of service has proved a ready means for the ruthless exploitation of human beings. What life will be like upon a decentralized basis wherein a better way of doing everything worth doing is imperative, is the lesson such honest learning as we have left has now to learn.

The comfort in this gospel of an organic archi-tecture for a more sensible people lies in the fact that the small thing may be the greater thing just as the big thing may be the small thing. Values to be valu-able will all be integral and human.

The modest three-thousand-dollar house will become fit associate for the house of machine-age luxury—the curse comes off the factory as associate for both and our American hinterland—the farm be-comes the most attractive unit of a city that grows to be everywhere or will probably be nowhere.

And in this more natural order of human growth the house will not go to the factory for pre-fabrication—No, the factory will go to the house. And when it does go in the hand of the competent Architect great economics and fresh new beauty will be the beneficial result.

Before that can happen, though, we will have a new kind of architect, differently educated, who sees architecture as of the ground and for the individual and into which the machine can enter only as a splen-did but subordinated tool leaving the whole house more humane and individual than it ever was before. In case you are inclined to scoff at this idea as Utopi-an or something, or merely language, such houses may be seen among the models of Broadacre City.

In short, wherever the center line of this cul-ture of the future is fixed, understood and respect-ed, it is not going to be the amount of money in-volved, or magnitude either, that gets respect in anything whatsoever.

The best thought for the best way with the least expenditure where and as *human* values go will be the new criterion for *building* or *living* or *being* any-where in our great country.

This means that no house is a machine for liv-ing in except as the heart of man is a suction pump. But it does mean that the house, if it is a home, is the epitome of the entire resource of this expert me-chanical era; those resources put to work to secure more life for more individuals as individual than life ever held for the individual before. More freedom, better quality—more colorful in effect so far as indi-viduality goes. I tell you *that* is of the true nature of true American Democracy.

Organic architecture has declared war upon the box and the box-man; upon housing à la mode—no matter if the housing (which only means with more deadly facility) more houses planned by the old order of thought for the old conditions however the old types are modified—can only stultify progress and be the same kind of waste Henry's old Model-T was just because Henry left off thinking at the engine and saw the old buggy as good enough to ride in. There deep in H. F. for all his shrewdness—and he is typi-cal—was the eclectic. For culture, he proves to be one when he spends his hard-money for a reproduc-tion of Liberty Hall in which to put heaps of Colo-nial paraphernalia worthless to growth. The old type of dwelling, Colonial or any other period, is not fit for the new machinery of production and can't be made so by all the fixing or fudging that mechanics or the mechanically minded can do, no matter who sells it to whom or where. The old house must be thrown away entirely and a new one, more fit to live in, conceived in the spirit of organic architecture.

So the United States of America is in danger of having to stop job-hunting and go to work to make work a joy to the worker again by getting some gen-uine human content back into work. That task is be-yond government. It must come from the people themselves. Call that desperately needed inner con-tent Art if you want to, a word so abused I prefer to say super-common sense. It is a kind of gospel of work we need right now more than anything else—even square meals. And if we are going to construct anything worth having we ourselves must find rem-edy for our malady. The malady is within—a malady for which fasting might be medicine: starvation the deplorable though not illogical end.

TO THE MEMORIAL CRAFTSMEN OF AMERICA

In a paper read on November 18, 1936, to the association of Memorial Craftsmen of America, Wright addresses a topic never before discussed in his writings or public speaking: cemeteries and monuments. He suggests placing the emphasis of cemeteries on the living, rather than the dead, and making them park-like features in the landscape, not cramped spaces with ugly stone monuments: "There is an essential difference where the living are concerned, and inasmuch as tombstones are really for the living instead of for the dead, I believe the monuments should give way to a sensible memorial. Monuments are merely a form of grandomania, and grandomania has gone so far with us now that we really should take steps so that it is discouraged." [Unpublished speech, November 18, 1936]

CONCERNING THIS BUSINESS OF DYING AND HAVING TO have "one of those things": I am glad you sent for an architect. You, Memorial Craftsmen of America, are chiefly occupied in distinguishing, or making distinguished, the houses of the dead: whereas the architect is busy (if he is busy at all) in making the houses of the quick distinguished: some not so quick nor so distinguished: some "dead at thirty awaiting burial at sixty."

I think these places we call cemeteries should be more pleasurable to the living as habitations for the dead—less dead to the living.

How to make them less dead?

Let's talk it over.

First: the first general curse on habitation for the living is placed there by the "realtor." It is the "lot," the interminable row of "lots," whereas an acre of ground to every house is the only sensible minimum now, if it never was before. The realtor comes first to the cemetery too: he seems to get everywhere first. The citizen alive gets a lot two by twice in some long row, and, dead, he gets another—as long as he is tall and as wide as he is long—when he moves down and out. Or is moved out and down.

There is no sense in this realtor's curse in either case, and I believe if the resting places of the quick and the dead are ever to be made more beautiful—ground and plenty of it must be more sensible and generously used for that purpose. The matter of improvement begins right there, and there is nothing much to do until the realtors are rounded up and most of them taken out to be shot at sunrise.

Now, we have several accepted ways of caring for our dead. And there is much to be said for all three of them. The first and simplest of all is the grave in native ground, made as attractive and beautiful as possible. The second and most pretentious is the mausoleum or sarcophagus, wherein the body reposes, embalmed in a marble casket, enshrined in fine building. The third and most scientific disposition of the whole matter is cremation—burning the flesh, grinding the bones to dust, and committing the dust to memorial urns, storing them in some grandiloquent columbarium. You memorial craftsmen are concerned with all three ways—according to the temperament of the deceased or the familiars. One of these ways is usually selected.

Concerning the first and simplest—the grave—we have more than plenty of ground, and more of it ought to be freely used for the living and also for the dead. This would enable us to use the horizontal headstone, and the extended pavement of stone slabs enscribed or tableted with bronze and surrounded with appropriate gardening, appropriate flowers, trees and shrubs. Make the city of the dead a proper *memorial* for the living. But where crowding has already taken place, I call to mind a design I made for the Martin family of Buffalo. I called it the Blue Sky Mausoleum, because the sloping lot became a terraced series of marble sarcophagi, making a white marble terraced pavement for the entire "lot." And the pavement rose on either side of a central marble aisle to an exhedra or marble seat a half-hexagon in shape, in the center of which stood the family monument suitably inscribed. The cover slabs of the concrete receptacles for the caskets,

which made the terraced paving of the entire lot, were also inscribed, to be read from the central aisle. The whole structure thus rising in gentle elevations on the hillslope. Lead and sulphur made the joints waterproof. A small, tall group of conifers stood behind the exhedra to give relief and contrast to the white marble pavement of slabs. Each slab was seven by three feet.

I mention this merely as a possible use of ground in already overcrowded cemeteries: a dignified way of making the accursed small lot more endurable. And if monuments must be, why not now extend the monument horizontally, keeping it broad and low instead of pushing it upward to make the usual inane forest of stone posts? Modern architecture declares this horizontal extension to be a better lead.

I believe the monument should give away now to the memorial. There is an essential difference where the living are concerned, and inasmuch as tombstones are really for the living instead of for the dead, I believe the monuments should give way to a sensible memorial. Monuments are merely a form of grandomania, and grandomania has gone so far with us now that we really should take steps to see that it is discouraged. Provincial vainglory and selfish pride should have a small place in the hamlets, villages and cities of the dead, but I know of no place in our hamlets and villages where we show all

Blue Sky Burial Terraces (Project). Buffalo, New York. 1928. Plan, elevation. Pencil on tracing paper, 35 x 30". FLLW Fdn#2801.007

UE-SKY SARCOPHAGUS   FOR D.D.MARTIN FAMILY   FRANK LLOYD WRIGHT ARCHITEC

Blue Sky Burial Terraces (Project). Buffalo, New York. 1928. Perspective. Pencil and color pencil on tracing paper, 23 x 18".
FLLW Fdn#2801.008

these to such bad advantage, in respect to these qualities, as on these poetry-crushing cemeteries of ours. The same thing is going on there between the Smiths, Joneses and Robinsons that goes on in the towns. These burial places show how little real feeling or creative imagination the living have to make these abodes for the dead at all fit for the living, or for that matter for the dead either.

I can imagine the ideal burying ground chosen for its natural beauty, heightened by park-like spacing of broad and quiet memory stones or tablets of bronze, or both together: mausoleums like the Getty Tomb at Graceland or the Ryerson Tomb there, or the beautiful Wainwright Tomb in St. Louis: beautiful appropriate edifices designed by my beloved master, Louis Sullivan. These places we call burying grounds should be places to which we might look with no repulsion or dread, a blessing too, instead of a curse on life. And, believe me, this is all a matter of *design:* appropriate spaciousness in the first place, an intelligent use of materials in the second place, and a fine

sense of the whole, dominant. If we are to be regimented in rows fifty feet on center while we are alive, for God's sake give us enough room to lie in, gracefully separate, and beautifully informal in arrangement when we are dead. This in order to have a little freedom to look forward to and a better sentiment toward death than we now seem to have: not that this would do us any good after we are dead, but because it would do us all good while we are alive to see our loved ones better treated at last. Finally, shouldn't every one of us be allowed a last line? That last line would shed much light upon the living, be a certain comeback from the dead. I have in mind Dorothy Parker's epitaph—she designed it for herself:

"Excuse my dust."

Everyone has a last line in him or her, and the headstone or the pavement or the marker is a good place for it. Humanize the cemeteries you memorializers! Humanize the burial places of your kind! They are now so much more dead than the dead can ever be dead!

197

APPRENTICESHIP TRAINING FOR THE ARCHITECT

The Taliesin Fellowship was well into its fourth year when Frank Lloyd Wright wrote this article for The Architectural Record. *By 1936 the fellowship's buildings at Hillside (the Hillside Home School) had been repaired, remodeled, and converted for use by the fellowship; the drafting room and rooms for sixteen apprentices, connected to the northern section of the original 1902 buildings, were under construction; sections of Taliesin, on the neighboring hill in this same ancestral valley, likewise had undergone repairs and conversion; a farm was established halfway between Taliesin, Wright's home, and Hillside—and named, appropriately, "Midway." New architectural work finally had begun to flow into the office, starting with a home for Edgar Kaufmann, "Fallingwater," in Mill Run, Pennsylvania, followed by an administration building for the S.C. Johnson & Son Company, in Racine, Wisconsin. During the lean years, from 1932 to 1935, when commissions were very limited, the fellowship worked on the Broadacre City model and related models, as well as carrying on the work of converting Hillside and expanding Taliesin for fellowship activities.*

In this article Wright explains the manner in which the training at Taliesin is carried out vis-à-vis conventional academic training. The core of the system is what he calls "apprenticeship-training." But he qualifies it from its original concept of centuries ago: "Apprenticeship, I believe, was something like this in the middle ages but with this important difference: the apprentice then was his master's slave. At Taliesin he is his master's comrade." [Published with two illustrations in The Architectural Record, *September 1936]*

WHY DO YOU—DOES ANY ONE—WANT TO BECOME AN architect?

If you can truthfully say you love building and want to know buildings how do you expect to become the kind of builder we should call "architect"?

Precisely what do you expect to learn in the schools that will help you to build good or great buildings?

Experience in actual planning and actual building with wood, plaster, stone, brick, steel, glass, synthetics, learning of the nature of materials by *working* with materials is needed, but where is creative inspiration, that essential qualification of the architect and of true architecture, where is inspiration to be found?

Of what possible use do you imagine schoolbooks and art history, school-styles and any mere technique whatsoever will be to you in becoming what we should call an architect? America needs organic architecture as she needs organic character in all her institutions where *experience* furnishes the only data and inspiration furnishes the only interpretation.

School education with its styles and history cannot be this inspiration for the young man in architecture today. At best, it can have only a small place in the development of his creative ability. The would-be architect must seek experience under inspired leadership—the guidance of men who do build from the inside out—and from the ground up spiritually as well as physically: men to whom the philosophy of structure is a natural consequence of learning from the great book of books—creation itself.

TALIESIN

I should say that present ideals and items of education are exactly wrong where genuine architecture or any art is concerned.

To justify the statement I need only point to the consequences, that is to say, point to the imitations and sterility that make of America a place wherein you may hardly find one building, wherewith any professional architect artist was concerned, manifestly inspired by the country itself or by any life in it that might be called indigenous.

So, Taliesin has rejected nearly all of the tenets that made and would maintain such a condition, setting up instead a simple experiment in which volunteers are working away at something so simple as to be amusing to the complex mentality that expects to get enlightenment by way of cerebratious student-information or Beaux-Arts training.

For some years past a small changing group of about twenty-five Fellows (young men and young women—all volunteers) has comprised the working group of apprentices to myself at Taliesin. During that time the novice has met, first, neglect, in the hope that he might "relax" and so by natural perception get a "break." The novitiate soon finds books and information, as such, left behind and that all stand in "atmosphere" free of pretense and hypocrisy and upon a "soil" which will nourish only such sincerity of character and purpose as each may possess, as a basis for talent.

Previous education is mostly in the way. All begin again (if they can begin at all) to think of building as an interpretation of life from the ground upward. They cannot avoid the implications of such thinking or get away from its effects. They are here together with me in a way of life and in surroundings that all point in the direction of such interpretation, and they are working comrades of one who has been "seeing it through" long enough to have some little wisdom from actual experience in getting the principles of an organic architecture into concrete form. In this, I think I have been tried by time almost as much as I have been a trial to time.

Apprenticeship, I believe, was something like this in the Middle Ages but with this important difference: the apprentice then was his master's slave. At Taliesin he is his master's comrade. He is engaged with him together with others like-minded in the spirit of creation. While up to the present time some ninety young men now practicing architecture around the world have been with me as employees, only during the past several years have any been here in the give and take of apprenticeship.

These previous young men came and went with no deeper intent than to pick up whatever they could and turn it over to their advantage as quickly as possible. I was willing, but not cooperative. Even so some few of them managed pretty well.

Now, I expect these more intimate young co-workers to be valuable as workmen knowing the nature of the whole, able to utter it in building, painting, carving, or able to write or sing or play it in terms of the spirit of our time and our manifold new opportunities.

Unfortunately, a novice must bring money with him to begin with, but we are not interested in getting him ready to earn money on the present basis of brokerage or wagery. I have seen the damage *that* can do to a good cause where all the new methods have so far outrun the understanding of the architect or artist and a feudal hangover kills his effort.

I believe the old-style practitioner—the broker—is dead anyway and a more creative individual capable of going through from start to finish

Administration Building for the S.C. Johnson & Son Company. Racine, Wisconsin. 1936. Perspective. Pencil and color pencil on tracing paper, 37 x 20". FLLW Fdn#3601.001

with his own building as *builder* is going to make America the Broadacre City. As architect he—or she—will do several buildings only—and completely—where predecessors did a hundred or so carcasses and turned them all over to the building equivalent of the hairdresser, the couturier, the master of ceremonies.

But the future architect in that Future that I believe to be the Present will be compensated as a creative factor in society, a single factor taking the place of realtor, contractor, decorator, landscapist and financier. That is to say, all responsibility for his client's buildings will be, not theoretically, but actually in this architect's hands. His predecessors have worked for six percent, say. This architect of the future works for thirty percent. What we are trying to do at Taliesin is to make a little human material fit for such responsibility where 30 architects will be needed instead of a single broker.

To this end the Taliesin novitiate is here in a fair way of life wherein "servant" has ceased to exist—where "service" is no sales-talk but is a condition; where all hands are in the mud of which the bricks are made and all hands are there from an early rising bell until all tumble into bed, worn out. The inexperienced have been getting the feel of materials into their hands after working on designs to be executed in the nature of those materials or finding new uses to be made of new materials, getting correlation of hand and brain where any plan, or any necessity for planning is concerned, meanwhile developing mastery over self by way of hard work and clear thinking along center lines that principle lays down—not only those laid down by Tradition.

Yes, again here is the unpopular gospel of Work and at a stage in our state where all work is prostitute to the cash-and-carry system. Therefore, I lay myself open to peculiarly invidious implications.

Again, work. Yes, but with new light for human-nature upon the nature of work and upon the nature of building as a proof of culture.

A dream? As usual. But real enough to those who get into action here. And here is *action*. Action, more action and some more action. Always. Emergency after emergency. Nothing much to work with but all the more necessity to work with thought, actuated by thought and to germinate thought.

Administration Building for the S.C. Johnson & Son Company. Racine, Wisconsin. 1936. Perspective. Sepia ink on tracing paper, 36 x 11".
FLLW Fdn#3601.006.

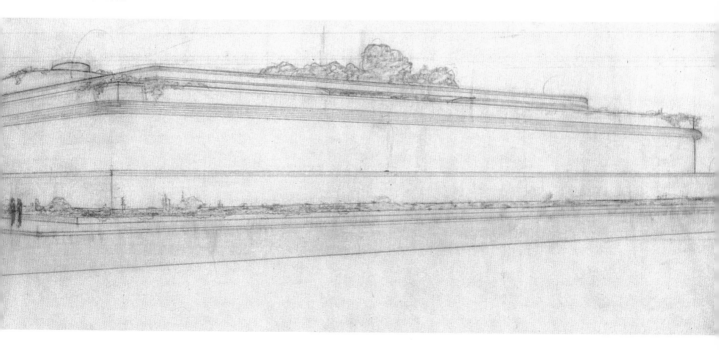

Workers are here, themselves becoming the thing they would do for their kind.

No longer "Education," you see, but "Culture" instead. Organic growth is slow growth indeed—but, it is *growth*. No garment to put on.

Not so many "graduates" are fit to enter this sort of thing now. I mean there are few still able to make the necessary surrender to reality. The many are either gamblers hopelessly in love with the romantic aspect of the gamble or have been educated to imagine that certain hard facts constitute reality, and "the many" are therefore in the same case as any squirrel who might mistake the shell of the nut for the kernel. That squirrel wouldn't live long.

And similarly the architects that made our present architecture are dead. Most of them were, at best, fragments—"designing partners." If anything was needed to prove that our Architecture is their corpse the late attempt at a style as a left wing of an organic architecture proved it.

Not a style at Taliesin. But a variety of daily effort all in the nature of Style. And all the while. The abstraction therefore is continually being made—afresh—by the apprenticeship.

We are learning to think and see in simples. And simples are always "the abstract," are they not?

The workers at Taliesin—when the spirit moves—make drawings recording abstraction as they see into what surrounds them and they make such abstractions as the lighter side of their labors. They are minded to learn to see *inside*. We occasionally exhibit these drawings in our galleries. And we often indulge in talk—sometimes encourage it—and we write, and play too, when the spirit moves.

To work with, meanwhile, we have Taliesin itself; we almost have a spacious new drafting room; we have a new theater; two galleries for exhibitions and many models; and we have it upon a two-hundred-acre farm where Wisconsin is most beautiful. Taking our work along with us we leave it all for the three winter months of each year to get fresh contacts with other soil and other scenes, while we work. Arizona desert for two years past. This year Russia. Next year, maybe, Japan. Because any real architect, now, must be a citizen of this world. No narrow nationalist can exist in any sense in the light of this ideal of architecture as organic expression of life as organic.

And the unpardonable sin at Taliesin is rest unless you are really doing something worthwhile while you are resting. We believe in recreation, not rest, and believe that change of work is recreation: a valid sport. We believe, too, that "reflection" is often clearest in perspective when action is swiftest and most certain. Organic growth is slow growth in this age of the quick "turn-over." But it is not merely some garment, put on.

A short-time ex-apprentice recently asked an apprentice still at Taliesin: "Is Taliesin interested in turning out human-beings or is it interested in turning out architects?" I should answer him by saying that, in spite of machinery, the human tide is so turning that unless we have the one we cannot have the other. The ideal of an organic architecture is such that *you are* the thing you do or you can't do anything. The builder who will take the place of the broker must interpret *life* in terms of building—out of *himself*. Not knowing life from within himself how is he going to make life objective by building?

PLAN: A MODERN HOME

In this article Wright aired his concerns about prefabricated housing, how it was used at that time and how it might instead evolve: "The pre-fabricated house problem is, including all its mechanical features—which should be automatic—essentially an architect's problem in organic architecture." He had initiated prefabrication into his designs in 1916 with the "American Ready-Cut System Built Homes," a number of examples of which were constructed in Chicago and Milwaukee. Wright continued to return to this concept, and at the time of this article was developing the Usonian house for the family of moderate income. [Published with one illustration in Inland Topics (Chicago), 1936]

THE CAPITALISTIC SYSTEM AS IT STILL EXISTS HAS MANY efficiencies to its credit but, as it stands, will never be able to present to the people a product with any artistic integrity whatsoever, unless inadvertent.

Inventive as it is, in its very vitals the system is antipathetic to all creative work in the arts because it has use for creative work only as in itself another commodity and will buy it only as it buys other commodities. In other words it will buy only when, somehow, it can find results ready-made to its hand for profit in an obvious market. So development of the essential quality of artistic integrity in anything whatsoever is nothing for the present system. And nothing forever. The system is not shrewd, it is only smart.

For a present instance, when the system, by way of its captains, was advised that a machine-made factory-built home now ought to "go" with the people, it got its "experts" busy with a few stylists—superficial speculators like stylists are always to be had for the asking—and all began on the thing as usual, from the outside. The last thing that seemed to occur to the system was that if the prefabricated house is to "go" at all it must be no makeshift but must be radical architecture in an organic sense as not only a good machine is but also as any natural thing is. Say, a tree. Integral and indigenous architecture. But, having been able to see or know architecture or have it only as an eclectic's makeshift, the system began to wonder and "questionnaire," whether Tudor, Mediterranean, Spanish or Modernistic (the latest style) would "go" best, and act accordingly. The nature of the materials to be used in the house and the process by which the house must be built as well as the nature of the life lived in it and the purpose of the whole altogether are obstacles to the stylist—Tudor or Modernist.

Inevitably the problem does not get more from the stylish than a shift to get by these obstacles to a style as handily as may be. The cleverest *manipulator*. Ah! There was the man the system wanted.

So the pre-fabricated house, so-called, has little or no chance at all for life in the hands of the system as the system "goes."

Attempts to date show this clearly enough. But now that the new epoch upon which we are entering is begun, some day a creative architect may get a model factory-made house—not merely a slum-cleaner but a home of the better class, built for somebody somehow, certainly not by the aid of the system. And if the house "goes" the system may swing around and take it probably to patent it to "protect" it. To "protect" it would mean to price it for what the traffic would bear, say a house costing $800—to be sold for $3,500.

Yet, I do not believe that many of the better American people interested in better homes are ever going to buy their houses as they buy their motor-cars, although I believe they should have the benefit of the same economies in construction that gave them the "protected" motor-car, the "protected" telephone and the "protected" radio. But another and a more valuable element than any found in these "protected" products enters into a man's home. A man's home is refuge for far more than the animal. Sleep, fodder and warmth well arranged, this most important thing, organic unity, yet remains to be achieved. To date, the house-owner has been put off in this matter by some monkeying or other with the look of the thing the other fellow did—"the other fellow" in every way and in every sense. And the home-maker got "the look of it" as the girls got dressed from a Sears Roebuck catalogue.

That this kind of selection-of-the-ready-made-by-way-of-fashion, or taste, has become character-istic and that "taste" may be—uncultured as the average American homemaker is to date—played upon to a large extent by the system, is obvious. As a matter of course this matter of ignorance—"taste" will be so played upon. But the larger interest in his home is already there in the citizen—asleep maybe, and the wasteful, servile thing he got into by way of ignorant "taste" is rotten ripe for change.

In spite of the testimony of the enormous sums of money spent foolishly to obtain appearances that may be mere show, there is a real nostalgia for beau-ty among the people of these United States.

Show the better American citizen the counte-nance of principle in a factory-made house, that is to say, show him a house that he can see is as naturally a home as he can see the motorship is a ship, see a plane is an aeroplane or see a car as good transporta-tion and I believe the house will "go," and that the ugly waste of the present building system will be ended by a system more natural to the machine-age.

Let's admit that none of the above mechanical objects of comparison are yet perfected as to form and are not perfected for much the same reasons I have given as working against the pre-fabricated house. But these mechanical features of our life are so infinitely better in degree as to be good enough to laugh at the factory-made house. When the American people do get their homes from the factory, made in synthetic materials, they will be better homes because they got them there that way—as they may be—and cheaper, too, because a wasteful, wretched, criss-cross building system has, necessarily, been junked.

But the buildings themselves must be so de-signed that genuine variety in unity is to be had in good proportion without stultifying the economics of standardization. And the new buildings must have an entirely new expansion of comfort and beauty owing to the very advantages of the new machine-construction and the synthetic materials in their make-up. The stylist stands in the way of all these potential assets, as does the system itself. So long as the new factory-made house is to be at the mercy of both stylist and system nothing much can happen except the usual exploitation unless it is a cabin for the Negroes or slum-cleaning apartments.

The pre-fabricated house problem is, includ-ing all its mechanical features—which should be automatic—essentially an architect's problem in organic architecture.

A more complete harmony is then inevitable because it is natural. Therefore only radical ideas and genuine ability grown up with respect for the nature of the component parts of the thing we call architecture can ever save the pre-fabricated house for the home-seller *as a home*.

Concerning the illustration—as a matter of

John Storer House. Los Angeles, California. 1923. Perspective. Pencil and color pencil on tracing paper, 17 x 8". FLLW Fdn#2304.002

fact the idea that a pre-fabricated house must be of steel or synthetic materials is only modernist propaganda. An interesting picture of a pre-fabricated mono-material house eliminating skilled labor in its construction is illustrated herewith. The house is pre-fabricated in concrete units knit together in erection by one-quarter-inch steel strands laid into interior grooves in the wall at the junction of the concrete units formed by the shape of the units themselves. This introduction of steel requires no skill, being practically automatic as to fixture. In this case the "factory" is easily transferable from site to site. The factory goes to the house instead of the house going to the factory.

SKYSCRAPERS DOOMED? YES!

The question "Are Skyscrapers Doomed?" was selected by the publisher of The Rotarian *as a topic of discussion for architects to consider. In the same issue of the magazine, another architect, V. G. Iden, had answered the question with a resounding "No!"*

But by 1936 Wright saw the trend of over-building and over-renting as a serious threat to human life. Therefore Wright's thesis in this article, as with all his writings about skyscrapers, was that skyscrapers crowded into densely overcrowded cities are an inhumane menace. Removed to the countryside or set in green parks, he argued, they can be beautiful as well as useful buildings. [Published with four illustrations in The Rotarian, *March 1936]*

THIS MODERN FEUDAL-TOWER, THE SKYSCRAPER, IS THE last and greatest symbol of the early get-rich-quick type of money-making method. The skyscraper exploits neighboring buildings in the same way that the businesses that build it often exploited neighboring business. But the fact that the feudal-tower is meant to make money was only "thrift" in the era in which we came to see the towering skyscraper as a symbol of success.

Fair enough, let us say. The best man wins. But what, exactly, does he win? What is this skyscraper thing anyway?

We are in a bad way to know something about our specific progress, now that we have succeeded. We may find certain implications in this outstanding example of "success" if we look at it for what it is.

Obviously, this race for the objective top represents considerable engineering ability: structural steel mills and the mechanical ingenuity of elevator companies, chiefly. Together, with considerable human inventive ingenuity, they enabled the thing to stand there accessible, with a real estate agent to sell the owner's original "lot" over and over again as many times as there are floors. But this free-for-all race for supremacy has taken place on the curb where the crowd is thickest: this, in order to exploit the crowd. But these tall business men, the skyscrapers themselves, standing skyward, tall and straight, landward as the ships come down the bay seaward . . . are they—were they ever—good business?

Well, when acceleration was on and the crowd was surging cityward, to surge upward seemed reasonable enough to most people and so the people surged, or, with a little skyscraping, were surged. To build the skyscraper, then, really was an easy way to hold the hot-spot of crowd-concentration by way of easy money for easy money.

But all exploitation must come to an end. This particular form of exploitation, having no ethical foundation whatsoever outside mere legality, and being as far out of human scale as humanity is now far gone beyond it on the road toward decentralization, the end of the skyscraper comes rather soon.

What is to become of these grandiloquent expedients in money-makers' grandomania?

To some of our people, exaggeration will always mean greatness—because they know no better grandeur. To such, the skyscrapers will be the great monuments marking the spot where pride once stood to say progress is necessarily commercial. Twentieth-century gravestones! Not milestones on the road to progress.

A well-known architect suggests that in the overbuilt areas they become the "housing" that government, at the moment, is seeking for its subjects. And since dwellings are underbuilt and offices overbuilt, it does seem reasonable enough that we should move the one into the other. As a matter of fact, there seems to be very little difference in our idea of cellular accommodation either for an office building, a hotel, or for housing. All look very much alike in our very best efforts. So, inasmuch as the best human element has already gone from the city where skyscrapers abound and the better element is getting ready to go to the country, why not let the slum be the scum for a while until all may be properly salvaged by the process of decentralization that is surely setting in?

I second the well-known architect's motion with proper emotion.

The skyscrapers were built to be amortized in thirty years. Some of them have not so far to go now, and the slums we have made by way of money-making will in some form last about that long notwithstanding our billions for relief. There is some poetic justice in this suggested picture of the skyscraper's future as a tenement. Strange though it must seem to good business, poetic justice is the very justice we all eventually do see dealt or do ourselves get.

Decentralization of the efficiencies of which the skyscraper is a conspicuous example is inevitable because, in any final showdown, the man means more than his horse or his tools. We, having had remarkable machine development as the engine of exploitation for profits, are now growing cautious: somewhat suspicious now about mechanical efficiencies as unmixed blessings.

Something has happened to make starvation a stark reality in the very midst of our plenty. The spectacle of empty skyscrapers being pulled down to save taxes while there is not shelter enough to go around; to keep prices up milk is poured into the streets, and hogs are drowned, corn is burned, cotton weeviled, when millions have not enough to wear and other millions are starving to death—all of this has made a good many people try to think who felt no need of thinking much before. Perhaps unmitigated machinery has much to do with this fiasco. We are suffering the internal pangs of revolution, now, so far as the ideas we once held concerning industry go.

We see that agriculture and industry can't go far separately by way of science to be of lasting benefit to society, and that neither can go alive without the arts. Art humanizes and gives living quality to all that man produces for consumption: mitigates machine production. The arts haven't been taken into the reckoning by the commerce that built so fast and so big . . . and so the product is empty of human significance. As a form of life it is sterile. It cannot reproduce no matter how it may be streamlined outside for "market."

I don't suppose many of our people realize that art deals with this matter of the human significance of things: of all kinds of things. Nor do many of our people know that above or below the belt the ultimate value to our social life of anything we do or make depends upon how much whatever we may produce fits harmoniously into place in some scheme of good life considered as a whole.

It isn't enough to do or to have things that are mere makeshifts. To be practical, they must have this quality of fitness to the purpose of life which is, in itself, a kind of life. We ought to know that because we can now see that the makeshift can only shift to make more shift and make less and less good life above the stereotype. The mechanical makeshift doesn't really arrive anywhere at all except into trouble by way of confusion, cross purposes—and ultimately, chaos.

This finer kind of order we call art, which depends upon comprehending the part and its use in relation to the use of the whole, is not found in the exaggerated part centralization has played in our time. The human being was left out. Such centralization as we know has made crowd exploitation all too easy. In fact, it has itself been that exploitation. Life values are flames, all human, and soon by such centralization as ours became all snuffed out.

When life is out of fix, it isn't quite the same as the old gas engine out of fix. The scientific or mechanical or political tinker isn't enough then. We are now where no one of them can help us very much if we are going to go on. We need this sense of the whole as a human interest at work upon some plan for the whole—a plan that as an expression of love of life has ways and means of using machinery to make life better worth living and, otherwise, not use deadly efficiencies at all.

Studying our present situation in this light we can only see that to spread out on the ground, more harmonious with it and with the new sense of space brought by universal mobilization and electro-communication, is now inevitable. We must see that our cherished institutions like the city, the skyscraper, the big knowledge factories, the big this and the big that, must resolve into thousands of lesser and little ones bringing up the individualities of many men instead of exaggerating the individuality of some one man or group of men who have nothing more than ambition and efficiency to recommend them. For the fact that neither are enough, let the skyscraper stand as a significant symbol.

Now it has been said by the expert—inevitably thoughtless—that skyscrapers are architecture. Not so. No commercial expedient, however good as a grand gesture, can be good architecture.

An imitation feudal-tower faked in masonry may be good scene-painting but not good architecture. Were it architecture you would see the tall building as a thing of steel and metals and glass, sheer and shimmering in the light from within or from without. A tall building in this age *might* be such a beautiful thing—might be indeed great architecture were it a free-standing child of space. But as a dubious commercial expedient, overdressed in material goods that do not belong to it, standing one side upon a street and another upon an alley—otherwise poaching upon the neighborhood preserves—well, however graceful and rich or even simple in itself the skyscraper may be, it has no place in the realm of architecture, though the effect might be pleasing enough in the town masquerade.

All these masonry-seeming tall money-makers, however they may be fashioned, belong to that exciting but relatively inconsequential form of event—the town masquerade. Any steel building inside that is a stone or a brick building outside is a ponderous anachronism destined to evil consequences—even when the steel does all the work and carries its false cover of masonry from one floor to another—without staggering.

But the very tall building might be a reasonable and socially desirable building. We will have such in the country some day as genuine architecture, standing free on all sides, fit companions to the trees and hills. But we should have them frankly and freely for what they are. They must be organic in character before we can call them architecture.

So far as true progress goes, then, the skyscraper as it stands is inherently a confession of impotence. Skyscraping is this ignoble confession at the moment of its proudest boast. Such engineering as it knows is completely wiped out by its designer's abortive attempt at architecture. Such economy as it knows is wiped out by its own excess. Such honor as it might have by way of progress has been betrayed by greed.

THE COUNTRY DOCTOR

In December 1936 Wright was struck by a severe case of pneumonia. He feared hospitals intensely, considering them to be houses of death that emphasized the dying more than the living. His wife, Olgivanna, was very much aware of this obsessive fear, and she decided that rather than subjecting him to the agony of hospitalization, she would keep him at home, at Taliesin. She called in Dr. Constantine Wahl from the neighboring town of Spring Green. Wright recovered under the careful watch and attention of Dr. Wahl, his wife, and the members of the Taliesin Fellowship. Once he was well enough to leave his room, Olgivanna arranged for him to go to Arizona to gain back his strength in the warm desert sunshine. Out of this illness, and the ensuing trip south, came the decision to make a winter home in the desert—Taliesin West. Part of her resolve to take him to Arizona annually was a remark made to her by another doctor, Dr. Michel Matanovich, an old family friend from her native Montenegro who was living in Phoenix at the time the Wrights went there in 1937. "If you will bring Frank to the Arizona desert and out of the Wisconsin cold," he told her, "every winter of his life, you will extend his life by twenty years, at the least."

The following article was Wright's form of praise and thanks for the care he received from "The Country Doctor." It also expresses his strong belief, in general, of reducing things to more individual, human units, in contradistinction to large, impersonal, and therefore less human, establishments. [Published four years after writing On Architecture (New York: Duell, Sloan, and Pearce, 1940)]

WERE I GOVERNOR OF THIS STATE THE COUNTRY DOCTOR of Wisconsin should have all the aid I could give him. But even the governor, I am afraid, would have to turn the job over to politicians in order to get anything done. Having just come through a serious illness by choice at home, with one of these rough diamonds rather than be carted off to the latest and best in hospitals, I have the rural doctor on my mind with gratitude for his hard sense—his faculties sharpened by personal experience. Faculties which proved right when precision instruments in more scientific hands went wrong. Dr. Osler once said he never discounted the diagnosis of a country doctor. And I hope all of you have read Ian McLaren's tribute to "the doctor of the old school." Alex Woollcott includes it in his new "reader."

What I would have done for him is no more than to endow every one of him with a small clinic of his own including an oxygen tank and the more indispensable modern instruments—free subscriptions to whatever scientific medico-surgical literature he might chose to subscribe.

And when he has grown less able to live on unpaid bills—a modest pension from the state.

I think it more important to increase his initiative and characterful contact with the sick of his region than to further emphasize exportations to the big hospital.

Yes—decentralization again instead of organized congestion.

I believe American country doctors to be the most valuable of all America's shock troops and would like to see more power and greater opportunity for usefulness coming to him where sick folk are at home.

The big "institution" is drawing from him rather than building him up—just as the big manufactured newspaper has killed the crusading editor.

The kind of self-reliance that, acting on his own judgement in emergency on emergency, breeds in the country doctor does something to his faculties "we the people" can't afford to lose.

Let us give the doctor of our Wisconsin countrysides—a break.

Blue loggia, Taliesin, Spring Green, Wisconsin. 1925. Interior perspective. Photograph by Hedrich-Blessing, courtesy the Chicago Historical Society. FLLW Fdn FA#2501.0239

CONCERNING THE U.S.S.R.

Wright's wife, Olgivanna, spent her early life in Russia; in Moscow during the winters and at her sister's dacha on the Black Sea in the summers. When Wright was invited to Russia in order to address the All-Union Congress of Soviet Architects, in June 1937, his trip was made more meaningful due to her skills as an interpreter and her ability to share with him her firsthand knowledge not only of the Russian language but also of the traditions, culture, peoples, and character of Russia itself. Expectedly, for her, Russia had drastically changed since her exodus in 1917 at the outbreak of the revolution. Just at the time that the Wrights were invited there, Stalin was waging his purge against the Russian peasant farmers who opposed his collective farming program. Hundreds of thousands died in that savage bloodbath, but the Wrights were obviously shielded from such events. Their associations and relationships were confined mainly to the Soviet architectural community. In this regard they had a most pleasant trip. His account of that visit, as he wrote for Soviet Russia Today, *praises the Russian peoples and their spirit and commends the attitude, if not the work, of its architects. Olgivanna, on the other hand, being fluent in the language, was more aware of the hardships and heartbreaks of the Soviet Union twenty years after its supposedly glorious revolution. Wright candidly expressed his views in this unpublished article, "Concerning the U.S.S.R.," as well as in an article for the Russian newspaper* Izvestia *in reply to their request for an article "about culture under fascism and culture in the U.S.S.R. for the twentieth-anniversary issue which will be read by at least twenty million people." When these articles and statements, along with others appearing in Soviet-American periodicals were read in the United States, they caused great consternation. Wright was accused of being a communist, of being what people at that time called a "red" sympathizer. The story of that Russian trip and its ensuing events was told in full by Wright when he revised and expanded* An Autobiography *in the early spring of 1943.*

In 1957 Wright was interviewed by Mike Wallace on national television. Wallace brought up these articles and the issues of Wright's visit to Moscow in 1937. He asked the architect, "How can you explain this enthusiasm for a country which even then, and certainly now, has instituted thought control by terror, political purges, by blood, suppression of intellectuals?" To which Wright replied, "Do you ever dissociate government and people? I don't find it difficult. I find that government can be a kind of gangsterism, and is, in Russia. . . . I think the people are unaware of all these things that are happening to them. I don't think they've appraised them at their true value. . . . Communism is utterly, from my standpoint, wrong."
[Unpublished essay, 1937]

IF CAPITALISM IS FAIR THEN UNIONISM MUST BE. IF MEN have a right to capitalize their ideas and the resources of their country then that right implies the right of men to capitalize their labors. In fact men must do so if any balance in the social order is to be preserved. That is why I said I should like to see our country unionized "to the hilt." The "hilt" meaning the government—I suppose. The right to capitalize implies the right to unionize. A non-fascist supreme court would declare and defend that obvious right.

But Russia has found a more simple way to carry on.

The "capital and labor" struggle is too complicated for the more human instincts of the more human point of view of that intensely humane racial group.

Capital and labor in the U.S.A. are two fists continually at each other—because the U.S.A. is "two-minded"—a country divided against itself. As I see the U.S.S.R., it is a two-handed affair, single-minded. A country united within itself.

The U.S.A., a senior country now, has its own problems and breakdowns steadily on the increase.

Olgivanna and Frank Lloyd Wright, on board the SS *Bremen*, en route to Russia. 1937. FLLW Fdn FA#6202.0001

The U.S.S.R., an infant, has its own problems and breakdowns steadily diminishing.

If conscience in the U.S.A. were still in human scale and clear, this new order in Russia would not appear a menace. As a people we would be keenly interested to learn the truth instead of press-wild to believe it must fail.

Ourselves unable, unwilling, or afraid to proceed the more simple way, we seem to resent even the thought that the simple way might be the better way and we shut our eyes, too tight.

Now I don't know what "Communism" is. For years I've tried to find out and no two advocates seem to describe it alike. As for Socialism—do you know what it is? Does even Norman Thomas know? What little hoping and thinking I've done concerning a social state yearns and leans toward democracy. Whatever is democratic I am inclined to trust. I love and cherish the ideal of freedom I read into the ideal our forefathers held for this country. But what is democratic? Certainly not the U.S.A. as it is drifting at present. England more so but still not so. France? Wait a little while and see. Japan? An imitation about where France is just now. Spain? A degenerate nation dismembered by hypocritical sympathizers. Germany? A natural consequence of inflicted inferiority. Italy? A natural consequence of degeneracy.

Holland, Switzerland, Sweden, Norway, Finland, and Denmark? Self-determining peoples nearer democracy than any. The Balkans? Just awakening to the dangers of "higher civilization." China? An antique giant trying to wipe sleep out of its eyes.

Russia? Well, compare her constitution with ours and go to see the *spirit* of her people—the *character* of her enterprise—the proud way her men and women walk the streets, sing in unison in the streetcars and work in factories and fields; their own enterprise: their own streets: their own factories: their own fields. Let those men and women tell you what they feel, and—yes, what they think too, concerning what they are doing and *why*, instead of taking what some little university boy turned press-reporter edited by a corporation-newspaper tells you.

Even the multitude of books so well and wisely written on the subject of the Soviet proceed to

Frank Lloyd Wright and Mr. and Mrs. Arkin, outside Moscow. 1937. FLLW Fdn FA#6827.0001

drink the tub of dye to find its color—never seeing it: never *seeing* it because the spirit alone can see the spirit.

The Russian spirit in this new way of life over there, where 90 per cent of the people are still what we call "illiterate," is vigorous and healthy beyond any nation on earth. As I walked the streets among them I felt "God help any nation, or nations either, undertaking to interfere with this."

Out of such liberation and consecration come heroisms: flyers over the North Pole, not stunting mind you, but as a natural consequence of their new way of life. Coming up are new heroisms in all walks of life. One hundred and forty-four states intensely alive and humane, colorful with individuality, all united in hope and purpose. Well, it does seem too good to be true. Says the press: "There is a nigger in the woodpile."

But how could the "press" see? The prejudice of self-interest is always blind. Fear sees only itself. Sees "red" in this case.

But so far as this country is democratic and not guilty, it must see the U.S.S.R. as a natural comrade of the U.S.A.

Concerning "the Reds," "Communists," Trotskyites, and campus intelligentsia in our country, they now seem to me the worst enemies of Russia. If as the Trotskyites say, Stalin is betraying the revolution, then—well, he is betraying it into the hands of the Russian people, which may be just too

bad for world-communism. But it doesn't seem bad for Russia.

Only about fifteen years away from the turmoil of revolution, inevitable reactions still in the bloodstream of the nation to be dealt with, enemies within her borders and surrounding her, that youth has found a wise and competent if relentless leader who begins the new Russia with the new-born being in the cradles of the crèche behind the workers, whether workers are in the factory, the field, or home.

Culture is a word everywhere used in practice by the Russians. There, in Moscow, stands the great new palace of culture designed by the Vesnin brothers: the Park of Culture and Rest with the Green Theater seating 20,000 people—400 acres in the very heart of Moscow: their splendid amplified cinemas, operas, the ballet, and the theaters: their incomparable free sanitariums and sanitoriums. And you ride with "culture" on the new subway as you pass through palatial station after station. They build culture in everywhere. Even their architects consider culture.

I don't recall ever hearing the word used in connection with our public enterprises, do you?

Russians with all their handicaps, work hard—but happy—toward the democracy we—a house divided against itself—profess and fail to practice.

Frank Lloyd Wright and Mr. and Mrs. Yofan, Society of Cultural Relations Banquet, Moscow. 1937. FLLW Fdn FA#6827.0002

FOR "IZVESTIA"

HERE IS TO YOU DEMOCRATIC RUSSIA, YOU THE INTERIOR nature of man working its way according to principle into a naturally beautiful way of life. You will soon see the architectural forms of hereditary aristocracy as just as false to any naturally beautiful way of life as the old aristocracy itself was false to human rights.

Fascism is the resort of nations in weakness or despair and may accept the old forms with modern improvements because Fascism is merely some man attempting to work out a pattern of life and impose it upon men from the outside. Nations living under capitalism or aristocracy too long become senile or bewildered, helplessly accepting the dictator. But Fascism does not know Principle. It knows only the approved fashion.

Russian Democracy must not have shed its blood to reject the aristocratic wrong only to spend its best energies in continuing the false forms of that aristocracy where culture is concerned—as it is being continued in architecture and the arts in Soviet Russia today. Soviet Russia can not afford to be too patient with that cultural lag. The cultural forms of the Czarist regime were betrayals of their originals and can only betray your new reality. They will make of your priceless youth a premature senility.

Capitalism too, helplessly accepts the false forms of hereditary aristocracy and applies them to whatever is new. Nothing is more capitalistic than the skyscraper and its elevator. With capitalism as with Fascism, the autocratic Beaux Arts sits in the shadow of government as a cultural lag to render cultural acts null and void—shirking reality as irksome, even vulgar. Neither the sterility of Fascism nor the blindness of capitalism should dominate in Russia today by way of this cultural lag.

Because Soviet Russia has begun her social life at the beginning and nobly takes her stand with the forces of Democracy, she must immediately seek true forms in the arts for all of her new life. And these forms cannot be traditional unless they were and still are organic where the new life lives. If Russia does not seek and find true new forms, she will build into her social fabric a time-lag from which she may never recover and that may prove fatal.

Unfortunately most of those buildings inspired by the European left wing in modern architecture are ugly structures badly built because no architect of the left wing is really enough of a technician to build original buildings. Some of these architects are painters experimenting with building as they would with any genre. So it is maybe difficult now for the Russian people to understand that the new Simplicity of organic architecture does not mean plainness. Organic form has true simplicity no matter how exuberant it may be or how completely rich in detail. Russia's first adventure in the direction of a modern architecture has resulted in many brutal concrete structures, not really simple in the organic sense. They are only plain.

Reaction was inevitable. But Russia will soon learn that she cannot find the necessary new forms in art and architecture by any renewed study of "classic" forms, because the new reality toward which life now turns for expression and in which Russia is socially a world leader was unknown to the ancients in their art. The modern thought of life and architecture as organic had no place in what the ancients did. They did not know this modern thought that the reality of a building does not consist in the four walls and roof but does consist in the space within them to be lived in; this thought that the reality of the vase is not the clay the potter shaped upon the wheel but the space he enclosed into which he might put something; the thought that not any fixed points but what lies between them in space established by the relation of each to each and each to all—relativity— is reality. In this nonfascist, noncapitalistic thought we have the true modern philosophy of art. A study of classic architecture cannot help us to express the thought because the ancients—if aware of it—did not learn to express it in the forms they made.

If Russian Democracy is to be itself and really live now, it must learn to express that thought in whatever it builds or makes. That thought is the end of the old materialistic life, beginning a life of the spirit. In addition to this fundamental change of thought there are now the miracles of glass and steel, electricity and machine power to use in giving it effect.

Russia must have food—quickly; Russians must not starve. They must have clothes and shelter; they must not freeze. But these things of life we call the arts they must now mean to Russia more than they could ever mean to Czarist aristocracy, or no real democracy will ripen for the Russian people. What has been done will revert to the type it overturned and the world will witness one more inversion. The old forms and uses of luxury must go out with the old sense of right which was wrong. Not only must a new success-ideal take its place but there must be a rationalization that the old luxury was also an unearned increment and is now even more harmful to the human spirit than was direct oppression.

So I am saying to the Russian people whom I love and am learning to respect: be yourselves *now*. Feel and think your way toward honesty of motive and noble purpose in building. In building, make honest uses of materials in forms suited to those materials and appropriate to the purpose of the building. Learn to understand these new functions and new materials like glass and steel and concrete as we are learning to understand the new freedoms of your social status.

Old Russian folkways, so far as they went, were wise in these things. The old aristocracy knew nothing of them and turned its back upon them. The palaces of the aristocrats, root and branch, were rot—as rotten as their lives. Their costumes and manners were no better. Their whole sense of beauty was as superficial as it was artificial—a subtle poison, and it destroyed them.

Tear the ugly Renaissance structures built by stupid kings and princes out of the Kremlin. Formal planning, the regimentation of classic orders, glittering chandeliers and vaulted ceilings are no mark of nobility. They are only the excesses of a privileged class—fashionable because they did not know how to use privilege for the good of mankind, and no more works of art than is a military uniform.

The buildings of a democracy will first know and love the nature of the ground upon which they stand. They will realize that the humble horizontal line is the line of human life upon this earth. Good or great building is the natural companion of trees and gardens and fields. Why should we know where those leave off and building begins? Study Russian nature for your forms, my Russians. Throw the musty text-books away. Close these morgues you were taught to call museums. Learn the basic principles of the new reality you profess as these principles apply to buildings, sculpture, painting, planting, and clothing. Only so can Democracy give fresh proof of quality—proof that it can feel and think for itself to create life anew on really noble terms.

It is only when principle is unknown or disregarded or its practice stale that vulgarity lifts its monstrous head to leer in the face of life, or dons a wig and silks, and minces. Russia, go slow with the unearned increment of that culture whose domination you have rightly rejected. Let Fascism have that delusion to go along with other shams to the ultimate shame that must belong to the makeshift. Russian architecture can grow by way of its living social principle. Fascist art has no chance for growth—dead at the root it can only wither.

This American hopes you will be true to Russian life, too true to take from your oppressors what you have not earned—putting on something poisoned by long abuse. You may die of it now as so many of your people died that you might choose the nobler thing—art and architecture true to the new reality. The Soviet Union must realize and represent the new realty—root, branch, flower, and fruit.

ARCHITECTURE AND MODERN LIFE

Architecture and Modern Life *was a book written by Frank Lloyd Wright and Baker Brownell and first published by Harper & Brothers, New York, in 1937. The chapters "Architecture and Social Life" and "Broadacre City, A Dialogue on the Nature of Structure in Architecture and Integral Life" were jointly authored; the chapters "Expression and the Modern World," "Society and the Future of Expression," and "A Balanced Society" were written solely by Brownell (and are not reprinted here), while "Some Aspects of the Past and Present of Architecture" and "Some Aspects of the Future of Architecture" are solely Wright's.*

In the opening chapter it is difficult to distinguish clearly the hand of the two writers. But in the passages addressing architecture and structure, the language is obviously Wright's.

The chapter "Some Aspects of the Past and Present of Architecture" reveals Wright's writing on the history of architecture in terms rarely equalled for beauty of language and insight. Many times in his later life he turned to this chapter, revised it, rewrote it, and continued to expand on it. Like his earlier essay "The Art and Craft of the Machine" (1901), Wright regarded this piece of writing as of great importance. In his chapter "Some Aspects of the Future of Architecture" he continued his thesis, but with more emphasis on some of the attributes of organic architecture. To explain the working out of an architectural solution for a particular problem or circumstance, he writes, "For our 'case in point' we shall take the Imperial Hotel at Tokyo and try to put into words something of the thought process that tended to make that structure organic."

The model for Broadacre City was about three years old at the time of the writing of this book. It had already had a wide exposure via exhibitions in several major cities across the country. The concluding chapter of the book is devoted to a dialogue between Wright and Brownell based on the concept and plan of Broadacre City. [Published by Harper & Brothers, New York, 1937]

ARCHITECTURE AND SOCIAL LIFE

THE HUDSON RIVER TUNNEL IS A GLISTENING CONDUIT through which a large amount of mankind is piped to New York in the morning and piped back to Jersey in the afternoon. It is smooth and looks aseptic. Its sides slide by in long motion, rhythms of light, the rustling of wheels. It delivers fifty thousand people every few hours silently, precisely, and with as much comfort as city people are permitted to have. What the railroad tunnels do as the climax of much contrivance and effort this vehicular tunnel does casually, as if it were the natural thing to slide under the Hudson river to New York.

Man is a fluid in metropolitan regions. He flows

through the rush hours, rolls along the bank-full streets. The tunnel is built for that fluidity. It is a homoduct, if God and the Oxford dictionary will permit the word, that interprets to some extent the social character of the times. It is architecturally the pressure to and fro of people, a structure of society worked out in the rock of the river bed. The violent ebb and flow of modern city life is here made smooth in a habit of concrete and steel. Does this distort the meaning of the word "architecture"? Not as this book means it. Architecture is architecture, not merely building, because it does interpret the structure of the society to which it belongs and in which it flourishes. Architecture makes social life articulate, tells its meaning, and is a chief fruit of culture. Mere building records the necessities of existence, but architecture is creative. It is itself a flux. It is the flow of human life in the channels cut by civilization in the rock face of earth.

But architecture not only interprets the nature of social structures, it may create them in the present and prophesy them in the future. In this respect architecture, an art, is different from engineering, a science. The engineer—at least as he is now trained—is responsible only for the physical character of the job to which he is assigned, regardless of other consequences, but the architect must have wider vision. As a creative artist he must consider the nature of human expression and the sensuous effects of his work. He must build into his structures the good life as a new kind of beauty. Like the engineer he will master materials and the activity of building, but he goes further. The engineer is responsible for facts: the architect is responsible for values too. His work is not so much *for* men as it *is* men.

A stainless, light-filled tower might rise above the city. It is clear and hard like a pinnacle of ice. It has left stone and its mass behind, as well as brick, tile, and other opaque earthenware. Only glass and stainless metal belong here above the jungle of the streets. It is some fabrication of thought and of things, of new materials and fresh values, as complex in the making as it is delicate and simple in result. It stands alone, like a virgin above the soiled frumperies of her older sisters below. It is expressive, timely, and a creation, no doubt, as well as an interpretation of human and aesthetic values. But creation is complex. Involved in this case there are not only new methods of engineering that eventuate in new forms of visual beauty; there are new accessories of convenience, new lighting patterns, new habits of office work and daily routine that amount to invention. There are new restaurants, perhaps, above the city, new patterns of eating, new dancing, new music. It is a more intrinsic recreation, if architecture is what it should be. In all this and more, the prophetic stainless building is involved.

The virgin stands icily above the city. She is remote and beautiful. But those who live and work on the streets below must pay a penalty for her purity. She is aristocratically apart, she breathes a better air, but her beauty and isolation must be rooted in the jungle below. She must feed on its darkness and congestion. Her presence in part, as things are, must create them. The physical building may be partly cause, partly consequence or condition in a much entangled pattern that includes both good and bad. It is creative. The tall, pure tower looks forward and backward; it is good, bad, but the quality of thought that can give such integrity to the building can and does work constructively in the social life of the times.

The stainless tower, like the great city itself, must be indeed a monument to the extreme concentrations of power, population, wealth, deadly facilities, that mark the modern era. It is tense and shining, but the instability of a people that knows no rest shows there. On streets laid out for a three-story town, an eighteen-story town must operate with a corresponding increase in velocity and interference. On human beings built for a slower pace of spasmodic action and repose the city lays a driving pressure and urgency. It seeks experiments and expedients in the emergency. It fails in sincere courage and vision. The natural integrity of life is broken down into intense activities each in its special compartment having little or nothing of the whole. The stainless tower is a part of this confusion but, though in it, is not of it. The internal integrity of its natural character that might be a factor in better social life seems of little avail for the moment. Architecture has hitherto made the structure of a society more fixed and more elaborate. Then excess brings inevitable change. An organic architecture such as this not only embodies social structures, but suggests other and better structures. Seeking an architecture more free in relation to change, more independent of the fixed symmetries imposed on life, organic architecture keeps itself free to continually begin at the beginning and continually live anew.

Architecture thus embodies social structures and suggests others when free to create them. When free it is organic, growing. Organic architecture continuously arises from within. It continuously begins at the beginning instead of growing more static as it grows older. Organic architecture alone has this power of growth in form.

This creativeness of organic architecture reaches out from life and back into life, in and out of varied parts of living. It means not merely the looks of buildings or the number of rooms, the size, the materials: it means also the effect that architectural forms have on people's action. For the lives of people take architectural forms that in turn affect the ideals of people and their action. As a house is built so the pattern of activity of those will be who live in it. Organic architecture controls their movement, their comings and goings. It clarifies and cultivates their sense of form in space, in color, in mass, and in action. Shall the housewife turn right or left after four steps, shall she move about with grace and ease, or shall she climb up and down from one floor to another floor or otherwise waste her steps in needless to and fro? Shall the child pause at the window for the view before he climbs fifteen steps to his play room? Shall confinement mark his life at home or shall his life be characterized by a sense of free action, spaciousness, and innate harmony? To these modest questions the house says "Yes" or "No." Many other questions it answers. Separately they are small matters, but together the very texture of living. The routines of life have their rhythms. They are a varied but eternal dance for which architecture provides a score. The kinaesthetic or muscular implications of architecture are an important though rarely recognized aspect of the art's creativeness. The rectangle, for example, was never well adapted to human movement. The hexagon is better. The folkways and habits of living, from the most lowly to the sublime,

are the ways of architecture. If architecture is empty, there is proof enough that life is empty.

The humble privy has become in recent years another example of what architecture may do as a creative social influence. This refers not so much to the aesthetic studies by Chic Sale, as to widespread work through the southern mountains and elsewhere generally in the improvement of public health and private decency by means of standardized designs for sanitation. Where conditions permit, the privy has come indoors as an integral part of any good building. Elsewhere, throughout wide regions, privies have been made safe to health and better looking by means of new design. Rebuilding, with public help, has created new folkways in this respect. The new designs reflect into the structure of society, and better health and more decent ways of living are the consequence. It is a lowly example and obvious enough, though to some it will seem beneath the dignity of architecture. But to those who believe with the modern poet that all significant experience may be the subject of art, even the building of a privy may involve architectural values. These human necessities are as legitimately involved in architectural values as eating or sleeping or dreaming.

Just as interpretation emerges as creation, so creation is prophecy. Architecture which is a genuine interpretation of the present is a prophecy of social structure yet to come. Unless architecture is this prophetic interpretation, we may still call it building but we may not call it architecture. For architecture is no mere reflection but as true interpretation of the present is naturally prophetic. It takes divine initiative, as it were, for in the old Biblical way it not merely foretells the future but, in embodying the advanced thought of its time, is a power that actually moves the world towards a better state.

If Radio City is a symbol of the good and evil of the present, Broadacre City envisions that way to life and beauty implicit in the future as the present: that future is always now. If Radio City is the man of today tipped up edgewise so that all may see his cellular imprisonment in the system that he serves, Broadacre City emphasizes the fact that the horizontal line of human movement on the ground is more important to man than the verticality of floor above floor. Without losing the elemental human virtues of the day of our forefathers, it avails itself of the inventions of the present, and offers a way to use them for humanity. Architecture is unique among the arts and professions in its ability to give to the present the possibilities of the future. It can make the future move. It can force tomorrow into the concrete realm of things touched and seen. It shows a complete cross section of our civilization in terms of this future within the present.

In a larger and perhaps more mystical sense of the word, architecture is itself whatever is organic. It is the organic pattern of all things. This remains the hidden mystery of creation until the architect has grasped and revealed it. We have said that architecture interprets structure and through structure creates form, prophesies new form: now we say that architecture in a more philosophical sense is whatever significance structure itself possesses. It is the significant structure of all created things as the mind may know them. It is at least the geometric pattern of things, of life, of the human and social world. It is at best that magic framework of reality that we sometimes touch upon when we use the word *order*. Architecture is this aura (or "oversoul" as Emerson might say) of structure. It is a true expression of the life of the human and social world. Buildings, merely, know nothing of it. Buildings are only material projects in some medium. In other media there are collateral projects and many illustrations. Music, economic activity, statesmanship, the dance, poetry are a few of the media in which other illustrations of this structure may occur. Only when buildings illustrate this structural integrity of all things are they architecturally expressive and good.

A battleship and a powerful newspaper, for example, are a good deal alike. They are parallel illustrations of a structural character that has great emphasis in modern society. They are timely, if time bound. They are angular, jut out boldly. They incorporate power and skill. Like airplanes, automobiles, electrification they are forms of the new world. Though our sentiments towards battleships may vary from dislike to admiration, it is true that the battleship in any case is expressive. It expresses the structure and purpose of society, or at least one aspect of it, and punctuates our power.

In this billion horse-power America, to continue the illustration, social structures are designed primarily to encourage action and to do work. In the entire western world, indeed, machine power is about the only mark of distinction. Other societies may rightly claim higher morality, more cleanliness, more religion, better art, more love, more wisdom and happiness: we are superior in power. We have more energy. We can do more work. America alone exploits more energy and uses more per capita than any people in human history. The battleship is an expression of that power. So is the big business newspaper. In a society where power and skin have so great a structural importance they are illustrations in different media of the same thing. They are forms identified with the structure of society. In this internal sense, too, is architecture structure.

The foregoing paragraphs have said that architecture interprets the structure of the society in which it is and as prophecy must create the future. These aspects of architecture will be developed by illustration and discussion through the first part of this book. In another and more metaphysical sense, architecture is itself the structure in all things. This will be considered throughout the book. The second part of the book will deal with the dominant characteristics of architecture in the past and present; the third part with the characteristics of the modern social world so far as they influence expression; the fourth part with the architecture of the future; the fifth part with society and the future; the sixth part with the nature of a balanced society; and the seventh part with the philosophy of society as architecture and of architecture as society.

Thus the following chapters are devoted to the theme that a natural architecture is not only the concrete expression of the life and structure of society but is social creation emerging as master building. It belongs to the materials used, and to the men who use them. It participates in their nature and their inherent patterns of relationship, but in turn it transmutes that nature and those structures from the realm of the potential into the realm of created things. It is not only part of their action, it is a bridge over which the past reached the present and the present will reach the future. For us in America, it is a new reality.

In the western world were three great architectures, the Greek, Roman, the Gothic, and now it will recognize another, the "Modern," or Organic. Each one begins in the basic act of building. The development of each one, to some extent, is responsible to the materials used, to the men who build, and to the society in which the building takes place. If the architecture of Egypt was an interpretation of flesh and death eternal, the architecture of Greece, earliest among western peoples, was a celebration of the sureness and immediacy of life, but with little or no sense of its organic character. If Gothic architecture was an expression of straining dreams, phantasy, escape from the ruthless life of that time, modern organic architecture, our theme, comes to mark again belief in life as a whole. It accepts, gratefully, its achievements. It goes along with the restless, seeking powers of man. It moves toward a more faithful reality than Realism or Romanticism could ever be.

Very different are the modes and men and materials of these architectures, as different as their varied expressions. In Egypt, for example, building belonged to stone. In Greece, building belonged to wood imitated in stone. And yet they both belong to stone in their physical antiquity. This is true although Greek buildings in their day were in spirit still gorgeously painted wooden buildings done in stone with little sense of the organic. As the Gothic towers of the builders of the thirteenth century tortured stone into forms that stone never should have, so they tortured life into unworldly aspirations. They not only emulated the forest in stone, but to escape the rough realism of the time, made stone soar in most incongruous flights. Modern builders may, and sometimes do, leave stone behind for lighter, tensile or more plastic stuff—steel, glass, and what we call synthetics. Forms today must be immeasurably changed by steel and glass. Modern organic architecture accepts and trusts the modern achievements of this world and regardless of old forms goes along with them to forms more faithful, not to realism or romanticism, but to reality.

The three great western architectures were embodied in stone. Now organic architecture is first to become independent of it—which is but one example of the difference today. In many other ways modern work might be an original and primary synthesis of the materials, the social interests, the technologies and power of the modern age instead of the confusion of all of them owing to the substitution of academic standards for the nature of growth and of organic change. Little of the work of this time is organic or even "modern," as we have here for the moment used the word.

The earth teems with tawdry buildings, cheap fashions, eclectic "styles," for the eclectics we have always with us. Eclectics are our characteristic mass product. Meantime American skyscrapers continue to imitate in steel the earlier forms in stone. They are nondescript, usually alien to the nature of their materials and the new reality that is organic. With their range immeasurably widened by steel and glass, modern buildings might achieve a new integrity, an organic architecture fearlessly accepting the laws of change inherent in all nature, including human nature. But few of them do. They are a babel of styles. Facility outruns thought and feeling. Intricate confusions surround the few examples of organic work. These examples are hard to find. All kinds of work are done today, both good and bad, to make a complex, contradictory world, and all of it is clearly modern, or at least contemporary. But we shall ignore the bad, for the purposes of this work, and use the word "modern" as referring to the great work that can be done and has been done in terms of modern values and conditions.

It is sunset and the dying sun spreads its last glory over the gas tanks—or are they oil tanks?—that mark the northern waters of San Francisco Bay. The air is misty rose, the water calm, as the sun leaves the darkening continent and sinks into the sea. To the north white forms arise—vague, bulbous, rose touched by the sun. Mist obscures their base. They float like great birds, balloons, the domes of Venice over the sea. They ride upon the air like escaped domes by Michelangelo, without distance seemingly, both near and far. Are they that soap bubble, named St. Peter's, repeated here in flocks upon a western shore? No, they are the gas tanks. Their aluminum painted sides glow with rose fire. They stand in vague rows and ranges off towards El Cerrito.

These gas tanks are features of a kind of world

that neither Greek nor Gothic, Egyptian, Renaissance nor any other older style could comprehend. Simple as they look there, rosy across the water, they are commands of steel, coal, petroleum, of railway men and miners, of new-found technics in a new kind of struggle to live. Their structure is the structure of that world. Their function is bound closely within that modern world's social pattern. These bland, unconscious gas tanks cannot be called art or works of art. If form follows function, however, and if expressiveness and plastic form are the ways of art, they well may stand ready to enter that portal by way of architecture. They are now the concern of architecture. They are deeply identified, like many other modern necessitous works, with such skill and power as we have today.

Modern organic architecture—to apply the term again to great work in the present and future—is not only comparable, then, to the other great architectures of the western world; in its expressiveness and its plasticity it must rise superior to them. It not only gives form or expression to the society from which it emerges, it plastically and rhythmically adjusts its structures to that contour, the contour of need. It has flow and continuity like movements in music or of a strong graceful person walking, for this is the meaning of plasticity; it intelligently serves, as Louis Sullivan has said; it does not suppress.

Modern organic architecture, in a word, is expressive and plastic because it begins with an integration of modern life. It gives when it accepts. It accepts when it gives. It formulates from within. It does not reformulate. The nature of this integration with modern life is identified with its nature. Why is this integrity new to America?

As architecture is integrated with modern life, so first it will appear as economy. It is clean. Nothing is stuck on. Nothing is present that does not contribute.

It has, second, honesty. Brick is brick and looks like it, feels like it, serves like it. So does iron, glass, wood, or steel. Pretense and fake, false fronts, loafing columns, false plaster of Paris echoes of honest craft from days gone by, are not present. Things not only are what they seem: they reveal more than they ever seemed.

Architecture, third, is functional. Its working parts are revealed as expressive features. It is never ashamed to confess its purpose. Purpose is exhibited. At its least, architecture is chaste and exact like a good machine: it is direct. But it is not a machine any more than a man's heart is a suction pump. Only when it is more than a machine is any building architecture.

It is, fourth, organic. Form and function are one. More than any appearance, or comment, or any mere convenience, it is something that is. It issues proudly from the practical nature of the thing as an entity. It has, by right, individuality. The complexities of materials and men, of social patterns and activity, have been organized within its frame, and it is responsible to their natures. It is a finer order than men could otherwise know or have dreamed. It reduces them to simples. They have informed it. And it is responsible to life alone for whatever life it has.

It has, fifth, such beauty as it knows inherent in its structure, and it has the magic of expression. It says something by way of itself that it alone may say. It has significance, and having significance has the countenance of truth.

These few truths of form and feature that we have called modern—although the word means only *à la mode* are not so much modern in themselves as they are modern where architecture is concerned. They are eternal. They assume that architecture is a plastic part of living in the present and all its works. They are fused with the moral and social implications of life, in contrast to current aesthetic eclecticism. Though this "organic" point of view is not, of course, a unique discovery of this age, it is a point of view that results always in freshness, vitality, and consequence. Though Laotze, the old Chinese philosopher, was aware of it, though Walt Whitman sensed it, the practice of the thought involved has, in architecture, been rare. It has still to grow up. The thought now penetrates to the basis of building in the nature of materials, methods and men and their human situation. Architecture may now safely abandon forms and their reforms held through habit or traditions: it creates forms anew out of the living reality of today. Or better, perhaps, it enters that reality and with both feeling and science imbues it with form and structure. It goes to the roots. That is its logic. It is radical. That also is its poetry.

The towers of America rise from the western plains and prairies as well as from the larger towns. In Wasco, Illinois, or Lily Lake, on Simpson's farm west of Clinton, Iowa, above the valley floor at Black Earth, Wisconsin, they may be seen. Towers mark the countryside. For three thousand miles from east to west and a thousand miles from north to south, are towers. Tower after tower pins down the continent on its base of soil and rock. From above they look like smoothed stakes driven there. They are the grain elevators of concrete and their smaller colleagues, the silos. If the towers of great cities and their imitators in smaller towns are restless fingers reaching towards God knows what, the gray grain elevators and farm silos are towers with more repose and at least some genuine significance. They stand along the waterfronts and the railroad sidings. They are simply built to contain, to hold in safety, the grain stores of a nation, with no thought of beauty or other consequence. They are, so to speak, merely the nation's granary. But they stand clean, reticent, secure, examples of firm orderliness, of refreshing simplicity. In this they belong to the new architecture that we have called organic. Man has taken many liberties with his towers. These, almost alone among them, have something of the significance and inevitable rhythm of a naturally created thing that is the basis of organic architecture. They stand, not classic certainly, nor as yet historic tradition. They are a wholesome negative. They have yet to make the affirmation that must be the substance of an indigenous American architecture.

SOME ASPECTS OF THE PAST AND PRESENT OF ARCHITECTURE

Building upon the land is as natural to man as to other animals, birds or insects. In so far as he was more than an animal his buildings became what we call architecture.

In ancient times his limitations served to keep his buildings architecture. Splendid examples: Mayan, Egyptian, Greek, Byzantine, Persian, Gothic, Indian, Chinese, Japanese.

Looking back at these, what then is architecture? It is man and more.

It is man in possession of his earth. It is the only true record of him where his possession of earth is concerned.

While he was true to earth his architecture was creative.

The time comes when he is no longer inspired by the nature of earth. His pagan philosophy is breaking down, owing to changing social conditions, to new science, new facilities, easy riches. The social world begins to turn upside down. Science takes the place of art. Things serve the man better than thoughts.

Nothing in his experience enables him to resist the disintegrating effect of money and machines. An enemy to his nature, likely to emasculate or destroy him, is embraced by him.

His creative faculties (art) are conditioned upon this earth. His possession of earth in this sense grows dim as his intellect (science and invention) discovers ways to beat work. Money shows him new ways to cheat life. Power becomes exterior instead of interior. His own acts—which are vicarious—are no longer inherent.

In these circumstances architecture becomes too difficult, building too easy. New facilities are here for which he has no corresponding forms. He seems for the moment powerless to make them. He is lost to the source of inspiration, the ground. He takes any substitute. Neither the pagan ideal nor its counterpart, Christianity, any longer lead him.

In the stress of circumstance a new ideal appears capable of leading him out of bondage into life again. Again the ground comes into the light as a brighter sense of reality dawns. It is the sense and nature of that which is within—integrity.

The room or space within the building is man's reality instead of his exterior circumstance. Though as old as philosophy, the new ideal takes on fresh significance in the ideal of architecture as organic. It must be integral to a life lived as organic.

New sense of the whole enters the life of man to bring order out of chaos. The old—"classic," eclecticism—is chaos, restlessness.

The new—"integral," organic—is order, repose.

All materials lie piled in masses or float as gases in the landscape of this planet much as the cataclysms of creation left them.

At the mercy of the cosmic elements, these materials have been disintegrated by temperatures, ground down by glaciers, eroded by wind and sea, sculptured by tireless forces qualifying each other. They are all externally modified by time as they modify this earth in a ceaseless procession of change.

Stone is the basic material of our planet. It is continually changed by cosmic forces, themselves a form of change. Contrasted with these great mineral masses of earth structure—this titanic wreckage—are placid depths and planes of mutable water or the vast depth-plane of the immutable sky hung with evanescent clouds. And this creeping ground-cover of vegetable life, more inexorable than death, is rising from it all, over all, against all, texturing with pattern, infinite in resource, and inexhaustible in variety of effect. This is the earthly abode of the buildings man has built to work, dwell, worship, dance and breed in.

Change is the one immutable circumstance found in landscape. But the changes all speak or sing in unison of cosmic law, itself a nobler form of change. These cosmic laws are the physical laws of all man-built structures as well as the laws of landscape.

Man takes a positive hand in creation whenever he puts a building upon the earth beneath the sun. If he has birthright at all, it must consist in this: that he, too, is no less a feature of the landscape than the rocks, trees, bears or bees of that nature to which he owes his being.

Continuously nature shows him the science of her remarkable economy of structure in mineral and vegetable constructions to go with the unspoiled character everywhere apparent in her forms.

The long, low lines of colorful, windswept terrain, the ineffable dotted line, the richly textured plain, great striated, stratified masses lying noble and quiet or rising with majesty above the vegetation of the desert floor: nature-masonry is piled up into ranges upon ranges of mountains that seem to utter a form-language of their own.

Earth is prostrate, prostitute to the sun. All life we may know is sun life, dies sun death, as shadow, only to be born again. Evidence is everywhere.

Material forms are manifest in one phase today, to be found in another tomorrow. Everywhere around us creeps the eternally mysterious purpose of this inexorable ground-cover of growth. It is mysterious purpose, desperately determined, devouring or being devoured in due course upon this titanic battlefield. Growth seeks conquest by way of death.

To what end is all in pattern?

Always—eternally—pattern? Why?

Why this intrigue of eye-music to go with sensuous ear-music?

What is this inner realm of rhythm that dances in sentient beings and lies quiescent but no less sentient in pattern?

There seems to be no mortal escape, least of all in death, from this earth-principle which is again the sun-principle of growth. Earth becomes more and more the creative creature of the sun. It is a womb quickened by the passions of the master sun.

Nevertheless, every line and the substance of earth's rock-bound structure speak of violence. All is scarred by warring forces seeking reconciliation, still marred by conflict and conquest. But in our era violence has subsided, is giving way to comparative repose. Streamlines of the mountain ranges come down more gently to the plains. Geological cataclysm is subsiding or becoming subservient. Divine order creeps out and rises superior to chaos. Pattern asserts itself. Once more, triumph.

Ceaselessly, the rock masses are made by fire, are laid low by water, are sculptured by wind and stream. They take on the streamlines characteristic of the sweeping forces that change them.

Already matter lies quieted, and with it violence and discord. It is bathed in light that so far as man can see is eternal. Penetrating all, itself penetrated by itself, is mysterious eye-music: pattern.

Meantime in all this lesser building within greater building there is other animation, still another kind of building: these are creatures of creation patterned upon similar patterns until plant, animal creature and earth and man resemble each other for purpose malign or beneficent. Insect, reptile, fish, animal and bird are there in all the elements using gifts of life in this mysterious yet strangely familiar resemblance that we call our world. The seemingly senseless destruction goes on in each.

Some law of laws seems to keep in full effect the law of change in this world-workshop. The crevices and secret places of earth, shadows of the great underneath are swarming with fantastic insects, also singing, working, dancing and breeding.

But with this singular creature, man? Gaining dominion over all, what will he do to maintain his dominion? What will be his essential "pattern"? What does the vulnerable master of cause and effect know of instrumental cosmic law? What may he create?

Man by nature desired to build as the birds were meantime building their nests, as insects were building their cities, and as animals were seeking their dens, making their lairs, or burrowing into the ground. And architecture became by way of this desire the greatest proof on earth of man's greatness, his right to be born, to inherit the earth.

If the man was poor and mean by nature he built that way. If he was noble and richly endowed then he built grandly, like a noble man. But high or low it was his instinct to build on this earth.

By innate animal instinct he got his first lessons. He got ideas of form from those nature-forms about him, native to the place where he lived. Consciously or unconsciously he was taught by birds and animals. Inspired by the way rock ledges were massed up against sky on the hills, he was taught by the stratified masses of the rock itself. Trees must have awakened his sense of form. The pagodas of China and Japan definitely resemble the pines with which they were associated. The constructions of the Incas married earth itself.

Man's faithful companion, the tree, lived by light. The building, man's own tree, lived by shadows. Therefore, early building masses naturally belonged to the sunlit landscape in which they stood. The stone constructions of the Incas belonged there. Those of the African, of the sea-islanders and of the cliff-dwellers belonged there. The more developed buildings of Persia, China, and Japan belonged there. Later a building had become consciously no less a child of the sun than trees themselves always were.

Probably man first lived in stone caves, when he did not live in trees, using selected sticks and seeking appropriate stones for tools. Concerning this point it is perhaps better to say he first lived sometimes in trees and sometimes in stone caves. As he moved north or south his type of dwelling changed with the climate. The north always demanded most from him in the way of building, if he was to preserve himself. And the Esquimaux learned to build their igloos of blocks of snow cemented with ice.

Farther south the builder was satisfied with some grass and leaves raised up on a platform of sticks, or with some kind of tent that he might fold up and take with him on his horse as he rode away. While still dwelling in caves the man perhaps learned to make utensils out of wet clay. He burned them hard for use. These utensils he seems to have made with a higher faculty. His instinct became an aesthetic sense of environment. It taught him something of form. He learned from the animals, the serpents, the plants that he knew. Except for this faculty he was no more than another animal.

Still clinging to the cliffs, he made whole caves out of wet clay and let the sun bake the cave hard. He made them just as he had made the vessels that he had previously put into fire to bake and had used in the cave in the rocks. And so, once upon a time, man moved into his first earth-built house, of *earth*.

This large clay cave or pot of the cliff-dwellers, with a lid on it, was among the first man-made houses. The lid was troublesome to him then and has always been so to subsequent builders. But previously better forms of houses had come from the sticks that had been conferred upon him by his friendly companion, the tree. The lighter, more scientific house-shapes were at first conical, made so by leaning upright sticks together at the top. And the builder covered the sticks with skins of the animals he had eaten. But later man made more roomy houses by squaring the interior space and framing the walls upright. To make the walls he put sticks upright and crossed them at intervals with other horizontal sticks firmly lashed to the vertical sticks, finally covering all with various forms of mats woven of tall dried grasses or grasses lashed directly to the framework. Some forms of these earlier houses in certain parts of Africa and of the South Sea Islands are beautiful architecture to this day.

Then the builder had to contrive the lid—by now it may be called a roof—by framing much heavier sticks together, sloping the sticks across the interior spaces from wall to wall to carry overhead masses of tall dried grasses laid on smaller cross sticks in such a way as to run the water off. He covered this over-head wood framing in the manner of a thatch. The shape of this cover (or roof) was what most affected the general aspect of his building. Sometimes the roof stood up tall within the walls. Sometimes in shape it was a low protective mound. Sometimes it projected boldly. But it always showed its wood construction beneath the final covering.

Walls at first of earth, stone or wood stood up and out heavily as most important. The roof was sel-dom visible, especially where war was in man's mind, as it usually was. Later the sense of roof as shelter overcame the sense of walls, and great roofs were to be seen with the walls standing back in under them. Man soon came to feel that, if he had no roof in this sense, he had no house.

Later he came to speak of his house as "his roof" and was fond of inviting strangers to come and sit or stay "under his roof." If other men displeased him he drove them "from beneath his roof." His roof was not only his shelter, it was his dignity, as well as his sense of home.

Civilization proceeded. Unless man had war in mind (as he usually did) the roof-shelter became the most important factor in the making of the house. It be-came the ultimate feature of his building. This remains true to this late day when changes of circumstances have made it the roof that he needs to fortify instead of the walls. The real menace of attack is now from the air.

The real science of structure entered into build-ing with this sense of the roof and of wood, or "the stick," because every roof had to be framed strongly enough to span the interior space from wall to wall. Sometimes, as a confession of inability, perhaps, or a forced economy, the roof had to be supported on in-terior posts or partitions. Various picturesque roof forms arose as different materials were used to span the space below. More pains had to be taken with these spans than with anything else about the build-ing. Although stone was used to imitate wood con-struction, the dome, the perfect masonry roof, soon arose among the myriad roofs of the world.

In all this work the principal tools in human hands were fire, the simple lever, and the wheel. But, in human hands, these soon grew into the might of the machine. Explosives soon came along to multiply the force of lever and wheel.

Early masonry buildings were mostly the work of men employing the simple leverage of inclined ways or using the bar as direct lever in human hands. The lever in some form (the wheel is the lever also) was used to make these early buildings.

Materials in primitive architecture were always most important. The character of all the earlier buildings was determined more by the materials available for construction than by any other one thing. Wood, brick, and stone always said "wood," "brick," or "stone," and acted it. Later the builder lost sight of nature in this integral sense. But these good limitations held until the so-called "Renais-sance" or "Rebirth" of architecture.

Being craftsmen, because taught by experience with materials in actual construction, the early builders could find a right way to work whatever ma-terials they found. They were ways that were best suited to the kind of buildings we can call architec-ture. Now the kind of building that we can call archi-tecture today is the building wherein human thought and feeling enter to create a greater harmony and true significance in the whole structure. Shelter and utility in themselves were never enough. The edifice was the highest product of the human mind. Man always sought reflection in it of his sense of himself as God-like. Man's imagination made the gods, and so he made a God-like building. He dedicated it to the god he had made. His architecture was something out of his practical self to his ideal self.

The gods were various, but as the God he made was high or low, so the buildings he made were no-ble or relatively mean.

As we view the widely different kinds of buildings built by red, yellow, white, or black men, we see that all were clustered into various aggregations under many different conditions. These aggregations we call cities, towns, and villages. In primitive times these clusters of buildings were occasioned by animal fear and social need of daily human contacts, or by obedience to rule. So we see buildings in clusters great, and clusters small. No doubt the cluster once represented a certain social consensus. The village once satisfied a real human need.

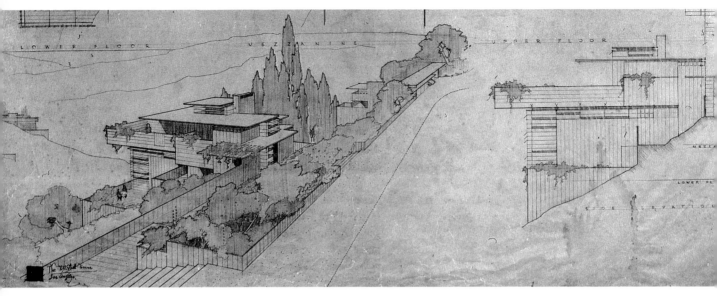

All Steel Houses (Project). Los Angeles, California. 1937. Detail of perspective. Pencil on tracing paper, 36 x 29". FLLW Fdn#3705.004

The warlike tribe had its village. The peaceful tribe tilling the ground also went to its village for the night. It was necessary to go for protection on one hand, and offense or defense on the other. And always, for the convenience of the chieftain as well as of his subjects, all was closed in around him. Man, the animal, has always sought safety first. As a man, he continually seeks permanence. As an animal he wishes to endure his life long. As a man he has invented immortality. Nowhere is this yearning for continuity or permanence so evident as in his architecture. Perhaps architecture is man's most obvious realization of this persistent dream he calls immortality.

Animal instinct has reached upward and found a higher satisfaction.

These various clusters of buildings grew from tribal villages into towns, from towns to cities, and from lesser to greater cities until a few cities had something of the might and character of great individual building. Sometimes a city became as various in its parts as any building, and similar in greatness.

But usually the city was an accretion not planned beyond the placing of a few features. These features probably were not designedly placed. The city happened much as any crowd will gather about centers of interest wherever the centers of interest happen to be. Sometimes a circumstance of transport or historical consideration changed this center.

And, usually, there was a difference in degree only between the village, town, and great city. The one often grew into the other so that original spacing suitable to the village became a serious fault in the subsequent city. Populous crowding took what places it could find. It often took them by force of circumstance. Real freedom of human life in such circumstances soon became a farce.

In early times cities and towns were surrounded by fortified walls because cities and towns were forts. When might made right, the chieftain, the baron, the pirate and the bandit throve. Often the most successful robber became baron, sometimes monarch. The ruffian could rule in feudal times and often did rule, as he often rules in our own time.

The "divine right of kings" was a relatively modern improvement. It was an assumption that wore itself out by attrition. But meantime, by way of baron and monarch, we see architecture more and more undertaken as the great empires of the rich and powerful rather than a service to the genius of a whole people or as the expression of race. Architecture became self-conscious. It began to be pretentious, affected and petty. Oftentimes as the robber chieftain became the baron and baron became monarch, the desire to build became vainglorious. It far outran necessity. All the great buildings thus built—many palaces and tombs, even churches, baths, theaters, and stadiums—were built as monuments to the powerful individuals under whose patronage they were erected. But conquering races were always coming down from the north as potentate rose against potentate. While baron contended with baron, neighboring cities were razed or enslaved by vandals, as they were called. This vandalism put new vandals into the places of weaker, older vandals. They called the weaker ones vassals. This is reflected in what remains of the architecture of periods when conquering mainly consisted in tearing down whatever the enemy might have built up. The more laborious and painstaking the building up had been, the more satisfactory was the pulling down.

In time, by way of the popular desperation caused by kingly discord and the baronial jealousies that employed men more for destruction than construction, government gradually became republican in form until in our day the people have subscribed to the idea of democratic government. This shows, at least, that the ultimate rise and progress of the whole people towards self-determination was proceeding, if slowly, through the human wreckage that we are viewing as ancient architecture. And however far away a satisfactory result may be, or however difficult it may be to imagine an indigenous architecture as its own expression, this struggle to rise does still go on among the peoples of the world. It is a seething in the mass. This, too, has affected the spirit that we call architecture. It is about to appear in new and more harmonious ways of building. Because they are more direct and natural, we are learning to call the new ways of building "organic." But to use the term in its biological sense only would be to miss its significance. The word organic should signify architecture as living "entity" and "entity" as individuality.

Let us now go nearer to the grand wreckage left by this tremendous energy poured forth by man in quest of his ideal, these various ruined cities and buildings built by the various races to survive the race. Let us go nearer to see how and why different races built the different buildings and what essential difference the buildings recorded.

Whether yellow, red, black, or white race took

precedence in the buildings that followed down the ages is not known. We have many authorities ready in this respect to cancel each other. History, necessarily post mortem, must be some kind of internal evidence discerned within what remains of the building itself. Remains of each separate race have for the most part totally disappeared. Some subsist merely as cuneiform writing on stone or as porcelain tablets. So conjecture has wide limits within which to thrive. But architecture appears, more and more with every fresh discovery, to have had common origin in the civilizations of the past. It seems now to be on the way out rather than on the way in.

In the evolution of the kind of building that we may call architecture, such primitive civilizations as remain have a high place. We may not neglect the contributions from the South Sea Islanders, from far south to the north, or of the Pacific savages who already made their implements look and feel stronger as utensils through the decoration they put upon them. The old Persian, the Dorian, and Ionic, and the old Byzantine all are architectures of vast importance. Their origins are lost to view. And all are tributary in our view of architecture. They proceed from one common human stock. But we begin with those great architectures in view from about 1000 B.C. to 1300 A.D. This is a period of time in which the greatest buildings of the world, traces of which are still visible to us, arose out of the soul and the soil of civilization. Civilizations are original cultural impulses whether they converge on some downward road or not.

Uncertain scholarship places the Mayan civilization centuries later than the height of Egyptian civilization. It was, say, 600 B.C., Germans and others dissenting. However that may be, Mayan and Egyptian both have more in common where elemental greatness is concerned than other cultures, unless we include the great work of the To, Cho, and Han periods of Chinese culture. These we may also place from 600 B.C. to 600 A.D. And as we have seen, architecture was in point of style relative to all that was used in it or in relation to it, that is to say, utensils, clothes, ornaments, arts, literature, life itself. All, manifestly, were of a family. They served a common purpose converging to a common end.

The Egyptian of that period was already more sophisticated than either early Mayan or early Chinese, and so might well have arisen at an earlier period in human development than either. Or, if primitive character is the more ancient, then the Mayan might be the elder. In Maya we see a grand simplicity of concept and form. Probably it is greater elemental architecture than anything remaining on record anywhere else. Next would come the early Chinese, especially their stone and bronze sculptures. In both Mayan and Chinese there was an assertion of form that could only have proceeded from the purest kinship to elemental nature and from nature forms of the materials used by both. Egyptian architecture, pyramid and obelisk excepted (they probably belong to an earlier period), had a sensuous smoothness and comparative elegance inspired by the sensuous human figure. Egyptian architecture was a noble kind of stone *flesh*. In the Egyptian dance, as contrasted with the Greek form of the dance, you may see this verified. The background of the architecture, the Egyptian landscape, was the sweeping simplicity of deserts relieved by greenery of the oasis. By his industry in the agrarian arts the Egyptian grew. He was astrological. He was a God-maker through myth. Egyptian individuality seems rounded. Its reward seems completely recorded by architecture. It is the most sophisticated of survivals from ancient origins.

But the Mayan lived amidst rugged rock formations. He contended with a vast jungle-like growth in which the serpent was a formidable figure. The Mayan grew by war. He was a great ritualist. He was a God-maker through force. Flesh lives in his architecture only as gigantic power. Grasp the simple force of the level grandeur of the primal Mayan sense of form and the Mayan enrichment of it. Grasp the cruel power of his crude Gods (to objectify one, a sculptured granite boulder might suffice), then relate that to the extended plateaux his terraces made and to the mighty scale of his horizontal stone constructions. You will have in these trabeations the sense of might in stone. Even a Mayan "decoration" was mighty. It was mostly stone built.

Yet, both Egyptian and Mayan races seem children of a common motherland. With a broad grasp compare the might and repose of the Mayan outlines with the primitive Egyptian form in its almost human undulations; so rounded and plastic is the Egyptian architecture against the endless levels of the undulating sands surrounding it that it is the pagan song in an architecture of human profiles cut in stone. Though it is modeled in stone like the human nude, it finds great and similar repose in the ultimate mass.

Then compare both Mayan and Egyptian architecture with primal Chinese nature-worship as seen in the outlines of early Chinese forms. They are influences, no doubt, coming in from the mysterious Pacific. A sense of materials is there. It is seeking qualities. It is form qualified always by the profound sense of depth in the chosen substance and in the working of it. You will then see that what the early Chinese made was not so much made to be looked at as it was made to be looked into. In whatever the Chinese made there was profundity of feeling that gave a perfect kinship to the beauty of the natural world as it lived about man, and that was China. It is an architecture wherein flesh as flesh lives not at all. The early art work of China is ethereal. And yet altogether these architectures seem to acknowledge kinship to each other, whether Mayan, Egyptian, Dorian or Chinese.

Early stone buildings—perhaps earlier than Egyptian or Greek—in the hands of the Byzantines became buildings quite different from Incan, Egyptian, or Chinese stone buildings. The arch was Byzantine and is a sophisticated building act resulting in more sophisticated forms than the lintel of the Mayan, Egyptian or Greek. Yet it is essentially primitive masonry. Byzantine architecture lived anew by the arch. The arch sprung from the caps of stone posts and found its way into roofing by way of the low, heavy, stone dome. Its haunches were well down within heavy walls. It was a flat crown showing above the stone masses punctured below by arches. St. Sophia is a later example. The stone walls of Byzantium often became a heavy mosaic of colored stone. The interiors above, roundabout and below, were encrusted with mosaics of gold, glazed pottery and colored glass. The Byzantines carved stone much in exfoliate forms, but the forms preserved the sense of stone mass in whatever they carved. Heavy wooden beams, painted or carved, rested on carved bolsters of stone or were set into the walls. Roof surfaces were covered with crude tiles. The effect of the whole was robust nature. It was worship by way of heavy material, masterful construction and much color.

The Romanesque proceeded from the Byzantine. And among the many other influences today our own country—so long degenerate where architecture is concerned—in the work of one of its greater architects, Henry Hobson Richardson, shows Romanesque influence.

St. Sophia is probably the greatest remaining, but a late example, of the architecture of Byzantium. In point of scale, at least, it is so. The Byzantine sense of form seems neither East nor West but belongs to both. It is obviously traditional architecture, the origins of which are lost in antiquity. Eventually becoming Christian, the Byzantine building was more nobly stone than any Gothic architecture. It was no less truly stone, though less spiritually so, than Mayan architecture. Into Byzantine buildings went the riches of the East in metals, weaving, images and ritual. Byzantium grew most by merchandising. Notwithstanding the dominance of the merchant class, a robust spirit lived in Byzantine work. It still grappled earth forcefully with simple purpose and complete individuality.

In the domed buildings of Persia we see the Byzantine arch still at work. Their buildings were the work of an enlightened people. Their architecture was probably the pinnacle of the civilizations that proceeded to the valley of the Euphrates and the Tigris from the supposed cradle of the white race. Persian architecture lifted its arches and domes to full height, in full flower, when great medieval western architecture was beginning to point its arches in stone. The Persian loved masonry. By the most knowing use on record of clay and the kiln he achieved enormous building scale by way of bricks and mortar. He worked out his roof by way of the kiln as a great masonry shell domed and encrusted with extraordinary tile mosaics. He made his brick domes strong by placing their haunches well down into massive brick walls. His masonry dome was erected as an organic part of the whole structure. And lifting this sky-arch high, with gently sensuous, swelling sides, he humanized it completely. The Persian liked his dome so much that he turbaned his head, we may imagine, to match it, and robed him-self from shoulders to the ground in keeping with the simple walls to carry the patterned enrichment. As ceramic efflorescence it flowed over his buildings, and as weaving and embroidery it overflowed upon his garments and carpets.

The Persian was born, or had become, a true mystic. And because he was a mystic, this particularly developed man of the white race naturally loved blue. He put blue within blue, blue to play again with blues in a delicate rhythmical pattern displaying divine color in all and all over his wall surfaces. He kept his wall surfaces unbroken, extended, and plain, so that he might enrich them with these sunlit inlays of his spirit evident in glazed colored pottery tile. His jars, less elegant than the Greek, were shapely and large and blue as no blue—not even Ming blue—has ever been blue. His personal adornments and ornaments were blue and gold. Subtle in rhythm and color, indelible in all, were rhythms as varied as those of the flowers themselves. Under his thought, walls became sunlit gardens of poetic thought expressed as geometric forms loving pure color. So also were the woven carpets under his feet with which he covered the red and blue mosaics of his floors.

And then the Persian surrounded his buildings by avenues of cypress trees and acres of living flower gardens. He mirrored his domes and minarets in great, placid, rectangular adjacent pools of fresh water coming flush with the ground and rimmed from the gardens by a narrow rib of stone.

Yes, the Persian liked his domed buildings so well that he not only dressed his head likewise but was continually making out of brass or silver or gold or enamel, similar buildings, in miniature, and he domed them too. Filling their basements with oil he would hang these little buildings by hundreds inside his buildings as lamps to softly light the glowing spaciousness of his wonderfully dignified interiors. His sense of scale was lofty, and he preserved it by never exaggerating the scale of his exquisite details. So these edifices stood out upon the plains, blue-domed against the sky among the rank and file of Persian cities as complete in themselves as the cypress trees around them were complete.

No ruffian ever ruled the Persians, but one did conquer them. His name was Alexander.

In the works of this imaginative race, sensitive to inner rhythms, superlative craftsmanship by way of the greatest scientific masonry the world has ever seen is yet to be found in the remains of the period ending about the eleventh and thirteenth centuries. The workman was the potential artist. He was not yet the time-bound slave of a wage system. And the architect was grandly and usefully a poet.

The *quality* of a man's work was then still his honor. These noble buildings were made of and made for well-made bodies, tall of stature, fine minds. Black heads and deep dark eyes were the perfect complement for this poetic sense of building and the garden, and of blue. So the Persian of old made his God of Beauty and passionately dreamed his life away godward.

What a romantic of the race was this Persian, what mystic romance this Persia! Aladdin with the wonderful lamp? The wonderful lamp was Persian imagination.

In these creations of Persian life the upward growth of imaginative philosophic building had come far toward us, far beyond primitive walls and roofs of mankind. It came probably as far as it was ever to come with the exterior sense of form. Yet it was much more developed than the pagan sense of mass which preceded it.

The opulent Arabian wandered, striking his splendid, gorgeous tents to roam elsewhere. He learned much from the Persian; the Hindu, learning from the same origins, was himself seemingly more involved. He raised his complex but less spiritual temples to his God in the manifold tiers and terraces and domes of masonry or copper or gold. They even rivaled the Persian in exuberance but seemed to lack the pure and simple synthesis of form and clear pattern and color achieved by the Persian. This architecture traveled South and East, by way of its genius, Buddha. It influenced China, Java, Bhutan, and Thibet.

The Hindu carved and grooved, fluted his groovings with moldings. Then he loaded his architecture with images where the Persian held his surfaces true, as he inlaid them with precious materials to give them sun-glory as strong walls. But a Persian building sang in sunshine as the nightingale sings in shadow.

Perhaps Persian architecture was the end of a quality of the spirit, a feeling for the abstract as form in architecture. Probably it was gradually lost, never to be surpassed unless the ideal of architecture as organic now reaches logical but passionate expression in years to come. These simple masses of noble mind and the exquisite tracery of fine human sensibilities remain in our grand vista to remind us of this phase of human architecture, called Persian. It is the natural dome among the more self-conscious roofs of the world of architecture.

Somber, forest-abstract made in stone, the architecture we call Gothic is much nearer to us and has taken to itself a long course of time in which to die. To the development of architecture in "Le Moyen Age" came stone embodying all earlier wood forms of architecture. The wood forms became more and more implicate and complicated as Gothic masonry perfected its science.

Stone craft as organic structure rose to its highest level. In the beautiful cathedral constructions of the Gothic builders, the "Gothic" of the Teuton, the Frank, the Gaul, the Anglo-Saxon, not only did the architect decorate construction but he constructed decoration. Some of this was not integral to structure. No stone arris was left unmolded. Stone itself had now blossomed into at least an affair of human skill, usually into a thing of the human spirit. The "Gothic" cathedral seems an expiring wave of creative impulse seizing humanity by way of stone. The noble material, becoming mutable as the sea, rose into lines of surge, peaks of foam that were all human symbols. In it images of organic life were caught and held in cosmic urge. It was the final movement in the great song of stone as in ages past we see man singing it in architecture. The human spirit, as organic or living entity, seems here to have triumphed over organic matter.

But this great architecture grew by feudal strength. The spirit called Gothic at this time pervaded the baron, the merchant, the guild, the peasant. In a religious age Mariolatry, the devil and hell became articulate in architecture, a dream of heaven. Flesh remained the rough, salty romance of the people. The merchant rapidly grew in power.

In all these great periods of human history the buildings themselves, in point of style, were related to everything put into them for human use or for beauty. They were related to anything else that was in any way related to them, even clothes and ornaments, the way of wearing them and of wearing the hair, the grooming of eyebrows, even making up the face. We may reasonably see these architectures altogether as having common origin, all flowing in the same direction. The features of all are truly the features of humankind. Human nature is their nature and human limitation their limitation. For, not only were ancient popular customs in perfect harmony with ancient buildings, utensils, and ornaments, but even human personal manners were affected likewise by environment and affected or reflected environment. Better to say that environment and architecture were one with nature in the life of the people at the time, whenever and wherever it existed as architecture.

This is the great fact in this great human-scape called architecture: architecture is simply a higher type and expression of nature by way of human nature where human beings are concerned. The spirit of man enters into all, making of the whole a God-like reflection of himself as creator.

In all buildings that man has built out of earth and upon the earth, his spirit, the pattern of him, rose great or small. It lived in his buildings. It still shows there. But common to all these workmanlike endeavors in buildings great or small, another spirit lived. Let us call this spirit, common to all buildings, the great spirit, architecture. Today we look back upon the endless succession of ruins that are no more than the geological deposits washed into shore formation by the sea, landscape formed by the cosmic elements. These ancient buildings were similarly formed by the human spirit. It is the spirit elemental of architecture. The buildings are now dead to uses of present-day activity. They were sculptured by the spirit of architecture in passing, as inert shapes of the shore were sculptured by cosmic forces. Any building is a by-product of eternal living force, a spiritual force taking forms in time and place appropriate to man. They constitute a record to be interpreted, no letter to be imitated.

We carelessly call these ancient aggregations "architecture." Looking back upon this enormous deposit to man's credit, and keeping in mind that just as man was in his own time and place so was his building in its time and place, we must remember that architecture is not these buildings in themselves but far greater. We must believe architecture to be the living spirit that made buildings what they were. It is a spirit by and for man, a spirit of time and place. And we must perceive architecture, if we are to understand it at all, to be a spirit of the spirit of man that will live as long as man lives. It begins always at the beginning. It continues to bestrew the years with forms destined to change and to be strange to men yet to come.

We are viewing this valid record of the inspired work of the red men, yellow men, black men or white men of the human race in perspective outline. What we see is a vast human expression having a common ground of origin. It is more a part of man himself than the turtle's shell is part of the turtle. A great mass of matter has been eroded by man's spirit. These buildings were wrested by his tireless energy from the earth and erected in the eye of the sun. It was originally the conscious creation, out of man himself, of a higher self. His building, in order to be architecture, was the true spirit of himself made manifest (objective) whereas the turtle had no freedom of choice or any spirit at all in the making of his shell.

Considering this, we may now see wherein architecture is to be distinguished from mere building. Mere building may not know "spirit" at all. And it is well to say that the spirit of the thing is the essential life of that thing because it is truth. Such, in the retrospect, is the only life of architecture.

Architecture is abstract. Abstract form is the pattern of the essential. It is, we may see, spirit in objectified forms. Strictly speaking, abstraction has no reality except as it is embodied in materials. Realization of form is always geometrical. That is to say, it is mathematic. We call it pattern. Geometry is the obvious framework upon which nature works to keep her scale in "designing." She relates things to each other and to the whole, while meantime she gives to your eye most subtle, mysterious and apparently spontaneous irregularity in effects. So, it is through the embodied abstract that any true architect, or any true artist, must work to put his inspiration into ideas of form in the realm of created things. To arrive at expressive "form" he, too, must work from within, with the geometry of mathematic pattern. But he so works only as the rug maker weaves the pattern of his rug upon the warp. Music, too, is mathematic. But the mathematician cannot make music for the same reason that no mere builder can make architecture. Music is woven with art, upon this warp that is mathematics. So architecture is woven with a supersense of building upon this warp that is the science of building. It also is mathematical. But no study of the mathematic can affect it greatly. In architecture, as in life, to separate spirit and matter is to destroy both.

Yet, all architecture must be some formulation of materials in some actually significant pattern. Building is itself only architecture when it is essential pattern significant of purpose.

We may look back now upon the character of the great works of man called architecture and see how, by way of instinctive abstraction, the hut of the African sometimes became in the sun very tree-like or flower-like or much like the more notable animal forms or hill-shapes round about it; how the cliff dwellers raised the clay up from under their feet into great square vessels for the sun to bake; and how they put smaller vessels into them, fire-baked into admirable shapes, for daily use or for fire-worship; how their vessels were marked by imaginative patterns, and how meanwhile they were making small human images to go into them or go along with them. We have seen how the Incas carried along earlier traditions, extending back to lost civilizations, and completed the rock strata of their region by noble structures of stone adorned by crude stone human images, and how they put stone and metal and pottery into them all and shaped them for use. Both buildings and their contents were enriched by adornment. They may be the record of greater, more ancient civilizations from which they were themselves only migrations.

We have seen how the Byzantines lifted stone up into the arch and then on up into the dome, asking their materials, even so, to be no better or worse than they were. We have seen how the Egyptians, another migration, worked stone ledges into build-

ings, and buildings into stone ledges; how they knew metals, pottery and weaving and adorned their buildings with the human image by way of painting and sculpture. Upon their walls, those pages of stone, were their hieroglyphics. But their buildings were in themselves hieroglyphs of truths coming to them from some ancient source of origin that seems common to all. This feeling seeps through all ancient architecture to us of the present day.

And we see how the later Greeks consciously evolved flower shapes in stone, but worked stone also as wood. After the Dorians and Ionians they seemed to have less sense of materials than other peoples. But the Greeks developed painting far and sculpture still further and put the building into the vase, as into the building they put the vase and the manuscript. The vase was the result of their search for the elegant solution, their supreme contribution to culture.

We have seen how the Persians came from similar distant origins, how they blue-domed their buildings under the canopy of blue and emblazoned them with blue and purple ceramic flower gardens, making their buildings flower gardens within flower gardens, and put into them illuminated enamels, pottery and weaving. They omitted human images except when illustrating their books.

We have seen how, more recently, the cathedral builders put the somber uprising forest into stone, until stone triumphant could endure no more and began to fall. But meantime they had been weaving into their stone forest great glass paintings and wood carvings, and finishing them with pictured woolen and linen textiles, painted wood and stone images, great music, stately ritual and many books.

We have seen how the pagoda of the Orientals grew to resemble the fir trees, and how their shrines harmonized with the pines around them, and how within their buildings was a wealth of nature-worship in gold and painting and sculpture. Writing and myriad crafts were at home among them, and these buildings too were loaded with images.

And now, finally, we may see how all this was man's sense of himself: how it all came to be by the simple way of human use and purpose, but how also, in all ages and all races, it was man's greatest work wherein his five senses were all employed and enjoyed. By way of eye, ear, and finger, by tongue and even by nostril he was creating out of himself greater delights for a super-self, finding deep satisfactions far beyond those he could ever know were he merely a good animal.

But we are compelled to see, looking back upon this vast homogeneous human record, that the human race built most nobly when limitations were greatest and, therefore, when most was required of imagination in order to build at all. Limitations seem to have always been the best friends of architecture. The limitation in itself seems to be the artist's best friend in the sum of all the arts, even now. Later, we must see how subjugation, sophistication, easy affluence and increasing facility of intercourse began to get things all mixed up until nothing great in architecture lived any more. All architecture became bastardized. Finally the great arch of the Persian dome was fatuously invited by a "greatest artist" in the name of art to live up in the air. It was tossed against the sky to stand on top of round columns. Unnecessary columns were placed against sturdy walls for mere appearance's sake. Roofs likewise became more ornamental than useful. Wood got to be used like stone, and stone like wood. Pottery began to be used like anything else but seldom used as itself. In short, mere appearance became enough. Integrity was given no thought. Also we are compelled to see how, when greater facilities of machinery came into use in the nineteenth century, the great art of building soon became utterly confused, degraded by mere facilities. The people began putting into their buildings so much piping and wiring, and so many sanitary appliances of every kind, that architecture of the earlier sort may be said to have died. Building had become so easy that architecture became too difficult.

No stream rises higher than its source. Whatever man might build could never express or reflect more than he was. It was not more than what he felt. He could record neither more nor less than he had learned of life when the buildings were built. His inmost thought lives in them. His philosophy, true or false, is there.

Inevitably, certain races were more developed than others. Some were more favorably situated. And we see that the influence in architecture of certain races profoundly or superficially affected other races. An instance: the artificial cornices and necessary columns of the Greeks still shape our public acts in the useless cornices and unnecessary columns of modern architecture "à la mode." Later work of the middle ages, called Gothic, still shapes our modern educational institutions and churches, and the modern homes of opulent tradesmen. They mark our public money-boxes called banks. It may be that the heights of architecture were reached so long ago that the various subsequent styles we now call "classic" and practice regardless, were already degenerate when they occurred.

Throughout this authentic human record, inscribed in the countless buildings erected by man's labor, now fallen or falling back again upon the earth to become again earth, a definite character may be discerned determining man's true relationship to time and place. The sum of man's creative impulses, we find, took substance in architecture as his creative passion rose and fell within it. It always was creative. We have now reached the point in time when such original impulses subside or cease. Inspiration is no more. Go back 500 years and nothing can be found in architecture worthy to be called creation, as architecture has been creative, except as folklore, folkways, folk building.

The last original impulse, called Gothic, has subsided and the "Renaissance," a period of rebirth of original forms that were also "rebirth" when first born, begins. Creative impulses grow dim, are all but lost. Only rebirth is possible to the culture of the period we are now to consider. It is probably an over-cultured period. Apparently, humanity had gone as far with its pagan ideal of architecture as it could go. The hitherto vast, uninspired merchant class has been gradually gaining the upper hand in society and will soon outbid the higher classes for power. It will then proceed to foreclose upon a decayed, uninspired higher class.

The handmaidens of architecture—music, painting, sculpture—during these 500 years are going on their way. Music, young, healthy, is growing up independently into Mozart, Bach and Beethoven. Painting based upon the work of Giotto and the early Italians begins to set up in this world

Herbert Jacobs House. Madison, Wisconsin. 1937. Perspectives. Pencil and color pencil on tracing paper, 33 x 22". FLLW Fdn#3702.002

of the "Reborn" as an art complete in itself. By way of many schools and phases it is to eventuate into the easel picture or the bogus mural. Sculpture begins the struggle for liberation from architecture that began with Buonarrotti. Undergoing many transforprimitive. At this period handicraft, still active and essential, is yet to die because men have found an easier way to accomplish the work of the world. Having found it, it is easier now for them to "immortalize" themselves.

From Italian sources, chiefly gathered together at Florence, where degeneration and regeneration of all arts were interlocked, Italian revivals of ancient Graeco-Roman architecture begin to reach the various European capitals as patterns. By importation or export these patterns are later to be exploited among the various western nations. Ancient Greek, itself a derivation, becomes the standard of a new "low" in western culture. The artificial cornice, the column and entablature, become the common refuge of a growing impotence.

Derivations of derivations, commercialized as Georgian "Colonial," or what not, are soon exports (or imports) to the new world, America. Later, all styles of all periods of "rebirth" were exported or imported by the Americans, as the Romans imported them and as the Japanese now import them, to be mingled, soon mangled, by the new machinery of endless reproduction. The saws, lathes, planers of modern mills are soon to strew the empty carcasses of these erstwhile styles far and wide until Queen Anne comes in and all sense goes out.

Where the primitive and splendid sense of structure or building construction was going on down the ages, the reality of all buildings for human occupation was found in the enclosing, supporting walls. But a deeper sense of architecture has come to light. This is due to a new philosophy, to the invention of new machines, and to the discovery of new materials. The new architecture finds reality in the space within the walls to be lived in. The new reality of the building is the interior space which roofs and walls only serve to enclose. This reality was not felt by primitive builders. Nor is it yet known to the pseudo-classic members of our academies today. Slowly dawning as the exterior or pagan sense of building dies, this interior ideal, or inner sense of the building as an organic whole, grows. It grows more consistent, carries more genuine culture with it as it develops: culture indigenous.

In modern building this ideal of structural cause as organic effect is destined to be the center line of man's modern culture. An organic architecture will be the consequence.

Ancient builders went to work "lavishly" upon the walls and roofs themselves as though they were the reality of the building, cutting holes in the walls for light and air. In the name of art they made such holes ornamental by putting molded caps over them, or by putting up unnecessary columns beside them, or by working needless moldings and insignificant ornament into or onto the walls. They built cornices. They surrounded all openings with more moldings to heal the breaches that had to be made in the walls to let in light and air, and to get in and out of. An architect worked with his building, then, much as a sculptor would work with his solid mass of clay. He strove to mold and enrich the mass. He tried to give to it some style that he had learned or happened to like. Exterior modeling and featuring thus became, by adoption, the so-called western academic concept of architecture. This academic—"classic"—concept was chiefly based upon Greek and Roman buildings. But meantime the Chinese, Japanese, Persians and the Moors, Orientals all, developed a somewhat different sense of building. Their sense of the building was also the mass of solid matter sculptured from the outside, but the Oriental sense of the building was more plastic, therefore more a thing of the spirit.

Being "plastic," the building was treated more consistently as a unit or consistent whole. It was less an aggregation of many features and parts, all remaining separate features, by, and for, themselves. In organic building nothing is complete in itself but is only complete as the part is merged into the larger expression of the whole. Something of this had begun to find its way into many Oriental buildings.

During these later periods of various "renaissances," even the Pope's authority at Rome, the religious capital, has been rivaled by the authority of the Italian artist and workman, as the Italian Renaissance grew upon Europe. And so the remarkable Italian city of Florence grew to be the artist capital if not the cultural capital of a world.

Paul and Jean Hanna House. Stanford, California. 1936. Aerial perspective. Pencil on paper, 36 x 22". FLLW Fdn#3701.001

But it became the artist capital of a western world that could only buy or sell. Already it was prostitute to imitation. It was a world prostitute to imitation because, with the exception of music and painting, and always excepting the newly born literature, society was unable to distinguish between birth and rebirth. It was unable to create anything much above the level of technique, scientific process or mechanical invention. The new world was learning to buy and sell its way to whatever it wanted in this matter of culture. By way of commercial reproductions of the styles affected by these European cultures society gratified such creative aspiration as remained.

Upon this prevalent rising tide that is called "commerce" comes the printed page, "letters," the book. Society becomes consciously literate as the printed book absorbs ever more of the cultural energies of mankind. Upon any large scale this scientific art of printing was the first application of the machine to human affairs. It is the machine that brings the book to humanity. And men, by means of the book, grew more literal. Life itself became and continues to grow more and more vicarious.

Human nature always seeks an easier way to do its work, or seeks a substitute. Human effort finds this "easiest way," or a substitute. The nineteenth century, especially, found both in machine development. As a consequence of this easy release all life, therefore all architecture, became less and less from within until society became content that art be something purchasable, something to be applied. The tendency of art in such circumstances is to become uncreative. It appears as some perverted form of literature or at least as no more than something literal. Realistic is the word. Machine power increased the deluge of literature and ready-made European "*objets d'art*." A newly literalized humanity becomes obvious to commerce as the new facility for exploitation. Yes, "realistic" is the proper word for the art work of the period. It was really no great art at all. Photography could take over the popular "art interest" of the period. It proceeded to do so.

Yet, the machine is to make opportunity new. The science of printing is to make the book a medium for human expression more facile than building and the book is to become a means of recording life perhaps more enduring than the great edifice ever was.

But, meantime, the printed word accelerates. An increasingly vicarious life and servile art is becoming universal in the western world. Foregathering to listen, to stand, to watch, or to ride is now sufficient. Fifty thousand people watch a football game. Ninety thousand watch a prize fight. A remittance man sits at the steering wheel of a hundred and twenty-five horse-power car, with the airs, and sensation, too, that the power is his own—is, in fact, him. Connection with the soil is giving way to machinery. Contacts between men are increasingly had by electrical devices. Intercommunication becomes instantaneous and far reaching, but actual human contacts become fewer and more feeble. Superficial release is provided by literature, now ubiquitous, and new ways and means to beat work are found. Culture as architecture and architecture as culture is on the way down and out. Structure no longer finds beauty by way of integral evolution. Nor does society think to ask for such.

The place where this great integrity was wont to be is fast becoming an empty place.

The machine can exploit externality. But as we have set it up the machine can do nothing nor let much be done from within. The machine reduces and reproduces such forms of old-fashioned representation in art as are most salable. Those most salable are naturally those most realistic or superficially elegant. Grandomania flourishes in consequence. Architecture as something ready-made is in the hand of the highly specialized and speculative salesman. Characteristic of this show-window period, architecture can only be a thing of mixed origins and haphazard applications. We may see it around us everywhere. Styles now abound. But nowhere is there genuine style. These are the days of the General Grant Gothic and the Pseudo-Classic. When Michelangelo piled the Pantheon upon the Parthenon and called it St. Peter's, he, a painter, had committed architectural adultery. It was destined to bring forth a characteristic monstrosity, namely, an arch set up into plain air on posts to shift for itself. It is an imitative anachronism that characterizes our public acts, as illustrated by our capitols, court houses, and town halls. A noble thing, the Persian dome has become ignoble. Now it is base. The same depravity sees a Greek temple as fitting memorial to Abraham Lincoln. He is the Greek antithesis. Nothing is Greek about his life or work or thought. A Gothicized French Château, incongruous pattern, is the unsuitable stall for some urban fire engine. Any Roman bath or sarcophagus will do to lend prestige to the sacrosanct bank on any town sidewalk anywhere. A Gothicized cathedral is set up at Yale to throw a glamour over college athletics. Another may serve to memorialize the grandmother of a successful speculator. All serve, unchallenged, this commercialized assumption or provincial gesture that the period calls culture.

In short, in this present time only the bastard survives even as a temple for the work of the Supreme Court of the United States. Stale survivals of every sort are "modern." Business turns to help itself liberally to "the classic." The "classic" goes to market as diamonds go.

Art and religion, in this inversion of human circumstances, lose prestige. Both these resources of the human spirit become purchasable and, as a natural consequence, life itself becomes purchasable. Meantime, science, far more useful to trade than either art or religion, grows in dominion. Neither art nor religion is longer a necessity to the people. The people have sought a replica. They have found and bought a substitute. The merchant has become the ruler for the time being of man's singing, dancing, dwelling and breeding. And the creative individual in the arts must become pauper, at this time when a Joseph Duveen is a knight, Andy Mellon a prince, and a Rockefeller, king.

In the preceding era, men of Florence were the guiding spirits and the light on the horizon, such as that light was. So, now in the twentieth century, social, economic, and artistic forms are determined by outward rather than by inner factors. Today the "civilized" world has come to the consequences of "renaissance." It has tried to live on a decadent precedent. Architecture and its kindred, as a matter of course, are divorced from nature in order to make of art the merchantable thing of texts, classroom armchairs and, above all, of speculative "price," that it now is. It is a speculative commodity.

The artist, now no more than the designing partner, the official streamliner, the interior decorator, the industrial designer, is entirely outside. Nothing could be more external than an interior decorator. Nothing could be more irrelevant than the exterior architect. Nothing could be more remote from life at the moment than citizens content to live in what either of them produces. Perspective is in reverse. The cart is before the horse.

A new type of patron of the arts has grown up out of this perversity. He is a Frick, a Widener, a Morgan, a Henry Ford, or a Bendix. Perhaps he is a Hart, Shaffner and Marx or Metro-Goldwyn-Mayer. He is, and he must be, some success in speculation upon some grand scale. Not for nothing was Joseph Duveen a knight.

By money power democracy has been perverted to inverted aristocracy. The new world has made social parasitism and vulgarity academic. What by nature can only be grown, may by such modern improvements be mere artifice freely bought to change hands at a price. Life itself must now be standardized because it is to be prefabricated, show-windowed, and eventually sold. Yes, and sold even now.

Trade and machine production are having their way and their say in the standardizations of our day. How can the young escape? As for the architect, who consents to buy and sell indulgences for his people, indulgences unwittingly provided by the traffic in foreign cultures to which he himself helped educate them: with him standardization has had its way too. Unwittingly, the Cass Gilberts, Ray Hoods, Corbetts and Walkers, the McGonigles and Popes carry on the work of the McKim, Mead and Whites, the D. H. Burnhams, Richard M. Hunts and the Henry Hardenbergs. They are merely useful tools of this devastating power.

The great and liberal arts that man nourished because they nourished him have gone. They have gone by this same route to the mill which is this remorseless standardization for profit. And the tide of literal representation by way of the press, radio and cinema, all rapacious maws for more fodder of the sort, rises unsteadily to new monopolies.

At this moment, 1937 A. D., any ideal at all organic in character becomes impractical if not slightly absurd: shopkeepers all. All in all are ruled by the expedient.

Only petty specialists in architecture and the sister arts are needed on the job made by our order of "business." Its wholly artificial power must be maintained upon an artificial basis. It is engendered and kept by indiscriminate use of indiscriminate increment. The whole man can no longer be used. He too is a "job."

Let us frankly admit it:

The universal modern "art" is really salesmanship.

Showmanship is perihelion. Everywhere, it is at a premium.

The show-window is the most important form of all artistry in these United States. Let it stand for the symbol of this era.

The mother of the arts, architecture, in such circumstances could have little or no issue. Neither impregnation nor conception upon any social scale is possible. And a restless movement begins the world over. Action is inevitable. It has now begun because, long ago, it was time.

In this human restlessness the new order of culture, structure to emerge as "organic," lies concealed as the child in the womb. Meanwhile, cultural decay of the individual proceeds by way of the commercialized mass-education we have learned to call academic.

Has this modern restlessness anything to turn to? Has it recourse? Yes. Organic architecture with its sense of structure, the sense of the whole, is one great recourse. Religion might be another. These two, now as always.

We have been describing what has happened to art. What, then, has happened to religion so far as it relates to art?

Religion, in its present form, is become "Christianity," the church. The church was the last great client of architecture. The last great urge of human creative energy, upward thrust of human creative power, flowered into stone as it built the great cathedrals. The church was Christianity. What of Christianity, now, as it passes for religion in this general confusion and debauchery of the creative powers of man-kind? Neither the teaching nor character of Christianity was such as to inspire the nature-worship of the creative mind.

Christianity took the church to man as a substitute for that law and order of the universe which should have been worked out by him from within himself, law and order made his own by way of the arts. But, as Christianity had it, the man was to be saved by his beliefs, not saved by his works. So, the church substituted beatitudes for beauty. Spiritually the man was invited to become a parasite upon the Lord. That quality in the man that stood tall inside him up against the roof of his mind, which must ever be his true self, can no longer be much encouraged even by the church.

And the ideals of Jesus, the gentle anarchist, remain generally feared because generally misunderstood or yet unknown.

This failure to see God and man as one has disaffected all art for it has betrayed architecture. There is no longer general realization of matter and spirit as the same thing. This is a fatal division of the house against itself. A great wave of ugliness has followed in the wake of this error. Bogus sanctuaries to God stand propped against the sky by steel, as though it were necessary to prove to some court of last resort that the final period of creative impulse on earth is dying of imitation or already dead by mutilation.

With Christianity for tenant today, architecture is a parasite, content with an imitation of an imitation like the spurious St. John the Divine in New York City. To go along with the imported cathedral are such inversions as the Lincoln Memorial, such aberrations as our capitols, such morgues as our museums, monuments, and such grandomania as our city halls. Abortions of sentiment, like the "Great White Whale" at Princeton, a Rockefeller cathedral on Riverside Drive are proof enough that the spirit of architecture has fled from a social era. Corpses encumber the ground. As for religion or art, a pig may live in a palace: any cat can scratch the face of a king.

Upon this, the American scene, emerges the new ideal-structure as organic architecture becomes interpretation of life itself. From within outward is no longer remote ideal. It is everywhere becoming action. With new integrity action insists upon indigenous culture. The new reality.

SOME ASPECTS OF THE FUTURE OF ARCHITECTURE

The chapter on the past and present of architecture ended with the ideal of an organic architecture—the new reality.

If architecture has any future more than revival or passive reform, we must speak of future architecture as organic. It is apparent that the pagan ideal of architecture—we call it classical—has broken down. In practice, then, speaking out from experience in the field, what does this term, organic architecture, mean? Already it has been said—*lieber meister* declared it—and biology knows and shows us that "form follows function." But the physicist cannot interpret the word "organic" as it applies to architecture. Not until we raise the dictum, now a dogma, to the realm of thought, and say: *Form and function are one*, have we stated the case for architecture.

That abstract saying "Form and function are one" is the center line of architecture, organic. It places us in line with nature and enables us sensibly to go to work. Now accepting that fundamental concept of architecture as interior discipline, how can we work it out in actual practice?

Let us rebuild a building with phrases as I have built one with bricks and mortar and men. I have built one, as I believe, naturally.

"Form and function are one" is the thought in the back of the mind that will now shape an attitude towards everything in our sight, including Mr. and Mrs. Domestic Client and progeny, or, it may be, towards the capitalist-captain, the unfeeling corporation, or the baron.

Before we begin to build, however, what is the "nature" of this act we call architecture? That quest will discover certain elemental truths with which building, as organic, is concerned. Form and function being one, it follows that the purpose and pattern of the building become one. They are integral. This, in a sentence, is the ages-old thesis, which, made new, we call the norm of organic architecture. This new integrity, "from within outward," is now evident as the modern architect's guide and opportunity. "Out of the ground into the light" is opportunity. The nature of materials is also his opportunity and no less limitation. All three opportunities are limitations but they are a condition of success. Human nature, too, is one of these materials, served by the building and serving it.

With the purpose or motive of the building we are to build well in mind, as of course it must be, and proceeding from generals to particulars, as "from-within-outward" must do, what consideration comes first?

The ground, doesn't it? The nature of the site, of the soil and of climate comes first. Next, what materials are available in the circumstances—money being one of them—with which to build? Wood, stone, brick, or synthetics? Next, what labor, or means of power, is available and advisable in the circumstances? Manual, machine, or both? The labor union or the factory, or both? Always with this "from the nature within" in mind, working in imagination towards a significant outward form, we proceed always within the circumstances.

Here we come well in towards the processes of thought that properly employ science in the erection of an organic building. But, still, the most desirable and valuable element in creation is lacking. It, too, is primary. We call it "inspiration." It seems to us a mysterious element. But it is of the "from within outward" and it is a qualification that gives finality to the whole structure as creative. To give life to the whole is "creative" and only that. We imply the structure of that life when we say form and function are one, or organic.

What, then, is life?

To answer that question the organic structure must now appear not only as "entity"; entity must appear as individuality. We are concerned with organism. We may say the organism is a living one, only when all is part to the whole as whole is to the part. This correlation, such as is found in any plant or animal, is fundamental to the life of organic architecture, as it is to any life whatever. But more important, and what finally makes any building live as true architecture, this building we are building must finally come to terms with the living human spirit. It must come alive where that spirit is concerned. Now what is this *"living"* human spirit?

First, it is a quality of the mind really informed with a sense of man's universe. It is a mind wholly in life as life is in it. It is the spirit in life for what life may be. It desires living to the utmost. Such spirit is seldom lost in any part of the whole. Such a mind never for long loses the direction of the center line of "sentient entity." The "living spirit" would, at least, be the spirit capable of that. Let us call the living spirit, then, the new-old integrity that in architecture, as in all else, is the bridge by which man's past reached the present and by which his present will reach the future, if his present is to have any future at all. If our present in architecture contains any future worthy of the living human spirit, it will cross over this bridge. I am trying to present that architecture here in words as architecture "organic": the living expression of living human spirit. Architecture alive.

As already said, such architecture is and, as a matter of course, must be actual interpretation of social human life. Such living architecture is a new integrity in these modern times. It enters a distorted world where capital has got ahead of labor; where individual qualities of the personality are rendered invalid by new dimensions for money.

We shall go on in thought now with this building we started to build.

We start with the *ground*.

This is rock and *humus*. A building is planted there to survive the elements. The building is, meanwhile, shelter and human dignity, though inevitably destined to succumb to time in due course.

Why should the building try to belong to the ground instead of being content with some box-like fixture perched upon the rock or stuck into the soil, where it stands out as mere artifice, regardless where it stands up and "off," as "Colonial" houses do, and just as all houses not indigenous must do?

The answer is found in the ideal stated in the abstract dictum, "Form and function are one." We must begin upon our structure with that.

The ground already has form. Why not begin to give at once by accepting that? Why not give by accepting the gifts of nature? But I have never seen a "Colonial" house that did or could do this. Inevitably that house looks as though it hated the ground, with vast vanity trying to rise superior to it regardless of nature, depending upon a detachment called "classical" for such human values as habit and association of ideas could give to it.

Well, then, rejecting the "classical"; what of the ground?

Is the ground a parcel of prairie, square and flat? Is the ground sunny or the shaded slope of some hill, high or low, bare or wooded, triangular or square?

Has the site features, trees, rocks, stream, or a visible trend of some kind? Has it some fault or a special virtue, or several?

In any and every case the character of the site is the beginning of the building that aspires to architecture. And this is true whatever the site or the building may be. It is true whether it be a dwelling among Wisconsin hills or a house on the bare prairie, the Imperial Hotel at Tokyo, or a skyscraper in New York City. All must begin there where they stand. For our "case in point" we shall take the Imperial Hotel at Tokyo and try to put into words something of the thought process that tended to make that structure organic.

A social clearing house, call it a hotel, became necessary to official Japan as a consequence of new foreign interest in the Japanese. A new hotel becomes necessary, because no foreigner, no matter how cultivated, could live on the floor, as the Japanese do, with any grace or comfort. It was also necessary for another reason: a Japanese gentleman does not entertain strangers, no matter how gentle, within his family circle. So the building will be more a place for entertainment with private supper rooms, banquet hall, theater and cabaret than it will be a hotel.

No foreign architect yet invited to work in Japan ever took off his hat to the Japanese and respected either Japanese conditions or traditions. And yet those aesthetic traditions are at the top among the noblest in the world. When I accepted the commission to design and build their building it was my instinct and definite intention not to insult them. Were they not a feature of my first condition, the ground? They were. The Japanese were more their own ground than any people I knew.

So while making their building "modern" in the best sense, I meant to leave it a sympathetic consort to Japanese buildings. I wanted to show the Japanese how their own conservation of space and the soul of their own religious Shinto, which is "be clean," might, in the use of all materials, take place as effectively for them indoors in sound masonry construction when on their feet as it had taken place for them when they were down upon their knees in their own inspired carpentry.

I meant to show them how to use our new civilizing-agents—call them plumbing, electrification, and heating—without such outrage to the art of building as we ourselves were practicing and they were then copying. I intended to make all these appurtenance systems a practical and aesthetic part of the building itself. It was to be given a new simplicity by making it a complete whole within itself.

Mechanical systems should be an asset to life and so an asset to architecture. They should be no detriment to either. Why shouldn't the Japanese nation make the same coordination of furnishing and building when they came to be at home on their feet that they had so wonderfully made for themselves at home on their knees?

And I believed I could show them how to build an earthquake-proof masonry building.

In short, I desired to help Japan make the transition from wood to masonry, and from her knees to her feet, without too great loss of her own great accomplishments in culture. And I wished to enable her to overcome some of the inherent weaknesses of her building system where the temblor was a constant threat to her happiness and to her very life.

There was this natural enemy to all building whatsoever: the temblor. And, as I well knew, the seismograph in Japan is never still. The presence of the temblor, an affair of the ground, never left me while I planned and for four years or more worked upon the plans and structure of the new hotel. Earthquakes I found to be due to wave movement of the ground. Because of wave movement, foundations like long piles oscillate and rock the structure. Heavy masses of masonry inevitably would be wrecked. The heavier the masonry the greater the wreck.

The feature of the ground that was the site itself was a flat 500- by 300-foot plot of ground composed of sixty feet of liquid mud overlaid by eight feet of filled soil. The filling was about the consistency of hard cheese. The perpetual water level stood within fifteen inches of the level of the ground. In short, the building was to stand up on an ancient marsh, an arm of the bay that had been filled in when Tokyo became the capital of the empire.

But the mud beneath the filling seemed to me a good cushion to relieve earthquake shocks. A building might float upon the mud somewhat as a battleship floats on salt water. Float the building upon the mud? Why not? And since it must float, why not extreme lightness combined with the tenuity and flexibility that are a property of steel instead of the great weight necessary to the usually excessive rigidity which, no matter how rigid, could never be rigid enough? Probably the answer was a building made flexible as the two hands thrust together, fingers interlocked, yielding to movement yet resilient to return to position when force exerted upon its members and membranes ceased. Why fight the force of the quake on its own terms? Why not go with it and come back unharmed? Outwit the quake?

That was how the nature of the site, the ground, entered into the conception of the building. Now, to carry out in detail these initial perceptions.

I took a preliminary year in which to acquire necessary data, making tests for the new type of foundation. Finally flexible foundations, economical too, were provided by driving tapered wooden piles, only eight feet long, into the strata of filled soil, pulling them out and throwing in concrete immediately, to form the thousands of small piers or concrete pins two feet apart on centers upon which the jointed footing courses were laid. Nine pile drivers dotted the ground, each with its band of singing women pulling on the ropes lifting and dropping the drive-head—twelve ropes, one for each pair of hands.

The good sense of careful calculation so far: now what about the superstructure?

The building was going native, so intensive hand methods have to be used and native materials too. The nature of the design therefore should be something hand methods could do better than machinery. It was impossible to say how far we could go in any direction with machines, probably not very far.

Evidently the straight line and flat plane to which I had already been committed by machines in America should be modified in point of style if I would respect the traditions of the people to whom the building would belong. The Japanese, centuries ago, had come nearer the ideal of an

Kathryn Winckler and Alma Goetsch House. Lansing, Michigan. 1937. Photographs by Hedrich-Blessing, courtesy the Chicago Historical Society. FLLW Fdn FA#3907.0012 and .0013

organic architecture in their dwellings than any civilized race on earth. The ideals we have been calling organic are even now best exemplified in their wood and paper dwellings where they lived on their knees. As I have already said, I wanted to help the Japanese get to their feet indoors and learn to live in fireproof masonry buildings, without loss of their native aesthetic prestige where the art of architecture was a factor. Trained by the disasters of centuries to build lightly on the ground, the wood and paper homes natural to them are kindled by any spark. When fire starts it seldom stops short of several hundred homes, sometimes destroys thousands, and ends in complete destruction of a city. After the irresistible wave movements have gone shuddering and jolting through the earth, changing all overnight in immense areas, islands disappearing, new ones appearing, mountains laid low and valleys lifted up taking awful toll of human life, then come the flames! Conflagration always at the end.

The cost of metal frames and sash at that time was prohibitive, but the plans were made for an otherwise completely fireproof building and the designs were so made that all architectural features were practical necessities.

The flexible light foundations had saved one hundred thousand dollars over the customary massive foundations. Now how could the building be made as light and flexible? I divided the building into sections about sixty feet long. This is the safe limit for temperature cracks in reinforced concrete in that climate. Wherever part met part I provided through joints.

To insure stability I carried the floor and roof loads as a waiter carries his tray on his upraised arm and fingers. At the center all supports were centered under the loaded floor-slabs; balancing the load instead of gripping the load at the edges with the walls, as in the accepted manner. In any movement a load so carried would be safe. The waiter's tray balanced on his hand at the center is the cantilever in principle.

This was done. This meant that the working principle of the cantilevers would help determine the style of the structure. So the cantilever became the principal feature of the structure and a great factor in shaping its forms throughout as the floor-slabs came through the walls and extended into various balconies and overhangs.

Tokyo buildings were top heavy. The exaggerated native roofs were covered deep with clay, and the heavy roof tiles laid on over the clay would come

loose and slide down with deadly effect into the narrow streets crowded with terrified humanity.

So the outer walls, spread thick and heavy at the base and tapering towards the top, were crowned there by a light roof covered with hand-worked sheet copper tiles. The light roof framing rested upon a concrete ceiling slab extended outward over the walls into an overhang, perforated to let sunlight into the windows of the rooms beneath.

Now as to materials. What would be desirable and available? Again we go to the ground.

A stone I had seen under foot and in common use in Tokyo building was a light, workable lava, called oya, weighing about as much as green oak and resembling travertine. It was quarried at Nikko and was floated down on rafts by sea to Tokyo and then by canal to the site.

I liked this material for its character but soon found that the building committee, made up of the financial autocracy of the empire, considered it sacrilege to use a material so cheap and common for so dignified a purpose. But finally the building committee gave in and we bought our own quarries at Nikko. We used oya (the lava) throughout the work, combining it with concrete walls cast in layers within thin wall shells of slender bricks.

Large or small, the pieces of lava could be easily hollowed out at the back and set up with the hollow side inside, as one side of the slab-forms for casting the concrete. In this way the three materials were cast solidly together as a structural unit when the concrete was poured into them.

Copper, too, was a prominent feature in our list of available handworked materials.

Thus the "Teikoku" (Imperial Hotel) after these measures were taken became a jointed steel-reinforced monolith with a thin integral facing of lava and thin brick, the whole sheltered overhead by light copper tiles. The mass of the structure rests upon a kind of pincushion. The pins were set close enough together to support, by friction, the weight calculated to be placed upon them. To the lengthwise and crosswise work in this particular structure all piping and wiring were made to conform. Both were designed to be laid in shafts and trenches free of construction. The pipes were of lead, sweeping with easy bend from trenches to shafts and curving again from shafts to fixtures. Thus any earthquake might rattle and flex the pipes as they hung but could break no connections. Last, but by no means least, an immense pool of water as an architectural feature of the extensive entrance court to the hotel was connected to its own private water system. This was to play its part in conflagration following in the wake of earthquake.

During the execution of these ideas I found the language a barrier. Men and methods were strange. But the "foreign" architect with twenty Japanese students from Tokyo and Kyoto University courses in architecture, some of whom were taken to Taliesin during the preliminary plan making, and one excellent American builder, Paul Mueller, made up the band that built the Imperial Hotel. Hayashi San, the general manager of the Imperial Hotel, was in direct charge of everything. The principal owner, the Imperial Household, was represented by Baron Okura. And there was a board of directors composed of five captains of Japanese big business—ships, tobacco, cement, and banking.

The original plans which I had worked out at Taliesin for the construction I threw aside as educational experience for the architect only and worked out the details on the ground as we went along. Plans served only as a preliminary study for final construction.

Those Japanese workmen! How clever they were. What skill and industry they displayed! So instead of trying to execute preconceived methods of execution, thereby wasting this precious human asset in vainly trying to make the workmen come our way, we learned from them and willingly went with them, their way. I modified many original intentions to make the most of what I now saw to be naturally theirs. But, of course, curious mistakes were common. I had occasion to learn that the characteristic Japanese approach to any subject is, by instinct, spiral. The Oriental instinct for attack in any direction is oblique or volute and becomes wearisome to a direct Occidental, whose instinct is frontal and whose approach is rectilinear.

But, then, they made up for this seeming indirection by gentleness, loyalty, and skill. Soon we began to educate the "foreigners" as they did us, and all went along together pretty well.

As the countenance of their building began to emerge from seeming confusion the workmen grew more and more interested in it. It was a common sight to see groups of them intelligently admiring and criticizing some finished feature as it would emerge to view. There was warmth of interest and depth of appreciation, unknown to me in the building circles of our country in our own day, to prove the sincerity of their pleasure and interest in their work.

Finally, out of this exercise of free will and common sense, with this unusual Western feeling of respect for the East and for Japanese life and traditions in view as discipline and inspiration, what would emerge?

A great building is to be born; one not looking out of place where it is to stand across the park from the Imperial Palace. The noble surrounding walls of the Palace rose above the ancient moat. The gateways to the Palace grounds, guarded by blue-tiled, white-walled buildings nesting on the massive stone walls, were visible above the moat across the way. It was architecture perfect of its kind and as Japanese as the countenance of the race. I conceived the form of this new associate—the Imperial—as something squat and strong, as harmonious with this precedent as the pines in the park. It should be a form seen to be bracing itself against storm and expected temblor. Appeal has already been made to imagination in a realm scientific; but pure reason and science must now wait there at the doorstep.

Wait there while something came to Japanese ground—something not Japanese, certainly, but sympathetic, embodying modern scientific building ideas by old methods not strange to Japan. No single form was really Japanese but the whole was informed by unity. The growing proportions were suitable to the best Japanese tradition. We have here in the individuality of the architect a sincere lover of old Japan, his hat in hand, seeking to contribute his share in the transition of a great old culture to a new and inevitably foreign one. Probably the new one was unsuitable. Certainly it was as yet but imperfectly understood by those who were blindly, even fatuously, accepting it as superior to their own. A great tragedy, it may be.

Looking on then as now, it seemed to me as though tragedy it must be. The Far East had so little to learn from our great West, so much to lose where culture is concerned.

I might ameliorate their loss by helping to make much that was spiritually sound and beautiful in their own life, as they had known it so well, over into a pattern of the unknown new life they were so rashly entering. To realize this ambition in concrete form, apparent in a structure that acknowledged and consciously embodied this appropriate pattern, was what I intended to do in this masonry building 500 feet long by 300 feet wide. It was a world complete within itself. It now may be seen. It is known far and wide as it stands on the beaten path around the world. Said Baron Takahashi to a conscientious objector from America, "You may not like our Imperial Hotel but we Japanese like it. We understand it."

Two years later—1923—in Los Angeles: news was shouted in the streets of awful disaster. Tokyo and nearby Yokohama were wiped out by the most terrific temblor in history. Appalling details came in day after day after the first silence when no details could be had. As the news began to add up it seemed that nothing human could have withstood the cataclysm.

Too anxious to get any sleep I kept trying to get news of the fate of the New Imperial and of my friends, Shugio, Hayashi, Endo San, my boys and the Baron, hosts of friends I had left over there. Finally the third or fourth day after the first outcry, about two o'clock in the morning, the telephone bell. Mr. Hearst's *Examiner* wished to inform me that the Imperial Hotel was completely destroyed. My heart sank as I laughed at them. "Read your dispatch," I said. The *Examiner* read a long list of "Imperial" this and "Imperial" that.

"You see how easy it is to get the Imperial Hotel mixed with other Imperials. If you print the destruction of the new Imperial Hotel as news you will have to retract. If anything is above ground in Tokyo it is that building," I said, and hoped.

Their turn to laugh while they spread the news of destruction with a photograph across the head of the front page in the morning. Then followed a week or more of anxiety. Conflicting reports came continually because during that time direct communication was cut off.

Then—a cablegram:

FRANK LLOYD WRIGHT, OLIVE HILL RESIDENCE, HOLLYWOOD, CALIFORNIA. FOLLOWING WIRELESS RECEIVED TODAY FROM TOKYO, HOTEL STANDS UNDAMAGED AS MONUMENT TO YOUR GENIUS HUNDREDS OF HOMELESS PROVIDED BY PERFECTLY MAINTAINED SERVICE. CONGRATULATIONS.
OKURA

For once in a lifetime good news was newspaper news and the Baron's cablegram flashed around the world to herald what? To herald the triumph of good sense in the head of an architect tough enough to stick to it through thick and thin. Yes, that. But it was really a new approach to building, the ideal of an organic architecture at work, that really saved the Imperial Hotel.

Both Tokyo houses of the Baron were gone. The splendid museum he gave to Tokyo was gone. The building by an American architect, whose hand he took to see him through, was what he had left in Tokyo standing intact, nor could love or money buy a share in it, now.

When letters finally came through, friends were found to be safe. And it appeared that not one pane of glass was broken in the building—no one harmed. Neither was the plumbing or the heating system damaged at all. But something else was especially gratifying to me. After the first great quake was over, the dead lying in heaps, the Japanese came in droves, dragging their children into the courses and up onto the terraces of the building, praying for protection by the God that had protected the Teikoku. Then, as the wall of fire that follows every great quake came sweeping across the city toward the long front of the Imperial, driving a continuous wail of human misery before it, the Hotel boys formed a bucket line to the big pool of the central entrance court (the city mains were disrupted by the quake) and found there a reserve of water to keep the wood window frames and sash wet to meet the flames. The last thought for the safety of the Imperial had taken effect.

Early in the twentieth century, a world in itself, true enough to its purpose and created spontaneously as any ever fashioned by the will of any creator of antiquity, had been completed within a sector of the lifetime of its one architect. Such work in ancient times generally proceeded from generation to generation and from architect to architect. Strange! Here expert handicraft had come at the beck and call of one who had, up to that time, devoted most of his effort to getting buildings true to modern machine processes built by machine.

Here in the Far East a significant transition building was born. Are really good buildings all transition buildings? But for the quality of thought that built it, the ideal of an organic architecture, it would surely have been just "another one of those things" and have been swept away.

While the New Imperial only partially realized the ideal of an organic architecture, the pursuit of that ideal made the building what it really was, and enabled it to do what it did do. The fact that were I to build it again it would be entirely different, although employing the same methods and means, does not vitiate my thesis here. It greatly strengthens it.

Now let us glance at what followed this natural approach to the nature of a problem as a natural consequence. Opposition, of course, followed until finally Baron Okura took full responsibility and saw the building through. There was the unfriendly attitude of Americans and Englishmen. Though none too friendly to each other, they opposed this approach. They had owned Tokyo up to now because, where foreign culture was being so freely and thoughtlessly bought, they were best sellers. The Germans were there, strong too, but they were almost out of the running by now. My sympathetic attitude, Japan for the Japanese, was regarded as treason to American interests. I encouraged and sometimes taught the Japanese how to do the work on their building themselves. The American construction companies were building ten-story steel buildings with such architecture as they had hung to the steel, setting the steel frames on long piles which they floated across the Pacific from Oregon and drove down to hard pan. I suppose they were built in this fashion so the steel might rattle the architecture off into the streets in any severe quake? These companies were especially virulent where I was concerned.

The Western Society of American Engineers gratuitously warned me that my "scheme for foundations was unsound." The A.I.A.—American Institute of Architects—passing through Tokyo when the building was nearly finished, took notice and published articles in Tokyo papers declaring the work an insult to American architecture, notifying my clients, and the world generally, that the whole thing would be down in the first quake with horrible loss of life.

Finally, when the building was about two-thirds completed, it came directly to the directors from such sources that their American architect was mad. Now every director except one (my sponsor, the Baron), so worked upon continually for several years, became a spy. The walls had ears. Propaganda increased. General Manager Hayashi was "on the spot." My freedom was going fast and I worked on, under difficulties greater than ever. Hayashi San, the powerful Okura, and my little band of Japanese student apprentices were loyal and we got ahead until the final storm broke in a dark scene in a directors' meeting. Then the Baron took over the reins himself to see me through with my work, and the building of the New Imperial went forward more smoothly to conclusion.

I have learned that wherever reason shows its countenance and change is to take place, the reaction in any established order, itself not organic, is similar. Therefore organic architecture has this barrier to throw down or cross over or go around.

As for government, I should say here that no permit to build the Imperial Hotel was ever issued by the government. I explained to the proper Imperial Department our intention, registered the drawings. The result was visitation by Japanese authorities, more explanations, head shakings. But the attitude was entirely friendly and sympathetic in contrast to the attitude that might be expected in our own country. Finally we were told no permit was needed, to go ahead, they would watch proceedings and hoped to learn something from the experiment. They could not say that most of the ideas did not seem right but, having no precedent, they could not officially act. They could wink, however, and "wink" the government did.

This "wink" is the utmost official sanction organic architecture or any thought-built action of the sort in any medium may expect from a social order itself inorganic and in such danger of disturbance if radical examination is permitted that even an approach in that direction is cause for hysteria. Institutions such as ours are safe, in fact remain "institutions" only upon some status quo, some supreme court, which inevitably becomes invalid as life goes on.

Now—so far as the architecture of the future is concerned, what is to be deduced from this particular and by no means typical instance?

Let us take an example with a broader application. The problem of the moderate cost home for that unfortunate—the "average American."

Suppose, then, we consider briefly a much broader application of the principles of an organic architecture: the moderate house for the citizen in moderate circumstances. For some reason—probably not a good one—five or six thousand dollars seems to be as much as the better part of the average citizenship of the United States can afford to pay for a house and the lot he builds one on. This lot is usually a fifty-foot lot for some other reason, certainly not a good reason. He may secure sixty or seventy feet, and has been known in rare instances to acquire title to as much as one hundred feet on some street front where sewer, water and gas, or electricity are available. The "lot"—the word is short for "allotment"—varies in depth from 125 to 200 feet, with a sixteen-foot "alley" at the end opposite the street end. Each lot on each side must range lengthwise along neighboring lots, so privacy is unlikely or impossible to any great extent. Corner lots are exposed to the street on two sides, with more taxes to pay accordingly and even less privacy than the inside neighbor has.

The result is a row of houses toeing an imaginary mark called a building line—a line predetermining how near the street the houses may come; and sometimes they must stay away several feet from the neighboring depthwise lot line. Oftentimes not: the feeling being pretty general that when a man buys a piece of ground it is his for better or for worse, not only from side to side but from the center of the earth to the top of the sky, although the "top of the sky" has been the subject of recent regulation.

Fortunately the owner's imagination, though ambitious, is limited. And he can go about as far as his neighbor goes and no farther. That is about all the actual discipline there is. Within that limitation each proceeds to be as original—"different" they call it—as each can be, with the net result, of course, that all look monotonously alike in their attempts to be "different" because the thought involved never changes. To be perfectly sincere—no thought at all ever enters into the affair from beginning to end. There is only habit, fashion—a certain association of ideas and the idiosyncrasy called "taste." The citizens talk of comfort and convenience without knowing very well what either really means. They spend two-fifths of the cost of the whole house to do as well as their neighbors in appearances, or to outdo them. Emulation or competition are in it all, but constructive thought does not enter. A certain shrewd common sense has to serve as it may, and such taste as may be.

Then the department store delivery wagon appears out front and the furnishings begin to come in from the chief source of furnishment. Countless items in the prevailing mode, all bought in some big establishment with the help sometimes of the interior decorator, whom even the undiscriminating are learning to call "the inferior desecrator."

So the interior is Marshall Field, Wanamaker or Kaufmann's at this level, instead of the Montgomery Ward and Sears Roebuck of the next level down—say the three-thousand-dollar bracket—house and lot. Now it is well to realize at this point that these houses so furnished are usually investments. They are homes, that's true, but they are homes afterward. Nothing must be done that detracts from the likelihood of profitable resale—on occasion. And American life is continually making that occasion for some reason, probably a good one this time.

A privy used to grace the backyard; perhaps there was a small stable for a horse and buggy, which necessitated a driveway along the north side of the house. And there was (still is) a north side which the sun never sees because the streets are all laid out square with the points of the compass—they had a reason for this but I could never find out what it was except that it was a surveyor's convenience. This scheme (or lack of one) gave every house a hot front or a cold front. The south belonged to one front alone. The morning sun shone in the east windows—the afternoon sun in those to the west. No one questioned the inevitability of all this, and only rarely is it ever questioned now. The net result of all the placing and fixing (and fussing, too, because they were awfully fussy about this) were the long rows of houses, all facing the street to the north or south or east or west, and set back to give thirty percent of the ground to that street for general effect. This dedication to the street is a marked characteristic of all American towns.

The "backyard" thus left was divided from the neighbor by a fence or hedge, or none. Modern plumbing came to take the privy into the house. The motor car came to add the so-called garage to every house in place of such stables as there were, and privacy was something none understood though some few did desire it. It would take too long to say how all this came to be. Of what use to say it now?

Into these inorganic circumstances so curiously, unthinkingly compounded to confound simple living comes this organic $5,500 house with the automobile as much a feature of life as the bathroom and the kitchen. When error has confused an issue hopelessly it is time to begin again. What can this house do to have a better beginning? Go to the country or go out in regional fields where ground is not yet exploited by the realtor. That is all. And it must go because to this house a garden is no backyard affair—an acre is necessary. The street cannot be desirable so far as this ground consideration is concerned except as a way to get to the place as unobtrusively as possible.

What, then, is desirable to this new house?

Well . . . *first*, free association with considerably more ground than the old house was allowed to have.

Second, sunlight and vista, a spaciousness conforming to the newly developed sense of space demanded by modern facilities. No north front because the house will not be set square with the compass.

Third, privacy, actual, not imaginary or merely makeshift.

Fourth, in the arrangement of rooms a free pattern for the occupation of the family that is to live in the house. As the families vary, so must the house. The rooms should be as much as possible on a single level for several reasons, all good.

It would be ideal to have all these requirements meet in some integral harmony of proportion to the human figure; to have all details so designed as to make the human relationship to building not only convenient but charming. For this building which we are considering is intended not to make shift with life but to give life more easy conditions that will cherish and protect the individual—not so much in fostering his idiosyncrasies and sentimentalities as in protecting his vital necessities and fine sentiment. Above all, we must see this new house as the cradle of continuously arising generations. So, while appeal to reason is intrinsic, it is insufficient. There must also be beauty—beauty of which man himself is capable, the utmost beauty of which he is capable without getting himself into trouble with the installment system and the tax collector. We are hinting at a new simplicity of appearances where this new home is concerned. It can only appear in a drawing or model.

We must achieve that new simplicity too, as well as establish a finer logic of use and want, but the new house won't pay two-fifths for it. It will pay nothing at all. Now, here we are with the acre essential to an individual human life on earth. The acre is level, with a few trees in one corner or more, but an acre fit for a garden. The house sees that garden to begin with, arranging itself about and within it so as to enjoy the sun and view and yet keep privacy.

The living room is where the familiar life is lived, so it must take first place. It is a room common to all, with a big fireplace in it.

Because of modern industrial developments the kitchen no longer has a curse upon it; it may become a part of the living room by being related to another part of that same room set apart for dining. An extra space, which may be used also for studying or reading, might become convenient between meals. In such a house the association between dining and the preparation of meals is immediate and convenient. It is private enough, too.

Next in importance to this decentralized central unit is the toilet unit, the bathroom. Only it should now be a triplicate bathroom, one section for man, one for wife, one for offspring. The fixtures are placed to have the economy of close connection but the three bath compartments themselves are large enough for dressing rooms, closets for linen, etc., even wardrobes, with perhaps a couch in each. The bedrooms adjoining this unit are small but airy. Both bedrooms and the triplicate bathroom would be alongside the garden, easy of access from the living room.

The indispensable car? It is still designed like a buggy. And it is treated like one when it is not in use. The car no longer needs such consideration. If it is weatherproof enough to run out in all weather it ought to be weatherproof enough to stand still under a canopy with a wind screen on two sides. Inasmuch as this car is a feature of the comings and goings of the family, some space at the entrance is the proper space for it. Thus the open car-port comes to take the part of the dangerous closed "garage."

While the car is yet far from being well designed, it has more in common with our sanitary appliances and modern kitchens than the older cars could have with the older houses. The proportions and lines of this organic house are those the industrialists are trying so hard to get into their products, succeeding only superficially in doing so. But they are doing so sufficiently to make congruous the house, car, kitchen and bathroom. Furniture too is coming to reflect this new sense of unity and congruity. They are calling it modernistic, or streamlined, or just modern.

Except for the more advanced triplicate bathroom unit, not yet executed, I have been describing here a particular house, the house of Herbert Jacobs built at Madison, Wisconsin. It was let by contract for $5500 to Harold Grove.

What I want to say in words the house itself alone can say. But perhaps enough has been said to suggest the ideals and processes of thought at work that are giving us an indigenous and, probably, a greater architecture in every respect than has existed before.

I could go on with many instances in the widely varying fields of our American activity and show how a new development in building design is bringing order out of chaos. I could show pretty clearly how a new technique of building is growing up into the American scene—a new technique as well as an integrity of design that does bring to the house builder and home owner the benefits of industrialism and the efficiencies of the factory. Instead of the criss-cross of the open field we are developing building schemes that utilize the economies of standardization without its curse, using the simple unit system applied to building, meaning buildings put together upon a horizontal and vertical unit system much as a rug is woven on its warp. The implications are as aesthetic as they are scientific and economic. I hope enough has been said to indicate that organic architecture has already gone far enough, that standardization is no real obstacle to freedom of individuality. Standardization is not a real obstacle in spite of the international style, the "permanent wave," the realtor, and "housing."

A future for architecture depends upon a new sense of reality, a different success ideal, a deeper social consciousness, a finer integrity of the individual—that there may be promoted the integration of a whole people with their own soil or ground. This will in turn bring about freedom from a false economy. It will bring about the end of labor, money, ground and buildings as speculative commodities. It will bring about the rise of cultured sentiment to take the place of educated sentimentality. It will abolish commercial standards that are only profit-taking. It will close institutes, museums and universities until new ones may be created to bring culture to youth by way of action in an atmosphere of truth and beauty. It will train youth to want and utilize its own ground. There is also necessary a new type of architect and a new structure of government that governs only where individuality may not exist. Such a government will function as a business of the whole people in matters common to the whole people, and only so, instead of as a policeman and a politician. A further essential is a popular realization of organic structure as the basis of all culture in the development of the whole life of a whole people. Such a future as this must grow slowly. Finally the abandonment of ultra-urban life is necessary. A new type of city must be realized. There will be organic structure in government, organic structure in society, organic structure in the economics of both.

THE MAN WHO. . . .

Frank Lloyd Wright wrote a series of twelve short stories, beginning in 1931 with the title "The Man Who. . . ." These quizzical and whimsical writings are unexpected of Wright. Along with their irony and sometimes strangely twisted humor, however, they each carry a characteristic message. The importance or pertinence of the messages vary as the stories themselves do. Some were published in Madison, Wisconsin, newspapers and in Coronet *magazine. But most of them are published here for the first time.*

THE MAN WHO ST. PETER LIKED

Those favored of God are those who plant and nurture the trees he made.

No Man who plants a tree can be wholly bad.

Whoever he is, he has been host to the future in good faith. He is for Mankind. So, I think he will go to his Heaven wherever that is.

This man who plants a tree is the man who makes all the difference to tomorrow between the shiftless, hopeless town or home and the shaded, fruitful village and the happy home.

Trees planted or trees saved are the best proofs we have that man is not vile . . . nor wholly selfish.

Thirty years ago, my uncle planted a group of firs at Taliesin. They are now fifty feet tall—a mass of deep green, summer and winter. I look at them and take my hat off to him. They prove him to have been a man of quality . . . so much better than any headstone or any tale of his deeds.

As for "Heaven" I am sure Saint Peter at the Gate asks "Did the man plant a tree?" "Yes, your reverence." "Did the tree live?" "Yes, your holy eminence." A pause . . . "Ah" says the venerable Saint. "I had almost forgotten." And he would add another question—"Did he plant the tree in a good place?" "Yes, your worship." "Then open the gate wide! Let the man come in and go where he pleases."

Were the answer "No" to the first question—"Did the man plant a tree?"—St. Peter would stand the man aside . . . outside . . . under suspicion . . . something must be wrong with him.

Were the answer "No" to the second question—"Did the tree live?"—St. Peter would say: "Too bad—good impulses but improvident . . . let the man sit down just inside the Gate . . . we will consider him. He probably neglected to water the tree."

Were the answer "No" to the last question—"Did the man plant the tree in the right place?"—St. Peter would sadly shake his wise old head and say "Never mind! Few do . . . it is enough that you now know you planted the tree in the wrong place." And the saintly gatekeeper would smile additional welcome.

Whoever plants a tree takes out insurance against Hell.

Nature will take care of him.

He is her own Son.

[Published in *Coronet,* December 1937]

THE MAN WHO WON

He was young and he was speaking. "The rich are rich because the poor are poor! As anyone may see therefore the poor are poor because the rich are rich?" And the candidate for governor quoted the Bible. The overflow meeting of country-folk looked at one another and nodded approval.

"Our glorious Commonwealth is controlled by wealth—wealth owns the newspapers—wealth runs the railroads—wealth fixes prices—wealth dominates education. Wealth to the wealthy. Aye to them that hath shall be given—but to him who hath not shall be taken away even that which he hath"—he thundered—and pounded the table. The countryfolk, elated, looked at one another. At last, their champion was here, their time—belated—was coming.

"The purse! The purse is the heart of the nation," he shouted. "Open the purse and you have good times or shut the purse and you have hard times. If money has hard times you have good times. If you have good times money has hard times. And whose money is it in that purse, my farmer friends? Whose money I ask you?" His angry cold-blue eyes reamed the crowd searching for someone brave enough to answer.

"Our money"—yelled some reckless renegade from the back of the hall—"Ours; all the money we haven't got."

"Right you are, my man," said the election-eer—"All the money you haven't got is in that purse."

"Let us open the Nation's purse and look into it," he said. "What do we see there? We see the labor of starving children—the labor of toiling masses—all the pay for all the work you should have done—all the sweat and privation that all of you (you the long-suffering underpaid millions) have made for all those who underpaid you; all the money you made for all those who now open and shut the purse—your government—at will. "Interest collected by sellers-of-money is in there; and then what do the sellers do? Make you pay for the use of your own money and so make you all slaves to yourselves. Blood money for the use of your own money is in there to enslave you to make more money for money. Money pretends to let you use your money cheap—your own money, mind you—so you can all make more money for money . . . all the money for them!" he shouted—quoted the Bible again and pounded the table.

"My friends," he roared, "take it from me (and my kind) all government is no more than an opening or shutting of the purse! Our pure form of God-given government can only come to fruition by opening the purse or shutting it. All the evils from which you suffer are because 'they' have too much money and you have too little money! What then is the remedy?" He ran his hands through his hair, gripped them as he glared at his awed, entranced listeners. . . . "I ask you, friends, what is the remedy? What is the sovereign remedy? Make 'em pay I say, make them PAY. Yes, tax 'em—tax 'em down to your own level," he roared. "Tax 'em all down, tax 'em all out and tax 'em all in again so you can tax 'em all out again some more. . . ."

Murmurs of approval—commotion in the crowd. Here was salvation—at last A MAN.

Warming up, but a little hoarse by now, the candidate pulled off his coat exposing the silk back on his vest—threw the coat aside, pulled off his satin tie and white collar—threw it away—rumpled his hair some more and leaned far over toward his spellbound audience:

"And you . . . are going to let them get away with it?" he hissed—between clenched teeth—"You, who are the body of this great Republic."

"Well . . . what about the brains?" came from a listener down on one side of the crowd—but produced no effect on the electioneer.

He again thundered, "You who are the body of this great republic."

"Well . . . how about the imagination," now came from a quiet voice at the rear.

Ignoring this, too, the electioneer shouted both down with again—"You who are the body of this great Republic, you have been given the sovereign remedy—a little white slip of paper—a slip of paper but—yet—a sacred thing—the great American ballot! The ballot!" he shouted. "The ballot! The ballot makes your citizen's right equal to any king's might! Use the little ballot, my farmer friends—use the sacred ballot! Use that little slip of paper right, and only over my dead body (and maybe yours) shall any wealth whatsoever prevail! Elect me and I promise you, one and all of you, right here, that to be open—and—(with hissing intensity through clenched teeth) the purse shall be s-s-s-shut, when it ought to be s-s-s-shut."

Wild applause.

Unqualified approval—

And they elected him.

But—as usual—nothing else happened.

[*Wisconsin State Journal,* May 15, 1936]

THE MAN WHO TOOK REFUGE

He had lines down each side his mouth. The line on the right side was deep enough to be called a "rut." When he smiled he looked alright. When he didn't smile he looked as though he ought to right away.

His mercurial Nature and the mobility of his features wrought this havoc with his face, a great disadvantage so he came to feel: anyone could see whether he was lying or telling the truth.

The next day after he had been shaving: "I'll fix it," he said suddenly and threw his razor out of the bathroom window.

"Let Nature take her course," said he. "Who am I that I should tamper with her work, alter her designs, frustrate any good intentions she may have had in my behalf? If the author of my being intended to expose me to every unkind wind that blows and to the mercy of every curious eye that winks he would have made me that way without meddling. Wouldn't he? Are whiskers, then, less ornamental than a head of hair? Whiskers protect the chest and throat. And while they may interfere with . . . oh well!" said he, "I can forego such nourishment."

"In any case I shall be protected."

"I can bluff them all."

"My secret thoughts can be no longer read."

"I have a fine nose and a better forehead. My eyes are fine: they will appear to good advantage when my cursed mouth is out of sight."

"I'll go in behind in ambush for others. I'll betray myself no more. No. With a beard, if I want to, I can betray my enemies."

He went his way—determined to *"let Nature take her course."*

His name (by no accident) being Samson, his trial of strength began.

The boys at the office kept pace with Sam's "ambush" as it grew day by day, Sam's nickname was now "Whiskers." But "Whiskers" bore up well under persecution because Samson had a cause.

Sam's whiskers came out red. His Grandfather's aunt and his great Grandmother's cousin had had red hair as he now knew for the first time. Like hereditary secrets dark or bright—this secret, too, had lain in ambush waiting for this fateful call to the impartial light of day.

"No matter," Sam muttered. "A red beard has character and it is fate."

"A red beard is more beautiful than a black beard and . . at any rate it's my own beard. *'Let Nature take her course.'"*

In due course the ambush was complete. No more was Sam betrayed. Betrayer he could be. "They" guessed—not. "They" saw his eyes and they were fine. "They" saw his nose was fine and they saw his forehead and they saw that it was the best of all. And no mouth said these features nay.

"She" saw that all these were fine and, womanly, wondered. She met him in the street car. She came and sat beside him—no choice but very close, warmed to him and he warmed to her. As they got off together he noticed a little curl on the nape of her neck and, well . . . soon she married him. But every single time she kissed him she would wonder?

Delila—"Lil" for short, was (not by accident) her name.

Lil, feminine and curious, kept on wondering what his mouth was really like—kept wondering if his chin was really firm. The third day . . . "Sam," she said, "You are so handsome, dear, but . . . I so hate 'whiskers' . . . Sweetheart . . ." she kissed him on the nose . . . "Shave?"—"Please!" she said: little curl nestling in front of one ear.

He was prone. Even so he sagged a little, but his emotions were by Nature's providence and his own Art, by now, concealed. So though she had cut him deep fond eyes, though shrewd, saw no inflicted misery in this downcast look of his. Had he been standing . . . she had all but cut him down.

He had no answer ready. Indeed . . . what answer was there?

"But . . . dearest," he began—and again—what was there to be said?

She blushed, whispered something to him . . . then: "Please! Now! Sam dear."

Lil pressed, feeling no strength of will in her Sam at all.

(Nemesis now), she said, "I got these for you myself. Yesterday," and she, (yes, Nemesis is always she)—stood there above him with "all" in hand. "There's hot water in the bowl dear—I have just put it there, myself."

And dumbly our Samson got up on his feet: "All is ever in vain"—he felt.

"All right, then," he said meekly—and meekly her Sam went into the bathroom and tri-weekly her Sam shaved.

The provident whiskers followed the razor he had before thrown out of the bathroom window!

"Nature" had taken her course . . . .

[Published as "The Man Who Grew Whiskers," *The New Freeman,* March 25, 1931]

THE MAN WHO PAID CASH

A scenario wherein a rich man meets an artist and, for a while, each has his say.

One day, because of the Artist's wife and the wife of the Rich Man, these two men met at an elaborate function. It is usually so. The wife of the professional man frequently has social privileges that take her where the wives of the rich like to go.

Power and culture thus seem to seek each other by way of "society"—furtively. The men were talking:

Said the Rich Man: Michelangelo was the greatest artist who ever lived.

Said the Artist: No, I think not. No "greatest" artist ever lived. (The Rich Man did not know what he meant.)

Said the Rich Man: I've just bought a Titian—a great picture! I'm having neon tubing mounted on it to bring it out. Great picture. Best thing Titian ever did!

Said the Artist: Impossible. No great artist ever did a "best thing." (The Rich Man did not know what he meant.)

The Rich Man persisted: I am fond of great pictures. Come see my collection sometime.

The Artist said: Thanks, but I would rather not.

The Rich Man: Well, and why not?

The Artist: Because I don't believe pictures by great masters should be privately owned—it is carrying ownership too far.

The Rich Man: "Too far?" What do you mean?

The Artist: Beyond human reason and cultural limits.

The Rich Man: Do you mean the man who painted the picture would feel that way about it?

The Artist: Yes, he would feel that way about it. The picture is still his. Any "masterpiece" is the artist's gift to posterity so how can it be yours?

The Rich Man laughed: Oh! Then let's see "posterity" come and get it.

The Artist (a little defiant): No need, let me see you keep it. Even now you would not dare destroy it, though you have paid for it.

The Rich Man: Well, I'll be damned! If the picture doesn't belong to me, who does own it?

The Artist (rudely): The rightful owners are those to whom the artist himself was a gift—those who appreciate his picture most—and that means several thousands, at least, who "own" it in a truer sense than you can ever own it. Your ownership only robs the rightful owners.

The Rich Man (quietly amused): But my friends can always see the picture.

The Artist: Your friends? A fair limitation that is!

The Rich Man: Yes, I call it fair enough. I paid for it. (Here the friendly wives came in and the matter seemed to drop. The Rich Man sat and thought.)

The good-natured Rich Man (to his wife): Hetty, our friend here thinks—and says—I'm a robber.

Hetty (his good-natured wife, sweetly): You are, aren't you, in the sense that all rich men rob the poor?

253

The Rich Man: No, no—our friend here means Titian would have the right to look down on me as a robber, because I paid $60,000 to "own" his picture and keep it where I want to keep it.

The Artist's tactful wife (to the Rich Man—with a sly glance at her husband): I should think that Titian might forgive you. So many great artists are waiting to be robbed.

The Artist (deliberately): Ah, but were Titian living and the $60,000 paid to Titian then I should have a weaker case. But our friend here paid $60,000 to no artist nor to art itself. "Owning" simply means paying money enough to let him keep it where he pleases, let whom he will see it, hoping he is "through." Meantime he is illuminated by the distinction of an art lover and a patron of the arts, gratis . . . probably at a profit . . . and—

The Artist's tactful wife (alarmed): Henry!!!—

[Published in *Coronet,* January 1939]

THE MAN WHO DRESSED

On the other side of the tall mirror his pretty blonde wife was dressing in modern colorful clothes. From his side: as he pulled on his black trousers:—"That was how the English dealt with the crotch," said Jerry, "a pair of black bags for a couple of perfectly good Irish legs." "Reckless of a man's anatomy they were, too," he muttered as he buttoned his suspenders . . . "As completely reckless as they were reckless of their poets," he added for good measure.

"Too tight in all the wrong places!"

And of course they were.

"Albion must have got the idea of these shoes, now, from a horse's hoofs.

"This hard-boiled collar, now. I could be hanged by the neck with the thing until dead, so I could," he said, as he fastened the starched band securely to the metal buttons in his hard-boiled white shirt.

"And this . . . tie—no use at all in the world. Idle decoration and in the wrong place again for all I can see," said he, surveying the tying of his black tie. He had seen a hanging once and again saw the gruesome figure with a rope around its neck. "Why not a red tie or green tie or a yellow one,"

said he grimly—"it would make hanging more picturesque."

Coming to his vest he buttoned the 44th button he had already buttoned in getting buttoned up. "Button to button," he sneered.

"There you are—you," said he, holding the black coat off in his hand—"There you are with a dozen more buttons. Where would it all be but for buttoning the buttons," he said to his side of the tall mirror.

Surveying himself with disgust: "A hearse or an advertisement for a paper-hanger, that's what I am. Too tight."

"Hush Jerry . . . hush" came over from his wife on her side of the mirror. Powdering her nose, "You aren't 'tight' yourself are you?"

"Well," he replied, "I am and all over me, too. Look at me!"

"And you, Nanette, would hush your lawful lord and master, would you?" Shaking a finger in her direction: "You women got out of bondage. You go out into the street now with less on you and that easier to wear than your 'undies' were ten years back. And what you wear, little dear, isn't pasted on you either except in the right places. You've seen to that and so you've got some chance to be yourself . . . And to be beautiful," he added.

Grumbling away as one cheated . . . "But let your husbands make the least little move toward their freedom—not to mention 'the beautiful' and would you 'blush' for them? You'd be 'down' in shame on any change in these grave clothes anywhere above or below the belt. Canny sect! Tis' we males must be 'respectable' now! Were I, your lawful lord and master—Mrs. MacGonigle, to wear one thing more sensible than this that might be patterned after the tin-can clothes our ancestors fought each other in with can-openers, well . . . It would embarrass you. You would be blushing for shame. You jailer you!"

He burst out . . . "Who got the human male to the rear now in this point of plumage?

"Every other decent male-animal wears the badge of his station, I'd have you know. The stag—his antlers; the boar—his tusks; the stallion—his arching neck—gorgeous coat. Look at his slowing mane and tail!

"As anyone can see the dress of any decent male-fowl is as gorgeous as the dress of his mate is meek and sleek and . . . quiet.

"See the peacock!" said he.

Jerry sat for a moment, himself quiet. Then . . . "How did it all happen?"—he roared.

Startled to attention, his Nanette said, "Why Jerry . . . it didn't 'happen.' It was simply 'evolution.' Once upon a time—your sword was your antlers or (a mischievous glance at the glass) it was more likely your tusks. And when your baleful sex laid the horrid sword aside you just had to behave. The human male always was over-rated, anyway," she said—"and oversexed, too," she added. "The 'peacocking' around of the male was always absurd. While fighting was to be done at any moment women let him go on with it, but there's no need now," said she—airily. "Women have no longer much cause to be afraid. So the male can take his place in the domestic arrangements . . . why make such a fuss about it, Jerry? Hand me my carmine-cloak with the ermine collar and 'hurry'—dear! . . . do come along; we are already late because of your ridiculous soliloquy."

Yes, his proper place reiterated, his Nanette scornfully swept him by in full evening regalia, blonde hair piled high on her head, waving a cigarette—scarlet lips and rouged cheeks.

Ruefully, the dubious Jerry picked up one more attribute of the hearse—his dun and dreary shaped-in overcoat—glanced with hate at his shaped-out black derby hat—it might have been cast-iron by the look of it—Jerry clapped his stovepipe hat (supreme triumph of the English in the toggery of Civilization), desperately over one ear. And—"came along."

Her husband was "dressed."
[Unpublished story, 1931]

THE MAN WHO SWORE

All his life long this kindly old man had been hearing the popular song "Conservative" close to his ears until the so-called "Conservative" would seem to be salt of earth, savior of all. God-man of the Democratic social order.

Who sang this popular song? . . . .

Well, yes, of course—but the old man had seen through "business."

Long ago, in his constructive work in this world he had discovered the busy man who calls himself "practical" to be merely some slave of some expedient. He had found that whenever this business-slave speaks of the Practical, he only means the Expedient. An old man, he had learned, finally, that such men cannot be trusted with an idea nor with any ideal. They murder either or both on behalf of safety. Their own safety, at that, somewhere around or on down the line. "Far too 'practical' to be trusted," he began. And a dreary monologue went on as several young men sat and listened to him.

"Boys," said he. "Boys—these time-serving slaves you call conservative do not even know what conservation means. They think it means holding tight to title, or sitting heavily on the lid of some issue in opposition to anything 'new.' On general principles, there they sit and ride.

"They call themselves conservative but letting good enough alone is the highest ideal of conservation these apostles of fear ever achieve because as a class they lack imagination—that's all." Said he: "Very well then, let's say their natural fear is the ballast in the hold of the ship, or they are the sand-bags in the balloon, or this particular "conservative" is the wooden plug in the bung-hole of the barrel, or the tribe are the paint on the post. In sociology let us say for the sake of argument—that they are themselves the same as the law of gravitation is in physics because nothing moves if they can help it unless by main strength it can overcome them and get away with it. They are watch-dogs of property, judges of the law, self-appointed policemen of the universe. Most of them are cowards, healthy, weighing about 185 pounds apiece, but all carrying more life insurance for a lifetime than they can well afford."

He paused a moment for bitter reflection:

"And I will venture to say that were you to inform these well insured gentlemen that no less than a true 'radical' could ever be genuinely conservative they would have the law on you—or have the

Kiwanis and the Rotarians out. Or maybe they would set the 100% Americans on you."

You see, to this exasperated man, the word Radical was a beautiful word. It meant roots, had roots, was roots. And yet the so-called conservative sees it as "red." The conservative always sees "red" whenever the sound of the word "radical" falls upon his ears . . . and looks him to his securities.

"No," said the grey-head warming up, "the so-called conservative is no conservative at all. He is not even preservative! In ninety-nine cases out of one hundred he's merely in the way of any conservation anywhere. Or preservation either for that matter. He is provocative of disaster, nothing more."

The monologue went on:

"The 'conservative' is seldom worth his ride. And this middle-of-the-road egotist will only ride, anywhere.

"It is my belief, boys, that any cause your so-called conservative espouses will leave off from sheer fatigue and stay right there where he is. Although he talks progress, 'staying right there where he is' is what he means by it. That is good enough and far enough for him.

"The Majority of course is conservative. But though it cannot realize it, it is itself only a stupid conspiracy against progress. Growth alone is truly conservative and Progress is forever in the keeping—for its very life, mind you, of the truly radical Minority—just as the thought the self-appointed conservators are sitting on . . . (or riding upon) today was, once upon a time.

"No, Conservation is no function of the crowd nor of the 'Conservative,' so called. I tell you: Conservation is not so easy."

"Why not?" said one of his young listeners.

"Well, because" (said the man more quietly now) "because in the first place, true conservation means keeping the 'life' in whatever is subject to the conservator's services. And, as the radical alone knows, life can't live without growing! That is why most causes that have any life at all in them grow away out of the hands of the would-be conservative—or else die there of suffocation; strangulation.

"Boys, to be honestly conservative you must first know in what the very life of the matter to be conserved consists. How can you know that unless down to the roots?"

Said another boy, "Then what is truly conservative?"

The old man said, "I know now that real conservation is a form of understanding—the understanding that is a kind of love: a sort of sympathy always necessary to keep life in line of growth. Only the true radical will fight for that and it's always necessary to fight and defeat the so-called 'conservative' in order to preserve any growth anywhere whatsoever. Keep away from that conservative my young man or he will destroy you!" (He said this fiercely.)

He raised his voice:

"This self-appointed 'Conservative'? See the expedient coward clinging to dead forms after the life has fled from them, imagining himself the preserver—on honorable terms—of what he calls Tradition! See him sitting, snugly gilt, in favored places. This mundane high-priest of 'things' safely sits with the thing he professes to love—by the throat. About as truly conservative as any other jealous 'husband,' I should say.

"Hard for the radical to reach him—as things are."

He seemed to feel better now and his voice dropped to quiet again:

"Time to go to the genuine Radical. Honor him as the true Conservative if you are ever going to put honest meaning into the word.

"Born of narrow self-interest, lid-sitting, stand-patting, professing 'conservatism' will take the life of anything. Eventually it will take the life of the Democracy itself."

And as he walked away down University Avenue swinging his walking stick recklessly, he contemptuously muttered a phrase—not heard.
[Unpublished story, 1931]

THE MAN WHO WOULD NOT GROW UP
A poetry-crushing department of Humanity, the young man thought as he looked at the oncoming faces—and then looked at the backs of the necks of the men who passed on by him. Bare faces coming and bare necks going—bare protruding ears—flesh

bare and unqualified as any in a butcher shop. James was sensitive. They said he was artistic.

Just then: "Get your hair cut!" came across to the lad from a group of boys across the street.

"Get your h-a-a-air cu-u-u-ut"—holding both hands to "cup" the insolence.

Not for the first time was there this disorder on University Avenue. One of those erect, forward-swinging lads, a rather wide hat-brim necessary because of longish hair, hair long enough to curl a little behind the ears and cover the back of his head rather down below the level of his collar. Jimmy seemed not to notice the cry.

Similar boys, when grown up, are suspected by Pie Club "get-together-men." The Pie-Club suspects that maybe such a man suspects himself of having ideas! Must be some poet—eh? The guy must be a Genius. Laughter.

Mobocracy can stand for many self-made implications but will not stand for that offensive one. Smile please as this youthful suspect now passed them by since you may not weep. It did not occur to anyone that Jimmy wore his hair the way he liked it "on principle," disliking unrelieved faces with no becoming hair—they were so "meaty." Never yet had Jimmy submitted to the barber's razor scraping the scruff of his neck—feeling it to be a barbarous indignity: desecration of nature not much better than the savage making the "tuft" on his smooth-shaven crown by scraping the hair off elsewhere. The razor, if you like, on his face, may be not even that but why go around on to the back of the neck to make that bare too. NO NEVER!

Wherever Jimmy and his kind go they not only bear ridicule but they have to fight ambitious barberhood. Jimmy's clothes, too—in the provinces (the provinces are everywhere)—mark him out from the crowd. He wore a blowzy coat because he despised the shaped-in ones with wide padded shoulders that all the young men thought "swell," tight sleeves set into the high shoulders to vulgarize and dummify any natural movement.

More trouble for him: clothes.

He had had to find a tailor who could properly make a loose garment: one of the few things only the English—originally they invented them—in

their England do well. In short, as already seen, the boy deserved what he got for simply trying to be himself and where every man was himself—and the devil for the hindmost, but this, in business way or in business only. Although he had thus been subjected to ridicule on account of this (an uncommon kind of sense) his sensibilities never quite got used to popular ribaldry. Strange to say! Every time, it broke on him like a bad egg. He despised himself for a coward. Nevertheless it always took some effort to change his thought and get back on good terms with himself.

We are all—even the most forthright—are we not—more or less uncomfortable when our own "kind" turns upon us? Is a young man like Jimmy really out of place in our country? Is one's individuality no longer a matter of one's own person perhaps as things are here? Anyway—is anyone's "person" worth the pains it takes to live up to one's sense of individuality in a mobocracy? Why not better to wear popular disguises in the popular way and get away from popular discrimination, or the lack of it, by conforming to them all, and by so doing, by disguise, save oneself for oneself?

These thoughts, in his own way, came now to our young "suspect" quite seriously. Earlier, even to think so would have seemed "selling himself out to senseless fashion." Now, however, he had got so far as to mention these subcutaneous doubts to his mother. This thought of giving up? What did it mean?

She, the fashionably faultless in her dress had secretly winced many a time at covert smiles and overt offenses in the direction of her unfashionable son. But he was her boy and mothers stood by their boys.

After confession the youthful mother smiled . . . a queer little smile—half sad, half relief—a little shamed. . . . "Well Jimmy," she said, "perhaps after all it isn't worth what it costs you. The street is a vulgar place. The street will never allow you any differences unless it can make sport of them. You see your 'difference' reflects upon them—their own ideas of style. Illiberality and intolerance are really common privilege in our great Republic, Jimmy dear. And you have made yourself a target for that

257

great privilege. And—really—why should they be considerate of your tastes when you are not considerate of theirs?"

"But, confound them, I let them alone," said Jimmy. "Why won't they take that view of me—just let me alone?"

"I know," she replied, "but they won't and who are you, my dear, that you should put yourself in a position to continually endure indignities from them?"

He was unprepared for this worst, this "who are you."

"All right mother," he said gently. "If you, too, feel that way about it."

Next day—Collegiate Barbershop.

As the previous incumbent was flipped up and out of the barber chair cut to the quick—shaved to the red—and—ah yes—raw to the eye . . . came his turn.

"Hair trimmed, I suppose."

This casual assumption from the barber struck on the boy like another "get your hair cut."

"Go as far as you like," he snapped.

His gentlemanly barbership tipped the lad back, tucked the white overall into his neck band—lathered his face to shave him first. This gave the new recruit time for reflection. Head on block, he looked sidewise at the grist, the grinding and those already ground. All looked to him infallibly better before the "get your hair cut" than they did afterward.

As the razor went over his face: "At last, this scraping every few days to the raw around behind the ears?—Down under the collar too?—Ugh!"

He thought of his mother's words—"Who are you—my dear—that you should put yourself where you must suffer indignities at their hands!" But the thought worked the other way now—in this position—this was the indignity indeed! That I should disgrace my sense of myself to please them? Rebellious. Even my mother, he thought.

Yes, who am I, maybe. But, who are they anyway? Rebellion.

Going to do something I despise to save myself a few jibes from them? Am I? Going back on myself to please them. Am I? Gibes must be effective!

No very pretty picture he made to himself there in the barber-chair. He had already seen the too much pains all the customers took with themselves to be nobody at all—or to avoid being anyone, somewhat. What continuous daily pains they took to look as they looked! Worse trouble and more of it than I ever took my way, thought James.

The barber tipped him up again with a jerk, tucked in to his neck another overhaul to begin on the hair of his head. Cold steel touched the back of his neck as the clipper thing wiggled into his back hair. At the unaccustomed touch the young man violently jerked the overall from his neck—jumped from the chair with a "NO" to the astonished barber—and, glancing at the clock on the wall, said—"have to run."

Grabbing collar and tie—he flipped the barber a coin and ran in the nick of time but with a "nick" in the back of his hair. Ran from the thought of continuously taking more trouble to surrender his sense of himself than he had ever taken to maintain it.

"Rome isn't worth the trouble Rome takes with itself—to make itself Rome. Let Rome howl," said James, "I'll be myself." [Unpublished story, 1931]

THE MAN IN ANGLICOR

As you will know for yourself, every lot owner's lot in Los Angeles is cast in the most extensive lot-lottery known to man. Every Anglican if not realtor is realtoristic, soon as fortune may be, to be Lottor or Lottee. To realtorate is the ambition of every Realtorite, Realterette or Realtorant. So all Anglicors are realtorificant. Other cities may be picturesque but Los Angeles is realtoresque. This artificial stimulant in the air got to the big Rotarian, Tony First—nativity, Middle West. And he instinctively hummed the "Toreador" from *Carmen* as he stood on the average block looking up, wistfully, at the usual prominent hill-top in the average Hollywoodian hill range.

Tony had money. So, needless to say, out there Tony was a marked man. Naturally a realtor soon happened beside him who said (any Spanish Toreador is comparatively backward with the bull) "Pretty—eh?" Said Tony, "It sure is."

"Like to go up?" ingratiated the inevitable. As Tony looked around he saw a long sleek car standing by the curb.

"All right, jump in!" said the friendly one. Tony, subconscious of the inevitable, jumped in.

And the chosen one was taken for a ride.

The big Rotarian came down from out the hills, a lot owner with a tip-top lot—a lottee now loudly singing the "bull-song." The Rotarian was about to become ideally prominent according to every true Anglicorian dream. Yes, our Tony was about to become the Hilltopian-Topper-of-the-Hills.

Although Tony First, he was born afterward, so he was going to take no chance on any chance realtor's recommendation beyond his newly acquired lot-lines. He had heard tales of the Money-Benefit-Mutual as practiced in Anglicor under the intoxication of perpetual sunshine.

So, at the time we meet the new lottee, Tony, he is looking for some architect to do the "Hill-topping." He fell in with this architect by accident. It is always the best way. The architect had come out to get well, or better off, and was registered at Tony's Hotel. The T-square man with the sophisticated hat looked good to the simple Tony. So with no extra recommendations either way—it is always the best way—Tony went to the point.

"See it up there," said Tony.

"If you mean your lot, I think I do," came from under the 'hat.'"

"Pretty from down here—Eh?" said the Rotarian.

"It is," said the T-square man.

They went up for it in the big car.

The steep bank of the narrow road torn out of the hillside might have caved in on them on the winding way up, but didn't. Or "in high," unwinding on the way down some wayward slip or loosening might have let Tony's big car down over the roadside into the clinging dwelling of some ambitious Anglican who—defeated in the race—got pushed over onto the slopes below, but it didn't. It is unfortunate (but it is true) that somebody always gets to the top first in Anglicor. And it is the especial reason why so many must cling desperately to the slopes and the hind-most must throng the big flats below.

Not for nothing is the average Anglicorian a Lottor or a Lottee. The Anglican's got no wings but altitude's his home. He gets that way with the name of his city—Los Angeles.

However that may be, the-about-to-be-permanent and his architectural accident got up to the lot by winding up and around and winding up and around some more and winding up around, finally winding up a little more again.

"No small tax, this, in gas and wear and tear on the machine—day by day," said the wise architect.

"No matter," said Tony. And this constant devotion; this real tax on the Anglican ambition is, at least, pathetically real out there in the Hollywood hills.

Finally his incipient "prominence" and a skeptical architect stood together on the top-lot. "Pretty, way off down there, Eh?" said Tony the prospect, referring to the prospect.

"Glorious view," admitted the architect.

"You can see this beauty-spot from pretty near everywhere down there—can't you?" said the proud owner.

The architect nodded.

By nature and habit the Realtoristocrats of Los Angeles—that is to say—the hill-toppers, all push up and out onto the very middle of every hill-top everywhere. They recklessly tear out the sides of the hills to get up to the houses, and throw the hill sides all over and down. So when they finally do get up to where the hill top was, not only is the hill top gone (not there any more because of the house) but the sides of the hill are gone too—because of the road.

Tony looked around him. "Now, Mr. Architect, right over here, right on the highest place on this hill is the very top. The middle of the house should come right in the middle of the top," he said, going to stand there himself.

"But, no . . . Mr. First," objected the architect. "On second thought I think the middle of your house should not come there in the middle of the hill where you stand there in the middle. To put it there in the middle would spoil your site."

"Spoil my site—hell!" (Tony, proud but huffy). "It's the S-I-G-H-T I'm after." And the big Rotarian roared his happy roar.

"Rather anxious to be one yourself, too, Mr. First, I suppose?" said the disingenuous T-square man gently with a disarming smile.

"Sure, I want to be the big picture," simply said the recently realtorified. "What do you suppose I bought this lot for, to dig a hole in it and bury myself?"

"No, evidently you bought this beautiful hill-top just to bury the hill top under you. And you are fooling yourself, Mr. First, just like all the others did, as you may see them around you here."

"What do you mean, fooling myself."

"I mean throwing real opportunity away—that's all: to show off!" (A bit reckless.)

Tony, getting hot: "Look around you, Man. Where do you see anyone with a chance like this 'throwing it away' like you say?"

"On every side of you to a man they have thrown away their opportunity because their beautiful hill-tops have gone under their houses. All they've got left is a more or less showy house. They might have had both hilltop and house together; might have been less realtoresque, but, picturesque."

"You may be a good architect and artistic"—the "istic" in artistic sounded sneerish as Tony said it—"and all that but, look here, I didn't get way up here on top of everything to get alongside anything at all. I'm practical."—That boast is the sure sign of the Rotarian no less than the realtorian.

Well—it was a clear case, so the draftsman of many sorrows made up his mind to take the line of least resistance.

This was the line of attack: "Mr. First! Your mind is finally made up to be just as prominent as anybody on any hill around here if not a damned sight more prominent. Am I right?"

Tony, the defiant, affirmed this.

"It's pretty hard to be prominent doing just the same thing all the other fellows are doing in just the same way they are doing it—isn't it? Why not 'get there' by being different from the others? Why not be a bigger and a better picture?"

The realtorfied looked his "accident" over, now interested, because after all where self-interest was concerned Tony was no fool. "A better picture, Eh?" he said. And he moved back toward the architect a little way, evidently interested in the "bigger and better picture."

"Just how do you mean?" he said.

"Why . . . put your new house just off and alongside the hill-top. You'll be living in the house as high up as the hill-top itself where you now stand. You'll add area to the top and see just as much as you could if you were on the top. House and hill-top will augment each other if you have the good sense to build off to one side of the hill-top."

"You talk like you know your stuff."

Tony was thinking.

"I get it!" he said. But a shade crossed his good-natured face and he inquired: "But, would they get it our way?"

"When we are through they might not only get in our way, they would see what they had missed too, their foolish way. . . ."

"All right, fine!" said Tony. "Go ahead!"

So, once upon a time, the man who bought a lot met with an accident . . . a serious architect in Anglicor.

[Unpublished story, 1931]

THE MAN WHO WAS SIMPLY GERTRUDE

Sincere Miss Stein sensibly solid, one hand square in square skirt pocket, eyes square upon the other holding many-many-square pages reiterating her brief for brevity as beauty, gave to me and to several hundred others her simple view of world literature: a view reduced by way of simples to simples. Simple as simple can be but not simples for simpletons nor so simple as to be simple at all unless you were that kind of simple yourself. As anybody can see simples of such simplicity are unsimple to the too simple and are too simple to the unsimple so that simplicity goes off outside the inside of the too simple whereas off goes the simple from inside the outside of the perfectly simple. Simples are only simple, then, to the truly simple outside and inside. But to be too simple either inside or outside is to defeat simplicity as simple—render it unsimple and so simples are of no use to the too simple nor of much use to the unsimple.

Anyone can see that.

And as I was saying—anyone can see, therefore, that the Stein simples are not Stein nor so simple but only simple to Stein—not so much simple to Stein as Stein is simple as they are simple as one word after another with the right word after that is simple—that is to say—as words are Stein-simple to Stein. The Stein thought, however, is not so simple as one Stein word next to another word by Stein is simple. Stein simples are therefore simple as Stein is simple but they are far too simple for the over-educated simpleton or simple to the simply too simple-minded. So, as I say, it is easy to see that consecutive as are the Stein simples and simple as the Stein words are next to one another to express the Stein simples, the Stein is unsimple except to the simples themselves as themselves truly simple.

And anyone can see that.

Nor is the reading of Stein simples from any manuscript truly simple Stein. Simples? One should know them well enough to say them simply to the simple. In fact if simples cannot be simply said to the simple or said simply to the unsimple but must be read by simple and unsimple alike then such simples are either not simple simples or the Stein is herself an unsimpled simple for all her simples.

What then are the Stein words? Something in type or something in the ear? Type in the ear is unnatural, sound in the eye is unnatural.

Phonetics must fascinate the Stein. I wonder if the man ever runs typed Stein simples backward for adventitious effects. The lines of one word next to another word could also be read upside down inside the outside or outside down upside the inside and suggest not only new phonetics but suggest new kinds of letters. As anyone can see, therefore, the possibilities once the barriers of more sense come down—are enormous.

Primarily a simple word was a sound, simple or unsimple to the ear. When it becomes type it is sight, and not sound. Any game of letters may be fascinating to play, but as to literature—who knows? Perhaps this emphasis on spontaneous words, word-playing in letters is needed and Miss Stein is our prophet. Instead of being merely prophetic as I think. So far as literature goes, the solid content of life, the Stein says, is gone. If that is simple truth, then let the simple artist in the simple man solace the man with the act of words, Stein or no Stein.

[Unpublished story, 1934]

THE MAN WHO WAS NO BAKER

"One does not need to bake a loaf of bread in order to judge of its excellence" is becoming a stock phrase in the critic's mouth.

Let's look this gift-horse, the critic, in the mouth and see what's in this phrase that seems to be all the teeth he has.

Bread may lie, of course, well within a critic's power of apprehension and so his judgement of bread be valid when a building or a symphony might utterly invalidate him. But, let's look at him, where his bread goes.

Some of him like bread white and fine, made only of the inner part of the kernel. Others like course bread made of the whole kernel. Others like bread mostly bran—the outer shell. The white-bread contingent can't see the case for brown bread at all. The brown-bread contingent sees the white bread clogging the intestines as an inert mass. Here you have "schools." Schools of preference and of some thought, mind you. And another school is forming that rejects bread entirely as inedible with meals; excellent bread is not excellent. Too much starch anyway say they. Here we have radical "conviction."

Now as to the way of baking the bread—some say white bread should be made like French bread—light and crusty. Some say it should be as near like "angel food" cake as possible. In the other school some say graham bread should be heavy or made with some molasses; they like Boston brown bread. Others say it should be mixed with other flour and prefer it made as light as possible. All disagree as to the matter of yeast. And there is salt-risen bread: bread with no yeast at all which seems to me most excellent. Finally, how about the bottom crust?

It is evident, then, that even in this bread business the critic may be pretty far afield in this matter of excellence and be no more to be trusted with the matter of excellence there than where he is concerned with the building or with the symphony. He can only say which bread he prefers and how he prefers it, say which school of thought he believes to be right by way of his familiarity with the taste of bread and his superficial outside view of it or other similar views he may have collected.

Nevertheless he becomes a champion of white bread, brown bread, black bread or no bread at all and straightway proceeds to tell you about it in a book with all doubts removed (and if he is good at it, including your own) automatically implying that bread excellence should be related to his broad view of bread because he has the proper view. Nor will he hesitate to tell you who the best bread baker is. Not being a good bread-maker himself nor concerned with the chemistry of its effects he has mentally sized up the whole matter and elected the bread that pleased him. He is eclectic, therefore, and elects the best bread by way of taste, taking up with some school of thinking concerning bread as food, or as not food, basing his selections on other preferences similarly made. What about this vicarious bread-book of his that is usually the consequence?

Now, say, an independent thinker enters with a deeper interest in bread.

This thinker will not be put off. What is the nature of bread? He goes into bread making—to find out . . . makes bread himself in order to experiment with the actions and reactions of different grains and methods of developing bread from the various grains as good food for good human beings. He learns the chemistry of the stomach, the secrets of the palate and really knows—eventually by inside experience—what good bread would be for a good human being.

And his labor is mostly in vain because the bread consumer says, "I may not know what good bread is but I know what I like."

And the critic says as much. He says, "I don't have to know bread to know excellent bread. I have a broad perspective of bread (meaning he has a breadth of view of bread surface). He says this breadth of view makes him a better judge of the excellence of bread than anyone else.

According to this conviction concerning himself and bread, he judges; and being a professor of sorts writes his book. By the way, what is he if not "crust"?

So the man who went inside to master the principles involved, this independent thinker who learned the nature of bread as good food for the good human being by learning the nature of the process, the nature of the human stomach and the nature of "taste"—idiosyncrasies aside—is impeached by this critic as "emotionally committed" to his own bread. The impeachment, however be it said, is because of depth, which was omitted from the critic's "breadth" of view.

Now such as this is most criticism as the critic proceeds to rouse popular recognition of the bread that by means of his view of bread surface he has superficially selected or elected as "best." He may have hit it. More likely he has missed it.

Various bread "opinions" begin to flourish as the various critics "judge." New schools are formed—blows are struck and nobody comes any nearer to the nature of good bread than before.

Meantime the independent partaker of the nature of bread by way of his very depth of experience has been set aside as "narrow" in his appreciation of bread because not only breadth but uncommon, or unfamiliar, depth of view is his possession. He does not elect or select by any idiosyncrasy of taste. By way of experience he has learned and by way of practical insight he knows.

The critic's head—then—is really the critic's bread? And Bread continues to be Bread.
[Unpublished story, 1935. Originally titled "These Critics"]

THE MAN WHO SUCCEEDED

He talked of salesmanship as the Pope might talk religion. At first he sold himself to his client in order to sell him the kind of architecture—outside or inside—the client wanted or said he wanted. To do this he had in stock—or up his sleeve—varieties to appeal to every taste: Medieval, Pseudo Classic, Tudor, Spanish, Baroque.

If this failed to land the prospect who may have seen and now wanted a house like an original one designed by some of his contemporaries, he said, "Oh! All right then. You like that house of Jones's? We will give you a house like that." And straightaway he sold copies of the work of his contemporary thus extending his stock in trade. In short, he took his own wherever he could find it like any eclectic and, like any eclectic, he could always find it when he needed it.

His idea of architecture was that it, too, was first of all a commodity. The first principle of Architecture was, "get the job."

Architecture? A commodity in stock, but if not in stock, "Well then, Madame, we will get you what you want just as you want it."

The client was really only a customer.

The man aimed at any sacrifice whatever to please any customer whomsoever. "The customer was always right."

To get the customer he employed a system by no means peculiar to himself—Publicity.

He mixed and he joined and he publicized and show-windowed.

That is to say he had a press agent and belonged to many clubs, especially to pie clubs, and to many leagues, lodges and country clubs.

His life was a predatory social affair. A golf course and liquor in a locker were among the minor implements of his trade. He took on a young partner to make the designs and draw the plans and took on another to "get out" the specifications and look after the building contractor. He called him an engineer.

The man himself was a good "performer" (in the show window) and could "hold" the self-interest of the business men by way of their own selfish interest: self-interest on self-interest. He was sufficiently familiar with finance to impress investment brokers and realtor bankers. And they knew, from him, that he would "stay in line."

Thus a school of money sharks swam in his shadow when he had grown big enough.

He swam in their shadow until he had.

He invented nothing. It would have been indiscreet.

He contributed no ideas. That would have been too great a hazard.

Ideas would have clogged his machinery and marked him "suspect."

He was timely. He was a machine.

Presently he exploited machinery and learned to call a house "a machine to live in."

He was wholly unfamiliar with machinery or with engineering or with materials except concerning such language as passes for expert advice or current professional testimony concerning them all. How was an honest business man or a decent real estate broker to know the ignorance beneath that? And if they had known it they would only have said "What of it? We get what we want."

The same premium was put upon him by them that is put upon the salesman in every other form of production in this because the prospect may be educated to want whatever the salesman has to sell for the prospector. And that was the kind of educating the prospect got.

This technique was "education."

This education was technique.

He filled—by various contacts—a superficial want he had himself created. Inner content being quite another matter quite beside the mark.

Later on he flattered himself that he was "modern." Because he was using modern methods he really thought himself modern. But he was only "à la mode."

He speeded up production and quantity.

But quality? That, too, was quite another matter. What would you?

Is he not now the famous time server of his day? The popular bootlicker of his time and generation?

He is.

He is "in line" and he knows how to stay there in order to knock architecture down to the lowest bidder like any commodity knocked down by any auctioneer to the highest bidder cheap!

He is no architect at all.

No, he is a functioneer.

But . . . he is a "success."

[Unpublished story, 1931]

THE MAN WHO WAS A PAINTER

The recent importation of more TIN CAN PROPHECY to the source of supply, this original home of the tin-can we call the United States, must have excited the tri-colored Swiss prophet as he endeavored to excite our citizenry and incite them to can themselves now, as logical conclusion of the canning already done.

So utterly urbanized was the canny prophet that he had probably never seen a cow nor ever been further afield than the fence. Apparently he had only heard of gardens while philosophizing, probably in some Paris cafe. All this pretentious Sunday-supplement "modernity" rattles empty: the rattle of phrases. The prophetic painter is pathetic in the role of architect though very noisy: noisily guessing more or less unhappily in the direction of a completely mechanized architecture which as a matter of course, like Ville Radieuse—radiance like that of bright tin—could only be for a completely mechanized people in order that they might live a completely mechanized life.

Of course, the present and the future are not two separate things, so the tin-can, undoubtedly a formidable commercial convenience in our lives, threatens our future. And if human life itself were now to be entirely canned life would become a still more desirable commercial commodity—at least so "the factors" themselves seem to be thinking.

But is thinking like that reason enough for the canning? The tri-colored Swiss comes over at the expense of the New Museum of New York City—Modern Art—itself an adventure inspired by volunteer propagandists for a "style" of architecture for the U.S.A., uniform with all countries. The museum brought the painter over to carry on the architectural propaganda begun in the travelling show the propagandists staged last year—also at New Museum expense. And it is well, now that the big town is dead or dying because of the modern advantages that once made it, to have this big-town provinciality out in the open, where some light may be let in upon the rattling. In any good light the rattling may be seen to be because the prophet is out of fix and the prophecy worth singularly little more than the rattle.

If there is anybody of age in this country with less sense where architecture is concerned than this provincial little museum corporation and its prophet "radieuse" he might be found among the tyros gathered about some student of Das Neue Sachlichkeit in some of our Eastern institutions of learning. I can see in all of us only nervousness mistaken for emotion—the usual haste to exploit modernity while exploitation lies so easy on the surface. No integrity either of thought or purpose can I find in the entire movement unless you count somewhat on the part of those who furnished money to carry the noise along—having been sold upon the idea that the can and the canning would be progress "à la mode" if the canning could be made to include all humanity. And call it a day.

The United States, still so provincial as to look "abroad" for culture, has been swindled before by way of provincial propagandists who have "been" abroad with similar sound-effects.

[Unpublished story, 1933]

937

WHAT THE CAUSE OF ARCHITECTURE NEEDS MOST

"**A**s I write—convalescent—it seems to me that what the cause of architecture needs most, to put it into plain homely English, is Love." By convalescent, Wright is referring to his recuperation from a bout with pneumonia, which left him considerably weakened, but not so weak as to be unable to spell out some of the ills of fellow architects and to suggest some solutions. [Published in Architectural Record, March 1937]

THE PRACTICE OF THE ARCHITECT IN THE OLD SENSE AS A cultured broker of cultural tastes must be making toward an inevitable out and the architect's more intimate and exacting practice of master builder, with his hands directly in the mud and money of which his buildings are made, be on the way in. Organic architecture demands this new master of building construction. I see evidence that architecture is gradually setting about making such.

Now I can only imagine what this guest-procession of young American architects, master builders, designers, brokers, streamliners, outliners and inliners will have to spread upon these liberal pages to edify their Continental kin, but I imagine the spread will much resemble what the Continental kin might be spreading upon similar pages in return.

I believe, however, marked evidence of progress toward clearer thinking and genuine organic handling will be seen.

This American "modern" is intensely ambitious. He knows no conscience. So zealous is he (for his "art"?) that he would not hesitate to kill his own grandmother with an axe rather than lower any prestige he has set up for himself at such sacrifice of love, honor, and friendship as he has made. There is no jealousy like professional jealousy. And some of these young "professionals" have gone prayerfully up into high mountains to discover the thing all seem to have more or less in common. Others to "discover" have made pilgrimages, to and fro. Some discoverers have taken it straight as gospel, by conversion. Others have taken their own wherever they could discover it ready-made. But all are discoverers prompted by intense ambition to succeed, and by very little continence where that success, so it seemed to them, was concerned. Some results—nevertheless—are honestly creditable—of that I am already sure.

Is all this climbing and pushing bad for architecture?

I think not, in the long run.

Meantime a branch to the left has been forced from the parent trunk of an organic architecture. You will know it when you see it. A branch to the right has also forced itself out. You will know that too when you see it. It would seem at the moment to be the misfortune of both branches that the trunk

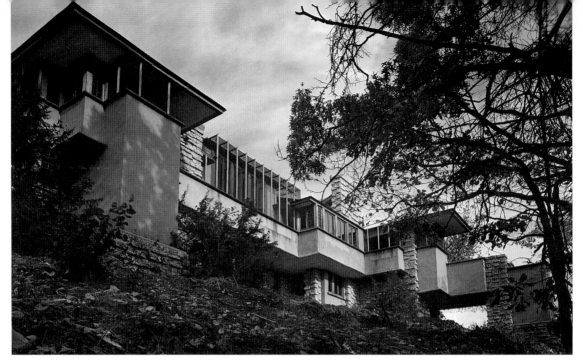

Taliesin. Spring Green, Wisconsin. 1925. Photograph by Hedrich-Blessing, courtesy the Chicago Historical Society.
FLLW Fdn FA#2501.0237

of the tree itself goes steadily on growing up. But, there is no essential disharmony, really, because all is Nature herself.

Were it not for inconsiderate illness, I should show herewith seven pieces of recent work from my own hand that, with the characteristic modesty which has endeared me to you all, I assume to be "the trunk of the tree going on growing up," this veteran being inveterate as you see. I sometimes wish veterans might be inviolable but I know it to be better for the Cause of Architecture that they should not be. So, this one is reconciled to violation as he is still ready to violate, which is a sign of health and strength at least?

As I write—convalescent—it seems to me that what the Cause of Architecture needs most, to put it into plain homely English, is Love: Love's inevitable devotions to a great art and less concern with these selfish ambitions our capitalistic system forces to be so ruthless: less publicizing: more patient self-sacrificing appreciation. When I think of the short-cuts taken by our young men today and consider the nine years in preparation and six of practice in silence that was my lot, it is to think

some modern improvement may have rendered that consecration "dated" or to reflect that perhaps such preparation may have unwittingly contributed, too much, to the "short-cut." This, from me, does sound rather "aged."

But the spirit of youth is ever the spirit of love. And love, I know, has its consecrations as surely as it is love. These consecrations are no longer possible to the eclecticisms of the old grand school any more than they are possible to the exploitations of the hard-as-nails new school. But where love is, there architecture will be growing strong in its own right.

Finally, to those of you who are America abroad and those of you who are abroad in America—these four commandments where your work is concerned. They are from a modern Sermon on the Mount:

The greatest virtue of the heart—Love.
The greatest virtue of the mind—Sincerity.
The greatest virtue of the will—Determination.
The greatest virtue of the spirit—Courage.

With these four simples you may discard the less civilized Ten Commandments our forefathers needed and begin a more civilized architecture where it must continuously begin—at the beginning.

FROM AN ARCHITECT'S POINT OF VIEW

The manuscript for this article, prepared as an address to the Chicago Real Estate Board on the occasion of the General Housing Conference of June 2, 1938, is prefaced by the comment: "Real Estate men here were still buzzing this week over a stiff indictment read to them by Frank Lloyd Wright, noted Wisconsin architect of Spring Green." But the indictment went much further than the real estate profession. Wright criticized the general state of the nation and its rising rate of unemployment. When he returned to the theme of real estate, Wright told the board: "If Real Estate were to go before some bar of judgement where human values were uppermost, it would be taken out and shot at sunrise as it stands. The good it has done is so little as compared to the injustice and misery it has deliberately caused for its own profit."
[Unpublished speech, delivered to the Chicago Real Estate Board, June 2, 1938]

THESE UNITED STATERS—OUR PROFIT-TAKERS—SEEM TO have no social sense. Our President accused them of having a horse and buggy mind. Triumph of understatement. They are really suffering from a feudal-hangover.

How can you, with reason, expect national prosperity when our nation is dominated by ideas of right and wrong that belong way back somewhere in the dark ages and call that domination Progress? Nevertheless these exploited inventions the profit-takers now own, go marching on by themselves to a tomorrow that is actually today.

Yes, we do have our modern improvements because of the profit-taker. But now it seems we must use them, in spite of the profit-takers, or give the improvements up. If the takers intend to bet on mobilization, bet on glass, on steel, and on electrification against their proper places in the lives of the American people, either they or the people must give them all up. Guess who will give them up?

Meantime we—the people—live in the midst of the scaffolding of a civilization, a scaffolding that defaces every countryside. Poles and wires, tracks and shods, stumpage and erosion, barbed-wire fences, sign boards and dumpage. How long will these blind illiberal uses of invention be used to make money instead of used to make men? Profit-taking put the scaffolding there where it is for a good purpose, I believe. But I believe, too, it is now time for those who put it there to take it down and let the finished work appear. But probably the people themselves must do that, for what social sense have the profit-takers ever shown?

Decentralization of industry (Education—capital E—is now our major industry standardization) is the only way to reach a proper use of the great

Living room, Taliesin. Spring Green, Wisconsin. 1925. Photograph by Hedrich-Blessing, courtesy the Chicago Historical Society.
FLLW Fdn FA#2501.0234

modern resources of enormous U.S.A. Already the point has been reached where our nation no longer owns its own ground, no longer owns anything, in fact, above some slight equity in it, or in an automobile, a radio, or some kind of machinery. And those corporate "makers" of ours can no longer sell outright what they make. They can only rent it to you by way of installment-buying and repossession. The average citizen has no longer any valid buying power. The sources of wealth—they are mainly human labor, and ground—have passed into impersonal corporate control or to the corporate citizen—not held for him as they should be.

Well, it is a headache now to the corporate bodies and a heartache now, as ever, for the body politic. Never mind—every problem carries with itself its own solution. And this one carries its own solution within itself. The very forces that, misused, enabled this exaggerated centralization to take place are now working, naturally, against it. See decentralization going on around you? See the motor car at first exaggerating the city, now tearing it down; see electrification, having aided congestion, now scattering it; see glass and steel, having given impetus to congestion by way of the skyscraper and its

brood, now giving rein by way of organic architecture (you call it modern architecture) to the new sense of space. And the modern city will someday be everywhere or be nowhere.

Concentration of Capital is already seeking a way back to the people in whose hands alone it can be fruitful. A nation consisting of actual capitalists and many millions of potential or fictitious capitalists is a gambler's paradise but just does not make economic sense. This fact is becoming sufficiently evident to our people now to soon take practical effect. And I imagine it will take effect not by way of more parties, either. Partisanship is old stuff, even in the provinces. Men and issues used to need a party, perhaps, but they do not need one now. A quiet revolution has taken place underneath the surface these nine years past and the people have seen that a party is a politician's bed first, and whatever else afterward and by whatever name you choose to call the party, new or old. The old term "conservative," too, no longer works as it did because the people now know enough to know that "standpatter" is what the word really means as it is used—and that only the radical (at the "root," of the root) can possibly be conservative. How (I ask you) are you going to keep the life in anything growing unless you know that growing thing, at the root?

Yes, it is getting harder for the newspapers to scare our people with the cry of "Red" or "Fascist." Our people do not see much sense in getting excited over our neighbor's pet forms of misgovernment when their own government doesn't know what to do with 30 million unemployed citizens any more than they know what to do with themselves.

Capital at the moment seems to realize that the safest place for it at present is in the homes for those people who have little or nothing—and we are seeing the big reservoirs of capital being tapped for that. Even the politicians—the more politic they are the better they see it—see their jobs in need of new parties—parties with fresh attitudes, bigger and better promises with fresher names for the same old things. As though parties and partisanship hadn't fooled the country long enough—and is now one of the things that is the matter with our kind of Democracy.

And so it goes on in the name of Progress, goes on as it has always gone on, I suppose. History repeating itself—because no organic basis for anything has yet existed where the ways of human life go on as they go.

We—the American people—need to realize that life is *organic* or it is just a *disease*. That essential knowledge is exactly what our major industry—education—has *not* brought to the American people. The people are left to discern that and work it out for themselves if they can. They can and they will.

Modern architecture's ideal is organic architecture. We are already building buildings that do use our advances in thought, materials and equipment. Why can't we have that sense of the whole in our social fabric by way of statesmen instead of politicians? Society is either organic and sound or inorganic and diseased.

And perhaps most of all we, the American people, need to know that government is necessarily "ipso-facto." We can't look to government to initiate better ways of doing things. Government, in a democracy, is executive to the will of the people. We hear of constructive legislation, but when we get it, or anything like it, such legislation will first have been the wish of the people. So—"it is up to us" and we seem to have run out of ideas.

How stupid to blame all our troubles on our President—when we made them and keep on making them for ourselves by our own cupidities and stupidities? He has done a lot to enlighten our ignorance, so it seems to me. But what can an executive do when the people run dry? Does this profit-motive dry up the sources of inspiration?

What is a Democracy anyway? Think it through to some logical conclusion! It needs doing. There is no longer excuse for our major industry (again, I mean "Education") to leave us so profoundly ignorant of what Democracy really means in execution and how much it does matter to us where we live as we now live. If we get that idea into our minds straight I have faith enough in ourselves to feel that we would, somehow, find a way out.

What do you say to a sub- or super-constitution that makes this matter of Democracy all a little clearer as a basis for our society than the one we have now? If Thomas Jefferson or Tom Paine could come back and look at the old one in the light of present events, aren't you pretty sure they would want to make it over? You see, it wouldn't be sacred to them. If they saw it was not a serviceable and practical basis for interpreting life in a Democracy they would throw it out, if we know them.

When this sense of the whole as organic enters the mind as an ideal—as it must (education notwithstanding) we will get the top, tops and the bottom beneath—all right. But—how now?

If Real Estate were to go before some bar of judgement where human values were uppermost, it would be taken out and shot at sunrise as it stands. The good it has done is so little as compared to the injustice and misery it has deliberately caused for its own profit.

If it has wisdom in its locker it should use it now to decentralize urban centers and reintegrate the people according to new space measurements brought here by motor, radio and telephone. When the people really get these new things for themselves, and that new space measurement will be one hundred to what "real-estate" made it as it now stands.

Taliesin. Spring Green, Wisconsin. 1925. Photograph by Hedrich-Blessing, courtesy the Chicago Historical Society.
FLLW Fdn FA#2501.0232

The fifty-foot lot is a curse upon life. Less than an acre to the person is even less than this country affords when it gets into its right mind and into its appropriate stride.

The horizontal line is the line of human life and of domesticity. Verticality is vertigo for human beings. Let's spread out.

The skyscraper is a landlord's ruse to enable a lot-area to be sold to the people over and over again as many times as steel can multiply it and engineers can make it stand up.

The motor car is only an out-grown horse and buggy yet in these United States and this United States, this specialist in motor cars.

The "real-estate" idea of a building was something from lot line to lot line, as high as the ordinance allowed, cut up into as small cells as the traffic would bear. The realtors were marketing congestion to congestion. Not so much longer—watch the reaction.

Exploitation of the herd instinct was once upon a time a good "realtor." It isn't so good now.

The fluttering flag, the barbecue and the bull—take your slice or leave it we have *had* that.

Promotion by commotion was good realtor circus, is good radio—good merchandising—good movies—but what now as the crowd spreads out thinner and thinner—freer and happier to be at home again with its feet on its ground?

The ground problem has been so changed by mobilization, electrification, glass and steel, that with it realty tactics must entirely change. The motor car, although it still resembles one, and like it is kept in a stable, is not a horse, gentlemen. But, you must conclude that the consequence of the use of the motor car have not dawned on the realtor mind if you watch them at work with it as though it were still a horse.

Absentee landlordism is a dam that had sprung a leak already. When that dam breaks the realtor may be swept away with it. Why not get ahead of the break now?

Three things that from any human viewpoint should not be speculative commodities: Land—Medium of exchange (money)—Ideas valuable to Society.

1. There must be no speculation in land.
2. There can be no speculation in money.
3. No speculation in the ideas by way of which society lives should be tolerated in a free society calling itself a Democracy.

There is more money to be made in real estate (such speculations abolished) than ever before, but it takes more money to make money and it takes much more vision to make it.

So a new type of promoter is needed in the U.S.A.; a promoter on the side of the American people—one who sees the humanities as something to be expanded and extended by his operations—not "altruistically," mind you, but automatically.

Why continue to pour sand into rat holes?

Just the same I can't conscientiously close this talk to American Real-Estate without saying that our old Chicago, being the only city in the United States to discover its own water-front, is going to be the most beautiful of cities, while they last (yes, they are going fast) except—probably—one. That one, judging from the plans, models and spirit of its people is—Moscow. (Chicago may resent the exception, but it will do so in ignorance of facts.) Chicago and Moscow have each a great spirit, differently approaching the one thing that matters most now—the growth of a free and independent people—free in their own right—citizens without fear, craving no one's charity. How wonderful to see a Civilization owning itself—and, what is a larger order and longer waiting, a *Culture* that can say its soul is its own and look itself in the face.

THE MAN AND THE ISSUE

This essay is devoted solely to the subject of politics, politicians, and elected officials in government. Wright laments the difficulty in getting capable and dedicated people—not merely politicians—into office who want and can effect changes that will heal national problems. He also takes the opportunity to endorse Wisconsin politician Tom Amlie. [Published in The Capital Times, *August 11, 1938]*

LOOKING FOR SOCIAL SIGNIFICANCE IN OUR "POLITICS" ANY student of structure must go mad, or laugh, a bitter laugh. Why longer, politicians? The late breakdown drove me, as millions of my fellow citizens, to study our policies in economics and government. Among other things the Broadacre City models were a result.

An architect is a student of structure and so a student of men and things where social structure is concerned. He must know his people's way of life because he interprets them. Today *structure* in this sense must be the American people's chief concern. But no American politician seems to know anything of structure and seems to care nothing about it. Himself an Expedient he goes to office and comes out again more "expedient" than ever. Business is Business, Politics is Politics, but Life is Life just the same. Though it may not "march on" it goes on inexorably heedless of the United States politician as he, himself heedless, now stands before us for a fall. The politician has proved himself no "red"—no: just yellow, that's all, especially if he is a Democrat; shamelessly a "hater" if Republican; illiberal or loftily Messianic if a Progressive. How the "Progressive" party ever got itself forward as "liberal" is legerdemain of newspaperdom.

Progression, we see, may be narrow as retrogression. The country goes to bed "broke," ill with partisanship—yet "progressives" call for more partisanship; another bed for another politician and beds for his friends. Don't we simply need men and issues now? Surely we do *not* need more politicians, *party* politics? Such have always left us in the lurch and would again leave us in worse straits than before. Witness our president's difficulties in doing anything constructive (or the difficulties suffered by anyone we ever had working for us for that matter) because of the "politics" of those who should be loyal to us by being loyal to our executive even should he make mistakes.

What Franklin Roosevelt has had to work against in working to enlighten the people who elected him concerning their own affairs sickens the American spirit of fairplay. Well, Tom Amlie wasn't one of those who made his chief's work harder. As a member of Congress he was the intelligent critic but nevertheless the loyal supporter of his superior officer. He didn't take advantage of the people's fool-sentimentality to double-cross that same people's executive, trying to represent the act as loyalty to something greater—the "grand old constitution" for instance.

Frank Lloyd Wright and Herbert F. Johnson at site of S. C. Johnson Administration Building test column, June 3, 1937. Racine, Wisconsin. FLLW Fdn FA#6801.0016

The people may be foolishly sentimental—they are—but I think they now know politicians well enough to show next election time how they feel about treachery no matter how nobly dressed or by what name it chooses to call itself.

I've read Tom Amlie's letters from Congress to find him interested deeply in the organic struc-

ture of our State. I should say Tom is a man's man who happened to be elected as a politician, maybe—and now deserves well of us because he went a little deeper into the matters that vitally concern us than most politicians care to or dare to.

Loving a liberal and seeking liberality I declare all partisanship illiberal at best, at worst treacherous, as we have seen. All politicians are purveyors of prejudice to prejudice; of course necessary in the getting and holding of their jobs. I recognize that Franklin Roosevelt couldn't have been president of these United States unless he were a politician nor could Tom Amlie have got to Congress unless he were a politician. Just the same I regret—and resent—the fact.

It is that fact, that we "the people, yes" ought now to challenge and change. We can change it. But we can't change it by more and better "parties." Nor can we do it by taking out good men—men who have given a good account of themselves by doing good work, interrupting one man's good work to put someone else in his place on the mere chance of that someone's doing better. Let's stand by the men who stood by the work of reconstruction needed by our country!

Let's give our hand up to men who have had the brains and gut-sense to see that discontent and criticism are well enough—but that lending a hand in trying circumstances is better than "walking out." To walk out or "strike" is a poor way to repay a people in emergency when the people need—most of all—work done, done well if possible.

I believe Franklin Roosevelt wisely tried well, if not always successfully, to get some of the needed work started and keep it going. A real man at that. And I believe Tom Amlie is such another man.

I am not saying there are no others. But when a man proves himself by his work why throw him out just to bet on change or to advantage some politician? I can visualize a time coming when we might not be able to get first-class help we so need at the seat of government because first-class men shun foregone futility. Let's forge parties and politicians for once and concentrate on the man and the issues: Tom Amlie is one of the men.

TO WILLIAMSBURG

It was not that Wright objected to the restoration of Colonial Williamsburg as a museum to show the American public the structures and life of Colonial times, but he did object to Williamsburg being held up as an example of what period or style in architecture befitted the United States. "I am familiar with all the aesthetics of that time and Williamsburg shows them in place but out of tune with the great work ahead to be done." This paper is a reply to the criticism he received when first he made these statements in a talk at William and Mary College. The adverse reactions, he assumes, must have come from "archaeologists of the 'restoration' or from fine ladies living in fine old Colonial mansions."

Just as the Chicago exposition of 1893 set up the neoclassic as an "example," and as a result the nation went wholeheartedly in that direction, Wright warned that the Colonial "example" at Williamsburg should not swing the course of architecture in that direction. [Unpublished essay, November 1938]

THE CAPTIOUS CAPTION-WRITER IS THE REAL "SENSA-tionalist" in this attempt of mine to interpret antique Williamsburg. No sensationalist in this matter of our culture, except as the sensible viewpoint is always a sensation, as things are with us, and the man in search of truth speaks truly—I am sorry to have offended those who cherish Williamsburg. I am myself as "colonial" as anyone living in our country today. In me a long line of preachers and governors dating back to "The Reformation" was finally carried out on the current of circumstance to the prairies of our great Middle West to grow up with the country—an architect.

I mention this and the fact that I have always felt a spiritual kinship with Thomas Jefferson to give me a certain credit, perhaps, where I now seem to have less than none.

From those who attended the talk at William and Mary I have not heard except by hearsay. But I must say I was never more in earnest nor ever more appreciatively listened to and applauded than then. The inimical reactions spreading through the East seem to come wholly from archaeologists of the "restoration" or from fine ladies living in fine old colonial mansions.

I say (as I said at William and Mary) that for one, I am truly grateful to Mr. Rockefeller for that work, made authentic by careful research and unlimited funds. The country needs it as a fine museum-piece showing the culture brought here by our forefathers as that culture then stood on the threshold of a great new life to come for the multimillions of English, Welsh, Irish, German, French, Italian, Russian, Norwegian, Swedish, Spanish, and the

Africans who now call this land home and misman-age it as a commonwealth. Many of the things I said have been misquoted. Most of them misunder-stood—but not, I think, by those accustomed to prefer reality to illusion.

Were I allowed but a single criticism of Williamsburg I should say the attempt to create an "illusion" by way of the restoration is where the matter goes wrong and is likely to do harm as it has done to little Margie Hoskins—William and Mary campus—who says she wants white palings, a scantling roof and white clapboards to surround her, "Yes," when the time comes. *The New York Herald-Tribune* credits her with sagacity beyond her years because she said it—and rests the case for Williamsburg right there with her. But there is a little Mary Jones, little Frieda Hof, little Gusta, little Olga, little Rosa Gallo, and little Rachel Finkelstein—what about them? A Richmond ed-itorial proposes cultural segregation—showing how far gone Thomas Jefferson's "liberality" can go? That is where I saw it going as I talked about it at the college—and why I said many of the things I said.

Of course the situation confronting us in Williamsburg is not new. It is old as civilization.

It is peculiarly aggravating, however, to find it so persistent where life is dedicated—afresh—to freedom—individuality inviolate . . . the United States of America. I suggest that opposition to the points of view I advanced arise from the fact that educationally (traditionally, that is to say) Art is an "aesthetic," therefore a matter of "taste." And that is another way of declaring art to be a matter of opinion. Subject to that "cultural lag" we have the English version of French culture brought over to an Indian-infested terrain—there to be named Williamsburg and be as true to "back-home" as the English could make it and they can always make it pretty much as their habit had it, and they can do it and do do it wherever they go on this earth.

Now the sermon I thought needed at the college was, at least, of a deeper sort. Art an ex-pression not of a new or old "aesthetic" but a vital expression of a way of life. That was what I meant when I said Colonial culture was "shallow," in re-

ferring to the evidences of that culture as recorded by the "colonials" at Williamsburg. I saw very clearly the refinements of taste in the objects of their search for the elegant solution which they modeled upon the search for that same thing by the French. I saw much to admire in the way they met the limitations of poverty by building more in intimate human scale. I am familiar with all the aesthetics of that time and Williamsburg shows them in place but out of tune with the great work ahead to be done.

Nor am I insensible to the birth of liberalism in such surroundings where Art was no more than an aesthetic—a borrowed one. It was time, and a pity that the liberality and ideality that demanded freedom and independence for life should have had no deeper sense of Art to guide it in making the new forms of which the new life was soon to find itself so much in need. As a memory Williamsburg may well be sacred. As an illusion it is silly.

The Williamsburg restoration conclusively shows us nothing of principle that could enter into the culture of the period to come—and soon we had the run of the colonial degenerating into Queen Anne, Medieval Gothic, General Grant Gothic—everywhere a wilderness of imitation for the new life to live in. Thus the inevitable cultural lag came to be and still persists. That it might cease to persist—I contributed my mite at Williamsburg in expounding there, not the new aesthetic, but the truth that great Art is *of* the life lived and not mere-ly something *on* it: that the new forms our life needs so much will be the result of no "aesthetic" what-ever, nor a continued search for "the elegant solu-tion"—but a brave and happier facing of reality—the evaluation of principle mastering the ways and means of our mechanisms in terms of better patterns for life—free; finding the beginning of all expressive art forms proceeding from the nature of the within, here and now, rather than begging the whole issue by preferring what our grandfathers had—quite thoughtlessly at the time. Since that earlier time a finer honesty in the realm of the spirit has been born to find its way into the affairs of our time by way of Architecture.

I preached that finer honesty at Williamsburg's

William and Mary as I have continued to build it for so many of my countrymen. I believe the cultural lag will never end for us in our day but may for the next generation but one—if we can be persuaded to abandon illusion, however sentimentally pretty and redolent of beloved memories it may be, put our shoulders to the wheel and move forward to more life and better life for all of our people.

Now the term "freakish" is most used by those who apply the term to whatever is unfamiliar. The unfamiliar is "strange" and strange is always suspect where there is no deeper reference than to some "aesthetic." But thought, sooner or later, had to enter into the ways of Art—notwithstanding artists and educational authority. Now the same overturn is occurring in that higher and more significant realm of life that occurred in the minds of our Williamsburg forefathers where political freedom was their concern and their objective. It is now our concern to take that spirit into the ways of living life we call our own. And that is what organic architecture is doing.

The remark "I am less and less willing to take off my hat to our forefathers—seeing what a mess they left us" probably needs some explanation. To see how culture failed them because it was merely an aesthetic is easy enough and no cause for a lessening of respect, because they were of their time, and there was then, nothing else. But it is more difficult to see by way of a deeper understanding brought about by an honest search for the organic structure of our state—or society—that the Colonial dream of freedom lacked the technique necessary to abolish the impositions that they, cooing here, rebelled against, only to allow these very feudal hangovers to persist as the economic basis of their beloved ideal—Democracy—then I feel a rebel, myself, against the consequences just exactly as they, my forebears, were rebels. But probably the hat should come off nevertheless, it is not much of a hat anyway, for how in the world could their foresight have equaled our hindsight?

And I repeat that were Thomas Jefferson alive today in the spirit—he would stand and say more bitter and caustic things to his worshippers (I called them "pallbearers" at Williamsburg) than I have the heart or capacity to say.

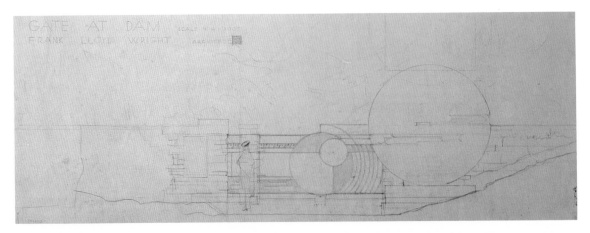

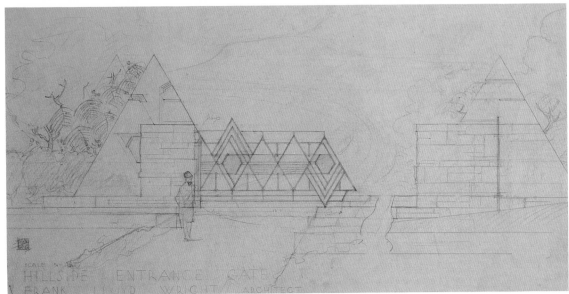

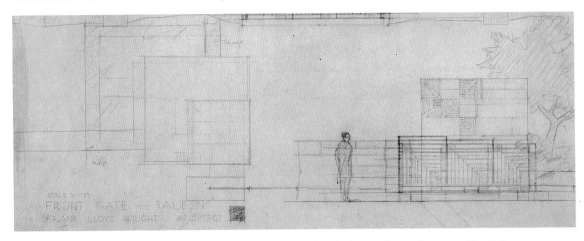

Taliesin Gates (Project). Spring Green, Wisconsin. 1939. Elevations. Pencil and color pencil on tracing paper, 36 x 25".
FLLW Fdn#3921.001/ 3921.002/3921.003

"THE ARCHITECTURAL FORUM"

In 1938, for the first time in his career, Frank Lloyd Wright was asked to design and contribute material to a monograph issue of an architectural periodical in the United States, The Architectural Forum. In a talk to the Taliesin Fellowship in 1950, he explained how the issue came to be:

> I have been writing this morning, trying to figure out for the Forum why my work always appears in the Forum. . . . It is wholly on account of Howard Myers. When we were getting a worm's eye view of society some fifteen years ago Howard Myers came to Taliesin on a special mission. I had not been publishing my work. I do not believe in indiscriminate publication—only when there was enough of it so that you could see its character. A single building—what can you tell about that? So when he came with this plea and said he would turn the whole Forum over to me, I could edit it, I could have as much of it as I wanted, as many illustrations—and he would go as far as I cared to go, if I would undertake it.[1]

The Forum prefaced this special issue with the statement:

> The Architectural Forum has the honor to present for January 1938 an issue devoted to the new and unpublished work of FRANK LLOYD WRIGHT. To have worked in close association with Mr. Wright in the development of this issue, which was designed and written by him, has been a stimulating experience which in some measure the editors believe will carry over to every Forum reader who devotes to these pages the study they merit.

Howard Myers was the editor-in-chief, and the success of this particular issue rests mainly in his persistent cooperation with Wright. The two of them became close friends, and ten years later, in 1948, Myers would be responsible for another monograph issue of the Forum devoted to Frank Lloyd Wright.

At the time this issue went to press, Wright was immersed in an extraordinary period of architectural productivity. Edgar Kaufmann's house, "Fallingwater," was complete and waiting final interior furnishings; the Johnson Wax Administration Building was nearing completion and would open by the following spring. The Paul and Jean Hanna house, in Stanford, California, was complete and furnished, awaiting landscaping. Herbert Johnson's "Wingspread" was also under construction. The Herbert Jacobs house, the first constructed Usonian house, was complete and likewise awaiting landscaping. The issue opened with photographs of Taliesin and the Taliesin Fellowship buildings at Hillside (The Hillside Home School).

Quotations from Henry David Thoreau and Walt Whitman were used throughout the issue as "by-lines." In the conclusion Wright explains his red-square logo with the following line from Whitman: "Chanting the square deific, out of the one advancing out of the sides; out of the old and new, out of the square entirely divine, solid—four sided—all the sides needed. I am time, old, modern as any."

And he quoted from the writings of Timitiazev, a plant physiologist: "The color red is invincible. It is the color not only of the blood—it is the color of creation. It is the only life-giving color in nature filling the sprouting plant with life and giving warmth to everything in creation." [Published with 117 illustrations in The Architectural Forum, January 1938][2]

To take this matter of an organic architecture a little deeper into the place where it belongs—the human heart—the design matter in this issue falls readily into the following sensuous expressions of principle at work. It is a sense of the whole that is lacking in the "modern" buildings I have seen, and we are here concerned with that sense of the whole which alone is radical.

1. The sense of the ground. (Topography, organic features. Growth.)

2. The sense of shelter.

3. The sense of materials. (Illustrated by characteristic early plans—showing interior living space becoming exterior architecture. Characteristic plans—early and late—abolishing walls, interior partitions, etc., and grouping or placing utilitarian features in such a manner as to allow space to be either magnified or uninterrupted so far as possible.)

4. The sense of space.

5. The sense of proportion. (With this you must be born. An instinct.)

6. The sense of order. (Related by cultivation to the sense of proportion.)

7. Ways and means, that is to say, technique. Last and least. Each man his own.

Characterizing these expressions in various forms—each an actual experience—plot-plans, plans, perspectives and photographs, some reminders of early buildings alongside later buildings. I have always considered plans most essential in the presentation or consideration of any building. There is more beauty in a fine ground plan itself than in almost any of its consequences. So plot-plans and structural plans have been given due place in this issue as of first importance. Furniture and planting are indicated on them. Next—the perspective study of the original concept. Then, photographs of finished structures and those in course of construction. Finally—certain details of these Usonian buildings.

Taliesin, a house of the north, is best seen under its blanket of snow, long icicles pendent from the eaves.

Twice destroyed by fire, it now stands on its 200 acres as rebuilt in 1925-26. The native product is the work of farmer masons, farmer carpenters, and farmer plasterers—and a farmer architect. Apprentices have added many features, completing and extending it to house—temporarily—in addition to the architect and family, some twenty-five young people, working alongside in architecture. Taliesin is a natural building, in love with the ground, built of native limestone quarried nearby. Sand from the river below was the body of its plastered surfaces, plain wood slabs and marking strips of red cypress finish the edges, mark the ceilings, and make the doors and sash.

Located four miles from the nearest village, forty from the nearest city, Taliesin must have its own water, sewer, heat, light and power systems and its own transportation system. What life and entertainment it knows are found pretty much within itself.

Such remnants (twice escaped destruction when the building burned) of the considerable collection of ancient works of art acquired during the building of the Imperial Hotel in Tokyo still stand on the piers and walls. Some of those that fell in the fire of '25 are built into its stone walls. In the vault is a fine collection, still, of Japanese prints.

Any modern building really out of the ground is timeless (fashion cannot harm it in the long run). The mother art—Architecture—may well associate with the timeless in sculpture, painting, and music wherever found without loss of significance or beauty to itself or to those arts. That is as far as "creed" at Taliesin goes.

The blacksmith's horses, the shoemaker's children, the architect's home all know a certain habitual "lag." Taliesin knows it, too. But its architect has here taken his own medicine in doses all but fatal.

The buildings of the Taliesin Fellowship, old and new, are a quarter of a mile away, just over the hill to the south.

Perhaps this house should stand as a proper example of the sense of the ground in the category of sensitiveness mentioned in the foreword.

It is also a good example of the use of materials and the play of space relations, the long stretches of low ceilings extending outside over and beyond the windows, related in direction to some feature of the landscape.

These low stretches are frequently relieved by high ceilings following the roof pitches—marked by wood strip: to emphasize contrasting planes with an eye to the repose of the whole. Landscape seen through the openings of the building thus placed and proportioned has greater charm than when seen independent of the architecture. Architecture properly studied in relation to the natural features surrounding it is a great clarifier and developer of the beauty of landscape. . . .

"Hillside," home and workshop of the Taliesin Fellowship is a reconditioning and extension of the Hillside Home School built for the Lloyd Jones sisters in 1902.

The original buildings, "Romeo and Juliet" one of them, were built of native brick sandstone quarried a mile away and of oak timbers felled and sawed on the timber lands of surrounding farms. The labor of digging, quarrying, and hauling was done by "the family." The then "assembly room" (now the living room of the Taliesin Fellowship) was intended as memorial to grandfather and grandmother. These Welsh pioneers settled on the site of the school some eighty years ago. Quotations from Isaiah (grandfather insisted on his sons and daughters learning the chapter from which they were taken) are carved in the oak beams of the room. The pioneer verses from Gray's "Elegy" are carved in the sandstone slabs over the fireplace.[3] The andirons "straight-line" pattern were made because they resembled Welsh hats, from cones the village blacksmith used in making iron rings. But there was a better reason. The old gymnasium the apprentices converted into the Taliesin Playhouse. A new drafting room 85' x 100' is ready to work in all but the finished floors. The other buildings are commenced or roofed over but the shops and guest inn are not yet begun. The original buildings were salvaged and extended when, as fate would have it (early in 1932), I had recourse only to the materials and in similar circumstances to those in which the early buildings were originally built.

We bought trees standing—logged them to the site, and from the sawn trunks dripping sap made the abstract forest we now call the drafting room, a photograph of which you see here. Forced to postpone construction when "relief" came in for our workmen in 1934, we have begun again to carry out the plan for the whole as a meanwhile steady job for the Fellowship itself—going ahead as materials are available. Within two years we hope to have the whole as you see it herewith.

The type of Architecture—Usonian type—is suited to the modeling of the surrounding hills, bespeaks the materials and methods under which and by way of which the buildings themselves were necessarily born. That they are not "modern" as use of steel, concrete, and glass would have made them is—I think—beside the mark.

"THE GARDEN WALL." House built for Dean Malcolm Willey—Nancy Willey, Superintendent. Cost $10,000. A well-protected brick house built upon a brick-paved three-inch concrete mat laid down over well drained bed of cinders and sand—the concrete mat jointed at partitions. To develop the nature of the materials a sand mold brick course alternates with a course of paving brick, the exterior cypress is left to weather and the interior cypress is only waxed.

The house wraps around the northwest corner of a lot sloping to the south—a fine vista in that direction. The plan protects the Willeys from the neighbors, sequesters a small garden and realizes the view to the utmost under good substantial shelter. Notwithstanding the protests of the builder and unusually many kind friends, the fireplace draws perfectly and the mat is perfectly comfortable in 30° below-zero weather. Nor does the frost show upon the inside of the outside walls. The house emphasizes the modern sense of space by vista inside and outside, without getting at all "modernistic." There is a well-balanced interpenetration (that is to say sense of proportion) of the sense of shelter with this sense of space, the sense of materials and the purpose of the whole structure in this dwelling. It is well-constructed for a life of several centuries if the shingle roof is renewed in twenty-five years or tile is substituted. Perhaps this northern house comes as near to being permanent human shelter as any family of this transitory period is entitled to expect. The furniture is of a like substantial character, missing items still being built and moved in from time to time as designs arrive and ways and means appear.

FALLINGWATER. The country lodge of Edgar Kaufmann built at Bear Run, Pennsylvania, is pretty clearly what it is shown to be in the photographs herewith. For the first time in my practice, where residence work is concerned in recent years, reinforced concrete was actually needed to construct the cantilever system of this extension of the cliff beside a mountain stream, making living space over and above the stream upon several terraces upon which a man who loved the place sincerely, one who liked to listen to the waterfall, might well live. Steel sash came within reach also for the first time. In this design for living down in a glen in a deep forest, shelter took on definite masonry form while still preserving protection overhead for extensive glass surface. These deep overhangs provide the interior, as usual, with the softened diffused lighting for which the in-dweller is invariably grateful, I have found.

The interiors would tell this story better than words but though they soon will be, they were not furnished at the time these pictures were made. Inasmuch as this furnishing is intimately part of the building, the interiors will appear at some later time.

This building is a late example of the inspiration of a site, the cooperation of an intelligent, appreciative client and the use of entirely masonry materials except for an interlining of redwood and asphalt beneath all flooring. Again, by way of steel in tension this building takes its place and achieves its form. The grammar of the slabs at their eaves is best shown by a detail. But the roof water is caught by a lead strip built into the concrete above near the beginning of the curve so what water dripping by gravity at the bottom of the curve—as it does—does not very much stain the curves. It is not the deluge of water in a storm that hurts any building: it is ooze and drip of dirty water in thawing and freezing, increased by slight showers. The cantilever slabs here carry parapets and the beams. They may be seen clutching big boulders. But next time, I believe, parapets will carry the floors—or better still we will know enough to make the two work together as one, as I originally intended.

This structure might serve to indicate that the sense of shelter—the sense of space where used with sound structural sense—has no limitations as to form except the materials used and the methods by which they are employed for what purpose. The ideas involved here are in no ways changed from those of early work. The materials and methods of construction come through them, here, as they may and will always come through everywhere. That is all. The effects you see in this house are not superficial effects.

"Fallingwater," Edgar J. Kaufmann House. Mill Run, Pennsylvania. 1935. Photograph by Hedrich-Blessing, courtesy the Chicago Historical Society. FLLW Fdn FA#3602.0043

TEXAS rolling prairie needs a house—a house with modern sense and idea of space—above all airy, naturally air conditioned. The breadths of vista down there are inspiring.

This house is so inspired. An extended central chimney stack exhausts hot air from all the rooms, especially the sleeping rooms. Except for these upper rooms the roof over the house is a screened-in deck like that of a ship. The floor areas below, exterior and interior, are unbroken except for gratings inserted at the wall lines under the door screens to intercept the sweeping water of sudden downpours.

When the house is open it may be wide open. When it is closed it may be completely closed except the roof deck. All top surfaces are insulated against a merciless sun and the roof deck is screened against it by shutters rolling back and forth on extended cantilever arms which also carry insect screens, the screening extending downward to include the lower terrace area in front of the living room.

The walls are of slender flesh-colored roman bricks—coped with copper to match the copper roofs.

All glass surfaces are continuous under wide thin projecting eaves—glass used more for vista than for light. These sheltering planes not only marry the house to the ground but afford a pleasant diffusion of light in the interiors. The copper itself is turquoise blue.

If Texas ever realizes that it needs a Texas house it will have a sheltering wing-spread over the ground similar to this one; an openness to rolling prairie vistas—like this one; a house protected from stagnation of summer air and sudden cold as this one—as clean and swift of line. Texas is yet young and architecturally Texas is yet untouched. But perhaps construction as permanent as contemplated here is unnecessary for the climate.

I believe—making provision against violent winds—a lighter more transient construction would serve well enough, something between Ocatilla, the architect's camp in the desert, and the San Marcos block building itself. The experiment would be worth making, local architects to the contrary notwithstanding.

Estimates on this house ran between 30 and 35 thousand dollars. Inasmuch as 20 to 25 thousand dollars was the cost limit fixed we reluctantly laid the plans aside and the job went local.

THIS plan for a skyscraper standing park-free in the city, the only urban skyscraper fit for human occupancy, is as nearly organic as steel in tension can make it, here doing for a tall building what Lidgerwood made it do for the long ship. The ship had its keel. This building has its concrete core. A shaft of concrete rises through the floors engaging each floor slab as one passes through the shaft at eighteen levels. Each floor proceeds outward as a cantilever slab extended from the shaft. The slab, thick at the shaft, grows thinner by way of an overlapping scale pattern as it goes outward until at the final leap to the rectangle it is no more than three inches thick. The outer enclosing shell of glass and copper is pendent from these cantilever slabs. The inner partitions nest upon the slab.

Quadruple in plan (four double-decked apartments to each floor, each apartment unaware of the

"Fallingwater," Edgar J. Kaufmann House. Mill Run, Pennsylvania. 1935. Photograph by Hedrich-Blessing, courtesy the Chicago Historical Society. FLLW Fdn FA#3602.0041

other as all are looking outward), the structure eliminates entirely the weight and waste space of masonry walls. The central shaft, standing inside away from lighted space, carries the elevators and entrance hallway well within itself. Two of the exterior walls of every apartment are entirely of glass set into sheet copper framing. But the building is so placed that the sun shines on only one wall at a time and the narrow upright blades, or mullions, project nine inches so that as the sun moves, shadows fall on the glass surfaces.

The building increases substantially in area from floor to floor as the structure rises—in order that the glass frontage of each story may drip clear of the one below, the building, thus, cleaning itself, and, also, because areas become more valuable the higher (within limits) the structure goes. The central shaft extending well into the ground may carry with safety a greatly extended top mass. This building, earthquake, fire and sound proof from within by structural economics inherent in its nature, weighs less than one-half the usual structure besides increasing available area for living purposes more than twenty per cent.

It is a logical development of the idea of a tall building in the age of glass and steel—as logical engineering as the Brooklyn Bridge or the ocean liner.

But the benefits of modernity such as this are not merely economic. There is greater privacy, safety, and beauty for human lives within it than is possible in any other type of apartment building.

Again the 1-2 triangle is employed—this time because in itself it has a flexibility in arrangement for human movement not afforded by the rectangle. The apparently irregular shapes of the rooms would not appear as "irregular" in reality—all would have great repose because all are not only properly in proportion to the human figure but to the figure made by the whole.

The building is a complete standardization for prefabrication. Only the concrete core and slabs need be made in the field. Our shop fabricating industrial system could here function at its best with substantial benefits to humanity. Owing to the unusual conformations the metal (copper) furniture would have to be a part of the building, as the furniture is designed to be.

Here again is the poise, balance, lightness and strength that may characterize the creations of this age instead of masonry mass which is an unsuitable, extravagant and unsafe hangover from feudal times.

"WINGSPREAD," the Herbert Johnson prairie house, now being built, is another experiment in the articulation which began with the Coonley House at Riverside, built 1909, wherein Living Room, Dining Room, Kitchen, Family sleeping rooms, Guest Rooms were each separate units grouped together and connected by corridor.

Notwithstanding the unprepossessing state of the building and the weather, several construction photographs are included here. The plan is oriented so that sunlight falls in all of the rooms and shows a logical expression of the zoned house.[4] (The first design for such a house was printed in the Taliesin monograph 1936).

At the center of the four zones the spacious Living Room stands. A tall central chimneystack with five fireplaces divides this vertical space into spaces for the various domestic functions: Entrance Hall, Family Living Room, Library Living Room, and Dining Room. Extending from this lofty central room are four wings—three low and one with mezzanine. The one with mezzanine floor and galleries is for the master, mistress and young daughter. Another wing extends

from the central space for their several boys; a playroom at the end, a graduated deep-pool in conjunction—another wing for service and utilities—another for guests and five motor cars. Each wing has independent views on two sides, each has perfect privacy—the whole being united by a complete house telephone system. Lighting is integral. Heating is integral, in the floor slab as in the S. C. Johnson Co. Administration Building and the Jacobs House at Madison.

This extended wing plan lies, very much at home, integral with the prairie landscape which is, through it, made more significant and beautiful. In this case, especially, growth will claim its own; wild-grape vines pendent from trellises; extensive collateral gardens in bloom; a great mass of evergreens in the entrance court; single tall associate of the building. Lake Michigan lies off to the middle distance seen over a wild-fowl pool stretching away in that direction from just below the main terrace of the house.

The farm unit is just opposite and in view. A gate lodge mounted on a street wall at the main highway is not in view. This structure is of the common type, proving itself to be a good one for a home in the climate around the Great Lakes. It is popularly known as brick veneer. Outside members are cypress plank, roofs tiled, floors of concrete, four-inch-square concrete-slab-tiles.

This house, while resembling the Coonley House, is much more bold, masculine and direct in form and treatment—executed in more permanent materials. The house has a heavy footing course of Kasota sandstone, the best brickwork I have seen in my life—and the materials of construction throughout are everywhere substantial. The house will be architecturally furnished in keeping with the character established by the building.

Construction is under a cost-plus system, in the architect's hands like the Administration Building for the S. C. Johnson Co. Construction being managed by Ben Wiltscheck, supervised by the Taliesin Fellowship.

Another prairie house in 1938 here joins the early ones of 1901–1910.

SINCE our favorite depression rendered the complete plans, specifications, and estimates for this winter resort a project merely—although the contract was ready for signature—the economical sum for completion was $480,000. I record it here so that ideas involved in that work may not be wholly lost.

I wanted to experience living in the desert so I might better make the plans. With my family and nine draftsmen I went into camp nearby the site to prepare the plans for this structure. The camp was actually built there by ourselves but as soon as we left, it was carried away by the Indians—so herewith also photographs of Ocatilla—the architect's camp.

San Marcos in the Desert was worked out upon a unit system adapted to the 1-2 or 60-30 triangle because, as you may have noticed, mountain ranges are all 60-30 triangles unless your eye is arrested by an effect produced by one that is equilateral. A cross-section of the talus at the base of the mountains is the hypotenuse of a 30-60 triangle. The camp itself first took the 60-30 form. Compounded, boarded up waist high, canvased on wood framing above that level and overhead, the openings were canvas on wood frames rigged with ship cord to open and shut. Open in the sunlight the camp resembled a fleet of ships sailing down the bay.

Concrete block construction was on my mind at the time having just seen it through with Albert McArthur in the Arizona Biltmore. I used the surrounding giant growth, Sahuaro, as motive for the building (see texture model erected in the compound of the camp) thus getting dotted lines throughout the construction. Here is another secret—the dotted line is outline in all desert creations. The building was laid out as a system of sunlit terraces conforming to the terrain and the Sahuaro entered into architecture. Dr. Alexander Chandler wanted echo-organ concerts as a feature.[5] This accounts for the tower seen beside the center of the whole: really a cluster of great organ pipes. Echo organs were planted on adjoining hills.

Sunlight poured into every room, bathroom, corridor and closet in the building. For once space concepts became a revel. The building was economical nevertheless—but too good to be true. I have found that when a scheme develops beyond a normal pitch of excellence the hand of fate strikes it down. The Japanese made a superstition of the circumstance. Purposely they leave some imperfection somewhere to appease the jealousy of the gods. I ne-

glected the precaution. San Marcos was not built.

In the vault at Taliesin is this completely developed set of plans, every block scheduled as to quantity and place. These plans are one of our prize possessions.

Dr. Paul Hanna of Stanford University has just moved into this house. We shall be able to complete the design only with the furniture and growth of the planting. Here the thesis changes, not in content—but in expression. Again we have a preliminary study for prefabrication—also made in humble native materials—principally redwood board-partitions erected on a concrete mat cut into hexagonal tiles. Another experiment because I am convinced that a cross-section of honeycomb has more fertility and flexibility where human movement is concerned than the square. The obtuse angle is more suited to human "to and fro" than the right angle. That flow and movement is, in this design, a characteristic lending itself admirably to life, as life is to be lived in it. The hexagon has been conservatively treated—however, it is allowed to appear in plan only and in the furniture which literally rises from and befits the floor pattern of the concrete slab upon which the whole stands. Heating being no serious matter on the Coast, we have allowed it to go "as is." This model for prefabrication was built by hand, not employing shop methods for which the work was primarily designed. The result is necessarily more expensive than need be were construction to have that advantage.

But the thesis goes far enough to demonstrate the folly of imagining that a true and beautiful house must employ synthetics or steel to be "modern," or go to the factory to be economical. Glass? Yes, the modern house must use glass liberally. Otherwise this house is a simple wood house under a sheet of copper—thin as paper, enough material in the whole construction only to make it substantial. Not a pound to waste. It might be said of this building that it is a plywood house, plywood furnished. To me here is a new lead into a fascinating realm of form, although somewhat repressed on the side of dignity and repose, in this first expression of the idea. I find it easy to take a definite unit of any simple geometric pattern and by modern technologies suited to the purpose, adjusted to human scale, evolve not only fresh appearances but vital contributions to a livelier domesticity. This house goes very far in conservation of space. I hope to demonstrate that no factory can take the house

"Wingspread," Herbert F. Johnson House. Wind Point, Racine, Wisconsin. 1937. Perspective. Pencil and color pencil on tracing paper, 40 x 17".
FLLW Fdn#3703.002

to itself but may itself go to the house. In the hands of one well-versed in the design of patterns for living it may come out continually refreshed by imagination—from within. You prefer what character, what atmosphere, Mrs. Gablemore, Mrs. Plasterbuilt, Miss Flattop? Very well, you shall have it. Only make up your mind as to qualities and character—forgetting that you have "been abroad"—asking only that you get desired character in the qualities you specify. Then you shall have all, with greater convenience and comfort than in the escapist architecture of your escapist lives, today. And have it so much better with so much less waste of money. I am speaking of modern architecture, Usonian, instead of Florentine Mission or Colonial. Or even the Museum style to which the "modern" seems converting the "classics." The new Reality of which I bespeak is in this house, with certain reservations needful at the moment. Appreciative clients not afraid they were going to be made ridiculous were essential to this experiment. Without such help as Paul Hanna and his wife Jean gave to this experiment with their lives, nothing could ever have really happened in that direction. University City would have had just another one of those things—nice things but nevertheless just "things." And we should mention Harold Turner the builder who "took" to

these ideas and did well with them considering the difficulties of this new venture into space-concepts erected in slight materials by new methods entirely.

THE HOUSE of moderate cost is not only America's major architectural problem but the problem most difficult for her major architects. As for me, I would rather solve it with satisfaction to myself and Usonia, than build anything I can think of at the moment except the modern theater now needed by the legitimate drama unless "the stage" is to be done to death by "the movies."

In our country the chief obstacle to any real solution of the moderate-cost house problem is the fact that our people do not really know how to live, imagining their idiosyncrasies to be their "tastes," their prejudices to be their predilections and their ignorance to be virtue where any beauty of living is concerned.

To be more specific, a small house on the side street might have charm if it didn't ape the big house on the avenue, just as the Usonian village itself might have great charm if it didn't ape the big town. Likewise, Marybud on the old farm might be charming in clothes befitting her state and her work, but is only silly in the Sears-Roebuck finery that imitates the clothes of her city sisters who imitate Hollywood stars with

their lipstick, rouge, high heels, silk stockings, bell skirt and cock-eyed hat. Exactly that sort of "monkeyfied" business is the obstacle to architectural achievement in our U.S.A. This provincial "culture-lag" does not allow the person, thing or thought to be simply and naturally itself: the true basis of genuine culture.

I am certain that any approach to the new house needed by indigenous culture—why worry about the house wanted by provincial ignorance—is fundamentally different. That house must be a pattern for more simple and, at the same time, more gracious living: new, but suitable to living conditions as they might so well be in the country we live in today.

This needed house of moderate cost must sometime face reality. Why not now? The houses built by the million, which journals propagate, do no such thing. To me such houses are "escapist" houses, putting on some style or other, really having none. Style *is* important. *A* style is not. There is all the difference when we work *with* style and not for *a* style. But so little honest thought has been allowed to penetrate to living conditions among us that to write about them and even to build for them seems foolish enough although seen to be necessary.

A pressing, needy, hungry, confused issue is the American "small house" problem. But where is a better thing to come from while government housing itself is only perpetuating the old stupidities? I do not believe the needed house can come from current education, from big business, or by way of smart advertising experts. I do not think it will be a matter of expert salesmanship at all unless common sense has dropped to that level in America. It is, first, common sense that might take us along the road to the better thing.

What would be really sensible in this matter? Let's see how far the Herbert Jacobs house at Madison, Wisconsin, is a sensible house. This house for a young journalist, his wife, and small daughter, is now under roof: cost $5,500, including architect's fee of $450. Contract let to Bert Groves.

To give the little Jacobs family the benefit of industrial advantages of the era in which they live, something else must be done for them than to plant another little imitation of a mansion. Simplifications must take place. Mr. and Mrs. Jacobs must themselves see life in somewhat simplified terms. What are essentials in their case, a typical case? It is necessary to get rid of all unnecessary materials in construction, necessary to use the mill to good advantage, necessary to eliminate, so far as possible, field labor which is always expensive. It is necessary to consolidate and simplify the three appurtenance systems—heating, lighting, and sanitation. At least this must be done if we are to achieve the sense of spaciousness and vista already necessary.

And it would be ideal to complete the building in one operation as it goes along, inside and outside. One operation and the house is finished inside as it is completed outside. There should be no complicated roofs. Every time a hip or valley or a dormer window is allowed to ruffle a roof the life of the building is threatened. The way windows are used is naturally the most useful resource to achieve the new characteristic sense of space. All of this fenestration can be made ready at the factory and set up as the walls. But there is no longer any sense in speaking of doors and windows. These walls are largely a system of fenestration having its own part in the building scheme—the system being as much a part of the design as eyes are a part of the face.

Now what can be eliminated?

1. Visible roofs are expensive and unnecessary.

2. A garage is no longer necessary as cars are made. A carport will do, with liberal overhead shelter and walls on two sides.

3. The old-fashioned basement, except for a fuel and heater space was always a plague spot. A steam-warmed concrete mat four inches thick laid directly on the ground over gravel filling, the walls set upon that, is better.

4. Interior "trim" is no longer necessary.

5. We need no radiators, no light fixtures. We will heat the house the Roman way—that is to say—in or beneath the floors, and make the wiring system itself be the light fixtures, throwing light upon the ceiling. Light will thus be indirect except for a few outlets for floor lamps.

6. Furniture, pictures and bric-a-brac are unnecessary except as the walls can be made to include them or be them.

7. No painting at all. Wood best preserves itself. Only the floor mat need be waxed.

8. No plastering in the building.

9. No gutters, no down spouts.

Now to assist in general planning, what must or may we use in our new construction? In this case five materials: wood, brick, cement, paper, glass. To simplify fabrication we must use the horizontal unit system in construction. (See lines crossing plans both ways making rectangles 2 x 4 feet.) We must also use a vertical unit system which will be the boards and batten-bands themselves, interlocking with the brick courses.

The walls will be wood board-walls the same inside as outside—three thicknesses of boards with paper placed between them, the boards fastened together with screws. These slab-walls of boards will be high in insulating value, be vermin proof, and practically fireproof. These walls like the fenestration may be prefabricated on the floor and raised up into place, or they may be made at the mill.

The appurtenance systems to avoid cutting and complications, must be an organic part of construction. Yes, we must have polished plate glass. It is one of the things we have at hand to gratify the designer of the truly modern house and bless its occupants.

The roof framing in this instance is laminated of 2 x 4's making the three offsets seen outside in the eaves of the roof and enabling the roof to be sufficiently pitched without the expense of "building up" the pitches. The middle offset may be used to ventilate the roof spaces in summer. These 2 x 4's sheathed and covered with a good asphalt roof are the top of the house, its shelter gratifying to the sense of shelter.

All this is in hand—no, it is in mind—as we will plan the disposition of the rooms.

What must we consider essential now? We have our corner lot—an acre—with a south and west exposure. We have a garden. The house is wrapped about two sides of this garden.

1. We must have as big a living room with as much garden coming into it as we can afford, with a fireplace in it, and book shelves, dining table, benches, and living room tables built in.

2. Convenient cooking and dining space adjacent to if not a part of the living room. This space may be set away from outside walls within the living area to make work easy. This is a new thought concerning a kitchen—taking it away from outside walls and letting it run up into overhead space with the chimney, thus connection to dining space is made immediate without unpleasant features and no outside wall space lost to the principal rooms. There are steps leading down from this space to a small cellar below for heater, fuel, and laundry. The bathroom is next so that plumbing features of both kitchen and bath may be combined.

3. Two bedrooms and, in this case, a workshop which may be a future bedroom. The single bathroom is not immediately connected to any single bedroom, for the sake of privacy. Bathrooms opening directly into a bedroom occupied by more than one person or

two bedrooms opening into a single bathroom have been badly overdone. We will have as much garden and space in all these space appropriations as our money allows after we have simplified our construction as proposed by way of modern technique.

These drawings represent a modest house that has no feeling at all for the "grand" except as the house extends itself parallel to the ground, companion to the horizon. That kind of extension can hardly go too far for comfort or beauty of proportion. As a matter of course a home like this is an architect's creation. It is not a builder's nor an amateur's effort and there is considerable risk in exposing the scheme to that sort of imitation or emulation. This is true because it could not be built except as the architect oversees the building and the building would fail of proper effect unless the furnishing and planting were done by the architect.

Showing it to you thus briefly may help to indicate how stifling the little colonial hot-boxes, hallowed by government or not, really are where Usonian family life is concerned. You might easily put two of them, each costing more, into the living space of this one and not go much outside the walls. Here is a moderate cost brick and wood house that by new technology of a lifetime has been greatly extended in scale and comfort. A single house. Imagine how the cost would come down were the technique familiar or if many were executed at one time—probably down to $3,500, according to number built and location. There is freedom of movement, and privacy too, afforded by the general arrangement here, unknown to the current boxment. Let us say nothing about beauty. It is an ambiguous term in the provinces of which our big cities are the largest. But I think a cultured American housewife will look well in it. The now inevitable car will seem part of it. Where does the garden leave off and the house begin? Where the garden begins and the house leaves off. Withal, it seems a thing loving the ground with the new sense of space—light—and freedom to which our U.S.A. is entitled.

Architectural interpretation of modern business at its best, this building is designed to be as inspiring a place to work in as any cathedral ever was in which to worship. The building is laid out upon a horizontal unit system twenty feet on center both ways and a vertical unit

of one brick course, three and a half inches. Glass is not used as bricks in this structure; the building becomes by way of long glass tubing crystal where crystal, either transparent or translucent, is most appropriate. In order to make the structure monolithic as possible, the exterior enclosing wall-material appears inside wherever it is sensible for it to do so. Main feature of construction is the simple repetition of hollow slender monolithic dendriform shafts or stems—stems standing on metal tips bedded at the floor level. The structure is light and plastic—reenforcing being mostly steel mesh—welded. The structure is earthquake proof and fireproof, cold and sound proof. Weight, here by way of steel in tension, appears to float in light and air, the "column" taking on integral character as a plastic unit of a plastic building-construction instead of being a mere insert for support. Clerical work is correlated in one vast room, 128 x 228 feet. The great room, air conditioned, is day-lit by rifts in the walls. The heating system of the main building is entirely in the floor slab. This building stands in unimpressive surroundings bounded by three streets, so main entrance is made interior to the lot; the motor car provided for as a modern indispensable. Ample parking facilities are under cover of this carport. The main building is set back from the streets on three sides; a colorful band of growth divides the main walls from the sidewalks, enlivening a dreary environment. Above, the carport becomes a playground for workers. A cinema seating 250 for daytime lectures or entertainment is placed at mezzanine level in the middle of the arrangement. An enclosed bridge connects the officers' quarters in the pent-house with a squash court rising above the garage. Herbert Johnson's office, stenographer and laboratory are at the apex of the pent-house; the other officers are in the wings extending from it. Below this arrangement of officers are the several hundred office workers. Sub-heads of various departments there function in a low gallery, mezzanine to the big room, where direct vision and prompt connection with the workers in the big room is had directly at convenient points by spiral iron stairways. The few enclosures within the big workroom are low glass walls, screened by Aeroshades. Thus the sense of the whole most stimulating to various parts is preserved. The officers' house at the center is wide open

Overleaf: **E. A. Smith House (Project). Piedmont Pines, California. 1939. Perspective. Pencil and color pencil on tracing paper, 22 x 23".** FLLW Fdn#3811.001

HOUSE FOR MR. AND MRS. E. A. SMITH . PIEDMONT
FRANK LLOYD WRIGHT . ARCH

to this big workroom below. The entire building construction, generally by way of cost-plus arrangements, is in the architect's hands—ably managed by Ben Wiltscheck, supervised by the Taliesin Fellowship.

FOREWORD CONCLUDED

Coming back from numerous meetings with young people in the colleges of most of our States, it seems to me that some kind of snubbing post for Usonian youth is urgently needed, where reality is concerned in this functionalistic drift toward realism and realistic. Neither realism nor realistic is the stuff of which the universal is made. As a matter of fact, the universal is made of intense and lively personal matter asking only that the matter have individuality. For a moment, risking offense, let me be personal, as an individual.

Already the architectural matter of this issue of the *Forum* will look out upon a modern-fashioning more in the likeness of the buildings, their interiors, building, and ways of furnishing them—originally designed by myself as early as 1895, getting into their modern stride by 1901 and continuing to this hour.

The ideas taking fresh form then have gone into a twentieth-century designer's world, worldwide.

With a change of labels from a bewildering variety of sources, the forms and features of these original designs are now—with certain sterilizations to make them safe for academic consumption—become modern architecture, modern industrial design, "streamlining" in general: mostly administered by minions "joined up" with our great American advertising order. It never sleeps.

At least enough success is prematurely result to make it apparent that the new simplicity unpretentiously making appearance as early as 1896 may be *the* fashionable eclecticisms of 1938–40. Then God help us all. We shall have sunk beneath the surface of an eclectic's world. Perhaps it is the only possible world.

But to this possibility the matter of this issue still says NO.

What disconcerts me is simply this: the early ideas and ways of planning buildings and building-ways of furnishing them do not seem so much changed for the better. "Effects" have been slenderized and hardened; they have been cleaned up a little, now and then, by unwisely leaving off protective copings, abol-ishing the sense of shelter by concealing it behind parapets; interiors and exteriors have changed superficially (they should have changed fundamentally) with the use of steel, glass, and synthetics; surfaces in general are smoothed out a little by omission of the articulation of materials and their logical protection from the elements. A severe negation of ornament is evident, not a bad negation when ignorance of the nature of ornament generally prevails, as it does. Reaction against that negation, however, is already visible. Sterilized, then, as the order that clings to standardization for life deems suitable, the work, internationally, has been counted sufficient for "new schools." Nothing radical has been done to carry it further afield.

Thus history repeats itself?

NEGATION is easy. Affirmation difficult.

The negation dubbed—by the Museum of Modern Art—"International Architecture" could make no headway unless there were truth in my accusation: "more reflection of surface than substance." How pernicious the notion of "functionalism" as a style! Why turn superficially to a style? The words "integral," "organic," "principle"—basic words concerning our ideal seem never to have occurred as necessary to such language as I have read trademarking that device. Yes, "device"—academic device at that—seeking to make a style when only style is needed. "No ornament?" That collateral fetish is the bastard begotten by intellectualists out of the dogma "Form follows function"; begotten because the abuse of a noble thing was mistaken for the thing itself.

"Form follows function" is but a statement of fact. When we say "Form and function are one"—only then do we take mere fact into the realm of creative thought. I should say that in that difference of statement lies the real difference between organic work, and that of the professed functionalists.

Melodic structure is absent in modern music for the same reason that genuine ornament is absent in "functionalism." True ornament is the inherent melody of structure and functionalism to date is a bad builder.

Russia trying out "functionalismus" proceeded to kick it out. That she should have mistaken it for modern architecture was tragedy for the Soviets.

I have at least ten years more (unless I get a Ford

**Office for Edgar J. Kaufmann, Kaufmann's Department Store.
Pittsburgh, Pennsylvania. 1937. Photograph by Hedrich-Blessing,
courtesy the Chicago Historical Society.** FLLW Fdn FA#3704.0001

up my back, or something) in which to practice the basic principles of an organic architecture. Slowly but surely, often through closed doors, these principles are making way against baldly ballyhooed, badly oversold practices of the unfunctional "functionalist" wing of our cause. For you who sympathize with this ideal of an organic architecture there is not only urgent need for real thought on our part to account for the deeper feeling behind it, but need also for the kind of technical knowledge in hand which only the application of actual principles by way of experience can give. Neither academic formulae nor sloganized dicta can really serve the cause at this time.

Organic architecture is profound architecture. Premature publicizing in this circus-era has some passing value but the fact appears that the deeper the matter, the more undesirable is premature publicity. Notwithstanding rescripts of university education every future architect must develop, in his own grasp, a technology of his own, his hands in work, however limited (the limitations will be his best friends) if technologies he employs are not to defeat the main purpose—a living architecture for our country as a free country.

We speak of genius as though it were the extrusion of some specialty or other. No, the quality is not there. Find genius, and you will find a poet. What is a poet?

If he is a poet he bestows on every object or
  quality its fit proportion—neither
  more nor less.
He is the arbiter of the diverse—the equaliz-
  er of his age and land.
He judges not as a judge judges, but as the sun
  falling round a helpless thing.

How America needs poets! God knows—she has enough profit takers, enough garage mechanics, enough journalists, enough teachers of only what has been taught, enough wage slaves. Without the poet—man of vision wherever he stands—the Soul of this people is a dead Soul. One must be insensible not to feel the chill creeping over ours.

We have technology and technologies to throw away, technicians to burn, but still have no architecture. To show, for them all, we have only a multiplicity of buildings imitating many insignificant countenances or making caricature of the countenance of principle. We need an architecture so rich in the life of today that just because of it life will be better worth living—even though a reeling capitalistic "system" fall flat of its own idiotic excess. Antiseptics are not enough to grow an architecture. Profit-taking as a motive for a civilization does not seem to be the ennobling basis for one.

But I believe, were the "system" aware of it, the capitalists especially would fortify themselves in Architecture that is Organic Architecture.

Having myself had the best and the worst of everything as preliminary to the ten years next to come, I hope none of the years will be wasted or thwarted where architecture, in what remains to us all of life, is concerned.

1. Frank Lloyd Wright to the Taliesin Fellowship, December 17, 1950. FLLW Fnd AV#1014.012, p.2.
2. The original *Architectural Forum* copiously illustrated all the buildings discussed in the article, only a few of which have been included here. The buildings and their dates are as follows: Romeo & Juliet (1886), Malcolm Willey house (1933), Fallingwater (1935), Stanley Marcus house (Texas project, 1935), Ocatilla (1928), St. Mark's Tower (1929), Wingspread (1937), S. C. Johnson Administration Building (1936), Herbert Jacobs house (1936), Paul and Jean Hanna house (1936).
3. The lines above the fireplace read: Oft did the harvest to their sickle yeild [*sic*], Their furrow oft the stubborn glebe has broke; How jocund did they drive their team afield! How bow'd the woods beneath their sturdy stroke!
4. "The Two-Zone House," published in *Taliesin,* vol. 1, no. 1, 1936.
5. Dr. Chandler commissioned San Marcos in the Desert (1927).

SPEECH TO THE A.F.A.

In this address delivered to six hundred architects at the Mayflower Hotel in Washington, D.C., on October 25, 1938, Wright opens with a detailed explanation of his thoughts about Colonial Williamsburg (see also pp. 273–274). He points out that wherever the English went, they brought with them the customs and culture of their native land. In this regard he sees it as tragic that the English, coming to the new continent, did not have the foresight to leave their old customs behind them and seek new forms for a new life on a new hemisphere. Many times he told his apprentices in the Taliesin Fellowship that had the Mayflower *brought one fine architect among its pilgrims to the new world, all would have proceeded differently. As it was, the Colonial, really an English assimilation of French and Italian tastes, became the "style" of the period. The restoration of Williamsburg, fine and well in its authenticity, tended to extend the life of the colonial tradition into modern life. In this regard, he states the case of the "floo-floo bird":*

> *The cultural influences in our country are like the floo-floo bird. I am referring to the peculiar and especial bird who always flew backward. To keep the wind out of its eyes? No. Just because it didn't give a darn where it was* going, *but just* had *to see where it had* been.

But he also expounds the cause of organic architecture and the need for the United States to find a culture of its own. Concerning his own work and efforts to this end, he writes:

> *I persisted with will and patience because there is something compelling in this country, and it is the people of this country. They are right-minded and sincere—at bottom, patient, long-suffering, generous, and wonderful. I love my people as I love architecture. You put those two loves together and what will you get? You will get a way of building born that is an honest way of building and a more genuine life by way of the building. You will see those things we call buildings blossoming into new forms, free patterns for new life and a wide life for all.*

Certainly this is a different direction than that proposed by the restoration of a Colonial village. Wright was addressing architects steeped in the "Graeco-Colonial" tradition, and speaking at a time when the nation was in dire straits with over 30 million unemployed. Indeed, throughout the article Wright refers to the Depression as a "breakdown." [Published in The Federal Architect, *June 1939]*

LADIES AND GENTLEMEN: I HAVE OFTEN SAID THAT IT IS impossible for a man to be a good architect and a gentleman at the same time. But—there you are—out there—so let each man judge for himself of this introduction I have just received and the remarks I am about to make.

I think the first thing we should, perhaps, do here tonight is to get this noisy Williamsburg matter (anyhow in our own minds) on straight. Now, I did *not* say "Williamsburg is all wrong." I did say that it was—Eastern newspaper editorials to the contrary—"quite all right"; but I don't think I meant, when I said that it was quite all right, what Rockefeller meant when he restored Williamsburg. It is an admirable restoration—authentic replica of the setting of our early historic settler's life. As a museum piece it is invaluable to us because it is placed where we can see it and see through it. We may read (as I read there) something of what really was the matter with our forefathers when they got here—the men who came here, rebels against oppression (later to become revolutionists) to find a new and better land. They came and lived within shooting distance of the Indians and brought that culture with them which we now see in detail at Williamsburg. We see that it was all just what they had there, back home. Of course, "back home" is what all Englishmen in foreign lands wish for. If you watch Englishmen conduct their lives as their lives run around the whole world you will find them doing just *what* was done and just as near as possible *as* it was done back home, whether they are doing it in India, Africa, Australia, or at the North Pole. Whatever they did at home, that same thing they do so far as they can do it—South, North, East, or West in the new land in which they find themselves.

Concerning Williamsburg. . . . They there ran true to form. We must say that the restoration *is* a fine museum piece and as such valuable to Americans if they would only let it be a museum piece and not an *illusion,* studying it for what significance it has where our life is concerned, not attempting to live in it, still. As an object lesson to the nation in architecture, it is valuable. Studying the exhibit at Williamsburg closely—from the inside—one may see why and how, now, this nation was contrived by the moneyed man for the moneyed man by the money-minded; see why property was the criterion by means of which this union was to survive, if it could survive at all. You can read in this "search for the elegant solution" that the culture which the colonists had on them, or with them, when they arrived was French culture unified by a century or two of English "taste." England had

little elegance of her own so turned to that of the French, imitated French culture and, inevitably, brought that imitation to these shores. That is plain truth concerning the culture of our colonists. Now, why not, indeed, have a fine restoration of that culture where we can look it in the face for what it is worth today and see what the culture was that lay in behind the culture of a mixed nation such as this one of ours? That early culture, as you will see, had little of reality in it but did have a certain reticence, a fine cleanliness when in poverty and a finer simplicity in general than is generally practiced now. But when, later, modern devotees of English colonial cultural became rich and could spend money like drunken sailors, it is easy to see how and why we got Queen Anne, Medieval Gothic, General Grant Gothic, etc., etc.—"the 57 varieties"—and easy to see why we have all these blind-as-bat government buildings to work in; why, and how, we got the kind of grandomania the government always so generously provides for us, for official purposes especially and for its popular heroes, regardless.

Facing reality as it soon did, how, in actuality, could that colonial culture prove itself equal to the strain soon to be put upon it? You may see the consequences all around you here in Washington. Now, with deeper thought, ignoring colonial *culture* you'll find something in the Colonial life of our forefathers that was clean, something sweet and straightforward, something out of the nature of the true liberal. The ideals of our forefathers were fine and high. And you will see that among them were great men—endowed with greatness and generosity, true aristocrats. That older nation from which they came knew that they were worth having, but didn't know how to keep them.

But unfortunately for the future of the ideals of freedom and democracy, old feudal hangovers from England came along with them. The colonials brought in the feudal land system, the feudal idea of money, the feudal notion of property rights in every thing on earth *as a speculative commodity.* Among these high minded men was one Tom Paine who did know something of a technical basis for the practice of individual human rights. But not until long after the colonial rebels had set up the constitution for this democracy was anything at all written into it concerned with the nature of human rights. Therefore—tonight—

standing here, an architect, I want to speak of the culture of organic architecture as opposed to this culture, we call it "colonial," brought to the great experiment here by our forefathers. It would be silly for me to say "modern architecture" in speaking to you because modern architecture means merely the architecture of today, or architecture à la mode. But, when you say "organic architecture" you immediately run up a flag to the masthead. You use a term that really compels thought. Now, of course, the architecture we had by way of the colonials, nobody has been compelled to think much about. It has not demanded nor has it received any thought at all. Even they had ceased to think about it. Sometimes I think it has gone as far as it has gone only to give a break to the inferior-desecrator and allow educated men to stop thinking, never allowing the nation to begin to make something of itself by way of its own life. Organic architecture is something that must come out of the ground by way of the life of the people—not out of universities. It comes out of the circumstances of the time, the place and the man. Universities do not know it, yet. They do, however, begin to suspect. Organic Architecture rejects Art as a mere aesthetic and clings to the creative evolution of principle.

So today Organic Architecture knows that during all these years we have suffered severely from a dreadful hangover—an illusory dream of culture—to such an extent that light and life have gone out of architecture, gone out of the building itself and the work that makes the building—perhaps for no better reason than because of the superficialities that came over to us in early days as culture, borrowed as they were even then by way of our colonial forefathers. I am not one so silly as to suppose that a man of Thomas Jefferson's calibre, were he living today, would wear knee breeches, buckles on his shoes, powdered hair, lace at throat and wrist and the other elegancies indulged in by gentlemen of his day. He was in advance of the thought of his time. He was leader of his kind in his day. He held in high esteem the generous, fine ideal called then, as now, "Democracy"—an ideal that is about as far from realization now as then, probably. Why has that ideal flourished so little here among us? Why have we so little of it that even England, from whom we received it as a reaction, now has more of it than we? Do we really know why? Can our universities tell us—do you imagine? Ask them!

Because of this deadly cultural lag (for that is what all this is and it is precisely what we suffer from), we have allowed ourselves to learn nothing of architecture. So we at this late day are now where we have to begin at the beginning, because the boys whom we sent to be cultured as architects were never allowed to begin at the beginning. As though some man who wanted to learn to fly had gone to a high precipice to jump off so they went to the top of a tall building to jump off. Well—we have had to begin where they fell. Now organic architecture has come to you out of your own country by way of the circumstances in which our national flag was planted, something natural and genuine out of our own ground has come to be in spite of current education and foolish sentimentality. It is the new reality—and it is a demand for finer integrity than "business" yet knows. You may treat it lightly; you may scoff; you may play horse with it if you wish—but it is the beginning, the rise of a center line of true culture for America.

I am talking of organic architecture for America. But America—I should say—now goes quite completely around the world; probably the America to which I refer can be found more abroad than found at home. This "organic" way is the spiritual way of doing things, a "spirited" way of being and doing that is already going around the world. Sad to admit, however, that if organic architecture is to come home and now live here at home, we must import what we exported. In this matter of architecture we have been turning to Europe for our own export because, it seems, the kind of eclecticism which has flourished so rankly among us can only get a genuine architecture that way. I am not reconciled to that. And yet I know it to be true. And I know that our "learning" is such that it can only arrive at the benefits which come from any pure philosophy of building or being when some hallmark from abroad is upon it: Oxford once but Paris now preferred. Any country other than our own country might do for us to imitate in this matter of culture. Nothing our own, nothing true to ourselves coming from the tall grass out on our great Midwest prairies, could get much credence in our "very best circles." It had to go "abroad" for recognition. So, our own creative effort in architecture has languished here in America as every great idea has languished or died as the price of too much "learning" where there should be *vision*. This peculiar trait of our kind of "learning" brings to mind Lieber Meister's definition of a high-brow: "a man educated far beyond his capacity." I think we as a nation have now been educated far beyond our capacity; educated out of thinking for ourselves, educated away from the things that mean life to the American people. Of course, we have unemployment and misery because we have no ideas by way of which to utilize our sciences and mechanical inventions; no ideas by way of which we might use these newer riches—glass and steel, no honest ideas by way of which these things could come into the possession of the life of the American people. No. Our American people today, being so badly over-educated still lack, most of all, what we properly call culture. The same lack of culture—"the cultural lag"—is here that exists in Russia today—which does not flatter us. Russia—a great nation, 91 percent illiterate (mostly serfs who had far less than nothing) is now free. Eating, during their lifetime, out of the hand of a superior class—seeing what culture the upper classes had—their tall ceilings, glittering glass chandeliers, sensual paintings, statues, with fountains playing on wide terraces: utter magnificence—now what? Can you talk to these freed serfs of simplicity? Can you talk to them of the things of the spirit and mind? You cannot. They want that which they did not have and were subject to when they were slaves—only now they want all of it twice as tall, want twice as many glittering chandeliers, more sensuality, more and bigger statues: more "magnificence," in short. And today, in what we call culture, how much better are we where this cultural lag is concerned? May *we* look down on *them* do you think? Not while Williamsburg is criterion.

Unfortunately nothing in education today genuinely suffices as a solution for this deadly wasteful lag because nothing is being done from the inside out. What have we done with our cultural lag? We have had our way (or will have it) if the education of the corporate, by the corporate, for incorporation doesn't loosen up a little; and it still stands: we've got

it to show for itself in the grandomania of our public buildings, in private "palaces" in these modern equivalents of barons, princes, and dukes, completely *commercialized*. And this deadly lag has not served life well in our case. We are bankrupt, culturally, by way of these hangovers from feudal times; impotent by a silly idealism; made ridiculous by a mawkish sentimentality that will keep on keeping men from demanding their own. The cultural influences in our country are like the floo-floo bird. I am referring to the peculiar and especial bird who always flew backward. To keep the wind out of its eyes? No. Just because it didn't give a darn where it was *going,* but just *had* to see where it had *been.*

Now, in the floo-floo bird you have the true symbol of our government architecture too, and in consequence how discredited American culture stands in the present time! All the world knows it to be funny except America. What prevented us and still prevents us from knowing it? Arm-chair education, let's say. Now, all this has parallels in history. The Romans were just as incognizant as we of the things of the spirit. They, too, had no culture of their own. England had none of her own and we, having none, got what we have as substitute second, third, or fourth hand from them all. Roman culture, for instance was Greek. The Romans did have, however, great engineers (you have all heard of the arch) but what did the Romans do with their greatest invention—the arch? You know well enough that for centuries they wasted it by pasting a travesty of Greek trabeation over it to conceal the truth of structure, until finally, some vulgar Roman, more "uncultured" than the rest, one day got up and said: "Hell! Take it all away! What's the matter with the arch? It's a genuine, beautiful and noble thing"—and finally they got it, got the common-arch as indigenous architecture. We, the modern Romans, probably are going to get architecture something like that same way. We are going to have a true architecture of glass—steel—and the forms that gratify our new sense of space. We are going to have it. No colonial Eden is able—long—to say us nay. Culture, given time, will catch up and assert itself in spite of reaction—even if asserting itself as reaction itself. This thing which we call America, as I have said, goes around the world today. It is chiefly spirit as yet

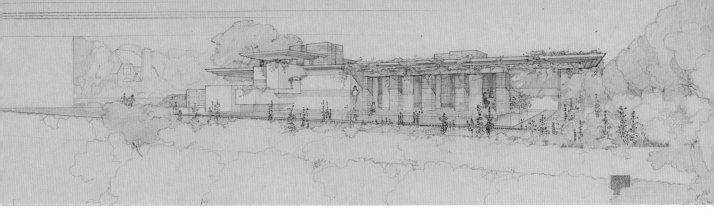

Blackbourn House for *Life* magazine (Project). Minneapolis, Minnesota. 1938. Perspective. Pencil and color pencil on tracing paper, 36 x 24". FLLW Fdn#3806.001

but that spirit is reality. Not by way of Government can we find encouragement of any help. No, we can have nothing by way of official Government until the thing is at least ten years in the past. What can Government do with an advanced idea? If it is still a controversial idea, and any good idea must be so, can Government touch it without its eye on at least the next election? It can not. I know of nothing more silly than to expect Government to solve our advanced problems for us. If we have no ideas, how can Government have any? That is a sensible question to ask, and the answer is that Government as a majority affair can never have any. So I see the tragedy of entrusting to Government billions to spend on billions. Why should Government ever be entrusted to build buildings? Inevitably buildings are for tomorrow. That is the last thing Government should be expected or allowed to do because in entrusting building to Government, we must go 10 or 100 years backward instead of 10 years ahead into the future. Tragic! But to talk against it is so much water over the dam. The driver may not know where to go but he is in the driver's seat. So what?

Perhaps you feel, as I feel in the circumstances, a burning indignation in my soul when I see the desecration everywhere with us in the name of culture and realize it as all our own fault. You know something of the degradation of the cultural fabric of your nation when you see our billions now being spent to give us human slums taken from the region of the body and poverty fixed as an institution in the realm of the American soul. That is what most of this so-called "housing" means to me and what it will come to mean to America in the future. I stand here and challenge our America to reflect that any honest, willing, *busy* workman of today with his family can own no home of his own at all unless by grace and

beneficence of "Government." That should make it time to sit up and raise hell with what made it that way. At least so I think and so you would think if you thought about it at all.

And I will tell you now that when any man in our nation has the courage to stand up and challenge the accustomed and is therefore accused of being a "sensationalist," do not trust that accusation. In the accusation there speaks, usually, the self-styled "conservative" in our country—than which I know of nothing more wearisome as obstruction to growth. By the term "conservative" as in popular use we've come to use it we mean—really, some stand-patter or a lid-sitter, some man who having got his, doesn't want and won't have a change. But truly speaking, a conservative is a radical by nature and character. He can be nothing else. The word "radical" means "of the root," and the word "conservative" means keeping life in the thing conserved—keeping it *growing* in other words. . . . And how can you do that unless you know and understand that thing at the beginning—at the root, that is. How can you consider yourselves "conservative" when you do not know that root, or when you consider that "root" to be money—and having made money are determined by hook or crook, to hang on to it? No . . . "They" so minded have got it all—all wrong. They now remind me of the darky who got the measure of a door by holding his hands just so wide apart. He ran down the street keeping his hands as he had them saying, "Git out de way, ev'ybody, I'se got de measure of a do'!"

Well—yes, the would-be conservative *has* got the measure of a door—and everybody must get out the way as best he can, but he hasn't the actual measure of *the* door. I suppose it is unbecoming, at least ungracious to talk in this way about the people out of whose hands we must all eat as things are with us. I suppose standing here I am biting the hand that feeds me. But perhaps less so than any other architect in America. Nevertheless directly or indirectly we are all eating out of the hand of the man higher up, as he is eating out of the hand above him until finally Government takes a hand. And we call it a system. Well, God knows it is no system. It is an adventitious hangover from feudal times: let's face it. If we had allowed ourselves to learn anything of culture, or if we had a genuine American culture on the way we would now insist upon a more organic structure for our society.

I am not talking to you like this out of any books at all. I am speaking here as an architect who has built more than 200 buildings for his own people, every one of the buildings an honest experiment in behalf of the man it was built for—always building, professedly and openly, as an experiment. To what end? That I might become famous as an architect? That I might make a reputation for myself which I might follow up with profit? No! Not that—I persisted with will and patience because there is something compelling in this country, and it is the people of the country. They are right-minded and sincere—at bottom, patient, long-suffering, generous, and wonderful. I love my people as I love architecture. You put those two loves together and what will you get? You will get a way of building born that is an honest way of building and a more genuine life by way of the building. You will see those things we call buildings blossoming into new forms, free patterns for new life and a wider life for all.

Every decent design for any building should be a design for better living—a better design for a richer, fairer way of life instead of being a shallow hangover from feudal times to please grandmother.

Perhaps this is as good a place to stop as any. I've said very little of what I meant to say. But I do want to say to you that there was—once upon a time—a great "modern" who was less neglected in his time than he would be were he living among us now—Victor Hugo. Victor Hugo had a prophetic mind. He wrote (in the great chapter on architecture which is not in most editions of *Nôtre Dame,* included in some under the title "The Book Will Kill the Edifice") to the effect that late in the 19th century and early in the 20th century, architecture would come alive again into the world after having lan-

guished and all but died for 500 years. I think he based the prophesy on the fact that the 19th century would have given us the new means, new ways he foresaw as "the machine," and that by that time (the 20th century), life would be impassioned again, intolerant of the back drag of old unsuitable forms. Now, bearing him out—in the wake of the printing press—came mobilization, the motor car, electrifications. The little village designed for horse and buggy or foot work, now gives over to a new scale at least 100 times that norm. Multiply the normal speed of movement today by God-knows-what, multiply—say steel and glass, the automobile, the radio, electrical communication—and what might we not have? And yet today the country is littered with the scaffolding of poles and wires, stumpage, dumpage, and ghastly derelicts of all kinds. We might move freely and speak to each other a thousand miles away by a little thing fixed in our coat lapel, provided patents had not been bought up and suppressed.

I wanted to put "cool" light in my latest building, offered the Johnson Wax building for a further experiment to an experiment already used successfully, but I found I could not have it. "General Electric" had bought the patent and was not prepared to give it to the public for two years—or until the way to commercialize the idea could be economically squared. That same thing in more important ways has been going on by utility companies making speculative commodities out of ideas by means of which society lives, moves, and has its being—and that way still is the only way our society has of getting these ideas at all. In fact, life itself is now a speculative commodity unless one has $2,500 a year or more. Then how can you still think of this as "a free country"? Now, what do you, as architects, think of all this?

The only justification I have for being here at all to talk is that I have earnestly tried to do something about it myself. The Broadacre City models were one of the things. And for that I asked of my country—three things—three things I needed for Broadacre City—in order that it might go.

First: Free land to those who could use it. No absentee ownership of land—the land to be held by the *improvements,* not the improvements held by some other holder of the land.

Second: A free medium of exchange. No monster we call money to go on working while we sleep—no more of this thing called money as an accretion, working endlessly for any man good or bad who gets a little of it regardless of his contribution to society. No—because here again is another speculative commodity so artificially set up that it can be thrown behind a vault door and still work for itself. That is wrong. That is a monstrosity.

Third: Let us have done with this making of speculative commodities out of common human needs, this patenting and selling of human ideas (the basis of life itself) by way of which society lives, loves, and has its being. These three things we should ask, we—architects (I am talking as an architect still, and for my country and the people of this country) in order that we may live our own lives *in deed* as well as in theory. As it now stands—architects—I ask you to observe—this country of ours does not own its own ground, unless the banks and insurance companies that do own it are the country. A nation that does not own its own ground has gone far toward extinction as a civilization. We are going there too fast now. If that is not food for thought for any architect—if that does not start him trying to work something out, I do not know what could.

All this may sound like socialism, communism, or what-not. I am no student of socialism, but I am a student of organic structure; and in searching for it in the bases of our civilization today I could not find it. I have read Henry George, Kropotkin, Gesell, Prud-home, Marx, Mazzini, Whitman, Thoreau, Veblen and many other advocates of freedom; and most of the things that applied in those great minds in the direction of freedom as conditions exist for us today point to a great breakdown. Before the long depression we, as architects, did not think much of this—but this is no "depression." It is certainly a breakdown. One that cannot be "fixed" by tinkering. Any architect speaking with understanding, making things stand up by way of the nature of materials and science of structure, his eyes open and on *entity,* must know in head and bones that this is so. Therefore these three freedoms—*free land, free money, free ideas*—we must have or there is no great life to come for this idea we love and are proud to call Democracy.

DISCUSSION

Q. Who should design government buildings—private architects or government employees?

A. Certainly not government employees, because no employee is free to do creative work. And I am not so sure about private architects as they stand at present. I think if we could forget about "official" designing, allowing buildings to be built simply, naturally, by builders—their hands in the mud of the bricks of which the buildings are made, a lot would come out of the ground a little more simply for the honest purposes of life—forgetting entirely "architecture" as we have now come to know it from the books. I think something good might then happen. I think we could somehow get many "traditions" off our necks in order that the great "traditions" might live and we would learn to see that in truth the cultural lag persists and obstructs our path by way of too many little traditions with no great sense at all of Tradition. Then I think what we call great-building might live again among us. But what hope when building has been turned over lock, stock and barrel to college boys who are now in training to the books?

Q. If private capital will only build for profit, and Government will not build except on the old lines, how shall we hope for change in building conditions?

A. That I leave up to you as it is now squarely up to all of us.

Q. You have made obvious criticism of conditions of today—have you anything constructive to offer?

A. I do not think what I have said has reached this gentleman behind the flag of December 7, 1887, hanging over the balcony over his head. So I ask you of what use for me to come here and speak to him? Perhaps he has not been listening. I have said constructive things but there must be a lot of destructive work, much satire before anything can be done in America today that is really constructive. I have planted organic buildings all around the world—over 200 of them I said—themselves in the nature of the thing. If they mean nothing then what can I say that would mean anything constructive?

Q. In domestic architecture, what do you say are the trends for small families?

A. Building small homes for the small families of little or no means is a very definite trend in the life

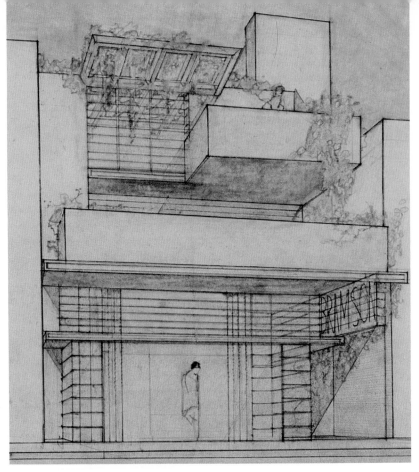

Bramson Dress Shop (Project). Oak Park, Illinois. 1937. Perspective. Pencil and color pencil on tracing paper, 16 x 15". FLLW Fdn#3706.001

of our country now. And—means or no means—I see that everybody is eager for space. The sense of space has become an American characteristic. Perhaps the new ideal of freedom we call Democracy had something to do with it. We will no longer be pigeonholed by way of classic colonialisms or by anything else, I think. My prescription for a modern house? One—a good site. Pick that one at the most difficult spot—pick a site no one wants—one that has features making for character; trees, individuality, a fault of some kind in the realtor mind. That means getting out of the city. Then—standing on that site, look about you so that you see what has charm. What is the reason you want to build there? Find out. Then build your house so that you may still look from where you stood upon all that charmed you and lose nothing of what you saw before the house

was built. See that architectural association accentuates character. Now, if you want a diagram. Just come in sometime!

Q. What do you think of the Jefferson Memorial?

A. Representative Amlie asking the question and he knows damn well what I think of the memorial but thanks to him for the "come on." That belated monstrosity is obviously across the grain of indigenous American feeling for architecture. It is the greatest insult yet and pure extravagance as such.

Q. The highest culture has always been achieved by nations which are almost on the decline, or at least have passed through the many stages of civilization. We are in that era now. Do you think we are justified in expecting the architects to do away with the culture lag?

A. You can wait for the lag to take itself off if you want to. I am not going to wait!

AN ORGANIC ARCHITECTURE

In the spring of 1939 Frank Lloyd Wright was invited by the Royal Institute of British Architects to deliver a series of four lectures and to hold the Sir George Watson Chair of the Sulgrave Manor Board. The last three lectures were prefaced by the showing of 16mm color films of Wright's homes and studios, Taliesin in Wisconsin and Taliesin West in Arizona (in construction at that time). The films were made by James Thomson, an apprentice of the Taliesin Fellowship. The four lectures were transcribed and published in 1939 in book form under the title An Organic Architecture: The Architecture of Democracy by Lund, Humphries, of London. The publisher introduced the lectures with the following observation:

> There is one feature of the lectures which no literary publication alone can convey, and that is the part which his audience played in making these meetings perhaps the most remarkable events of recent architectural affairs in England. No architectural speaker in London has ever in living memory gathered such audiences. The atmosphere was charged with a strange expectancy, not merely caused by the natural curiosity of men to meet in person a seer, the greatest architect of his country, nor even caused by that Athenian curiosity which Englishmen share with their fellow Americans for anything new. Indeed, these audiences, largely of young architects, came with some knowledge at least of Mr. Frank Lloyd Wright's buildings, so that their historical significance rather than their newness may be said to have concerned them. What was far more fundamental to the temper of the audiences than the curiosity or a desire to evaluate works was the modern English architect's hunger for criteria. The audiences, or at least the larger parts of them which were not composed of complacent "traditionalists," were out not just to hear an architect expound his faith, but to catch from his faith every gleam of light that could serve to clarify or direct their own beliefs and practice. And in this Mr. Frank Lloyd Wright can have disappointed few. His critics and questioners were not from the rearguard forces of classicism, as might have been expected, but were people who, being inside the modern movement themselves, were able sympathetically and critically to relate Mr. Frank Lloyd Wright's ideas to their own. It is these, above all, to whom the lectures were given, and who can feel some partnership in the faith that has carried Mr. Frank Lloyd Wright consistently through half a century of practice.

Wright commented on many occasions about the vitality and enthusiasm of the audience, how they not only directed pertinent questions to him, but also argued and discussed among themselves his answers. It was definitely an inspiring audience, and the lectures reflect some of the magnetism and vivacity that prevailed in the hall during those four evenings.

Along with the lectures were many other honors, dinners, and occasions in and about London. With Wright were his wife, Olgivanna, and their daughter, Iovanna.

The next year, sitting in his living room at Taliesin West in Arizona listening to the radio New Year's Eve, 1940, Wright suddenly heard the announcement that King George had selected him, upon the recommendation of the Royal Institute of British Architects, as the King's Gold Medalist for the year 1941. A letter followed from Windsor Castle stating: "The King has been pleased to approve that Mr. Frank Lloyd Wright should be His Majesty's Gold Medalist of the Royal Institute of British Architects, for the year 1941. The Medal will be presented after the war. Signed, Keeper of the Privy Purse." Wright was deeply touched that England, in the midst of a terrifying world war, would look across the sea to a man born on the Midwest prairie and so honor him. [Published with 23 illustrations by Lund, Humphries & Co. Ltd., 1939]

FIRST EVENING

THANKING OUR CHAIRMAN FOR HIS WARM WELCOME, I observe that "we, the British," do things with such imposing formality that already I feel, as I stand here, I ought to be prepared to deliver a studied, formal lecture. Not knowing very well what formal lectures are, however, having attended none in my lifetime, I do not quite know how to give you one. At the outset I may as well confess that I have come here with a minority report: an informal Declaration of Independence. Great Britain had one from us, July 4, 1776: a formal Declaration of Independence which concerned taxes; this one concerns the spirit.

Am I, then, a rebel, too? Yes. But only a rebel as one who has in his actual work, for a lifetime—or is it more?—been carrying out in practice day by day what he believes to be true. British myself—father Yorkshire, mother Carnarvon—fate took me out to the prairies of the Middle West of the United States of America—Usonia let us say—and there in the tall grass I grew up and learned to build, with due credit to a great master, Louis Sullivan.

We were doing fairly well in the States going on toward expression of ourselves as a people with an architecture of our own, when as luck would have it we got our first World's Fair, the World's Fair of 1893. And there, for the first time the United States of America saw architecture as a great orchestration, and loved it, without giving much consideration to its nature, not knowing that it all came to them on tracing paper from dry books, or that as "traditional" it all lay oblique against the grain of our own integral indigenous effort. We had many too-well-educated architects at that time—you know their names, you who are familiar with architecture—and it became quite simple on their part, scholars—all—thus finding architecture ready-made, to sell it on a large scale, conveniently enough, to the American people. Architecture forthwith became a great business in the old forms of grandomania as architects themselves—scholars all—became active brokers. Our "great" architects were, what was not then known, "designing partners," in behind the scenes. Most architectural firms were composed of several men—"architects." There was the "designing" partner who designed the buildings, there was the man who was an engineer and managed somehow to get the imitative buildings—damned things—built by the aid of a contractor—the damn'd. And then there was the general salesman—the jobgetter. I think it was our great architect Henry Richardson who said that "the first principle of architecture was to get the job"!

Therefore, most architecture in our Usonia, after this 1893 World's Fair disaster, was a kind of mongering of that sort. For myself I could never see that such ready-made architecture obtained any great results or had anything to do with our life as our life was lived. I felt sure, even then, that architecture which was really architecture proceeded from the ground and that somehow the terrain, the native industrial conditions, the nature of materials and the purpose of the building, must inevitably determine the form and character of any good building. All this crowding in on the scene, therefore, was a great distress to me. Louis Sullivan, my old master, with whom I had been growing up, had already demonstrated his thought as

Apprentices clearing ground prior to construction; Frank Lloyd Wright's office is seen in the background. Taliesin West, Scottsdale, Arizona. 1937. FLLW Fdn FA#3803.0267

independent and worthy of the attention of his people but this world's-fair wave of pseudo "classic" now an 'ism, swept over and swept us all under. It was years and years before we began to emerge from the undertow of that tremendous backwash. Meantime, keeping on as I could, little by little, step by step, year by year an entirely new idea of building had taken hold of me. I am calling it new, but the idea dates back to at least five hundred years before Jesus. Although I did not know it then, the principle now at the center of our modern movement was very clearly stated as early as that by the Chinese philosopher Lao Tze. The first building which I consciously built as an honest endeavor on my part to express this "new" idea of building was Unity Temple—Oak Park, 1904.

What is that new idea of a building? Well—I have come over here to you hoping to show you something that may make it easier to get this ideal of modern architecture a little straighter in your minds than it seems to me to be. Because of this early endeavor a new countenance definitely showed itself on our Midwestern prairies—the unfamiliar countenance of principle. The countenance soon went abroad by way of Germany and Holland but the principle seems mostly to have stayed at home. You are all familiar now with that countenance as it appeared in several subsequent World's Fairs, Paris first. And in many other modern buildings you may see in every country such appearances as are called modernistic. But the principle is still, so I think, little understood or not at

all practiced. In these conversations therefore I shall endeavor to state as clearly as I can, the center line of principle animating—originally—this ideal so that organic architecture may stand firm against this now world-wide wave of imitation of itself. Unhappily I feel that this great ideal which I so long ago, early in my life came to love and diligently practiced has been betrayed, unintentionally betrayed, but— nonetheless—betrayed by its would-be friends who fell to imitating it without understanding it.

Architecture in Usonia has always imported your traditional forms into our country. First and foremost we had with us (always) the old English Colonial tradition as a stumbling block; the tradition which was responsible for such cultural life as we knew; we had this Colonial tradition to fight then, and we still have to fight it because to this day many of our private and most of our public buildings in the United States try to express this early tradition of yours here in England. And when I come to you in London as I now do, I see nearly everything man-made we possess above our ground here with you in the original. But of course— let us admit it—it was never original with you . . . was it? With you at the time of its adoption it was an eclecticism, too, elected French, I believe. Our Colonial architecture was your Georgian? And your Georgian was French proceeding from Florence—Italy? It is this Italo-French-English architecture which is being largely reproduced in America today. The government is building Cape Cod ("codfish-colonial") houses on

Entry and Frank Lloyd Wright's office, Taliesin West. Scottsdale, Arizona. 1937. FLLW Fdn FA#3803.0112

the prairies of the Middle West to this very day. In Kansas, the Dakotas, and Nebraska you may see these little "Colonial" hot-boxes recently put up by our government regardless, it seems, of nature or of the nature of architecture or of good sense: put up in the name of beneficent "housing."

If we are to live our own lives we must be true, but true to what? Seemingly in this matter of architecture true to the dwindling end of a culture arriving on our shores already degenerate, never having had in it at best more than the moot question of taste, little or no knowledge; no sense of the whole, nothing of real integrity of concept or structure by way of which a new nation might proceed to grow into its own way of life, and by ways of its own establish a culture belonging to itself instead of humbly accepting senility as the fashion.

Now, that old "Colonial" inheritance as we see it in the light of modern times—was tragic. Therefore the Declaration of Independence I bring you today is no mere negation. It is affirmative denial of the validity of any such thing as that servility on this earth and it is assertion of the right of life to live. In England you may proceed with the old traditional forms by which we were corrupted if you like. They are dead but more legitimate here; they are more or less yours, but they are not ours. I declare, the time is here for architecture to recognize its own nature, to realize the fact that it is out of life itself for life as it is now lived, a humane and therefore an intensely human thing; it must again become the most human of all the expressions of

human nature. Architecture is a necessary interpretation of such human life as we now know if we ourselves are to live with individuality and beauty.

The "classic" of course made no such statement; the "classic" ideal can allow nothing of the kind to transpire. The "classic" was more a mask for life to wear than an expression of life itself. Then how much more so was pseudo-classic? So modern architecture rejects the major-axis and the minor-axis of classic architecture. It rejects all grandomania, every building that would stand in military fashion heels together, eyes front, something on the right hand and something on the left hand. Architecture already favors the reflex, the natural easy attitude, the occult symmetry of grace and rhythm affirming the ease, grace, and naturalness of natural life. Modern architecture—let us now say *organic* architecture—is a natural architecture—the architecture of nature, for nature.

To go back now for a moment to the central thought of organic architecture, it was Lao Tze, five hundred years before Jesus, who, so far as I know, first declared that the reality of the building consisted not in the four walls and the roof but inhered in the space within, the space to be lived in. That idea is the entire reversal of all pagan—"classic"—ideals of building whatsoever. If you accept that concept of building classical architecture falls dead to the ground. An entirely new concept has entered the mind of the architect and the life of his people. My own recognition of this concept has been instinctive; I did not know of

Drafting room from Wright's office, Taliesin West. Scottsdale, Arizona. 1937. FLLW Fdn FA#3803.0110

Lao Tze when I began to build with it in my mind; I discovered him much later. I came across Lao Tze quite by accident. One day I came in from the garden where I had been working and picked up a little book the Japanese ambassador to America had sent me and in it I came upon the concept of building I have just mentioned to you. It expressed precisely what had been in my mind and what I had myself been trying to do with a building: "The reality of the building does not consist of walls and roof but in the space within to be lived in." There it was! At first I was inclined to dissemble a little; I had thought myself somewhat a prophet and felt I was charged with a great message which humanity needed, only to find after all, that I was an "Also Ran." The message had been given to the world thousands of years ago. . . . So what? I could not hide the book nor could I conceal the fact. For some time I felt as a punctured balloon looks. But then I began to see that, after all, I had not derived that idea from Lao Tze; it was a deeper, profound something that survived in the world, something probably eternal therefore universal, something that persisted and will persist for ever. Then I began to feel that I ought to be proud to have perceived it as Lao Tze had perceived it and to have tried to *build* it! I need not be too disappointed.

As I found, so you may find, that that concept of architecture alive today as *modern,* is first of all, *organic.* "Organic" is the word which we should apply to this new architecture. So here I stand before you preach-

ing *organic* architecture; declaring organic architecture to be the modern ideal and the teaching so much needed if we are to see the whole of life, and to now serve the whole of life, holding no "traditions" essential to the great TRADITION. Nor cherishing any preconceived form fixing upon us either past, present or future, but—instead—exalting the simple laws of common sense—or of super-sense if you prefer—determining form by way of the nature of materials, the nature of purpose so well understood that a bank will not look like a Greek temple, a university will not look like a cathedral, nor a fire-engine house resemble a French château, or what have you? Form follows function? Yes, but more important now *form and function are one.* When this deeper concept enters the mind it all means this—that imposition upon our life of what we have come to call the "57 varieties" is dead wrong; that classicism, and all ism, is really imposition upon life itself by way of previous education. So I became rebellious where education is concerned, particularly the education of an architect. I believe that architects are born. I much doubt whether they can really be made. I think that if an architect is born and you try to *make* him you are going to ruin him at the present juncture because there is not enough data upon the tables with which you can indoctrinate him and let him live and work. If you are going to teach him, if you are going to tell him, what are you going to tell him and who is going to teach him? What have you in the universities, the academies and the schools—yet—to give to the young architect that is really out of life in this deeper, more valid sense, as he should himself be? What experience have you in architectural schools that is not something *on* life: some armchair theory or an aesthetic pattern of some kind? What I have now said and am going to say of this concept inevitably means the end of architecture and of all art as some fashionable *aesthetic*. Just *that* is our trouble now with the modern movement itself. Instead of taking these principles, following them faithfully and endeavoring to interpret life according to them, it is only the new countenance that is seen, and having been and being bred as eclectics, young architects take the new countenance by selection and election, giving us, by way of it (if they have their way), another style, the 58th variety. Just too bad, because it is no better than before except for novelty and a certain superficial simplicity making plain surfaces and flat roofs an aesthetic.

So far as this 58th variety is concerned, you have some fresh examples in London. You have felt its impact here, and I think that while some of the motives and a certain devotion to the new ideal are there, and the courage and self-sacrifice of the effort therefore to be commended, the principle being absent results are likely to be, for the moment only, disastrous. What they do to London is—well, perhaps London deserves it; I do not know!

Taliesin Fellowship members, Taliesin West. Scottsdale, Arizona. 1940. FLLW Fdn FA#6505.0016

Seriously . . . going back again into the nature of this thing that I would champion, getting back to the minority report—the "Declaration of Independence," we may now ask, independence of what? Well, let me say again, independence of all imposition from without, from whatever sources not in touch with life; independence of classicism—new or old—and of any devotion to the "classics" so-called; independence of further crucifixion of life by current commercialized or academic standards and, more than that, a rejection of all imposition whatsoever upon life; a declaration of independence not only where the cultural lag of our own "old-colonial" traditions is concerned, but also where our educational eclecticism still stands. I am declaring resolute independence of any academic aesthetic, as such, whatsoever—however and wherever hallowed.

We used to guess, to "feel," to predicate and predict, but now we know somewhat. Strange as the assertion may seem, unbecoming and egotistic as it may seem, we do *know*. We now know that we can trust life in this deeper sense. We *know* that life is to be trusted. We *know* that the *interpretation* of life is the true function of the architect because we know that buildings are made for life, to be lived in and to be lived in happily, designed to contribute to that living, joy and living beauty. But, as a matter of fact, all these words—truth, beauty, love—have been so badly oversold by our advertising agents in Usonia (I imagine the same thing applies to England, because I am beginning to see, as I go about among you, that almost everything we do and have, is just about a little England, somehow, somewhere) that I have avoided using the noble words as "suspect" until this moment. Were we to inquire seriously and deeply into the English practice, too, in these verbal matters we should find you guilty not only in much the same sense as ourselves but in many other directions where culture is concerned, I am sure . . . my lords, ladies and gentlemen!

Now, looking backward at the old order it comes to this . . . does it not . . . that instead of going to the fountain-head for inspiration, instead of going to the nature-principle by way of our trust in life and love of life, going there for inspiration and for knowledge, where have we been going? Going to the armchairs of universities, going to their hallowed musty books, going to the famous armchair men who were tutored by armchair men, themselves famous offspring of the armchair. We have been getting mere instruction and dubious formation in this vicarious, left-handed way until the whole social fabric, educated as it is far beyond its capacity, is unable to bear up, longer, under the strain of reality. "Lieber Meister's" definition of a "highbrow" was "a man educated far beyond his capacity," and I can assure you that Usonia is educated far beyond capacity, and that education is not even on speaking terms with true culture at the present time. How much better off you are at the moment remains to be seen by yourselves, my lords, ladies and gentlemen.

And so comes this open challenge to England, no less a challenge to our own nation, yes . . . a challenge to the world at large: this new reality to face and to work out to larger purpose and a better end.

Now, reality is not new except as we are new to reality.

How new we are to reality I think you can all see by looking about you in city streets, in town suburbs or country. And you can see this not only in architecture; you can see it in dress, customs—utilities confused; you can see it just as well in the state of the world at the moment—hysterical, uneasy, an unhappy sense of impending danger and total loss. Everything material is at sixes and sevens with anything spiritual. In short, life itself is at a loss, not at a premium. Glance at yourselves with your "conscription." What does that indicate? What does the whole condition of this world at the moment indicate but the need for some trust in life; for some sense of direction such as our ideal of an organic architecture can give. It is a great peacemaker as well as a great pacemaker because it is constructive.

Out of the ground into the light—yes! Not only must the building so proceed, but we cannot have an organic architecture unless we achieve an organic society! We may build some buildings for a few people knowing the significance or value of that sense-of-the-whole which we are learning to call "organic," but we cannot have an architecture for a society. We who love architecture and recognize it as the great sense of structure in whatever is—music, painting, sculpture,

or life itself—we must somehow act as intermediaries—maybe missionaries. But I know well how dangerous the missionary spirit is; I myself come of a long line of preachers going back to the days of the Reformation. I have seen missionaries miscarry in Japan and I have seen the harm others like them are doing round the world; but for an architecture to come to social being in this sense of an organic architecture we who practice it must inevitably become missionaries to a certain extent. Architects, however, would do better and well enough were they to stick to their own last and do their own work quietly in their own way. I do not suppose that I myself have much right to be standing here preaching and talking to you of all this except as I have done this thing for a lifetime and swear never to try to tell you of something that I myself have not practiced and so do not really know. This talk to you this afternoon, therefore, is not in the least academic. Like many another personal adventure story it will bristle with the personal singular. Never mind. I know of no form of egotism quite so backhand as British humility in the second person plural. Notwithstanding the pain and quite infinite disgust I may occasion certain tenderly nurtured British scholars—these talks are for you for what they may be worth to you.

Language, of course, difficult as it is, is comparatively easy to use; it will always be easier to phrase an ideal than to build it. You will know, if you try it, how difficult it is to build form from the ground, independently, truthfully and sincerely. Until it is done, however, this whole mad world will be just as jittery, jealous, envious, mean and unsatisfactory to live in as it is now.

I do feel, standing here and talking to you from out the field, a busy practicing architect, that here . . . in this ideal of form as organic lies the true center line not only of architecture itself but of indigenous culture throughout the modern world. What we call America already goes round the world. It is a spirit no longer a matter of Usonia, only. I find it here among you and I find it wherever I go. I know it is abroad in the whole of the world and that it needs only the definite lines of actual principle to form this new life that we call modern but which after all is so old, old as life itself, into vital entity—the new integrity. Yes—*integral* is criterion now.

And I will try, in several subsequent lectures, to show how this simple principle of an organic architecture has already gone to work, try to indicate what it is doing and show—on the screen, at least—the difference between buildings informed by that spirit and such buildings as our great cities still put up by government or "by order" and which our great nations build to express the dignity of official authority.

For such an instance, a world-wide one, let us take Michelangelo's dome: the dome of St. Peter's at Rome. Michelangelo was no architect; he was a painter—not a very good one; he was a sculptor and a good one. But he would build buildings and concerning one building in particular he had a grand idea. Now, you must see a dome as an arch, and know, as you do, that an arch is always thrusting outward at the bottom. Any arch whatsoever, must find something to resist that thrust or it comes down. Michelangelo seemed not to care so much about that. Probably he did not know much about it anyway. But this form "the dome" intrigued the man. Originally a dome had haunches well down within the building itself and so was valid architectural structure. But Michelangelo thought it fine to put his grand arch up in the sky on the top of tall posts. He did it. The result was a fantastic, aesthetic sculptural effect, actually nonsensical; a ponderous anachronism. Before the dome had been completed, cracks appeared in its base, and chunks of masonry began to fall. There was a hurried call in Rome for blacksmiths and every one of them got quickly to work to forge a great chain to put round the Angelo dome. The chain got there just in time. It is there yet. Well, the moral is that this singularly bastardized expression of architecture, be-corniced and be-plastered, false, untrue to itself, became the symbol of official authority the world over. We have it everywhere in Usonia. We have it for the nation's Capitol and for the state house and for the county court houses. Even the district likes a dome up on its pilastered offices and big business has tried to steal it although getting along very well, thank you, with medieval mass.

Now as unthinking as that, just as inorganic as that, is all this unthought-out academic building in which we find life embedded today. We no longer think about it at all. Even these buildings we live in, or for, are no longer *thought-built*. In fact, they never were. They were merely *taste-built*. Take your great St. Paul's. Sir Christopher Wren, darling of England (certainly he had the adoration of the people of his day), has built a dome for you patterned after the Michelangelo dome. Sir Christopher had the hardihood to boast that his dome would have stood alone without the chain—but at the same time he used the chain. I mention this as one little minor incident which stands out to show the sort of thing against which organic architecture has had to fight and for no good honest reason must continue fighting.

You may well see that it is quite a "job," this one the young in spirit have on hand; quite a work they now have to do? Some fight this, to clear away our dead past by clear thinking to make way for direct and honest building out of what ground we have to what light there is. No, it is all not so simple, nor is it too difficult. But it cannot be done by the architect alone while our social structure itself is in the same senseless chaotic state. But our spirits are still alive in this rubbish heap professional aestheticism has left to us. The old order passes and the new meantime is groping, growing, hoping to find some way through the heap to something more integral and consistent with the laws of nature; the love of human nature square with human life. We will see what can be done.

SECOND EVENING

As the first line of this, our second talk, and as you see from Jimmie Thomson's fine film, you have no lecturer before you tonight. A worker is in from the field. I could wish that workers came more often from the field to your platform to talk to you straight from experience; talk, firsthand, straight from the shoulder—about what is actually happening out in the world. Over the entrance to the new drafting room we are building at Taliesin, which you have just glimpsed in winter and summer, we are to have the following words carved in the oak wood over the doorway: "What a man does, that he has," and I believe that statement is—not the starting point perhaps, but at least a proper profession of direction for what we call this new adventure into reality, an organic architecture. As I explained in my last lecture, this new architecture is—in truth—an earnest search for reality.

Men and all their things have become so encrusted, so disguised by the pseudo-classic mask which is being worn everywhere people are educated, that the search is arduous.

I suppose essentially the wearing of the mask was and still is defensive tactics of a sort. Having for five hundred years, at least, really created nothing cultural of our own, we have expropriated what we thought was best to take or—more likely—merely what we admired most, and we did the best we could with it. We did very well indeed? England did very well? And France did very well because France sent to the Italians themselves for help to get her Renaissance all on straight! But the English, though less delicate and elegant, did very well with it in England by living in it in the English way and domesticating it. They gave this curious French renaissance of the Renaissance a very homely aspect indeed. What I like most and admire most in your country today is that homeliness which you have known so well how to achieve—in spite of renaissance, mind you, not because of it. It is hard to achieve such homeliness with the new, until God has "made it click" as they say in Hollywood. But we are achieving it, surpassing it, I think, in the Usonian buildings we are now building. The first condition of homeliness, so it seems to me, is that any building which is built should love the ground on which it stands. Too much of the old traditional architecture, certainly the pseudo-classic architecture, and, I would say, what Georgio-colonial architecture we have—a Renaissance of the renaissance of the Renaissance—really hates the ground and looks as though it did so. The house just stands there that way, that's all, and it is the same stance whether it be on a slope or whether the ground be flat, wooded or bare rock. No matter what the topographical conditions are, there the outlines of the same tradition are observed, lengthwise, crosswise—up and down. Usually the entrance is in the center. There are rooms right and rooms left, a wing here and a wing there. You take it all that way or you leave it! If you adhere to that sacred but stupid "tradition" you are, if not admirable, certainly respectable. If you depart from it at all you are a danger, or in danger. But now that is no longer living as we understand living. The reflex of which I have spoken is coming in, and it appears in all the buildings you have

just seen on the screen this evening. If major and minor axes show in such buildings today, it is because that sacrifice happens to be natural in the circumstances. Sometimes major and minor axes are natural, but major and minor axis architecture, as we know it and call it "classic," was never intended to serve life; it was mainly an imposition upon it. We know that now.

The imposition was not made consciously, but there it stood—monarchic and not democratic—not of the life within the building, which if natural would be in the reflex. To put it very simply, that natural reflex expresses very directly the feeling we now have at Taliesin about what constitutes the basis of our buildings. In buildings we are building there the movement has developed and grown up as the trunk of the tree sends out branches and foliage. We practice these principles and ideals every day grappling with life and with nature at first hand in every way possible to us. But nevertheless we have had a too far left wing or branch and we have had a too far right wing or branch. The left wing has taken the aspect of the thing that we loved to practice and with painter-like perspicacity has made of it a mere scene, a superficial style; in other words we have come, by the left, to another superficiality trying to escape reality by the same old practice of art as an aesthetic instead of the feeling that now that the time has come when buildings may be scientifically built, science and art and even religion must find expression, as one, in what we build. The right-wing sees the manner and knowing something of the means proceeds to exaggerate both. Education unfortunately for us now, in our need, has produced only those young men who can do things by election and selection, rather than from within by creative impulse and instinct guided by tested principles.

So, the left wing of this movement, as it has grown up, you may see in the States and every other nation today in the buildings called "modernistic." You have some of them in London, and we have remarked upon what they have done to London. In Russia too there are some. You may see what they did to Russia. The Russians taking one good look at them promptly threw out or were not very kind to the men who built them because, after all, the Russian character being rather wild and romantic, she was impatient of any such importation. And yet, strange to say, having thrown out the one aesthetic aspect of the thing because they did not like it they are now subscribing to an old one, another and a worse. They have gone back to "classic" architecture because knowing nothing, yet, of *organic* architecture they thought these left-wing two-dimensional buildings were modern architecture. And there is danger that in London, you are going on to think the same thing. We at Taliesin see these new buildings, hard, unsympathetic in aspect, thin, as useful negation in appearance but, essentially, merely the expression of another aesthetic, though a better one and not greatly nearer the truth of architecture and no nearer the heart of life than the ornamenta and grandomania that preceded the modernistic.

Inasmuch as modern architecture may be anything built today, and we are talking of organic architecture, let us always say organic architecture. Now let me reiterate—the word "organic" does not, cannot apply to so-called classic architecture in any form whatsoever, and it does not apply to any of the "period" buildings, even the "Georgian" in which we live today. The term does not apply to anything else we happen to have. It would apply however to the old Japanese buildings; Japanese domestic architecture was truly organic architecture. It would apply to certain other periods in the architectures of the world. Egyptian architecture was in a sense organic architecture, an expression of the feeling for human form. The Gothic cathedrals in the Middle Ages had much in them that was organic in character, and they became influential and beautiful, insofar as that quality lived in them which was organic, as did all other architectures possessing it. Greek architecture knew it—not at all! It was the supreme search for the elegant solution.

Working with apprentices as I do, I have observed that when this idea of architecture as organic begins to work in the young mind something happens: something definite happens to life. Something larger happens to one's outlook upon life. One becomes impatient of these unfounded restraints, these empirical impositions, these insignificant gestures as in grand opera, these posturings which all the buildings of the pseudo-classic and pseudo-renaissance assume to be art and architecture. One begins to want something a little nearer to the ground, more *of* life not so much *on* it. We begin to want to live like spirited hu-

man beings. So the first rejection in this new movement, which took place at the beginning, was "the styles," next came the obvious major and minor axis of "classic" architecture. Symmetry and rhythm we wanted, because both are life, but symmetry occult, graceful, rhythm throughout as gracious as may be, but never putting on airs for itself alone at any time anywhere. Always in human scale in all proportions. But the new movement—it is genuinely a "movement"—as an assertion of these principles starting as it did in the tall grass of the western prairies, has in the main become more or less abortive. I myself could be, as I stand here, a bitterly disappointed old man. I am not. I am quite happy and still interested in the thing that I love, because I recognize that any new movement concerning the philosophy of building or being, must because of the character of the education which still prevails amongst us, be exploited, and probably temporarily exploded. We cannot blame young architects brought up at the plan-factory drawing board or by book or become architects by armchair precepts, for getting no further than exterior precedent with new principles. There is very little precedent yet safe to go upon. If they can find a precedent at all they will soon though not intentionally exploit the precedent. So naturally enough we soon have only another drawing-board architecture of a slightly different type of fallacious façade. And, also, we have with us by emulation what, among ourselves, we have come to call the "reformed" or the "deflowered" classic. Today at least that has been our modern movement's influence on the ancient classic orders. The "classic" not yielding a jot where thought is concerned, but by scraping off exterior detail simplifying its aspect to conform to the new aesthetic. Buildings by architects of the old classic school have come to appear more like the appearances of the new simplicity which have arisen. And so we do have some improved effects? I think we all like "deflowered" classic much better than we like the old ornate classic.

So far, so good. And that good is directly due to our new movement. Someone has said, and I think very well said, that radical liberals do their work not so much by growing strong in themselves as by making all others more liberal. Now that much has already happened to our credit. Today we have much in the appearances of the world as direct consequence of the thrust and power of this new idea. But it is not unreasonable to suppose that having that now, we are going further afield with it and putting definite working principles even into our schools. Yet, I wonder whether we are going to have any schools in the near future in the same sense as of old or at present. And I wonder too whether we are going to have cities in the old sense in which we once had cities. Personally I believe both schools and the city to be distinctly dated. The great city, haphazard at best might be possible for what existed at the time, has become scientifically impossible. The horse and buggy, foot-work . . . the enemy just outside the gates? Well once upon a time, close the gates and the enemy could not get in. When life was primitive and things very different mechanically the overgrown city had validity as a necessity. But what validity has the overgrown city now? If we were less habituated, if we were less like sheep, if we had not been made, by years of habitude to imposition, to like it, we could not stand it longer. It is all one's life is worth now to live in any great modern city. Someone has said that to cross the street in New York now, one must have been born on the other side. To get into the now senseless aggregation and to get out of it again takes too much life out of the man. We should soon have in authority developed minds that comprehend the modern sense of spaciousness so characteristic of today now that scientific mechanization is being made available to everyone, rich or poor. We should soon be able to realize that the door of this cage—this thing we call the great city—is at last—open. The door is open and we can fly. We can go from the cage and it can go from itself never to return. We should realize too that gathered together now, in cities, we are frightfully vulnerable; we can easily be destroyed in masses. The enemy still exists; peoples still hate one another so destructive forces are more than ever at large. Once upon a time we defended ourselves by city walls and gates in the walls. We could shut out the enemy. But we cannot deal longer with the enemy in that simple way. More important than this misfortune there is growing up by way of speed and instantaneous interchange a new sense of spaciousness, a new need for the outside coming into the building and for the inside going out.

Garden and building may now be one. In any good organic structure it is difficult to say where the garden ends and where the house begins or the house ends and the garden begins—and that is all as should be, because organic architecture declares that we are by nature ground-loving animals, and insofar as we court the ground, know the ground and sympathize with what it has to give us and produce in what we do to it, we are utilizing practically our birthright. We can go to any place anywhere then and happily be ourselves. But in the overgrown village called a metropolis, now, we have to watch our step, dodge cars, literally take our lives in our own hands to get from somewhere to anywhere—wasting all of our nervous energy and half our time merely to get there and get back again—get back again maybe—keeping up this senseless urban concentration in a pig-piling and scraping, the basis for which disappeared when all these scientific inventions that now threaten us from above and from every side, were made. Do you not think we could with reason expect our architects to take all this in constructively, so that we could get away from all that or have it on more directly humane terms and as soon as possible? By no means is it possible for us to satisfactorily make over our great cities. Reflect that congestion has only just begun! The motorcar Englishman will soon be three out of five. No, by no means is it possible for us to "make over" the old style buildings still called "classic." A fundamental new thought with scientific constructive insight into the nature of the thing to be done and the way of the doing, must save modern humanity from the torture of its self-inflicted misery: that thought is ready to go to work as organic architecture.

It is not enough merely to be sincere about this thing. I think the time has come when one must be intelligent; you, young architects—so many of you there against the walls—you must be able to grasp the meaning of this crisis and learn to proceed from generals to particulars to solve these entirely new equations. Then this movement toward an organic architecture will be a genuine, upward, forward movement of life itself because as its center line, I am sure, henceforward lies the truth of any culture of indigenous character for any people, and anywhere. I am sure it applies in England just as it applies in the United States.

I am chagrined somewhat, to come back here—as I have already said—only to see that nearly everything we have above ground has proceeded from London, has come to us from the United Kingdom; nearly all of our abuses of such culture as we have, nearly all of our bad architecture and a great many of our bad personal habits. Professional humility and overworked pronunciation among them. But I am happy to say that I now see that a great many of our good things came from you too. I could not deny that nor wish to do so. I am glad to say that our English inheritance is the best thing we have, provided we can understand it, see it in perspective—and not be too "awfully had" by it. That is an English expression, is it not? I once heard somebody say in Tokyo: "You know, my dear, I was *awfully had* yesterday, yes, yes *had* awfully." You see I remember it! Now I think we Usonians have been "awfully had, my dear" by our educational, Oxfordian, Cambridgeistic servility concerning "you all" and what you have got in the way you have it. I think Usonians now have something which you in England have yet to get. I think you need that something most of all.

Standing here as I do again today, I am really an emissary of the ground, preaching the salt and savor of a new and a fresh life. I urge you to be a little less self-consciously educated and conservative, to be a little more liberally reasonable, and all of you—every architect included—should—daily for seven minutes if possible—do a little more serious and a little deeper thinking on the subject of what constitutes organic character in economics, in statesmanship, in architecture, yes and why not in salesmanship? True architecture my noble lords, ladies and gentlemen . . . is poetry. A good building is the greatest of poems when it is organic architecture. The fact that the building faces and is reality and serves while it releases life, makes daily life better worth living and makes all the necessities happier because of useful living in it, makes the building none the less poetry, but more truly so. Every great architect is—necessarily—a great poet. He must be a great original interpreter of his time, his day, his age. This afternoon I went to the Architectural Association and spoke to 250 or more young people, just one little handful among all those young architects you are making to help carve out your future for you. There they

were. They were being educated—and how? I do not mean this as a reflection upon them or their teachers in particular, because that condition is one that is now found throughout the world. It is worse in Usonia than it is in England. It is worse with us than it is with you because there is less excuse for it with us.

But what should those boys be doing now if this movement toward organic expression of organic society is to grow? Where should they be? Not there at all. Having ground they should make a plan and working drawings for the work they want to do and the way they want to do it. Somebody should give them that piece of ground; there are so many splendid pieces lying waiting, just for them, here in England. The boys should then go out on that ground and inspired by it—build. And during the building while scheming and scheming while building, meantime designing and drawing, learn something actual with the sweat of the learning on their sun-tanned brows. That, I take it, may not be "education," but it would be culture. And culture is far better—now.

Today, I think, our Usonian educational system and the thing we call culture are not even on speaking terms with each other. And since you, our England, has been our teacher how can it all be different here with you? I have said that it is quite unlikely that a man can be a gentleman and a good architect too, and that is probably true, if we take the accepted sense of the term "gentleman" and the new sense of the term "architect." But you do not see that out of all the professionalizing in this world and out of no professionalist, no life can come now? He—poor man—is *ipso facto*. He was made what he is by what was, but he cannot leave that now, to experiment. He cannot go forward, any more than government can do so. Government—by nature—must be *ipso facto* also. Both, as they stand, and if they are to stand at all, can follow but cannot lead. We in our country for instance have expected our President to have ideas and have browbeaten him senselessly—ceaselessly—because he cannot think of anything we would like to save us. Senseless hatred from those he sought to save was Franklin Roosevelt's fate and I suppose it will be the fate of anybody in a similar position today. Nations have run out of ideas because the individuals composing them have none.

Now you may properly ask where is all this fresh

impetus to come from? Where are we going to find this salt and savor of life that comes fresh from the ground with the needed ideas, coming with capacity for broader applications of those new ideas in order to make of life the thing that really life ought to be under this democratic ideal that we profess and wear as a label? You in England probably have more of the democratic instinct or, let us say, the actual practice disguised by certain superficial dissemblances, than we have in the United States. Of that I am not sure, but I do feel—since knowing you better—that it is possibly true. Why then do you not trust life? Why does not great England on behalf of this great upward swing of life, on behalf of this desire to serve and interpret and develop humanity with fresh integrity; why does England not trust life? After all, it is a good and lordly gesture, is it not? Yes, it would even be a "gentlemanly" thing to do.

Awfully painful this assumption that life is a thief and a liar until it somehow, to your satisfaction, proves itself innocent. That is no proper attitude for gentlemen to take. But it seems to me to have become your attitude. And your attitude is adopted nearly all over the world, as I have seen it. When I got here I was immensely disappointed to see the fear that exists among you. Where is the great old England, standing up, afraid of nothing, magnanimous, splendid, not afraid of life, because she was living? If she still lives why be afraid of anything today, even of a great idea? Certainly not afraid of an aeroplane carrying bombs. After all, airplanes are only a stunt. They can do a deal of damage and perhaps kill a great many women and children, if the world really has sunk so low that warfare must consist in killing women and children. If so then why not kill them all? But I digress a little now; I should not have touched upon this, I know. It was only that I hoped to find something among you over here, that I know *is* here but see submerged for the moment. I know it is here because I am one with it, I know that what I feel, what I desire, what I love and hope for, is just as English as it is Usonian. It is probably also German, probably Italian too. And I happen to know that very largely, way in underneath, it is Japanese. So what? The ideal of an organic architecture for an organic society as the center line of a new culture is inevitably a great peacemaker in the world, because it is genuinely *constructive.*

I have sometimes been called an iconoclast but no such term properly applies to me. I never wanted to destroy anything living nor wanted to take even the dead away unless death became a threat to life. I have had a better thing in a better way in my hand to plant, with the planting of which the living dead interfered. That reasonable destruction by order of nature is the only justification there is for destruction. Perhaps it is all the justification we need.

I am speaking of this new movement, tonight, as the ideal of a life organic, of buildings as organic, of an economic system truly organic. A statesman would be a great architect in this sense of knowing life at its best to be organic. I am speaking to you, therefore, of a great humane ideal. If we are to be served by it, if we are to see it grow, continue to move and come forward, let us divest life and the movement itself, especially of all these equivocal appearances either "left" or "right," and let us get youth to work at it as the center line runs—true. And youth never was nor ever will be a matter of one's years.

Now I have talked enough. Really talking is of very little value, I feel. I am always ashamed to be doing it publicly but . . . still . . . I do it. After I have given a talk of this kind I go home depressed thinking to myself: "Here I am at it again trying, trying, trying, and what is the use?" That, "what is the use" is too English I think. You English listen, you approve, you say, "Yes, that is true," and you do nothing at all about it because a deep pessimism concerning life seems settling down among you if you don't watch out.

I rather gathered from Mr. Wright that cities are a bad institution and that what we ought to do is to go out into the country and live there. Should not we by that means destroy the country and, without making it exactly like a ribbon-developed road, make it lose the character which we want it to have?

That is a sensible question and the supposition that the city is a bad institution now is a natural one. But, as for destroying the country, of course we are not talking about such buildings as now constitute the city moving to the country. God forbid! We are talking about the countryside itself developing into a type of building in which will lie naturally building becoming part of the countryside, building belonging there naturally with grace. Such buildings will exist. There are already a few of them. I too should hate to see these London buildings of yours in the English countryside. English life is all cooped up in them for all your little garden plots outside. These buildings of yours look to me far too pessimistic. They have no appropriate sense of the countryside and lack any modern sense of life whatever. If London were to be preserved as a museum piece by parking its insignificant undesirable portions it would become a great treasure for the future. I should dislike to see it destroyed bit by bit by builders. I should like to see the slums and insignificant parts removed and the precious, historical aspects of old London itself preserved for posterity in a great park, when the people, having learned how to build, go further afield, and all the countryside of England becomes one beautiful modern city, in the new sense, wherein the country was the more beautiful because of the buildings, yes, even the factories. Then they could come back to London and see it for what it once was. That is possible.

What would you do if you had to build something new in an old city? Would you put your own architecture into it or would you think of something which would fit what was there already?

I think that question deals with the problem of the moment: how to continue, in this transitory period, to live in an old city without destroying it with new ideas or abortive old ones. If I were asked to build a building in London as I have said, I should not know what to do. But if I built at all I should try to build something at least not outrageous, something which would least insult and mortify my sense of London. Just what that would be, how do I know! All that is possible now, in the buildings you build in your city, is a kind of merciful mitigation. Nothing thoroughbred of strength and purpose and character can be city-born nowadays. But you can do something to ease off dying and make this old city quite comfortable while it approaches inevitable dissolution.

How would you suggest bringing the countryside into a garden that is a plot 60 or 100 or 200 feet wide? That is a problem which in England is a very great one, as we have everywhere the development of very small plots.

The plot of 60 by 100, or any line-up of plots, is a hideous thing, making larger life impossible at the

beginning. Why should there be such small plots, even in England, for anybody? As for us if everybody in the United States of America had an acre of ground at his disposal, we should not fill the state of Texas alone, and you would be surprised. I am sure, how much everybody might have if you took the population of England and worked out how much ground area would be available to the family provided it was all properly available. When people are huddled together as they are in London it seems as though there was not enough room in all the world for them. But not far away from here, at Richmond, there is a 1,000-acre park! I sat next to a gentleman the other day at dinner who spoke of his 4,000-acre estate. There is plenty of room in the British Isles for British life and British scenery to be none the less desirable.

Is not this ideal of yours entirely against the basic principle of humanity? Is not the basic principle of humanity to herd? Surely human beings still have the desire to herd and not to spread themselves as far as they can from their fellow human beings?

Did I say "as far as they can"? But I think the young gentleman asked a very sensible question. He asserts the herding instinct of humanity as "basic." He thinks we are still like sheep and still have these animal attributes. So we have. But I believe culture—in spite of urban education—has done something for us, and think that culture should and will go on to do more by way of agricultural training. If we are to grow and develop as human beings, by way of that spirit which has been a gift to us, we shall grow less and less like animals and in the light of modern times do less and less "herding." This new philosophic principle of reality, and these great opportunities now for the first time given to humanity by science, resulting in this gorgeous sense of speed and space, is so loved by us, even though we are animals, that by way of these scientific gifts we are going to seek to herd more intelligently, and so, herd less and less. I do not say that we should go as far from each other as possible, but I do say we should go sufficiently far for this modern sense of space and life to be ours, at no one else's expense.

Is it not inevitable that organic architecture will also develop a body of pattern and that there will be dogmas and principles which are not altogether obvious and must be inculcated into students? If the movement is not to dissipate itself in a hundred and one directions, must not it be given some direction and some basic structure?

That is a moot question, and I think an easy way to answer it is by saying: Yes and No. We were all, in Britain as probably in Usonia, educated as eclectics and that inbred eclecticism is become our special touch upon life. And so, general and specific imitation is yet inevitable. People *will* take these ideas and principles and exploit them on the one hand and formulate them for academic training on the other hand. Academies will soon be making *a* style where only *style* itself is needed. In fact, "they" have already done so. But what we have to keep in mind is that we no longer want a style, if that is what you mean by "basic structure." Humanity needs style all the time, therefore needs individuality perpetually fresh and new with every instance in any and every generation in every nation on earth. The law of change is immutable law; the only law we have not taken into account. It is the only law we have not learned to consider and respect when we proceed to make FORM. We have tried to stem and hold in check the tides of life. Now, why go on with it? Why not see that if pattern is to be made at all it must be free pattern, the one most suited to growth, the one most likely to encourage and concede growth to life? That means, I think, the end of the word "institution" as we have it set up. The moment we have any vested or sentimental interest we feel we have to protect it, to guard it, to fend off its enemies by holding it tight. Our thinking, our philosophy, everything we have, is like that "to have and to hold." I am sure you would be surprised to see how effective it might be to reverse that process. If education would learn to do that by way of some true human culture, forgetting its "to have and to hold" precepts and practices, allowing organic culture to come through with its great liberal sense of life, you would find that life can be trusted, perhaps that life is all that can really be trusted. And how interesting you would find its variety of manifestation!

We young people, after a very lengthy training, come out of our schools possibly with some feeling that it has not all been as satisfactory as we should like it to have been, and we go, for instance, to work under a borough engineer or someone like that. While serving the community as far as we can in our position, how are we, after all this education,

to uneducate ourselves in order to serve the community better?

There is only one way to uneducate ourselves. Of course, all things with us are literally and mentally now in pigeon-holes or compartments. For an instance we have the engineer, the architect, the landscape architect, the interior decorator, etc., etc. But, under this thing that I have been talking to you about, a man soon gains a sense of the whole and a feeling of complete responsibility as a unit in the whole develops in him, not to be pigeon-holed. The only way he can "uneducate" himself is by going to work with this new sense growing up in him, getting out to work somewhere where life is actual, not theoretical. In that way, holding to the larger view, he will be likely to forget everything he was taught because what he was taught just would not work.

If you tonight, and on the other occasions when you address numbers of people who are interested in building, achieve in each person a realization of the organic principles of building and life, how would you suggest that we can in this country bring about that realization among the millions of people who have not met you and are not at present architecturally minded? How can we achieve, in a country such as this, within our lifetime, what you would wish to bring about?

Why worry about one's lifetime or too much about the future? Everything that *is*, is right now. If opportunity is mine and I do well with it, next to it another will come to me. The future—beyond that part of it that is seen today—is something we cannot assure nor should we think too much about it. We should consider our present; we should act in the present for the future, the present being the future so far as we can now see. I think we should not be too much concerned about how long growth is going to take or about how difficult it is going to be either here and now or hereafter. If we see it as good it is for us to *act*, now. . . . If my words have conveyed my thought and inspired one single mind tonight I shall be satisfied. One mind is enough.

You have inspired me tonight. You have given me a feeling of space, a feeling that I want to expand and feel things as you feel them. Some day I hope to be given a commission to build something. Assuming that I get that commission, I shall first of all have to please my client and give him what he wants. What I want will probably not be what he wants. If I can get a combination of the two, I shall then be faced with the task of getting my scheme passed by the local authority. Those two obstacles are paramount amongst the difficulties which we architects over here have to face. I am sure that in your early buildings you have faced similar difficulties.

I have and, while vexatious, they are really only difficulties to be overcome.

What I want to know is how you were able to break away originally from what had gone before and evolve the new style of architecture in face of what I call these difficulties.

First, to go back to your fear of your probable client. It is a reasonable fear and one which stands as a specter before many a young man throughout the world today. Fortunately, it did not exist for me. I had to break away from nothing. Things were as they were, I was as I was, and I built as I wanted to build. My client came to me to build for him, so he was mine too. I do not think any architect *could* build for a client across the grain or against his own knowledge or feeling or goodwill. Nor is that to be your job, as I see it. In a case of the sort I think you should say: "I am sorry but I cannot build for you," and wait until some right opportunity does come. Then it will surely come. No man can build a building for another who does not believe in him, who does not believe in what he believes in, and who has not chosen him because of this faith, knowing what he can do. That is the nature of architect and client as I see it. When a man wants to build a building he seeks an interpreter, does he not? He seeks some man who has the technique to express that thing which he himself desires but cannot do. So, should a man come to me for a building he would be ready for me. It would be what I could do that he wanted. I have opened the door and shown many a man out of my office when I found he sought mere novelty and did not understand what I would be doing for him. Only the other day it was the name that interested a client. He was not up to this organic endeavor in building, I knew. And I knew that building for him would be only putting something into his hands that he could not properly live in. So do not despair of the break-away on any account. Every man has his own and his own will come to him, though he may have to wait a long time in England!

Architects are the only people who are taught to plan; no other people in the community are taught anything about planning. It should form a small part of everyone's general education, especially in the case of people who take up politics. I think a Prime Minister or a President who does not know how to plan in the abstract cannot possibly be expected to be able to plan for a community, and I think that the fact that architects are the only people who have any knowledge at all of planning is very unsatisfactory from the point of the community.

I think that is a fact and very unsatisfactory. I believe every man or woman should have included in his or her culture—I will not say their education—some knowledge of planning and of reading a plan. Any really cultivated man or woman should be able to read a plan as easily as a book. When that is the case ideas will flow more freely. What we have been talking about tonight presupposes architecture as the center line of any truly indigenous culture. That being so, it should be just as natural for young boys and girls to learn the nature of the plan and themselves to plan as it is for them to learn to play the piano or the harp, or read Dickens or even read Walt Whitman.

England and America are democracies and we like to think that they are free countries, yet our building is regulated and can be hindered to a large extent by by-laws, regulations and all sorts of conditions. Germany and Italy are under dictatorships; yet we see splendid building schemes going on there and being completed in a very short space of time. Can you suggest a reasonable compromise between those two states of affairs?

I could suggest a basis for compromise, but I do not think that would settle the matter. The building codes of the democracies embody, of course, only what the previous generation knew or thought about building, and the ensuing generation finds the code a stumbling block. When I was called to build the building in Tokyo I could not get a permit to build it. Nor could I get a building permit to build any one of the buildings you have seen in the film tonight. With regard to the building you have just seen finished, the S. C. Johnson Wax building, I could not get full permission to build that either. And we are just building in Philadelphia a little group of houses called the Ardmore Experiment.[1] That experiment could not be passed under the building codes, so we managed to have the code abrogated. It is sometimes necessary to say: "After all, buildings are for life and life goes on. If you want to confine all that the next generation or this generation is going to know about building to what the past generation knew, go ahead and stop our building." But they do not quite like to take that responsibility. We are a little more liberal in Usonia, probably, than you feel you can afford to be here. But this anachronism of which you speak, however, does not arise entirely from the fact that we are democracies and other countries fascist. It arises because we are not genuine democracies: we are in too many ways undemocratic in thought. Democracy is on our lips, an oration on the pages of school books. But we put little of it into active practice. And the illiberal administration of these building codes is due directly to the antiquated educational processes that have produced the men who made the codes.

The desire to hold to rules and regulations that prevent progress is not characteristic of a democracy but, of course, committee work is slow work at best and democracy is a kind of committee at work. Dictatorship is free to abrogate and to say: "This is a good idea; let us have it," and you might wish you hadn't got it. But under the system that you have in England and even the one we have in America it is only rarely that our "rulers" dare to say that, until the matter goes to committee. They, and we, seem to think their countries are democracies when rule is by committee . . . an idea of democracy extremely peculiar, as you will see if you analyze it. Even so. . . . No, I do not think hindering codes are a question of dictatorship as against democracy, but are a matter of present confusion of ideas in our democracies. And fear of any individual's free-will (except the dictator's) on the part of dictatorships. Really there is no good reason why a democracy should not have, and be free to will and to possess the best. Is not democracy the highest form of aristocracy that the world has ever seen—the aristocracy of the man, the individual, his qualities as a man making him the aristocrat? Let us put that kind of democracy into practice somehow in place of snobocracy and the code will be no impediment to better building. It seems a long way to go.

You mentioned in your lecture that there was one justification for destruction, namely, building something better. Do not we come up against that same moot point—who is to decide what is something better? A certain friend of ours on the Continent thinks he has been doing that for some time.

Yes—who is to decide what is better? Well, in a democracy the man decides his own for himself. I would not say that any tribunal would be competent to pass upon the "better" for him. Nor do I think it should be a case of "tribunal," a matter of judgeship or of judging. The time comes when nature herself, the nature of things coinciding with the nature of the man, cries out, demands and determines in its own way. For instance, I think we are there now in this matter of architecture, because of circumstantial changes brought to pass by science.

Do not you think we should design buildings to suit the people who have to live in them and not to please ourselves?

Yes, but as we see suitability, if we are consulted. People who live in buildings know strangely little about buildings, as a rule. They think they know what they want. Sometimes they do. If they come to you, wanting you, believing that you know, they do know that much. But, if they come to you to tell you *how* to build what they want, that is something else. That could not work. In building according to this ideal which I have just propounded I am sure it would not work. Any architect builds a building to please his client, certainly; otherwise why is he architect and the man his client? But were you as an architect to go out seeking a job, go after a piece of work, try to persuade a man to let you build a building for him, then perhaps you would have to please your client against your will, do what he told you, and serve you right, too! But to put yourself there in his power is unethical, of course.

To think and plan nowadays an architect has to have a thorough knowledge of the very complex technique of building, which is becoming more and more complex. Can the average intelligence master all that, or must specialists be employed?

The matter of "experts" seems embedded in "the system" as it exists today. The specialist has arisen because the capitalistic system which we practice needs cogs to make its wheels keep turning. It is true that buildings have become extremely complex, but they have become complex because the system creates its own complexities and confusions. There is no very great difficulty in creating an organism, an entity, in the way of a building in which all needed services are incorporated features of the building. But that type of building, call it creation, cannot be under any "specialistic" system such as that to which you refer. Such creation must occur by single-minded mastery on the part of the creator of the building, and that alone is organic building. We cannot in organic building have a group of specialists; we have to relegate the expert to the back-yard of the building . . . or to oblivion. I like what Henry Ford said about the expert—"if he had an opposition which he wished to destroy he would endow it with experts." I believe that today the expert is the absolute enemy of the thing about which I have been talking to you, and that the more you let him come in and the more you think you are going to get from him the worse off you will be. So I believe an architect should learn the principles underlying the installation of electricity, he should know what constitutes good plumbing, he should be able to invent and arrange and bring all this together as a complete organism. We are talking of an entity when we speak of an organic building; we are not talking of a shell being set up and appurtenance men cutting it half down in order to get their work into it—then the plasterer coming in, daubing it all up—the painter coming in to patch up defects, and so on.

Think of those old five-process buildings! Now we are building one-process buildings and have dispensed with some of the appurtenances; for an instance the heating is underneath the floor now. It had become so difficult to build a building that it was almost impossible to think of building one. And this new thought that I am bringing to you tonight demands first a general simplification in the process of building. The architect must learn to think "in simples" before he can build a modern building worth building.

Much as we might despise and condemn most of the buildings in the suburbs of London, the people living in them think that they are wonderful; they love their houses. Do you suggest that we should take the liberty, the burden and the responsibility of advising them that they are quite wrong, to satisfy our own ideals of what a house should look like?

If I thought the houses were quite wrong, I should certainly tell the people living in them so, if they asked for my opinion. But I do not think I would walk in on them, just to tell them so.

THIRD EVENING

First of all as "hors d'oeuvre" I shall show you some more of the apprentice Jimmie Thomson's film of our work at Taliesin North and West. The modern world is become so picture-minded that it is difficult to get much understanding of anything without pictures. (The film being shown.) The pictures on the screen now show you what we call the Taliesin Fellowship, and show first of all the desert camp on a great Arizona mesa which the boys, together with myself, are now building to work and live in during the winter-time. We work in Wisconsin for only seven months of the year—summer—and for the other five months—winter—we leave that region, where it becomes about 30° below zero and go out to where the sun is shining in the vast desert of the great far West. We have only half-finished building the buildings you see now. Many of the building units have canvas tops carried by red-wood framing resting on massive stone walls made by placing the flat desert stones into wood boxes and throwing in stones and concrete behind them. Most of the canvas frames may be opened or kept closed. In addition to my study which you see to the left there is a large general workroom and there are thirty cubicles for the boys. Instead of sculpture, as you see we have used native rocks written on centuries ago by the American Indians and which we found on our own piece of ground. The camp has grown out of that ground, according to the spirit of environment and climate, although perhaps you may not feel it in that way as I do when you look at it in these pictures. Here comes a detail of the furniture. The furniture goes with the buildings—spawned by it really—but unfortunately, as you have seen, although their skins are, the costumes of our people living there are not yet got into line with the structure. The canvas overhead being translucent, there is a very beautiful light to live and work in; I have experienced nothing like it elsewhere except in Japan somewhat, in their houses with sliding paper walls, or *shoji*.

The film now shows you the native background for our camp buildings, the wonderful skylines with the finest sunshine anywhere unless in Greece. The great cacti you see standing about like monuments are called saguaro. They are one of the few prehistoric plants still existing; they were there when the ichthyosauri were there too. Some of them, still growing, are about six hundred years old.

The pictures now are—in summer—of our real home, Taliesin, Wisconsin. Every boy there has to take his turn at the work which has to be done about the place, and the girls do the same. A boy may be in the kitchen one day and next day driving a tractor, the next day laying stone, but nearly every day he spends some time in the drawing room making plans. It is amazing what the boys accomplish with just a little direction. The leadership rotates from fortnight to fortnight and so all the seniors take a turn in leading the others. We have as little organization as possible—too little, I suppose. We are trying to develop initiative in these young people. We build all the time that we are not drawing or maintaining ourselves and we find it, as a way of life, very interesting. Some of these youngsters will refuse tea in the afternoon in order to keep on working when they are especially interested in what they are doing, as they usually are. It is that special interest in his work which I think immensely important in the education of an architect, getting a feeling of the stone and wood and a sense of construction into his hands on the way to his mind.

Music is a great feature of our lives and, as you see in this portion of the film, we have a little quartette now playing Bach as they often play Beethoven—the two greatest architects I know anything about. All that we ask is action, more action and then some more action. It need not be violent, however, as you see we all enjoy ourselves as work goes along, and part of it takes place in the drafting room every day or any evening.

Taliesin itself is a natural house built of the stone of the region, as you now see, and surrounded with hollyhocks. I believe the hollyhock is considered a weed; at any rate it seems to volunteer all over the world. I have been told that it originated in Asia Minor and in southern Europe but I think the English have made it feel more at home than has any other nation. Most of our ornaments at Taliesin are ancient Chinese like those you are seeing now. They seem to have the modern spirit which characterizes modern

buildings and the more ancient they are the more of that spirit they seem to have! There is room for an argument there, I suppose. Continually we try to keep awake an enquiring, experimental frame of mind. The girls work just as the boys do; we try to make no distinction between them at work although that is sometimes difficult.

I do not want you to have the idea that Taliesin is a school, or a community. It happens to be our home and where we work, and these young people are my comrade apprentices: no scholars. They come to help, and if they can learn—well, we are very happy. There are very many things to do because we have several hundred acres of "farm," and in addition we are practicing architects; we are building at the present time some fifty or sixty buildings all over the United States, so that we are fairly busy. But at the same time we were building this camp in Arizona and extending our own home at Taliesin, we were building the Johnson administration offices, an enormous air-conditioned building, modern in every sense; you will see something of it later, and a number of modest-cost houses as well.

The film stops and Mr. Wright begins his lecture.

The modest-cost-house movement is now the thing we are engaged upon for most of our time. It is really amazing to find how low-cost housing in America is the crying need of the hour; I imagine that we could keep on building such houses indefinitely. I feel that it is the most important field that we have and it has been neglected by our architects. I therefore undertook to build a little $5,500 house in Madison, Wisconsin, and I succeeded in building it without an extra, with nothing whatever for the owner to pay in addition to his $5,500. This "Jacobs House" was a floor-heated laminated-wood-wall house abolishing the hollow spaces made by most wood construction and which, as you know, are an invitation to vermin to come and live with you. Once there, it is hard to get rid of them. The cellular spaces also make the building good kindling wood for fire. We have, therefore, made a thin but solid wall house and by the configuration of the laminated wood walls get strength enough to carry the roof. Most of these houses are of one story but they could be two stories if necessary and are simplified—greatly in plan—all appurtenances made one with the house.

Having built this house some of my colleagues, I am told, said that this was just a stunt and that I would never build another. But, being of the opinion that to build these houses is the one most important thing in our country for an architect to do, I pledged myself to do forty of them. We are now on our twenty-seventh, and I want to assure you that there is nothing more interesting or more important in this world today than trying to put into the houses in which our typical best citizens live something of the quality of a genuine work of art; but nothing is more arduous, nothing is more exhausting and difficult. It would be an exaggeration to say that into one of these little low-cost buildings goes as much thought and effort as goes into a building like the Johnson office building which cost a million dollars. But in any case the effort is disproportionate to the reward as architects practice now. If I were rich or well endowed I would go on building these houses for the rest of my life because from them, I am sure, would begin to flow the better public and industrial building we need so much. But I think something might be done to make an architect's service better worth while on both sides if the importance of it were realized.

Tonight we shall attempt to go on with the practical applications of this new ideal which I have been trying to lay before you. I want to say that I went in so strongly for designing these small houses because I believe that to be one of the most practical of all applications of architecture, in noble sense, today. And it is quite surprising, as well as gratifying, to find how architecture-conscious our young people have become in Usonia concerning this deeper thought in architecture. I go about somewhat among our youngsters, refusing to go more than seven or eight times a year. I have gone to our various universities to talk directly to them about this matter of a center line for indigenous culture and have tried to explain it as simply as I could. The response—I may truly say—has been tremendous. They one and all seem hungry for something, they do not know what but know they are in shallows now. They all feel that what grandmother had and the way grandmother had it was all right because grandmother was all right, but—not just the thing for them now. And that applies to buildings just as much or

even more than anything else. Still more than all does it apply to the life that is just in sight.

Here, owing to the young minds of our nation, you will soon find practical applications of the idea from coast to coast—from Canada to the Gulf. Many examples are already to be found in every state of our Union. Perhaps in England your young people are only just beginning to feel the impact of modern science where and as they live, of mobilization—the motorcar, telephone, telegraph, the radio and television, flying and all these other modern agencies which have made our life in America hold such potentialities, a great spaciousness, a change in human scale which is still resisted by all the ideals which we possessed concerning buildings and life in them. But the young have begun to understand that "the door of the cage we call a city has been left open," and they can go out as they are qualified to go. In our United States of America we are beginning to find practical realizations of freedom in the fact that spaciousness is the great modern opportunity, that human scale *is* grown entirely different and that we no longer need—nor will we—live on little plots of ground with our toes in the street and a little backyard behind us with a few plants in it, shaking hands out of the windows on either side with neighbors good and bad. I have said that an acre to the individual should approximate the minimum and if there are seven in a family that family should have seven acres. An approximation we are trying to bring home to the people of our United States. A practical effort of great importance, I feel sure.

It is difficult to get this application or any keen realization of it because of education, the school training of most of our architects, as I have before said again and again—being backwash. We are just a little newer England, East of Buffalo. New York, that's all, with other nationalities thrown in for good measure. But our old Colonial traditions, fine as they were, were soon, so far as the country went on westward, exploited and exploded. We no longer wear the knee-breeches and the silk stockings and the buckles with the lace at our wrist and neck that went with our forefathers' buildings. Wherever and whenever we build them I wish that we might be compelled to do so. It would be much more consistent with what is being done in certain parts of our East. But really Usonian life has gone far and away by the East now and if English travelers want to see "America" as it really is they must forget all about that. Now, America begins *west* of Buffalo. The greatest and most nearly beautiful city of our young nation is probably Chicago. Eventually I think that Chicago will be the most beautiful great city left in the modern world.

For practical applications of our ideal of an organic architecture these grand western plains with their great sense of space afford us room enough in which to carry out, letter and spirit, my own practical proposal of Broadacre City. To introduce Broadacre City as a "practical application to date" now, may take us too far afield into the future—reserved for our last lecture. But it seems important now. . . . The Broadacre City proposal suggested a new human spacing— as already said—the acre to the individual. To accommodate everyone in our nation on that scale—let me say again, would require only one single state. We should have to take the state of Texas, but the state of Texas would accommodate everybody that we have with a minimum of an acre of land for each and leave the rest of Usonia empty of people. While the proposals cannot be carried out in our lifetime at least it is not, therefore, unreasonable to suppose it practicable to educate people to again proceed in that manner to the ground. I do not believe in a "back to the land" movement; I think that any backward movement would be folly; but if we can go forward to large-scale practical application now with all that science has provided for us—or laid up against us—going forward intelligently to the new forms which *must* be made for the accommodation of life so that men may live more generously, more spaciously and more fully, we shall be dealing—practically—with the actual problem of construction now on our hands. And that is why I shall introduce Broadacre City to you here tonight. The future we see is our present. Any reference to Broadacre City is a kind of preachment I suppose. I think that I received the urge to preach from England, because my forebears were preachers going back to the days of your Reformation. I am aware that it is a bad thing, but here it is and there you are. So if I am to tell you tonight how far we have got with our ideal—I must hold up Broadacre City to you—a little.

You will all hear more about it within a year or two.

I have just spoken to you of the modest-cost house. We have got that movement toward Broadacre City to show already. We never know just where the next development in that connection is going to be. It happens to be at the moment that we are building in Broadacre style a group of eight houses on forty acres, and for whom, do you suppose? For the university professors of the State University at Lansing, Michigan. I call that heaping coals of fire on my own head but practical progress; our professors—philosophy, etc., etc.—are getting Broadacre religion too! In Wheeling, West Virginia (old Colonial stronghold east of Buffalo) we are to build another group which we will call Usonia III. Taliesin is Usonia I and Lansing is Usonia II.

Again, I do not know whether some of you here tonight for the first time are familiar with this word "Usonia" for our country. "United Statesers" doesn't sound well and we are not really entitled to call ourselves "Americans," because we have not a monopoly of that title. The South Americans, as I found when I was in Rio de Janeiro several years ago, resent our use of it; the Brazilians say that they are the Americans. We have therefore to settle a dispute to find a good name for ourselves. Your Samuel Butler called us "Usonians." I think Usonian an excellent name, having its roots in union, as we have our national life in it. So I use the term and hope to get the country used to it in good time. Well—to get back again to practical application of the idea, these various little centers springing up in the Broadacre style are the newer Usonia, expressing the inner spirit of our democracy, which by and large is not yet so very democratic after all, as you may know. I believe there is more the feeling and practice of democracy here in England than with us.

But we are comrades now with England: no longer the little one lost on the prairies, we are coming back to stand shoulder to shoulder with you and I hope we are going some day to take you somewhere in Usonia to see this new expression of life in a democracy—Broadacre City.

If we have found it so very hard to cut through the crust of dead tradition, so hard to throw traditions away in order that the great Tradition may live; you may have some idea how hard it will be to establish such reintegration of life as Broadacre City means. When we try to move we encounter the resistance that will reach you too, indeed I am not sure it does not reach us from you. Were it not for current popular education, Oxfordization in our country, we should be miles along the road toward the realization in that idea of perhaps the greatest architecture the world has ever seen and probably the grandest expression of human life, too, the world has ever seen. But that realization cannot take place except by inches, little by little, overcoming the cultural lag, the educational tenets of yesterday imposed upon life today. In education today what have we—actually—to help realization of Broadacre City? Well, our own country is filled—and this is incidental to my topic, Broadacres, although it may not seem to be—with young but helpless white-collarites all walking the streets looking for a job and not knowing a job when they see it unless it happens to be one of those particular perquisites of education such as selling bonds or stocks or being made agents for selling something somehow, somewhere or becoming an acceptable son-in-law. It has never occurred to these young men, our better-educated young men, scholars and gentlemen at that, to go back to their own countryside, or to go out to the old farms, to go again, enlightened now, to native ground to make life there so beautiful as they might, making their land and buildings and way of life there homely and surpassingly lovely. Were they so minded that would mean the beginning of the actual building of Broadacre City if they would qualify. There in the beauty of vernal countryside today they might so easily have on liberal terms anything a great city has to give them except the gregarious pressures of humanity upon humanity, and such excesses of the herd instinct as are there inevitable. But, tragic as it all is, we must face the fact that even the United States of America now no longer owns its own ground. Its ground has gone into the hands of brokers, banks, insurance companies and other money-lending institutions of our country, until today to find any true popular ownership of ground is rare indeed unless we can get it back again to the people by some such plan as Broadacre City presents.

That senseless unthinking drift toward urbanization, that ceaseless drift from the green country to the hard pavements and overgrown factory industry—that it is that stands principally in the way of what we want to do in Usonia now and where we want to go from where we are, that is to say to Broadacre City. Because of this seemingly hopeless drift toward destruction at the depth of depression—1932—we began to work out at Taliesin this better way of life, a free and a better pattern for living it in a democracy—based upon a true capitalistic system. We thought we ought not to talk much about these things until we could really say what might be a better way of doing the thing we talked about, and so we began a great model, really a cross-section of our complete civilization studying that in much detail. We conceived and modeled in this way better ways of doing nearly everything to be done in it than ways being followed then or now. Soon, however, we came up against the fact that it is useless to attempt to free humanity by way of architecture (organic) so long as humanity itself is inorganic, therefore in jail. So long as nothing else—social—is free, the social mind being essentially in darkness and the economic system knowing only the profit system, nothing of the nature of money, we were faced with one tremendous obstacle after another. Who knew the nature of money? No one seemed to know. Was that ever taught us in school? It seems to have been accepted as an abstraction even by kind old Karl Marx.

And we found that we must have ground free in the sense that Henry George predicated free ground—I am not speaking of the single tax—and we found that we must have not only free ground but free money, that is money not taxed by interest but money only as a free medium of exchange, and as ground would be free to those who could and would use it. Then we ran against another dark-place iniquity, lurking there: the ideas by way of which society lives, moves and has its being, all become speculative commodities. A little further on we began to realize that everything we had to live on—this, remember, was during the 1929–1935 Depression—was some form of *speculative* commodity. We found that life itself with us had practically become a speculative commodity; yes, the matter had gone down so far as that. Of course, having everything in life down on the level of speculative commodity, you would naturally enough have a nation of gamblers; and you would have gambling not only as the principal money-getting device but the great romance of being of a whole people. And that is what the capitalist system (call it capitalistic but it isn't really) became in America. It is very largely so today, perhaps not knowing how to become essentially capitalistic or probably now unable to become so.

An organic architecture may belong to a genuine capitalist system, the base of that system broad upon the ground, but it encounters all this imposition, these gestures, these pretenses, these general inhibitions, these sanctified falsifications—because that is what they are—of the main issue, that issue being a better life for a better man. Now, we realized soon that one cannot spend one's life building buildings for humanity, loving humanity, loving the art of building and inspired by modern opportunity, seeing what it might be and what it might do for humanity, without realizing the iniquity of these establishments or institutions about which I have just been speaking. And I assure you I am not talking out of books; nor am I advancing theories. I am giving to you as simply as I can with the usual bristling personal pronouns the result of a prolonged practical unscholarly effort on our part to build a better basis for building in a better way a better life for a democracy. I am telling you how these certain things we encountered make it unlikely that any such effort should ever generally succeed until changes are effected in our so-called "System" by more intelligent education. I bring that point up tonight because it is really practical, and the sap in the veins of any organic architecture of creative scope and character. How, I ask you, are we to build great free buildings, buildings out of the ground into the light with a new fine sense of spaciousness—apostrophe to freedom for a free people—unless life is itself—free? How are things in detail, economic and social, to be able to add up to a free life and make it happy to live in modern circumstances, realizing the advantages modern science has given us—the enlarged scale of living, the swift clean beauty of speed, of the richness of broadened community contacts and a general or common interest the world over? Nothing does happen or can happen in one corner of the world at any

moment today which may not the next moment be known everywhere. A single decade is today the equal of a past century in point of elapsed time.

Organic architecture in the Broadacre City plans perceives that all our scientific progress has its great romance, its possible beauty. But these must make their way to our lives as a blessing instead of a curse dead against almost everything we call culture and especially against the current of popular education. Again our major effort encounters the terrific cultural back-drag of the scholar. Is the back-drag justified in the United States of America? Is it even justified longer in old England? It is perhaps justified—temporarily—in Russia, where it is seen in a most painful state today. There in the U.S.S.R. we have a great nation, the majority recently serfs. A nation ninety-one percent, I believe, illiterate, therefore young and able now to emancipate themselves. I suppose they are doing what they please, asking for what they want and getting it. Serfs mainly, before they were liberated, they had had less than nothing, eating out of the hand of a superficial upper crust of culture which finally, as it went on, had nothing of great Russia herself in it: becoming merely an eclecticism imported from the European common stock. Those pilastered buildings with lofty ceilings hung with glittering glass chandeliers, Greek statues on balustraded Renaissance terraces with baroque sculptured fountains playing against the tonsured green, in short a form of grandomania which had seized the Western world for five centuries, examples of which you see all over the "great" cities of our civilized world. And dire poverty beyond conception ate out of the hand of that spurious thing. But what do they want now that they are free? What is it "they" are determined to have? Well, they are now determined to have just that very same thing. Talk to them of simplicity? No. Talk to them of organic architecture? Why . . . they would reply, "No, give us this thing that we want." And we find it in the classic! So Russia is getting a revival of the Renaissance now, that was a greater degradation of life than any imposition she revolted against. Every subway station on the underground railway in Moscow more or less resembles a palace with glittering chandeliers, when the subways are popular. Everywhere you go in Russia, soon you may see that kind of thing again especially in the great palace dedicated to WORK. Economic and social freedom here outran culture, hence their own desperate cultural lag.

But really how much better off are we, the great enlightened! How far have we gone, my lords, ladies and gentlemen, with the realization of this great new simplicity I have been putting up to you? Has this new demand for integrity of the form and character of the thing that we must live in and the way that we must now live in it gone much further on with us? Life has not yet gone very far forward with us when we are still back with the Franco-Georgian tradition, and with these great old Renaissance palaces you treasure. Again I ask where did you get them? Ask yourselves where they came from to you in England. I know, as every architect who thinks must know, that buildings of that insane period are no longer treasures, that they were a mere mask upon a meretricious life and are in no sense revealing or evolutionary where modern life is concerned except as a horrible example. We know, if we care to know, that they lack integrity in every sense.

Now, concerning the practical applications of this movement—and it is a world-wide movement at last—I have justly said that many of the buildings built in its name betray the movement. Nevertheless it is a nobler human movement toward a finer integrity on earth than we have had before—this movement that so inevitably has from the very beginning encountered the resistance of the trained, habituated mind of the popular scholar. But, worse than all, it has encountered this self-satisfied superficial bugaboo of "cultivated" taste. I want to reiterate and emphasize that the better buildings of the movement reject that matter as first rejection of all. It is not that the architects of organic buildings do not value good taste: we do believe in developing it, conserving it and respecting it but only when it is in its place—a minor place now, because we believe that if ever this complete circle, science, art and religion as one, is to be struck—we shall have to stop dividing life all up on the surface from the outside and give far less respect to merely taste-built buildings at present and in future. Let us have what good taste there is, but first, I say, let us have the rightminded application to structure of the right idea in the right circumstances. Then by the in-

stinct that is taste carry the expressions of life we call art as high in the scale of things beautiful as you please, beautiful as you know how to make them. God knows how beautiful buildings can be made now, as compared with those either standing or yet to stand inspired by any erudite trifling with outworn, outmoded traditions, whatsoever.

I think I have drifted afield (one of the risks of extemporaneous discourse) and left largely unsaid what I started to say of what has been accomplished to date in the designs of Broadacre City. I shall have to take that up as "continued in our next" because I have talked too long already. But now, I am willing to stand here and "take it from you."

Why do you consider that Chicago is going to be the most beautiful city in the world?

First of all because it has a generous park system, the greatest on earth. You may drive nearly the whole day without going away from the boulevard and park system of Chicago. And the parks are as well looked after as your own London parks which is very well indeed. Another reason is that, thanks to an architect, Dan Burnham, Chicago seems to be the only great city in our States to have discovered its own waterfront. Moreover, to a greater extent than any other city it has a life of its own. Chicago takes pride in building things in a big substantial broad way. Even when the city goes in for gangsters it does so on a big scale, although I think you'll find more gangsters in New York City than in Chicago and a more dangerous gangster mind there too. I deplore its narrow provinciality but I like to go occasionally to New York. But, well, I like Chicago.

Mr. Frank Lloyd Wright has said that houses should be built in order that people might live happily in them and that those houses should be suited to the needs of the family. A working-class family with several children who have to live in three or four rooms can still be very happy, and, since they live in such a small space, they become like sailors on board ship; they learn to respect each other's requirements, and when they go out into the world they are good-natured and have very many qualities which stand them in good stead. I doubt very much whether it would be any advantage to them to have an acre or two, because they could not keep it in order. If the population of England was spread out at the rate of an acre per head, England itself would be ruined as a playground for those who live in the town and take their holidays enjoying the country; there would be semisuburban conditions all over the kingdom. It is different in America, with its large areas.

Another point is that there is no better man than the Cockney soldier and no one who can bear hardship with greater fortitude and cheerfulness. I think that is due to the fact that he has lived what I may call a battleship existence through living in crowded quarters; his wife can lean out of the window and talk comfortably to her neighbor. There is much to be said for such a life. People who may be perfectly happy in such conditions may be led into desiring to have a motorcar and into feeling that they must spend something every time they want to have some pleasure, and I do not think that that is at all necessary. In Colonial times in America the family lived on the farm and made becoming hats out of coonskin with the head in front and the tail hanging down the man's back, and they had buckskin coats and trousers.

Yes Sir, and with that coon-skin cap modern architecture may be said to have begun for the United States of America.

I think that we should have people who will go back to the land and live on farms, making everything for themselves. It means that the women will have to work from morning till night, but they can do it easily if their minds are not on other things. The men will have to work all day as well, and they will not be able to afford to buy newspapers or have a radio or anything of that kind. Provided they are willing to do without those things they can live in the country.

Is that drudge-a-day life the beau ideal, then, of modern civilization—the battleship existence of which you speak? If it is then I think the speaker perfectly right, and suggest that the more we can compress our people the better; the less space we give them the more effective the result will be. And in that case I really do not see why they should need as much space as they have got now; why not put the pressure on still stronger and deprive them of still more, so that they may fight even better? Because they have not known a better life, probably will not know it in this generation or the next, or the next, I suppose where ignorance is bliss, 'tis folly to be wise!

The existence the speaker describes is, however, to me a negation of life rather than any affirmation of it. I deplore the circumstances in which such lives must be spent. It is just that kind of thing that the modern movement and life itself go up against. It is

true that human life may be satisfied or habituated under pressures to adapt itself to whatever circumstances, even the bombing of women and children as modern warfare. But is life to end there? Why did Englishmen go to the new country we call ours now? Why have we this great new nation and this new country? It is because, long ago, Englishmen said No to that idea of yours, sir. Some of them would not accept it. Were they worse men than the Cockney soldier? Even the slums, on your assumption, may be very fruitful. Maintaining them might produce excellent results of which we are not yet aware. Perhaps were we to abolish "the battleship life" of the slums it would do a great deal to abolish war, which would be a great disaster to the human race, would it not? Perhaps the admirable Cockney is a soldier just because of his "battleship existence." Perhaps humanity itself now labors under fearful threat of war because of this ideal disciplinary character of the "battleship-life" lived by citizens in tight quarters and in slums.

I feel, however, that to be humane we must stand for the philosophy of freedom rather than for any philosophy of battleship sacrifice whatever, because what has the fighting Cockney soldier achieved in life, so far, by his fighting except *the need for more Cockney soldiers?*

What worth having has civilization to show gained from these human sacrifices? What? Unless more and more airplanes flying overhead destroying women and children in masses, now legitimate as modern warfare? I can think of nothing more degraded in this world.

I suggest that Mr. Wright's remarks on Russian architecture are rather unfair in view of the fact that the architects of any experience in Russia today are a legacy from the Czarist regime, and that the younger element have not had the experience yet whereby they can produce this new architecture.

I would not wish to say anything unfair to Russia. I admire the spirit of the Russian people, and I believe in the potency of that spirit. I know but little concerning their politics or policies. But I was there two years ago talking with the younger architects, making their acquaintance, and then learned a little of what was going on. It seems their leader, Stalin, said: "Yes, we want simplicity in building for a better life, but remember that this generation fought the war of the revolution; give them what they want now. We will tear it all down again in ten years." I think that, too, is in a way, a fine spirit in advance of our sentimentality that would preserve it indefinitely. Nevertheless I do not believe such temporizing with the future—right.

With the idea of an acre for each person there will be a good many people in agreement, but it would be interesting to know what kind of community life people will have in these circumstances. People cannot merely subsist for themselves; they must have some kind of community life, and I should be interested to know the kind of community life which Mr. Wright has in mind. In Northern Ireland the farms are very small and the people there breed pigs and have sold them with some difficulty in the past, but now the State has worked out a means of educating them in the breeding of their pigs, in the buying of their pigs and in selling them through central agencies, and now the only reason they have for going into the country towns is to go to the "pictures," or to buy a pair of braces, or something like that. The old community is going and a new order is being superimposed on these people. It is very much a matter for a town planner or architect to try to find out what kind of community life these small scattered farmers in Northern Ireland will live, and the same problem will arise in a community where there is an acre to each person.

We who eat pigs should have a care for the breeders of pigs, but we live in a period of transition, and it will take many decades of transition for the outlines of what I have given you as Broadacre City— pigs in place—tonight, to become visible. You must not think the kind of buildings we now have are going to remain, or that community needs as they are now will remain as they are now. They are all going to change as a new and finer type of building in a freer community we do not yet foresee except that it will be more of the country, is growing up. The more of such buildings we have in the country the more beautiful community life will become and the less you will be aware of the fact that buildings are there at all as intrusion.

As for the definite future pattern of the community life in such circumstances, who knows just what any community life of the future is going to be like? The old relationships are bound to change. The motorcar has already vitally affected the rural community life of our States. Even Northern Scotland won't escape in due course. Nearly every man in the States will soon have a car, and today I know of no pig-farmer (we call them dirt-farmers) in my own neighborhood who has not his family motorcar, and perhaps two. I know of none who have no telephone. All have a radio. I know of some who do not care, now, to leave the farm to go into a town to eke out the remainder of their days. The Usonian farm—notwithstanding its mortgage—is by way of becoming the little principality, the unit most desired in our life, just when it is being taken away from the farmer. To say that it has already become so would be untrue. But definitely that is the direction in which things are moving, with no aid from architects and only a makeshift economics. A realization is growing that community life in the sense that it is now lived in small hamlets, villages and cities is going to be no longer necessary, nor as charming as it used to be when it becomes unnecessary. Ease of intercommunication is making ten miles today what two city blocks used to be. As I have said, many times, an entirely new space-consciousness is entering into all of life, town or country. A new human scale has come in that is bound to change community life, changing everything within it. So what community life? If you had parking space and driving space enough for everyone in London even now there would be no London at all, because all there is of London would barely provide the parking space and driving space essential even now. Reflect that the motorcar Englishman has only just begun on London. What will your own urban community life be like ten years from now? What will be the community twenty-five years from now? As architects we must look beyond the tolerances and ignorances of the moment, rural or urban, and try to see the future. If we are not able to see beyond the present and to plan accordingly for the future, I think community life, pigs and goods plus God or leisure, will remain a battleship life and we shall stay where we are—eventually to fight for existence in trenches in our city parks or rot in bombproof cellars.

Mr. Wright said in his lecture that he would leave London as it is, and yet in reply to the last question he said that existing buildings would disappear. That seems a little inconsistent.

I do not see inconsistency. The better parts of London, like so many of our great cities, constitute now the greatest museum piece in the world. Great cities, or the more valuable and historic portions of them, might be just that, were we to keep them as they are as we decentralize. I suggested, our last session I believe, that London, its insignificant parts and slums removed to make room for trees or grass, would make a wonderful park in which the citizens of the newer London might take their recreation, certain parts still habitable. It would not be possible to rebuild London, because a habitable London on modern terms would disappear in the process; there would be no London, so why not leave historic London as historic London?

So I see no inconsistency in what I have said. London buildings, not valuable history, are unfit to go to the country; the dreary miles of gloomy dwellings seem to me more like miserable coops for humanity than buildings with a modern sense of life and space. So destroy all those. Let them disappear because, nevertheless and notwithstanding, there is plenty of room in England for a Broadacre City. I do not believe the assertion that there is not enough room in England for the modern life of which I have spoken. I will mention again the thousand-acre park nearby at Richmond, and the incident of sitting at dinner next to a gentleman who mentioned his four-thousand-acre estate. There are thousands such, where natural beauty would be enhanced not destroyed. I would not destroy the beauty of such estates by taking buildings into them, as London building is now or as London builders are. But I do advocate on the part of architects the development of a fresh sense of the ground, developing landscape rather than destroying it by way of building. There is such a thing as that—I build it, but it is hard to explain in a few words just how I do it. I know such union of countryside and building is coming, and to the enhancement of each, I believe.

It seems to me that if you take away these buildings which you say that you will rebuild, you will destroy your museum piece.

No, I would destroy nothing but London's shame. I suggest you maintain all that is truly "historic." I would destroy the rows and rows of commonplace houses in which people try to live, not those where there was once a glorious life. I would preserve the better houses and palaces, historic old streets and lanes and public buildings and churches.

But if you take away all the squalor and unpleasantness of London, and leave just the historic buildings, what is left of London?

Enough. We occasionally go to the graveyards of our ancestors, so why not to the remains of their cities? But vision which will cut through the weight of their past to the freedom of our future does not come in a moment.

I am not satisfied with the answer given with regard to communal life. If the people of England are to be dispersed over the country in the way suggested, it will require the area of a square with sides 260 miles in length, which will take up most of the country, and even if they are dispersed they will require to join in communities of some kind if any of the country is to be left free. There are some places where houses cannot be built, as on the tops of mountains.

The mountain sites would make the nicest building sites. And I doubt the gentleman's arithmetic. I advocate building (perhaps high buildings) on those portions of the land least useful for other purposes. It is possible to build a building anywhere in this new sense of organic building. You could not build Georgian or Elizabethan or Tudor houses there, but you could build wide-spread ground-built houses such as I have described, or upstanding slender isolated ones.

But let's say, to help along the argument, that the country is coming to the citizen instead of the citizen going to the country. I do not wish to "disperse" any city; decentralization is not dispersal—that is wrong . . . it is reintegration. And whether you believe what I have been saying or do not, the great implements science has put into the hands of humanity are themselves carving out this new city that is to be everywhere and nowhere. They are going to build something like Broadacre City. Architects are not going to build it, I fear, because I see that as they are educated they are not competent even to see it. And so these natural agencies, these tremendous scientific forces, will build it without them but will not lack master builders.

Dispersal is not going to take place, I think. The matter will be more a process of the gradual absorption by integration of inevitable consequences. Little by little people are going to become more and more dissatisfied with increasing urban pressures. Mass education is going to lose its hold on the people as organic culture comes to take the place of such sterilizing education. When culture does come changes are going to take place rapidly because any true form of culture now will work with the law of change, not try to stand against it or fall to its knees shedding tears.

I would ask you all why civilization is everywhere so jittery and miserable today? Is it not because there has been no great vision, no real thought, which wisely accepted the law of change and went along with it, making patterns for life so free that to the life concerned the law of change need not mean unhappiness and torture? The time must come to take this inexorable law as a matter of course into the philosophy and the concrete forms expressing our era. I am one of those who firmly believe that that time is here.

I want you to go a little further than that and come down to practical details. These individuals may be happy on their acres, but they will have to cooperate among themselves.

Yes they will—why not?

But having got the people where you want them. . . .

Not, sir, where *I* want them, but where *they* want to be. If more practical education has not first taken hold of the man to teach him somewhat of the ground and make him a lover of the gifts of the ground (he is a ground animal), nothing much can be done with him except deport him or build a skyscraper in some country park letting him live in that to cooperate in the style to which he is accustomed, all of which is practical enough in the new scheme of Broadacre City, itself a pattern for a free communal life.

When these people are where they want to be, they will have between them some sense of cooperation. Music, the theater and art all need cooperation in some form or other.

Yes—naturally. But in the future more on the air, or chiefly perhaps, because people may not want to leave their complete homes to go to something which they can enjoy much better at home.

In the film we saw your boys playing music on the hill, and they seemed to like it better than the radio.

We could not have music on the radio unless we continued to make it ourselves. I think we need and will always have both at home. But, inevitably, there will develop a new form of community life, but just

what it will be except as Broadacre City tentatively outlines it as free to grow, who can say? Not I. Who is going to say how humanity will eventually be modified by all these spiritual changes and physical advantages, sound and vision coming through solid walls to men, each aware of anything in or of the world he lives in without lifting a finger, making it unnecessary to go anywhere on earth unless it is a pleasure to go. The whole psyche of humanity is changing and what that change will ultimately bring as future community I will not prophesy. It *is* already greatly changed. I see this more plainly in my own country than you can see it in yours. The result of our education is the folly which does not wish to see change nor allow for it as a law of growth. So the young man today is helpless. Knowing nothing of the changing life of organic growth spiritual or material—he is a parasite. Not born a parasite, perhaps, but if he is not so born he is made one to breed one. What then are we to do with community life, say, in a parasitic world for parasites? Well, I can't say. But community life will take care of itself given these amplified, enlivened, widened horizons and conditions I see as inevitable. And for one I believe that community life to come will be much more alive just because it will be less an escape from life. I do not think you or I can know all the details. All either of us need know is the general direction and after that what is coming next in sight.

What part is the appeal to romance going to play in the architecture of the future?

From my point of view as a modern architect, the center of what we call romance has shifted; I find it lying no longer upon the periphery of things. So it is no longer much concerned with taste. I find it as a new sense of reality, a new adventure in a thrilling search for reality. If there is anything more romantic than that, it has not appeared in my life, and I do not think that it will appear in yours—the hazards, the great rewards, the incomparable beauties, the unreasonable punishments, all go to make life romantic. No longer escapist gestures, no longer taste-built, taste-formed ideas, but an earnest lifelong search for that thing growing out of the nature of the thing, not from anything applied to that thing from without.

And now I must ask, at long last, to make an end of this discourse. I have allowed you to go far afield from the original intention for conversation number three and cut well into number four.

FOURTH EVENING

At our last session—the third—we went so far afield with our discussion and got so far into the future that the topic intended for tonight —"The Future"—has been about exhausted. So I shall have to, probably, "sum up." But, as before, we shall begin by showing another and the final installment of the James Thomson Taliesin film. We preface the pictures of our latest buildings as designed at Taliesin by showing you the boys (and girls) working on the farm while carrying on their work in the draughting rooms. As you see, architecture is not simply a drawing-board matter with us; it is a way of life. By doing this outdoor work the boys (some girls too) get the nature of ground into their system and find sweat on their brows excellent for promoting ideas. When I am myself weary of ideas and seem getting a little stale, I go out and pound stone on the new roads, work on the buildings or go out in the fields. I come back refreshed—better able to carry on. We have a 200-acre farm upon which we all work. I have been told that we at Taliesin have been accused of being "escapist," but this rigorous sort of thing as you see it on the screen doesn't look especially escapist, . . . or does it? These pictures appear here preliminary to the conversation that is coming, but they are really collateral. At this moment you see apprentices painting the rebuilt barn by spraying it with red paint. The red barn is one of Wisconsin's greatest assets in her landscape. Nearly all the barns in Wisconsin are similar red (oxide of iron). Now you are seeing the work of rebuilding going on after the dam conserving our water power was washed out and we had to rebuild it. We do not so much mind if something does occasionally fail, because it gives us opportunity to do it over again, and do it better the second time. We learn that way. I am happy to say that although all these Taliesin young people are using machinery and edged tools, sometimes doing things not very safe, during all the six years we have been working there have been no casualties of moment. That speaks well for the correlation of these youngsters. And we are all "self-starters" at Taliesin; we take care of ourselves lengthwise and crosswise, heating, lighting, transport and water system, and have little or no paid help. We feed ourselves, from the ground partly, and entertain ourselves. And we provide for the coming winter in summer. One reason why men from the north are conquerors of the men of the south is because they are perpetually surrounded by circumstances which are inimical to life and have to fend for themselves, meantime providing for themselves when winter comes. The north can never "let go" as the south may, because emergencies are always to be met. On the screen now is a building in The Glen, Bear Run, Pennsylvania. The house is called Fallingwater. Concrete cantilever slabs projecting from the rock bank over the stream carry the living space out over the waterfall. The structure has the usual sense of space. The slabs appear rather gentler than usual because all edges of the copings and overhangs and the slabs of the eaves are all rounded. The slabs are genuine reinforced slabs throughout, doing the work they seem to be doing. Natural stone has been used together with them. The building is very much part of its site. When building such structures it is our custom always to send one of our apprentices to the building on which we are engaged, and there they gain actual experience as work on the building goes along in the draughting room and in the field.

Next we come to a wooden house on a Californian hilltop, built with thin but solid walls of laminated wood, the conformation of the walls devised for strength, the Hanna House—we call it Honeycomb House because the structure was fashioned upon a hexagonal unit system. The hexangle is better suited to human movement than the rectangle.

Next comes one of our houses on Long Island, near New York, cypress-wood boards and battens inside and out, red brick walls likewise. We have used no plastering here. We have eliminated plastering from our buildings wherever possible, using wood boards or plywood instead. Sometimes synthetics are used, and increasingly steel and glass.

Here you see the latest prairie house, the Johnson House at Racine, Wisconsin. We call that house "Wingspread." A house with a great living room with a tall chimney standing up through the center, wings extend from it in four directions; to the left you see the wing (a mezzanine coming into the open living room as a balcony) with rooms for the owner and his wife and his young daughter; to the right is a wing on the ground level for the four boys, a playroom at the far end; another wing is for the servants and their activities and still another for guests and automobiles. The clear-cut sweep of the building is like the many other houses I have thought appropriate to our Midwestern prairies. The ground below the many projecting trellises is planted with wild grape vines. The outside woodwork is two-inch cypress plank, while the brick walls are red and the stone a pink Kasota sandstone. There is the usual feeling of breadth and human spaciousness about it all, and from the house itself the surrounding landscape looks particularly charming. No one noticed that we had a particularly beautiful site until the house was built. Then they began to realize how beautiful it really was. When organic architecture is properly carried out no landscape is ever outraged, but is always developed by it. The side walls of the swimming pool are undercut. The average swimming pool looks to me like a glorified bath tub. There is less sense there of the water than of the basin it is in. With the pool sides undercut you see no walls in the pool but only the water and reflections. This house—"Wing-spread"—has something of the clean-limbed sense of power adapted to purpose which you find in a well-poised plane or ocean liner, but it is no mere aesthetic, it is constitutional, I assure you. This probably is one of the most complete, best constructed and most expensive houses it has ever been my good fortune to build.

Lastly, you are seeing construction photographs of the windowless, floor-heated, completely air-conditioned office building of the S. C. Johnson Wax Company at Racine, Wisconsin, here shown ready for the glass tubing to go in on the skeleton frames. We had to carry out tests before the Wisconsin Building Commission would let us go on with this structure. The dendriform columns you see now are being tested for the Wisconsin Building Commission. They proved to be about six times stronger than needed. I believe this also is one of the best built buildings, technically, anywhere in the world. And I regard it as not only a thoroughly modern piece of work but more nearly exemplifying the ideal of an organic architecture than any other I have built. But perhaps that is only because it is the latest one. There is no feeling of weight when you are inside, mass has vanished, no sense of being enclosed either as you have not been cut off from outdoor light or a sense of sky anywhere.

Now to go on with our last "conversation." Perhaps what you have seen on the screen has given you a little idea of this new way of building about which I have been talking; this feeling for a building as something out of the ground for the life lived in it, a building conditioned by the nature of the materials and the purpose of the thing done, as something actually having a fresh integrity—not theory but practice.

Before we started to look at the screen this evening I said we had dealt with the subject matter of the lecture proposed for this evening, at the last session getting so far afield into the future that perhaps we ought to come back tonight, bring out the keg of nails and with a heavy hammer drive home some technical details. I was again somewhat shocked this afternoon when an ornamentally bewhiskered young man who came to the hotel to interview me, said that he had heard me accused of being "escapist" and would like to have me affirm or deny it. Well, it is probably time I put up some defense, but really I don't know exactly what an "escapist," in his sense of the term, is, nor what it means to be one. I might call him one if I knew. But if he means escaping from the oppression of the dead past into a life more suited to the living present, I plead guilty to the soft impeachment. The basis of the "escapist" accusation may be that at Taliesin we live a pretty self-contained life, devoting ourselves to a life of our own in our own way; you have just seen something of its character on the screen. And if that is escaping from life then I do not know what life is. We intend to head straight into it, all courting it, not afraid of it but eager to explore reality. In fact, I believe Taliesin to be a little research station on the way toward just that—*reality*. We at Taliesin see reality as romance today. We have already found that romance lies no longer on the periphery of life as we see it now man-made, but is something deeper to be independently found within life by living it. I daresay that that is an escape too, but, if so, let's all escape! But, rather, I guess the accusation had reference to some cult of the mind because sentimentality went too far and the "anti's" want to go too far the opposite way now.

Well, during the preceding several evenings I

have said a great deal (but finally you have done considerable talking yourselves) about an architecture in the equivocal circumstances in which we live at present; now we have with us or against us—really—in every branch of culture the precious aesthetic, the high sentimentality in false consideration for the old, the consequent foolish academic unwillingness to bury the dead. Now why this universal reluctance to let the dead past bury its dead? I confess to being in love with fine sentiment myself, but I deny that I am therefore either escapist or a sentimentalist. Since coming to London I have found, as I expected, that the cultured Englishman is the best comrade and most charming company in the world, and I find this dear old London of yours full of pathetic charm and a lively antiquarian interest. I have not been through a museum of any sort for many years and I like it. As such I do not want to see London changed much. I should hate, too, to see this fine museum piece of yours patched up. Why not save it as it is? Why let architects or bombers destroy it?

There was a pleasant little fracas at the English Speaking Union the other evening between your Professor Richardson and others (myself on the side lines). Question: whether London was in more danger from builders or bombers? I took the stand, then, that it is really immaterial. I don't think it matters so very much because I believe London is in danger from neither; London is only seriously in danger from this thing we call Life, life itself, because, let us face it, my lords, ladies and gentlemen, architectural London is senile. London is senile. How can we deny it longer? Now had you a grandmother hopelessly senile, what would be your attitude toward her? It would be one of amelioration and of mitigation, wouldn't it? That should be your humane attitude, and you probably would not embalm her and preserve her in a glass case if she died. As I see it something like that should be your attitude toward London—amelioration, mitigation, honoring old London and leaving it at that, but at last and soon preserving the best of it as memorial in a great green park.

This may seem on the face of it, too simple a solution of all these vexing technical difficulties with the conflicting interests of human nature. But decentralization and reintegration is the one eventual, in-evitable solution not only for London but for every overgrown village in the world today. I know it is hard to accept what I am saying as true, but I am sure that if you do not take the matter of getting away from London into your own hands the natural, mechanistic, scientific forces which are carving out the future whether your architects like it or not (of course they won't like it) will build you a city of the future more akin, I believe, to Taliesin's proposal for a Broadacre City as we discussed it or tried to—somewhat—at our last evening together, than anything we have yet had opportunity to consider as a definite modeling of an advanced idea of good modern life.

Yes, tonight we will recapitulate and—as usual —reiterate. There has been much reiteration in these talks, necessarily. Not one of them has been intended as a proper lecture upon the subject of architecture. Every one of them has been as spontaneous a discussion of its need and place in society as anything may be, not enough studied, but felt very deeply indeed. I stand here before you now for the last time, feeling more deeply than ever about what I have just said to you, about the city for one thing, and also concerning the nature of life in this jam it has got itself into all over the world today. We "humans" are really in a dreadful fix. We are not even so well conditioned as to be between the devil and the deep sea for all our military pomp and show—perhaps because we have gone so far with just that—that we are so utterly bewildered we don't know where we are. The young people whom I meet and talk with as I have gone about our country somewhat, your country too, now, young "educated" people, talking to them as I am talking to you (educated people) now—are all bewildered, eager to know direction forward as I am sure you are. They are pretty sure there must be a better life for them somewhere just as you are sure. As I have said, all of them are educated in the style of some façade and very far indeed beyond their capacity, in Usonia, undoubtedly no more so than in older countries like yours. And all for what? Surely it cannot be that they are educated just for more cannon fodder? Surely it cannot be that they are educated merely for false gods to make just another cog on the too-many wheels of a capitalist system which—let us face that fact too—is really no capitalist system at all. I wish we had a true capitalist system! I believe in a capitalistic system which has its base laid broad upon the ground, its apex high as you please. But here we have one with its apex on the ground and its base well up in the air; something has been going wrong for democracy! For all the swarming everywhere there is no real potence. The potential forces of peace are far greater than those of war, but they have never yet been marshaled in all the colorful beauty of their charm. Love for Joan of Arc will far outlive hatred of Napoleon.

I know little about politics. I confess that I respect politicians not at all. But as an architect studying structure I find it deplorable that no sense of structure as something organic exists today in their minds to make them statesmen so as to help save the life of the world. And I am certain if that sense of structure does not get into action among you soon where will civilization be found? At an end.

Scholarship aside, we can readily understand how architecture got into the fix it is in today when we realize that architecture has been for 500 years merely the application to construction of the revival of some kind of superficial aesthetics, and I believe that same thing goes all the way along the line of our education where our culture ought to be. We have got into the fix we are in in the States because—as I have insisted—the "aesthetic" we accepted came along to our shores as the "Colonial tradition," having in it no knowledge of organic principles, knowing nothing at all upon which a new life on new ground in new circumstances could fashion the new forms it needed to be something organic in character itself. Some form of Colonialism was all we had for culture and you got what you had in much the same way that we got ours. This "ism" went round about the world (and pretty much the same) as some kind of renaissance of many another renaissance . . . many too many. So for 500 years at least, that mere application of taste to circumstances from the outside in a pagan sense, in all the affairs of life, has been what the world of architecture and no less therefore the affairs of men has had to live and grow upon.

In the meantime, what great creative work have we to show as an actual working basis for the life which we have led or as proof of its validity? Not much. No, it was truly an escapist life we have led.

We will find there in that life just application of the word "escapist" if the word has any meaning at all. All of our culture has been this poor secondhand attempt to, on the left or on the right, escape from the actualities of existence by way of taste-created fashionable *illusions.* Spurious education has confirmed the fashionable illusions from generation to generation, confirmed them by book, by order and by reward. Economically, as architecturally, nearly everything with which we started to build the democracy of our United States—like our inherited cultural lag—was a feudal hangover, some unsuitable hangover from feudal times. We began with the great idea of making life an even break for every man, giving every man an equal opportunity before the law. I think it must have been an error when it was written into the Declaration of Independence that every man was born free and equal, because that is pure nonsense. . . . I think that what was meant was that every man is born free and equal before the law. . . . That being so, it did not take long for these hangovers of a feudal age now so freshly set up as the economic basis for the new democracy to allow the wolf and the fox and the rat in human form to be the winners in that new set-up, and they are quite completely the winners now. So were we headed off from any expression of a democratic life very quickly, doomed to defeat even before we began. No wonder we are now stalemate, out of work and utterly bewildered.

Yes, some thinking, some real thought, must enter not only into architecture but also into this thing which we call the economic basis of social life.

No longer satisfied—as bystanders—with looking in from the outside we must enter within as masters by way of some sense of structure such as I have been reiterating during these four evenings. Some deeper thought on our part, even though we are educated, must get inside, penetrate, and from the inside work out the practical new forms suited to genuine democratic life, rational structural forms that will make democracy not something upside down or leave it something merely on the lips, but make it an actual way of life and work, *alive,* and affecting, throughout, every human being today right where he stands.

Occasionally I scan the newspapers and have noticed the way in which democracy is being held up as opposed to fascism. But I think the more you analyze communism, the more you analyze fascism and democracy, the less you will be able to see any substantial differences between them in practice after the theory has evaporated. Now something radical is missing in all this hullaballoo of the *hoi polloi* "press," and so "radical" we must now be. We need honest radicals. England I am happy to say has been hospitable to such. But to mention the word in our pseudo-capitalistic country is like waving a red flag; educated people expect everything to come tumbling down upon them. Ten-to-one they will call the police, "disperse you" or have you arrested. But let us be rational . . . radical only means trying to find out what lies at the root—the word "radical" means "of the root." How much do we of today know of the root? Notwithstanding our "penchant" for history how much have we been taught of roots, the roots of our economic order for instance? Professors in Usonian universities who begin to meddle at the root of anything like that may lose their jobs. Many of them, meaning no harm and not wishing to injure life or humanity, but hoping to benefit it, seek by research to find out something about roots in order that they may teach, but they encounter this opposition from their employers—the system—in a free country, in our own democracy! I know a number of such.

None will say that is admirable, but is it even sensible? Is it longer tolerable? What has brought all this prejudice and fear down upon our heads like tons and tons of collapsed bricks? Why have we not yet the courage of the free? Why are we not yet able to see for ourselves and to stand alone? Why do we not know the nature of these vital things we have been discussing, the inner nature of this thing which we call architecture for one instance? All other life-concerns are the same as that great one or would be in any true democracy! What is architecture anyway? Is it a vast collection of the various buildings which have been built to please the varying tastes of the various lords of mankind? No. I think not. I know that architecture is life; or at least it is life itself taking form and therefore is the truest record of life as it was lived in the world yesterday, as it is being lived today or ever will be lived. So architecture I know to be a great spirit. No, it is not something which consists of the buildings which have

been built by man on his earth. Architecture is that great living creative spirit which from generation to generation, from age to age, proceeds, persists, creates, according to the nature of man, and his circumstances as they both *change*. That really is architecture.

Now in this broad sense do the professors handling the subject for us know much about it? Do they do much for us? We are talking about architecture now as something which has again to come right-side up—for a right-side-up society. Architecture is something we must have right-side up or miss the beat of the rhythms that life has to bring to us, or forever lose something vital and valuable; something for which all that science has been doing so much to accomplish at such frightful cost to us, cannot compensate. Science has done more than much to accomplish miracles which might bless our lives but which are now becoming curses, because culture without creative architecture cannot come along with them to make them blessings. Without creative architecture as the center line of all culture we cannot utilize what science has already done, nor show how to use bountiful scientific results intelligently in even a material way, to say nothing of using them creatively and beautifully.

What prevents this realization and the cultural utilization of science in creating a better tomorrow today? What prevents true statesmen (architects of the social order) from arising among us at a time like this? Why are peoples the world over at the mercy of scheming industrialists and wily politicians? Why do national intrigue and financial plotting come to be accepted as normal statesmanship? Why is it now accepted by civilized nations that women and children may be mass-murdered in their own homes by wholesale mechanical "improvements" as an accepted form of warfare in modern civilization? That murder is lower than anything degraded I can think of in past history. In that crime being tolerated by civilized nations you may see what the status of thought or thinking in such life as ours has come down to be. No nation, no, nor any combination of nations being able to say No to such desperate degradation, what future can we hope for? Well . . . economically our so-called capitalist system may need such degradation and worse to keep going on. That alleged system is of course primarily a matter of money—but, believe it or not, nobody, the "system" least of all, really understands money. During the breakdown in the United States— they liked to call it a depression there, but it was a breakdown—I do not think anyone in our country (or in yours, either) ever heard during that dreadful time one single enlightened official suggestion as to the why or wherefore of the circumstantial mystery called money, nor listened to any sensible remedy in the circumstances. And this was so simply because "they" did not understand the nature of the thing— money. No, "they" did not and do not even yet understand the nature of money. Dear beneficent old Karl Marx and noble Henry George did not understand it either; they accepted it as established abstraction or as something from God. And we have so accepted it. I only mention money as one instance of the lack of any *sense of structure* in economics or society and in this search for organic structure for which I am pleading in architecture. Nowhere is any such thinking in simples operative and effective as we might truly call *practical* today.

Now this costly confusion because of the recent terrible breakdown of all the old theories—economic, social, aesthetic—certainly calls for something from within to come forth and indicate a better way of use and wont; promulgate a way according to nature which primarily will not be afraid of the law of change because that law must be recognized as the necessary inevitable *law of growth*. I believe that what has done most damage to youth in their euphemistic educational training in both our cultural and economic system, is the fact that the "isms" of institutionalism have become habitual and we must fight the "istic" of the "ites" who are all against the vital laws of organic change instinctively—the cowards regarding all changes whatever as enemies. So indeed we are become now all somewhat afraid of change and feel secure only if we know we can keep hands on what we have as we now have it. The more money power we get and keep the more we become stupid stand-patters rather than promulgators of the good life for its own sake. Let our universities realize and teach that *the law of organic change is the only thing that mankind can know as beneficent or as actual!* We can only know that all things are in process of flowing in some continuous state of becoming. Heraclitus was stoned in the streets

of Athens for a fool for making that declaration of independence, I do not remember how many hundreds of years ago. But today modern culture has made no progress in that direction because we took no heed of that courageous declaration and because we became so institutional, so limited in outlook, so filled with fear of life rather than inspired by willingness to trust it, that I am afraid deep distrust of life now is stronger in the United States of America and in England today than ever before. We are afraid . . . cowards . . . yes . . . because we are so busy having and holding (or trying to) that we have not got hold of something deeper and substantial which we must now find, or watch ourselves disappear as a civilization. It is that same something which we must find that I have kept on trying to drive home to you in all these informal egotistic talks. It is that same substantial something which organic architecture has found and although we have so little of it to show, it is finding its place and planting, little by little, round the whole world. But, except for rare exemplars, what can we do with an organic architecture in general as the architecture of a whole people so long as we have no whole people, but have only a society so superficial as ours has become; so ignorant of cause and effect as to be afraid of everything life really is? I have learned in my lifetime that there is only one trust worthy of any man and that is trust in life itself; the firm belief that life is (worlds without end, amen) that you cannot cheat it nor can you defeat it. So far as what education chooses to call culture goes we have been trying all these centuries to beat life and to defeat it, pretty nearly succeeding too. "Authority" has seldom trusted life at any time. We certainly have not trusted life in architecture, nor have we trusted it in economics, and we have not trusted it in politics or statesmanship. We have not trusted it anywhere, no—not even in religion! We talk about God, and we have built all these great architectural sacrifices to God, God being anything other and elsewhere than the life we know and the daily life we live. No wonder we are as we are and not as we must be in order to go on alive—or go dead, to Heaven! And it is of no little significance that one must be dead to go there.

As I go back to my home and to my knitting, go back to Taliesin trying to put these simple things of

Frank Lloyd Wright. London, England. 1939. FLLW Fdn FA#6005.0004

the spiritual life on earth into objective concrete form, trying to bring out subjective truth to make forms and patterns for living more worthy of life, I can only leave with you what I have been saying these past several evenings to help overcome this terrific cultural . . . architectural lag that our science exposes and shames, every nation the same so it seems to me.

The cultural lag has been greatly aided by our wily, wanton, prostitute, social sentimentality. Nor can any aesthetic whatsoever, no matter how mechanistic and hard it may imagine itself to be, save us now. We have to get people, states and buildings *thought-built!* Unless the things of life concerning culture, a natural architecture being first among them, are now thought-built from within, I think we are at the end of the last chapter in . . . is it a great civilization I wonder? Are we perhaps at the tail end of something, dwindling to a conclusion? How many of you can feel that unless we find this upward way from within, life is on the upward rather than the downward grade? For myself, I feel we *must* learn the nature of this organic character and integrity in all that we do *now* or perish. If we do not soon learn to call that learning "culture" we shall soon learn to call what we now call culture, a curse!

Here these suggestive democratic preachments, I am afraid, come to an end. We have no time tonight for many questions. In any case I am not going to let you take me so far afield as you did at our last meeting. But if I have said something tonight which you think not true perhaps you will tell me. I have—all along—seemed to belittle the nature of our time and the great achievements of science, but I have intended to do neither because I believe human nature still sound and recognize that science has done a grand job well; but well I know that science cannot save us. Science can give us only the tools in the box, mechanical miracles that it has already given us. But of what use to us are miraculous tools until we have mastered the humane, cultural use of them? We do not want to live in a world where the machine has mastered the man; we want to live in a world where man has mastered the machine!

At least, or at long last, I have brought you this message; what we call organic architecture is no mere aesthetic nor cult nor fashion but an actual movement based upon a profound idea of a new integrity of human life wherein art, religion and science are one: form and function seen as one, of such is democracy.

Well . . . if you are not ready with questions tonight, I think I would better go. . . .

Thanking you, my lords, ladies and gentlemen—all of you out there, from the bottom of my heart for giving me such indulgent, appreciative audience . . . good-by and good hope!

---

1. Wright called this project "Suntop Homes," a design for four quadruple unit buildings, only one of which was built. The work was commissioned by Otto Mallery and built in Admore, Pennsylvania in 1938.

ARCHITECTURE AND MODERN LIFE: DIALOGUE

The following conversation is the final chapter of Architecture and Modern Life. *Although not "written" by Wright, it is included here as an appendix because the dialogue surveys many of the most prescient ideas of this period in Wright's writings.*

Wright: We have nearly finished this book, Baker Brownell, and our points of view have been too much in accord. Can't we turn up some features of this subject on which we might find ourselves in interesting disagreement?

Brownell: I have always had the impression that we agree on major things but disagree on all minor ones. But there are at least two things left to examine. One is the nature of structure in society and architecture, and the other is a study of ideal structure as it would be in existence, as, for instance, in Broadacre City. Our book has moved along from one aspect of structure to another in society and architecture. Now what is structure?

Wright: Well, since we have been talking about architecture and structure, it might be interesting to examine an example of structure where it is really an interpretation of a social condition—democratic, of course. It is the ideal we profess, isn't it? So let us consider this example of democratic structure.

Brownell: Before we do that, I wish to ask this question: What is structure? Is it here in the room? Is it out there in the hills and pastures? Your room here, due to some structure that you have given it, moves out among the cedars and birches on the slope. It is part of them. As I look out of the window at the hills of the Wisconsin River across the way from Taliesin, they seem to me to have structure. So does that Ming jar standing on the stone pier of your terrace. The ideas that we are now discussing also have structure—at least I hope so. But what is structure?

Wright: It is pretty hard to take the word "structure" apart. Webster makes a failure of it. The word itself stands as a necessary symbol of a factual condition.

Brownell: I admit that structure in things is a fact, but that does not tell much about its nature, it seems to me.

Wright: When we say "structure" we speak of the nature and character of an organism, do we not?

Brownell: The character of an organism . . . there is something in your phrase that reveals a great deal about structure. But doesn't it reveal something that you see rather than something that you think or make conceptually clear? Can't we simplify and sharpen it? It seems to me that when we speak of structure we are speaking of the composition of parts to make a whole.

Wright: The word composition can hardly be used in connection with structure in the organic sense. Its features, parts, fibers, tissues become a constitution in a genuinely creative sense.

Brownell: Do you mean by constitution, the relationship of the parts to each other? Or do you mean something more integral, more spiritually one than that? Do you mean, perhaps, form?

Wright: Yes, that, but more. Form is the inevitable result of structure. There is no structure without form, no form without structure.

Brownell: Then is structure an abstraction of form?

Wright: What do you mean by "abstraction"?

Brownell: An abstraction, I suppose, is taking a part out of something and treating it as if it were a whole. Abstraction of form is the pure design of the relationships of the parts to a whole without the concrete body or matter. If you carry it far enough, it usually tends to become mathematical.

Wright: But to me abstraction—to make anything in the abstract—is to make clear in some pattern the spirit of the thing.

Brownell: Is that spirit mathematical? I mean spirit in some pattern.

Wright: Spirit perhaps is always what you might call mathematical. But certainly in abstraction it is the structure or pattern of the thing that comes clear, stripped of all realistic effects, divested of any realism whatever. Abstraction is stark form, we might say.

Brownell: Yes, but I would say further that structure is the very simple thing that we mean when we say that it is the arrangement of the parts in a whole.

Wright: That, of course, it is. But the definition I think we are seeking must go deeper than that.

Brownell: You are giving structure a metaphysical kind of reality which it may or may not have. What is stock form?

Wright: I am endeavoring to give it reality, which is always metaphysical, as well as sub- and super-physical. There is no division into parts where reality is concerned.

Brownell: I think that you are spiritualizing it. I don't mind your doing that, but structure in the broadest sense is a much simpler thing.

Wright: But your assumption is only a part of structure.

Brownell: What is the other part?

Wright: The other part is the necessity for it and the actual substances of which the correlation of parts is made. Even more important are the inter-relationships that are the "in between" of Laotze.

Brownell: There, I think, you have changed to another conception of structure—namely, not merely the pattern but the force and support of an organization. In fact, structure seems to be becoming a great many things.

Wright: Well, I am speaking of structure with an "interior" sense of the whole.

Brownell: You mean, then, that the structure is not only the bones but the flesh of the body, and now also the inner system of it?

Wright: And not only the inner system of it but the reason for it as well—the each in all and all in all making them necessary to each other. Let's throw that in, too.

Brownell: That sounds like a kind of cross between Plato and Gertrude Stein. It has wonderful possibilities. And back of that, if I may go on collecting your definitions of structure, it seems to me you have identified structure with the total concrete reality of the body. Surely, that is no longer structure. Do you mean, for example, that the structure of the blue Ming jar is the whole jar?

Wright: You continue to talk of construction. To me structure is the very basis of what I call reality. When I speak of structure I have in mind reality, the essential constitution of whatever may be constructed. Something intrinsic, not merely extrinsic. Perhaps that word "constitution" more than any other single word comes close to my meaning. The *constitution* of the thing is *how* the thing is made integral. It is the fashion. We speak of our constitutions, and when we so speak we mean the way we are made, do we not? And when we speak of our constitutions we are speaking of something integral, that which characterizes the fashioning. It is structure that enables us to be what we are, how we are, for what we are.

Brownell: Constitution is good, it is perhaps what you have called the character of an organism. But we are puttering around the word "structure" too much. Shouldn't we be more concerned about structure in architecture, in society and in other concrete things? I, for my part, have moved away from Plato since my youth. I would be inclined to say that neither structure nor form has reality, as you call it, except in concrete, complete things.

Wright: Well, Baker Brownell, you started this with a request for some analysis of the word structure. And Plato's eternal "idea of the thing" is still valid, so far as I can see. I should say structure is what Plato meant by "Eternal Idea"—the essential framework of reality.

Brownell: All right then, I did start it; but now I want to end it. Our "structure" thus far has been so abstract and evanescent that it can't even be seen. Why not try to consider structure as we always must find it in experience, namely, in concrete objects and individual things? Take the big Ming jar again. It stands on the pier of your terrace. It is a plastic flowing blue. The sun behind it glints around the edges. The jar is cylindrical in shape, tapered at the two ends, with an abstract design of some sort in relief around the sides. I suppose it was made to be a tea jar. Now it is standing here above the Wisconsin River, aristocratically alone, and more precious, seemingly, because it is alone. What is the structure of the Ming vase? Is it the elements which constitute it? If so, what do those elements include?

Wright: First they include the idea of a serviceable jar for storing tea, then the forces put to work upon materials to shape them to the desired end. There must first be this ideal of function and of purpose. In this case the function is storing tea, a jar from which tea may be sold, and so a jar that can be man-handled. Before clay is touched there is in mind this definite concept as to what is to be achieved. Now how? By way of the potter's clay and the potter. This beginning is a feature of structure. We call it concept. To me it is an element of structure because structure begins there. If we are to speak of structure as organic structure it is essential to include conception. So far as reality is concerned it is the most "real" or essential

feature of the whole creative process. Structure is, of course, the product of this process.

Brownell: We can and perhaps should think of the universe as a set of dynamic relationships or processes. Pragmatists, I think, would do that in contrast to the Platonists and the Rationalists. They would make structure an order of activities and would think of pattern and static design only as metaphors, so to speak, or translations of the order of the making process.

Wright: Nature could not have static structure first if she would. Structure does not come into the world ready-made. There must have been a concept and then a process or development of structure accordingly.

Brownell: That sounds like Platonism again, with the form or concept prior to the process. But perhaps you think of the "concept" as the process of a person's thought. I myself would not personalize nature in that way. Nevertheless we do think of the physical universe as having two great aspects. One is its structure and the other is its process. Probably they, too, are relics of Platonism. In any case, the process is determined by the character of the structure.

Wright: Physicists may prefer that order for convenience, but structure where character is concerned is not first.

Brownell: Would you say that the automobile begins to run before it is made? Isn't the running of the automobile based on the prior fact that the automobile has a structure of parts patterned to each other?

Wright: If we were talking of the function of the car, yes. But we are talking about the making of the car, not its functioning. Then, certainly it must begin to run before it is made. The making process in regard to the automobile is really a kind of extension of the past into the present of this process of the running of the automobile.

Brownell: In that case you may be stepping out of the field of discourse—namely, the automobile. The physicist in his conception of the world as a whole probably has no right to step out of the field of discourse, however, nor is it possible for him to do so. It is true that for him action or proceeding cannot be secondary to design and plan. They are one.

Wright: They are one. That is my own contention. So here we are again and once more. We have the plan. Then we proceed to include within that plan the nature of materials and the shaping of the parts. We proceed definitely within certain limitations, towards a conceived end, part to part, as parts are to the whole.

Brownell: By "plan" I suppose you mean, as I think Plato would, that there is a difference between the becoming or the process in a structure and the design or form. I hope you will pardon me for bringing in these old academic references, but Plato, I think, would say that design or form can be abstracted from the becoming or process of action, and that the universal form only is the real whereas the action in time is not.

Wright: No, I do not mean to say, nor do I think, that a difference can really exist between the process of making the structure and the design or form. Otherwise how could I assert, as I do, that form and function are one? I say that structure is not only involved as much with procedure as with any other elemental scheme of action, but defines and limits action, as it is in turn defined and limited by it. Structure is integral to action as action is to structure.

Brownell: There still is the difference, however, at least the difference that physicists talk about, between structure and process. The automobile has a structure such as the chassis, the wheels, the engine. But it also has a process—it goes.

Wright: No. Physicists must have separate pigeon-holes and separate labels—the more the better. I am not talking about process as the subsequent functioning of some form. I mean that initial process that proceeds to make a thing what and how it is, as it functions. The subsequent process that makes it go is inevitably bound up in the nature of the whole structure. But it is not this proceeding to which I refer. All structure has its process, before it can have any proceeding as entity. First the concept, then the process, finally the ultimate proceeding or functioning.

Brownell: Let us return to the Ming tea jar on your terrace. The structure of the designs in relief on its surface is not a process.

Wright: But it is. That feature proceeds from generals to particulars. It has definite motivation and the motivation eventuates into appropriate pattern.

Brownell: But the pattern, when we have it, is not getting anywhere. It does not do anything.

Wright: It does. It is alive. It is a realized form expressing the purpose of the jar while it reinforces the walls. It is a rhythmical expression of this jar maker's joy in his job.

Brownell: Do you mean that it is rhythmical as a process, a cumulative kind of activity? Is rhythm always a time rhythm—namely, doing something, going somewhere?

Wright: I don't know just what you mean by "time rhythm." But time is as surely involved in all rhythm as interval is essential to emphasis. I cannot conceive of rhythm which would be essentially timeless—that is, without intervals or emphasis. Once you say "interval" we have the image of time at once, a space between something. The moment we fix points we imagine time. It is an unfortunate matter of fact, I believe, that it is impossible for our finite minds to conceive of anything except as this element of time in some form enters into it, nor any sense of space except as we fix limits.

Brownell: Then you would say, perhaps, that these buildings of yours are not "frozen music," they are music, music that never was frozen, never can be. But it seems to me that there are timeless elements in our experience.

Wright: If there are timeless elements in our experience, Baker B., we could not be conscious of them. We might have a feeling that they were so, but we could not mentally grasp them as such. We could make no image of them.

Brownell: Perhaps we could not express them or perhaps we could. The whole purpose of the arts is to express those timeless moments.

Wright: Not consciously, I think. The whole purpose of art is to objectify those subjective elements and feelings which all people may have, but which many people cannot express for themselves. An intuitive nature might perceive them and yet only an artist nature be able to objectify them. Perhaps it is a matter of horizon. One man's is wider than another's. And what is one man's today is not his tomorrow. Within this horizon creative art must take place, whatever may lie outside, in which you call the timeless. What is it to be an artist? Simply to make objective in form what was subjective in idea. It is to make things within and yet beyond the power of the ordinary man. The artist may feel no deeper, may see no further but has the gift that enables him to put that insight into form in whatever medium he uses. Without this specific power he is not an artist but merely a man of feeling and of appreciation unable to create.

Brownell: It is not a matter of seeing further or feeling deeper, nor is it only the power to make those discriminations articulate. A dog gives form to his feelings and insights, such as they are, when he barks. But this formulation of experience, at least natural experience, is not enough for art. It is expressive, but art is the expression of more than he expresses. The ability to see and feel and to be sensitive to experience is a gift of great importance, but the artist is not primarily an extremely sensitive photographer's plate able to catch impressions beyond ordinary human susceptibility, and his function is not merely the natural expression of those impressions. He may do that, but he does more. The artist—and I mean the artist in everybody as well as the great man of art—reaches beyond the relativities and the incompleteness of life that we call "time" and things temporal; he creates or finds what nature does not give and what the world of fact cannot record; he finds what is not relative or incomplete but is final. He gives to reality a final timeless significance that nature alone cannot give. Art tries to make articulate the timeless elements in our experience. It is action, yes; it is creative action; but it creates something that is not given in anyone's natural experience, however sensitive that experience may be. The artist creates something beyond natural experience. I rather think structure, as I mean it here, is that timeless synthesis. Only the artist, or the artistic or religious spirit in every man, can do those things. Only he can create those timeless forms.

Wright: Whether the forms created are timeless or not is of little consequence to the artist himself. He is that thing which he does. He does not try to lift himself by his own boot straps, if he is wise.

Brownell: Of course he is that which he does. That is the point, the very agency of his timelessness. The whole meaning of art is to transcend the time order.

Wright: Transcending the time order—that, indeed, he does. But his effort is to get order here and now. In other words, to make it actual in *the present.* That is the important thing to him. He dips into the universe probably without being self-consciously aware of it. He is in tune with it because he is of it, if indeed he is not it himself. He comes with something for the here and now. He has made of the "universal," as you call it, the very thing we should call the "here and now." That is his function, his "business," as we might and do say.

Brownell: We have come to the same place by different roads. The here and now, which I would call the wholeness of the concrete experience, is the important thing. In that here and now he integrates all the future and all the past. That is what I mean by the timeless moment of artistic experience.

Wright: But my point is that that is not so important to him, if he is truly an artist, because he *is* that thing. He does not have to think much, if at all, about it. If he consciously thought and thought about it when he wanted to do some work, if he deliberately tried to be in tune with infinity, he would never create anything at all. He would be an actor playing to the gallery. No, the creative artist just wants to make these things, with which he is working, the best and most beautiful things that can be made in his medium for his purpose, and he wants to do that because it is a joy to him. He likes to be useful, too, in his way if he is an architect. But more likely he will use rather than be useful.

Brownell: I think that is not so much in disagreement with what I have said as you may imagine. I mean precisely that the immediate significance of it is the important thing to the artist. That is what I mean when I say that he abandons the past and the future, or rather carries them into the living present.

Wright: Oh yes. He *does* carry the past and future into the living present. But it is for others to come along and pick up the concrete object, find the significance of it, realize the critical interpretations of it, and eulogize it, perhaps. But the artist does not care very much about that, although the man himself—there is one in every artist—might be pleased.

Brownell: No, that is not quite what I mean by significance. I mean by significance here its relation to itself and its completeness of value in its own field of reference. It may be nothing more than a splotch of red color or the blue glisten of the sun on the Ming tea jar. He finds it directly and immediately important to him.

Wright: I don't think that would be very intelligent on the part of any artist. The only significance the splotch of red or the blue glisten has for him lies in this interrelationship which alone can give it any significance at all.

Brownell: It is the immediacy of it that counts. Intelligence for him is secondary.

Wright: Intellect is his tool box, but intelligence is never secondary. Perhaps you mean intellect.

Brownell: The words are not very different, nor important. You may take intelligence either as the perception of relations or as the process of reason; in either case it is secondary in the artist to the immediacy of experience. Knowing about things, to the artist, is secondary to participation in them.

But it is late in the morning now. The hours that we have been talking about have gone through the cedars and the birches on the hillside in their usual order. The future hours are no doubt marching on us also in their regular procession. You have returned from Dodgeville where you visited Gene Masselink who was hurt last night. But the sun is blue-green on the side of the Ming jar on your terrace. A mourning dove in the trees below is calling. The stony pasture on the hill across the way has turned bright under the sun. It is bright now. And this moment is this moment. All past and future is here, and only here.

Wright: Perception is only a property of intelligence and knowing about things is not enough. One must realize them. Participation in that sense only is action. I prefer to think of art as that integral action. What we call art, to be sure, is the means of making something, making sound, forms, giving fresh impressions of something. But primarily the artist is a maker, a free fashioner. A poet says it with words. A painter says it with color and line. The architect says it with stone or bricks and mortar, or steel and glass and an industrial system, usually to ennoble a utilitarian purpose or make the mundane a thing of beauty. But they are all of a stripe. All are of the same fiber. And they are pretty much of the same character, too. But rarely do they ever recognize the same quality of thought or the same inspiration in a different medium. This concerning them has often puzzled me.

Brownell: I think you are saying, and saying very well, that art is practice. You are saying that art is the action involved in creating beautiful structures. It is a dynamic conception of art. I rather think it can be called a plastic conception of art in the sense that plasticity means the flowing together of action in time. And I believe, strange as it may seem, that art is practice. Artistic action, however, has its value primarily in that magic ability to integrate the past and the future in this burning present moment. Art is activity which has beauty and value in itself. In this respect the medium makes little difference since, through any medium that the artist may use, he gets something of the same final value.

Wright: Art is, as thought is, the highest form of action. But it does make a difference that artists should be blind except as they put their eyes to their own particular key-hole. If I were to put into a building a certain quality of feeling and thought, and if a musician were to put the same qualities into music, and a painter put them upon his canvas, the musician would come into my building and never recognize them there. The painter would do the same thing by either the building or the music. That looks like the dumb, halt, and blind to me. And then and to that disability the fact that to three-fourths of the people neither building, painting, nor music would have any significance at all—and you have something that looks tragic.

Brownell: I don't think that it makes so much difference whether they recognize each other's work. The important fact is that each one is getting the same thing out of his activity so far as he gets it at all.

Wright: Not the same. Too limited. Each is speaking a different language, understanding no universal language.

Artists in different mediums seem to understand each other as a Frenchman would understand an African or an African a Chinaman. Any artist should be more interested in qualities than in any specific language in which they were expressed, even his own language. Qualities really worry him and delight him most, and although qualities in the concrete are, after all, infinitely various and different from each other, to the artist mind they should be recognizable wherever they are.

Brownell: To get back to the question of structure. I wonder if structure does not mean something rather deeper than either one of us so far has actually said?

Wright: It begins to look as though it depended upon who uses the word.

Brownell: I mean that the artist in his approach to structure is breaking down those divisions to which we have been accustomed in Occidental philosophy or in religion.

Wright: He should be breaking down divisions but setting up new unities perpetually. But he can do so only if he has experience of the organic point of view.

Brownell: Structure in other words is the integration, not only of time but of those abstractions that we have called spirit and matter.

Wright: Do you think matter an abstraction?

Brownell: I think it is if you separate it from spirit.

Wright: How can the separation be effected or effective?

Brownell: It cannot be effective, but it has been effected ever since Plato made it long ago, or the Indic philosophers before him.

Wright: Isn't that separation the cause of what we call artificiality?

Brownell: I think it is, very definitely. It is intellectual artifice.

Wright: Yes, it is itself intellectual artifice but I think it is the basis of our superficiality. Is not such artificiality the very characteristic feature of our present failure?

Brownell: I would agree that our present failure comes almost directly from the Platonic separation of spirit from matter, as we have seen it come down through the medium of the western church.

Wright: Education with a capital "E" seems to be based almost wholly upon Artificiality with a capital "A."

Brownell: That is true. Formal education is the machine producing a modern disaster.

Wright: Let's say the modern disaster.

Brownell: I would accept that, except that there are so many other modern disasters.

Wright: Name one comparable in extent and fatality!

Brownell: I would name this, the separation in economic life between the activity of production and the activity of enjoyment.

Wright: But that separation is only the consequence of the initial separation.

Brownell: I believe they are concomitant. They both came out of the same parent. I think we can see our entire living process not as a series of preparations and sacrifices for something not present, but as a living and immediate value in the process itself.

Wright: You speak of value. You believe in "values" then?

Brownell: Well, values are another thing. They are nearest to us, but hardest to explain. We don't know them, we find them. We find them in concrete things, in that Japanese print tacked on your draughtsman's board, in the color of glass of the window pane, in the design of this room and the fire deep in its place in the wall.

Wright: But do you really believe in "values" so called?

Brownell: All human beings must believe in values.

Wright: I doubt that. I think our concept of values devastating.

Brownell: Perhaps our concept of it, because we usually think of value in terms of postponed values.

Wright: Don't you think that when we assume values we evaluate—simply pronounce judgment and really establish nothing?

Brownell: Quite true, we often do.

Wright: Is it not another kind of price system in the wrong realm?

Brownell: Possibly, but the fact remains that if value means interest in things, which I think fundamentally it does mean, we cannot escape values in life.

Wright: Well, one may use the word value in different senses—to value is to cherish—but to value in the sense that I think you are using the word, is a determination of relative position or of desirability.

Brownell: No, I would disagree there. I think you mean the act of evaluating, which involves a critical attitude, and that I don't mean in this case.

Wright: Both are worthless, of course. But what do you mean?

Brownell: I meant simply that we take attitudes toward things of like and dislike, of love and hate, funny and sorry, good and bad, and the like.

Wright: All of those "values," if so they are, are as likely to be matters of ignorance as of enlightenment.

Brownell: I think they are neither matters of ignorance nor enlightenment but matters of human attitude. They are deep in our fiber and we cannot escape them and don't want to.

Wright: I want to escape attitudes, my own and those of others. I often do escape them. Mine as well as others.

Brownell: Then you agree with Santayana when he says that the spiritual life is the disintoxication from values?

Wright: No, I seldom agree with Santayana and do not now.

Brownell: I thought so. Yet I think your whole life is characterized by tremendous drives in terms of values.

Wright: You are using the word values in another language now, probably your own.

Brownell: No, I mean you love things and you hate them. You find things that are beautiful and things that are not beautiful.

Wright: Beautiful or not beautiful to you—certainly. But how can a man love without hating, and hate without loving, if beauty is in question?

Brownell: You do both.

Wright: Yes. Love and hate are each one side of the same shield.

Brownell: That is a matter I shall not touch now.

Wright: Where now are "values" in this connection?

Brownell: Values are the fact that you are not indifferent to these things.

Wright: I do not see how "values" come in or come into being in that connection.

Brownell: This seems to me what values are.

Wright: You mean loves and hates? Acceptances and rejections, in other words?

Brownell: Just that.

Wright: Well, I think I would not use the word values in that connection—desirabilities you mean.

Brownell: That is all right, desirabilities and undesirabilities, if you will. It does not make much difference.

Wright: When I think of values I think of something that I have weighed and found wanting, or weighed and found satisfactory. They are estimations for what they are worth today and they will change tomorrow. They are temporal and never anything but tentative.

Brownell: I would say that is the classical standard of values so far as you refer to the weighing process. So far as you think of them as temporal and tentative, it seems to me that you perhaps mean personal taste. But I doubt if either one is the essential nature of value. They are single points of view toward value.

Wright: Values as the word is used must imply appraisal. It must be some estimate by some one to some end?

Brownell: No, I would say not to some end necessarily—simply the fact that you like something or you don't like it.

Wright: You are dissociating it, then, from "judgment" and making it an entirely personal matter?

Brownell: Unquestionably. I think the economic system is based on one type of value, which I think is a bad one, namely the idea of postponed values and postponed rewards. Whether it is personal is another question that depends on what is meant by personality.

Wright: Value then becomes not only an idiosyncrasy but a personal idiosyncrasy. Somehow I fail to get your idea as to what constitutes value—in other words, the *structure* of value, otherwise.

Brownell: Possibly because what I am talking about is so simple.

Wright: Yes, but the word, as you use it, is of a language that you have become accustomed to using. Have you not given the word a significance which is perhaps uncommon?

Brownell: That may be true. I don't insist on the word *value*. I merely insist that deep in all our lives is the fact that we take to some things and we don't take to others. Some things are beautiful and some things are not. We like some things. We don't like others.

Wright: So you are only using the word *value* then in the sense of to prize or cherish, or to prefer, or to accept or reject, and to denote your own acceptances and rejections. A matter then purely relative.

Brownell: I will not argue over the word. But I am not sure that value is relative, in the deeper sense. Otherwise, the word *taste* would do. I say that I am not sure. As for the word, I would just as soon give it up, but whatever word we—

Wright: I have learned that to proceed in life upon the basis of such idiosyncratic—pardon the word—conventions as "values" is to step from one wobbly stepping stone to another wobbly stepping stone, eventually to find yourself where you didn't want to be.

Brownell: I quite agree with you.

Wright: "Value" can only mean something we have established as for us or against us, and every such establishment is subject to the law of change. Inevitably all our "valuations" are nine-tenths worthless because they are being continually altered by experiences. Our own and that of others. It is so much safer to have as few so-called "values" as possible because values soon become baggage. I prefer to travel light with as little baggage as possible. I don't know really how much baggage of the sort I am trailing along right now, in spite of myself. But as soon as I can make it clear to myself that I have committed an "evaluation" and by way of "judgment" considered a matter settled for myself, I, like the man in the nursery rhyme who jumped into the bramble bush and scratched out both his eyes, jump into another bush and scratch them in again.

Brownell: You mean, I think, that one must always be creating afresh in terms of his likes and dislikes.

Wright: What I mean is that one must never sit in judgment. Our judgments are dangerous. Yet the educational and economic order dotes upon them and trusts them. Jesus went to "Judgment," but, in the sense we use the word, did Jesus judge? One of his sayings that I remember is—"Judge not that ye be not judged." Nevertheless "judging"—in other words evaluating—creating "values" became, notwithstanding his wisdom, the basis of all these institutions of ours which crucify life today instead of liberating it, and which seem to have formed a crust upon life which life is now struggling to break through. Therefore, I am inclined to be suspicious of so-called "values," yours and mine, too, unless you mean something by the term which goes deeper than I am wading.

Brownell: You cannot quarrel with me on that. I am quite willing to give up the word "value" if you wish. And I shan't quarrel with what you say in regard to the disastrous effect of so-called academic scholarship.

Wright: No, I did not say "academic scholarship." I was thinking of our entire modern philosophy of modern education when I spoke of the *crust* which life is trying to break through.

Brownell: And still I make no protest.

Wright: Yes, but it has economic phases. It is not called "academic" then. Nevertheless it goes all through the fiber of society owing to this mistaken idea of need of evaluation which then becomes just another name for institution. Extrinsic instead of intrinsic.

Brownell: I think that what you really are saying is something that I agree with thoroughly, namely, that values are often used second-hand and are fixed and are not fresh and new.

Wright: It is always dangerous to make them except firsthand. Even then the *attitude,* it seems to me, is wrong. Why sit in judgment? Why not humbly enter into action for the sake of experience, and by way of that experience enter into another action and another and another? Why attempt to formulate, reduce, catechize and arrange something that, in its very nature, is best fluid and inevitably remains in a state of change?

Brownell: You have said that beautifully. But I am not going to permit you to set me up as a straw man to attack when the meaning of what you are saying is what I am trying to say. We simply happen to be using different words. I have said that I would give up the use of the word.

Wright: Well, here we are again right where we have been all along. Now let's start and try to disagree about something. Let's start fresh and see if we cannot come out with disagreement.

Brownell: I am not sure that agreement is so deplorable. There can be adventures in agreement too. But one more word on structure. I think that we are groping for something deep in the idea of structure. Doesn't it lie below these artificial, rational distinctions between subject and object, inner and outer form and matter, flesh and spirit, and similar ideological divisions?

Wright: I am afraid structure will have the last word after all.

Brownell: It always does. Isn't the structure that we are talking about the integrity of concrete things? Our actual experience of those concrete things has none of those ideological divisions.

Wright: Well, yes. Certainly the integrity of common things. Whenever we start we seem to slide into deep water, at least as deep as that. Let's say the concrete integrity of things and let it go at that for the moment. This afternoon the thing will be further along.

Brownell: Now, Frank, you are an architect. You have insight into the forms of building and of living. You create designs for living and you mould brick and glass and stone, wood, air, concrete and light, steel, space and plaster into organic forms and plastic structures that are pertinent to life and are beautiful. You think in stone and glass, with a little contempt, I imagine, for these strange, shifting things that we call words. We have used many of them in this book, restless, undisciplined, disordered words, for that is their nature.

Now we want a few words more, such as they are, on structure in architecture and society, and particularly on your project, or dream, Broadacre City. You have done things in glass and steel. Now tell us what you are doing. You will find it harder, I think, to tell the things that you are doing, than to do them.

Wright: I'll try. But accuse me of no dream, please. You have heard of the little boy, have you not, who, curious, cut out the head of his drum to find out where the sound came from, and had neither sound nor drum? You don't want to place me in a similar position, I am sure. But nevertheless the little boy did find out a very important thing, and that was that the sound was not in the drum.

Brownell: And that analysis destroys it.

Wright: Yes, but sometimes we destroy that we may build. The danger does not prevent our human desire to poke around in this scrap heap we call our minds to see what curious and pretty things we can fish out. For one, I feel that, cerebration aside, thinking about things, considering them in their relationships quite sincerely for what one may be searching for—if we are searching for this thing we call reality— is worth a man's time. It is because mere cerebration, in the form of association of ideas, has passed for thought, that architecture is in a pretty hard case and that a Broadacre City is necessary.

Taste, association of ideas, is insufficient. A man, to build, must know. And I believe he may know the direction at least. He may learn to reach the center line of movement by way of thought and progress in line with what we call growth. So, in this state of becoming in which we all find ourselves, we may take the course, not of least resistance perhaps as things go and yet, yes, as a seed in the soil warmed by the sun reaches upward to the light, so it is natural for the man to take this course rather than any other. Therefore, why not the line of least resistance? We shall call it truth, come what may.

Brownell: I love this great house of yours, these limestone fireplaces in each large room, these long slopes of the house and the hill. And when I am here I sense somehow that not only have you made the house in the way you live, but that you live in the way that you have made the house. It seems to me that so simple a sort of thing as that, the relationship between the structure of architecture and the structure of social life, or of human life in general, has a deep meaning.

Wright: *Organic* structure, of course, has that integrity, whether social or architectural or what we call life.

Brownell: And isn't it the same structure, both of the house and of your life?

Wright: Yes, it is the life I have put in the house that really is the house. And in any building, which may be called architecture, you will find life put into it, interpreted as we have said. Your social structure will be made articulate, manifest in the terms of building we have been calling Architecture, if you have a civilization that is on speaking terms with culture. What we call a house, or place of worship, or a place to work in or a place to dance in or sing in, well—such places cannot exist at all as any form of life unless they are interpretations of human life. They express and bless human beings.

Brownell: Do you mean that the house is a manifestation of the activities of life? If the activities are broken, scattered, disintegrated, the houses of men will be broken, scattered, disintegrated. If the activities of life are whole and wholesome, if they are significantly one in structure and meaning, the buildings that house those activities—

Wright: Yes, I mean that. I mean that whatever a social or individual life may be, architecture will express that and something more.

Brownell: But it is not only the individual house for the individual man or family. We are living in a crowded and complex world. We must think of housing not merely individuals and families, but housing many individuals and many families who must live in relationship to each other. I think that your Broadacre City project has been largely an endeavor to synthesize building with the modern social problem. Let me ask several questions about Broadacre City. I think that the idea is based on the relationship of buildings and people to the land. Am I right?

Wright: Yes, as a matter of course. Intrinsic relationship, not extrinsic. Life has drifted by way of artificialities, "values," false abstraction, and by way of resultant academic standards into an urbanism that has gone or is going sterile. Man cannot be taken, still less can he take himself, away from his birthright, the ground, and remain sane any more than he can take himself away from the air he breathes, the food he eats, the water he drinks. His spirit is conditioned completely upon normal relationship of his life to what we call the life of nature. Being natural he is fruitful, happy, safe. The moment he attempts the unnatural he is punished. He has taken awful punishment. He must yet take worse punishment. Perhaps whole civilizations, this one in particular, must disappear because of the fatal artifice which humanity seems to consider to be civilization. Humanity even speaks of its digression in this respect as culture.

Brownell: And civilization, that high-powered and supposedly high-valued word, really means in its derivation, *citification.*

Wright: No, let us use again the word "disaster." When I say man's birthright, I mean his right to a place in the sun certainly. But he can have no place in the sun except as he has his feet on his own ground. Now, by his own ground I don't mean some plot, two by twice, that he has bought and paid for somewhere. I mean as much ground as he can utilize in his share of making life fruitful and beautiful as a whole.

Brownell: As to the size, the ground area, and number of people in your Broadacre City project, what about that?

Wright: Because we are in the United States of America I laid out Broadacre City on the assumption that an acre of ground for every individual was minimum. Meanwhile, certain sections were set aside to be used for the growing of preferred trees as crops: these areas to come into use as population expanded or increased. Were a man properly educated, that is to say, were he brought up in the gospel of work rather than the prevailing gospel of as much as possible of something for as little as possible, he could, with his feet on his own ground, become an independent unit in a society completely capitalistic. Youth would be brought up to be not as the millions of citizens who are merely potential capitalists, frustrated now, and who, were they to realize their actual position, would find the game and the cards all stacked against them by the winners. No, he would be brought up in a new recognition of the principles of sanity and coveting its effects.

Brownell: That doctrine of work, which you speak of, is much misunderstood. I think even you too may misunderstand it. Carlyle, for example, thought of work as a sacrificial necessity. How tragically wrong he was; and Carlyle was my boyhood favorite! A man, from Carlyle's point of view, who found pleasure in his work was not a good workman. On the other hand, I think your use of the word "work" may not be Carlyle's use. It seems to me that our western doctrine of work, which descends from the old separation between the preparation for heaven and the enjoyment of the reward after death or at the end of a long life of work, is a most disastrous doctrine. It underlies, psychologically at least, many of the disasters of our modern times. Work, I think, should be redefined as activity which includes consumption as well as production, which is enjoyable and significant in itself as well as significant for the results that it brings about after the work is performed. Until we have a life in which work has both kinds of value, namely, instrumental value and final value, until then we shall not have a life that is worth while. As I see it, your idea of Broadacre City involves an idea of work which is both productive and significant in itself as well.

Wright: Work. Significant, yes, because productive. And because productive or fruitful work, joyful. Carlyle was unfortunate. Such an opinion of work as you mention was his perhaps because he was sick, or because he was a Scotch Presbyterian or because of an untoward domestic situation. At any rate he was an old scold; he was not only unhappy, but proud of it. But we must admit, however, that he was a tremendous worker. Didn't he rewrite *The French Revolution* completely from beginning to end when a servant had thrown the original away?

Brownell: Yes, we admire Carlyle's nobility, but his doctrine of work is nevertheless the expression of a bad point of view.

Wright: Yes, and yet I wonder if Carlyle would call the writing of his *Sartor Resartus* and his essays in *Past and Present* work?

Brownell: I don't see how he could.

Wright: He might call the rewriting of *The French Revolution* work. I think Carlyle means drudgery by his use of the word *work*. Drudgery and work are not synonymous terms.

Brownell: Sacrificial drudgery.

Wright: Sacrificial, yes; by that I think you mean work chiefly a penance for the good of the soul or a disagreeable duty. And work *has* gone wrong for us in our day because of that, but more, I believe, because it has been made a speculative commodity. Work is and must be done in exchange for money. And money has become more than ever that thing by means of which alone, every man is enabled to get that in which any man may take pleasure or whatever he desires.

Brownell: In the same way our idea of freedom today, even when expressed by men as liberal as George Bernard Shaw, is of purchased freedom at the price of sacrificial work. It makes freedom the same as leisure, in other words an insignificant freedom.

Wright: Right. Or it is only a licence by way of earnings, to do as one wishes, which is seldom if ever freedom.

Brownell: Freedom seems to me to be the ability to work productively and enjoyably and at the same time to control, so far as possible, the conditions under which one works.

Wright: Or, let us say, as we are speaking of art, to find one's self in what one does.

Brownell: Shaw said not long ago in an article on democracy, "The practical form of freedom is leisure." Then he went on to say something like this, "Genuine democracy can exist only when the necessary slavery to nature—that is, the task of productive work, without which we would all perish, is equally shared, and the leisure left when that is done equally shared in consequence."

That is a perfect example of the kind of fallacy that I think permeates our Occidental ideology. It is the main trouble with our life. It is a common misconception of freedom and of work. Of course, I don't want to dispute Mr. Shaw's statement that unpleasant work as well as pleasant leisure should be more equally shared. None of us would dispute that very much. I do wish, however, to dispute the idea that the practical form of freedom is leisure and that productive work is a necessary slavery to nature. The idea has a long history of error.

Wright: It has. Go ahead, dispute the idea. It is not only fallacious. It is the popular error that will put an end to our own history.

Brownell: The Occidental ideology—and Plato started this thing—is based on the sharp cleavage between production and consumption. It is based on the idea that production is a sacrificial, though menial, effort put forth in order that consumption or aristocratic enjoyment may take place later. Work was Adam's punishment. Our Christian heaven is based on much the same conception. This world is a preparation for something that comes later, postponed to the future. "Success" has the same theory. It is a theory of postponed rewards. We must have a future, but—

Wright: My turn to agree and applaud. And yet isn't anticipation nine-tenths of enjoyment? Anticipation is tied up with this deadly charm of gambling. Every man, woman, and child in the United States is born and bred a potential gambler. We have fostered the gambling spirit. It is a form of anticipation but an abuse of it.

Brownell: You can have your anticipation. I shall take the immediate or direct reality.

Wright: Is reality then also divisible into Past, Immediate, and Future? If so, I should say that anticipation is very much the better part because out of the past it stands in the present because of the future.

Brownell: I think you are suffering from the cleavage of which I spoke. The immediate, or the direct, is just that timeless synthesis of art that I urged on you this morning. But as I move about in your buildings and see your work and listen to some, but not all, of your words, I feel sure that you are not really suffering from that fatal cleavage, at that. But Mr. Shaw is. This beautiful design of space in your room, reaching through the open walls into the sun, denies my charge against you, though some of your words seem to say otherwise. But to return to "work" and "freedom":

It seems to me that the real problem of both society and art is not to give leisure or unoccupied time, but to make human activity significant. If activity is significant it must be both free and functional. If it is functional without freedom it is likely to be some form of slavery. If it is free without function it can be little more than frivolous. Mr. Shaw bounces from slavery to frivolity. One is about as bad as the other.

Wright: And what, then, is this bouncing of Mr. Shaw? Activity without art?

Brownell: What he says would indicate that as his philosophy. Contrary to Mr. Shaw I suggest that art and society must come together in the ideal of human activity. When human activity is significant and is well directed we may say, I think, that social ideals and artistic ideals both are attained. That is a pretty broad definition and you probably would force me to qualify it, if you had a chance.

Wright: Yes, go on. Are you not giving me that good chance?

Brownell: This significant activity, or art, is possible only in a society where work can have functional significance and also appreciative significance. It is, namely, a society where the activity of producing is also in part the activity of consuming or enjoying. In society in which productive work is sharply separated from enjoyment by means of techniques such as mass production, centralization, specialization, standardization, will fail in terms of human values although it may produce a great deal of cheap goods. A society of this sort is marked not only by the decline of self-sustaining industry but by the decline of native, self-sustaining art, of folk art, or amateur art in the best sense of the word. Extreme professionalism, expertism or virtuosity in the arts takes the place of generally distributed and diffused artistic production. The great mass of people take their art, their sport, their enjoyment in general as a spectacle to be purchased rather than an activity to be lived.

Wright: More approval. And let me say that architecture is in a basic strategic position in this integrity of production and enjoyment, of art and of life of which you speak. It is itself an expression of that very integrity, as in Broadacre City, or architecture is only a liability.

Brownell: Now tell me about Broadacre City. How many people will there be in each city? What will they do for a living? How will they live? The afternoon is moving on. The cattle on the hill over there are lying bunched up under the ridge. They are chewing their cuds, no doubt. What philosophers they are! Probably they too think it's time to hear about Broadacre City.

Wright: Before we proceed with the details of Broadacre City, let us get a little clearer the basis upon which it was conceived. Broadacre City is no city at all in the sense that you are using the word. Broadacre City is everywhere or nowhere. It is the country itself come alive as a truly great city. It is out of the ground into the light by way of man's sense of himself in his work. With his feet on his own ground each man is not only a potential but an actual capitalist. So you see, while the present condition under which he lives is money-bound first and is everything else afterward, in Broadacre City a man's own capabilities in his work become his wealth and by means of that wealth he obtains, more directly than is possible now, those things of which he dreams and that he desires. He is not and never can be unemployed or a slave in any sense. The true wealth of our nation would be increased enormously instead of funneled down to the little drip that we are in the habit of calling our financial resources.

Brownell: Does that mean that he lives in a comparatively self-sustaining system?

Wright: Not comparatively self-sustaining. Absolutely self-sustaining, if he is a true self. A true self still lives in most men notwithstanding the ravages of such libertine individualism as the once famous Liberty League called upon in the name of freedom.

Brownell: Still he must buy tools, automobiles, power, with money, must he not?

Wright: Not with money as a speculative commodity, but by some simple social medium of exchange which enables the fruits of his labor in connection with natural resources to be exchanged for the fruits of another man's labor in that connection.

Brownell: That means that we must know more about the actual structure of this Broadacre City. How do the people live?

Wright: Wait a little. Let's proceed from generals to particulars. Let's discuss why they must live there, first. To understand why, we must know more about the actual nature of this thing we call money, for one thing. A simplification of our entire economic concept is essential, beginning with that abstraction as well as with the use of the ground. Simplification is not so difficult as it seems because a natural economic order is yet possible to us in America, and possible, I believe, without bloodshed or any greater suffering on the part of any one except those who would unjustly and unfairly try to prevent a just measure of life for other men. They suffer in that attempt anyway, dying a thousand deaths where they need die but once.

Brownell: Do you mean that we may have a local revolution in respect to Broadacre City and ignore the course of economic life outside?

Wright: No revolution local or outside. There is no need of revolution nor of isolation. I think Broadacre City is really in process of arriving right now as an organic necessity of our times. I believe the recent depression—let's call it by its right name, break-down—of the past seven years has produced the revolution quietly beneath the surface

of things. This revolution will eventuate in what I am calling, for lack of a better term, Broadacre City. He can see that the present impositions upon life have gone almost as far as they can go. These impositions have given us, in general, a factory worker's and an industrialist's and, in particular, a *speculator's* view of a universe. Acting on these views has resulted in the exaggerated urbanism we suffer from. This urbanism has increasingly crucified life in the name of "service" and "freedom." Efficiencies we have worshiped we are finding to be extravagant exploitations of the very life we—some of us—sincerely enough expected them to serve.

Brownell: But admitting that that has failed in human terms, do you think that Broadacre City will come as a natural consequence?

Wright: All that Broadacre City needs, in order to come into existence, is the application of the principles of an organic architecture to the life of our people, and the interpretation of that life in terms of Architecture. We need structure in the sense we have used the word where we now have only a badly planned set-up. We cannot say we have a system.

Brownell: That seems rather indefinite. If, for example, every person is to have an acre or so of land, how can you provide for his keeping his land?

Wright: I do not know by what method except that his work upon and improvements will hold it. He will not be allowed to alienate his land. He may designate his successor. But other things are even more important. Perhaps first and foremost we need to begin with a new success ideal.

Brownell: True.

Wright: And this different sense of life which insures that new ideal, I believe, is coming. We, as a people, have lately been "behind the scenes." As I now occasionally go about among young people, talking to them in these universities of ours, I think I see that new ideal coming. Every man I meet and talk to, from the intelligent workman to the richest of the rich men feels dissatisfied, more or less uneasy, uncertain. In short, not happy.

Brownell: I think most of them would like to have what you say, but they think that the inevitable evolution of economic life is towards greater concentration and away from what you say.

Wright: They did think so up to this time. But I believe now the majority of our thinking people have gone deeper and are beginning to think and feel otherwise.

Brownell: But it is time that we know more of the picture of Broadacre City. How do they live? How many people are there? What is it like?

Wright: No picture please. Not yet anyway. Let us first see where we are now. We are now in a society built like some badly planned factory, run like a factory, systematically turning out herdstruck humans as machinery turns out shoes. Our society is a cultural weed of a dangerous kind: dangerous to ourselves and to others. When life itself becomes a restless tenant, as it has become on our farms no less than in big cities, the citizen must lose sight of the true aims of human existence and voluntarily accept substitutes. His life, now unnaturally gregarious, tends towards the blind adventure of a crafty animal. To live, or "get by," is some form of graft, coupled with some febrile pursuit of sex. Only in these does he find or see relief from the factual routine in this mechanical uproar of mechanical conflicts of this mechanical life of his—conflicts that seem to hypnotize him while they crucify him.

Brownell: That is what I mean by the separation of enjoyment from significant production.

Wright: A citizen pays as he is paid. He is bought as he buys. As he buys and sells so he is bought and sold. He is struggling to maintain a heartless, worthless artificiality. His faculties, his vital sap, meantime ebb. The citizen's entire life, for lack of some basis natural to him—therefore organic—is exaggerated and sterilized by way of machinery instead of blessed. American life itself has now become some form of anxious rent. The citizen's own life is rented, his family evicted if he is in arrears. This stricture is what we please to call a system; God knows it has no structure. It is a stricture that is no system but is only an adventitious circumstance. Should this anxious lockstep of man fall out with the landlord, the money lord, the machine lord, man is a total loss. The "system" goes to smash, and he perpetually fears the smash.

Brownell: Still, the people in Broadacre City would use machines, would they not?

Wright: Yes, all the powerful modern machines at work upon the resources are the premium paid to human greed. Machines and resources would be naturally his. Both are now turned against him and involuntarily are turning against him in the city. They could be his own now, by way of no revolution, but by way of a simple understanding of the nature of what he is, what he does, and where he is. They could go now to work for him in the circumstances if the right structure could be found, the right pattern that would not soon again become another stricture.

Brownell: How would the necessary machines be produced and how would the citizen of Broadacre City purchase them?

Wright: They would be produced much as they are produced now except under happier circumstances, produced by such people as those who use them. I think it unnecessary to change radically any of the methods and processes which have given us our great advantages except to make them more radical and humane. But we must arrive at some understanding as to a beneficial and natural human basis on which to make use of them. That means a rational social structure in place of the adventitious stricture.

Brownell: But doesn't efficient production of big machines involve the big factory and the big industrial city?

Wright: No longer. The big factory and the big city were the inevitable consequence of the present exploitation we call centralization. Such as this was "the great efficiency."

It was to bring to all human beings everything which they desired. It has brought them to the beginning of the end.

Brownell: But isn't centralization involved with division of labor and specialization, which are necessary to efficient production of cheap machines?

Wright: Yes, centralization is dependent on men as cogs, or in the elimination of them as factors in production so far as possible and their increase in consumption. But what do you mean by "cheap"? If you mean machines that cost an exploiter the least money, if you mean getting ten machines for the price of one, then "cheap" we clearly have at a pretty stiff price.

Brownell: I mean by "cheap" machines those which the average person in the average community can buy if he needs them.

Wright: The "average person" in the community in Broadacre City could have all the machinery that was profitable to him as a human being to use as one. And we must use the word "profitable" here in a little broader sense than the mere money sense of a price system has given it.

Brownell: How would he get the machines?

Wright: He would make them, as he makes them now, but he would make them under circumstances and in a situation where there would be pleasure in the making and true profit to him in the making as well as in the using.

Brownell: Would he make them through methods of industrial organization?

Wright: Probably, if cooperation is organization. And it is a form of it. I see nothing wrong with organization if it is organic. I see everything wrong with the exaggeration of organization, and with inorganic organization which is only aggregation or organization run to seed. Some forms of organization are primitive impulses and valuable instruments of any social life.

Brownell: What do you think of the influence of new technological methods such as the use of electrical power in place of steam?

Wright: I think that these new facilities and extended powers together with our other advantages, mobilization, glass and steel, are what make Broadacre City possible.

Brownell: Would this city be a large city?

Wright: As I have said, this city would be everywhere and nowhere.

Brownell: It would be a decentralized city?

Wright: Certainly. Decentralization of all those interests in which individuality is concerned is a basic condition fundamental to Broadacre City. But centralization of all that does not involve individuality would be a matter of what we now call government.

Brownell: Can you produce U. S. Steel by decentralized methods?

Wright: Yes, of course; more effectively, so far as human life is concerned and the benefit that it derives from steel, than steel is produced now.

Brownell: There would still be the Garys and the Pittsburghs, would there not?

Wright: No, there would not be. The Garys and the Pittsburghs have served their term. We do not need them now. Together with other crude scaffolding and hardships by way of which we have reached this crisis they would disappear.

Brownell: Do we return to the home forge and the village smithy?

Wright: No, indeed. We keep all the advantages which concentration upon making money has unwittingly pushed to over-development. We've got them. Why not keep them? I see no reason why we should throw one of them away. By means of them we could have many more. But the test of achievement in any civilization is not the amount of money that some men make because of it, but what the eventual result that civilization is found to yield where a human life is concerned. These results are human if at all valid. Or, instead of valid, let us again say intrinsic.

Brownell: What would the average citizen do in Broadacre City? What would be his pattern of work and enjoyment?

Wright: As a matter of fact there would be no "average citizen" in Broadacre City. Broadacre City aims to eliminate the "average citizen."

Brownell: What would the "unaverage citizen" do?

Wright: Let us understand, first, that we are concerned here with a future for individuality in organic sense. I believe individuality to be the prime integrity of the human being as integer of the race. Without such integrity I believe there can be no real culture whatsoever, no matter what we may choose to call civilization. I have called this city Broadacre City because it is a broad freedom for the individual, honestly democratic, based upon the ground—the minimum of one acre to the person. To date our capitalism has miscalled personality individuality. Our eclecticism, which must be called mere personality instead of true individuality, has, by way of what we call taste—have used taste as a substitute for culture—obstructed where it has not obscured the integrity of individuality. And we, on account of that vicious, fundamental misunderstanding, have become the prey of our captains turned playboys, our kept universities, our high-powered culturemongers (such as the arch-salesmen, Sir Joseph Duveen, et al.) and we—the people, yes—stand in danger of losing our chance at this free life. Nevertheless, our charter of liberty originally held it out to us. And now I see a pattern for that free life in Broadacre City. It is a life that reckons with the law of change as a desirable circumstance, not as fatality.

Brownell: That is a good statement of the ideal of life in Broadacre City. But is there anything in your plan that explains how it will come into existence?

Wright: First the ideal, which, thanks to your pretended dumbness, I have now outlined somewhat. Now, then, we come to the plan.

Brownell: Not all of it was either pretense or dumbness: I am trying to see the thing in the concrete. What is the plan? Will there be shops, roads, hydrants?

Wright: Ask me rather, first, "What is the nature of this plan?" And I will say it is a free pattern. It is of the ground and with the ground. Wherever this free pattern is applied it varies with the ground and as the conditions of climate and life vary. The ground may happen to be suited to one kind of life or to many kinds. The common spirit of the people involved is disciplined automatically from within by means and methods and materials which are all organic.

It is a great unity in diversity I have sought.

The changes that Broadacre sees and accepts as natural and desirable have already made the big city no longer efficient or endurable. But the city struggles, as it must, against the change. For example, let us say that the present city spacing was based fairly enough on the human being on his feet or sitting in some trap behind a horse or two. So all now is too small, too mean for the automobile. And originally the city was a group life of powerful individualities true to life, conveniently enough spaced. But by way of instantaneous communications and easy mobilization this better life has already left the modern city. Not only such genius as the city has known for many a day is recruited from the country, but success in the city means life in the country. What, then, is the overgrown city for? Almost all necessities that once chained the individual to city life are dying away and the present citizens must die there as these needs die. It is only as life has been taken from him and he has meekly accepted substitutes offered to placate or fleece him that any citizen voluntarily remains in the city. The fundamental unit of space-measurement has so radically changed that the man now bulks ten to one in space, and a thousand to one in speed when seated in his motor car. Mobilization is rapidly becoming universal.

This circumstance alone would render the present form of our cities obsolete. Like some dead dwelling the city is inhabited only because we have it. We feel that we must use it and cannot afford to throw it away to build the new one we now know we need. But compulsion is here. I imagine we'll soon be willing to give all we have, to get this new freedom that might so easily be ours. We will give what we have left to get it for our posterity, even if we may not have it ourselves. Devouring human individuality invariably ends in desolation, some kind of desertion such as is under way. Invariably, as history records, greed ends in destruction of the devourer. The city is in this case the devourer, and the impulses that exaggerated the mechanical forces that built it are senile in nearly every phase.

Brownell: Now what of the new Broadacre City?

Wright: The principles underlying the free pattern called Broadacre City are simply those of an organic architecture. Organic architecture now comes with a demand for finer integrity in order to unite modern improvements with natural resources in the service of men. Integration is here, as set dead against centralization. By the natural working of organic forces and ideas man is now to be brought forward to his inheritance, the ground, that he may become a whole man again. There is no longer much excuse for him to remain the parasite that spasmodic centralization has succeeded, almost, in making of him. The practical solution is this matter of social structure or free pattern. And definitely it is a matter of what we call organic architecture. So we must begin to learn to see life as organic architecture and begin to learn to see organic architecture as life. Broadacre City is not only the only democratic city; it is the only possible city looking towards any future for these United States.

Brownell: The big bell has rung three o'clock. The sun has moved around and is now a spot of silver foil on the side of your Ming tea jar. I grant that the big city has the seeds of death for itself and for people in it. But until we know the actual structure of Broadacre City, we have not yet made articulate in materials the new structure of society that you suggest. I suppose that you mean a Broadacre City type of community to be perhaps not more than 5,000 or 10,000 people.

Wright: No, any number of people, so long as the ground holds out, and our states insure that there is no danger of its running out. On the plan of Broadacre City nearly all of the inhabitants of the United States today could be accommodated today in the State of Texas alone.

Brownell: Do you assume that commercial farming will give way to self-sustaining farming?

Wright: Commercial farming is certainly a failure. It must give way to something. Why not natural farming, if you can imagine such a thing? Such farming would be self-sustaining farming.

Brownell: What would that be?

Wright: The answer to that question cannot be yet. We are getting too far into minor details before we clean up the big ones. The general scheme we have not yet finished in outline.

Brownell: But it is hard to understand principles unless we can see them in concrete experience.

Wright: Well, let us proceed then to concrete experience. We have spoken of the new scale. We have spoken of the new simplicity: spoken too of the new space consciousness. Organic architecture in relation to organic living has been the real theme of this book, although well concealed by too many words. What, then, is all this to be like in terms of people, of town organization, of buildings and materials? What, then, will Broadacre buildings be like?

Brownell: That is the question.

Wright: The answer cannot be complete in words. That is why I have made plans and models. But something may be said.

Let us first take the problem of the poor. That means the housing problem receiving so much philanthropic attention from higher up at the moment. Beneficent though it is, it can only result in putting off by mitigation the day of regeneration for the poor. The majority of the poor are those damaged most by this growth of unearned increment as it piles up into vast fortunes by way of some kind of rent. Where is the place of the poor in this city now built by triple rent, that is to say rent within rent upon rent

for rent? A vicious circle. There is always some dignity in freedom, even though one's own way may sink to license or filth. But what dignity can there be in the cell of a soulless economic repetition? What dignity is there in spiritual poverty, even though some posy be stuck in a flower box, like a gratuity, for each poor man by those who, having bested him, would now better him?

Why not make more free to the poor the land they were born to inherit as they were born to inherit air to breathe and daylight to see by and water to drink? Else why are they born? I am aware of the academic economist's reaction to any land question. Nevertheless, Henry George clearly enough showed us the basis of poverty in human society. Some organic solution of this land problem is not only needed, it is imperative. Broadacre City proposes one and it is not the Single Tax.

What hope is there for a great or even a good architecture while land holds the improvements instead of the improvements made by the man holding the land? For any organic economic structure this is the wrong end about. Our architecture in the circumstances can only be for some landlord. But by some form of exemption and subsequent sharing of the increase in land values, we can now make his acre available to each so-called poor man, or rather make more than an acre available according to his ability to use the land. And let us begin to call his "education" that training which makes him competent in respect to this birthright of his—the ground. He has been industrialized to the limit. Now agrarianize him. Somewhat. Stop "classicizing" his progeny.

Brownell: And then what house for him? And where and how may he go to work to build it?

Wright: Having ground—what house? See the plans. They are truly ground plans. And where? Well, you will see in the models that mobilization is already his by way of a mobilized traffic lane that used to be the railroad, or some bus or perhaps a second-hand Ford, or perhaps a new one of his own, as the prices for Fords and other cars are going now. Emancipated from the rent that he must now pay in the city in order to work at all (everything he earns he must spend to keep him on the job), the machine worker goes back by way of this machine to his birthright in the ground. Ten miles or twenty is now easy for him. So where? Anywhere almost. He may go to work, perhaps, for some manufacturing employer in some decentralized factory unit near by. Fifteen miles is near by now by any modern standard of space or of time.

Now as to "how." Let us say that the poor man—the man at the machine is usually the poor man—buys the modern, civilized, standardized privy (it is a duplicate or even triplicate bathroom) manufactured and delivered complete in a single unit, even as his car or bathtub is manufactured and ready to use when connected to a standard tile septic tank or a cesspool. These costly civic improvements that cost so much are growing less necessary every day. Pass the hat, please, for Mr. Insull! The free man plants this first unit on his free ground as a focal point to which a standardized complete kitchen unit appropriate to the general plan of Broadacres may be added. As the months go by, the rent saved may buy other standardized units, harmonizing with the first. He earns them by work he has been trained to do on his own ground or trained also to do in the factory units scattered about within, say, fifteen to thirty miles. Near by. The units would be suited in general scheme of design to assembly either on flat land or on hillside and be so designed as to make a well planned whole when put together. These various organic units cheaply become the machine worker's by way of his labor either in the factory unit near by or on his own ground or the ground of others. The benefits of standardization thus become his, just as the automobile has become his by the cheapening power of a mass production that serves him. Serves him now as a man and not as a machine. Such is the pre-fabricated house in Broadacres.

Being no longer intimidated by starvation—he can eat— he may say "yes" or "no" without fear. His menage may grow as his devotion and labor grow. His family joins in this life on and of the ground in new circumstances—a new freedom altogether. He buys each building unit as he needs it in a group scheme that has had the benefit of expert study, in design and production, by the world's best minds. Not only may this group of units be variegated and so harmonized by design as to do no outrage to the landscape, but even now it may be so cheap that his rent for three months in the present city in order to "keep on the job" would buy him the first units needed for life in Broadacre City.

Brownell: Who do you think will do these things—will produce these units? The government? Or will you leave it to private industry?

Wright: Either by private or cooperative industry or by governmental cooperation general manufacturing might be done. I see no reason why in Broadacre City there should be any discrimination one way or the other. The organic nature of the circumstances would determine "how."

In a year or two any man could own a house scientifically modern and aesthetically complete along any one of an infinite variety of lines and plan schemes, and his house would never become a regimentation. It would always be good to look at and at the same time be his own house. All could be hooked up in his own way with such a garden as he might make, outbuildings harmoniously added as he would need them.

Brownell: Will there be any way of controlling his own bad taste in selecting house design?

Wright: His own bad taste in selecting house design would be controlled by the fact that there would be no bad designs and that he would no longer be educated in bad taste. Even if he wanted bad ones he could find only good ones because in an organic architecture, that is to say architecture based upon organic ideals, bad design would be unthinkable. Impossible. With some proper aid in the way of tax exemption, here within reach of the poor man is a natural home of his own. In quality, so far as it went,

his own home would be no inferior associate of the house of the man better off or further along next door. His devotion to work as a man would bring home comforts and graces to him as a free man. And the machine could give him this freedom in a five hundred dollar house, say, as it gives him his hundred and fifty dollar automobile now standing in his forty dollar garage. This could all be his on a higher level of quality than ever before if the benefits of mass production were made available to him by voluntary cooperation.

Brownell: It seems to me you are thinking at one time of organic architecture as an ideal and at another time as a compulsion.

Wright: I am thinking of it as both. Is not any ideal a very real compulsion?

Brownell: Only ideally, I am afraid.

Wright: Do you mean by "ideally," fancifully? Some personal fancy? The only discipline that can ever characterize any democratic society, I believe, is discipline from within, and that can only be what I call the discipline of an ideal.

Brownell: But I am wondering if there is here an adequate instrumentation of the ideal. What will make it actual? And for that matter, how can you save people from their own bad taste?

Wright: Two questions at once. I will answer the latter. Save people from bad taste? By allowing them to grow up more naturally, cultured as well as "educated" (perhaps instead)—providing meantime designs for manufacture that are organic designs. They may be had even now. Where then would be bad things that a man could buy to outrage the sensibilities of others? Where could he get inferior designs? You may ask where he would get superior designs. In the changed circumstances, he would probably make them himself. Or, if not, he would have a wide range of choice in designs made by those who could. He would himself, however, determine various relationships that would still give individuality to the whole arrangement. In any case, bad units he could not find. Nor could he assemble those he could find in any way to do violence to the unity of the whole. Because the scheme, I would remind you, is organic in character.

Brownell: I think your ideal is noble, but I cannot help but feel you are ignoring the kind of human animals we are, with our bad taste and our commercial architects. Still it is true, I suppose, that today it is impossible to buy an ugly automobile, and so tomorrow it may be impossible to buy an ugly house. I wait with hope.

Wright: I do not take our present bad taste and commercial architects to Broadacres. As for nobility—what is it? As for commercial architects, commercial architecture would have no place in Broadacre City, nor anything else purely commercial. So that unnatural type of animal would not be there. I referred at the outset to a new success ideal. I don't think Broadacre City would be fit for humans that have been more or less degraded by the circumstances in which they now live. Something would have to be done for them while they last. Some preparation for their end. Time for development is essential for the betterment of anything human. Betterment cannot be imposed. Seldom ever is it a gift. Broadacres sets up preparation first and foremost, as you may see by studying the plan.

Brownell: That development is very important. I am doubtful, however, whether education can do much more than make articulate the standards and values already practiced in a society.

Wright: As education stands at present, you might be right. But culture remains. Let us turn the job over to culture. From generation to generation is organic growth: and that growth is culture.

Brownell: You mean culture as a verb, I take it, a kind of action, not a noun.

Wright: I have no concern with culture as verb or noun. It is an act. It would be folly to take a man away as he is, take him from tending a machine which his whole thought, all the cultural life he had experienced, and put him onto ground which he did not understand and with which, to begin with, he could do nothing. I repeat, organic growth is slow growth. There is no short cut. The quick turnover is cut out. But, only growth is safe. Broadacre City is a safe city.

Brownell: An illustration of your Broadacre City occurs to me which you will probably not accept, but which seems to me a good example of a functional relationship of land to life in towns. In early New England they built their villages with a limited amount of land to each person, and when there was no more land available, they allowed no more people to settle in the village. They started a new village somewhere else. Their building and their land were functional in respect to their lives.

Wright: So far as they went—so good. They did well in the circumstances. But that they were really functional in the organic sense I do not believe. It was the same building they were accustomed to and wanted, by habit only; furthermore, it was probably the only one they could get, and they borrowed money to buy their ground. They did their best with it. But their life was destined to pass away because it had no genuine organic basis in relation to the whole.

Brownell: It was good within their limits because there was nothing else they could do.

Wright: It was good within its limits, but not good enough today according to present possibilities in the light of an organic architecture.

Brownell: I see Father Menifer with his twenty protégés marching upon you. They have left their big bus down the hill and have come to see Taliesin. Everyone has a camera, it seems. I can't see who is conducting them. It looks like Jim Thompson. Now he has detoured them. They are going towards the play-house. That will give us a few minutes more. It is nearly four o'clock.

Your big Ming jar has turned greenish in the afternoon sunlight. It is a Ming jar, I hope, after all I have said about it.

Wright: You are safe. Yes, it is a Ming tea jar. I brought eight back with me from Pekin (now Peiping) but four have been destroyed by weather, or the fire of 1925 . . . they are gone.

Brownell: But this one is left. It has changed color in the different sun. On the hill across the way the shadows of the rocks and trees have disappeared, so far as I can see, withered quite away on the steep slope. And our efforts to find the nature of structure and of structure made manifest in the social and architectural pattern of Broadacre City have also matured, though not, I hope, withered away. Perhaps the simplest conclusion we can make, in view of what we have said many times throughout the book, is that we cannot hope for a good architecture until we have a good society.

Wright: The discussion may have matured somewhat. But I doubt the maturity. As for the hope for a good architecture, we can have a good architecture meantime by way of good architects working for good individuals. We may have valuable exemplars without waiting for the entire mass to come along and make them a mass product.

Brownell: They can act as lights for the way.

Wright: Naturally such creative exemplars so act. If we ever do have an organic social order worthy of an organic architecture, it will come to us with the other because of the perception, devotion, and better understanding of such appreciative people as are ours. As for creative work we call the results works of art—I cannot see that thing coming from the bottom up.

Brownell: Nor from the top down.

Wright: Why not?

Brownell: I think one is as vicious as the other.

Wright: Why? Why should the top of a society be vicious, if that top is not artificially top, therefore sterile? Unable to go to seed? Nature produces her seeds at the top unless we are speaking of pumpkins and then they are well inside.

Brownell: I don't mean that the top is vicious. I mean the method of coming from the top down.

Wright: But the blossom at the top or tip has preceded the fruit. It is organic. Better things could not come from any other source or from any other direction than from the genuinely best or bravest of our people.

Brownell: There are many instances where great movements have been created by the changing conditions. The best and bravest are many, many people awaiting only those conditions to call them forth.

Wright: True enough. The few in the many, as the many are in the few. Just as you will find all great movements motivated by great individuals. Great individuals expressing the many.

Brownell: The great individual reflects the implicit ideals of the many who are unable to express them.

Wright: Yes, but I think the ideals of the few creative intellects, which are really the minds of the body politic, are reflected no less by that body. Perhaps greatly more. What I refer to is again from the top down, but the organic top of a bottom from which it proceeded or was produced.

Brownell: But isn't that the same as "from the bottom up," which is something that you repudiated a moment ago? Then you were about to go Platonic again—aristocratic segregation. But now, when you say "the organic top of a bottom from which it was produced," it is hard to tell which way you are going. Perhaps you are going both ways.

Yet I think that your attitude is probably consistent after all. If you discriminate between the great artist's self-confident isolation from herd standards in the process and method of his work, and the artist's necessary integration with his people in function, ideal, and the deep expression of their lives, and if you give the greater emphasis to the latter, then I am sure that you are consistent. The artist is the instrument of a people's expression. But I wouldn't call that "from the top down."

Wright: Perhaps we are involved with the immortal "which came first, the hen or the egg?" I don't mean that top which is top by virtue of adventitious circumstance. I don't mean the top by way of an artificial aristocracy, one of birth and of privileged place. Nor do I mean those advantaged by money who have their place by virtue of something not their own. When I speak of "the top" I mean the organic top. I mean humanity's best and bravest minds, natures, and characters produced out of itself by way of itself, in the course of events to come down by way of itself that others may become top in due course. There can be no other interpretation of life as organic.

Brownell: That's better. I would answer what you were saying a moment ago by quoting your own fine doctrine of art, namely, that art is making manifest the implicit character of the materials of which it is created. I think the great individual is simply making manifest the characteristics of the people from which he comes.

Wright: I don't think you should use the word "simply" in that connection if you mean by simply "only." Growth cannot come by way of any interpretation and expression of the stupidities, limitations, inferiorities of a people. It comes down to all that find the best and the highest of which they, the people, are capable, leading them, reacting upon them. And the matter goes still further: things of which the people themselves are frequently unaware until they see them, ideas which exist for them only as potentialities, are laid out for them by somebody a little further along than they, a little more articulate and certainly vastly deeper in the experience of life. The great artist lays it out for them where they can see it, touch it, apprehend it as life itself.

Brownell: Just as a beautiful carving in wood is determined by the limitations of the nature of wood, so the great individual is determined by the limitations of the people from which he comes.

Wright: But my point is that he is not limited by the determinations of his people. The limitations of his own human nature and the characteristics of the people of whom he is a part are as much the artist as themselves, but they are to him no limitation. However, if he is too far from the nature of the people he cannot serve them; if he is too much of them he cannot serve them; only if he is to them as your head is to your body or your mind is to your corporeality, can he do anything at all for them as artist. They see in parts. He must see and grasp the whole. His work is the flower of his race proceeding from that race as seed from the soil, dropping down into it again to germinate and produce other flowering.

Brownell: Again we come to the same point of view, but by different roads, and I think that perhaps is our conclusion.

Wright: A conclusion proper enough, although Broadacre City still remains to be seen as an architect's model, not coming much nearer because of words, notwithstanding all your skill. As for the artist, I might add that until the artist is more the society he serves than the society is itself, he is not a great artist.

INDEX